Community Voices
Academic, Work, and Public Readings

Marcia F. Muth
University of Colorado at Denver

New York Boston San Francisco
London Toronto Sydney Tokyo Singapore Madrid
Mexico City Munich Paris Cape Town Hong Kong Montreal

Senior Vice President and Publisher: Joe Opiela
Acquisitions Editor: Susan Kunchandy
Executive Marketing Manager: Ann Stypuloski
Production Manager: Charles Annis
Project Coordination, Text Design, and Electronic Page Makeup: Nesbitt Graphics, Inc.
Cover Designer/Manager: Wendy Fredericks
Cover Art: ® Jane Sterrett/SIS, Inc.
Photo Researcher: Photosearch, Inc.
Manufacturing Manager: Dennis J. Para
Printer and Binder: Phoenix Color Corp.
Cover Printer: Phoenix Color Corp.

For permission to use copyrighted material, grateful acknowledgment is made to the copyright holders on pp. 579–584, which are hereby made part of this copyright page.

Library of Congress Cataloging-in-Publication Data

Muth, Marcia F.
   Community voices : academic, work, and public readings / Marcia F. Muth.
      p. cm.
   Includes index.
   ISBN 0-321-09331-3 — ISBN 0-321-09331-3
  1. College readers. 2. English language—Rhetoric—Problems, exercises, etc. 3. Report writing—Problems, exercises, etc. I. Title.

PE1417.M88 2003
808'.0427—dc22
                                        2003021619

Copyright © 2004 by Pearson Education.

All rights reserved. No part of this publication may be reproduced, stored in a retrieval system, or transmitted, in any form or by any means, electronic, mechanical, photocopying, recording, or otherwise, without the prior written permission of the publisher. Printed in the United States.

Please visit our website at http://www.ablongman.com

0-321-09331-3

1 2 3 4 5 6 7 8 9 10—PHH—06 05 04 03

Contents

Preface for Readers and Writers xi
Reading and Writing in the Academic, Work, and Public Communities 1

Part 1: The Academic Community

Introduction: Reading and Writing in the Academic Community 9

A. Community Voices
Charles Dickens: Nothing but Facts from *Hard Times* 11
Malcolm X: Prison Studies 16
Mike Rose: Lilia 19
bell hooks: Keeping Close to Home: Class and Education 22

B. Community Perspectives and Issues
Parker J. Palmer: The Quest for Community in Higher Education 33
Janet Donald: Learning, Understanding, and Meaning 43
Stanley N. Katz: The Pathbreaking, Fractionalized, Uncertain World of Knowledge 52
Carol Aslanian: The Community College Pathway for Underprepared Students 59
Deborah Tannen: The Roots of Debate in Education and the Hope of Dialogue 65
Linda Lee: The Case Against College 73

C. Community Ethics
Robert Harris: Anti-Plagiarism Strategies for Research Papers 77
Betsy Levonian Morgan and Ann J. Korschgen: The Ethics of Faculty Behavior: Students' and Professors' Views 87

D. Texts and Documents from the Academic Community
College Application Essay
Leo Stoscheck, Student Writer: Application Essay 94
Letter of Advice from a Parent
Paul J. Vermette: Improving Understanding and Increasing Grades: 4 Tips for Fall Freshman at Columbus Day, An Open Letter to My Son at College 96

Essay in Response to Reading
Elizabeth Peet, Student Writer: The Logos, Constant Change, and Wisdom: Heraclitus and Unification   101

Informative Essay
Cristina Tang, Student Writer: The Cell Cycle and Cancer   105

Speculative Essay
Margaret Harris, Student Writer: So Many Numbers—What Do You Do with the Data?   109

Interpretive Essay
Bert O. States: Troping through Proverbia   112

Theoretical Essay
John C. Meyer: Humor as a Double-Edged Sword: Four Functions of Humor in Communication   119

Persuasive Essay
Mark A. Small and Robin Kimbrough-Melton: Rethinking Justice   126

Research Reflection
Brooke Kush, Student Writer: Researching Bedlam and Madness in the Early Modern Era   133

Documented Problem–Solution Essay
Matt Woodard, Student Writer: Fueling the Revolution   135

Research Paper
Valerie Gamble, Student Writer: The Evolution of Coral-Zooxanthellae Symbioses: Implications of Coral Bleaching   141

Review of a Book
Review of *Sticks and Stones: The Troublesome Success of Children's Literature from Slovenly Peter to Harry Potter* by Jack Zipes   149

Gordon W. Russell: Review of *Why We Watch: The Attractions of Violent Entertainment*, edited by Jeffrey H. Goldstein   151

Abstract
John C. Simon, Thane K. Pratt, Kim E. Berlin, James R. Kowalsky, Steven G. Fancy, and Jeff S. Hatfield: Temporal Variation in Bird Counts within a Hawaiian Rainforest   154

Executive Summary
David Blacker: In Memoriam: Understanding Teaching as Public Service   156

Literature Review
Alyssa N. Bryant: ERIC Review: Community College Students: Recent Findings and Trends   159

Report of Field Research
Reasie A. Henry, Janice G. Weber, and David Yarbrough: Money Management Practices of College Students   165

Report of Laboratory Study

S. M. Carr, H. D. Marshall, K. A. Johnstone, L. M. Pynn, and G. B. Stenson:
How to Tell a Sea Monster: Molecular Discrimination of Large Marine
Animals of the North Atlantic   171

Examination and Examination Answers

Leslie Hankins, Professor, and Anderson Muth, Student Writer:
Hitchcock Final with Answers   180

Grant Proposal

Kathryn Sorrells: Communicating Common Ground   183

Graduate School Application Essay

Melanie Dedecker, Student Writer: Statement of Purpose   189

Academic Address

Harry Mairson: In Praise of the Research University: Remarks
at the Brandeis Commencement, May 1996, School of Science
Ceremonies   192

Web Site

Purdue University: Online Writing Lab (OWL):
http://owl.english.purdue.edu   197

Part 2: The Work Community

Introduction: Reading and Writing in the Work Community   203

A. Community Voices

Lisa Liu, as told to David Bacon: The Story of a Garment Worker   205

Barbara Ehrenreich: Evaluation   208

Marty Jones: And the Weiner Is . . .   213

Sam Walton with John Huey: Running a Successful Company:
Ten Rules That Worked for Me   216

B. Community Perspectives and Issues

Dave Ulrich: Six Practices for Creating Communities of Value,
Not Proximity   221

Robert A. Lutz: It's Okay to Be Anal Sometimes   228

Daniel Eisenberg: The Coming Job Boom   233

Lee G. Bolman and Terrence E. Deal: Cracking the Hidden Code:
Becoming a Cultural Sleuth   240

Jeremy Rifkin: The New Culture of Capitalism   247

Sally Helgesen: When Life Itself Becomes Incredibly Complex   256

C. Community Ethics

Dave Zielinski: Are You a Copyright Criminal?   264

C. Fred Alford: Don't Just Do It to Save Lives   271

D. Texts and Documents from the Work Community

Job Announcement
U.S. Army: Discover How Far You Can Go   280
Wilson Quarterly: Editorial Internships   282

Résumé for Job Hunting
Elizabeth Falvo, Student Writer: Marketing Résumé   284
Brad Roepstorff, Student Writer: Technology Résumé   285

Career Advice
Jayne Swanson: Model Format for Cover Letter (Inquiry or Application)   287

Organizational Welcome to Employees
Olive Garden Italian Restaurant: Welcome to the Family   289

Executive Summary
David G. Baldwin: How to Win the Blame Game   298
Patricia B. Seybold: Get Inside the Lives of Your Customers   298
Michael E. Porter: Strategy and the Internet   299

Article in Professional Journal
Mark Simpson: Are Incentives for Drug Abuse Treatment Too Strong?   301

Memorandum
Georgia Lesh-Laurie: Memo to CU-Denver Community   307

Letter
Bill Marriott: Holiday Greetings   308
J. Katherine Brown-Rowe: Dear Customer   311
Stephen E. Gibson: President's Message, February 11, 2000   312
Stephen E. Gibson: President's Message, February 12, 2001   316

Review of an Artifact
Michael Webb: Steel Belvedere   319

Industry Report
Marcia Mogelonsky: Young Adults: New Customers/New Foods   325

Project Report and Public Information
T-REX Transportation Expansion Project: Introduction to T-REX, Construction Photos, and Traffic Updates   332

Instructions
Hewlett-Packard: LaserJet Toner Cartridge Recycling Program   337

Organizational Promotion
United Illuminating Company: Romeo and J l et   341

Advertisement

Glenbrook Life, Allstate Financial Group: Dedicated, Focused, and Diversified   343

Web Site

Technical Standards, Inc.: www.tecstandards.com   347

Part 3: The Public Community

Introduction: Reading and Writing in the Public Community   353

A. Community Voices

Severn Cullis-Suzuki: The Young Can't Wait   355

Studs Terkel: Organizer: Bill Talcott   357

Katharine S. Miller: Wanted: "Civic Scientists" to Educate the Public, Press and Policy Makers   362

Bill Moyers: Journalism & Democracy: On the Importance of Being a "Public Nuisance"   366

B. Community Perspectives and Issues

Suzanne W. Morse: Five Building Blocks for Successful Communities   374

Stan Hutton and Frances Phillips: Tuning In to the World of Nonprofit Organizations   379

Jill Nelson: A Beginning   386

Stephen R. Covey: The Ideal Community   390

Kathleen Hall Jamieson: Preface to *Everything You Think You Know About Politics... And Why You're Wrong*   397

Jaime A. Zobel de Ayala II: Anticipating the Community of the Future   405

C. Community Ethics

Anthony R. Pratkanis and Elliot Aronson: Our Age of Propaganda   412

Peter J. Gomes: A More Excellent Way   420

D. Texts and Documents from the Public Community

Civic Declaration

Thomas Jefferson: The Declaration of Independence   426

Maude Barlow and Jeremy Rifkin: The Treaty Initiative to Share and Protect the Global Water Commons   431

Civic Address

President George W. Bush: Address to a Joint Session of Congress and the American People, September 20, 2001   433

Martin Luther King, Jr.: I Have a Dream   439

Call to Action

Christie Brinkley: Why You Need to Vote   443

Donna Dees-Thomases: Dear Friend   445

Appeal to Supporters

John Head and Arnie Grossman: SAFE Colorado: Sane Alternatives to the Firearms Epidemic   447

National Rifle Association Foundation: Become a National Sponsor   449

Susan L. Huntington: Dear Ohio State Graduate   451

Richard Whittaker: Dear Subscriber   453

Republican Presidential Roundtable: Invitation to the 8th Annual Republican Senatorial Regain the Majority Dinner   455

Appeal to Voters

Centennial Supporters: City of Centennial: Yes   457

City of Greenwood Village: A New City?   459

Senator Wayne Allard: Announcement Remarks   465

Tom Strickland: Strickland Announces Candidacy for U.S. Senate   468

Letter to Officials

Rice for Peace: Dear President Bush   471

Rick Ashton: Dear Denver Public Library Customer   473

Newsletter

Greenwood Village, Colorado: Newsletter   475

Christine M. Ladisch: Message from Chris, CSR Today   477

Civic Argument

Maude Barlow and Tony Clarke: The Standpoint: How Common Principles and Goals Can Save the World's Water   479

Civic Debate

Fuel Economy Overview: Evolution of the Current Policy   490

Senator John Kerry, Massachusetts, and Senator Christopher S. Bond, Missouri: Pro & Con: Should Congress Set Higher MPG Requirements for Cars and Light Trucks?   495

Position Paper

American Civil Liberties Union: Briefing Paper: Hate Speech on Campus   504

Editorial

Denver Post: The ER Nightmare   510

Letter to the Editor

Sandra S. McRae: Irony in the Morning   512

Linda Doran: Grateful to *News* for Good News on Teens   513

Sarah Davidon: Orange You Feeling Threatened?   513

Anthony J. Fabian: A Tax, Not a Fee   514
Opinion Piece
Lynn K. Rhodes: Think You Can Teach? Pass This Test   515
Report
David Popenoe and Barbara Dafoe Whitehead: Sex without Strings, Relationships without Rings: Today's Young Singles Talk about Mating and Dating   518
Public Advice
American Automobile Association: Your Driving Costs 2003: Figuring It Out   530
Nolo: Law for All: How to Make a Budget and Stick to It   543
Promotional Brochure
College of Arts and Media, University of Colorado at Denver: Artistic License   548
Flyer
AmeriCorps/VISTA: Change Lives ... Including Your Own   552
Proposal
Cornell College: Living & Learning Program   554
Anderson Muth, Peter Strutt, Drew Ahrold, Joe Seabloom, Brian Fenoglio, and Ben Merrill, Student Writers: Proposal for a Cornell College Living & Learning Group   555
Grant Proposal
The National Fund for the United States Botanic Garden: Grant Proposal   559
Web Site
Smoke Free Movies: www.smokefreemovies.ucsf.edu   566
College Drinking: Changing the Culture: www.collegedrinkingprevention.gov   568

Guide to Themes, Topics, and Rhetorical Strategies   573
Credits   579
Index of Authors and Titles   585

Preface for Readers and Writers

Community Voices: Academic, Work, and Public Readings has grown from my own experience as a reader and a writer. Each writing task I've faced as a teacher, editor, textbook author, freelance writer, grant writer, volunteer, or civic activist has prompted questions. What kind of document is needed? Who will read it? What are they concerned about? What will they expect of my document? What does it need to cover? How should it be organized? What tone and style should it use? What format and conventions should it follow? As a working writer, I've learned to ask, "Can you supply a sample that illustrates what you want?" As a teacher, I've grown accustomed to saying, "Let's take a look at your draft."

Based on these experiences, I've tried to design this book so that it will help you answer your own questions about your writing assignments, tasks, and opportunities. As a result, *Community Voices* is brimming with sample texts and documents written by students, professors, businesspeople, workers, professionals, observers, partisans, and activists—in short, all sorts of people who are writing in the general academic, work, and public communities where most of us read and write during our lives. Although these three general communities may differ in expectation and execution, they also share forms, conventions, and situations that challenge writers.

Both the introductory community readings and the texts and documents that illustrate community applications should be rich resources for you as a reader and a writer. Organized by community, the texts and documents reflect common writing tasks and common types of writing, each defined by its purpose, form, situation, authorial preference, or tradition. These selections provide ample opportunity to read, analyze, and practice the types of writing they illustrate.

In addition, each set of community texts and documents is introduced by reflections, analyses, and commentaries—a dozen readings that identify and define the expectations, views, and concerns typical of the general community. How each community defines and justifies itself can help to explain what readers are likely to expect and what writers are likely to provide in their texts and documents.

Opportunity for Student Writers

Although this book includes 36 introductory readings, a dozen for each community, and more than 80 sample texts and documents, you may wish that it illustrated other types or supplied different samples of the types included. You're invited to send me your original texts and documents, written in response to your community expectations or to the writing activities suggested here. I'll gladly consider including your texts and documents as I plan future editions of the book.

Please contact me through the publisher: Marcia Muth, Author of *Community Voices,* c/o Rhetoric and Composition Studies, College Textbooks, Pearson Longman, 1185 Avenue of the Americas, New York, NY 10036. Include your text or document, a short explanation of how you came to write it, contact information so that I can reach you, and your instructor's name and institution if you are writing an academic assignment. Thank you, in advance, for sharing your writing challenges and solutions with me.

Community Organization

Community Voices: Academic, Work, and Public Readings is organized as its subtitle suggests. It is divided into three parts, each concentrating on one of three general communities of readers and writers.

Part 1: The Academic Community. Part 1 focuses on the intellectual orientation of the academic community, especially its concern with generating and exchanging knowledge.

Part 2: The Work Community. Part 2 concentrates on the practical orientation of the workplace, promoting products, providing services, and accomplishing organizational missions.

Part 3: The Public Community. Part 3 conveys the varied interests and powerful values that motivate nonprofit organizations, special-interest groups, volunteers, thoughtful citizens, and the passionate advocates who engage in civic exchanges, public service, service learning, and similar activities.

Community Introductions

The general introduction to the book and the concise introductions to the three parts will help you turn your attention to typical writing situations and readers' expectations that characterize each community. Although these introductions are brief and generalize about very broad communities, they should help you begin to examine your own specific communities of writers and readers more critically.

General Introduction. The initial overview introduces all three communities, orienting readers and writers to the organization of the book.

Part Introductions. Each part begins with a brief introduction to reading and writing in the community under consideration. This introduction includes a general overview of the community's orientation and a short preview of the readings that follow.

Community Readings

In each part, a dozen introductory readings explore the community's values, assumptions, and concerns: what motivates each community, what changes it may anticipate, and what tensions may trouble it. As a group, these readings convey expectations, orientations, and issues that influence writing practices reflected in community texts and documents. These readings are grouped into three sections, which precede a wide range of sample community texts and documents.

A. Community Voices. These four accounts relate the experiences and observations of participants, often sharing their stories firsthand.

B. Community Perspectives and Issues. In these six readings, analysts, observers, and participants define the nature of the community. They convey its central concerns, values, and aspirations. They also explore its challenges, conflicts, trends, and possible changes.

C. Community Ethics. These two ethical explorations turn to values, preferences, and ideals—and the tough business of applying them in daily practice.

D. Community Texts and Documents. Each collection of community texts and documents illustrates how the expectations of readers and the decisions of writers take shape in a wide variety of materials. These selections, identified by type, can serve as occasions for response, examples for analysis, or springboards for writing. They are useful examples, however, not ideal models, so you have plenty of opportunity to critique them and to consider which of their features work well and which do not. Though these materials cannot illustrate all the possibilities accepted within each community, all the preferences of individual readers, or all the choices available to writers, they do present typical purposes, forms, variations, and options.

Introductory Notes, Reading Responses, Writing Activities, and Community Links

Throughout this book, selections are preceded by introductory notes and followed by activities for reading and writing. You can use these materials to prepare for class sessions, to help you complete assignments, or to enrich and deepen your reading and writing as a community participant.

Reading Introduction. A brief note introduces each reading and each sample text or document. These notes may identify the original context of the selection, supply background information about the reading or its author, or suggest what you will encounter as you begin to read.

Reading Responses. These questions follow each selection and ask you to consider matters such as these: the reading's purpose; its appeal to readers and their likely expectations; typical features, including visual components; and specific strategies used by the writer. You may respond to these questions individually, perhaps in a reading journal or notebook, or discuss them during class using notes jotted in the margins or highlighted examples.

Writing Activities. The writing activities generally encourage you to identify, analyze, and apply the forms and strategies used in the reading. All of them ask you to engage in typical activities of writers—summarizing, listing, outlining, explaining, analyzing, evaluating, reacting, or drafting a similar text or document.

Community Links. Readers in each community expect writers to advance certain priorities and to conform to certain expectations. Even so, the texts and documents typical of the three general communities share many features, conventions, and themes. The Community Links guide you as you examine expectations and applications across community lines. These Community Links will direct you to related selections that may illustrate comparable features or alternative solutions to a challenge shared by readings across two or three communities.

Guide to Themes, Topics, and Rhetorical Strategies

Placed at the end of the book, the guide identifies readings that are linked by theme, that approach related topics from different community viewpoints, or that share writing strategies or forms. Here, you can identify related and contrasting readings that may illustrate the choices of different writers or the preferences of different communities.

Flexible Organization

As the features of the book suggest, readers might examine the orientation and texts of each community in turn, moving through the parts in sequence. On the other hand, readers might concentrate on a single community—for example, the academic community—using the Community Links and the Guide to Themes, Topics, and Rhetorical Strategies to identify and compare related readings from other communities. Alternatively, readers might use the Guide to Themes, Topics, and Rhetorical Strategies to identify readings by type, looking at letters, reports, arguments, or other clusters of readings, regardless of community orientation.

Acknowledgments

I'd like first to thank the following student writers whose previously unpublished work appears in this book: Drew Ahrold, Melanie Dedecker, Elizabeth Falvo, Brian Fenoglio, Valerie Gamble, Brooke Kush, Ben Merrill, Anderson Muth, Elizabeth Peet, Brad Roepstorff, Joe Seabloom, Peter Strutt, and Matt Woodard. I'd also like to thank Leslie Kathleen Hankins, Department of English; Matt Johnson, Assistant Dean of Students and Director of Residence Life; and Jayne Swanson, Director, Career Services, all of Cornell College, Mt. Vernon, Iowa, for generously providing materials that appear here. Other student and faculty writers are acknowledged in the credits.

    I am grateful to those who have helped me to gather varied and engaging samples of student and professional writing—many more than this volume could accommodate. Special thanks go to Martha Condon, Department of Biology, and other faculty at Cornell College; R. James Goldstein, Department of English, Auburn University; and Anderson Muth, Elizabeth Peet, and Melanie Dedecker who have helped me to locate lively student texts. Thanks go as well to Chris Anson, Director of Campus Writing and Speaking Program, North Carolina State University, and Bob Schwegler, College Writing Program, Department of English, University of Rhode Island—my co-authors on *The Longman Writer's Companion* and *The Longman Pocket Writer's Companion*—for enriching my ideas about communities of readers and writers. I also have benefited from the exchanges of a large electronic community that has stimulated my thinking and guided me to a variety of resources. Thanks particularly to the generous and insightful members of the electronic lists organized through the WPA (Writing Program Administrators), TECHWR-L (for technical communicators), APCC (Association of Professional Communication Consultants), and Tomorrow's Professor (sponsored by the Stanford University Center for Teaching and Learning).

During several years of collecting readings, I have very much appreciated the exemplary assistance of the Arapahoe Library District, Arapahoe County, Colorado, especially the patient and tireless staff at the Smoky Hill Branch in Centennial. I am grateful as well for the efficient aid of Auraria Library, which serves the University of Colorado at Denver, and for the ready advice and valuable suggestions of Mary Finley of the University Library at California State University Northridge. As always, I am indebted to the lively community of writers and readers who have gathered in my writing workshops, offered through the School of Education at the University of Colorado at Denver.

Thanks also are due to the insightful reviewers whose comments have encouraged me while strengthening this book: Lisa Bickmore, Salt Lake Community College; Laura Gray, University of Arkansas; Miles McCrimmon, J. Sargeant Reynolds Community College; Lyle W. Morgan, Pittsburg State University; Robin Morris, Cape Fear Community College; Tami Penley, Mountain Empire Community College; Gayle Price, Gardner-Webb University; Robert Rongner, Whatcom Community College; Anthony J. Viola, Ohio State University; and John M. Yozzo, East Central University.

At Longman, Susan Kunchandy, my cheerful and ingenious editor, has encouraged this project from the very beginning. Others on the Longman team have included Rebecca Gilpin, who has coordinated details large and small, and Charles Annis, who has guided the book through production. Special thanks go to Caroline Gloodt for her especially patient work on permissions and to Julie Tesser for image research. Julie DeSilva, the book's able and inventive project manager, and others at Nesbitt Graphics, including production coordinator Karen Papa and designers Jerilyn Kauffman and Catherine Bradish, have facilitated a smooth production process while creatively representing the textual features and the visual components of widely varied selections.

Finally, I am grateful to my family for their ongoing support and patience. My son, Anderson, has continued to share his triumphs and challenges as a college, workplace, and public writer. My husband, Rod, has consistently demonstrated to me the many reasons why writers should treasure their readers. Thanks to both of you—my smallest but most valuable community of writers and readers.

Reading and Writing in the Academic, Work, and Public Communities

When you write, you can change how someone else thinks, acts, or reacts. To use this tremendous power effectively, you need to figure out how to make contact with your readers—how to recognize what they expect and how to provide what they need. Although readers may have individual preferences, most readers reflect the values of their communities: groups of writers and readers who make contact through written materials and who share similar purposes and expectations.

This book considers the writing typical of academic, work, and public communities—three general communities where most people are likely to read and write, often throughout their lives. Your own situation is probably a good example. Are you taking a college course? Are you working on campus or off? Do you belong to a campus, service-learning, or other volunteer group? If so, you are already reading and writing within these three communities.

Meeting Community Expectations

As a college student, you sometimes may be baffled by the requirements of your instructors. Why, you may wonder, do they so often expect you to analyze texts, summarize readings, or integrate information from sources? Why are they so fussy about the details—the clear thesis statement for an essay, the precise headings for a lab report, or the exact sequence and punctuation of information in a list of references? Though your specific assignments will vary with the instructor, the course, and the discipline, most will reflect the general values of the academic community. As a result, most will want you to join the search for knowledge by engaging actively with readings, evaluating information critically, and accepting the intellectual challenge of wrestling with ideas. They'll also want you to show respect for the thinking and research of others, expressed through the careful identification of your sources. They'll want you to show that respect by using the documentation form appropriate for a particular field—cracking the code that conveys to readers in the field all the details needed to expand or refine their knowledge about your topic by turning to your sources. In short, your instructors will expect you to read and to write in ways that acknowledge the values of the academic community.

At work, you're likely to find a similar pattern. When your supervisor asks you to write a letter to a client, fill out a customer contact form, or draft part of a report for your team, you'll be expected to follow a certain format and to represent your company or organization in a specific way. You'll need to prepare information to meet the needs of others—attracting the prospective client, conserving your busy supervisor's time, or clearly identifying alternatives for your work group. Instead of concentrating on the discovery, interpretation, and presentation of knowledge as you do in college courses, you'll focus on advancing the organization's mission, solving problems with products or services, or building solid relationships with clients or customers.

Even in widely varied public contexts, you'll find that readers share expectations. Their ideas are likely to reflect their personal needs and concerns, their past experiences, and the mission of any civic or voluntary organization involved. Their expectations may also reflect external guidelines such as the time limit for public comments at a board meeting, the requirements for grant proposals specified by the funder, or the maximum length allowed for letters to the editor. Public readers know that you may write as a partisan or an advocate, but they also expect you to present information clearly, use evidence fairly, express opinions reasonably, and treat others respectfully, whether they agree or disagree.

In each wide community, these general agreements shape the expectations of readers and the practices of writers. They are the foundation of the community's specific conventions—the working agreements held by writers and readers about how things ought to be done. Understanding how readers and writers interact in your community will help you refine your purpose as a writer, discover your most effective approach to a broad topic, adjust your tone, and concentrate attention on the needs of your readers. You'll unleash your power as a writer as you increase your sensitivity to different communities of readers.

Building Skills across Communities

Most readers and writers are likely to be involved in several communities simultaneously. For example, right now you probably attend classes, participate in social or interest groups, and have a job. Similarly, employees of your college or university may apply academic values in some situations (as they teach and conduct or report research) and workplace values in others (as they select their health benefits or enroll their children in the campus day care center). Further, expectations, values, and conventions may be shared, applied, or examined in several communities. For example, academic researchers may study the activities and values of other communities as part of their search for knowledge. On the other hand, researchers or trainers in the work and public sectors may organize their work or evaluate their efforts by the same standards that academics would use.

As you attend college, prepare for professional employment, or engage in public exchanges and activities, you'll need to build strong writing skills. Fortunately, these essential skills are respected in all three broad communities. What you learn in one community often will transfer readily to another. For instance, if you learn to write an effective academic abstract, summing up your research paper, you can easily transfer this skill when you need to draft an executive summary for your report at work or a concise opening for your group's political brochure. All three tasks require that you identify and convey the essentials in short form.

In addition, however, each task requires that you pay attention both to the general expectations of readers in the wide community and to the specific expectations of your immediate group of readers. If you learn how to analyze what the academic community values and what your particular college instructor requires, odds are that you can also figure out what your team at work expects or what the school board wants from the parents contributing to a report on standardized testing. Knowing how to discover, anticipate, and respond thoughtfully to readers' needs is an asset in any community.

Recognizing Common Situations and Shared Conventions

Although each community may favor specific texts and documents that meet its readers' needs, writers in the three general communities face many comparable situations. For example, a letter to the editor on a civic issue and a workplace letter to a client may look alike, not just because they follow the same format, but also because they face a similar challenge—succinctly identifying issues and respectfully engaging or persuading readers. A lab report for a campus biology course may be less complex than a lab employee's report for a pharmaceutical company, but both probably will cover procedures and results. In the same way, directions for readers may concentrate on the "how to" basics whether they are academic assignments, product instructions, or guides for community activists.

All three communities share many common expectations about writing. Whether your readers are on campus, at the office, or on a civic committee, they'll probably appreciate thoughtful, orderly texts with clear sentences and carefully chosen wording. They'll expect you to treat them respectfully, considering their needs and anticipating their questions or concerns. They'll hope that your points appear in a sequence that they can understand and that your ideas connect logically. When you explain general ideas, they'll appreciate appropriate examples, though different communities may value or tolerate different types of illustrations. They'll want to be able to read your sentences easily and understand them without a struggle, though some readers will advocate the brevity and directness of the active voice while others will favor the passive voice for its focus on what's done, not who did it. Finally, they'll expect you to use apostrophes correctly and to spell accurately even if they have slightly different ideas about how to use commas.

Analyzing Your Community

Within each general community, readers and writers share common expectations, aims, and attitudes. In addition, particular groups of readers and writers within a general community may share specific interests and hold very specific expectations about their exchanges with each other and with those outside their group. You also may bring your individual or personal interests to your community and situation: your own goals, concerns, and passions as a reader and a writer.

As you gain experience reading and writing within a community, you'll learn its expectations by observing its preferences and seeing the models it values. You'll find out how others respond to texts, documents, and exchanges—

what they value and approve and what they find inappropriate. In this way, you'll develop conventional expectations—awareness of what others think a particular type of writing is supposed to be or do. Then, when you begin planning your own draft, you'll be able to figure out the basics that define your community: Where are you? What do you want or need to do? Who are your readers? What do they want or need? How are you expected to accomplish your goals as you meet their needs?

If you are responding to an assignment or a writing task from your teacher, supervisor, or civic group, you can analyze it for pointers about what's expected. If you feel uncertain, you might read examples of the same type to see what they do and how they work. You might also answer questions like these to determine your community's expectations.

- **What is the purpose of your assignment?** To interpret a reading? To present your own research or to synthesize the studies of others? To explain a product or service? To promote your solution to a problem? To persuade a colleague, a customer, or a public official?
- **Who will read your assignment?** One person or several? Your instructor or your classmates? Your work colleagues, your supervisor, or your customers? Your fellow committee members, prospective members, or outsiders who may not share your group's goals?
- **How do you want readers to respond?** To think, to act, or to react? To understand your point? To accept your logic or evidence? To buy your product or service? To implement your proposal? To join your cause? To respect your viewpoint even when they disagree with your conclusions?
- **How should you organize and shape your writing?** What parts will readers expect? What sequence will they prefer? What approach or tone will they find most compelling?
- **How should you present your main point?** Where should you identify or state it? How should you support it? What kinds of evidence will readers expect? How much detail and development will they want?
- **What characteristics do readers admire?** How do they define good writing? Will they look for clear sentences or punchy motivational lines? Logical arguments or emotional appeals? Powerful language or neutral expression? Plain wording or fancy flourishes?
- **What format is typical for the text or document?** Simple paragraphs? Headings to guide the reader? Indented or centered elements for a letter or résumé? A specific layout or design for a brochure? Illustrations, tables, graphs, or other visuals? Source citations with a list of references? Links in an e-mail message or a Web page?

Using *Community Voices*

To help you learn how to analyze and address different communities effectively, this book is divided into three parts. Each part is devoted to one of three general communities of writers and readers: academic, work, and public. Each part has the same structure so that you know what to expect throughout the book and can easily move among the three communities. First, each part opens with a short introduction to reading and writing in that community. This introduction identifies the primary characteristics of the community and briefly previews the readings that follow. Next, each part includes a dozen introductory readings that describe the community. Finally, each part presents a wide variety of community texts or documents that illustrate the expectations and conventions of its writers and readers.

When you read a selection, use the reading introduction that precedes it to discover its original context or its background. Use the Reading Responses, Writing Activities, and Community Links that follow it to help you respond to it, write about it, apply it, or relate it to other readings. Should it lead you into your own field research, be sure to follow any college or workplace guidelines for research involving other people.

The introductory readings for the academic community establish its focus on knowledge: its preoccupation with intellectual exploration and its reliance on the past studies in a field to set boundaries for the development of original thought. On the other hand, the opening selections about the work community establish its concentration on the organizational mission, whether to sell a product, promote an organization, or provide a service. In contrast, the readings introducing the public community identify participants' varied motivations: a sense of civic duty, a desire to volunteer, devotion to a cause, zeal for public service, or the satisfaction found in service to others. Such motivations establish the public community's focus on values, its admiration for forthright advocacy, and its zeal to act rather than to contemplate.

The texts and documents for each community illustrate how its focus and orientation take shape in a variety of materials. You can approach these materials as examples for analysis and response or as guides for drafting similar texts. These selections cannot illustrate all the writing possibilities within each community, but they do present typical forms, variations, and options. In addition, they illustrate both the shared approaches and the distinctive strategies that their writers use as they try to achieve their objectives, establish connections with readers, and communicate effectively in varied situations.

Part 1

The Academic Community

Introduction: Reading and Writing in the Academic Community

A. Community Voices
B. Community Perspectives and Issues
C. Community Ethics
D. Texts and Documents from the Academic Community

Introduction: Reading and Writing in the Academic Community

The academic community focuses on knowledge. In this wide community, participants develop, probe, and exchange ideas: they read, write, and discuss. They teach and learn, motivated by a passion simply to know—and eventually to know more clearly and more exactly. Scholars and researchers investigate issues, sharing their expertise, questions, and discoveries with students and with academic colleagues, practitioners in the field, and other interested readers. This community shares and exchanges knowledge in many ways: through classroom interactions, books, journal articles, essays, research reports, electronic discussions, and presentations at conferences sponsored by disciplinary and professional organizations.

As you enter the academic community as a student, you read, discuss, and study to learn the history, assumptions, issues, habits of thoughts, and methods typical of this community. When you declare a major and select an area of concentration, you move into increasingly specialized fields, each with its own ways of defining and conducting the search for knowledge. Although the broad values of the academic community are pervasive, the ways that physicists or historians or economists pose questions, seek knowledge, defend their viewpoints, and share research findings will differ, each reflecting the expectations of the discipline.

Despite the differences among the many academic fields, most academic readers expect thoughtful reasoning and specific conclusions supported by pertinent evidence. They respect the traditional methods, studies, and findings in their fields. When they read academic texts, they expect to find accurate background information that justifies issues in light of previous studies, engaging problems that extend prior learning, respectful acknowledgments of other views and approaches, tested methods of investigation, carefully reasoned analyses and interpretations, and substantial source citations that recognize and honor the existing work in the field.

Academic writers strive to satisfy these expectations of readers by identifying, organizing, supporting, and substantiating their findings in familiar ways. They show their regard for the broad community values as they try to advance knowledge and share what they learn with their readers. They define issues and problems worthy of investigation, using the approaches and forms generally accepted in the wide community and within a specific discipline. They ask questions and seek answers, relying on pertinent, detailed evidence. They try to follow accepted procedures and methods, whether in the chemistry lab, at an archaeological dig, or in the library. They document their sources in conventional ways, showing their respect for the ideas and work of others. They examine meanings, causes, reasons, connections, and interpretations, sharing what they have learned and challenging others to expand this understanding.

Readings in the Academic Community

Twelve readings in three sections introduce the values, concerns, and expectations of the academic community. First, four community voices speak as Dickens, Malcolm X, Rose, and hooks tell their stories about education—examining what and how people learn. Then, six readings present perspectives and issues from the academic community. Introducing the section, Palmer finds a powerful community in the processes of teaching, learning, and sharing. Next, Donald examines assumptions, shared and distinct, within academic disciplines. Katz considers the uncertain yet stimulating search for knowledge, while Aslanian turns to practical education at community colleges. The prominence of debate concerns Tannen, and Lee directly challenges the assumption that college is an appropriate experience for all. Finally, two readings explore ethics in the academic community: Harris examines plagiarism while Morgan and Korschgen report their research on faculty ethics.

Next, a wide variety of academic texts and documents illustrates the many ways that the academic community exchanges ideas. The section begins with an application essay and a parental letter of advice, both typical markers as students enter this community. Then varied essays and other selections illustrate the many types of texts students may learn to write as they join the broad academic community. Essays by students, scholars, and researchers show how academicians may explain, respond to readings, inform, speculate, interpret, theorize, and persuade as they investigate and exchange ideas. Other sample texts respond to particular situations using accepted forms such as reviews, abstracts and executive summaries, literature reviews, and research reports. An examination, a proposal, and an application to graduate school illustrate ways of responding to different kinds of academic assessment. Finally, a characteristic academic address—the commencement speech—and an academic Web site conclude the readings in the academic community.

Community Voices

NOTHING BUT FACTS FROM *HARD TIMES*

Charles Dickens

Charles Dickens (1812–1870) was a popular British novelist noted for his powerful social commentary. Published in 1854, his novel Hard Times *explores the shortcomings of an educational system—and a way of life—that reduces everything to the "facts." In the following selection from the beginning of the novel, Dickens dramatically illustrates how Mr. Gradgrind implements his system and how it shapes his young students.*

Chapter I: *The One Thing Needful*

1 "Now, what I want is Facts. Teach these boys and girls nothing but Facts. Facts alone are wanted in life. Plant nothing else, and root out everything else. You can only form the minds of reasoning animals upon Facts: nothing else will ever be of any service to them. This is the principle on which I bring up my own children, and this is the principle on which I bring up these children. Stick to Facts, sir!"

2 The scene was a plain, bare, monotonous vault of a school-room, and the speaker's square forefinger emphasized his observations by underscoring every sentence with a line on the schoolmaster's sleeve. The emphasis was helped by the speaker's square wall of a forehead, which had his eyebrows for its base, while his eyes found commodious cellarage in two dark caves, overshadowed by the wall. The emphasis was helped by the speaker's mouth, which was wide, thin, and hard set. The emphasis was helped by the speaker's voice, which was inflexible, dry, and dictatorial. The emphasis was helped by the speaker's hair, which bristled on the skirts of his bald head, a plantation of firs to keep the wind from its shining surface, all covered with knobs, like the crust of a plum pie, as if the head had scarcely warehouse-room for the hard facts stored inside. The speaker's obstinate carriage, square coat, square legs, square shoulders—nay, his very neckcloth, trained to take him by the throat with an unaccommodating grasp, like a stubborn fact, as it was—all helped the emphasis.

3 "In this life, we want nothing but Facts, sir; nothing but Facts!"

4   The speaker, and the schoolmaster, and the third grown person present, all backed a little, and swept with their eyes the inclined plane of little vessels then and there arranged in order, ready to have imperial gallons of facts poured into them until they were full to the brim.

Chapter II: *Murdering the Innocents*

5   Thomas Gradgrind, sir. A man of realities. A man of facts and calculations. A man who proceeds upon the principle that two and two are four, and nothing over, and who is not to be talked into allowing for anything over. Thomas Gradgrind, sir—peremptorily Thomas—Thomas Gradgrind. With a rule and a pair of scales, and the multiplication table always in his pocket, sir, ready to weigh and measure any parcel of human nature, and tell you exactly what it comes to. It is a mere question of figures, a case of simple arithmetic. You might hope to get some other nonsensical belief into the head of George Gradgrind, or Augustus Gradgrind, or John Gradgrind, or Joseph Gradgrind (all suppositions, non-existent persons), but into the head of Thomas Gradgrind—no, sir!

6   In such terms Mr. Gradgrind always mentally introduced himself, whether to his private circle of acquaintance, or to the public in general. In such terms, no doubt, substituting the words "boys and girls," for "sir," Thomas Gradgrind now presented Thomas Gradgrind to the little pitchers before him, who were to be filled so full of facts.

7   Indeed, as he eagerly sparkled at them from the cellarage before mentioned, he seemed a kind of cannon loaded to the muzzle with facts, and prepared to blow them clean out of the regions of childhood at one discharge. He seemed a galvanizing apparatus, too, charged with a grim mechanical substitute for the tender young imaginations that were to be stormed away.

8   "Girl number twenty," said Mr. Gradgrind, squarely pointing with his square forefinger, "I don't know that girl. Who is that girl?"

9   "Sissy Jupe, sir," explained number twenty, blushing, standing up, and curtseying.

10 "Sissy is not a name," said Mr. Gradgrind. "Don't call yourself Sissy. Call yourself Cecilia."

11 "It's father as calls me Sissy, sir," returned the young girl in a trembling voice, and with another curtsey.

12 "Then he has no business to do it," said Mr. Gradgrind. "Tell him he mustn't. Cecilia Jupe. Let me see. What is your father?"

13 "He belongs to the horse-riding, if you please, sir."

14 Mr. Gradgrind frowned, and waved off the objectionable calling with his hand.

15 "We don't want to know anything about that, here. You mustn't tell us about that, here. Your father breaks horses, don't he?"

16 "If you please, sir, when they can get any to break, they do break horses in the ring, sir."

17 "You mustn't tell us about the ring, here. Very well, then. Describe your father as a horsebreaker. He doctors sick horses, I dare say?"

18 "Oh yes, sir."

19 "Very well, then. He is a veterinary surgeon, a farrier, and horsebreaker. Give me your definition of a horse."

20 (Sissy Jupe thrown into the greatest alarm by this demand.)

21 "Girl number twenty unable to define a horse!" said Mr. Gradgrind, for the general behoof of all the little pitchers. "Girl number twenty possessed of no facts, in reference to one of the commonest of animals! Some boy's definition of a horse. Bitzer, yours."

22 The square finger, moving here and there, lighted suddenly on Bitzer, perhaps because he chanced to sit in the same ray of sunlight which, darting in at one of the bare windows of the intensely whitewashed room, irradiated Sissy. For the boys and girls sat on the face of the inclined plane in two compact bodies, divided up the centre by a narrow interval; and Sissy, being at the corner of a row on the sunny side, came in for the beginning of a sunbeam, of which Bitzer, being at the corner of a row on the other side, a few rows in advance, caught the end. But whereas the girl was so dark-eyed and dark-haired that she seemed to receive a deeper and more lustrous colour from the sun when it shone upon her, the boy was so light-eyed and light-haired that the selfsame rays appeared to draw out of him what little colour he ever possessed. His cold eyes would hardly have been eyes but for the short ends of lashes which, by bringing them into immediate contrast with something paler than themselves, expressed their form. His short-cropped hair might have been a mere continuation of the sandy freckles on his forehead and face. His skin was so unwholesomely deficient in the natural tinge, that he looked as though, if he were cut, he would bleed white.

23 "Bitzer," said Thomas Gradgrind. "Your definition of a horse."

24 "Quadruped. Graminivorous. Forty teeth, namely, twenty-four grinders, four eye-teeth, and twelve incisive. Sheds coat in the spring; in marshy countries, sheds hoofs, too. Hoofs hard, but requiring to be shod with iron. Age known by marks in mouth." Thus (and much more) Bitzer.

25 "Now girl number twenty," said Mr. Gradgrind. "You know what a horse is."

26 She curtseyed again, and would have blushed deeper if she could have blushed deeper than she had blushed all this time. Bitzer, after rapidly blinking at Thomas Gradgrind with both eyes at once, and so catching the light upon his quivering ends of lashes that they looked like the antennae of busy insects, put his knuckles to his freckled forehead and sat down again.

27 The third gentleman now stepped forth. A mighty man at cutting and drying he was; a government officer; in his way (and in most other people's too), a professed pugilist; always in training, always with a system to force down the general throat like a bolus, always to be heard of at the bar of his little public-office, ready to fight all England. To continue in fistic phraseology, he had a genius for coming up to the scratch, wherever and whatever it was, and proving himself an ugly customer. He would go in and damage any subject whatever with his right, follow up with his left, stop, exchange, counter, bore his

opponent (he always fought All England) to the ropes, and fall upon him neatly. He was certain to knock the wind out of common sense, and render that unlucky adversary deaf to the call of time. And he had it in charge from high authority to bring about the great public-office Millennium, when Commissioners should reign upon earth.

28 "Very well," said this gentleman, briskly smiling, and folding his arms. "That's a horse. Now, let me ask you girls and boys: Would you paper a room with representations of horses?"

29 After a pause, one half of the children cried in chorus, "Yes, sir!" Upon which the other half, seeing in the gentleman's face that Yes was wrong, cried out in chorus, "No, sir!"—as the custom is in these examinations.

30 "Of course, No. Why wouldn't you?"

31 A pause. One corpulent slow boy, with a wheezy manner of breathing, ventured the answer, Because he wouldn't paper a room at all, but would paint it.

32 "You *must* paper it," said the gentleman, rather warmly.

33 "You must paper it," said Thomas Gradgrind, "whether you like it or not. Don't tell *us* you wouldn't paper it. What do you mean, boy?"

34 "I'll explain to you, then," said the gentleman, after another and a dismal pause, "why you wouldn't paper a room with representations of horses. Do you ever see horses walking up and down the sides of rooms in reality—in fact? Do you?"

35 "Yes, sir!" from one half. "No, sir!" from the other.

36 "Of course, No," said the gentleman, with an indignant look at the wrong half. "Why, then, you are not to see anywhere what you don't see in fact; you are not to have anywhere what you don't have in fact. What is called Taste is only another name for Fact."

37 Thomas Gradgrind nodded his approbation.

38 "This is a new principle, a discovery, a great discovery," said the gentleman. "Now, I'll try you again. Suppose you were going to carpet a room. Would you use a carpet having a representation of flowers upon it?"

39 There being a general conviction by this time that "No, sir!" was always the right answer to this gentleman, the chorus of No was very strong. Only a few feeble stragglers said Yes: among them Sissy Jupe.

40 "Girl number twenty," said the gentleman, smiling in the calm strength of knowledge.

41 Sissy blushed, and stood up.

42 "So you would carpet your room—or your husband's room, if you were a grown woman, and had a husband—with representations of flowers, would you?" said the gentleman. "Why would you?"

43 "If you please, sir, I am very fond of flowers," returned the girl.

44 "And is that why you would put tables and chairs upon them, and have people walking over them with heavy boots?"

45 "It wouldn't hurt them, sir. They wouldn't crush and wither, if you please, sir. They would be the pictures of what was very pretty and pleasant, and I would fancy———"

46   "Aye, aye, aye! But you musn't fancy," cried the gentleman, quite elated by coming so happily to his point. "That's it! You are never to fancy."

47   "You are not, Cecilia Jupe," Thomas Gradgrind solemnly repeated, "to do anything of that kind."

48   "Fact, fact, fact!" said the gentleman. And "Fact, fact, fact!" repeated Thomas Gradgrind.

49   "You are to be in all things regulated and governed," said the gentleman, "by fact. We hope to have, before long, a board of fact, composed of commissioners of fact, who will force the people to be a people of fact, and of nothing but fact. You must discard the word Fancy altogether. You have nothing to do with it. You are not to have, in any object of use or ornament, what would be a contradiction in fact. You don't walk upon flowers in fact; you cannot be allowed to walk upon flowers in carpets. You don't find that foreign birds and butterflies come and perch upon your crockery; you cannot be permitted to paint foreign birds and butterflies upon your crockery. You never meet with quadrupeds going up and down walls; you must not have quadrupeds represented upon walls. You must see," said the gentleman, "for all these purposes, combinations and modifications (in primary colours) of mathematical figures which are susceptible of proof and demonstration. This is the new discovery. This is fact. This is taste."

50   The girl curtseyed, and sat down. She was very young, and she looked as if she were frightened by the matter-of-fact prospect the world afforded.

Reading Responses

1. What point does Dickens make about an education that sticks just to the facts?
2. How does Dickens use description and dialogue to make his point? Which parts of this opening scene do you find most powerful and vivid?
3. What alternatives to Mr. Gradgrind's system does this opening scene suggest? What—besides the facts—might be valued and nurtured in an educational system?

Writing Activities

1. Write your own definition of a horse.
2. Following Dickens's model, write your own short narrative about your early education. Select an event—something that happened to you or that you observed at school—that reveals particular attitudes about education today. Rely on vivid, concrete details and dialogue to convey the scene and to make your point clear.
3. Write an essay that explains several points that you wish to make about an educational system based on facts alone. Use examples from the scene from *Hard Times* to illustrate your points.

Community Links

Read Liu's account of her work in "The Story of a Garment Worker" (pp. 205–207). Compare and contrast her account with Dickens's presentation of education by facts.

PRISON STUDIES
Malcolm X

◆

Malcolm X (1925–1965) began life in Omaha, Nebraska, as Malcolm Little. Following a prison term, he changed his life, becoming a Muslim minister, an ardent spokesperson for Black Muslims, and eventually the founder of the Organization for Afro-American Unity. This selection from The Autobiography of Malcolm X *(1964), written collaboratively with Alex Haley, explains how Malcolm X began what he called his "homemade education."*

1   Many who today hear me somewhere in person, or on television, or those who read something I've said, will think I went to school far beyond the eighth grade. This impression is due entirely to my prison studies.

2   It had really begun back in the Charlestown Prison, when Bimbi first made me feel envy of his stock of knowledge. Bimbi had always taken charge of any conversation he was in, and I had tried to emulate him. But every book I picked up had few sentences which didn't contain anywhere from one to nearly all of the words that might as well have been in Chinese. When I just skipped those words, of course, I really ended up with little idea of what the book said. So I had come to the Norfolk Prison Colony still going through only book-reading motions. Pretty soon, I would have quit even these motions, unless I had received the motivation that I did.

3   I saw that the best thing I could do was get hold of a dictionary—to study, to learn some words. I was lucky enough to reason also that I should try to improve my penmanship. It was sad. I couldn't even write in a straight line. It was both ideas together that moved me to request a dictionary along with some tablets and pencils from the Norfolk Prison Colony school.

4   I spent two days just riffling uncertainly through the dictionary's pages. I'd never realized so many words existed! I didn't know *which* words I needed to learn. Finally, just to start some kind of action, I began copying.

5   In my slow, painstaking, ragged handwriting, I copied into my tablet everything printed on that first page, down to the punctuation marks.

6   I believe it took me a day. Then, aloud, I read back, to myself, everything I'd written on the tablet. Over and over, aloud, to myself, I read my own handwriting.

7   I woke up the next morning, thinking about those words—immensely proud to realize that not only had I written so much at one time, but I'd written words that I never knew were in the world. Moreover, with a little effort, I also could remember what many of these words meant. I reviewed the words whose meanings I didn't remember. Funny thing, from the dictionary first page right now, that "aardvark" springs to my mind. The dictionary had a picture of it, a long-tailed, long-eared, burrowing African mammal, which lives off termites caught by sticking out its tongue as an anteater does for ants.

8   I was so fascinated that I went on—I copied the dictionary's next page. And the same experience came when I studied that. With every succeeding page, I also learned of people and places and events from history. Actually the dictionary is like a miniature encyclopedia. Finally the dictionary's A section had filled a whole tablet—and I went on into the B's. That was the way I started copying what eventually became the entire dictionary. It went a lot faster after so much practice helped me to pick up handwriting speed. Between what I wrote in my tablet, and writing letters, during the rest of my time in prison I would guess I wrote a million words.

9   I suppose it was inevitable that as my word-base broadened, I could for the first time pick up a book and read and now begin to understand what the book was saying. Anyone who has read a great deal can imagine the new world that opened. Let me tell you something: from then until I left that prison, in every free moment I had, if I was not reading in the library, I was reading on my bunk. You couldn't have gotten me out of books with a wedge. Between Mr. Muhammad's teachings, my correspondence, my visitors—usually Ella and Reginald—and my reading of books, months passed without my even thinking about being imprisoned. In fact, up to then, I never had been so truly free in my life.

10   The Norfolk Prison Colony's library was in the school building. A variety of classes was taught there by instructors who came from such places as Harvard and Boston universities. The weekly debates between inmate teams were also held in the school building. You would be astonished to know how worked up convict debaters and audiences would get over subjects like "Should Babies Be Fed Milk?"

11   Available on the prison library's shelves were books on just about every general subject. Much of the big private collection that Parkhurst had willed to the prison was still in crates and boxes in the back of the library—thousands of old books. Some of them looked ancient: covers faded, old-time parchment-looking binding. Parkhurst, I've mentioned, seemed to have been principally interested in history and religion. He had the money and the special interest to have a lot of books that you wouldn't have in general circulation. Any college library would have been lucky to get that collection.

12   As you can imagine, especially in a prison where there was heavy emphasis on rehabilitation, an inmate was smiled upon if he demonstrated an unusually intense interest in books. There was a sizable number of well-read inmates, especially the popular debaters. Some were said by many to be practically walking encyclopedias. They were almost celebrities. No university would ask any

student to devour literature as I did when this new world opened to me, of being able to read and *understand*.

13 I read more in my room than in the library itself. An inmate who was known to read a lot could check out more than the permitted maximum number of books. I preferred reading in the total isolation of my own room.

14 When I had progressed to really serious reading, every night at about ten P.M. I would be outraged with the "lights out." It always seemed to catch me right in the middle of something engrossing.

15 Fortunately, right outside my door was a corridor light that cast a glow into my room. The glow was enough to read by, once my eyes adjusted to it. So when "lights out" came, I would sit on the floor where I could continue reading in that glow.

16 At one-hour intervals the night guards paced past every room. Each time I heard the approaching footsteps, I jumped into bed and feigned sleep. And as soon as the guard passed, I got back out of bed onto the floor area of that light-glow, where I would read for another fifty-eight minutes—until the guard approached again. That went on until three or four every morning. Three or four hours of sleep a night was enough for me. Often in the years in the streets I had slept less than that.

Reading Responses

1. How does Malcolm X tell his "literacy story"? What are the main events in the story? What are the complications? What is the outcome?
2. What impression of his education in prison does Malcolm X convey? What differences does he suggest between his prison education and his education through eighth grade?
3. What is the effect of Malcolm X's voice, speaking as "I" and occasionally referring to "you"? Identify passages or word choices that contribute to your sense of his purpose and credibility.

Writing Activities

1. Write your own "literacy story," telling about a significant series of events that shaped your learning in or out of school.
2. Write an essay that defines your own education, whether it is a formal school education, a "homemade education" like Malcolm X's, or some other type.
3. Play Alex Haley's role, interviewing someone and then writing an account of that person's education or studies. Use quotations from the interview and your own interpretive comments to make a central point about the person's education.

Community Links

Compare and contrast several accounts of people facing challenges and overcoming hardships or obstacles, such as Malcolm X's "Prison Studies" (pp. 16–18) or Rose's "Lilia" (pp. 19–21) from the academic community, Liu's "The Story of a Garment Worker" (pp. 205–207) from the work community, and Cullis-Suzuki's "The Young Can't Wait" (pp. 355–356) from the public community. In what ways are the accounts you select similar or different? How do you account for these similarities or differences?

LILIA
Mike Rose

◆

In Lives on the Boundary: The Struggles and Achievements of America's Underprepared *(1989), Mike Rose tells the stories of many students in the writing program at the University of California at Los Angeles. In the following selection, which concludes his book, he presents Lilia's story.*

1   I sit with Lilia, the tape recorder going. "We came from Mexico when I was four years old. When I went into school, I flunked the first grade. The first grade! I had to repeat it, and they put me in classes for slow learners. I stayed in those classes for five years. I guess there was a pattern where they put me in those really basic classes and then decided I would go through my elementary school years in those classes. I didn't learn to read or write. My parents got my cousins—they came here prior to us, so they knew English really well—and they had me read for them. I couldn't. They told my parents I didn't know anything. That's when my parents decided they would move. They moved to Tulare County. My aunt was there and told them that the schools were good and that there was work in agriculture. I picked grapes and cotton and oranges—everything—for six straight summers. I kinda liked it, out there with all the adults, but I knew it wasn't what I wanted for the future. The schools *were* good. The teachers really liked me, and I did very well. . . . Between the eighth and ninth grades I came to UCLA for six weeks in the summer. It was called the MENTE program—Migrants Engaged in New Themes of Education—I came here and loved the campus. It was like dreamland for me. And I made it my goal to come here."

2   The school that designated Lilia a slow learner is two miles from my old neighborhood on South Vermont. She arrived as a child about eight years after

---

Source: Reprinted with permission of The Free Press, a division of Simon & Schuster Adult Publishing Group, from *Lives on the Boundary: The Struggles and Achievements of America's Underprepared* by Mike Rose. Copyright © 1989 by Mike Rose.

I left as an adult. The next generation. We make our acquaintance in an office of the University of California at Los Angeles. Lilia is participating in an unusual educational experiment, one developed by some coworkers of mine at UCLA Writing Programs. Lilia and fifteen other freshmen—all of whom started UCLA in remedial writing courses themselves—are tutoring low-achieving students in Los Angeles area schools. The tutoring is connected to a special composition class, and Lilia and her partners write papers on their tutorial work and on issues of schooling. Lilia is writing a paper on the academic, social, and psychological effects of being placed in the remedial track. Her teacher suggested she come to see me. I can't stop asking her questions about growing up in South L.A.

3   Desire gets confused on South Vermont. There were times when I wanted so much to be other than what I was, to walk through the magical gate of a television cottage. But, strange blessing, we can never really free ourselves from the mood of early neighborhoods, from our first stories, from the original tales of hope and despair. There are basic truths there about the vulnerability and power of coming to know, about the way the world invites and denies language. This is what lies at the base of education—to be tapped or sealed over or distorted, by others, by us. Lilia says the tutoring makes her feel good. "Sometimes I feel that because I know their language, I can communicate. I see these kids and I see myself like I was in elementary school." Lilia stops. She asks me what it was like in South L.A. when *I* was there, when I was going to school. Not much different then, I say. Not as tough probably. She asks me if I've ever gone back. I tell her I did, just recently. . . .

4   The place was desolate. The power plant was still standing, smaller than I remembered it, surrounded now by barbed wire. All the storefront businesses were covered with iron grating; about half of them, maybe more, were shut down. The ones that were open had the grating pulled back the width of the door, no further. The hair and nails shop was closed. The Stranger's Rest Baptist Church was closed. Teddy's Rough Riders—an American Legion post—was battered and closed. The Huston Mortuary looked closed. My house had been stuccoed over, a dark dirty tan with holes in the walls. 9116 South Vermont. My old neighborhood was a blighted island in the slum. Poverty had gutted it, and sealed the merchants' doors. "It's worse now," I tell Lilia, "much worse. No one comes. No one goes." At Ninety-sixth Street two men were sitting on the curb outside a minimart. East on Ninety-first a girl sat in the shadows of steps tucked back from the pavement. At Eighty-ninth Street, a woman walked diagonally in front of me, moving unsteadily in a tight dress, working the floured paper off an X-L-NT burrito. As I drove back by my house, I saw a little boy playing with two cans in the dirt. Imagination's delivery. Fantasy in cylinders and tin.

5   Lilia is telling me about one of her fellow classmates who had also been designated a slow learner. "She said it was awful. She had no friends because everyone called her dumb, and no one wanted to be seen with a dumb person. . . . Because they were calling her dumb, she started to believe she was really dumb. And with myself and my brother, it was the same thing. When we were

in those courses we thought very low of ourselves. We sort of created a little world of our own where only we existed. We became really shy."

6   What we define as intelligence, what we set out to measure and identify with a number, is both in us and out of us. We have been socialized to think of intelligence as internal, fixed, genetically coded. There is, of course, a neurophysiology to intelligence, but there's a feeling to it as well, and a culture. In moving from one school to another—another setting, another set of social definitions—Lilia was transformed from dumb to normal. And then, with six powerful weeks as a child on a university campus—"opening new horizons for me, scary, but showing me what was out there"—she began to see herself in a different way, tentatively, cautiously. Lilia began the transition to smart, to high school honors classes, to UCLA. She could go back, then, to the schools, to the place where, as she says, she "knows the language."

7   The promise of community and equality is at the center of our most prized national document, yet we're shaped by harsh forces to see difference and to base judgment on it. The language Lilia can speak to the students in the schools is the language of intersection, of crossed boundaries. It is a rich language, filled with uncertainty. Having crossed boundaries, you sometimes can't articulate what you know, or what you know seems strange. What is required, then, is for Lilia and her students to lean back against their desks, grip the firm wood, and talk about what they hear and see, looking straight ahead, looking skyward. What are the gaps and discordances in the terrain? What mix of sounds—eerie and compelling—issues from the hillside? Sitting with Lilia, our lives playing off each other, I realize that, finally, this is why the current perception of educational need is so limited: It substitutes terror for awe. But it is not terror that fosters learning, it is hope, everyday heroics, the power of the common play of the human mind.

Reading Responses

1. How does Lilia tell her story? How does Mike Rose tell his story? What is the purpose of each account?
2. Who are the various audiences identified and addressed in this selection? Based on Rose's approach, what would you conclude that these audiences might want, need, or expect?
3. What is Rose's main point? How does he use Lilia's story and his own to support and explain that point?

Writing Activities

1. Write a brief summary of Lilia's story. Next, write a brief summary of Mike Rose's story. Be certain that each summary includes the main impression conveyed by the story.

2. Write your own account of crossing boundaries. Use your experiences and observations to illustrate a boundary that you have crossed and the consequences of that crossing.
3. Write an essay that considers Rose's concluding sentence about what "fosters learning." What is his assertion or claim? In what ways do you agree or disagree with him?

Community Links

Read Ehrenreich's "Evaluation" (pp. 208–212), which presents her conclusions about her experiences crossing boundaries to work in low-wage jobs. Both Ehrenreich and Rose use their own experiences and observations to support their broader conclusions about the academic or work community. Briefly analyze how this strategy works, using examples from both essays.

KEEPING CLOSE TO HOME: CLASS AND EDUCATION

bell hooks

◆

In this essay from Talking Back: thinking feminist, thinking black, *bell hooks examines the effect of her college education on her relationships with her family and her home community in Kentucky. Her essay raises issues of gender, race, and class, themes that she has examined in other books written during her career as a faculty member at several academic institutions, including Yale University, Oberlin College, and City College of New York.*

1   We are both awake in the almost dark of 5 a.m. Everyone else is sound asleep. Mama asks the usual questions. Telling me to look around, make sure I have everything, scolding me because I am uncertain about the actual time the bus arrives. By 5:30 we are waiting outside the closed station. Alone together, we have a chance to really talk. Mama begins. Angry with her children, especially the ones who whisper behind her back, she says bitterly, "Your childhood could not have been that bad. You were fed and clothed. You did not have to do without—that's more than a lot of folks have and I just can't stand the way y'all go on." The hurt in her voice saddens me. I have always wanted to protect mama from hurt, to ease her burdens. Now I am part of what troubles. Confronting me, she says accusingly, "It's not just the other children. You talk too much about the past. You don't just listen." And I do talk. Worse, I write about it.

2   Mama has always come to each of her children seeking different responses. With me she expresses the disappointment, hurt, and anger of betrayal: anger

that her children are so critical, that we can't even have the sense to like the presents she sends. She says, "From now on there will be no presents. I'll just stick some money in a little envelope the way the rest of you do. Nobody wants criticism. Everybody can criticize me but I am supposed to say nothing." When I try to talk, my voice sounds like a twelve year old. When I try to talk, she speaks louder, interrupting me, even though she has said repeatedly, "Explain it to me, this talk about the past." I struggle to return to my thirty-five year old self so that she will know by the sound of my voice that we are two women talking together. It is only when I state firmly in my very adult voice, "Mama, you are not listening," that she becomes quiet. She waits. Now that I have her attention, I fear that my explanations will be lame, inadequate. "Mama," I begin, "people usually go to therapy because they feel hurt inside, because they have pain that will not stop, like a wound that continually breaks open, that does not heal. And often these hurts, that pain has to do with things that have happened in the past, sometimes in childhood, often in child-hood, or things that we believe happened." She wants to know, "What hurts, what hurts are you talking about?" "Mom, I can't answer that. I can't speak for all of us, the hurts are different for everybody. But the point is you try to make the hurt better, to heal it, by understanding how it came to be. And I know you feel mad when we say something happened or hurt that you don't remember being that way, but the past isn't like that, we don't have the same memory of it. We remember things differently. You know that. And sometimes folk feel hurt about stuff and you just don't know or didn't realize it, and they need to talk about it. Surely you understand the need to talk about it."

3 Our conversation is interrupted by the sight of my uncle walking across the park toward us. We stop to watch him. He is on his way to work dressed in a familiar blue suit. They look alike, these two who rarely discuss the past. This interruption makes me think about life in a small town. You always see some-one you know. Interruptions, intrusions are part of daily life. Privacy is difficult to maintain. We leave our private space in the car to greet him. After the hug and kiss he has given me every year since I was born, they talk about the day's funerals. In the distance the bus approaches. He walks away knowing that they will see each other later. Just before I board the bus I turn, staring into my mother's face. I am momentarily back in time, seeing myself eighteen years ago, at this same bus stop, staring into my mother's face, continually turning back, waving farewell as I returned to college—that experience which first took me away from our town, from family. Departing was as painful then as it is now. Each movement away makes return harder. Each separation intensifies distance, both physical and emotional.

4 To a southern black girl from a working-class background who had never been on a city bus, who had never stepped on an escalator, who had never trav-elled by plane, leaving the comfortable confines of a small town Kentucky life to attend Stanford University was not just frightening; it was utterly painful. My parents had not been delighted that I had been accepted and adamantly opposed my going so far from home. At the time, I did not see their opposi-tion as an expression of their fear that they would lose me forever. Like many working-class folks, they feared what college education might do to their

children's minds even as they unenthusiastically acknowledged its importance. They did not understand why I could not attend a college nearby, an all-black college. To them, any college would do. I would graduate, become a school teacher, make a decent living and a good marriage. And even though they reluctantly and skeptically supported my educational endeavors, they also subjected them to constant harsh and bitter critique. It is difficult for me to talk about my parents and their impact on me because they have always felt wary, ambivalent, mistrusting of my intellectual aspirations even as they have been caring and supportive. I want to speak about these contradictions because sorting through them, seeking resolution and reconciliation has been important to me both as it affects my development as a writer, my effort to be fully self-realized, and my longing to remain close to the family and community that provided the groundwork for much of my thinking, writing, and being.

5 Studying at Stanford, I began to think seriously about class differences. To be materially underprivileged at a university where most folks (with the exception of workers) are materially privileged provokes such thought. Class differences were boundaries no one wanted to face or talk about. It was easier to downplay them, to act as though we were all from privileged backgrounds, to work around them, to confront them privately in the solitude of one's room, or to pretend that just being chosen to study at such an institution meant that those of us who did not come from privilege were already in transition toward privilege. To not long for such transition marked one as rebellious, as unlikely to succeed. It was a kind of treason not to believe that it was better to be identified with the world of material privilege than with the world of the working class, the poor. No wonder our working-class parents from poor backgrounds feared our entry into such a world, intuiting perhaps that we might learn to be ashamed of where we had come from, that we might never return home, or come back only to lord it over them.

6 Though I hung with students who were supposedly radical and chic, we did not discuss class. I talked to no one about the sources of my shame, how it hurt me to witness the contempt shown the brown-skinned Filipina maids who cleaned our rooms, or later my concern about the $100 a month I paid for a room off-campus which was more than half of what my parents paid for rent. I talked to no one about my efforts to save money, to send a little something home. Yet these class realities separated me from fellow students. We were moving in different directions. I did not intend to forget my class background or alter my class allegiance. And even though I received an education designed to provide me with a bourgeois sensibility, passive acquiescence was not my only option. I knew that I could resist. I could rebel. I could shape the direction and focus of the various forms of knowledge available to me. Even though I sometimes envied and longed for greater material advantages (particularly at vacation times when I would be one of few if any students remaining in the dormitory because there was no money for travel), I did not share the sensibility and values of my peers. That was important—class was not just about money; it was about values which showed and determined behavior. While I often needed more money, I never needed a new set of beliefs and values. For example, I was profoundly shocked and disturbed when peers would

talk about their parents without respect, or would even say that they hated their parents. This was especially troubling to me when it seemed that these parents were caring and concerned. It was often explained to me that such hatred was "healthy and normal." To my white, middle-class California roommate, I explained the way we were taught to value our parents and their care, to understand that they were not obligated to give us care. She would always shake her head, laughing all the while, and say, "Missy, you will learn that it's different here, that we think differently." She was right. Soon, I lived alone, like the one Mormon student who kept to himself as he made a concentrated effort to remain true to his religious beliefs and values. Later in graduate school I found that classmates believed "lower class" people had no beliefs and values. I was silent in such discussions, disgusted by their ignorance.

Carol Stack's anthropological study, *All Our Kin*, was one of the first books I read which confirmed my experiential understanding that within black culture (especially among the working class and poor, particularly in southern states), a value system emerged that was counter-hegemonic, that challenged notions of individualism and private property so important to the maintenance of white-supremacist, capitalist patriarchy. Black folk created in marginal spaces a world of community and collectivity where resources were shared. In the preface to *Feminist Theory: from margin to center*, I talked about how the point of difference, this marginality can be the space for the formation of an oppositional world view. That world view must be articulated, named if it is to provide a sustained blueprint for change. Unfortunately, there has existed no consistent framework for such naming. Consequently both the experience of this difference and documentation of it (when it occurs) gradually loses presence and meaning.

Much of what Stack documented about the "culture of poverty," for example, would not describe interactions among most black poor today irrespective of geographical setting. Since the black people she described did not acknowledge (if they recognized it in theoretical terms) the oppositional value of their world view, apparently seeing it more as a survival strategy determined less by conscious efforts to oppose oppressive race and class biases than by circumstance, they did not attempt to establish a framework to transmit their beliefs and values from generation to generation. When circumstances changed, values altered. Efforts to assimilate the values and beliefs of privileged white people, presented through media like television, undermine and destroy potential structures of opposition.

Increasingly, young black people are encouraged by the dominant culture (and by those black people who internalize the values of this hegemony) to believe that assimilation is the only possible way to survive, to succeed. Without the framework of an organized civil rights or black resistance struggle, individual and collective efforts at black liberation that focus on the primacy of self-definition and self-determination often go unrecognized. It is crucial that those among us who resist and rebel, who survive and succeed, speak openly and honestly about our lives and the nature of our personal struggles, the means by which we resolve and reconcile contradictions. This is no easy task. Within the educational institutions where we learn to develop and strengthen our writing and analytical skills, we also learn to think, write, and talk in a manner that shifts attention away from personal experience. Yet if we are to reach our people and all people, if we are to remain connected (especially those of us whose familial backgrounds are poor and working-class), we must understand that the telling of one's personal story provides a meaningful example, a way for folks to identify and connect.

10   Combining personal with critical analysis and theoretical perspectives can engage listeners who might other wise feel estranged, alienated. To speak simply with language that is accessible to as many folks as possible is also important. Speaking about one's personal experience or speaking with simple language is often considered by academics and/or intellectuals (irrespective of their political inclinations) to be a sign of intellectual weakness or even anti-intellectualism. Lately, when I speak, I do not stand in place—reading my paper, making little or no eye contact with audiences—but instead make eye contact, talk extemporaneously, digress, and address the audience directly. I have been told that people assume I am not prepared, that I am anti-intellectual, unprofessional (a concept that has everything to do with class as it determines actions and behavior), or that I am reinforcing the stereotype of black people as non-theoretical and gutsy.

11   Such criticism was raised recently by fellow feminist scholars after a talk I gave at Northwestern University at a conference on "Gender, Culture, Politics" to an audience that was mainly students and academics. I deliberately chose to speak in a very basic way, thinking especially about the few community folks who had come to hear me. Weeks later, Kum-Kum Sangari, a fellow participant who shared with me what was said when I was no longer present, and I engaged in quite rigorous critical dialogue about the way my presentation had been perceived primarily by privileged white female academics. She was concerned that I not mask my knowledge of theory, that I not appear anti-intellectual. Her critique compelled me to articulate concerns that I am often silent about with colleagues. I spoke about class allegiance and revolutionary commitments, explaining that it was disturbing to me that intellectual radicals who speak about transforming society, ending the domination of race, sex, class, cannot break with behavior patterns that reinforce and perpetuate domination, or continue to use as their sole reference point how we might be or are perceived by those who dominate, whether or not we gain their acceptance and approval.

12   This is a primary contradiction which raises the issue of whether or not the academic setting is a place where one can be truly radical or subversive. Concurrently, the use of a language and style of presentation that alienates most folks who are not also academically trained reinforces the notion that the academic world is separate from real life, that everyday world where we constantly adjust our language and behavior to meet diverse needs. The academic setting is separate only when we work to make it so. It is a false dichotomy which suggests that academics and/or intellectuals can only speak to one another, that we cannot hope to speak with the masses. What is true is that we make choices, that we choose our audiences, that we choose voices to hear and voices to silence. If I do not speak in a language that can be understood, then there is little chance for dialogue. This issue of language and behavior is a cen-

tral contradiction all radical intellectuals, particularly those who are members of oppressed groups, must continually confront and work to resolve. One of the clear and present dangers that exists when we move outside our class of origin, our collective ethnic experience, and enter hierarchical institutions which daily reinforce domination by race, sex, and class, is that we gradually assume a mindset similar to those who dominate and oppress, that we lose critical consciousness because it is not reinforced or affirmed by the environment. We must be ever vigilant. It is important that we know who we are speaking to, who we most want to hear us, who we most long to move, motivate, and touch with our words.

13   When I first came to New Haven to teach at Yale, I was truly surprised by the marked class divisions between black folks—students and professors—who identify with Yale and those black folks who work at Yale or in surrounding communities. Style of dress and self-presentation are most often the central markers of one's position. I soon learned that the black folks who spoke on the street were likely to be part of the black community and those who carefully shifted their glance were likely to be associated with Yale. Walking with a black female colleague one day, I spoke to practically every black person in sight (a gesture which reflects my upbringing), an action which disturbed my companion. Since I addressed black folk who were clearly not associated with Yale, she wanted to know whether or not I knew them. That was funny to me. "Of course not," I answered. Yet when I thought about it seriously, I realized that in a deep way, I knew them for they, and not my companion or most of my colleagues at Yale, resemble my family. Later that year, in a black women's support group I started for undergraduates, students from poor backgrounds spoke about the shame they sometimes feel when faced with the reality of their connection to working-class and poor black people. One student confessed that her father is a street person, addicted to drugs, someone who begs from passersby. She, like other Yale students, turns away from street people often, sometimes showing anger or contempt; she hasn't wanted anyone to know that she was related to this kind of person. She struggles with this, wanting to find a way to acknowledge and affirm this reality, to claim this connection. The group asked me and one another what we do to remain connected, to honor the bonds we have with working-class and poor people even as our class experience alters.

14   Maintaining connections with family and community across class boundaries demands more than just summary recall of where one's roots are, where one comes from. It requires knowing, naming, and being ever-mindful of those aspects of one's past that have enabled and do enable one's self-development in the present, that sustain and support, that enrich. One must also honestly confront barriers that do exist, aspects of that past that do diminish. My parents' ambivalence about my love for reading led to intense conflict. They (especially my mother) would work to ensure that I had access to books, but would threaten to burn the books or throw them away if I did not conform to other expectations. Or they would insist that reading too much would drive me insane. Their ambivalence nurtured in me a like uncertainty about the value and significance of intellectual endeavor which took years for me to

unlearn. While this aspect of our class reality was one that wounded and diminished, their vigilant insistence that being smart did not make me a "better" or "superior" person (which often got on my nerves because I think I wanted to have that sense that it did indeed set me apart, make me better) made a profound impression. From them I learned to value and respect various skills and talents folk might have, not just to value people who read books and talk about ideas. They and my grandparents might say about somebody, "Now he don't read nor write a lick, but he can tell a story," or as my grandmother would say, "call out the hell in words."

15   Empty romanticization of poor or working-class backgrounds undermines the possibility of true connection. Such connection is based on understanding difference in experience and perspective and working to mediate and negotiate these terrains. Language is a crucial issue for folk whose movement outside the boundaries of poor and working-class backgrounds changes the nature and direction of their speech. Coming to Stanford with my own version of a Kentucky accent, which I think of always as a strong sound quite different from Tennessee or Georgia speech, I learned to speak differently while maintaining the speech of my region, the sound of my family and community. This was of course much easier to keep up when I returned home to stay often. In recent years, I have endeavored to use various speaking styles in the classroom as a teacher and find it disconcerts those who feel that the use of a particular patois excludes them as listeners, even if there is translation into the usual, acceptable mode of speech. Learning to listen to different voices, hearing different speech challenges the notion that we must all assimilate—share a single, similar talk—in educational institutions. Language reflects the culture from which we emerge. To deny ourselves daily use of speech patterns that are common and familiar, that embody the unique and distinctive aspect of our self is one of the ways we become estranged and alienated from our past. It is important for us to have as many languages on hand as we can know or learn. It is important for those of us who are black, who speak in particular patois as well as standard English to express ourselves in both ways.

16   Often I tell students from poor and working-class backgrounds that if you believe what you have learned and are learning in schools and universities separates you from your past, this is precisely what will happen. It is important to stand firm in the conviction that nothing can truly separate us from our pasts when we nurture and cherish that connection. An important strategy for maintaining contact is ongoing acknowledgement of the primacy of one's past, of one's background, affirming the reality that such bonds are not severed automatically solely because one enters a new environment or moves toward a different class experience.

17   Again, I do not wish to romanticize this effort, to dismiss the reality of conflict and contradiction. During my time at Stanford, I did go through a period of more than a year when I did not return home. That period was one where I felt that it was simply too difficult to mesh my profoundly disparate realities. Critical reflection about the choice I was making, particularly about why I felt a choice had to be made, pulled me through this difficult time. Luckily I recognized that the insistence on choosing between the world of

family and community and the new world of privileged white people and privileged ways of knowing was imposed upon me by the outside. It is as though a mythical contract had been signed somewhere which demanded of us black folks that once we entered these spheres we would immediately give up all vestiges of our underprivileged past. It was my responsibility to formulate a way of being that would allow me to participate fully in my new environment while integrating and maintaining aspects of the old.

18   One of the most tragic manifestations of the pressure black people feel to assimilate is expressed in the internalization of racist perspectives. I was shocked and saddened when I first heard black professors at Stanford downgrade and express contempt for black students, expecting us to do poorly, refusing to establish nurturing bonds. At every university I have attended as a student or worked at as a teacher, I have heard similar attitudes expressed with little or no understanding of factors that might prevent brilliant black students from performing to their full capability. Within universities, there are few educational and social spaces where students who wish to affirm positive ties to ethnicity—to blackness, to working-class backgrounds—can receive affirmation and support. Ideologically, the message is clear—assimilation is the way to gain acceptance and approval from those in power.

19   Many white people enthusiastically supported Richard Rodriguez's vehement contention in his autobiography, *Hunger of Memory,* that attempts to maintain ties with his Chicano background impeded his progress, that he had to sever ties with community and kin to succeed at Stanford and in the larger world, that family language, in his case Spanish, had to be made secondary or discarded. If the terms of success as defined by the standards of ruling groups within white-supremacist, capitalist patriarchy are the only standards that exist, then assimilation is indeed necessary. But they are not. Even in the face of powerful structures of domination, it remains possible for each of us, especially those of us who are members of oppressed and/or exploited groups as well as those radical visionaries who may have race, class, and sex privilege, to define and determine alternative standards, to decide on the nature and extent of compromise. Standards by which one's success is measured, whether student or professor, are quite different for those of us who wish to resist reinforcing the domination of race, sex, and class, who work to maintain and strengthen our ties with the oppressed, with those who lack material privilege, with our families who are poor and working-class.

20   When I wrote my first book, *Ain't I A Woman: black women and feminism,* the issue of class and its relationship to who one's reading audience might be came up for me around my decision not to use footnotes, for which I have been sharply criticized. I told people that my concern was that footnotes set class boundaries for readers, determining who a book is for. I was shocked that many academic folks scoffed at this idea. I shared that I went into working-class black communities as well as talked with family and friends to survey whether or not they ever read books with footnotes and found that they did not. A few did not know what they were, but most folks saw them as indicating that a book was for college-educated people. These responses influenced my decision. When some of my more radical, college-educated friends freaked

out about the absence of footnotes, I seriously questioned how we could ever imagine revolutionary transformation of society if such a small shift in direction could be viewed as threatening. Of course, many folks warned that the absence of footnotes would make the work less credible in academic circles. This information also highlighted the way in which class informs our choices. Certainly I did feel that choosing to use simple language, absence of footnotes, etc. would mean I was jeopardizing the possibility of being taken seriously in academic circles but then this was a political matter and a political decision. It utterly delights me that this has proven not to be the case and that the book is read by many academics as well as by people who are not college-educated.

21   Always our first response when we are motivated to conform or compromise within structures that reinforce domination must be to engage in critical reflection. Only by challenging ourselves to push against oppressive boundaries do we make the radical alternative possible, expanding the realm and scope of critical inquiry. Unless we share radical strategies, ways of rethinking and revisioning with students, with kin and community, with a larger audience, we risk perpetuating the stereotype that we succeed because we are the exception, different from the rest of our people. Since I left home and entered college, I am often asked, usually by white people, if my sisters and brothers are also high achievers. At the root of this question is the longing for reinforcement of the belief in "the exception" which enables race, sex, and class biases to remain intact. I am careful to separate what it means to be exceptional from a notion of "the exception."

22   Frequently I hear smart black folks, from poor and working-class backgrounds, stressing their frustration that at times family and community do not recognize that they are exceptional. Absence of positive affirmation clearly diminishes the longing to excel in academic endeavors. Yet it is important to distinguish between the absence of basic positive affirmation and the longing for continued reinforcement that we are special. Usually liberal white folks will willingly offer continual reinforcement of us as exceptions—as special. This can be both patronizing and very seductive. Since we often work in situations where we are isolated from other black folks, we can easily begin to feel that encouragement from white people is the primary or only source of support and recognition. Given the internalization of racism, it is easy to view this support as more validating and legitimizing than similar support from black people. Still, nothing takes the place of being valued and appreciated by one's own, by one's family and community. We share a mutual and reciprocal responsibility for affirming one another's successes. Sometimes we have to talk to our folks about the fact that we need their ongoing support and affirmation, that it is unique and special to us. In some cases we may never receive desired recognition and acknowledgement of specific achievements from kin. Rather than seeing this as a basis for estrangement, for severing connection, it is useful to explore other sources of nourishment and support.

23   I do not know that my mother's mother ever acknowledged my college education except to ask me once, "How can you live so far away from your people?" Yet she gave me sources of affirmation and nourishment, sharing the

legacy of her quilt-making, of family history, of her incredible way with words. Recently, when our father retired after more than thirty years of work as a janitor, I wanted to pay tribute to this experience, to identify links between his work and my own as writer and teacher. Reflecting on our family past, I recalled ways he had been an impressive example of diligence and hard work, approaching tasks with a seriousness of concentration I work to mirror and develop, with a discipline I struggle to maintain. Sharing these thoughts with him keeps us connected, nurtures our respect for each other, maintaining a space, however large or small, where we can talk.

24 Open, honest communication is the most important way we maintain relationships with kin and community as our class experience and backgrounds change. It is as vital as the sharing of resources. Often financial assistance is given in circumstances where there is no meaningful contact. However helpful, this can also be an expression of estrangement and alienation. Communication between black folks from various experiences of material privilege was much easier when we were all in segregated communities sharing common experiences in relation to social institutions. Without this grounding, we must work to maintain ties, connection. We must assume greater responsibility for making and maintaining contact, connections that can shape our intellectual visions and inform our radical commitments.

25 The most powerful resource any of us can have as we study and teach in university settings is full understanding and appreciation of the richness, beauty, and primacy of our familial and community backgrounds. Maintaining awareness of class differences, nurturing ties with the poor and working-class people who are our most intimate kin, our comrades in struggle, transforms and enriches our intellectual experience. Education as the practice of freedom becomes not a force which fragments or separates, but one that brings us closer, expanding our definitions of home and community.

Reading Responses

1. Which expectations of the academic community does hooks challenge or question? Why doesn't she agree with these expectations?
2. What techniques does hooks use in her essay to help readers understand the differences between home and school?
3. How does hooks suggest that students can stay connected with their past?

Writing Activities

1. Make a brief outline of hooks's essay, noting the topics covered in paragraphs or paragraph clusters. Then briefly summarize the main point of her essay.

2. Write a personal essay about the differences between your academic community and your family or home community. Use both contrasting anecdotes and your own analysis or explanation to identify and interpret these differences.
3. Write an essay directed to new or prospective students with backgrounds similar to your own. Based on your experience coming to college, advise them about ways to cope with the changes they are likely to encounter.

Community Links

Hooks considers ways to sustain connections between home and the academic community. Consider her points in relation to Helgesen's "When Life Itself Becomes Incredibly Complex" (pp. 256–262) or Nelson's "A Beginning" (pp. 386–389), both concerned with ways to balance the demands of the work or the public community with personal needs.

Community Perspectives and Issues

THE QUEST FOR COMMUNITY IN HIGHER EDUCATION

Parker J. Palmer

◆

Parker Palmer's essay is the afterword that concludes Creating Campus Community: In Search of Ernest Boyer's Legacy. *This book gathers eight essays, all honoring Ernest Boyer's contributions to community in higher education. During his sixteen years as president of The Carnegie Foundation for the Advancement of Teaching, Boyer encouraged colleges and universities to build or renew a sense of community on campus. Palmer's essay brings closure to the book's theme, honoring Boyer's principles and showing how individuals can contribute to and benefit from a sense of academic community.*

1 Academic culture is a curious and conflicted thing. On the one hand, it holds out the allure and occasionally the reality of being a "community of scholars"—colleagues with common roots in the depths of the intellectual tradition working together to seek new insights into the world's wonders. On the other hand, it is a culture infamous for fragmentation, isolation, and competitive individualism—a culture in which community sometimes feels harder to come by than in any other institution on the face of the earth.

2 This cultural contradiction is vexing, partly because people feel resentful when they are promised one thing and given something quite different. When the academy fails to achieve sustained community in even minimal form, its capacity to pursue its core mission is weakened.

3 That mission can be summed up in three words: *knowing, teaching,* and *learning.* And all three of those words name enterprises that are essentially communal. This claim seems simple and straightforward, but the truth is that we tacitly understand the academy's three-fold mission in highly individualistic terms. Knowing is often regarded as an act of personal genius, something done by very smart people working largely in isolation. Teaching and learning are often regarded as a one-on-one exchange of information, a transfer of knowledge from a teacher who is quite smart to a student who is not—at least not yet!

4 However, when knowing, teaching, and learning are understood and pursued in these ways, we not only distort intellectual history but we fail to develop genuine intellectual capacity in the next generation. Knowing has always been and always will be a dialectic between individual insight and shared communal understandings—a back-and-forth of dissent and consent around what

33

we see and what it means, without which our sight would be even dimmer than it is. Teaching and learning have always been and always will be a complex dance between teachers, students, and subjects, a communal engagement with each other and with the world without which authentic education cannot happen.

5   Community in higher education is not optional but essential if we wish to pursue our mission with full integrity. In service of that mission, I want to explore the quest for community on three levels of academic life: community across the entire staff of an institution; community in the classroom and other teaching and learning venues; and community between the academy and the world around it.

Community Across the Staff

6   I spent my undergraduate years at Carleton College in Minnesota, and among the remarkable teachers I had on that campus were Dacie and Roy Moses. Neither of them had a Ph.D., and I am not even sure whether either of them had graduated from high school. Dacie, who was in her sixties when I was a student, worked behind the desk in the college library. Roy had been a skilled carpenter in his younger years, but early on, while he was helping a neighbor build a barn, a huge beam had fallen on him, leaving Roy permanently disabled and largely homebound.

7   The Moses' house on the edge of campus was a home-away-from-home for many Carleton undergraduates, including me. If you were having trouble with a professor, trouble with romance, trouble with your parents, or—most likely—trouble with yourself, stopping by Dacie's and Roy's for a round of cribbage, coffee, cookies, and conversation was the best therapy you could get.

8   In what sense were Dacie and Roy my teachers? What I learned from them was the very incarnation of the abstract ideas we were studying in our liberal arts courses. I learned that generosity is stronger than arrogance. I learned about the dignity of common work. I learned about the value of honest relationships. I learned about the transcendence of the human spirit.

9   There are many things that make me proud of my alma mater and grateful to her. But nothing makes me prouder or more grateful than the fact that, after Roy and Dacie died, the college purchased their home and turned it into a permanent house of hospitality, honoring the fact that—rightly understood—everyone who works at a college is a teacher.

10   The notion that "we are all teachers" is not romanticism. Instead, it is a simple reality related to what educational researchers have called the hidden curriculum. What students learn in college comes not only—and certainly not principally—from lectures, readings, and discussions, that is, from the content of the formal curriculum. It comes from the way individual and collective life is lived on a campus—from the way the people employed there do their work, conduct their relationships, make their choices, and otherwise reveal their true values, which may be quite at odds with the values espoused in the classroom.

11   We should celebrate the congruities we find between academic rhetoric and practice, and we should be conscious and critical of the many incon-

gruities. It is cause for celebration when we teach courses on ecological problems *and* have a buildings and grounds crew that takes leadership in a campus recycling program; when we exhort students to become good citizens *and* have a faculty that conducts its decision making in a civil manner; when we advocate good customer relations in business courses *and* have a registrar's staff that deals understandingly with students when they are trying to enroll in overcrowded courses.

12 But when we find incongruities at points such as these, we can be sure of one thing: students are learning at least as much from what we do as from what we say. We need to work hard on aligning the hidden curriculum with our educational purposes—as hard as we work on our formal course offerings. Above all, we must work to bring all staff into a shared sense of community and mission, for only so will people be willing to embrace the reality that we are all teachers.

13 This, in turn, requires a realistic understanding of what community among staff might mean. Every educational institution has gaps, large and small, between administrative, academic, student services, and professional support staff—gaps in power, status, income, job security. Although some of these gaps can and should be narrowed or closed, others will always be with us. Community among staff cannot have a utopian meaning that flies in the face of reality, or the rhetoric will discourage rather than empower people.

14 So what might community mean in a real-life situation? I believe that certain experiential markers allow individuals to feel that they are in community with others despite any gaps that might exist. Here are five such markers that are within our reach, if we choose to reach for them:

1. I feel in community when I believe that I play a meaningful role in a shared educational mission, and others see me doing so. The first part—belief—is my own responsibility, and it often requires inner work to embrace the meaning of my own role. The second part is the responsibility of others: leaders who articulate the shared mission, staff development activities that assume a shared mission, and colleagues in other departments who act as if we had a shared mission.

2. I feel in community when I am affirmed for the work I do on behalf of the shared mission if it contributes to that mission. If what I do falls short, I am told about that as well and offered help to improve my performance. That is, I am not ignored in either the successes or the failures of the work I do.

3. I feel in community when I know that I can take creative risks in my work and sometimes fail—and still be supported. I understand that not any old risk will do. The risks must be worth taking to advance the shared mission, and the failures must be such that I can learn from them. But within those limits, the safety to fail in a good cause and still be supported is one of the marks that I am in community.

4. I feel in community when I am trusted with basic information about important issues relating to the shared mission. For example, instead of the silence that often surrounds budgetary cutbacks or realignments, I am told that decisions need to be made and why—and I am given adequate information

about when, how, by whom, and on what basis they are being made. Nothing undercuts my sense of community more quickly than being kept in the dark about basic issues until "the day after."

5. I feel in community when I have a chance to voice my opinion on issues relating to the shared mission or my part of it—and I am given meaningful responses to what I have to say. I do not need to have my way all the time or even most of the time, but I need to know that my voice is wanted and heard.

15   In sum, I feel that I am in community when I feel seen, known, and respected—when I am taken seriously and appreciated, not just for the function I perform but for who I am as a person. Community is about power *and* rewards *and* relationships *and* meaning—and there will always be imbalances among us in those regards. But we can go a long way toward community by understanding that imbalances in one area can often be corrected, or at least relieved, by rebalancing in another.

16   There are many practical steps we can take to help community happen. This is not the place to spell them out in great detail, but here are three possibilities that can be realized either on small college campuses or within human-scale units of a large university:

- People often spend decades working alongside each other without knowing much, if anything, about who the others are, how they are, why they are here, or where they are going. The absolute minimum in building community is to learn at least a little bit about each other's stories. We could begin small staff or committee meetings with a simple autobiographical question that each person has a few minutes to answer aloud: "Tell us about an important older person in your life." "Tell us about the first dollar you ever made." "Tell us about the best vacation you ever took." Questions like these are nonthreatening and can be answered on any level of vulnerability a person chooses. But the cumulative effect of asking and answering them over a period of months and years is the growth of interpersonal understanding and a deepening sense of community.
- Though much of our work in institutions must be done through a division of labor, with different people pursuing different specializations, it is possible from time to time to find work that can be shared for the sake of community building. In a school where I once worked, there was an annual mass mailing to alumni and other constituents to solicit financial support. The mailing could have been done by a machine or by an outside "service provider." Instead, we gathered the entire staff once a year, for the better part of a day, and together we folded papers and stuffed envelopes, sang and laughed and told tales, and enjoyed each other's company.
- Every institution could profit from examining its own processes of information sharing and decision making through the lens of exclusion and

inclusion. In many colleges and universities, for example, the proportion of adjunct faculty has increased dramatically over the past decade. But during that same decade, information sharing and decision making has proceeded apace, as if all the faculty were full-time, either tenured or on a tenure track. The good that would come from including adjunct faculty as trust holders of the institution cannot be overestimated—and its impact would be felt not only in improved morale but in teaching effectiveness as well.

Community in Teaching and Learning

17 Closely examined, the phrase "community in teaching and learning" is redundant; without community, there can be no teaching or learning worthy of the name. But it is a redundancy worth uttering because teaching and learning are so often reduced to a one-to-one exchange of information in which "community" is regarded as neither achievable nor desirable. Students are gathered in one place, called the classroom, not for the sake of community but merely to make it unnecessary for the professor to deliver the information more than once.

18 By now we have more than enough research (to say nothing of personal experience) to know that the fastest and deepest learning happens when there is a dynamic community of connections between teacher and student and subject. The student who feels related to a subject is motivated to do the hard work called learning. That relationship is often mediated by a professor to whom the student feels connected in the first place and strengthened by building relations with other students who are engaged in the process.

19 As I argue at length in my book *The Courage to Teach* (1998), the danger in insisting on making community a key component of teaching and learning is that people will try too quickly to translate community into a technique, for example, collaborative learning. But good teaching can never be reduced to technique. If you want to prove the point, simply collect a dozen student stories of good teachers they have had and notice how seldom technique is mentioned—and how, when it is mentioned, there is great variation among the techniques that good teachers use.

20 To say that community is key to teaching and learning and then translate that into small circles of students engaged in analyzing case studies or solving problems is to diminish the possibilities inherent in the idea and to marginalize faculty whose disciplines or personal gifts do not lend themselves to this approach.

21 We need a more capacious view of what community in teaching and learning might mean, which is why I have found myself talking less about *community*—a word that is so easily reified—and more about *a capacity for connectedness*. If we could ask ourselves critical questions about our own capacity for connectedness and our strategies for developing that capacity in our students, we might discover more and more ways to create community in the classroom without confining the concept to its most conventional forms.

22   As an acid test of my point, let me take the much-maligned pedagogy called lecturing, which is often criticized these days as tragically anticommunal, little more than the egocentric performance of a "sage on the stage," as contrasted with the community-building mentoring of a "guide by the side." That caricature began to fall apart for me as I thought back over my own education, which was graced, from time to time, by a lecturer who created a palpable and powerful sense of community in session after session after session.

23   How can a lecture course create community when, for fifty minutes, the classroom is dominated by one voice? The answer, of course, involves the motivations of the lecturer, what he or she is saying, and the ends he or she intends to serve. A lecture that emerges from "a capacity for connectedness" and evokes that same capacity in the listener has certain characteristics that distinguish it quite clearly from a lecture that cuts the connections off.

24   The latter is exemplified by the lecturer who tells you what the right questions are and gives you all the right answers, asking only your assent. But when a lecturer generates new questions right before your eyes, giving you a glimpse of where questions come from, then wrestles with those questions in open and vulnerable ways, a sense of connectedness is created among the listeners, who find themselves engaged in their own inner dialogue.

25   Similarly, when a lecturer simply rehearses "the facts of the matter" in a given field of study, expecting the listeners to commit them to memory, connectedness is shut down. But when a lecturer portrays the human drama from which those facts were generated—when we learn not just the content of Marx's ideas but the personal and social dynamics that animated his mind—we are connected with the lecturer, the subject, and one another in surprising ways.

26   The communal consequences of a good lecture are much like those of good theater. When you attend a skillful production of a great drama, you are not a passive member of the audience. Far from it. You are deeply engaged in body, mind, and spirit with what is happening on stage. You need not be a member of the cast to be a participant in that community of meaning, for your own life is being evoked by the words of the playwright and the interpretations of the actors.

27   My insistence that a variety of teaching techniques have the potential to help create community should not be taken as a license to teach however one will. It should give us pause to note that the practice of lecturing is much more widespread in the academy than the practice of creating community through lecturing! There is a litmus test here, and it is a rigorous one. Does my pedagogy come from a place of connectedness in me so it can evoke in my students those connections that make learning possible? Or am I using my pedagogy in a way that distances me from my subject and sets me apart from my students, thus diminishing the chances that my classroom will become a place of live encounter?

28   If we could ask those questions openly and answer them honestly, we would take a meaningful step toward creating more community among teachers and students at the heart of academic life—without reducing community to one size that fails to fit all.

Community with the World

From its very inception, higher education has had an uneasy, even hostile, relation to the world around it; we tend to hold academic values in ways that set us apart. In fact, we sometimes hold our values as weapons against the world—a tendency driven deep into our institutional DNA.

Here is how the Columbia Accountability Study (1995) characterizes the evolutionary starting point of the modern university:

> Since their medieval origins, universities have claimed special status, not as a privilege but as an essential prerequisite to carrying out their mission. Universities arose from non-institutional gatherings of scholars. A great teacher would attract a following, often from faraway places. Soon the out-of-towners found themselves in need of protection, and so they banded together in guilds to obtain immunities from local interference, service obligations, and taxation [Graham, Lyman, and Trow, p. 5].

Do we still need protection today, so many centuries later? I do not want to minimize the dangers of external assaults on academic freedom (though I agree with the wag who said that academic freedom in recent decades has meant little more than the freedom to be academic). But the protection we most need today is not from the outside world but from ourselves: from our own tendencies toward arrogance and isolation, from our own self-protective and self-defeating insularity, from our many ways of widening rather than closing the gap between the academy and the world around us.

We can hold our values in ways that connect us creatively with the world rather than set us apart. We can reach out for partnerships with others, and when we do, we may find that our values are more widely shared than we imagine.

"The world" is a very large place, so I need to be selective in illustrating the kinds of partnerships I have in mind. I will offer just one example as I bring this afterword to a close: the story of Princeton Project 55. It is a story that is not as well known as it deserves to be and is instructive on at least two fronts: it gives us a model of creating community between the academy and world, and it tells us something about transforming academic politics in order to get a job done.

As they approached their fortieth reunion, the Class of 1955 at Princeton University decided to give their alma mater an unusual gift. Instead of a bell tower or a meditation garden or a major contribution to the endowment, they offered their influence and expertise in building a bridge between the university and the world—a bridge that would allow new generations of Princeton students to link their education with their emerging vocations and with a wide range of societal concerns.

The influence and expertise of the Class of '55 is considerable. Among their number are some who are quite visible in American public life, others who are not known publicly but who hold positions of real power, and still others whose lives have been quietly devoted to high purposes. Not every college could claim so many names in the first or second categories, perhaps, but every college has among its alumni countless people who know and serve the world well.

36 For several years prior to their fortieth reunion, members of the Class of '55 worked to generate both money for this project and, more important, administrative and faculty commitment to a partnership between the university and its alumni in the service of Princeton students. Using their connections, class members began to create internships and service-learning opportunities for undergraduates, and the faculty and administration began to explore the implications of such a program for finances, the academic calendar, course credit, curriculum, and pedagogy.

37 What ensued is impressive by any measure. In 1990, Princeton Project 55 launched its first initiative, with fourteen summer interns and eight year-long fellows being placed in significant positions with public interest organizations. Since that time, Project 55 has placed almost seven hundred students or recent graduates as interns and fellows in twenty cities around the country, while leveraging nearly $6 million in stipends and salaries for these students. The leaders of Project 55 estimate that these students, through their work with public interest organizations, have touched the lives of some five million Americans. (Supporting documents and additional information on Project 55 can be found on the Web at http://www.project55.org/Index.html.)

38 These data are impressive. But even more impressive to me is that, from the outset, the Class of '55 started using its authority in the life of the university to open a new dialogue about curriculum and pedagogy—about community at the heart of academic life.

39 In 1995, the group—which had by then expanded to include alumni from every decade since the fifties—issued a discussion paper titled "Princeton University in the 21st Century: Paths to More Effective Undergraduate Education." In the preface, the writers announce their intentions in words both substantive and bold, words of a sort not often uttered by alumni to their alma mater:

> This paper makes the case for a new approach to undergraduate education at Princeton, an approach that takes account of research that:
>
> • Increasingly illuminates how individuals learn most effectively;
> • Reflects a growing consensus on what students need to know to function more effectively as individuals, citizens, and workers; and
> • Suggests the curricular and pedagogical approaches most responsive to new knowledge and new needs.
>
> It is time for even the greatest of our institutions of higher education and research to think in different ways. As they do so, the first requirement will be for clarity about, and a shared definition of, basic institutional purposes. So that readers will understand our perspectives in what follows, we note our belief that Princeton's purposes should be:

- Nurturing (not merely "teaching") reflective, caring, able citizens;
- Discovering important knowledge and truths; and
- Serving society's civic, economic, and social needs.

Secondly, we intend this paper to be a strong argument for experiential education at Princeton. The contemporary definition of experiential education is:

> Learning activities that engage the learner in the phenomenon being studied. It assumes (and we cannot stress this point too strongly) that the experience is closely linked to a course, is overseen by a teacher, and is subjected to active, collaborative reflection with peers and others in the classroom and elsewhere on campus.

Exploring all that we might learn from Princeton Project 55 is beyond the scope of this book. But the most important insight the story offers, it seems to me, is this: among all the constituencies of our academic institutions, alumni may be in the best position to help us create more community between the academy and the world and to do so in ways that respect core academic values. They are also the constituency least often called upon for purposes such as these—or for any purpose other than financial support!

Ever since I learned about Princeton Project 55, I have been pondering a critical question: Why do we who care about educational reform either ignore the alumni or wait for them to approach us, as the Class of 1955 approached Princeton? Why do we not reach out to the graduates of our institutions for assistance in building bridges between the academy and the world?

What alumni can bring to this bridge building is not only energy, knowledge, contacts, and financial resources. They also bring a new force to the politics of academic reform, which is much in need of new forces! In very short order, Project 55 broke through the historic resistance of many academic institutions, especially elite institutions, to anything that takes them out of their comfort zone. They were able to do so for at least three reasons: (1) the alumni are a legitimate constituency of the university; (2) their approach to the university was deeply respectful of its integrity and yet appropriately critical of its limitations; and (3) they represent real power in the university's life.

As we pursue our efforts to fulfill the promise of the academy by deepening the communal relations of administration, faculty, staff, and students, let us not forget the needs of the larger world—or our own need for the new perspectives and energies that exchange with that world can bring. Perhaps we have planted the seeds of our own transformation by educating generations of students who left the academy, became good citizens of that larger world, and can now turn around and help us become good citizens, too.

Update, August 2003. Since members of the Class of '55 launched Princeton Project 55 (PP55) in 1989, over 1,000 fellows and interns have been placed in nonprofit organizations, leveraging over $14 million in stipends. Most of the former fellows and interns continue to be actively involved in their communities through careers and/or volunteerism. PP55's discussion paper cited by Palmer led to the Princeton University Community-Based Learning Initiative. Also, PP55 has encourgaged alumni of other colleges and universities to develop public interest efforts. PP55's "The Alumni Network" program, started in 1999, has 19 affiliates so far, including alumni groups from Bucknell, Dartmouth, Franklin & Marshall, Georgetown, Harvard, Syracuse, and Yale. For these and other PP55 programs, visit www.project55.org.

References

Graham, P. A., Lyman, R. W., and Trow, M. (1995). Accountability of colleges and universities: An Essay. In *The Accountability Study*. New York: Columbia University. Available at: http://Info.library.emory.edu/FryeInstitute/Readings/17141501.pdf

Palmer, P. J. (1998). *The courage to teach*. San Francisco: Jossey-Bass.

Reading Responses

1. Why does Palmer believe that building community is a critical matter for academic institutions? What might he want to accomplish?

2. Palmer uses many examples to illustrate his main points. Identify and analyze one or two that seem especially effective to you. For each, consider how the example is woven into the essay, how it supports a broader point, and why it is likely to appeal to readers.

3. While Palmer strongly advocates academic community, he also challenges preconceptions that readers might hold about who is included in an academic community, how community is evidenced in the classroom, and how an academic community might relate to the outside world. Why does Palmer use this approach in his essay? How does this approach contribute to the effectiveness of his essay?

Writing Activities

1. Write a few sentences summarizing each section of Palmer's essay. Combine these section summaries. Next, add an appropriate introduction and conclusion to sum up his overall idea. Revise your combined summary as needed, adding transitions so that the sentences connect clearly and rewording to avoid repetition.

2. Write a brief tribute to an outstanding "teacher" you have known on or off campus during your lifetime as a student. Describe this "teacher," and identify what you have learned from this person as Palmer does in his tribute to Dacie and Roy Moses (paragraphs 6–9).

3. In paragraph 14, Palmer asks "what might community mean in a real-life situation?" and then answers this question by supplying five markers of community and three practical steps that could encourage community (paragraphs 14–16). Write your own "real-life" list from a student viewpoint—either identifying markers of community for students or suggesting steps students on your campus might take to build community.

Community Links

Reread Palmer's five markers of an academic community and his three practical steps to encourage community (paragraphs 14–16). Compare and contrast his lists with those of Ulrich (pp. 221–227), Morse (pp. 374–378), or Covey (pp. 390–395). According to two or more of these writers, what shared principles unite academic, work, and public communities? What differences divide them?

Learning, Understanding, and Meaning

Janet Donald

◆

Many discussions about different college majors simply distinguish the content covered in each field, just as course titles and descriptions do in an academic catalog. In this selection from Learning to Think: Disciplinary Perspectives, *Janet Donald develops an alternate approach. Relying on years of research about teaching, learning, and thinking, she identifies different ways of thinking that are typical of different academic disciplines or fields of study. She considers how academic learning communities can help students develop intellectually by looking more deeply at what the scholars and teachers in a discipline expect of students: what students need to learn, how they are expected to think, and how teachers can help them develop their thinking processes.*

One important part of learning in the university is that students talk to each other and test each other's understanding. You can listen to a lecturer expounding on a subject and you can understand it as it goes along, but when you come to discuss it with someone else or to try to apply it to problems or to an experiment, to work with it, you might find that you do not know it as well as you thought. Having to cope with someone else's uncertainties is a stringent test of your own understanding. —Physics Professor

Thinking processes are the most important thing students would pick up from the course, and yet they are probably the least explicitly examined for or taught. The procedure of learning is a process of constant reexposure and gradual growth in the facility with which one is able to think.
—English Professor

1 The English and physics professors quoted here present us with the ultimate challenge in this book: how to encourage understanding and change the learning context so that it becomes more supportive of higher-order learning. In the previous chapters we have seen ways in which the disciplinary context may aid learning or constrain it. We have seen how higher-order learning might be promoted in different domains. We also recognize that each discipline or discursive community presents a competing way or ways of giving meaning to the world. Students will therefore learn different ways of organizing and explaining their experience depending on their decision to concentrate on one discipline rather than another. They may become contextual knowers and constructivists because of their varied experience, or they may turn away from the apparent chaos to a nonintellectual life. Their learning will depend to a great extent on the message that faculty and institutions give them about the nature of intellectual endeavor. [...]

Comparison of Learning in the Social Sciences and Humanities

2 Complexity, antinomies, and diversity characterize the four disciplines investigated in the social sciences and humanities: psychology, law, education, and English literature. Each deals with phenomena at a broader or more inclusive level than do the natural sciences. Scholars in these areas ask questions that require multifaceted answers. Why do people behave in the way they do? Who is responsible? How can we help people learn? What is genuine authority? These questions are abstract yet socially driven; human, subjective experience is the genesis of study.

3   What do these disciplines have in common and what differentiates them? What is to be learned by students entering these fields? (See Exhibit 9.1.) In psychology, students must learn methods of empirical analysis and theory construction. In law, the methods of analysis depend on a history of practice that must be learned. In education, students need to understand the disciplines they are responsible for teaching, and how to design instructional practices to fit learners' needs. In English, students must analyze texts for their meaning and apply an aesthetic criterion in addition to others. [. . .]

Comparison of Thinking and Validation Processes Across Disciplines

4 Thinking in different disciplines shows conspicuous trends from deductive to interpretive. At the most structured and delimited end of the continuum, deductive reasoning is used—inference based on a general law or premise leading necessarily to a conclusion. Less structured disciplines tend to use inductive reasoning, moving from the particular to the general and based on frequency of occurrence or probability. Further along the continuum are specific cases and arguments built around the cases (Exhibit 9.3). The methods essential for understanding are specific to each field. In physics, engineering, and chemistry, for example, the problem constitutes the framework for thinking but the process of thinking varies. The unknown in physics comes in the form of hypothesizing potential situations. In engineering one must solve a problem without having all of the information needed; the problem solver must extrapolate. In chemistry the thinking process is a matter of transforming problems into a recognizable structure. In each of these disciplines, however, structure and procedure prevail.

5   In biology and psychology, the methods employed are more varied, appropriate to the greater variation in phenomena studied; hypothesis development and testing are central. The concept-mapping research revealed a lower ratio of links to concepts in the biology and psychology courses (.92 and .64, respectively) than in physics and chemistry (1.33 and 1.15, respectively), which indicates a looser or more data-dense structure in the biological sciences and psychology. In these disciplines the problems or hypotheses must first be identified, and various consequences are possible based on the framework or system applied. At this intermediate level of structure, methods of thinking

Exhibit 9.1 Comparison of Learning in Social Science and Humanities Disciplines

Discipline	Nature of Discipline	What Is to Be Learned	Expectations of Entering Students	Instructional Methods
Psychology	Ranges from hard to soft, highly structured to complex; multifaceted, pure to applied, young, preparadigmatic; intermediate convergence	New abstract vocabulary, theoretical frameworks; analytic reasoning; research methods: observation, experiment, measurement, analysis, theory construction	Ability to think logically, independently, abstractly	*Found*: lecturing, seminars, discussion, reading reference material. *Optimal*: applying science to human experience, problem solving, organizing conceptual frameworks
Law	Ancient advanced faculty, insular; soft; applied, profession dominates academy; intermediate (limited) convergence	Abstract technical terminology; logic, analysis, analogy; how the reasonable person would act; statute and precedent; professional practice, skills and values	Ability to describe a legal situation, choose information relevant to the case, think logically	*Found*: Socratic questioning in lectures, casebook. *Optimal*: open to a variety of opinions and values, teams working on case studies, joint venture exercise, computer exercises
Education	Soft, applied, comprehensive, diverse; metascience science, social science, amalgam of disciplines, or professions	Understanding the conceptual frameworks of the subject matter disciplines, the institutional context, how to represent and adapt subject matter to learners, how to design instructional processes for optimal learning	A relatively fragmented knowledge of their subject areas; ability to think logically, in an internally consistent manner, independently	*Found*: class discussion, cooperative learning, group projects, student development activities, student-selected topics. *Optimal*: interviewing or following a learner, constructivist framework, apprenticeship
English literature	Soft, unbounded, pure, argumentative, interpretive, divergent	Technical language, assessment of value of literary texts, decoding text, training in sensibility, modes of perceiving	Intuition and sensibility rather than logic	*Found*: lectures, tutorials, group work, performance. *Optimal*: reengaging in controversies, semester devoted to analysis of inquiry processes

46 The Academic Community

Exhibit 9.3   Comparison of Thinking and Validation Processes Across Disciplines

	Terms Used to Describe Thinking	Examples of Thinking	Validation Processes
Physics	Problem solving, analysis and synthesis, visualization, deductive logic	Experimentation, scientific explanation, what if?	Matching evidence to systematic theorizing A reasonable answer, plausible, within expected limits
Engineering	Problem solving Design Mathematical modeling of physical systems	Problem solving where all the needed information is not known Using procedural knowledge	Does it work? approximate or within certain limits
Chemistry	Deductive and inductive problem solving	Transforming a nonroutine problem Guided inquiry	Experiment—range of methods of analysis match varying levels of specificity
Biology	Inductive, phenomenological, inferential Uses powerful metaphors	Varied consequences of various hypotheses Regulatory networks	Questioning results and conclusions
Psychology	Skeptical investigation Research methods—experimental technique Understanding oneself Analytic reasoning	Writing reports Evaluating previous research in a field Identifying problems to be investigated Questioning assumptions in an argument	Interrater reliability Empirical testing

Law	Thinking like a lawyer Solving puzzles Legal analysis using syllogism and analogy Factual Investigation	Analyze facts, appreciate the shifting legal results produced by factual nuances Derive legal conclusion in the light of legal doctrine	Human authority Evolving tradition Legal evidence Witnesses Logic versus value Winning a case—convincing a judge to accept an argument
Education	Pedagogical reasoning Expert processes Transforming text Evaluating Reflecting	Representing ideas in the form of new analogies or metaphors Specific problem solving in the classroom	Practical judgments Comparing options and triangulating evidence Authenticity and utility Ecological validity
English literature	Hermeneutics Interpretation Literary analysis-criticism Imagination Rhetoric	Close reading; taking meaning from text Bridging gaps and integrating textual elements Analyzing the organizing principle that unifies a work's elements and identifies its uniqueness	Critique of others' claims Rhetorical reflexivity weakens validity Peer review, credibility, and plausibility Testing the parts against the whole

include a review of possible frameworks from the literature, and proof of thinking is found in the reports written by students on their labs or experiments.

6   Law and education also require multifaceted puzzle solution and transformation. The examples of thinking shown in Exhibit 9.3 illustrate the need to recognize the particular situation and respond to it. In law this takes place in a larger framework set out by statute and precedent; in education the subject matter discipline and pedagogical knowledge provide the framework. These applied social sciences do not lack structure: in the concept maps, the ratio of links to concepts parallels that of the physical sciences, 1.36 in law and 1.15 in education. From our examination of the structure of knowledge in law and education, *statute* and *precedent* are more codified forms of knowledge than the pedagogical content knowledge that links the instructional process with different subject matter disciplines. The would-be teacher has a more difficult search for a framework to apply.

7   At the least structured and most inclusive end of the continuum, varied forms of criticism supply potentially conflicting frameworks for thinking. In English literature, the hunt appears to be wide open, with a variety of perspectives to work from, but at the same time attention to historical accuracy and aesthetic sensibility are demanded. The logical structure displayed in the concept mapping research showed a ratio of one link per concept, thus structure is balanced by data. Given this context, the student must focus on the text while scanning for modes of interpreting it, then compare the effects of different forms of criticism or synthesize the results from different perspectives.

8   Differences between the pure and applied disciplines reside primarily in the necessity in the applied areas of building active models or frameworks. The function of application is to put a theory or model into practice, and this requires situational learning in which students have the opportunity to test their own cognitive frameworks or structures in a context where they must perform. Thus in engineering programs, learning in design or project courses is evaluated by means of student products, whereas in law, moot court and joint venture exercises are venues for testing skills. In education, students must show how they have tailored their own learners' experiences in the classroom; in English drama, performance describes the central outcome. The combination of being a hard and applied discipline puts greater performance pressure on engineering students, as engineering students and professors commented.

9   The different validation processes used in the disciplines show a trend in where authority resides—from the objective empirical to peers. In more structured disciplines, evidence is matched to theory. Psychology occupies a middle position, where empirical testing and interrater reliability are both used as proof. Further into the human sciences, proof rests in evidence that will convince an authority in law, or test results in education, or in internal consistency rendering work plausible in English literature. In engineering and in education, one major criterion equilibrates the empirical and the judgment of others: Does it work? In law and in English literature the criterion is more specifically oriented to convincing others of one's case. In our studies of the validation processes used in the physical and social sciences and the humani-

ties, differences were statistically significant; the thinking processes *are* particular to each discipline. However, consistencies in the use of certain specific thinking processes across disciplines suggests that there are thinking processes a student in any discipline needs to acquire.

10 Greatest agreement across disciplines was found in the importance of students' learning to *identify the context* and *state assumptions,* and *change perspective,* and their learning the selection, representation, and synthesis processes (Exhibit 9.4). *Identifying the context* may include setting up the general framework for a problem, recognizing what kind of problem they are dealing with, finding where a framework fits the processes being studied, or recognizing the history of the period in which text was written. *Stating assumptions* is critical to solving a problem, recognizing bias, perspective, or the framework being applied, or considering the steps to be taken or individuals to be taken into account. The general importance of *changing perspective* is consistent with the need for a constructivist or postmodern approach to knowledge.

11 All disciplines acknowledge that because of the abundance of information and phenomena, students must learn to select. Representation describes the structure in each discipline. The general importance of representation as a thinking process lies in its providing conceptual frameworks. Because these are tacit in some disciplines, representation may not be talked about as frequently as inference is, but it is essential to constructivist thinking. Synthesis plays a particular role across the disciplines. It results in laws in physics. Engineering professors approach synthesis as a goal for their students, training them in design skills in team projects. In education, synthesis is important for bringing together all the elements of the classroom situation. In English literature, although multiplicity and paradox are the hallmarks, the search for form is central.

12 Are these more general thinking processes? They originate in different methods of inquiry or conceptualizations of thinking; for example, *identifying the context* is the mark of the expert, whereas *stating assumptions* is a defining characteristic of critical thinking. Selection has been cast in the more general role of defining intelligence, while representation and synthesis are found in the problem-solving literature. *Changing perspective* and *confirming results* are found more generally in methods of inquiry—in expertise, problem solving, and critical thinking. [. . .] The general agreement on the importance of these thinking processes suggests that they are foundational to postsecondary learning. What if professors in the different disciplines advised students that these were processes they needed to learn whatever course of study they were pursuing? What if these processes were deliberately taught and assessed in each course?

13 Trends across disciplines in representation parallel the degree of structure in them. In *organizing principles,* there is a continuum from strong to weak schemas—from laws in physics, models in engineering, theories in psychology, small working models in education, to the questioning of structure in English. Professors could use these examples to explain the nature of organizing principles in their discipline in contrast to those in others. Types of illustration show

Exhibit 9.4 Most Important Thinking Processes Used Generally Across Disciplines

Process	Definition
Identify the context	Establish surrounding environment to create a total picture.
State assumptions	State suppositions, postulates, or propositions assumed.
SELECTION:	
Choose relevant information	Select information that is pertinent to the issue in question.
Order information in importance	Rank, arrange in importance or according to significance.
Identify critical elements	Determine units, parts, components that are important.
Identify critical relations	Determine connections between things that are important.
REPRESENTATION:	
Recognize organizing principles	Identify laws, methods, rules that arrange in a systematic whole.
Organize elements and relations	Arrange parts, connections between things into a systematic whole.
Illustrate elements and relations	Make clear by examples the parts, connections between things.
Modify elements and relations	Change, alter, or qualify the parts, connections between things.
Change perspective	Alter view, vista, interrelations, significance of facts or information.
SYNTHESIS:	
Combine parts to form a whole	Join, associate elements, components into a system or pattern.
Elaborate	Work out, complete with great detail, exactness, or complexity.
Generate missing links	Produce or create what is lacking in a sequence, fill in the gap.
Develop a course of action	Work out or expand the path, route, or direction to be taken.
Confirm results	Establish or ratify conclusions, effects, outcomes, or products.

a slightly different pattern. Physics uses graphs, engineering has similar but more extensive systems, and psychology has metaphor and examples, as does education, along with stories that link and relate. In English literature, the process is reversed, because representation is in the text rather than superordinate to it as in other disciplines. Inference also varies depending on the degree of structure in the discipline, with physicists doing experiments, engineers solving problems, psychologists formulating general principles from evidence, and English literature searching for possible meanings. Verification processes differ so much that they are defining characteristics of the disciplines. The degree of structure and the need to develop thinking abilities are themes that continue in the challenges to instruction.

Reading Responses

1. What is Donald's purpose? What does she hope to accomplish by writing about learning in different academic disciplines?
2. Donald uses several common methods of presenting information: comparison and contrast (pointing out similarities and differences), classification (grouping in categories by types), and definition (explaining essential or characteristic qualities). Find at least one example of each method. Why does Donald use these strategies? How effectively do they work?
3. Analyze one of the exhibits in this reading. What is the exhibit designed to show? How is it organized? How does it relate to the text?

Writing Activities

1. Imagine that you want to explain part of this reading to a fellow student who is worried about how to choose a major. Select one paragraph, and paraphrase it for this student by translating Donald's explanation into your own words and your own sentence patterns. (You do not need to reword the names of specific fields such as English or physics.) Be sure to cover all of Donald's points as clearly as possible, even if your paragraph is as long as hers or even longer.
2. Write an essay comparing or contrasting the approaches to learning in two courses you are taking or have taken in different disciplines. Draw a conclusion about the two approaches based on several specific points, such as types of course topics, teaching methods, habits of thought, classroom activities, or assignments.
3. Using Donald's first exhibit (p. 45) as a model, prepare your own exhibit comparing the kinds of learning expected of you in two or more of your classes.

Community Links

Compare and contrast Donald's exhibits with other visuals that are used with readings in the work and public communities. (See the Guide to Themes, Topics, and Rhetorical Strategies at the end of the book for lists of other readings with such materials. Select one or two of these to consider in detail.)

What characteristics do Donald's exhibits share with other visuals? What characteristics differ? How do you account for these similarities and differences?

THE PATHBREAKING, FRACTIONALIZED, UNCERTAIN WORLD OF KNOWLEDGE

Stanley N. Katz

◆

This article originally appeared in the Chronicle of Higher Education, *a print and online newspaper reporting on events, issues, and trends in higher education. Here, Stanley Katz, past president of the American Council of Learned Societies, considers what is expected of the university, an issue likely to concern* Chronicle *readers, especially faculty and administrators at colleges and universities.*

1   Many years ago, the philosopher Alfred North Whitehead remarked, "The task of the university is the creation of the future, so far as rational thought, and civilized modes of appreciation, can affect the issue." But for many of today's academics, rationality is in question, civilization is anathema, and universities have not created, for themselves or for their societies, the future Whitehead envisaged. What, then, are we about? If, as Stanley O. Ikenberry, former president of the American Council of Education, has claimed, American universities are "at the top of their game," then just what game are they playing, and what's the prize?

2   One way to approach those questions is to look at how our universities support the intellectual infrastructure of our country and the world. The task of building and maintaining intellectual infrastructure is much more daunting today than it was for Whitehead and his colleagues, although the resources for undertaking it are unbelievably richer. In the United States and elsewhere, universities have both created some of the changes they face today, especially those related to the production of new knowledge, and been affected by others—for example, the growth in some demographic groups and the democratization of American society.

3   The biggest of the changes, however, is probably in how we Americans think about universities: what we expect of them. Up to the middle of the last century, we asked higher education to provide basic and professional education for young people, to discover and preserve the knowledge of the past, and, especially in the sciences, to create new knowledge. We thought of knowledge, however, in a unitary fashion, and did not distinguish as sharply as we do today between the practical and useless kinds (although it is true that many years ago the philosopher George Santayana spoke out for the "utility of useless

knowledge"). Knowledge grew slowly and incrementally, and we were mostly content to leave its creation to university academics and industrial laboratories.

4 But all of that has changed. One could argue about starting points, but the rapid pace of discovery in atomic science that took off in the 1930s and 1940s may have been the formative process. For one thing, the Manhattan Project and the postwar establishment of the National Science Foundation in 1950 began large-scale government support of scientific research. For another, cold-war competitiveness initiated the state-sponsored expansion of our university system (just as the earlier GI Bill launched the tremendous growth in the number of students in higher education). Money and the rapidly growing scale of the system created the modern research university, in which the production of knowledge and its publication became virtually the sole criterion of academic success—the be-all and end-all of the growing cohort of research universities.

5 And produce knowledge they did, at an incredible rate and with astonishing successes—with the revolution in cell biology perhaps the largest. They were able to do so, first and most obviously, because of the scaling up of the educational system. Not only were more research institutions of all kinds (including independent research institutes and industrial laboratories) created, but also an increasing number of well-trained Ph.D.'s, postdocs, and graduate students (both domestic and foreign), and an infrastructure to support them (journals, libraries, national, and international learned societies). Second, more money was poured into universities from more sources than had ever before been available to the academic research community. Most came from state and (especially) federal government sources, though private philanthropic foundations, corporations, and even individuals also made major contributions.

6 The quantity and quality of knowledge production in the second half of the 20th century was stupendous. Lewis Thomas once remarked that more had been learned about medicine during his working career than had been learned in all of history up to that time. And it may be that he was right. The era witnessed an explosion of knowledge of staggering proportions, and much of that was generated in the academy, most of it in the research universities. That was just as true across the humanities, social sciences, and professions as it was in the physical and life sciences.

7 But there was a cost. The increase in knowledge depended on a phenomenon first identified by Adam Smith—task specialization. In every field, the growing number of investigators led to narrower and more precise specification of the problem to be addressed. The traditional fields were subdivided into finer and finer parts, while, at the same time, whole new fields of investigation (to some extent in all areas but, because of funding, particularly in the sciences) were created, sometimes as old fields were merged into new ones, for example in the creation of biological physics and medical engineering. New learned societies emerged to professionalize these sub- and supra-fields, and new journals emerged to communicate their findings. In every field, specialization won the day over generalization.

8 To cite a trivial example, I was trained in American history, with a specialization in colonial history (which in those days meant from the arrival of

Europeans until the Revolution or the post-Constitutional period). My minor field was all of English history. I was trained to be able to teach any course relating to American history, and at the beginning of my career I was also teaching TudorStuart English history. I tried to keep up with all the new work in those fields. Within five years, I had begun to concentrate on colonial-American legal history, and soon I was struggling simply to keep up with that. It has gotten a lot more specialized since then.

9   Nevertheless, universities were held in high regard by the public during most of the period following the Second World War—for their training of undergraduates, for their professional education, for their research accomplishments. The public was also receptive to the books, speeches, and interviews of the most articulate university scholars, though those appreciated were not necessarily those held in highest esteem by their academic confreres. Similarly, university presidents and other institutional officials were also once public intellectuals and, sometimes, nationally important figures.

10   So, the current university has clearly been doing many things right, although it is hard to generalize about the 125 or so research universities that sustain the intellectual infrastructure in the United States. Differing substantially from one another, they are, in most respects, awesome institutions. They have superb faculties and student bodies (both substantially internationalized). They train their students well in most respects. They produce pathbreaking research in large quantities. They have magnificent laboratories and libraries. They engage, to some extent, in serving the interests of their communities through work in the schools, continuing education, extension services, and the like. To excel in teaching, learning, and service has long been the professed ambition of American higher education, and today's institutions largely live up to it.

11   Yet, current triumphs notwithstanding, the high-water mark of general admiration for the research universities may well have come by about 1980. The national political atmosphere of the 1980s was hostile to intellectuals to an extent not seen since the dog days of McCarthyism in the early 1950s—populist anti-intellectualism once again became respectable. For that and other reasons, public intellectuals have become thin on the ground. On the whole, professors did best in print culture; as new media have developed, their overwhelming commercial character increasingly has had little use for intellectuals unless they are very good looking and can shout with the best of the commercial talking heads. And today's university presidents are rarely widely known beyond the fringes of their own campuses—for good reason. Hired to be managers and fund raisers rather than educational leaders, they have largely ceased speaking out on major educational issues, not to mention their silence on most other issues of public import and interest.

12   Indeed, I think the public (and public officials) have come to see research universities as self-aggrandizing money machines populated by professors who have lost interest both in teaching and in creating immediately useful knowledge.

13   The institutions have, sadly, become too large, arrogant, rapacious, and impersonal for outsiders to understand and sympathize with (despite their best

efforts to generate loyalty through the introduction of quasi-professional sports). The public's sense of the professoriate is now similar to Robert Maynard Hutchins's castigation of his own University of Chicago faculty at its annual Christmas dinner in 1943—you are engaged in "making molehills out of mountains."

14 But it's not just the public view that has altered. Even if the abstract goals of the universities have not changed, their behavior and, especially, their management have changed profoundly over the past half century. Here the central fact is not that there are more research universities, but that each institution has become so much larger, more complex, and harder to finance. It is not so much that there are more students (nearly 50,000 on just the Twin Cities campus of the University of Minnesota and more than that number on the Columbus campus of Ohio State University, for example), but that there are more departments, centers, schools, buildings—and correspondingly more faculty and staff members.

15 Universities are very big businesses, usually the largest employers in their local communities, and, like any large organism, they must spend more and more time nourishing themselves. The raising of funds for research, physical-plant maintenance, faculty salaries, and other costs requires personnel, energy, and attention on a scale that dwarfs the needs of institutions even a few decades ago.

16 A second type of change is hard to define precisely—the transformation of the intellectual atmosphere on our university campuses. At one end of the political spectrum is the emergence of cultural politics as a dominating force. That is primarily a function of the emergence of identity politics that has made a wide range of policies and ideas hard to discuss freely—gender, sexual orientation, and race and ethnicity, for instance. While there is broad support on our campuses for diversity as a goal, the academy has fallen into a self-censorship that makes it hard to express thoughtful disagreement about relevant policies. At the other end of the spectrum is the emergence of a variety of politically and religiously conservative ideologies, which to a lesser extent constrain the development of a truly civilized campus community of discourse. Should it really be so hard to determine whether it is appropriate for freshmen to be exposed to some of the ideas of the Koran?

17 Why does that matter for what universities contribute to the national intellectual infrastructure? Mainly, I think, because the institutions are intellectually out of focus and out of control. Earlier they were organized around a limited number of schools and departments, and there was substantial consensus as to what ought to be taught and what ought to be researched. Faculty members were primarily loyal to their own institutions. There was a better balance between teaching and research—and let us not forget that one of the most important tasks of teaching is training new generations to carry on the intellectual mission of the academy.

18 But, most of all, enormous damage has been done to the creation and sustenance of our intellectual infrastructure by the increasing inability of teaching faculties to agree upon what constitutes Whitehead's "civilized modes of appreciation." Both the organization and the content of the academic life of the

mind have become fractionalized, anomic, and increasingly uncertain. Too many individual professors are running their own research programs, frequently institutionalized as centers, buying out their teaching time, and setting their own agendas, more frequently in response to funding sources than to colleagues or students. The result is that departments and even administrations have little impact on research direction, and there is increasingly a struggle to mount plausible curriculums for undergraduates and even for graduate students.

19 An analogous phenomenon afflicts faculties more generally, since most faculty members in universities confine their teaching to their own increasingly narrow research fields. Less and less effort goes into constructing intellectually comprehensive and coherent curriculums to help students make sense of the highly sophisticated knowledge they are taught. The dominance of research as the primary criterion for faculty hiring, reward, and promotion has increased the pressure for professors to publish—more and more frequently in narrowly professional areas. Contributions tend to be framed in technical jargon and sharply focused. More and more, specialists address other specialists.

20 Not only does that lessen the chance that they will reach general audiences, but it also means that the very language they use in their written work is different from their speech to students, who are not up to or interested in the publishable production of their teachers. And, of course, this problem is exacerbated by the increasing proportion of teaching done by graduate students (who are shooting for a professional foothold) and by non-tenure-track adjunct professors.

21 And, in many fields, changes in the sociology of knowledge have created profound problems in communicating research beyond the inner core of professional academic elites. One example would be the "turn to theory" prevalent in the humanities during the 1970s, 1980s, and early 1990s; another would be the increasingly theoretical bent of the social sciences, especially economics and political science.

22 In literature and related fields, the impact of French philosophy in the United States (in the form of postmodernism and deconstruction) produced, along with much original and exciting work, texts that were so jargon-ridden and abstruse that even many professionals had a tough time understanding them. Many works in the humanities became altogether incomprehensible to even the most sophisticated general readers. In political science, to take another example, emphasis on the economistic "rational choice" approach to political analysis has produced highly abstract statistical modeling that is not only hard for laypersons to understand, but is driving out the traditional study of legislatures, cities, and other organizations that genuinely interests nonspecialist academics and the general public, and is frequently the basis for public policy.

23 These problems have been accentuated by continuing administrative attempts to gain control of the university budget by what amount to neo-liberal economic strategies to impose rigorous expenditure responsibility on individual schools and departments. The result has frequently been to privilege those academic units that have the greatest access to external funding, and to punish

those more traditional departments, especially in the humanities, that survive on their portion of the general university budget. A more profound effect is to lessen the communal sense of the institution, to reward individual departmental initiative rather than commitment to general university purposes.

24 In the end, what is the impact of all this on the larger intellectual structure of American life? There are clearly many things that universities are doing better than ever before. Despite Hutchins's sarcasm, universities are generating more knowledge (and better knowledge) than they have in any previous period of human history. We know more and more about most things—even if we also learn more and more about less and less. Academic scientific and technical knowledge is the basis for an incredible range of techniques and products that serve to better our country and the world. If we are truly living in a "knowledge economy," then the university contribution to the economy is profound—even if it does not result in the quick turnaround to product and profit that some outside the academy demand. We have, in sum, become extremely efficient in producing many types of knowledge.

25 But it could be argued that, in other respects, universities are not holding up their end of their implicit compact with society. I would say that we are neglecting undergraduate education in a serious way, although probably not for the reasons many populist critics of higher education have contended. They have charged professors with teaching too few hours, ignoring students and pursuing useless research, out of bad politics and bad motives; such critics have ignored the context in which change has occurred. It is interesting to note, however, that public complaint about this aspect of higher education, intense during the early 1990s, seems mainly to have disappeared. Today, beyond understandable anguish over the cost of higher education, critical voices are, for some reason, less frequently heard.

26 Nevertheless, we should not forget: If "general education" is one of the bases for democratic citizenship, and I believe that it is, we need to think much harder about what we are offering our students. The opportunities are immense, since today's universities educate such a large and representative segment of the relevant age cohort. But both the material structure and intellectual direction of the professoriate work against a reform of undergraduate education. The challenge of the university is to train an elite cohort (these days increasingly selected on egalitarian terms) to lead society politically and socially, as well as to run its businesses and laboratories. Such young people are currently very well trained in specialized techniques, but not so well prepared in those general critical thinking skills that have always been thought basic to liberal education.

27 It may also be the case that the theoretical complexity of the knowledge currently generated by research universities is too inaccessible to large numbers of citizens outside the academy. That is true in the sciences and the humanities and the social sciences, though it may well be that the tradition of high-level popularization of scientific thought is healthier than in the social sciences and humanities. There is a sense in which the modalities for communicating with the public are less vibrant than they used to be. If so, that is probably as much a factor of the dominance of highly commercialized new media as it is of the unwillingness or inability of academics to translate their work for the general

public. And the current crisis—economic and intellectual—in serious publishing is surely another sign of the same phenomenon.

28   So in some respects the glass is overflowing, but in others it is less than half full. The intellectual accomplishments of universities are undeniably rich and valuable to our larger society. One obvious cost of the accentuation of research, however, has been a relative decline in the quality (though an increase in the quantity) of undergraduate education. But the larger question may be whether the recent turn to the hyper-professionalization of knowledge in research universities has not subtly and adversely affected the tone of the university's impact on society. We may be contributing more to information than to what Whitehead thought of as "rational thought."

Reading Responses

1. How does Katz use the quotations in his first paragraph to introduce his article? Why does he ask questions several times in the article rather than simply making statements?

2. Katz uses many examples as he examines changes in the task and expectations of the university. What are some of the ways that Katz organizes these examples? Select several paragraphs, and identify the types of details Katz mentions and the ways he arranges them.

3. Why does Katz continue to relate the changing expectations and tasks of universities to American society in general rather than restricting his discussion to the academic institutions where most of his readers probably work or teach? Given this focus, how does he reflect or acknowledge in the article possible concerns of his readers?

Writing Activities

1. Briefly outline Katz's essay, noting his main topics and subtopics.

2. In your own words, write a short summary of Katz's essay, concisely stating his thesis or central idea and his major supporting points.

3. Drawing on the information that Katz provides and your own experiences, write an essay about the current task of the university from the viewpoint of a student. Support your points with examples from your experiences in class or on campus.

Community Links

Consider how the knowledge-oriented academic community connects with other communities using as sources readings such as Katz's essay, Aslanian's "The Community College Pathway for Underprepared Students" (pp. 59–64), or Miller's "Wanted: 'Civic Scientists' to Educate the Public, Press and Policy Makers" (pp. 362–365).

THE COMMUNITY COLLEGE PATHWAY FOR UNDERPREPARED STUDENTS

Carol Aslanian

◆

This article, written by Carol Aslanian, an expert on adult learning, with the assistance of Heather Larson, originally appeared in The College Board Review. *Each academic year, the three issues of this publication are distributed by the College Entrance Examination Board to high school and college teachers and administrators who subscribe or whose institutions belong to the College Board. Its articles, like Aslanian's update on the role of community colleges, report on current trends and issues in education.*

1 The changing profile of American society has produced an economically diverse and multiethnic population—a population that brings with it wide variance in educational attainment and youth who are typically underprepared to enter college. As the national population diversifies, technology continues to advance rapidly. New skills and new information demands for the workplace are leading millions of Americans to college repeatedly throughout their lifetimes.

2 In the decades to follow, we will witness an increasing need for highly skilled and educated workers from every class of our society, and the current education system will be responsible for preparing all Americans for the demands of the future.

3 In his address to the National Community Reinvestment Coalition in March 2000, Alan Greenspan stressed the importance of community colleges as suppliers of the complex and ever-changing job skills the American workforce requires. His remarks on the outlook of the economy for the beginning of the new century emphasized the need to educate all people who have not previously participated in postsecondary education in order to both strengthen our workforce and improve our economy. He urged community leaders to "enhance our stock of human capital," noting that while completing a high school degree once provided sufficient skills to last a lifetime, today's workers must be trained along many dimensions and willing to continually learn new skills to cope with technological developments.

4 As Robert McCabe, a specialist in community colleges, has written, 80 percent of new jobs will require some postsecondary education. Even simple jobs will become high-performance positions, requiring workers to reason through complex processes rather than follow rote instructions. Workers will need better skills, not only to perform their jobs, but also as a foundation for lifelong learning. However, less than one-half of all Americans 18 years of age or older have any postsecondary education and far fewer have acquired a college degree (30 percent). Clearly, it will be critical to advance the competencies and educational levels of all Americans—young and old—throughout their lives.

5 Fortunately, the proportion of high school graduates entering college over recent decades has increased steadily, and today stands at roughly 65 percent, a trend that will help advance educational attainment levels for Americans. It is noteworthy that one-half of high school graduates entering college choose to enroll at a community college, perhaps because more than one-half of these students are first-generation students (often from working-class families and minority backgrounds). Many of them, however, enter community colleges unprepared for the rigors of college work and in need of remedial programs and special services. As the nation aims for higher proportions of high school graduates to move on to institutions of higher education, colleges will be challenged further to assist the even less prepared lower third of the high school graduating class.

6 Another important factor is that many of the first-generation students today, and most likely increasing proportions in the years ahead, will be of minority backgrounds—African Americans, Hispanics, Asian Pacific groups, Native Americans. By 2050 they will make up nearly half of the United States population. Current statistics demonstrate, unfortunately, that minorities tend to have higher poverty rates that correlate with lack of educational preparation. Given the changing demands of the workforce, it is imperative that people of all backgrounds have access to an education that will afford them the knowledge and skills necessary to perform the jobs of the future.

7 Officials in Maryland recently predicted that by 2010 there would be "across-the-board labor shortages particularly acute in information technology, the health sciences, and K–12 education." At the same time, the state recognized that the education levels of minorities, who composed 32 percent of the state's population, were quickly being outpaced by the labor market. Moreover, Maryland predicted that 60 percent of all job openings through the year 2005 would require candidates to possess postsecondary education. Obviously, the challenge to Maryland demonstrates a strong need for further education for a large segment of the population. By examining comparable patterns across the nation, the government and institutions of higher learning have come to recognize the urgency of attracting and serving the postsecondary needs of underserved and underprepared populations.

Postsecondary Education in Transition

8 The growing importance of community colleges is documented by the fact that among the 13 million undergraduates today, nearly one-half are enrolled at a community college. This proportion, too, has been increasing steadily and is likely to grow even further as community colleges quickly transform themselves into colleges of choice for both recent high school graduates and returning adult students.

9 Community colleges continue to serve the widest student population range of any sector in higher education. The students range from high school dropouts who enroll in community college courses to acquire high school credentials while also earning college credit, to men and women with advanced degrees who return to obtain more in-depth training or to change careers. On average, more than 20 percent of community college students already have a

degree. But most important, community colleges are able to address the needs of the growing number of unprepared students: single parents, first-generation students, minority students, and older returning students. These students tend to be more exposed to nonacademic pressures such as financial problems, family responsibilities, and old age. Such pressures often lead them to withdraw without having completed their courses or credit requirements. They are also in need of the remedial programs offered by community colleges, particularly in light of a growing number of states that ban remedial courses from public four-year colleges and universities. This is often due to the colleges' desire to improve quality, coupled with legislators who want to reduce the cost of remedial programs. Some states, such as Louisiana and Nevada, have gone on to tighten their admissions standards to reduce the number of students in remedial classes. Consequently, more people are applying to community colleges. This in turn leaves community colleges facing even larger numbers of underprepared students who need to make their way onto the college campus to prepare for the workforce.

Community Colleges and Underprepared Students: A Good Match

10   Community colleges offer a solid solution for connecting the growing numbers of ill-prepared students—young and old—to the education and training they need today and in the future. They make higher education most accessible to these groups in a number of ways. Community colleges are less costly than four-year institutions. This is an important consideration to the underprepared because many come from poor backgrounds. Community colleges also have an open-entry admissions policy, which allows ill-prepared students to begin their postsecondary education. Moreover, community colleges have features that help these students succeed in their course work. The assistance comes in a program to improve their basic skills in preparation for traditional college-level courses. Another feature is the small class size and tailored support services, which provide a setting that is conducive to the instructional needs of these students. Further, the colleges' rich and varied curriculum enables the students to prepare for immediate jobs. Work-study programs and field training offer real-life experiences that these students often need. But for those students who do not choose to go to work immediately, community colleges offer transfer programs that lead to four-year universities. Given their advanced status in higher education in regard to technology, community colleges also help narrow the digital divide faced by lower-income, less prepared students. The institutions provide state-of-the-art computer skills and information technology to students who otherwise would be left out. Most important, community colleges are well located throughout the nation, offering courses convenient to where students live and work and providing varied course schedules to meet student time constraints.

11   What makes these students select one institution over the other? Those who choose a community college are influenced by the advice and support of family members and guidance offered either by their secondary school or the commu-

nity college staff. These factors are pivotal in helping them to decide whether to attend college, especially those from poor backgrounds. Those community colleges most successful in attracting students to their campus often make special efforts to ease and guide students onto the campuses. If the special circumstances and needs of underprepared, often low-income students are overlooked, their attempts to pursue higher education become nearly impossible.

12   Some community colleges have established innovative programs to deal with the special circumstances of underprepared students. Bridge programs link community colleges and high schools to help students overcome academic deficiencies and motivate them to move on to postsecondary education. The programs have high school students visit the community college campus for special orientation and tutoring, thereby helping them begin to learn how to adjust to a college campus. In contrast, for new entering freshmen, the Emerging Scholars Program at St. Louis Community College creates a system of rewards for academic achievement among underprepared students; it has also proved beneficial for minority students. Strongly promoted all year on campus, the program uses a number of strategies, including supplemental instruction, peer tutoring, directed advising, and study groups, to help developmental students remain enrolled and ultimately achieve college-level competencies. It culminates in a banquet at the end of the year with guests who include community leaders and state legislators. The banquet honors 15 developmental students who maintained a 3.5 GPA or higher in transfer courses. The program raises self-esteem, honors student commitment to education, and provides encouragement throughout the year. It also raises students' expectations of themselves—an important motivating factor for students who may begin higher education with insufficient confidence.

Community Colleges Address Student Achievement

13   Community colleges have come a long way in serving underprepared students and helping them reach their goals. Many community colleges offer support services that consider the students' academic background and economic standing, as well as external societal views. They have done much to meet student needs by establishing personal counseling services, maintaining high standards of academic instruction, promoting personal contact with mentors, supplying successful minority role models, employing familial support, providing transfer assistance, seeking financial aid opportunities, and offering activities that create a greater peer support system.

14   In a recent study at Pellissippi State Technical Community College of Knoxville, Tennessee, minority students themselves identified the types of assistance they believed would benefit their performance in college classes as well as later achievements. The college responded by supplying relevant and timely career information, providing transportation opportunities to improve access to the campus, designing minority-focused courses, offering speakers and programs to reflect cultural differences, providing tutoring services as necessary, and establishing childcare services at convenient times and locations.

15   An absence or shortage of financial aid to underprepared students affects not only enrollment rates but, more importantly, retention and transfer rates.

Studies have indicated that many students, for example, may be denied financial aid because they overestimate actual income on financial aid forms.[1] There is also a greater need for many first-generation students to support themselves or their families while trying to obtain education credits, causing finances to be a top reason for not completing credits or higher degrees.

16   In fact, some students may begin the college process burdened with financial obligations such as loan defaults or debt. It is even more important for these students to receive financial aid awards and guidance so that their basic living requirements do not interfere with the need to obtain knowledge and skills to improve their careers and lives. Greater financial assistance to minority and first-generation students has been shown to have a positive effect on achievement in higher education. In one study[2], for example, Hispanic community college students who received higher levels of financial aid awards in the form of grants were enrolled for longer periods of time, earned more semester hours, and more often received some form of a credential. These financial awards were found to relate more to Hispanic students' retention than their high school grades or cumulative grade point average at the community college.[3]

17   Strong alliances between community colleges and four-year institutions are necessary for assisting those students who seek a baccalaureate. Programs that focus student goals on a four-year degree, as well as aiding with the transfer process, will contribute to higher retention rates and more degree awards by community colleges. They can also boost underprepared student achievement in higher education. Several examples are noteworthy.

18   One, in California, is a successful transfer program in which the University of California has made greater access for community college students one of its highest priorities. The program lays out funding commitments for the state and accountability commitments for the university. The partnership calls for a 6 percent annual increase in community college transfers to UC through 2005–2006. The components of the program include transfer admissions agreements that guarantee admission for community college students with a required GPA in appropriate lower-division coursework; outreach programs that foster academic development of students with exceedingly difficult challenges; a Web-based planning system for transfer students; and increasing personal contact between UC representatives and community college students.

19   Similarly, Seattle Central Community College is trying to make transferring easier with its Transfer Advising Center. Recognizing that many of their students are first-generation college attendees, it offers visits from university representatives, workshops on completing applications and financial aid forms, and personal attention, especially to fears and misconceptions about academia. In addition, some educators are planning to hold classes intermittently at the University of Washington in order to acclimate community college students to the university setting. Seattle Central also offers an online program that allows community college students to enter the grades and courses they've taken to decipher which degree requirements they have fulfilled, as well as next steps in the transferring process.

20   Transfer assistance programs like these are obviously vital to student achievement in higher education. As more and more organizations and institutions aspire to create these programs, success rates among underprepared stu-

dents in community colleges are climbing, and the necessary formulas to attain such achievement in community colleges are beginning to become apparent.

21   What tasks await attention? One is the issue of identity. Challenges that every student entering college experiences are often magnified for underprepared students who feel out of place. Community colleges must cultivate a sense of belonging for them, as well as an environment where all students are appreciated and encouraged to reach their potential. Such goals can be accomplished by a school policy that encourages and stresses acceptance and achievement. Social organizations and student support groups help acclimate such students to a new campus and help give a sense of belonging.

Educators of America's Workforce

22   Community colleges have come a long way in supporting the achievement of underprepared students. The colleges have provided a tremendous commitment to these students over the years, because of their open admissions policies and ability to adapt to the needs of special populations. As more and more students enter college poorly prepared, community college administrators must remain committed to their unique needs to ensure that they gain the skills necessary for personal and career satisfaction, as well as job effectiveness. By offering transition services to assist the underprepared and tracking enrollments and outcomes, community colleges have become the educators of America's workforce. As we proceed into a new century with its increasingly complex and unpredictable challenges, community colleges are well positioned to respond with new programs and practices. They will ensure that all Americans have the opportunity to prepare themselves for the future.

Notes

1. Nora, Amaury, "Campus-Base Aid Programs as Determinants of Retention among Hispanic Community College Students." *Journal of Higher Education,* 1990, 61 (3) 312–327.
2. Rendon, Laura, and Nora, Amaury, "Hispanic Students: Stopping the Leaks in the Pipleine." *Educational Record,* 1987–88, 68 (4), 79–85.
3. Avalos, Juan, and Pavel, D. Michael, "Improving the Performance of the Hispanic Community College Student." Source: ERIC Clearinghouse for Junior Colleges, Los Angeles, CA. May 1993.

Reading Responses

1. What does Aslanian present as the primary role of the community college? What is her main point about community colleges?
2. What kinds of authorities and sources does Aslanian mention in her article? How do their areas of expertise contribute to her argument?
3. In the section "Community Colleges and Underprepared Students: A Good Match" (p. 61), what benefits for students does Aslanian identify? Given the many examples included here, how does Aslanian connect one

point to another? How does she vary her presentation so that the section doesn't read like a grocery list?

Writing Activities

1. Using your responses to question 3 above and any class discussion of the question, write a brief analysis of the section "Community Colleges and Underprepared Students: A Good Match." In your analysis, identify and illustrate several of Aslanian's strategies as a writer. Be sure to cite your source, supply page (or paragraph) numbers to identify the exact locations of examples from the article, and quote accurately.
2. Working by yourself or with a small group, compare and contrast Aslanian's assumptions about the role of higher education with Katz's assumptions in "The Pathbreaking, Fractionalized, Uncertain World of Knowledge" (pp. 52–58). Write a brief summary of each point of view.
3. Investigate resources on your own campus for students who have some of the needs identified in Aslanian's article. Write a short guide to several of these resources, directed to other students who may not be aware of available campus services, programs, or assistance. Plan your guide so that it focuses on meeting a specific need or assisting a certain type of student. Describe specific resources that might meet that need or appeal to that type of student. Include what the resources provide, how to locate or access them, and how they might benefit those who use them.

Community Links

After reading Aslanian's article and Eisenberg's "The Coming Job Boom" (pp. 233–239), draft your own thesis statement about education and employment. Synthesize or combine ideas and details from both articles to support the points you want to make. Be sure to cite your sources and quote or paraphrase accurately.

THE ROOTS OF DEBATE IN EDUCATION AND THE HOPE OF DIALOGUE

Deborah Tannen

Throughout her career as a linguist, Tannen has examined conversations in many contexts—among friends, men and women, and colleagues at work. This selection is part of the concluding chapter of The Argument Culture: Moving from Debate to Dialogue, *which examines the adversarial approach common in public exchanges. In this excerpt, Tannen examines the roots of this combative approach in our educational system.*

1   The teacher sits at the head of the classroom, feeling pleased with herself and her class. The students are engaged in a heated debate. The very noise level reassures the teacher that the students are participating, taking responsibility for their own learning. Education is going on. The class is a success.

2   But look again, cautions Patricia Rosof, a high school history teacher who admits to having experienced that wave of satisfaction with herself and the job she is doing. On closer inspection, you notice that only a few students are participating in the debate; the majority of the class is sitting silently, maybe attentive but perhaps either indifferent or actively turned off. And the students who are arguing are not addressing the subtleties, nuances, or complexities of the points they are making or disputing. They do not have that luxury because they want to win the argument—so they must go for the most gross and dramatic statements they can muster. They will not concede an opponent's point, even if they can see its validity, because that would weaken their position. Anyone tempted to synthesize the varying views would not dare to do so because it would look like a "cop-out," an inability to take a stand.

3   One reason so many teachers use the debate format to promote student involvement is that it is relatively easy to set up and the rewards are quick and obvious: the decibel level of noise, the excitement of those who are taking part. Showing students how to integrate ideas and explore subtleties and complexities is much harder. And the rewards are quieter—but more lasting.

4   Our schools and universities, our ways of doing science and approaching knowledge, are deeply agonistic. We all pass through our country's educational system, and it is there that the seeds of our adversarial culture are planted. Seeing how these seeds develop, and where they came from, is a key to understanding the argument culture and a necessary foundation for determining what changes we would like to make.

Roots of the Adversarial Approach to Knowledge

5   The argument culture, with its tendency to approach issues as a polarized debate, and the culture of critique, with its inclination to regard criticism and attack as the best if not the only type of rigorous thinking, are deeply rooted in Western tradition, going back to the ancient Greeks. This point is made by Walter Ong, a Jesuit professor at Saint Louis University, in his book *Fighting for Life*. Ong credits the ancient Greeks with a fascination with adversativeness in language and thought. He also connects the adversarial tradition of educational institutions to their all-male character. To attend the earliest universities, in the Middle Ages, young men were torn from their families and deposited in cloistered environments where corporal, even brutal, punishment was rampant. Their suffering drove them to bond with each other in opposition to their keepers—the teachers who were their symbolic enemies. Similar in many ways to puberty rites in traditional cultures, this secret society to which young men were confined also had a private language, Latin, in which

students read about military exploits. Knowledge was gleaned through public oral disputation and tested by combative oral performance, which carried with it the risk of public humiliation. Students at these institutions were trained not to discover the truth but to argue either side of an argument—in other words, to debate. Ong points out that the Latin term for school, *ludus,* also referred to play or games, but it derived from the military sense of the word—training exercises for war.

6   If debate seems self-evidently the appropriate or even the only path to insight and knowledge, says Ong, consider the Chinese approach. Disputation was rejected in ancient China as "incompatible with the decorum and harmony cultivated by the true sage." During the Classical periods in both China and India, according to Robert T. Oliver, the preferred mode of rhetoric was exposition rather than argument. The aim was to "enlighten an inquirer," not to "overwhelm an opponent." And the preferred style reflected "the earnestness of investigation" rather than "the fervor of conviction." In contrast to Aristotle's trust of logic and mistrust of emotion, in ancient Asia intuitive insight was considered the superior means of perceiving truth. Asian rhetoric was devoted not to devising logical arguments but to explicating widely accepted propositions. Furthermore, the search for abstract truth that we assume is the goal of philosophy, while taken for granted in the West, was not found in the East, where philosophy was concerned with observation and experience.

7   If Aristotelian philosophy, with its emphasis on formal logic, was based on the assumption that truth is gained by opposition, Chinese philosophy offers an alternative view. With its emphasis on harmony, says anthropologist Linda Young, Chinese philosophy sees a diverse universe in precarious balance that is maintained by talk. This translates into methods of investigation that focus more on integrating ideas and exploring relations among them than on opposing ideas and fighting over them. [...]

Sharing Time: Early Training in School

8   A commitment to formal logic as the truest form of intellectual pursuit remains with us today. Our glorification of opposition as the path to truth is related to the development of formal logic, which encourages thinkers to regard truth seeking as a step-by-step alternation of claims and counterclaims. Truth, in this schema, is an abstract notion that tends to be taken out of context. This formal approach to learning is taught in our schools, often indirectly.

9   Educational researcher James Wertsch shows that schools place great emphasis on formal representation of knowledge. The common elementary school practice of "sharing time" (or, as it used to be called, "show-and-tell") is a prime arena for such training. Wertsch gives the example of a kindergarten pupil named Danny who took a piece of lava to class. Danny told his classmates, "My mom went to the volcano and got it." When the teacher asked what he wanted to tell about it, he said, "I've always been taking care of it." This placed the rock at the center of his feelings and his family: the rock's connection to his mother, who gave it to him, and the attention and care he has lavished on it. The teacher reframed the children's interest in the rock as informational: "Is it rough or smooth?" "Is it heavy or light?" She also suggested

they look up "volcano" and "lava" in the dictionary. This is not to imply that the teacher harmed the child; she built on his personal attachment to the rock to teach him a new way of thinking about it. But the example shows the focus of education on formal rather than relational knowledge—information about the rock that has meaning out of context, rather than information tied to the context: Who got the rock for him? How did she get it? What is his relation to it?

10   Here's another example of how a teacher uses sharing time to train children to speak and think formally. Sarah Michaels spent time watching and tape-recording in a first-grade classroom. During sharing time, a little girl named Mindy held up two candles and told her classmates, "When I was in day camp we made these candles. And I tried it with different colors with both of them but one just came out, this one just came out blue and I don't know what this color is." The teacher responded, "That's neat-o. Tell the kids how you do it from the very start. Pretend we don't know a thing about candles. OK, what did you do first? What did you use?" She continued to prompt: "What makes it have a shape?" and "Who knows what the string is for?" By encouraging Mindy to give information in a sequential manner, even if it might not seem the most important to her and if the children might already know some of it, the teacher was training her to talk in a focused, explicit way.

11   The tendency to value formal, objective knowledge over relational, intuitive knowledge grows out of our notion of education as training for debate. It is a legacy of the agonistic heritage. There are many other traces as well. Many Ph.D. programs still require public "defenses" of dissertations or dissertation proposals, and oral performance of knowledge in comprehensive exams. Throughout our educational system, the most pervasive inheritance is the conviction that issues have two sides, that knowledge is best gained through debate, that ideas should be presented orally to an audience that does its best to poke holes and find weaknesses, and that to get recognition, one has to "stake out a position" in opposition to another. [. . .]

The Culture of Critique: Attack in the Academy

12   The standard way of writing an academic paper is to position your work in opposition to someone else's, which you prove wrong. This creates a *need* to make others wrong, which is quite a different matter from reading something with an open mind and discovering that you disagree with it. Students are taught that they must disprove others' arguments in order to be original, make a contribution, and demonstrate their intellectual ability. When there is a *need* to make others wrong, the temptation is great to oversimplify at best, and at worst to distort or even misrepresent others' positions, the better to refute them—to search for the most foolish statement in a generally reasonable treatise, seize upon the weakest examples, ignore facts that support your opponent's views, and focus only on those that support yours. Straw men spring up like scarecrows in a cornfield.

13   Sometimes it seems as if there is a maxim driving academic discourse that counsels, "If you can't find something bad to say, don't say anything." As a result, any work that gets a lot of attention is immediately opposed. There is an

advantage to this approach: Weaknesses are exposed, and that is surely good. But another result is that it is difficult for those outside the field (or even inside) to know what is "true." Like two expert witnesses hired by opposing attorneys, academics can seem to be canceling each other out. In the words of policy analysts David Greenberg and Philip Robins:

> The process of scientific inquiry almost ensures that competing sets of results will be obtained. . . . Once the first set of findings are published, other researchers eager to make a name for themselves must come up with different approaches and results to get their studies published.

How are outsiders (or insiders, for that matter) to know which "side" to believe? As a result, it is extremely difficult for research to influence public policy. [. . .]

14 One reason the argument culture is so widespread is that arguing is so easy to do. Lynne Hewitt, Judith Duchan, and Erwin Segal came up with a fascinating finding: Speakers with language disabilities who had trouble taking part in other types of verbal interaction were able to participate in arguments. Observing adults with mental retardation who lived in a group home, the researchers found that the residents often engaged in verbal conflicts as a means of prolonging interaction. It was a form of sociability. Most surprising, this was equally true of two residents who had severe language and comprehension disorders yet were able to take part in the verbal disputes, because arguments have a predictable structure.

15 Academics, too, know that it is easy to ask challenging questions without listening, reading, or thinking very carefully. Critics can always complain about research methods, sample size, and what has been left out. To study anything, a researcher must isolate a piece of the subject and narrow the scope of vision in order to focus. An entire tree cannot be placed under a microscope; a tiny bit has to be separated to be examined closely. This gives critics the handle of a weapon with which to strike an easy blow: They can point out all the bits that were not studied. Like family members or partners in a close relationship, anyone looking for things to pick on will have no trouble finding them.

16 All of this is not to imply that scholars should not criticize each other or disagree. In the words of poet William Blake, "Without contraries is no progression." The point is to distinguish constructive ways of doing so from nonconstructive ones. Criticizing a colleague on empirical grounds is the beginning of a discussion; if researchers come up with different findings, they can engage in a dialogue: What is it about their methods, data, or means of analysis that explains the different results? In some cases, those who set out to disprove another's claims end up proving them instead—something that is highly unlikely to happen in fields that deal in argumentation alone.

17 A stunning example in which opponents attempting to disprove a heretical claim ended up proving it involves the cause and treatment of ulcers. It is now widely known and accepted that ulcers are caused by bacteria in the stomach and can be cured by massive doses of antibiotics. For years, however, the cure and treatment of ulcers remained elusive, as all the experts agreed that ulcers

were the classic psychogenic illness caused by stress. The stomach, experts further agreed, was a sterile environment: No bacteria could live there. So pathologists did not look for bacteria in the stomachs of ailing or deceased patients, and those who came across them simply ignored them, in effect not seeing what was before their eyes because they did not believe it could be there. When Dr. Barry Marshall, an Australian resident in internal medicine, presented evidence that ulcers are caused by bacteria, no one believed him. His findings were ultimately confirmed by researchers intent on proving him wrong.

18   The case of ulcers shows that setting out to prove others wrong can be constructive—when it is driven by genuine differences and when it motivates others to undertake new research. But if seeking to prove others wrong becomes a habit, an end in itself, the sole line of inquiry, the results can be far less rewarding. [. . .]

Moving from Debate to Dialogue

19 Many of the issues I have discussed are also of concern to Amitai Etzioni and other communitarians. In *The New Golden Rule,* Etzioni proposes rules of engagement to make dialogue more constructive between people with differing views. His rules of engagement are designed to reflect—and reinforce—the tenet that people whose ideas conflict are still members of the same community. Among these rules are:

- Don't demonize those with whom you disagree.
- Don't affront their deepest moral commitments.
- Talk less of rights, which are nonnegotiable, and more of needs, wants, and interests.
- Leave some issues out.
- Engage in a dialogue of convictions. Don't be so reasonable and conciliatory that you lose touch with a core of belief you feel passionately about.

20 As I stressed in earlier chapters, producers putting together television or radio shows and journalists covering stories might consider—in at least some cases—preferring rather than rejecting potential commentators who say they cannot take one side or the other unequivocally. Information shows might do better with only one guest who is given a chance to explore an idea in depth rather than two who will prevent each other from developing either perspective. A producer who feels that two guests with radically opposed views seem truly the most appropriate might begin by asking whether the issue is being framed in the most constructive way. If it is, a third or fourth participant could be invited as well, to temper the "two sides" perspective.

21   Perhaps it is time to reexamine the assumption that audiences always prefer a fight. In reviewing a book about the history of *National Geographic,* Marina Warner scoffs at the magazine's policy of avoiding attack. She quotes the editor who wrote in 1915, "Only what is of a kindly nature is printed about any country or people, everything unpleasant or unduly critical being avoided." Warner describes this editorial approach condescendingly as a "happy-talk,

feel-good philosophy" and concludes that "its deep wish not to offend has often made it dull." But the facts belie this judgment. *National Geographic* is one of the most successful magazines of all time—as reported in the same review, its circulation "stands at over 10 million, and the readership, according to surveys, is four times that number."

22   Perhaps, too, it is time to question our glorification of debate as the best, if not the only, means of inquiry. The debate format leads us to regard those doing different kinds of research as belonging to warring camps. There is something very appealing about conceptualizing differing approaches in this way, because dichotomies appeal to our sense of how knowledge should be organized.

23   Well, what's wrong with that?

24   What's wrong is that it obscures aspects of disparate work that overlap and can enlighten each other.

25   What's wrong is that it obscures the complexity of research. Fitting ideas into a particular camp requires you to oversimplify them. Again, disinformation and distortion can result. Less knowledge is gained, not more. And time spent attacking an opponent or defending against attacks is not spent doing something else—like original research.

26   What's wrong is that it implies that only one framework can apply, when in most cases many can. As a colleague put it, "Most theories are wrong not in what they assert but in what they deny." Clinging to the elephant's leg, they loudly proclaim that the person describing the elephant's tail is wrong. This is not going to help them—or their readers—understand an elephant. Again, there are parallels in personal relationships. I recall a man who had just returned from a weekend human development seminar. Full of enthusiasm, he explained the main lesson he had learned: "I don't have to make others wrong to prove that I'm right." He experienced this revelation as a liberation; it relieved him of the burden of trying to prove others wrong.

27   If you limit your view of a problem to choosing between two sides, you inevitably reject much that is true, and you narrow your field of vision to the limits of those two sides, making it unlikely you'll pull back, widen your field of vision, and discover the paradigm shift that will permit truly new understanding.

28   In moving away from a narrow view of debate, we need not give up conflict and criticism altogether. Quite the contrary, we can develop more varied—and more constructive—ways of expressing opposition and negotiating disagreement.

29   We need to use our imaginations and ingenuity to find different ways to seek truth and gain knowledge, and add them to our arsenal—or, should I say, to the ingredients for our stew. It will take creativity to find ways to blunt the most dangerous blades of the argument culture. It's a challenge we must undertake, because our public and private lives are at stake.

Notes

1. *going back to the ancient Greeks* (paragraph 5): This does not mean it goes back in an unbroken chain. David Noble, in *A World Without Women*, claims that Aristotle was all but lost to the West during the early Christian era and was rediscovered in the me-

dieval era, when universities were first established. This is significant for his observation that many early Christian monasteries welcomed both women and men who could equally aspire to an androgynous ideal, in contrast to the Middle Ages, when the female was stigmatized, unmarried women were consigned to convents, priests were required to be celibate, and women were excluded from spiritual authority.
2. *Ong credits the ancient Greeks* (paragraph 5): There is a fascinating parallel in the evolution of the early Christian Church and the Southern Baptist Church: Noble shows that the early Christian Church regarded women as equally beloved of Jesus and equally capable of devoting their lives to religious study, so women comprised a majority of early converts to Christianity, some of them leaving their husbands—or bringing their husbands along—to join monastic communities. It was later, leading up to the medieval period, that the clerical movement gained ascendancy in part by systematically separating women, confining them in either marriage or convents, stigmatizing them, and barring them from positions of power within the church. Christine Leigh Heyrman, in *Southern Cross: The Beginnings of the Bible Belt,* shows that a similar trajectory characterized the Southern Baptist movement. At first, young Baptist and Methodist preachers (in the 1740s to 1830s) preached that both women and blacks were equally God's children, deserving of spiritual authority—with the result that the majority of converts were women and slaves. To counteract this distressing demography, the message was changed: Antislavery rhetoric faded, and women's roles were narrowed to domesticity and subservience. With these shifts, the evangelical movement swept the South. At the same time, Heyrman shows, military imagery took over: The ideal man of God was transformed from a "willing martyr" to a "formidable fighter" led by "warrior preachers."
3. *"incompatible with the decorum"* (paragraph 6): Ong, *Fighting for Life,* p. 122. Ong's source, on which I also rely, is Oliver, *Communication and Culture in Ancient India and China.* My own quotations from Oliver are from p. 259.
4. *regard truth seeking as* (paragraph 8): Moulton, "A Paradigm of Philosophy"; Ong, *Fighting for Life.*
5. The example of Danny and the lava (paragraph 9): Wertsch, *Voices of the Mind,* pp. 113–14.
6. *"The process of scientific"* (paragraph 13): Greenberg and Robins, "The Changing Role of Social Experiments in Policy Analysis," p. 350.
7. *"Without contraries is no progression"* (paragraph 16): I've borrowed the William Blake quote from Peter Elbow, who used it to open his book *Embracing Contraries.*
8. *His findings were ultimately confirmed* (paragraph 17): Terence Monmaney, "Marshall's Hunch," *The New Yorker,* Sept. 20, 1993, pp. 64–72.
9. *His rules of engagement* (paragraph 19): Etzioni, *The New Golden Rule,* pp. 104–106. He attributes the rule "Talk less of rights . . . and more of needs, wants, and interests" to Mary Ann Glendon.
10. *In reviewing a book* (paragraph 21): Marina Warner, "High-Minded Pursuit of the Exotic," review of *Reading National Geographic* by Catherine A. Lutz and Jane L. Collins in *The New York Times Book Review,* Sept. 19, 1993, p. 13.
11. *"Most theories are wrong"* (paragraph 26): I got this from A. L. Becker, who got it from Kenneth Pike, who got it from . . .

Reading Responses

1. What assumptions of our culture does Tannen challenge? What does she advocate?
2. Why, in the concluding chapter of her book, does Tannen turn to a discussion of the educational system? What might Tannen want the educational system to do?
3. What does Tannen assume about the educational experiences of her readers? How are her assumptions reflected in the examples she selects?

Explain whether you find particular examples convincing, considering in what ways they are or are not persuasive.

Writing Activities

1. Based on your own educational experience, write an essay agreeing or disagreeing with one of Tannen's points. Use examples from your experience to support your main point.
2. Go to the library, and examine several copies of *National Geographic* to see how it implements its "policy of avoiding attack" (paragraph 21). Then select another popular magazine that you like to read or that you find at the library. Skim through some of its recent issues, and read several of its articles to see whether it avoids, tolerates, or encourages attacks. Compare or contrast the two magazines, concentrating on your conclusions about their editorial policies about adversarial attacks, debates, or other argumentative approaches.
3. Working individually or in a small group, conduct some informal research on the types of academic papers commonly assigned at your college. Look back at assignment sheets from past courses or other classes, print out assignment sheets from courses with Web sites, or survey archives of assignment sheets at the tutoring center, department offices, or other locations on campus. What percentage of assignment sheets do and do not require the typical oppositional paper that Tannen describes? What types of assignments seem to call for oppositional papers? Write a report presenting your findings. Address your report to other students, faculty, or the entire college community.

Community Links

Compare and contrast Tannen's perspective with that of Bill Moyers in "Journalism & Democracy: On the Importance of Being a 'Public Nuisance'" (pp. 366–372).

THE CASE AGAINST COLLEGE
Linda Lee

◆

This opinion piece appeared in the Full Circle column of Family Circle, *a popular magazine with millions of readers, primarily women. Most of the articles in this magazine provide information about aspects of women's lives, including household activities, health, and families. The Full Circle page, however, features brief opinion pieces about topics or issues likely to concern readers. The author of this column,*

Linda Lee, also wrote Success Without College. *Her opinion piece uses her son's experiences to support her viewpoint about college.*

1   Do you, like me, have a child who is smart but never paid attention in class? Now it's high-school graduation time. Other parents are talking Stanford this and State U. that. Your own child has gotten into a pretty good college. The question is: Is he ready? Should he go at all?

2   In this country two-thirds of high school graduates go on to college. In some middle-class suburbs, that number reaches 90 percent. So why do so many feel the need to go?

3   America is obsessed with college. It has the second-highest number of graduates worldwide, after (not Great Britain, not Japan, not Germany) Australia. Even so, only 27 percent of Americans have a bachelor's degree or higher. That leaves an awful lot who succeed without college, or at least without a degree. Many read books, think seriously about life and have well-paying jobs. Some want to start businesses. Others want to be electricians or wilderness guides or makeup artists. Not everyone needs a higher education.

4   What about the statistics showing that college graduates make more money? First, until the computer industry came along, all the highest-paying jobs *required* a college degree: doctor, lawyer, engineer. Second, on average, the brightest and hardest-working kids in school go to college. So is it a surprise that they go on to make more money? And those studies almost always pit kids with degrees against those with just high school. An awful lot have additional training, but they are not included. Ponder for a moment: Who makes more, a plumber or a philosophy major?

5   These are tough words. I certainly wouldn't have listened to them five years ago when my son was graduating from high school. He had been smart enough to get into the Bronx High School of Science in New York and did well on his SATs. But I know now that he did not belong in college, at least not straight out of high school.

6   But he went, because all his friends were going, because it sounded like fun, because he could drink beer and hang out. He did not go to study philosophy. Nor did he feel it incumbent to go to class or complete courses. Meanwhile I was paying $1,000 a week for this pleasure cruise.

7   Eventually I asked myself, "Is he getting $1,000 a week's worth of education?" Heck no. That's when I began wondering why everyone needs to go to college. (My hair colorist makes $300,000 a year without a degree.) What about the famous people who don't have one, like Bill Gates (dropped out of Harvard) and Walter Cronkite (who left the University of Texas to begin a career in journalism)?

8   So I told my son (in a kind way) that his college career was over for now, but he could reapply to the Bank of Mom in two years if he wanted to go back. Meanwhile, I said, get a job.

9   If college is so wonderful, how come so many kids "stop out"? (That's the new terminology.) One study showed only 26 percent of those who began four-year colleges had earned a degree in six years. And what about the kids who finish, then can't find work? Of course, education is worth a great deal

more than just employment. But most kids today view college as a way to get a good job.

10   I know, I know. What else is there to do? Won't he miss the "college experience?" First off, there are thousands of things for kids to do. And yes, he will miss the college experience, which may include binge drinking, reckless driving and sleeping in on class days. He can have the same experience in the Marine Corps, minus the sleeping in, and be paid good money for it and learn a trade and discipline.

11   If my son had gone straight through college, he would be a graduate by now. A number of his friends are, and those who were savvy enough to go into computers at an Ivy League school walked into $50,000-a-year jobs. But that's not everyone. An awful lot became teachers making half that. And some still don't know what they want to do.

12   They may, like my son, end up taking whatever jobs they can get. Over the last two years, he's done roofing, delivered UPS packages and fixed broken toilets. His phone was turned off a few times, and he began to pay attention to details, like the price of a gallon of gasoline.

13   But a year ago he began working at a telecommunications company. He loves his work, and over the last year, he's gotten a raise and a year-end bonus. He tells me now he plans to stay there and become a manager.

14   So, just about on schedule, my son has had his own graduation day. And although I won't be able to take a picture of him in cap and gown, I couldn't be any more proud. He grew up, as most kids do. And he did it, for the most part, in spite of college.

Reading Responses

1. What is Lee's main point? How does she introduce her point to readers?
2. What common assumptions about the value or purpose of a college education does Lee question? What evidence does she provide to support her own point of view?
3. How does Lee direct her argument to specific readers? Cite examples to show how she appeals to their values, assumptions, or experiences.

Writing Activities

1. Write a brief summary of Lee's position, including the major points in her argument.
2. Write a response to Lee's argument. Briefly acknowledge points in her article that you agree with, but also present and support your own viewpoint.
3. Write your own opinion piece, "The Case for College," based on your experiences and opinions about the value of a college education to you.

Community Links

Lee does not specifically address the academic community or write as a member of that community, but she challenges assumptions about attending college. Read some other selections that challenge preconceptions such as Simpson's "Are Incentives for Drug Abuse Treatment Too Strong?" (pp. 301–306) from the work community or Jamieson's "Preface" (pp. 397–404) or Rhodes's "Think You Can Teach? Pass This Test" (pp. 515–517), both from the public community. Compare and contrast one or two of these selections with Lee's opinion piece. Consider questions such as these: How does each reading tackle the problem of challenging readers' preconceptions? What approaches or strategies do the readings share? What differences may reflect community expectations?

Community Ethics

ANTI-PLAGIARISM STRATEGIES FOR RESEARCH PAPERS
Robert Harris

♦

A major ethical issue in the academic community is plagiarism, *the presentation of someone else's work as one's own. Taking credit for someone else's creation or transmission of knowledge challenges deeply held values of the academic community. Students, scholars, or professional writers plagiarize deliberately if they present a paper or passages from someone else's work as their own. Inexperienced or careless researchers may plagiarize inadvertently if they omit quotation marks, quote inaccurately, rely on inexact notes, or confuse their own writing with wording from a source. To help prevent plagiarism, Robert Harris, author of* The Plagiarism Handbook, *posted this article on the VirtualSalt Web site.*

1   The availability of textual material in electronic format has made plagiarism easier than ever. Copying and pasting of paragraphs or even entire essays now can be performed with just a few mouse clicks. The strategies discussed here can be used to combat what some believe is an increasing amount of plagiarism on research papers. By employing these strategies, you can help encourage students to value the assignment and to do their own work.

Strategies of Awareness

2   **1. Understand why students cheat.** By understanding some of the reasons students are tempted to cheat on papers, you can take steps to prevent cheating by attacking the causes. Some of the major reasons include these:

- Students are natural economizers. Many students are interested in the shortest route possible through a course. That's why they ask questions such as, "Will this be on the test?" Copying a paper sometimes looks [like a] shortcut through an assignment, especially when the student feels overloaded with work already. To combat this cause, assign your paper to be due well before the end-of-term pressures. Remind students that the purpose of the course is to learn and develop skills and not just "get through." The more they learn and develop their skills, the more effective they will be in their future lives.

- Students are faced with too many choices, so they put off low priorities. With so many things to do (both of academic and recreational nature), many students put off assignments that do not interest them. A remedy here would be to customize the research topic to include something of real interest to the students or to offer topics with high intrinsic interest to them.
- Many students have poor time management and planning skills. Some students are just procrastinators, while others do not understand the hours required to develop a good research paper, and they run out of time as the due date looms. Thus, they are most tempted to copy a paper when time is short and they have not yet started the assignment. If you structure your research assignment so that intermediate parts of it (topic, early research, prospectus, outline, draft, bibliography, final draft) are due at regular intervals, students will be less likely to get in a time-pressure panic and look for an expedient shortcut.
- Some students fear that their writing ability is inadequate. Fear of a bad grade and inability to perform cause some students to look for a superior product. Sadly, these students are among [those] least able to judge a good paper and are often likely to turn in a very poor copied one. Some help for these students may come from demonstrating how poor many of the online papers are and by emphasizing the value of the learning process (more on this below). Reassuring students of the help available to them (your personal attention, a writing center, teaching assistants, online lab sites, etc.) may give them the courage to persevere.
- A few students like the thrill of rule breaking. The more angrily you condemn plagiarism the more they can hardly wait to do it. An approach that may have some effect is to present the assignment and the proper citation of sources in a positive light (more below).

2. **Educate yourself about plagiarism.** Plagiarism on research papers takes many forms. Some of the most common include these:

- Downloading a free research paper. Many of these papers have been written and shared by other students. Since paper swappers are often not among the best students, free papers are often of poor quality, in both mechanics and content. Some of the papers are surprisingly old (with citations being no more recent than the seventies).
- Buying a paper from a commercial paper mill. These papers can be good—and sometimes they are too good. If you have given students an in-class writing assignment, you can compare the quality and be quite enlightened. Moreover, mills often sell both custom and stock papers, with custom papers becoming stock papers very quickly. If you visit some of the mill sites, you might just find the same paper available for sale by searching by title or subject.
- Copying an article from the Web or an online or electronic database. Only some of these articles will have the quantity and type of citations that academic research papers are expected to have. If you receive a well-

written, highly informed essay without a single citation (or with just a few), it may have been copied wholesale from an electronic source.
- Copying a paper from a local source. Papers may be copied from students who have taken your course previously, from fraternity files, or from other paper-sharing sources near campus. If you keep copies of previous papers turned in to you, they can be a source of detection of this particular practice.
- Cutting and pasting to create a paper from several sources. These "assembly-kit" papers are often betrayed by wide variations in tone, diction, and citation style. The introduction and conclusion are often student-written and therefore noticeably different from and weaker than the often glowing middle.
- Quoting less than all the words copied. This practice includes premature end quotation marks or missing quotation marks. A common type of plagiarism occurs when a student quotes a sentence or two, places the end quotation mark and the citation, and then continues copying from the source. Or the student may copy from the source verbatim without any quotation marks at all, but adding a citation, implying that the information is the student's summary of the source. Checking the citation will expose this practice.
- Faking a citation. In lieu of real research, some students will make up quotations and supply fake citations. You can discover this practice by randomly checking citations. If you require several Web or other electronic sources for the paper, these can be checked quickly.

4   Visiting some of the sites that give away or sell research papers can be an informative experience. If you have Web projection capability, you might do this visiting in class and show the students (1) that you know about these sites and (2) that the papers are often well below your expectations for quality, timeliness, and research. There is a list of many of these sites at Termpapers.com at http://www.termpapers.com and at "Internet Paper Mills" at http://www.coastal.edu/library/mills2.htm.

5   3. **Educate your students about plagiarism.** Do not assume that students know what plagiarism is, even if they nod their heads when you ask them. Provide an explicit definition for them. For example, "Plagiarism is using another person's words or ideas without giving credit to the other person. When you use someone else's words, you must put quotation marks around them and give the writer or speaker credit by revealing the source in a citation. Even if you revise or paraphrase the words of someone else or just use their ideas, you still must give the author credit in a note. Not giving due credit to the creator of an idea or writing is very much like lying."

6   In addition to a definition, though, you should discuss with your students the difference between appropriate, referenced use of ideas or quotations and inappropriate use. You might show them an example of a permissible paraphrase (with its citation) and an impermissible paraphrase (containing some paraphrasing and some copying), and discuss the difference. Discuss also quoting a passage and using quotation marks and a citation as opposed to

quoting a passage with neither (in other words, merely copying without attribution). Such a discussion should educate those who truly do not understand citation issues ("But I put it in my own words, so I didn't think I had to cite it") and it will also warn the truly dishonest that you are watching.

Discussing with students why plagiarism is wrong may be helpful also. Clarifying for them that plagiarism is a combination of stealing (another's words) and lying (claiming implicitly that the words are the student's own) should be mentioned at some point, but should not be the whole emphasis or you risk setting up a challenge for the rebels (those who like to break the rules just for fun). Many statements on plagiarism also remind students that such cheating shows contempt for the professor, other students, and the entire academic enterprise. Plagiarizers by their actions declare that they are not at the university to gain an education, but only to pretend to do so, and that they therefore intend to gain by fraud the credentials (the degree) of an educated person.

Perhaps the most effective discussion will ask the students to think about who is really being cheated when someone plagiarizes. Copying papers or even parts of papers short circuits a number of learning experiences and opportunities for the development of skills: actually doing the work of the research paper rather than counterfeiting it gives the student not only knowledge of the subject and insights into the world of information and controversy, but improves research skills, thinking and analyzing, organizing, writing, planning and time management, and even meticulousness (those picky citation styles actually help improve one's attention to detail). All this is missed when the paper is faked, and it is these missed skills which will be of high value in the working world. A degree will help students get a first job, but performance—using the skills developed by doing just such assignments as research papers—will be required for promotion.

4. **Discuss the benefits of citing sources.** Many students do not seem to realize that whenever they cite a source, they are strengthening their writing. Citing a source, whether paraphrased or quoted, reveals that they have performed research work and synthesized the findings into their own argument. Using sources shows that the student in engaged in "the great conversation," the world of ideas, and that the student is aware of other thinkers' positions on the topic. By quoting (and citing) writers who support the student's position, the student adds strength to the position. By responding reasonably to those who oppose the position, the student shows that there are valid counter arguments. In a nutshell, citing helps make the essay stronger and sounder and will probably result in a better grade.

Appropriate quoting and citing also evidences the student's respect for the creators of ideas and arguments—honoring thinkers and their intellectual property. Most college graduates will become knowledge workers themselves, earning at least part of their living creating information products. They therefore have an interest in maintaining a respect for intellectual property and the proper attribution of ideas and words.

5. **Make the penalties clear.** If an institutional policy exists, quote it in your syllabus. If you have your own policy, specify the penalties involved. For

example, "Cheating on a paper will result in an F on that paper with no possibility of a makeup. A second act of cheating will result in an F in the course regardless of the student's grade otherwise." If you teach at a university where the penalty for plagiarism is dismissal from the university or being reported to the Academic Dean or Dean of Students, you should make that clear as well. Even the penalties can be presented in a positive light. Penalties exist to reassure honest students that their efforts are respected and valued, so much so that those who would escape the work by fakery will be punished substantially.

Strategies of Prevention

12 The overall goal of these specific strategies is to make the assignment and requirements unique enough that an off-the-shelf paper or a paper written for another class or a friend's paper will not fulfill the requirements. Only a newly written paper will.

13   1. **Make the assignment clear.** Be specific about your expectations. Should the paper be an individual effort or is collaboration permitted? Must the paper be unique to your course, or do you allow it to be submitted to another course as well? (In scholarly publishing, such multiple publication is usually called self-plagiarism. If you require a unique paper, be sure to prohibit photocopied papers and insist on original typescripts or printouts.) What kind of research do you require? How should it be evidenced in the paper, by quotation or just summary? It has been claimed that a major source of poor student papers (not just plagiarizing) is the unclear assignment. You might ask another faculty member to read your paper assignment and discuss with you whether or not it is clear and detailed enough for students to fulfill in the way you intend.

14   2. **Provide a list of specific topics** and require students to choose one of them. Change topics from semester to semester whenever possible. Unusual topics or topics with a narrow twist are good because there will be fewer papers already written on them. If you provide a substantial enough list of topics (say two dozen), most students will find something that can interest them. You can also allow for a custom topic if the student comes to discuss it with you first.

15   3. **Require specific components in the paper.** For example, "The paper must make use of two Internet sources, two printed book sources, two printed journal sources, one personal interview, and one personally conducted survey." Or, "You must make use of Wells' article on 'Intelligent Design Principles,' and some material from either the Jones or Smith book." Or, "Include a graph which represents the data discussed in the first section." Requirements that will strongly inhibit the use of a copied paper include these:

- Use of one or more sources written within the past year. A requirement like this will quickly outdate most paper mill products.

- Use of one or more specific articles or books you name or provide. The articles could be available online (from the Web or one of your university's proprietary databases) to save the effort of photocopying and distribution.
- Incorporation of some information you provide (for example, a data set).
- A personal interview with an expert or authority. An interview creates both a current and a checkable source.

If a student begins with someone else's paper and has to work additional material such as the above into it, you'll probably be able to tell. (For example, the fit will be awkward where the new material has been stuffed in or the writing styles will differ.)

4. **Require process steps for the paper.** Set a series of due dates throughout the term for the various steps of the research paper process: topic or problem, preliminary bibliography, prospectus, research material (annotated photocopies of articles, for example), outline, rough draft, final annotated bibliography, final draft. Some of these parts can be reverse engineered by the determined cheater, but most students should realize that doing the assignment honestly is easier than the alternative.

The rough draft serves several functions. A quick glance will reveal whether whole sections are appearing without citations. At the draft stage, you have the opportunity to educate the student further and discuss how proper citation works. You can also mark places and ask for more research material to be incorporated. If you are suspicious of the paper at this point, ask for the incorporation of some specific material that you name, such as a particular book or article. Keep the drafts and let students know that you expect major revisions and improvements between drafts. (This is actually a great way to improve students' writing, quite apart from the other goal of preventing plagiarism.)

5. **Require oral reports of student papers.** Ask students questions about their research and writing process. If students know at the beginning of the term that they will be giving a presentation on their research papers to the rest of the class, they will recognize the need to be very familiar with both the process and the content of the paper. Such knowledge should serve as a strong deterrent against simply copying a paper. Regardless of how many times a student reads over a copied paper, much of the knowledge of the research, the drafting, leaving out, and so on will still remain unknown. Alternative to an in-class presentation is a one-on-one office meeting, where you can quiz the student about several aspects of the paper as needed.

Many students have been caught by simple questions like, "What exactly do you mean here by 'dynamic equivalence'?" Few students use words they cannot pronounce, so having them read some of the paper aloud can be interesting as well (although you may be merely exposing the mindless use of a thesaurus). If you suspect a student has copied a whole paper, complete with citations, asking about the sources can be useful. "Where did you find the article by Edwards? It sounds fascinating. Can you bring me a copy at the next meeting?" Or, "This quotation seems slightly out of context. What was Follet's main point in the chapter?"

20   **6. Have students include an annotated bibliography.** The annotation should include a brief summary of the source, where it was located (including call number for books or complete Web URL), and an evaluation about the usefulness of the source. (Optionally, as a lesson in information quality, ask them to comment on why they thought the source credible.) The normal process of research makes completing this task easy, but it creates headaches for students who have copied a paper from someone else since few papers include annotated bibliographies like this. Another benefit of this assignment is that students must reflect on the reliability and quality of their sources.

21   **7. Require most references to be up-to-date.** Many of the free term papers online (and many of the ones for sale) are quite old, with correspondingly old references. If you require all research material to be, say, less than five years old, you will automatically eliminate thousands of online papers. Such a recent date restriction is not usually workable for some subjects, such as history or English literature, but you can always require a few sources of recent date.

22   **8. Require a metalearning essay.** On the day you collect the papers, have students write an in-class essay about what they learned from the assignment. What problems did they face and how did they overcome them? What research strategy did they follow? Where did they locate most of their sources? What is the most important thing they learned from investigating this subject? For most students, who actually did the research paper, this assignment will help them think about their own learning. It also provides you with information about the students' knowledge of their papers and it gives you a writing sample to compare with the papers. If a student's knowledge of the paper and its process seems modest or if the in-class essay quality diverges strikingly from the writing ability shown in the paper, further investigation is probably warranted.

Strategies of Detection

23   **1. Look for the clues.** As you read the papers, look for internal evidence that may indicate plagiarism. Among the clues are the following:

- Mixed citation styles. If some paragraphs are cited in MLA style, while other references are in APA, and perhaps one or two are in CBE or Chicago, you are probably looking at a paste-up.
- Lack of references or quotations. Lengthy, well written sections without documentation may have been taken from general knowledge sources, such as encyclopedias, popular magazines, or Web sites.
- Unusual formatting. Strange margins, skewed tables, lines broken in half, mixed subhead styles and other formatting anomalies may indicate a hasty copy and paste job.
- Off topic. If the paper does not develop one of the assigned topics or even the topic it announces, it may have been borrowed at the last minute or downloaded. Similarly, if parts of the paper do develop the subject, but other parts seem oddly off, the product may be a cut and paste.

- Signs of datedness. If there are no references after some well past date (e.g., 1985), or if a data table offers a company's sales from 1989 to 1994, either the student is using very old material or the paper itself is rather old.
- Anachronisms. If the paper refers to long-past events as current ("Only after the Gulf War is over will we see lower oil prices" or "Why isn't the Carter administration acting on this?"), you almost certainly have a recycled paper on your hands.
- Anomalies of diction. Many undergraduates do not understand the concept of levels of diction. They think all words are equally welcome in every paper. As a result, when those who plagiarize with the cut-and-paste method perform their deeds, they often mix paragraphs of varying levels together—the sophisticated scholar's paragraph precedes the breezy journalist's commentary, which may be followed by the student's own highly colloquial addition. Similarly, you may come upon some suspiciously elevated vocabulary usages. "Thesaurusitis" is one source of this, to be sure, but a common source of such vocabulary is another writer, who should have been quoted rather than simply copied. "What do you mean by 'ineffable'?" can sometimes provide you with inexpressible information. Lastly, if you find that the paper uses several archaic terms, or words no longer used in the way the paper uses them, you may be looking at some very old text.
- Anomalies of style. Is the prose style remarkable? Are there two-page paragraphs that remind you of a nineteenth-century encyclopedia? Is there ornate rhetorical structure? Does the introduction get in its own way and stumble around, only to give way to glowing, flowing discourse? Is there a mixture of British and American punctuation or spelling, with consistent usage within large sections?
- Smoking guns. This category might be called "blunders of the clueless," since it includes obvious indicators of copying. Reported in the past have been labels left at the end of papers ("Thank you for using TermPaperMania"), title pages stapled to Web printouts (complete with dates and URL in the corners), title pages claiming the paper is by Tom Jones when subsequent pages say "Smith, page 2," and papers with whiteout over the previous author's name.

Few of these clues will provide courtroom proof of plagiarism, of course, but their presence should alert you to investigate the paper. Even if you do not find the source of the paper, you may be able to use these clues profitably in a discussion with the student in your office.

2. **Know where the sources of papers are.** Before you begin to search for the source or sources of a suspect paper, you should know where to look. Here are the major sources of text in electronic form:

- Free and for-sale term paper sites. As mentioned earlier, there is a list of many of these sites at Termpapers.com at http://www.termpapers.com and at "Internet Paper Mills" at http://www.coastal.edu/library/mills2.htm.

- The free, visible Web. This category includes all the publicly mounted Web pages, which are indexed by search engines.
- The free, invisible Web. This category includes the contents of sites that provide articles free to users, but that content may be accessible only by going directly to the site. That is, the articles are not indexed by search engines and therefore cannot be located by using a search engine. Some magazines, newspapers, reference works, encyclopedias, and subject-specific sites are in this category.
- Paid databases over the Web. This category includes commercial databases for consumers (such as Northern Light's Special Collection) and databases that libraries subscribe to, containing scholarly journals, newspapers, court cases and the like. Providers like Lexis-Nexis, UMI Proquest, Infotrac, JSTOR and others are in this group. To find information from this category, you must have access to the database (through password or an on-campus computer) and search on the database directly.
- CD-ROM resources. Encyclopedias and some databases are available on CD-ROM.

3. **Search for the paper online.** If you suspect the paper may have come from the Web, you might try these strategies to find it:

- First, go to Findsame, at http://www.findsame.com, a powerful content-search engine, and type or paste in a suspect paragraph. Findsame will return a list of matching pages, ranked by percent of sameness. You can even view your suspect text and the matching texts side by side for comparison.
- You might also try HowOriginal at http://www.howoriginal.com and PlagiServe at http://www.plagiserve.com for two more text-matching tools.
- If you find nothing with these tools, try several of the large-database, full-text search engines like Google, Northern Light, or Fast Search, and perform an exact phrase search on a four-to-six-word phrase from a suspect part of the paper (find a phrase that has two or three relatively unusual words in it). Remember that no search engine covers more than about a third of the visible Web, so you should try several engines before you give up.
- Next, locate some appropriate databases on the invisible Web, depending on the subject of the paper. You can find many of these databases by consulting the "World Wide Web Research Tools" page on this site. If indicated, visit some of the online encyclopedias as well. Here, you will have to use keyword searches rather than exact phrase searches, but using a string of appropriate keywords can be very powerful.
- Now go to your library's online database subscriptions and search on subject-appropriate databases using keyword searches.

26   **4. Use a plagiarism detector.** If you do not find the paper this way, you might want to turn to some commercial services that provide plagiarism detection. Here are some of the services:

- Plagiarism.com at http://www.plagiarism.com. Educational materials and a software screening program that creates a test of familiarity for a student to complete. The company says that no student has been falsely accused. CD-ROM program.
- Plagiarism.org at http://www.plagiarism.org. Online service that checks submitted student papers against a large database and provides reports of results. Also monitors term paper mills.
- Wordcheck at http://www.wordchecksystems.com. Keyword matching software. Requires local database of papers or texts to match.
- Integriguard at http://www.integriguard.com. Compares submissions against a database of other papers and Web sites.
- Eve at http://www.canexus.com/eve/index.shtml. Inexpensive software agent that searches the Web to compare a suspect paper with Internet content. Shows site and degree of match.

It is sometimes said that the best plagiarism detector is the student who handed in the paper, because he or she already knows whether or not the paper is genuine, or what part is fraudulent. Therefore, you can sometimes enlist the student's help. You must be very careful about accusing a student of cheating unless you have clear proof, because a false accusation can be both cruel and reason for litigation. But if you ask the right questions in the right way, you will often be successful. Here are some example questions that may help reveal the truth:

- "I was quite surprised by your paper, so I did some investigation into it. Before I tell you what I found out, is there anything you want to tell me about it?" With the appropriately serious demeanor and tone, a well phrased question like this will often result in a confession. If the student is innocent or just hardened and replies, "No," you can always reveal some innocuous fact and go on.
- "I'm curious to know why your writing style is so good in some parts of the paper and so poor in others. And why have you not shown such great writing on the in-class essays?"
- "This long passage doesn't sound like your normal style. Is this a quotation where you accidentally forgot the quotation marks?"

Reading Responses

1. What is Harris's purpose in this article?
2. Who does Harris expect to be his primary reader? How does he address this reader? What does he assume about the values, judgments, and concerns of his readers?

3. How does Harris organize and present his article? What features of his presentation are especially well suited to the Web?

Writing Activities

1. Conduct some informal research about plagiarism attitudes, guidelines, and penalties on your campus. You might examine your student handbook, departmental guidelines, assignment sheets, or other course materials. You might also interview other students, faculty, administrators, or members of the campus judiciary body. Prepare a brief report explaining what you discover. If you quote or paraphrase any material, be sure to do so accurately, and cite your sources.
2. Propose a specific policy or make a specific recommendation about some aspect of the plagiarism issue. Explain your proposal, supplying logical, persuasive reasons and pertinent supporting evidence that will appeal to your readers. You may address your proposal to other students, an instructor, a department, a campus administrator, parents, a particular student organization, a campus judiciary group, or some other specific readers affiliated with your campus.
3. Imagine that you have been asked to contribute some advice about plagiarism to a campus Web site for prospective students. Explain what you consider an important and useful point about how to adjust to college expectations and avoid plagiarism. Address your readers directly, taking into account their possible experience, age, values, and concerns. Present your advice clearly, designing and organizing it as one section of a Web site.

Community Links

After reading Harris's discussion of plagiarism, turn to Zielinski's article, "Are You a Copyright Criminal?" (pp. 264–270). In what ways are these selections similar or different? How does each address concerns typical of its community?

THE ETHICS OF FACULTY BEHAVIOR: STUDENTS' AND PROFESSORS' VIEWS

Betsy Levonian Morgan and Ann J. Korschgen

———◆———

As Betsy Levonian Morgan and Ann Korschgen explain in the short abstract introducing their article, they studied student and faculty perceptions of the ethics of sixteen faculty behaviors. Their article appeared in College Student Journal, *a publication devoted to research and theory about college students and college teaching. It follows the article format and citation style recommended in the* Publication Manual of the American Psychological Association *(APA). The article also uses conventional symbols and abbreviations, such as < for "less than" and N for "number of responses,"* t *for results of a* "t *test" comparing means (or averages) of responses,* p *for "probability," the likelihood that the result is due to chance, or SD for "standard deviation."*

We examined differences in professors' and students' perceptions of the ethicalness of faculty behavior. The sample of 115 professors and 157 undergraduates responded to 16 items regarding faculty behavior. Faculty and students differed significantly on 4 of the 16 behaviors and showed a strong trend on another 3. Faculty saw ensuring popularity with an easy test, accepting a textbook rebate, and using profanity as more unethical than did the undergraduates. The students viewed failing to update notes as more unethical than did the faculty. We argue that future research should explore students' views on the distinction between professors' undesirable and unethical behaviors.

1. Many educators and social commentators have explored ethical issues in higher education (e.g., Alexander, 1986; Finn, 1989; Robinson & Moulton, 1985; Thompson, 1991; Wilshire, 1990). Professional associations, such as the American Association of University Professors (AAUP, 1987) and the American Psychological Association (APA, 1992) have issued responsibility standards that apply to their general membership and special considerations that cover the unique situations that confront their academic professionals. Despite the fact that scholars have noted that teaching is rife with ethical dilemmas that require a "conscious reflection on values" (e.g., Svinicki, 1994, p. 277), there is relatively little empirical research on ethical issues in academia (Tabachnick, Keith-Spiegel, & Pope, 1991). Research on faculty behavior has focused on "hot topics" such as sexual harassment and largely ignored the more daily ethical dilemmas involved in teaching and instructor-student interactions. In particular, there is sparse research on students' perceptions of faculty behavior.

2. Tabachnick, Keith-Spiegel, and Pope (1991) conducted a survey of ethical problems in higher education utilizing a 63-item questionnaire that asked faculty to identify and rank potential ethical issues. Although their study was limited to academic psychologists, research on ethical issues involved in teaching per se suggests that many of the themes are generalizable across disciplines (Keith-Spiegel, Wittig, Perkins, Balogh, & Whitley, 1993). In a related follow-up, Keith-Spiegel, Tabachnick, and Allen (1993) culled 51 items from their original work and explored students' views of professors' actions. Unfortunately, due to differences in the response scales used, they could not make direct statistical comparisons between students and faculty. However, they did find indications that faculty and students were similar on most of the items.

3. The present study compared faculty and student perceptions of faculty behavior using items from Tabachnick, Keith-Spiegel, and Pope's (1991) work. We expected that agreement would be high for faculty and students.

Method

Procedure

We sampled faculty (N = 115) and undergraduates (N = 157) at a medium-sized public Midwestern university. We mailed questionnaires to a randomly selected sample of 234 faculty members (representing half the faculty). The 115 responses represented a response rate of 49%. The students were enrolled in a general education introductory psychology course and received course credit for their participation. To insure that the students had reasonable familiarity with university life, they must have completed at least two semesters of college in order to participate in the study.

Respondents rated the ethicalness of 16 faculty behaviors on a 5-point scale that ranged from 1 (*unquestionably not ethical*) to 5 (*unquestionably ethical*). We selected the items from a larger list of issues developed by Tabachnick, Keith-Spiegel, and Pope (1991) and we focused primarily on student-teacher relationships and professional ethical issues for college teachers. We chose items that appeared to be appropriate across all disciplines.

Sample Characteristics

Faculty. Of the 115 faculty respondents, 62% were men and 38% were women. The median age was 47 and the age range was 28–63. The sample was predominantly European-American (96%). The majority of the faculty was from a college of liberal arts (62%), 12% were from the college of business, and an additional 25% were from colleges of science, and health/physical education. Respondents indicated that, on average, they spent 81% of their workload on teaching related activities. In general, despite a higher percentage of female faculty, the sample approximated the demographics of the faculty pool.

Students. Of the 157 student respondents, 94 were women (60%) and 63 were men (40%). The median age was 19 and the age range was 18–28. The sample was predominantly European-American (92%). Seventy percent of the sample was sophomores and the remaining 30% were juniors or seniors. The students represented a cross-section of majors.

Results

To adjust for the use of multiple tests, we considered differences significant if they achieved the probability level of .003 or better. In contrast to the expectation of high agreement between faculty and students, we found significant differences on 4 of the 16 behaviors and a strong trend in another 3 behaviors. Although both faculty and students viewed most of the behaviors as unethical, there were differences detected in the degree of perceived ethicalness.

Table 1 shows the mean score on each behavior for the faculty and student samples. Faculty saw ensuring popularity with easy tests ($t = -5.04, p < .001$), accepting a textbook rebate ($t = -5.14, p < .001$), and using profanity in lectures ($t = -6.68, p < .001$) as more unethical than did the student sample. Additionally, there was a strong trend for faculty to see sexual involvement with a student as more unethical than did the students ($t = -2.91, p = .004$).

Table 1 The 16 Ethical Issues in Academia Items[a]—Student and Faculty Comparisons

	Faculty Sample (N = 115)		Student Sample (N = 157)	
	M	SD	M	SD
Behaviors that faculty viewed as more unethical				
1. Giving easy courses or tests to ensure your popularity with students.	1.33	.81	1.85[c]	.89
2. Accepting for yourself a publisher's monetary rebate for adopting their text.	1.57	1.01	2.24[c]	1.14
3. Using profanity in lectures.	2.29	1.13	3.25[c]	1.20
4. Becoming sexually involved with a student.[b]	1.41	.78	1.72	.98
Behaviors that students viewed as more unethical				
5. Failing to update lecture notes when re-teaching a course.	2.58	1.11	2.10[c]	1.02
6. Telling colleagues a confidential disclosure told to you by a student.[b]	1.56	.72	1.32[c]	.62
7. Teaching material you haven't really mastered.[b]	2.62	1.04	2.26[c]	1.01
Behaviors that did not yield significant differences				
8. Ignoring strong evidence of cheating.	1.20	.55	1.39	.79
9. Teaching full time while "moonlighting" at least 20 hours per week.	2.66	1.24	2.94	1.09
10. Selling unwanted complimentary textbooks to used book vendors.	2.46	1.31	2.48	1.19
11. Allowing students to drop courses for reasons not officially approved.	2.56	1.06	2.79	1.19
12. Omitting significant information when writing a letter of recommendation for a student.	2.11	.88	2.00	.98
13. Insulting, ridiculing, etc. a student in his or her absence.	1.36	.68	1.35	.74
14. Ignoring unethical behavior by colleagues.	1.93	.88	1.77	.82
15. Allowing a student's "likability" to influence your grading.	1.51	.79	1.77	1.03
16. Grading on a strict curve regardless of class performance level.	2.42	1.25	2.13	1.05

[a]From Tabachnick et al. (1991).
[b]Evidence of a strong trend (p. < .005)
[c]Adjusting for multiple t tests, differences considered significant at the p. < .003 level.

Note: Ratings are on a 1–5 Likert-type scale. The lower the number the more unethical the behavior.
Note: Items administered in the following order: 8, 1, 9, 10, 2, 11, 12, 5, 6, 13, 3, 4, 7, 14, 15, 16.

Students saw the use of old lecture notes ($t = 3.66, p < .001$) as more unethical than did faculty, and had a strong trend toward viewing the breaking of confidence ($t = 2.85, p = .005$) and the teaching of unmastered material ($t = 2.89, p = .004$) as more unethical than did the faculty.

Discussion

10 Overall, we detected more differences between students and faculty than previous research would suggest (Keith-Spiegel, Tabachnick, & Allen, 1993). However, the findings are logical when we consider the daily context of both students and faculty. For instance, students' understandable self-interest is evident in their concern over course issues such as outdated lecture notes. On the other hand, faculty are more aware of factors (such as emergency hires) that refocus the moral principles that may underlie "unwanted" behaviors such as "teaching material you haven't really mastered." Students appear less perturbed by some of the "political" issues in academia such as allowing likability to influence grading, giving easy tests for popularity sake, or sexual relations between faculty and students. However, although there was a difference of degree, both faculty and students viewed most of the behaviors as unethical. For instance, both faculty and students [saw] ignoring evidence of cheating and insulting a student in his/her absence as strongly unethical.

11 Recently, researchers have examined students' "pet peeves" regarding faculty behavior (Murray, 2000). Appleby (1990) and Perlman and McCann (1998) have tapped students' views of undesirable faculty behaviors. The lists include behaviors such as poor organization, intellectual arrogance, poor testing, and keeping students past the end of class. When contrasting the work on ethics in education with the work on pet peeves, we believe that it is important to conduct further empirical research into students' motivation and ability to distinguish between undesirable behaviors and unethical behaviors. We need to explore whether students discern the underlying moral principle at hand when considering their concerns regarding professors' behaviors. In focus group work with students in this area (Morgan, Korschgen, & Gardner, 1996), we detected few arguments that centered on classic moral reasoning (e.g., Rest, 1986). Future research on this topic may be well served by using senior students due to their increased experience with college situations. In a practical sense, we believe that professors should know if students perceive a behavior as more than just a "pet peeve." We see judgments of morality to carry a more severe implication than those regarding unwanted behaviors. Professors' attention to students concerns (undesirable or unethical) should improve the quality of the classroom interaction and, consequently, student learning.

References

Alexander, J. (1986). The university and morality: A revised approach to university autonomy and its limits. *The Journal of Higher Education, 57,* 463–476.

American Association of University Professors. (1987) Statement on professional ethics. *Academe, 73,* 49.

American Psychological Association. (1992). Ethical principles of psychologists and code of conduct. *American Psychologist, 47,* 1597–1611.

Appleby, D. C. (1990). Faculty and student perceptions of irritation behaviors in the college classroom. *Journal of Staff, Program, and Organization Development, 8,* 41–46.

Finn, C. (1989, December 13). Ignoble and self-serving practices subvert the moral authority of higher education. *The Chronicle of Higher Education,* B1, B3.

Keith-Spiegel, P. C., Wittig, A. F., Perkins, D. V., Balogh, D. W. & Whitley, B. E., Jr. (1993). *The ethics of teaching.* Muncie, IN: Ball State University.

Keith-Spiegel, P. C., Tabachnick, B. G. & Allen, M. (1993). Ethics in academia: Students' views of professors' actions. *Ethics and Behavior, 3,* 149–162.

Morgan, B. L., Korschgen, A. J., & Gardner, J. C. (1996). *Students' and professors' views on the ethics of faculty behavior* (Report No. HE030225). East Lansing, MI: National Center for Research on Teacher Learning (ERIC Document Reproduction Service No. ED409752)

Murray, B. (2000, January). Professors' most grating habits. *Monitor on Psychology,* 56–57.

Perlman, B. & McCann, L. I. (1998). Students' pet peeves about teaching. *Teaching of Psychology, 25,* 201–203.

Rest, J. R. (1986). *Moral development: Advances in research and theory.* New York, NY: Praeger.

Robinson, G. M., & Moulton, J. (1985). *Ethical problems in higher education.* Englewood Cliffs, NJ: Prentice-Hall.

Svinicki, M. (1994). Ethics in college teaching. In W. J. McKeachie (Ed.), *Teaching tips: Strategies, research, and theory for college and university teachers* (9th ed., pp. 269–277). Lexington, MA: D. C. Heath.

Tabachnick, B. G., Keith-Spiegel, P. C., & Pope, K. S. (1991). Ethics of teaching: Beliefs and behaviors of psychologists as educators. *American Psychologist, 46,* 506–515.

Thompson, D. L. (Ed.). (1991). *Moral values and higher education: A nation at risk.* Provo, UT: Brigham Young University.

Wilshire, B. W. (1990). *The moral collapse of the university: Professionalism, purity, and alienation.* Albany: State University of New York Press.

Notes

We thank Kristin Bever and Joseph Monroe for their help with the data collection. [...]

 Reading Responses

1. Why did Morgan and Korschgen conduct their study?
2. How did they conduct the study? Who participated, and what were participants asked to do?
3. The items in the authors' survey are listed in Table 1 (p. 90). If you had participated in their survey, how would you have rated these items using their five-point scale (1 = not ethical; 5 = ethical)? (When you look at Table 1, you will see that it uses some conventional abbreviations: N for the number of responses, M for the mean or the average of the participants' responses, and SD for the standard deviation, a calculation that indicates whether the responses are clustered close together or widely separated. If you want to see how other students responded to an issue, look under Student Sample. The M column across from each behavior supplies the average of the student responses to that item. For example, if three students rated an item with a 1, a 2, and a 3, the M or average of the ratings would be 2. The lower the average rating number, the more un-

ethical the participants found the behavior; the higher the number, the more ethical.)

Writing Activities

1. Write a brief summary of the study's findings, explaining in your own words what Morgan and Korschgen found. Next, add your own reaction to the findings, noting any results that surprised you or caught your attention.
2. Select one of the ethical issues included in the study from the list in Table 1 (p. 90). Write a short position paper on this issue, explaining your views on the ethical considerations involved. Supply logical reasons and persuasive evidence to support your opinions.
3. The sections in this article have standard headings and are arranged in a standard sequence based on the advice of the APA manual and other guidelines for organizing academic research studies. Imagine that you want to launch a new journal that will publish student research studies. To give your journal as much credibility as possible, you plan to require student writers to follow the conventional format. Using the article by Morgan and Korschgen as a model, write guidelines for students who want to organize their papers in this same way. Explain what sections to include, what sequence to follow, and what to discuss in each section.

Community Links

Examine several of the research papers or reports included in this book. (Skim the table of contents or refer to the Guide to Themes, Topics, and Rhetorical Strategies at the end of the book to find examples in all three communities.) Compare and contrast two reports or studies from different communities. Consider what the two have in common and how they differ. In what ways might community expectations account for their similarities or differences?

Texts and Documents from the Academic Community

College Application Essay

APPLICATION ESSAY
Leo Stoscheck, Student Writer

◆

At the end of March 2001, this application essay was broadcast on Morning Edition, *the news and information program presented across the country on National Public Radio (NPR). Leo Stoscheck's essay was one of five essays selected from more than 150 submitted by listeners during the preceding month. Each of the five writers read his or her essay on the air during the week in a feature scheduled to coincide with the arrival of college acceptance letters in students' mailboxes across the country. Although each application essay reflects the personality and experiences of its writer, all essays of this type face the same test: persuading an admissions officer or committee to reply with a letter of acceptance.*

1   It's late December and my family and I have finally returned home from three months living in the city. A small house built by my parents twenty-five years ago and the hundred acres surrounding it on this easterly facing hill in upstate New York, this is my home. As we all trudge up the steep and winding path towards the pond with ice skates in hand, I glance up at the bright full moon. I begin to recall memories of my seventeen years growing up on this land. I skate around the pond like I have done every winter. I have lived on this hill, in these woods and fields, my entire life. The moon illuminates the trees, the ravines, the surrounding hills and valleys, the land that has taught me much of what I know and has shaped me into the person I am today. Under full moons my family and I have followed the tracks of deer, explored forgotten trails, and cross-country skied for miles. We have swum in cool waters on warm August evenings at moonrise just as the fog settled over the pond. Over the years I have developed a deep rooted connection to this land: from my bones to the veins running through my body like the ravines and small creeks mapping the surface of this hill. After living in the city for three months I am struck by the silence. It has always been quiet here. The only sounds I hear now are the blades of our skates scraping the frozen pond.

2   But this pond is not always frozen. In spring it teems with life. Often on early spring nights my mom would hand me a flashlight and head outside into

the warm darkness. The peepers were calling and she was out to look for them. I would run after my mom, catching up with her on the dew-drenched path, through the crown vetch leading up the bank to the pond. Crouching on all fours we would stalk the tiny and elusive frogs for hours. Believing that one of them was calling out from just under our noses, we would flip on our flashlights only to see a wavering blade of grass. Eventually, if we got lucky, we'd catch sight of one with its throat bulging larger than the frog itself. Holding our breaths, we would remain crouched there, enthralled, until the little frog jumped into the darkness. The trill whistle of thousands of spring peepers resonated deep within me. My world was full of life. Until I was fourteen years old and attended school for the first time, the land we lived on was my classroom and its occupants my teachers. So much was learned from building a terrarium, hatching a wood frog egg found in a cold puddle, and observing its entire life cycle; or from observing the strange spiraling flight of a male woodcock's mating ritual in the field above our house. I found a dead deer once while walking in the woods. I collected the bones and reassembled the skeleton. Mine was a living education.

3   As I grew older, though, the vast woods and fields that were my classroom seemed to be shrinking. All I had known was woods, fields, and streams, and so I assumed in my young mind that most of the world looked this way. But as I spent more and more time away from home, in school and in the city, my perception began to shift. The untouched wilderness of my childhood, once endless, now seemed to be a small island surrounded by the concrete world of humans. The night I knew this to be true was when I heard the coyotes for the second time in my life. Only recently had the Eastern Coyote returned to our area since they were eradicated. Their undaunted howls filled me with a renewed hope for the resiliency of the natural world. I awoke that night to the distant sound of a fire siren in the valley. There was nothing remarkable about this, but then I heard the excited yaps and howls of coyotes in the fields below our house, calling back. Witnessing Nature calling out, trying to communicate with a machine, forced upon me the ultimate realization that it is almost impossible to escape the far-reaching influence of man.

4   As I unlace my skates and head back down the steep, slippery pond bank I have a renewed awareness of this land that bore me and my deep-rooted connections to it. I glance up at the moon before turning toward the glowing windows of the house. I am still young and foolish. I cannot say where my life will take me. I do not know if one day I will return to this area and settle down. I do know, however, that part of me will always be here in this land that showed me the value of silence and reflection; educated me; and ultimately led me to realize its very fragility.

Reading Responses

1. What is the main idea that Leo develops in his essay?
2. What impression of himself does Leo convey? How does he create this impression?

3. How does Leo use description in his essay? Which descriptions do you find most effective? Which of the senses (sight, sound, taste, touch, and smell) do these descriptions draw upon?

Writing Activities

1. A friend or relative is planning to apply to a college that requires an application essay. This college does not specify a required topic but expects the essay to reveal the personality of the writer and show why he or she should be admitted. Write an e-mail message or a letter to this person, explaining how to write an effective essay.
2. Imagine that you are the admissions officer at the college where Leo applied. Write him a letter of acceptance that includes an explanation of why his essay persuaded you to admit him.
3. Write the application essay that you wish you had written when you applied to college. Or write an application essay for a semester abroad, an internship, a summer program, or some other academic opportunity. Use your essay to show why you should be accepted for that opportunity.

Community Links

Read Melanie Dedecker's "Statement of Purpose" (pp. 189–191). In what ways is her essay applying to graduate school similar to or different from this college application essay?

Letter of Advice from a Parent

IMPROVING UNDERSTANDING AND INCREASING GRADES: 4 TIPS FOR FALL FRESHMAN AT COLUMBUS DAY, AN OPEN LETTER TO MY SON AT COLLEGE

Paul J. Vermette

◆

Paul Vermette, a professor at Niagara University, wrote this letter to his son during his first semester at college. It combines typical parental advice with specialized tips, drawn from the professor's experience as both a student and a teacher. Later, the letter was published in College Student Journal *so that other students could also benefit from the advice.*

Dear Matt,

   Please notice that this is the first letter that I have written to you that has a title!!!!! Thinking about your situation at St. John Fisher made me think about all the Fall Freshman at Niagara that I have taught . . . and perhaps failed to help as much as I could! If you let me, I will share this note with other Freshmen in other colleges . . . and maybe help them too.

   This weekend (the second one in October) is infamous at College: some of us always fear that many of our students simply would NOT come back from their trip home on the extended break . . . or . . . they would feel so bad about all the difficult adjustments that they're facing that they would come back feeling "defeated". Many talented students don't negotiate all the "firsts" that they encounter in college and end up being down on themselves. Having a few strategies to use may help you weather the inevitable storm that is coming.

   Things are going well for you and I think that you can make the best out of these suggestions. I offer you a few simple pieces of advice that (a) you can implement easily and quickly (b) will make your school work different and perhaps more enjoyable and (c) no doubt will raise your grades!!!!

   Now, first of all there is a precondition to this set of 4 TIPS. Most of the time we parents offer ideas such as "get enough sleep", "eat fruits and vegetables", "go to class" and "don't get in trouble". These are wonderful suggestions and valuable: take note of them. However, the precondition that I offer is different: Go talk to your professor about your work and your efforts, preferably during her or his office hours AND before a big test (Don't be late or fail to show for an appointment). This short chat assures the prof that you actually are serious about your work (which you are), puts a name on a face, gives the prof a chance to assess how much you do know about the course AND provides him or her with an opportunity to offer advice about study techniques for that specific content.

   This last point is important. If you ask a prof "Do you have any suggestions that would help me do better in the course?", the answer often is "study more" or "do the reading". These hints are fine, but you already know these things. What might be offered is something like this: "make sure that you understand the chapter subtitles—they're critical", or "I make all my test questions similar to the samples offered in the book, so look at those" or "There is at least one question about every term I put on the board on every test" or "Note that in the syllabus, there is a key question for every class: you might want to be able to answer them!". When a prof says something like this . . . you ought to take serious note of it!!! They all want you to pass (and prosper); very few, if any, really want the students to fail. Trust them; they won't lead you astray.

   I once did a study of college profs with Dr. P here at Niagara back in 1989 . . . almost everyone of them gave definite in-class hints as to test items every day!!!! All I had to do was look for emphasis during class and I could identify these examination points. Later, in discussion, I found out that the professors hoped that the students would be able to identify them too.

   So, the precondition is simply: Go and have a chat so that everybody is a little bit clearer about your willingness and ability to do well. Oh, yeah, and eat the green vegetables.

98   The Academic Community

9   Now here are the four (4) tips that are guaranteed to raise your achievement. I anticipate that you will face ESSAYS and PAPERS that require you to use information to defend an argument and MULTIPLE-CHOICE TESTS that expect identifications of causes or results or which seek comparisons. These tips all are useful in getting ready for those kinds of challenges. Give them a chance (or two). As they used to say in an old TV commercial, "Try them . . . you'll like them".

10   (1) DISTRIBUTE YOUR PRACTICE AND STUDY TIME. This is simple: set up a schedule so that you have a plan! (remember Fred Ward in "Tremors"; he was always making a new plan, but at least he had one!) If you are going to do three hours work, you're better off spreading the work across three one-hour sessions than doing all three hours at one shot. Organize your very busy schedule so that you have a few work times for each course spread across the week. (Note that your football coaches break practice into shorter work periods and that you review and extend new plays and old plays every day: this is the same principle at work in sports.)

11   This is a powerful factor in learning: spreading out your study time gets you organized, keeps you attentive, makes you feel like you're accomplishing something, increases efficiency, and means that you are using knowledge all the time. Note, too, that these distributed practices are ACTIVE . . . where you DO something to learn each time. The next three tips are all examples of sample activities that could be done during the study/learning sessions. To start, know that putting things into your own words is a good idea. So, in the space below, transform this first hint (about distributing practice) into your own words:

12   (2) For a second tip, TRY ELABORATING YOUR NOTES, which means of course, having some notes! These can be from lecture (which is tough), discussion (which is almost impossible), from reading (which can take forever), or from someone else's notebook (which can help you make friends or be illegal): if you choose this last suggestion, TAKE NOTES on his or her notes, DO NOT just copy them! Taking your own notes (and in your own words) helps because it makes the mind active and aggressive. Copying notes is passive (Bart Simpson writes 100 times a day that he will not do something, yet I bet that he never can remember those sentences!)

13   How can you elaborate on your notes? First of all, you can IDENTIFY main ideas and extend their meanings. For example, if the notes say "South Vietnam never did have a democratically elected leadership," you could jot down "key point #1" or "bet this had to be hidden by the US government" or "LBJ would disagree". In all three cases you've identified something, and in the final two elaborated on them. This also works for text material as well as notes.

14   Another way to elaborate is to BUILD CHUNKS of notes: you look down at what you wrote and put it in sections. CHUNKING can really help because OFTEN one's notes are a mess . . . just a bunch of stuff written down during class. For example:

15   "Religions . . . satisfy human needs for . . . big picture . . . Man doesn't know . . . animism in Africa . . . wounded buffalo? Five pillars tell Moslems how, but what tells them why? And why do they believe? All Christianities are Ok with after-life concept . . . fear of nothingness . . . human self-delusion or self-

[margin notes: Spread out study time. / Be Active in taking notes.]

Improving Understanding and Increasing Grades **99**

assurance? People need to know why they exist and what they are for . . . the reason for humanness".

16 Making sense of this could result in chunking about "big questions of humanity" or "ways that different religions help". Thinking about what chunks to use makes your mind try to make sense of the notes.

17 My favorite way to elaborate on notes is simply to TRANSFORM them, usually into drawings. Putting the notes in your own words is helpful, but drawings stick in memory better (for most of us). Try your hand at it right now. Read the following statements, then draw them in the margin.

18 "The US fought a ground war against an invisible enemy, one that would "hit and run" its enemy and then blend into the people and the countryside like ghosts."

19 "Films showed Viet Nam metaphorically, as if it couldn't have been a real event (like WWII). For the families of the 50,000 dead US soldiers, this might have been the ultimate injury, the pinnacle of despair for their losses."

20 Another elaboration technique is to INVENT COMPARISONS, especially analogies like "ghosts" used in an example above. Having to think about comparisons requires deep processing of material and leads to comprehension. For example, generating or answering the question, "how is football the same (or different) from a ground war?" would help you grasp important relationships bout the US use of ground power in Viet Nam.

21 In regards to religions, you could make a note in the notebook margin that says "Hinduism is like strait jacket: all binding rules" . . . or "Koran is like Bible: both tell stories, give big picture, set rules . . . and promise a future to the good people." Another example would be as follows: Your notes state that "The US was split down the middle between hawks and doves: hawks wanted war to prove we're right and doves thought peace could only be brought along by stopping violence. Hardly anybody was in the middle": try your hand making a comparison or an analogy (hint on this one: the concept of fences come to my mind!)

22 (3) If you like to distribute your active practice and use elaborations, you might also like this piece of advice: MARK UP YOUR BOOKS!!! Adler calls this "an act of love" and it means that you were actively reading the materials. DON'T be super cheap and try to make your used book appear to be clean and new so that you can [get] an extra $1.23 back from the bookstore next semester!! You can underline, yellow out or number parts of your book, and here are a couple of other ideas:

23 (a) Identify information in a paragraph as EVIDENCE for something, and try to figure out what that something was . . . the clues will be in previous paragraphs. Authors don't just put stuff in a book sort of randomly; everything in there is either a major point (a thesis statement) or supporting EVIDENCE. For example, the lead sentence in a paragraph in the middle of the page says, "Furthermore, the TET offensive also made the US war publicity machine look bad. People had thought that the US was winning . . . and now doubt was raised." Before going any further, you can try to make sense of this point. This statement is evidence that (a) publicity was important; (b) some thing called the TET offensive had several implications; (c) there was some kind of sequence of events that TET was part of.

24   If you can finish connecting those ideas, you've learned some important content and prepared for a test item seeking to examine those connections.

25   (b) You can also mark up your book by ARGUING WITH OR CHALLENGING the author: remember books are written by people trying to convince readers of their theories (as I am trying to do in this letter). Try arguing or questioning the following statement . . . and do so by scratching your ideas right in the margins of this paper.

26   "Obviously, the opposition to the WAR was fostered by communists living in the United States and who had been frustrated by their own inept attempts at a local revolution."

27   As I calmed down, I would write stuff like . . . "name three such opposition leaders" . . . "does this mean they were hired by USSR?" "what local revolution" or "I thought dissent was freedom of speech . . . communists don't like personal freedoms."

28   All of these strategies make you actively deal with the knowledge, using it for some purpose and changing it somehow. You will remember and understand more if you do these things . . . and if you distribute your sessions, you'll see your grades fly high. But, I promised you four tips; here is the last one:

29   (4) If you really want to do well in college, go EXPLAIN these TIPS to another human being. This is a good way to make friends or to meet people. You can always claim that it is part of a psychology or education project ("My father is doing research on 'explanation' and he'd like you to give me twenty minutes while I explain . . ."). If you do this explaining thing twice, you will (a) have distributed practice (b) remembered and understood all the TIPS (techniques) and (c) have several new acquaintances. IF those persons are also classmates and join you in using these strategies (perhaps in a cooperative study group!) you all will see your grades rise.

30   In this space, tell the name of the partner(s) and a brief summary of how the explanation process went:

31   It's been fun writing to you and I hope you enjoy reading the letter and trying the ideas out. Also, I await your reply as to whether I can share it with other students. You know that my first two years in college were dismal academically . . . and things didn't improve until I changed my study habits (patterns and strategies). I've done pretty well in school with average ability . . . but I have always used good technique since my personal "turnaround".

32   All my best . . . Love always . . . you're always in my mind and in my heart. . . . let me know how these ideas work out, especially the "explaining to others" one.

33   Dad

34   PS. If you look carefully, you'll see that the letter has an introduction, a precondition, 4 tips (including 4 types of elaborations), 2 ways to mark a book, and a challenge (assignment). Try to identify each of these and you'll see my chunks (and the outline of the letter). Moreover, you could take a pen and use the "marking" strategy to argue with me in the margins . . . which would help you remember the strategy (and my point).

Reading Responses

1. Why did Vermette write this letter? Why did he publish it as an "open letter"?
2. Identify the features listed in the first sentence of the PS to the letter.
3. Which aspects of the letter are personal? Which reveal the writer's academic background and expertise?

Writing Activities

1. List Vermette's tips and strategies, stating them in your own words. For each, add your own examples and illustrations.
2. Write an addition to Vermette's letter, explaining another strategy that is useful to students.
3. Write a letter to your child (real or imagined). Based on your experience thus far getting into college and taking college courses, advise your child about how to handle this major life transition. Supply both parental booster comments and specific advice about strategies for coping and learning.

Community Links

Compare Vermette's letter with advice for the work community, such as "Model Format for Cover Letter" (pp. 287–288), or with advice from the public community such as the brochure from the American Automobile Association, "Your Driving Costs 2003: Figuring It Out" (pp. 530–541) or Nolo's "How to Make a Budget and Stick to It" (pp. 543–547). What seem to be the general characteristics of texts that supply advice? What features—such as format, organization, degree of formality, or tone—vary with the community, the type of text, or the situation?

Essay in Response to Reading

THE LOGOS, CONSTANT CHANGE, AND WISDOM: HERACLITUS AND UNIFICATION

Elizabeth Peet, Student Writer

♦

For her course in ancient philosophy, Liz Peet was assigned an essay explaining a major concept presented by a classical Greek philosopher. To support their explanations, students were not to use outside secondary sources but to rely on primary or original evidence—the selections and fragments from classical sources collected in their philosophy book. (Liz identifies these sources by citing the fragment number and page number in her textbook.) In addition to explaining the concept, students were to evaluate and respond to the philosopher's thinking. Liz wrote about the logos, an idea held by the Greek philosopher Heraclitus who was born about 540 B.C. and identified change, not permanence, as reality.

Elizabeth Peet
Ancient Philosophy
March 10, 2002

The Logos, Constant Change, and Wisdom: Heraclitus and Unification

1   Heraclitus, one of the most respected ancient philosophers, believed that everything was connected through the logos. His idea of unity, or the logos, encompassed all things, including constant change and wisdom. Although the logos is considered one stable entity, it is the constant change that stabilizes it, and all things, such as wisdom, are known through the logos. Heraclitus' idea of unity and the logos, along with constant change and wisdom, creates a unique philosophical ideal that tries to explain the truths of the universe. And for the most part, I think his idea is solid and does a good job of connecting things. However, the fact that the logos has no properties specific to it and there is no need to explain an origin with it causes me to doubt the actual soundness of the theory.

2   To understand any view of Heraclitus fully, it is necessary to know well his idea of the logos. The logos is Heraclitus' explanation of what is. It is the cosmic law and is used to describe the structure of the cosmos, and it cannot be violated. The logos is unity and the thought that everything is one. All things are connected, even things that are apparently unconnected (such as opposites). There is no beginning and no end, and the logos is all around all the time.

3   The main idea behind the logos is unity, for "all things are one" (H 44. CCR, p. 29). This unity is very strong and can also be described by the idea of opposites. Opposites can be used to explain Heraclitus' logos because he claims that the things that are apparently unconnected, like opposites, actually are the most connected. This is because opposites could be relative to each other or could be opposite of each other at the same time. For example, Heraclitus says that the sea is both pure and polluted: "to fishes drinkable and bringing safety, to humans undrinkable and destructive" (H 50. CCR, p. 29). The terms of the sea are relative to what we take to be good and bad, safe and unsafe. So although opposites appear unconnected, they are not only connected to form a unity but define each other.

4   Another way to think of the logos is as fire. Fire is a constant, unified idea that does not change but is constantly changing. Fire always holds the same properties but the actual flames are always different. Fire always holds heat, it can burn things, and it can be both helpful (for example, when cooking food) and harmful (when it burns you). Although fire always is the same in its prop-

erties, there is never a same fire. Flames of a fire are always new and different even when they are the flames of the same fire. This idea of fire explains a very important aspect of Heraclitus' logos: constant change.

5   The idea of constant change is critical to Heraclitus' argument for the logos. Although fire is the physical sign for the logos, there are two other elements that are included in it. Water and earth (along with fire) create the ever-changing universe. These three elements are constantly changing into each other. "Fire lives the death of earth and air lives the death of fire, water lives the death of air, earth that of water" (H 73. CCR, p. 31). This passage explains that the change (or death) of every element is actually just the birth (or beginning) of a new element. The beginning and end are unified and therefore, Heraclitus argues, there is no beginning and no end.

6   One argument against the idea of constant change being unified and beneficial is the idea that because of constant change, nothing can be. Things are always forming and changing so there can never be one set thing. Heraclitus refutes this argument by explaining that it is this constant change that creates stability. It is an undeniable fact that things always change; therefore the claim that things change constantly cannot be denied. If constant change cannot be denied, then the idea of constant change is solid and stable. The passage, "changing, it rests," explains this (H 75. CCR, p. 31). Change occurs so frequently that it is stable enough to be called resting.

7   It is easy enough to see the connection that the logos has with constant change, but if the logos is all encompassing, then where does something like wisdom fit in? To Heraclitus, wisdom is understanding. Heraclitus argues that thinking is shared by all and all can "know themselves" and "think it rightly" (H 28, 29. CCR, p. 27–28). But although everyone thinks, a wise person is neither willing nor unwilling to be hailed as Zeus (H 27. CCR, p. 27). By this Heraclitus is claiming that a wise man does not think he is above others, even when he actually may be. This idea of the wise being better than the unwise is shown in passage twelve, which says that the "wise is set apart from all" (H 12. CCR, p. 26) even though this is not recognized.

8   Another trait of wisdom, according to Heraclitus, is that wise men, those who love wisdom, inquire about many things (H 31. CCR, p. 28). But it is not inquiry and learning only that makes a person wise. If learning taught insight, "it would have taught Hesiod and Pythagoras, and moreover Xenophanes and Hecataues" (H 14. CCR, p. 26). Here Heraclitus is explaining that the philosophers before him are unwise because they do not agree with his idea of the logos, and it is the understanding of the logos that makes a person wise.

9   Although these basic ideas of the logos seem easy enough, Heraclitus argues that people are still too ignorant to understand and perceive it (H 1. CCR, p. 25). In this passage Heraclitus is obviously showing his concern for the perception of the logos. He feels that people are willfully ignorant. Although the logos is all around them at all times, they would rather believe popular thought because it is popular than think for themselves (H 2. CCR, p. 25). Thus people remain "at odds with the *logos*, with which above all they are in continuous contact," and ordinary, everyday things "appear strange to them" (H 7. CCR, p. 26). Here, Heraclitus is making clear that there is something

obvious around people every day, but they just do not see it. This lack of perception is a problem because, without recognition and understanding of the logos, one cannot be wise.

10   Heraclitus presents a very solid concept of unification that does a good job of including and explaining almost everything. He claims that the logos is everything and even different ideas such as constant change and wisdom can be clarified through it. There are a couple of problems with his theory though. The logos is an unexplainable thing. He gives it no properties specifically and assumes that, since there is no beginning or end, he does not have to explain an origin. This, in my opinion, is a problem. If the logos cannot explain an origin or be defined as something with properties of its own, then it appears to be nothing. Everything must have properties special to itself in order to be something. If the argument is made that something is the ideas that construct it, then the logos cannot actually exist in itself, only the ideas can. Ideas can exist independently of any one thing connecting them, so if a logos exists, then it must have properties. In other words, logos, if void of any properties special to itself, cannot exist because it would just be ideas that already exist without it. Also, if it does not arise from something, it cannot exist, since everything must come from something.

11   I like Heraclitus' proposal of a logos. He claims that through it anything can be explained because everything is unified. And unification is always a nice idea since it means we are all connected in ways beyond our control. The fact that Heraclitus feels he can explain everything from constant change to wisdom through the logos is a bonus since it is usually difficult (if not impossible) to explain either of those independently. However, in order to accept his explanation of how things fit into the logos, someone must first accept the idea of the logos. This is more difficult because the explanation of the origin and the traits of the logos are not clear. I suppose, though, that my questioning, whether valid or not, would lead Heraclitus to consider me wise, since only "a fool is excited by every word (*logos*)" (H 9. CCR, p. 26).

Reference
Cohen, S. Marc, Patricia Curd, and C. D. C. Reeve, eds. "Heraclitus." *Readings in Ancient Greek Philosophy from Thales to Aristotle.* 2nd ed. Indianapolis: Hackett, 2000.

Reading Responses

1. What are the main points that Liz explains about the logos? What questions does she raise about these ideas?
2. How can you distinguish Liz's explanation of the logos from her personal evaluation of the idea? Based on your experience as a college student, when is the first-person (*I*) acceptable in college papers and when is it considered informal or inappropriate?
3. If you were asked to help Liz as a peer reviewer, what advice would you give her about her essay? What do you like about the essay? What are its strengths? What changes would you suggest?

Writing Activities

1. Based on the information in Liz's essay, write a short definition of the logos.
2. Based on the information in Liz's essay, write a short personal response evaluating the idea of the logos.
3. Write your own explanation of a key term used in one of your classes. Use your textbook as a source to help you explain the term. (Be certain that you quote or paraphrase accurately and that you cite your source.) Besides explaining the term, include your personal response to the term or your evaluation of it.

Community Links

Read several of the other selections that define or explain terms such as the Declaration of Independence (pp. 426–430) or Barlow and Clarke's "The Standpoint" (pp. 479–489). Analyze several of the definitions or explanations. How are they similar, and how do they differ? How does each try to meet the expectations of its readers?

Informative Essay

THE CELL CYCLE AND CANCER

Cristina Tang, Student Writer

♦

JYI, the Journal of Young Investigators, is a Web journal whose reviewers and authors, called student science journalists, are undergraduate students. Here, students can submit their essays and research studies in scientific, mathematical, and engineering fields. Other students can gain valuable experience by serving as the editors who review and recommend articles for publication, just as faculty and researchers serve as reviewers for other scholarly journals. The journal's Web site at www.jyi.org posts current and past issues as well as information about submitting articles. Cristina Tang's JYI article explains the body's process of cell division, including its importance for curing cancer.

1   The human body can be thought of as a small laboratory (weighing no more than ~3 kg at birth) where millions of chemical reactions can take place at the same time, in the right order, and in the right compartment. It is also probably the only "machine" that knows to save fuel when fed in excess and to

bring out the reserves when starved, one that can protect itself when attacked by viruses and bacteria, one capable of adjusting and withstanding changes of weather and most importantly, one that is able to learn, think, and create on its own. The human body is a highly integrated and organized system, able to respond to a wide range of stimuli in order to perform all the functions that are vital to our survival. Moreover, since errors and malfunctions in this "organic factory" can have damaging results, ranging from discomfort to life-threatening illnesses, many reactions and processes that take place within our cells are under very tight control.

2   An example of one of the many complicated-yet-elegant processes that continuously occur in our bodies is the cell division cycle. As you read this sentence, many of the cells in your body are dividing into two. However, behind this seemingly simple step is a complicated series of reactions and changes, such as DNA replication and protein synthesis, which involve a dazzling array of proteins working in concert to achieve a common goal.

3   The cell division cycle is generally divided into four phases. In normal cells, progress from one phase to the next is always strictly controlled at so-called "checkpoints." Checkpoints can be considered safety measures for the cell, preventing the control system from dictating the start of another cell cycle event before the previous one has finished, or before any damage to the cell has been properly repaired. In addition to internal signals provided by the checkpoints, completion of the cell division cycle is also dependent upon external cues. When cell division is unregulated and independent of external cues, it has the potential of leading to one of the most devastating diseases that afflicts almost one in five people in first-world countries: cancer.

4   The cell division cycle has been divided into the G_1 (growth) phase, followed by the S (synthesis) phase, G_2 phase (second growth), and the M (mitotic) phase. Cells that are not dividing (quiescent) are said to be in the G_0 phase. When cells receive external cues (i.e., growth factors released by neighboring cells) to initiate division, they move from the quiescent state into the G_1 phase. In the G_1 phase, cells prepare for division by producing more proteins. In the S phase, cells replicate their DNA, creating two identical copies so that each daughter cell can each inherit an exact copy. In G_2, cells continue to grow and synthesize all the proteins the daughter cells will need after division. And finally, in the M phase, the cell separates its DNA and divides into two.

5   All cells must accurately replicate and segregate their chromosomes during cell division. To accomplish these tasks in an ordered and sequential manner, all the events related to cell division must be coordinated throughout the duration of the cycle. For example, if a cell divides before it has reached a certain size, then the daughter cells would become smaller with every subsequent division. How do cells regulate the processes of the division cycle? The answer lies within a set of interacting proteins that form the cell cycle control system. This system of proteins, as the "chief commander" of the cycle, directs and coordinates other proteins involved in particular tasks such as in DNA replication. However, in spite of its "power" to act on other proteins, the control system must still follow feedback signals coming from the cell cycle itself. There are

other proteins in the cell cycle involved in surveillance control mechanisms. These proteins can stop or delay the progress of the control system at the cycle checkpoints. In fact, several defects or syndromes that lead to increased susceptibility of developing cancer are the result of the loss or inactivation of a gene encoding a protein in the surveillance system.

6   The control system of the cell cycle is based on two families of proteins: the cyclins and the cyclin-dependent kinases (Cdk). Cdks induce other proteins to perform their functions by phosphorylating (adding a phosphate group) key amino acid residues, and cyclins bind to Cdks to control their ability to phosphorylate those target proteins.

7   Many proteins are involved in the surveillance system. There are several ways by which they can delay or terminate the progress of the cell cycle. Some proteins, for example, can promote the rapid degradation of cyclins and others can prevent the entry of Cdk-cyclin complexes into the cell compartments where they are needed to promote cell cycle progression. The first checkpoint a cell encounters before entry into the cycle is at the transition between G_0 and G_1. A protein suspected to be involved at this point is encoded by the retinoblastoma (Rb) gene. The Rb protein inhibits the passage of the cell past the "start" point of the cycle by shutting off the transcription of genes required for cell division and sequestering the proteins that regulate DNA replication. The importance of this gene in the regulation of cell division is made evident by the fact that many common types of cancer, such as lung, breast, and bladder cancer, are missing both functional copies of the Rb gene.

8   Once the cell has entered G_1, it can continue unchecked until the beginning of the S phase. The G_1/S metaphase then ensures that the DNA is intact before replication. The protein p53 stops progression of the cell cycle when even the smallest DNA damage occurs. This protein is produced in greater quantities when the cell is exposed to DNA-damaging agents (e.g., UV radiation) and induces the synthesis of another protein that inhibits the function of the Cdk-cyclin complex. In humans, absence of one good copy of this gene is associated with Li-Fraumeni syndrome, which is characterized by the propensity to develop tumors in several tissues. This predisposition to cancer is related to the cell's increased chances of producing daughter cells that carry mutations that can lead to the formation of tumors, since without control from p53, the cell is more likely to progress from the G_1 to S phase even when DNA is damaged.

9   More cell cycle checkpoints can be found at the G_2/M transition and within the M phase. At the G_2/M checkpoint, for example, failure to complete DNA replication causes specific proteins to inhibit the action of the Cdk-cyclin complex by preventing their entry into the nucleus. Within the M phase, control mechanisms ensure that the cell does not divide until all the chromosomes have moved toward opposite poles of the cell.

10 Because of the large network of proteins involved in cell cycle progression and regulation, we are still far from understanding the details of its functioning. However, intense cancer research has uncovered many genes and the roles they play in this cycle. Hopefully, through a gradual understanding of the mechanisms underlying this complex system, we can find the long-awaited cure for this disease.

References
Hunter T. and J. Pines. "Cyclins and Cancer. II: Cyclin D and CDK inhibitors come of age." *Cell.* 79(1994): 573–582
Hatakeyama M. and R.A. Weinberg. "The role of RB in cell cycle control." *Prog Cell Cycle Res.* 1(1995): 9–19
Hartwell L.H. and T.A. Weinert. "Checkpoints: controls that ensure the order of cell cycle events." *Science.* 246(1989): 629–633
Kastan M.B., et al. "Participation of p53 protein in the cellular response to DNA damage." *Cancer Res.* 51(1991): 6304–6311
Srivastava S., et al. "Germ-line transmission of a mutated p53 gene in a cancer-prone family with Li-Fraumeni syndrome." *Nature.* 348(1990): 747–749
Evan G. and T. Littlewood. "A matter of life and cell death." *Science.* 281(1998): 1317–1322

Reading Responses

1. Why, according to Cristina, is the cell-division cycle important?
2. What strategies does Cristina use to explain the cell-division cycle in ways that even readers with little scientific background can understand?
3. How does Cristina organize her discussion? How does this organization assist readers without scientific backgrounds?

Writing Activities

1. Using your own words, briefly summarize Cristina's main point.
2. Write a brief analysis of Cristina's word choices, comparisons, and other methods of explaining a technical topic to readers who may not have technical backgrounds.
3. Using Cristina's essay as a model, write your own informative essay, explaining a complex topic that is familiar to you but possibly not to readers. Show why understanding this topic is important to readers or significant in some way. Explain the processes, stages, or components that make up this topic as clearly as possible using nontechnical explanations whenever possible.

Community Links

Compare Cristina's explanation of the process of cell division with other process explanations such as those in Hewlett-Packard's "LaserJet Toner Cartridge Recycling Program" (pp. 337–340), the American Automobile Association's "Your Driving Costs 2003: Figuring It Out" (pp. 530–541), or Nolo's "How to Make a Budget and Stick to It" (pp. 543–547). What do these explanations have in common? How do they differ? To what extent do the differences reflect community expectations?

Speculative Essay

SO MANY NUMBERS—WHAT DO YOU DO WITH THE DATA?

Margaret Harris, Student Writer

◆

Like the preceding essay by Cristina Tang, this essay by Margaret Harris was published in JYI, *the* Journal of Young Investigators, *on the Web at www.jyi.org. The* JYI *articles are written and reviewed by undergraduate students who are studying in a range of disciplines in the sciences, mathematics, and engineering. This speculative essay introduces a problem and speculates about its possible solutions but stops short of proposing a solution.*

1 The genetic instructions for making you, a human being, are written in three billion DNA base pairs and tucked inside the nucleus of every cell in your body (except red blood cells). Of those three billion, only 2% are actually part of your roughly 35,000 genes. The remainder may hold your chromosomes' structure together, play unknown roles in regulating protein production, or simply take up space as "junk" DNA, the detritus of humankind's long evolution from earlier species.

2 If all that information—junk, genes, and all—were printed on paper, it would fill 200 volumes each the size of a Manhattan telephone book. If you started to read this weighty collection tomorrow, you'd be at it for another 9.5 years. And if you took all three billion DNA base pairs and laid them end-to-end, as you would inevitably be inclined to do, they would reach pretty much anywhere on Earth you wanted—several times over. When describing the size of these numbers, "staggering" is an understatement.

3 Computers have, to a certain extent, solved the problem: *The Complete Works of You, Vols. 1–200,* would fit comfortably onto a reasonably-sized computer hard drive. Three billion pairs means three gigabytes (GB) of disk space—a big number, certainly, but nothing modern computers can't handle.

4 But what happens if researchers want to look at more than one genome at a time? What if they want to examine, say, a few thousand, in order to seek out and compare the genetic quirks that make us unique—or give us rare diseases? What if they want to add their own comments every few lines, as an aid to others' understanding? What should they do with the data?

5 Different field, same problem: The next generation of fiber optic cables will be fast enough to transmit the informational content of the entire Library of Congress from New York to Paris in about a millisecond, quicker than you can say "overdue fine." But what happens once it gets there? What do you do with the data?

6   Consider the weatherman, the poor chap on TV who predicts flurries and gets a blizzard. Creating better mathematical and computer models of weather patterns—or any other near-chaotic, complex, and time-dependent system—requires not only tremendous number-crunching power and an immense amount of storage space, but also some means of organizing and displaying the data in a meaningful way. Teasing predictions out of such a system is, in the understated jargon of science, "nontrivial," not easy. How do they deal with the data?

7   The data problem is not new. Researchers have used computers for scientific purposes since the days of vacuum tubes and relays, and the need for effective data storage and access has always been a driving force behind computer architecture. So far, the results have been impressive; an empirical axiom, Moore's Law, states that computing power will double every 18 months, and historically the doubling period has often been even shorter.

8   In recent years, however, changes in the scientific process have led to such a rapid proliferation of data that advances in storage are no longer keeping up with the sheer volume of data. The biggest culprit is genomics, a new field whose reams of raw data gobble up storage space on desktops and mainframes alike—both in high-profile efforts like the Human Genome Project and in studies of smaller gene fragments, or other species. Unlike older areas of biology, genomics is largely driven by discoveries rather than by hypotheses. In discovery-driven science, researchers mine collected data for anomalies and trends, instead of using the more traditional process of formulating a hypothesis or theory and testing it experimentally. For example, a genomic scientist might track the expression of various genes in yeast samples at different temperatures, to see if differences in temperature led to changes in the yeast's life cycle. The result is a data-storage-and-access nightmare; even a humble fungus has some 6300 genes for researchers to monitor over its six-hour life cycle, and it's easy to extrapolate that humans are almost unimaginably more complex.

9   Other fields also use the discovery approach to research, and they face similar problems with data. Neuroscientists, for example, often compare large amounts of data in an effort to find patterns and trends, and for them data storage and access has proved even more problematic. In one experiment at Duke University, volunteers' brains were scanned as they looked at various words. The resulting images, depicted in false color to show regions of activity in the brain, were recorded on high-density DVDs. This would have been ideal, since DVDs are efficient information-storage platforms. However, once the images were in place, the DVDs were stacked in a closet. Although a closet full of disembodied brain images might sound creepy to a layman, it bothered the scientists even more: How do you compare images and data when all the raw information is literally closeted and no two scans will fit on the computer at the same time?

10   The scientific data problem is inherently interesting to computer scientists. This is especially true because information proliferation will eventually bring Moore's Law of progress up against a formidable theoretical barrier: The quantum-mechanical limit to how much information and how much computing power can fit onto a silicon wafer. Research on quantum computing—an effort that hopes to use the quantum properties of atoms or nuclei to mimic

some functions of a computer's processor and memory—is at least partly aimed at overcoming this physical barrier.

11   Suggestions for a shorter-term "fix" are not hard to find. In one typically clever proposal—with the catchy title "A Petabyte in Your Pocket"—researchers at the University of Wisconsin-Madison and the Oregon Graduate Institute suggested that a new method of structuring databases could offer unheard-of storage capacity without resorting to exotic quantum- or DNA-based computers. Another approach proposes trading two-dimensional CDs and computer chips for three-dimensional "information cubes;" the addition of a z-axis to the x and y would allow more information to be encoded at a single point.

12   Whatever the solution, though, the underlying problem is not going to disappear anytime soon. Until then, the question remains: What do you do with the data?

Reading Responses

1. What is the problem that Margaret explains? Why is it so troublesome for researchers? Why doesn't she propose a solution?
2. Why does Margaret provide so many examples and illustrations? How do these examples contribute to her point?
3. How does Margaret draw readers into her essay? What strategies does she use to help even readers with little scientific background to grasp the issues?

Writing Activities

1. Write another section for this paper, adding a different example that is familiar to you.
2. Consider a similar situation in which you encounter too much data—for example, conducting searches on the Web, shopping in a large mall or superstore, or channel-surfing the sports channels on satellite television. Write an essay advising others in the same situation about how to handle too much data.
3. Write your own speculative essay, explaining a problem and speculating about possible alternatives. Although you need not propose any specific solution, be certain that you supply enough explanations and examples that readers understand the nature of the problem and the complications that it creates.

Community Links

Compare and contrast Margaret's essay with other readings that include speculation such as Barlow and Clarke's "The Standpoint" (pp. 479–489) or any of the grant or other proposals. In what ways do these writers base their speculations on concrete, realistic details and examples? In what ways do they abandon the realm of concrete detail to imagine other possibilities? How do they persuade readers to make the jump from the problems of reality to the speculative solutions or ideas that they consider?

Interpretive Essay
TROPING THROUGH PROVERBIA
Bert O. States

◆

This essay appeared in The American Scholar, *a journal sponsored by the Phi Beta Kappa Society. This quarterly publication is directed to general readers who are interested in books, reviews, and engaging discussions of a variety of literary, cultural, and scientific topics. Bert States, a Professor Emeritus at the University of California, Santa Barbara, takes the reader along on a visit to Proverbia.*

Proverbia is a land of laws and regulations based on the wisdom of its forefathers, so much so that the speech of Proverbians is strangely ornamented with their matter and in conversation the Proverbians often seem to be practicing law rather than life. As a result, there are so many interpretations and variants of the laws that if one is not to your liking, you can generally find another that is, and it will frequently conflict with other laws bearing on the same conduct and behavior.
—Traveler's Guide to Mythical Lands

1 Proverbia is a country most of us visit more frequently than we realize. What we bring home from it each time is a compact nugget of usage called a proverb, which has the remarkable power of justifying anything we may wish to undertake ourselves or anything we may wish to forgive or condemn in others. Proverbs, our mythical guide tells us, are "strangely ornamented" sayings, which rise in our speech like the caps of waves breaking on the shore of conversation. I take that back. Most proverbs sneak into speech like foxes into the hen house. Ada and Ida are talking, and Ada says something like, "Well, if a job's worth doing, it's worth doing well" or "We should let bygones be bygones," and Ida says (in either case), "Oh, that's so true, and we should practice what we preach." Neither will notice how the drift of meaning has suddenly been condensed into a molecule of philosophy born long before either of them. In a flash, a whole world slips into speech through a narrow opening—the world of received wisdom, which, it turns out, is really a world of contradictions.

2 Proverbs are a sort of instant wisdom, an endorphin for all occasions. Normally, proverbs are metaphorical, on two counts: they contain both a figurative and a literal level of meaning, and they are models of verbal economy. As Walker Percy puts it in my favorite definition of metaphor, a metaphor is "a big

thing happening in a small place." And "a proverb," as one of them runs, "is shorter than a bird's beak," and of course it is the beak—or the brevity—that enables the proverb to hit the mark, just as it enables the early bird to catch the worm. Proverbs belong to the literature of wisdom, and insofar as they are figurations ("A stitch in time saves nine," "A bird in the hand is worth two in the bush"), they usually stand in relation to that wisdom as explicit example to implicit precept. This is easy enough to see in the two proverbs above, which simply ask you to make a generalization from sewing and bird catching to analogous situations in daily life in which timeliness or possession are advisable. But it is not always that simple. For example, proverbs like "The eye is bigger than the belly" and "Two heads are better than one" introduce an inverted variation on the straight figurative proverb. That is, they are outright falsehoods taken on the literal level, but are understood to be true if you take "eye" and "belly" as figures for "appetite," and "heads" as meaning "minds" or "persons," rather than body organs. And what leads you to do this is that the falsehood makes no sense unless you bump it up another level in the associative process. Moreover, many proverbs are not figurative at all, but simply state a precept without offering an example or an illustration ("Generosity is its own reward," "First things first," "Knowledge is power"). In either case, the appeal of a proverb depends on the authority of wisdom unleashed, as Percy says, "in a small place," which is to say, in as few words as possible. Like rolling stones, proverbs gather no moss.

3   Still, one could claim that all proverbs are metaphors, whether they actually contain a metaphor or not; that is, they are a way of carrying old moral or behavioral processes into some new situation or set of facts, as one would speak in a time of loss or penury the maxims of patience or endurance coined for other situations. Normally one would also find a strong "poetic" metaphor, something borrowed from the household or field, to drive the parallel firmly home. But either way, the proverb functions more like a scientific analogy than like a poetic figure of speech, working much as the formula πr^2 works in finding the circumference of any circle anywhere in the world.

4   To put it another way, poetic metaphor is usually concerned with theme rather than thesis, reflection or recognition rather than practical action or behavior; and when a character in a play speaks a proverb, you can never be sure that the author is endorsing it as good advice for people outside the play or even for the character who speaks it. For example, Troilus defends the keeping of Helen in Troy by citing such proverbs as "What is aught but as 'tis valued?" and "We turn not back the silks upon the merchant, when we have spoil'd them." Shakespeare may have personally "believed" in these proverbs (on some occasions), but in the play (given his portrait of Helen and his "lecherous" view of war) his sympathies are probably closer to those of Hector, who is more a realist than a chivalric moralist. Poetic metaphor enjoys the correspondence, because it is true, expressive, and apt; whereas the business of the *proverbial* metaphor, and by extension all proverbs (whether they contain metaphors or not), is continually to demonstrate that what was good for yesteryear's geese is equally good for today's young ganders.

5   One of the differences between straight metaphors and proverbs is that metaphors are more striking for their originality and freshness; they make us

work a little harder, and this seems to be a more pleasant experience than being told exactly what to think. When metaphors die—that is, pass from their literary homes in poems and books into the public domain (the process called lexicalization)—they become idioms: idiom being what we know so well that we see straight through it, as in Shakespeare's "Not a mouse stirring." Indeed, as Francis Sparshott has put it, "a language is nothing but a necropolis of dead metaphors." Or, as Stanislaw Lec, another aphorist, put it, "In the beginning there was the Word—at the end just the Cliché."

6   Proverbs, on the other hand, are never original but more often than not have been passed down, like jokes, from unknown sources. "A proverb," as a famous one goes, "is the wit of one and the wisdom of many." But one might take issue with this proverb, or with half of it, anyway. We can easily grant the point that a proverb is the "wit of one" when we have direct evidence of its source. But most of the time, I'll wager, a proverb is no more the work of one "wit" than a cow path is the work of one cow. Surely many proverbs must come about by stages. That is, a proverb doesn't begin life as a *proverb* (with someone standing on a rock and saying, "Hear hear, I'm about to make a proverb!") but as a response to a recurring situation. For example, there is a good possibility that "A stitch in time saves nine" came from one or more housewives in one or more places who noticed, one or more times, that less work is involved if you patch the elbow of a coat or sweater when the hole is still small. Certainly no argument here. And if the situation comes up frequently, it will undoubtedly provoke language ("John, let me stitch that snag before it gets bigger"), and language used as a response to a recurring situation will itself become recurrent, as all married people know. The response is not yet a proverb, but it is on its way to becoming one when it achieves the economy that comes with repetition and, somewhere along the line, perhaps, the added spice of a sharp parallel structure capped by rhyme. Such "improvements" are retained and passed on in ever widening distribution, perhaps in different forms in different locales, and at length the response settles into language as a proverb that can be applied to situations that have nothing to do with stitching elbows but a good deal to do with nipping lots of things in the bud.

7   The proverb form is as versatile as any other literary or cultural form, and can even be adapted to include new forms of wisdom. For instance, there is a species we might refer to as original or ironic proverbs, utterances that sound like proverbs but are inversions of typical proverbial wisdom ("He who hesitates is probably right," "Two wrongs are only the beginning," "One good turn gets most of the blanket"). There are also satirical applications of the proverb principle to "new" situations ("The hardness of the butter is proportional to the softness of the bread," "To succeed in politics it is often necessary to rise above your principles," "The sooner you fall behind, the more time you have to catch up"). These examples, incidentally, are from my e-mail joke service, and I apologize for the theft. I am somewhat heartened, however, by the likelihood that they were collected from unidentified sources and thus are, like all proverbs, common property (as one of the entries tells us, "To steal from one person is plagiarism, to steal from many is research").

8   Proverbs always seem to be looking for metaphors that try to squeeze or reduce large emotional stirrings or forms of behavior, virtue, or human folly into small objects or creatures that you might find around the house or barnyard ("Silence catches a mouse," "Curiosity killed the cat," "The devil is in the dice," "At length the fox is brought to the furrier"). In all of these a homely figure is set against the intangible ground of a behavioral abstraction (silence, curiosity, evil). These seem to be persuasive ("Common proverb seldom lies") because the very detection of a correspondence between two things, as so many experiments in cognitive psychology have shown, is an influential factor in the formation of our attitudes about those things. One thing rubs off on another, as when you rub two sticks together with sufficient agitation the result is fire, or enlightenment. Proverbs, however, are not intended to enlighten as much as they are intended to light the way toward the right course or to justify what one would have done anyway, as when the conqueror who is about to take a city finds a proverbial way to see his action as God's will or manifest destiny rather than the result of his own ambition.

9   The real virtue of the economy of proverbs, however, is not to be found in the form and figuration of the proverb itself, but in what we might call the foveal, or focused, energy of proverbs as an extreme perspective on experience. That is, of all literary forms, proverbs most lack the dimension of peripheral vision, by which I mean the tendency to see all things as posed against other things. Literature—certainly not in all its forms—has a good deal of peripheral vision because it is (at its best, anyway) a delineation of the possible, not of the right or the wrong. This can be simply illustrated by turning again to Troilus's proverb "What is aught but as 'tis valu'd." Taken from the play and put in a *Book of Proverbs* under, say, WEALTH, alongside such variants as "Money isn't everything," it becomes a received truth—moreover, one that does not change with time, because it is itself a conclusion made about time. In the play, however, it is poised against alternative recommendations, so we are forced to take it in a relative way. The consequence of this is that the play—even though it is the most vociferously cynical play in all of Shakespeare—achieves a kind of openness. You can interpret it almost any way you like, by virtue of its containing opposite kinds of advice and conviction. There is an even more famous case of this in *King Lear*, in which we find one character (Gloucester) saying, "As flies to wanton boys, are we to the gods. They kill us for their sport," and another character (Edgar) saying, "The gods are just, and of our pleasant vices, make instruments to plague us." In short, a head-on contradiction. You can probably read the whole play from either point of view, as you wish, but it makes more sense to think that Shakespeare was simply telling us that human disasters are caused by conflicting beliefs. We might say that such works are evasive, in the sense that metaphor is evasive, or, if you will, that they are ironic, in the sense that they create a context composed of opposing views. What is open about the proverb, on the other hand, is not its possible meanings, or interpretations, but the unlimited range of its possible application to any experience that can be cut to its pattern.

10   The truth is that, as almost all its scholars have noted, a book of proverbs is a shameless repository of contradictions. If you read it straight through

looking for advice on how to live your life, as you might Dale Carnegie or the Bible, you would be hopelessly confused before you got through the "A"s. What conclusion would you reach: "Easy come, easy go" or "Waste not, want not"? "Dumb men get no lands" or "Talk is talk; but 'tis money buys land"? "In trust is truth" or "In trust is treason"? "Absence makes the heart grow fonder" or "Out of sight, out of mind"? Luckily, there are no proverbs urging murder, adultery, sloth, avarice, or wrath as antidotes to goodness, chastity, industry, generosity, and forgiveness. And it would be hard to imagine a proverb like "Where virtue is, vice follows," or "More is better," simply because it would be hard to imagine a sector of the world where these values are held. In other words, such positions do not require ironic redress, because they defeat themselves in their own perverse advertisement. Still, there is ample room in Proverbia for cynicism as an antidote to optimism ("The world is full of knaves," "Ill weeds grow apace," "A bad penny always turns up," "There is a scorpion under every stone"). The logic behind such inclusiveness, however, is itself ironic, because, taken as a whole, a book of proverbs, constituted thus of opposites, forms as it were the master drama of human relations, in which "Nothing is certain but uncertainty itself." But out of this uncertainty arises a certainty of a different kind, necessarily ironic, since it requires that all individual proverbs be considered as neither true nor false but *contributory to a total vision*. Thus it turns out that contradiction isn't the product of conflicting proverbs; contradiction is a product of human experience, in which conflict is inevitable and resilience indispensable. A book of proverbs is like a pharmacy where all varieties of medicine are stored. But medicines that serve as cures for one disease might kill if taken for another. So a book of proverbs is, in Kenneth Burke's term, a rhetoric of motives, and this is the respect in which it literally contains, in small, the plot of every imaginable novel or fiction.

11   As we have seen with Troilus, proverbs fit snugly into literature, particularly the literature of the sixteenth and seventeenth centuries. You will find lots of Shakespeare in proverb books and even more proverbs in Shakespeare. Yet Shakespeare's world is "proverbial" not simply in the number of proverbs his people speak but in the quality of life in it. Everywhere we find a predisposition toward what Foucault calls *taxonomia*, or "an algebra of complex representations," in which one continually hears "the insistent murmur of resemblance." As a generous example let us look at Polonius's advice to Laertes, in *Hamlet*. It is well known that Shakespeare is leaning on the traditional practice of fathers giving advice to departing sons, and the sense of every one of Polonius's precepts can be found in standard proverb collections. But there is something different about the "algebra" of representation, and it takes us to the salient distinction between proverbs and literary tropes as forms of expression. For example, Polonius's "Give thy thoughts no tongue" sounds like a proverb and might even pass as one, but when you come to the second half of the utterance ("Nor any unproportion'd thought his act"), something unproverbial happens; it is probably best referred to as the emergence of *embellishment*, or the making of a distinction between speaking your mind, on the one hand, and doing something only rashly thought out, on the other. In a literary work, such embellishments are part of our expectation, but for proverbial purposes we need two proverbs rather than one to express this distinction.

12   Elsewhere in Polonius's speech we come closer to pure proverb: "Give every man thy ear but few thy voice," "Costly thy habit as thy purse can buy," "Apparel oft proclaims the man," and "Neither a borrower nor a lender be." And you will find variations on all of these in the proverb books. But even here we have taken the sayings out of a context that is not only thick in embellishment but marked, overall, by the performance of an artist (Shakespeare) who is using proverbial wisdom to a mimetic end. Something else is being done with proverbs, and the something else is the illustration of a human being (Polonius) caught in the "unproportion'd" act of making proverbs. Moreover, Shakespeare's text is rich in figurative language that impresses us not only for its moral sense but for its portraiture of worldly diversity. The speech yields a great canvas of human behavior, like Jaques's seven ages of man speech in *As You Like It*, and when we arrive finally at

> This above all: to thine own self be true,
> And it must follow as the night the day
> Thou canst not then be false to any man

we pass from proverb to something closer to moral philosophy. By indirection we are reminded that one of the central characteristics of proverbs, as of folk literature at large, is the absence of character in the speaking voice—not certainly in the Aristotelian sense of character as ethos, or ethical truth, but in the sense of an individualized speaker to whom we can assign psychological traits, such as Polonius's garrulousness, pomposity, addiction to proverbial wisdom, and genuine concern for his son's welfare. In other words, proverbs travel light and cannot afford the divergencies of poetry.

13   Finally, there is the question of how proverbs suffer their life in time. What seems to happen is that proverbs, like metaphors, pass into the world of idiom, because their figurative aspect becomes transparent from overuse, somewhat like the passage of Chinese pictographs into less graphically descriptive characters. Some examples of proverbs that have "degenerated" into idiom-like expressions might be "Still waters run deep," "The walls have ears," "Let sleeping dogs lie," "Look before you leap," "Little pitchers have big ears," and so on. These are idiomatic in that you no longer "see" what you're saying or hearing, just as you don't "see" parts of human anatomy when you speak of elbow room, the leg of a table, the foot of the stairs, or the head of the class. In short, the gap between figurative and literal meaning has disappeared and we are left with the unobtrusive shell of a usage that once had a true metaphorical status, as "leg" did when it was first applied to "table." One might call them "dead proverbs," I suppose, but I suspect that the graphic life of a proverb is rather short, in any case, and that its active life is a direct function of its application to fresh (but of course timeless) situations, of which there are always plenty. One would assume that proverbs, like slang, have a period of use in which the vehicle itself is "catchy" insofar as it can be applied to different tenors, or situations. But after a while the catchiness wears thin and the power of the utterance shifts to its idiographic or "reminder" value. How many times could you hear "the early bird gets the worm" and still see birds or worms in your mind's eye?

But you would still know precisely what was meant. In other words, your understanding of the utterance would be automatic, assuming you are a native of the culture.

On the other hand, metaphors in literary works are hermetically contained by the virtual space of the work itself. The famous joke about the rube who tried to save Desdemona's life at a performance of *Othello* is a "proverbial" way of illustrating fiction's independence from the real world and the timelessness of its own world. Metaphor in fiction has a virtually eternal life, thanks to, among other things, the fact that for pragmatic purposes most fiction is almost useless. There is the other story, of course, about the lady who disliked *Hamlet* because it contained so many clichés, but again that is a joke about the lady's getting confused over the difference between literature and culture. There are no clichés or dead metaphors in Shakespeare, but many of his metaphors have died when they were carted outside and put to uses for which they were not intended. Figurative language in Shakespeare, and in literature at large, is always at the service of a complex context that involves character, plot, vision, sound, balance, antithesis, climax, and, above all, the intrinsic relation of the parts to each other and to the whole—in short, to a complete virtual world that has only an analogical relation to our own. The proverb on the other hand, is a kind of free agent, with no obligation to a virtual home. It grows out of the same bustling world of manners and morals as literary fictions, but its business is far more urgent: to supply that world with ongoing proof that essentials never change, that history eternally repeats itself, and that every proverb in the book is true until the end of time. And time, as another proverb tells us, "devours all things"—including, presumably, all proverbs.

Reading Responses

1. What does the essay's title, "Troping Through Proverbia," mean? If you did not know the title's meaning when you first read it, what did it suggest to you?
2. How does States introduce the topic of proverbs? Where does he state the thesis or central idea of his essay?
3. How does States define a proverb? What characteristics of proverbs does he discuss in the essay?

Writing Activities

1. Carefully read one or two paragraphs from the middle of States's essay. Analyze how the paragraph or paragraphs are developed. What are the functions of the first sentence, the middle sentences, and the last sentence? Write a brief analysis, explaining what pattern States uses in your sample and how this pattern affects readers.
2. Write another section for the essay, discussing proverbs used by your family or friends. Begin your section by making a general observation or stating a general principle or characteristic that applies to your collection of proverbs.

Next, discuss the proverbs, supplying examples and explaining what they convey or how they function when used by your family or friends.

3. Write your own interpretive essay about a particular type of expression. Introduce it, define and explain it, and investigate what it does or how it functions in different situations, using examples. You might, for example, explore the slang expressions used by a certain group or team, common campus greetings or farewells, introductory party chatter, or the emoticons used in a particular online community.

Community Links

Compare and contrast the use of details and examples in this essay by States with Bolman and Deal's "Cracking the Hidden Code" (pp. 240–245) about the work community or Hutton and Phillip's "Tuning in to the World of Nonprofit Organizations" (pp. 379–385). How do these writers use details and examples in similar or different ways? What do their strategies suggest about the expectations of their communities?

Theoretical Essay

HUMOR AS A DOUBLE-EDGED SWORD: FOUR FUNCTIONS OF HUMOR IN COMMUNICATION

John C. Meyer

———♦———

This essay appeared in Communication Theory, *one of the journals published by the International Communication Association. Most of the members of this association are scholars and teachers whose specialties range from interpersonal to popular to visual communication. As the journal's title indicates, its articles are about theory, concentrating on principles that underlie communication rather than practical applications. The selection here is the first part of John Meyer's essay, which explores three theories of humor. The abstract preceding the essay summarizes the entire essay, including the second part, which explains four functions of humor.*

The compelling power of humor makes it a recurrent topic for research in many fields, including communication. Three theories of humor creation emerge in humor research: the relief theory, which focuses on physiological release of tension; the incongruity theory, singling out violations of a rationally learned pattern; and the superiority theory, involving a sense of victory or triumph. Each theory helps to explain the creation of different aspects of humor, but each runs into problems explaining rhetorical applications of humor. Because each theory of humor origin tries to explain all instances of humor, the diverging communication effects of humor remain unexplained. Humor's enactment leads to 4 basic functions of humor in communication. Two tend to unite communicators: the identification and the clarification functions. The other 2 tend to divide 1 set of communicators from others: the enforcement and differentiation functions. Exploration of these effects-based functions of humor will clarify understanding of its use in messages. Humor use unites communicators through mutual identification and clarification of positions and values, while dividing them through enforcement of norms and differentiation of acceptable versus unacceptable behaviors or people. This paradox in the functions of humor in communication as, alternately, a unifier and divider, allows humor use to delineate social boundaries.

1   Humor in communication is a subject that seems difficult to analyze. After all, if one has to explain a joke, it is probably no longer funny. Yet, the compelling, mysterious power of humor leads scholars of all stripes to return to it again and again as a focus for study, because humor is so pervasive—while being most enjoyable and pleasant. Not only is humor pleasant; its recurring presence in rhetoric suggests that communicators believe it is also persuasive. What is it about humor that makes it so rewarding and so influential? Humor is generally viewed as a social phenomenon. For instance, people laugh less when watching a funny television show alone than during the same show with a group all laughing hilariously. Persons who are perceived to appreciate humor readily are generally more popular with others (Wanzer, Booth-Butterfield, & Booth-Butterfield, 1996). Such social properties make humor a natural focus for communication study. Central to all communication is the audience—those to whom a message may be directed. The audience gives attempts at humor their success or failure. This receiver-centered nature of humor, focusing on the intended effect of a message on the hearers, suggests that a rhetorical perspective on humor will lead to insights into how humor influences audiences.

2   Much research has sought to determine the causes of humor, why it exists, and why humor is funny. This essay focuses on how rhetors use humor when constructing messages. Such uses of humor are found to break down into two basic functions: unification and division. These functions result in four "theories of use," or key functions of humor in messages, rather than theories of humor origin. Politicians especially find humor a useful tool for uniting their audience behind them and dividing them from the opposition; thus, communicators use humor for various rhetorical purposes. However, the audience or receiver of the message determines how it is interpreted and what actual function the humor use serves. This essay refers to such communication effects as functions of humor, while maintaining that communicators try to include humor for intended purposes, seeking to effect a desired humor function. Before discussing functions, however, it is useful to review briefly the major theories of humor origin to understand how humor's four key communication functions (identification, clarification, enforcement, and differentiation) emerge from them.

3   Several major theories claim to comprehensively explain how humor originates in the minds of those experiencing it. Humor is viewed as a cognitive experience involving an internal redefining of sociocultural reality and resulting in a "mirthful" state of mind, of which laughter is a possible external display

(Apte, 1985). Laughter is a primary indicator of the experience of humor, but it is not the only one. Smiles, grins, or even sudden exhalations can indicate such experience. The perception- or audience-centered nature of humor is highlighted by the fact that, other than through such nonlinguistic indicators, the only evidence of humor experience comes from statements by the person experiencing it. Communication is a key factor in nearly all theories of humor because of its resulting from a message or interaction perceived by someone. At times, simple observations or thoughts can provoke humor, but theorists acknowledge the cognitive and symbolic nature of humor (McGhee, 1979). Some symbols must be processed in one's mind to perceive humor in a given situation, whether one is communicating or merely observing. Humor has been claimed to emerge in three basic ways in human thought: through perceptions of relief, incongruity, and superiority (Berger, 1993; Raskin, 1985).

Theories of Humor Origin

Relief

4   From the perspective of the relief theory, people experience humor and laugh because they sense stress has been reduced in a certain way (Berlyne, 1972; Morreall, 1983; Shurcliff, 1968). The physiological manifestations or "symptoms" of humor are most important to this view, which holds that humor stems from the relief experienced when tensions are engendered and removed from an individual. Humor then results from a release of nervous energy. This tension reduction may engender humor by reducing the state of arousal (the "jag" theory) or increasing the arousal (the "boost" theory), depending on the perspective (Berlyne, 1972). Some elaborations of the relief theory hold that humor may result from releases of energy that subconsciously overcome sociocultural inhibitions (Freud, 1960; Schaeffer, 1981). This release or arousal does not depend so much on symbols, allowing for the existence of humor indicated by happy laughter for no discernible reason, or children's laughter (Eckardt, 1992). Yet tellers of jokes or humorous stories may purposefully build tension, even using an incongruity, for the express purpose of releasing tension by resolving the incongruity (Maase, Fink, & Kaplowitz, 1984).

5   Communicators take advantage of this source of humor by telling a joke, often at the beginning of their remarks, to defuse a potentially tense situation. Often tension results from dissonance people experience after making a decision or sensing the approach of incompatible and undesirable thoughts or actions. Because people desire and find it pleasing to reduce dissonance (Festinger, 1957), speakers who do so can create humor. People feeling threatened by budget cuts in their organization, for instance, laugh with relief at a joke told at the start of a luncheon meeting on the budget to the effect that, "Well, it turns out we still can afford to have lunch—but I don't think the cook is accepting complaints." Remarks like this make the situation seem more elastic, or more manageable, by showing that difficulties are not so overwhelming as to be out of control after all (Burke, 1984). Using jokes to reduce tension in situations points to a common application of the relief theory of humor by communicators. Simple and even awkward laughter during conversations has

been found to relieve tension and facilitate further interaction between the parties (O'Donnell-Trujillo & Adams, 1983).

Incongruity

6 From the perspective of the incongruity theory, people laugh at what surprises them, is unexpected, or is odd in a nonthreatening way (Berger, 1976; Deckers & Divine, 1981; McGhee, 1979). An accepted pattern is violated, or a difference is noted—close enough to the norm to be nonthreatening, but different enough from the norm to be remarkable. It is this difference, neither too shocking nor too mundane, that provokes humor in the mind of the receiver, according to the incongruity theory.

7 Rather than focusing on the physiological or emotional effects of humor, the incongruity theory emphasizes cognition. Individuals must have rationally come to understand normal patterns of reality before they can notice differences. The mental capacity to note, understand, and categorize incongruous changes is necessary for the perceiver to experience humor, as it is viewed from the incongruity perspective. Only with this ability can humor arise from any sort of perceived incongruous relation, including an unexpected event or object, a physical or moral defect, an odd or disproportionate object, or any observable deviation from an implied standard (Grimes, 1955b). Comprehending these situations and their implications is required before humor, or a cognitive state of mirth, can be experienced.

8 Surprise, of course, is a key ingredient in humor from the incongruity perspective (Shurcliff, 1968). People laughed, for instance, at a comedian responding to criticism with a loud "Excuuuuse me!" because that is not normally how one is expected to respond to criticism; such a response is surprising, whereas an attempt to defend oneself or deny responsibility might not be. This use of surprise in humor is evident when one becomes irritated when telling a joke to someone who already knows the punch line. The joke is less funny because it is familiar; the element of surprise is lost, as the joke's pattern is now known and recognized by the receiver. Yet, people will often experience humor when hearing a joke told again, watching a funny routine again, or seeing a comedy multiple times. Incongruity theorists hold in such cases that people obtain humor from the "surprise" of a new perspective being enjoyed multiple times even when they know the basics of an impending humorous message. Veatch (1992) makes incongruity through "affective absurdity" the centerpiece of his humor theory, which holds that a humorous situation must involve a perceiver simultaneously having in mind one view of a situation that seems normal, and one view where there is a violation of the moral or natural order. When it seems that the situation is normal, yet something is wrong, humor occurs (Veatch, 1992). If one or the other of these perceptions is absent, the perceiver will not find humor. This perspective stresses the need for a rational development of a set of expectations that must be violated before humor can be perceived, explaining why mental sophistication is required for humor's appreciation and humor's consequent rarity in the animal kingdom (Apte, 1985). Such a crucial role for incongruity also suggests why

humor is a social phenomenon, because much humor stems from violations of what is socially or culturally agreed to be normal.

9   Examples of incongruity humor are numerous (Chapman & Foot, 1977; Meyer, 1990; Schutz, 1977). Politicians use humor from incongruity to portray opponents' actions as irrational. In 1992, President George Bush tried to portray opposing vice presidential candidate Al Gore as "Mr. Ozone," alluding to his advocacy of strict environmental regulations. Ten years earlier, President Ronald Reagan pointed to incongruities in governmental attempts to control crime: "We have the technological genius to send astronauts to the moon and bring them safely home. But we're having trouble making it safe for a citizen to take a walk in the evening through a park" (Reagan, 1982). Another Reagan commonplace that used incongruity for humor recurred frequently during his campaigns: "A federal program, once started, is the nearest thing to eternal life you'll ever see on this earth" (Reagan, 1976). He placed "eternal life," something usually associated with religion, in the context of government programs, an unusual association and hence an incongruity. Popular television shows like *America's Funniest Home Videos* or *Seinfeld* long have taken advantage of the humor found when people enact highly unusual or inappropriate behaviors.

Superiority

10 The superiority theory notes that people laugh outwardly or inwardly at others because they feel some sort of triumph over them or feel superior in some way to them (Feinberg, 1978; Grotjahn, 1957; Gruner, 1997, 1978; Morreall, 1983; Rapp, 1951; Ziv, 1984). Laughing at "ignorant" actions on the part of others, as adults often laugh at the sayings or doings of children, illustrates this perspective. Such events engender a state of mirth within individuals, which may result in outward laughter. Hostile laughter also is thought to be explainable by the superiority theory (Bergson, 1911; Singer, 1968). Mirth is first felt due to superiority, and then it may be expressed through laughter—sending an explicit message of superiority. The disagreeable feelings of threat to our identity from being laughed at stem from such humorous messages of superiority. Often superiority is not a pleasant type of humor for those subjected to it.

11 This theory also allows for open displays of humor to be used as social correctives (Bergson, 1911). Duncan (1962, p. 187) noted that such "disciplining by laughter" was one of the functions of the royal fool throughout the ages. Foolish antics were laughed at to show that such behaviors or beliefs were unacceptable in serious society (Apte, 1985). From a superiority theory perspective, humor results, not just from something irrational or unexpected, but from seeing oneself as superior, right, or triumphant in contrast to one who is inferior, wrong, or defeated. Fine (1976) has described how sexual humor sets and enforces the relevant social norms in a culture by ridiculing "lower" forms of behavior or language from the perspective of society's mainstream.

12 Laughing at faulty behavior can also reinforce unity among group members, as a feeling of superiority over those being ridiculed can coexist with a feeling of belonging (Duncan, 1982). Two important effects of superiority

humor follow: Human society is kept in order as those who disobey are censured by laughter, and people are made to feel part of a group by laughing at some ridiculed others. As examples of mild forms of superiority humor, television shows like *Candid Camera,* as well as many situation comedies, allow audiences to laugh at people caught in unenviable or idiotic situations.

The author would like to thank students in his Humor in Communication seminars, as well as the editor of *Communication Theory* and two reviewers for their contributions to this essay. An earlier version of this essay was presented at the National Communication Association annual convention, New York, NY, November 1998.

References
Apte, M. (1985). *Humor and laughter: An anthropological approach.* Ithaca, NY: Cornell University Press.
Berger, A. A. (1993). *An anatomy of humor.* New Brunswick, NJ: Transaction.
Berger, A. A. (1976). Anatomy of the joke. *Journal of Communication, 26*(3), 113–115.
Bergson, H. (1911). *Laughter: An essay on the meaning of the comic.* New York: MacMillan.
Berlyne, D. E. (1972). Humor and its kin. In J. H. Goldstein & P. E. McGhee (Eds.) *The psychology of humor* (pp. 43–60). New York: Academic Press.
Burke, K. (1984). *Permanence and change.* Los Angeles: University of California Press. (Original work published 1934)
Chapman, A. J., & Foot, H. C. (Eds.). (1977). *It's a funny thing, humour.* New York: Pergamon Press.
Deckers, L., & Devine, J. (1981). Humor by violating an existing expectancy. *Journal of Psychology, 108,* 107–110.
Duncan, H. D. (1962). *Communication and social order.* New York: Bedminster Press.
Duncan, W. F. (1982). Humor in management: Prospects for administrative practice and research. *Academy of Management Review, 7,* 136–142.
Eckhardt, A. R. (1992). *Sitting in the earth and laughing: A handbook of humor.* New Brunswick, NJ: Transaction.
Feinberg, L. (1978). *The secret of humor.* Amsterdam: Rodopi.
Festinger, L. A. (1957). *A theory of cognitive dissonance.* Evanston, IL: Row, Peterson.
Fine, G. A. (1976). Obscene joking across cultures. *Journal of Communication, 26*(3), 134–140.
Freud, S. (1960). *Jokes and their relation to the unconscious.* New York: Norton.
Grimes, W. (1955b). A theory of humor for public address: The mirth experience. *Communication Monographs, 22,* 217–226.
Grotjahn, M. (1957). *Beyond laughter: Humor and the subconscious.* New York: McGraw-Hill.
Gruner, C. R. (1997). *The game of humor.* New Brunswick, NJ: Transaction.
Gruner, C. R. (1985). Advice to the beginning speaker on using humor—What research tells us. *Communication Education, 34,* 142–146.
Maase, S. W., Fink, E. L., & Kaplowitz, S. A. (1984). Incongruity in humor: The incongruity theory. In R. N. Bostrom & B. H. Westley (Eds.), *Communication Yearbook 8,* Beverly Hills, CA: Sage.
McGhee, P. E. (1979). *Humor: Its origin and development.* San Francisco: W. H. Freeman.
Meyer, J. (1990). Ronald Reagan and humor: A politician's velvet weapon. *Communication Studies, 41,* 76–88.
Morreall, J. (1983). *Taking laughter seriously.* Albany: State University of New York.
O'Donnell-Trujillo, N., & Adams, K. (1983). Heheh in conversation: Some coordinating accomplishments of laughter. *Western Journal of Speech, 47,* 175–191.
Rapp, A. (1951). *The origins of wit and humor.* New York: E. P. Dutton.

Raskin, V. (1985). *Semantic mechanisms of humor*. Boston: Reidel.
Reagan, R. (1982, September 9). Landon Lecture Series address. Kansas State University, Manhattan, KS.
Reagan, R. (1976, January). *Campaign address*. Keene, NH: Audiotape.
Schaeffer, N. (1981). *The art of laughter*. New York: Columbia University Press.
Schutz, C. E. (1977). *Political humor*. London: Associated University Presses.
Shurcliff, A. (1968). Judged humor, arousal, and the relief theory. *Journal of Personality and Social Psychology, 8,* 360–363.
Singer, D. L. (1968). Aggression arousal, hostile humor, catharsis. *Journal of Personality and Social Psychology Monograph Supplement, 8,* 1–14.
Veatch, T. C. (1992, October). *A theory of humor*. Paper presented at the Speech Communication Association annual convention, Chicago.
Wanzer, M. B., Booth-Butterfield, M., & Booth-Butterfield, S. (1996). Are funny people popular? An examination of humor orientation, loneliness, and social attraction. *Communication Quarterly, 44,* 42–52.
Ziv, A. (1984). *Personality and sense of humor*. New York: Springer.

Reading Responses

1. What issue does the author plan to explore in his entire essay? What issue is discussed in the selection here?
2. What is the purpose of the abstract that precedes the article?
3. Meyer is addressing an academic audience interested in theories of communication. In what ways has he written his essay to appeal to these readers?

Writing Activities

1. Briefly explain, in your own words, the three theories of the origins of humor that Meyer reviews.
2. Spend some time observing interactions and events around you, looking for examples of humor. Write an essay that describes one humorous event. Then, use one of the three theories to account for the humor in the situation.
3. Write your own essay about one function of humor on the college campus. Identify the function of humor that you select—one general way that humor may act or one thing that it may accomplish in a campus situation—and use examples to explain the function to readers.

Community Links

Meyer, like Donald in "Learning, Understanding, and Meaning" (pp. 43–51), explores a topic by classifying or categorizing types. How do their approaches, intended for academic readers, compare or contrast with that of Lutz in "It's Okay to Be Anal Sometimes" (pp. 228–232), directed to the work community?

Persuasive Essay
Rethinking Justice
Mark A. Small and Robin Kimbrough-Melton

◆

This essay appeared originally in Behavioral Sciences and the Law, *a journal published six times each year. The special topic of the issue was International Perspectives on Restorative and Community Justice; Mark Small and Robin Kimbrough-Melton's essay appeared first, opening discussion of the topic. "Rethinking Justice" is a persuasive essay, but as its title suggests, it raises many points that need consideration in order to find new ways to administer justice effectively.*

Changes in the way people marry, bear children and live together, combined with the changing nature of support for families, has put pressure on the justice system to adjust to new family and community realities in order to accomplish justice goals. Although the entire legal system is implicated by the changing nature of families and communities, most scholars and practitioners have focused on the judicial system and those courts most relevant to family issues: namely, the juvenile, family, and criminal courts. As scholars and practitioners began to 'rethink justice,' whole new reform movements of therapeutic jurisprudence, restorative justice, and community justice (among others) have emerged to offer new paradigms for the administration of justice. In this essay we discuss ways in which families and the justice system interact to strengthen and weaken each other to accomplish justice goals. Copyright © 2002 John Wiley & Sons, Ltd.

1 The changing nature of family and community life poses significant challenges for the administration of justice in the 21st century. Changes in the way people marry, bear children and live together, combined with the changing nature of support for families, has put pressure on the justice system to adjust to new family and community realities in order to accomplish justice goals (Kimbrough-Melton & Small, in press). Although the entire legal system is implicated by the changing nature of families and communities, most scholars and practitioners have focused on the judicial system and those courts most relevant to family issues: namely, the juvenile, family, and criminal courts. As scholars and practitioners began to 'rethink justice,' whole new reform movements of therapeutic jurisprudence, restorative justice, and community justice (among others) have emerged to offer new paradigms for the administration of justice.

2 To be successful, any rethinking of justice is going to require more than an extended discussion and debate among scholars and practitioners as to what might be proper new roles for offenders, victims, families, and communities in the judicial system. Significant and lasting changes in the administration of justice will only come about when there is sufficient political will and a corresponding public acceptance to enact necessary legislative changes. As many legal change advocates often discover, creating meaningful and systemic change

within the administration of justice to respond to the changing nature of family and community life is frequently a slow and cumbersome process.

3   The common threads among judicial reform movements on how various justice systems might be redesigned to accomplish justice system goals have included a reconsideration of the roles of both families and communities in the administration of justice. A revised role for families especially has been seen as a critical component in restorative and community justice approaches.

4   Historically, few efforts were made to address the potential harm experienced by families when a family member became involved with the legal system. Conversely, because the legal system is not designed to maximize the potential help family members may offer, family members often are underutilized as a resource to bring about desired behavior change. Given the seemingly permanent changes in family structure and the probable corresponding consequences for the administration of justice, there is a clear need for understanding how family involvement in the legal system might be better orchestrated to accomplish justice system goals.

5   Typically, when a court exerts jurisdiction over an individual, a series of events are set in motion that have the potential to impact a family. The impacts experienced by a family may be positive or negative, direct or indirect, intended or unintended. Rarely are these family impacts understood in their totality—either by family members themselves or by those in charge of the administration of justice. As a result, administration of justice personnel and families often view each other with suspicion, and at times, outright hostility.

6   Unfortunately, initial contact with the legal system does little to ease this sense of mistrust and misunderstanding. Initial contact puts many individuals and their families at immediate risk of untoward family consequences. For example, assuming an arrested person is a positive resource for the family, once incarcerated, there is the potential disruption of the ability of the person to carry on in his or her respective family roles, perhaps as breadwinner or caretaker. Aside from the debilitating effect on the member, the family unit similarly is deprived of a contributing member. If nothing else, the normal function and routines of families are disrupted as they react to the crisis of a family member becoming entangled with the legal system. If there is removal of a truly essential family member (e.g., a single mother), inadequate attention may be paid to the potentially devastating impact on remaining family members, especially children.

7   Because most people often are uneducated about the legal process, individuals and their families who come into contact with the legal system may express fear and powerlessness regarding the proceedings. The family may be blamed for the member's predicament, so the stigmatizing pall cast over the member extends to the rest of the family as well. Conversely, in some communities, there is such a high degree of contact with the criminal justice system that shame has lost all effect as a measure of informal social control. In these communities, a degree of incarceration is expected as a rite of passage for young adults.

8   Should services be offered to a legally entangled family member, a number of obstacles diminish the odds that they will be successful. First, assessments

frequently reflect only the availability of services, not the treatment needs of the individual. Services, broadly defined, are often limited and delivered in such a way as to discriminate against the poor. Additionally, they are stigmatizing and may at best, promise only limited short-term solutions. Little or no efforts are made to sustain the treatment services once the person exits the legal system. Treatment services are offered through a fragmented delivery system that seemingly operates beyond the ability of the courts to change. The needs of affected family members are largely ignored. For some, the entire process and outcomes of treatment services confirm the impression of a punitive and racist system.

9   Despite these flaws, the system also has positive family impacts. A harmful family member may be removed from the family. Accurate assessments and appropriate treatment services can change disruptive family behavior. The court can give family members a meaningful voice for dispositional orders, empowering families through due process and strengthening family relationships. Finally, an active court may help develop necessary family and community resources.

Rethinking Justice

10   Because goals vary across justice systems, any move toward more family-centered and community-engaged legal systems must begin with a recognition of how a particular justice system's goals relate to family and community involvement. For example, the juvenile justice system has long functioned on the assumption that adult guidance provided through the family and/or the community is a necessary precondition to reduce recidivism. Similarly, in dependency and family courts, the family and community are seen as resources to ameliorate any harmful effects that may follow a family member's legal entanglement. In contrast, when punitive goals are paramount, as in criminal courts, the effects on families and communities of the judicial processing and disposition of the offender is of minor importance.

11   Despite the range of importance given to family and community matters by different courts and their respective jurisdictions, all courts are linked in various degrees to family treatment services. Thus, any movement toward reform in the direction of taking families and communities seriously in the administration of justice necessarily will involve answering some tough questions on how best to integrate treatment (broadly construed as including all social services) within the administration of justice (broadly construed as encompassing the full range of legal involvement from pre-arrest investigation to post-release). A non-exhaustive list of some of these tough questions follows, with some practical considerations offered to help set a context for rethinking justice.

To What Extent Should Family and Community Interests Be Considered by the Legal System?

12   Family and community interests should be considered to the extent that they further goals of the legal system. Thus, the extent of consideration will vary

depending on the particular legal agency and the specific legal goal sought to be accomplished. For example, in criminal cases, family interests will receive more consideration in situations where maintaining family integrity is likely to lead to successful rehabilitation of an offender or when community safety merits family involvement. Given the potential positive or negative impacts on a legal actor's family as a consequence of involvement with the legal system, some consideration might be given family interests regardless of the proceeding. For example, it is hard to imagine cases in which a child would not be impacted by legal proceedings involving a parent. Ultimately, with sufficient deliberation, some uniformity of opinion might be reached to determine the conditions under which different family interests are accorded weight in specific legal proceedings.

What Are the Risks of Increasing Family and Community Involvement?

13 There are risks to the family, the legal system and the community for increasing family and community involvement in legal proceedings. For families, there is the risk that extralegal involvement by additional family members will exacerbate preexisting familial conflicts. For example, when courts script family members in supervisory roles, the family member essentially replaces the judge as a coercive agent—a role in conflict with being a supportive family member. Additionally, for the legal system, equal protection issues may arise when services or particular dispositions are afforded only those with significant family ties (e.g., those with family support systems receive more favorable probation and parole treatment). Finally, communities may be at risk from the consequences of reforming legal proceedings to bring other family members into the legal system who otherwise would be left out. One example of this net widening would be parents who are held in contempt during truancy proceedings of their children. Thus, careful deliberation should be given to the risks of increasing family and community involvement in legal proceedings.

What Happens to the Integrity of the Justice System When Courts Assume New Roles?

14 Judicial integrity is directly related to whether judges are perceived to dispense justice with objectivity and fairness. There are consequences for this popular perception when courts assume roles that blend traditional judicial functions with new responsibilities aimed at solving social problems. For example, courts may lose moral authority if they become too involved in treatment (e.g., victims of domestic violence are devalued when offenders receive treatment services in lieu of retribution). Alternatively, traditional due process and fairness concerns may be compromised when courts act as a broker for mental health services and allow services to some, but not others. Although drug courts and other venues of community justice are experimenting with new judicial models, a deeper understanding is necessary for guiding what might be the optimal mix of justice and treatment goals.

What Strategies Are Available for Courts Interested in Involving Family Members and Community Institutions?

15 As courts ponder new and fruitful ways to consider family interests, any success will be partially determined by the strategies utilized to involve family members. A familiar though still uncommon strategy is to consolidate cases so that a single judge has oversight over an entire family. In some jurisdictions, this may require enacting new legislation. Of the carrot and stick approaches to getting family members involved, the use of contempt orders by judges often is easier to invoke than the use of incentives. The limited options for judges interested in involving family members necessitates more in-depth discussion of how new and existing strategies might be developed.

How May Courts Increase Limited Dispositional Alternatives for Individuals and Family Members?

16 Unsurprisingly, most courts do not have at their disposal a full continuum of treatment and sanction options to fashion dispositions. Moreover, there are few resources and fewer court appointed personnel who have time to develop more comprehensive treatment networks. Still, as courts experiment with strategies to engage community organizations, there may be opportunities to expand available disposition options. Additionally, given limited options, supreme importance should be placed on the successful dissemination of what does work.

What Are Barriers to Reforming the Legal System to be More Responsive to Families and Engaged with Community Organizations?

17 Of barriers and obstacles, there are many. First, and perhaps foremost, there is judicial reluctance to engage in broader social roles. For many judges, the family and community are largely invisible during legal proceedings, with most judges believing that to be proper. To accomplish change in judicial attitudes, the following might be considered.

(i) An expanded roles for judges would need to be explicit within the Judicial Codes of Ethics.

(ii) Judicial training for expanded social roles could take place in the Judicial College or workshops. Specific techniques may include training in a strengths-based approach, or education relating to how judges may better relate to defendants to accomplish change.

(iii) Legal education in law schools should reflect new judicial roles.

(iv) An advocacy movement to make the case for broader social roles for judges, perhaps based on efficiency and administrative arguments.

(v) Increased federal spending for judicial reform.

(vi) Policy makers and key stake-holders must be convinced of the effectiveness of system change.

How Involved Should Judges Be in Treatment Decisions?

18 Because judges are genuinely interested in seeing behavior change, not merely getting compliance with court orders, there is a great deal of interest among judges in acquiring a general understanding of how treatment works. In addi-

tion, there is a corresponding interest in understanding the role family members can play in treatment. Unfortunately, there is not much known about the effectiveness of either, especially the involvement of families in treatment dispositions. True, there are new models of drug courts, mental health courts, and family group conferencing, but these are mostly untested, particularly in terms of family involvement.

19   A more recent interest by some judges (notably drug court judges) is an understanding of how individual and family strengths could be used in court ordered dispositions. Currently, most judicial systems are not set up to emphasize individual and family strengths. Oftentimes, treatment reports to judges limit the judicial options because of a focus on the deficits of the individual, rather than on any strengths possessed by the individual or the family, or within the broader community. Even with knowledge of family and community strengths, there are open questions about when family and community services are integrated best into the system, including questions about the family consequences for involvement at various legal stages from predisposition to release from incarceration.

20   The need for judicial understanding of treatment is taking on greater urgency as judges look for ways to improve the current triage approach whereby quick determinations are made about who is going to get court time versus who will be 'processed.' Compounding the difficulty of getting a fix on treatment efficacy is the changing nature of the administration of treatment services (e.g., managed care).

Should Courts Lead in Community Justice Projects?

21   There is considerable debate about the proper role of courts in the community. Unlike law enforcement or corrections, there has not been widespread activity by courts to lead community development of justice related projects. To be sure, there have been some community justice programs and models to emerge from those programs, but for the most part, judges have been silent. For those courts who are willing but unable to lead community justice projects, attention should be focused on increasing their capacity.

New Challenges for Families and the Justice System

22   Although the courts and the accompanying justice system were founded on assumptions about family life that no longer hold true (e.g., less than 7% of households have a male breadwinner and stay-at-home wife and mother), family involvement remains instrumental in fulfilling some goals of the legal system. For example, courts that involve family members and relevant community organizations advance the goal of deterrence, as family and community members will be more watchful if, in part, they are responsible for the successful behavior of each other. Additionally, to the extent rehabilitation is a goal in a particular case, treatment of an offender will be more effective if family and community members are involved. Retribution is served as family and community members may feel greater satisfaction if involved in justice decisions. Conversely, retribution is also served as family members may suffer by criminal

punishment of an individual family member, either directly (e.g., parental responsibility law) or indirectly through the loss encountered when a family member is incarcerated. At a more fundamental level, family involvement in the administration of justice ultimately increases community safety. An obvious example is the enhanced safety of community when there is a social support system available for released convicts.

23   In addition to serving goals of the justice system, family and community involvement arguably is normatively demanded. The value of families to society suggests that considering the legal impact on families is a necessary endeavor to preserve and protect family integrity. Ignoring family dynamics in a particular case denigrates the dignity of families as meaningful social groups. Moreover, the creation of strong families helps build strong neighborhoods and communities. Thus, there is a need to understand the ways in which families and the justice system interact to strengthen and weaken each other.

24   In recognition of the importance of family and community involvement in advancing justice goals, the movements to reform justice all emphasize an increased judicial awareness of how the legal impact on one family member affects other family members and the pivotal role nonlegal community institutions play in the furtherance of justice goals. As current efforts to rethink justice evolve into more sustained movements of reform, families and community organizations should play an increasingly important role.

Reference

Kimbrough-Melton, R. K., & Small, M. A. (in press). *Families in the justice system: Challenges of the new millennium.* Washington, DC: Bureau of Justice Assistance.

Reading Responses

1. What is this essay's overall argument? What changes in the judicial system would Small and Kimbrough-Melton be likely to encourage?
2. How does the essay try to persuade readers to consider changes in the justice system? Why do you think that the authors did not simply list a series of "shoulds" or "musts," telling readers just what ought to be done?
3. Examine the headings in the essay to discover how they are used. Where do they appear? How many levels of main headings and subheadings are used? How might the headings help readers follow the essay?

Writing Activities

1. Using your own words, summarize Small and Kimbrough-Melton's discussion of one of the questions in the essay's headings.
2. Write a short essay that presents your own view about the interaction of families and the justice system. To demonstrate a reasonable, balanced ap-

proach, however, devote one section to possible problems that may arise from family–judicial interactions and another section to possible benefits of this interaction. Although you may use "Rethinking Justice" as a resource, develop other examples that seem significant and pertinent to you.

3. Write your own "rethinking" essay, urging readers to reconsider the status quo in some area that concerns you. Using "Rethinking Justice" as a model, identify the perspective that is important to you, acknowledge potential problems that might result from change, discuss some of the "tough questions" that should be considered, and then summarize your viewpoint.

Community Links

Contrast this persuasive academic essay with other texts that try to persuade readers to a particular viewpoint such as Lesh-Laurie's "Memo to CU-Denver Community" (p. 307) or Gibson's two messages about the Liberty Newport Tiger Fund (pp. 312–318) from the work community or Cullis-Suzuki's "The Young Can't Wait" (pp. 355–356) or the Declaration of Independence (pp. 426–430) from the public community. Analyze two or three of these selections, considering which persuasive strategies they do or do not share.

Research Reflection

RESEARCHING BEDLAM AND MADNESS IN THE EARLY MODERN ERA

Brooke Kush, Student Writer

◆

When her Shakespeare class read Hamlet, *Brooke Kush conducted research on Bedlam Hospital. This London institution, the oldest mental hospital in England, began treating patients long before Shakespeare's day. Brooke wanted to discover the contemporary treatments for madness and melancholy and then apply this information to the play. In the following research reflection, Brooke considers her experience as a researcher and briefly explains what she learned. Her reflection was submitted to her instructor as a short essay, but it might have been recorded in a research journal or research file.*

Brooke Kush
Shakespeare 2
19 September 2001

Researching Bedlam and Madness in the Early Modern Era

1. My experience as a researcher for this project was interesting, yet overwhelming. I knew that I wanted to mostly focus on Bedlam Hospital since it was so near the Globe Theater and nearly in the heart of London—Shakespeare's town. I wasn't sure exactly what I was going to find out about how Shakespeare himself would have treated the mad, and I didn't find much, unfortunately. But, I did discover how his society and his time treated people who today probably would have been mostly treated in outpatient settings.

2. Reading about Bedlam was difficult for me because of the topic as well as the fact that there isn't a whole lot of information about it. There were very few primary documents about the hospital, and even the hospital's Web site wasn't that impressive. What information I did find about the hospital was quite disturbing. The way that the "melancholy" or "mad" people were treated in Shakespeare's time was atrocious, especially by today's standards of helping the ill. Patients were often chained to the wall, tortured under the premise that it was for their own good, left screaming in the darkness alone, sometimes doused with cold water or spun around on rotating chairs. For a while, the headmaster of the hospital carried on a black-market business of allowing rich males to rape the young female patients.

3. As far as early modern views of the insane, the lines of thinking were not much better than at Bedlam itself. People with mental or physical disabilities were thought to be either related to Satan or innocent people who were cursed with abnormal or sinful human behavior characteristics. Words in Shakespeare's time that were thought of as "politically correct" ways to describe the clinically insane were idiot, stupid, witless, crazy, mad, fool, and melancholic.

4. Textually, I discovered that had Hamlet and Ophelia not been royalty they could have been categorized as "freaks" at Bedlam hospital. Talking to oneself, dressing in black, hearing voices, seeing "visions," and having a pale complexion were all characteristics that both Hamlet and Ophelia exhibited. Luckily, they escaped with being left alone (for the most part) in terms of their complex mental illnesses.

5. Overall, this was one of the more interesting readings I've done of *Hamlet*, knowing all that I do now about how people with mental illnesses were treated.

Reading Responses

1. How does Brooke evaluate her experience as a researcher?
2. What information did Brooke find, and what information was unavailable? Why do you suppose this was the case?
3. Why doesn't Brooke formally cite her sources in this essay?

Writing Activities

1. Summarize in your own words what Brooke learned about Bedlam.
2. Begin your own research journal—a file or notebook that you use for personal reflections, observations, ideas, and comments during a research project for a class, at work, or for a civic group.
3. Investigate a name, an institution, or a location that has turned up in your personal reading, a textbook, or class discussion. Report on your investigation in three ways. On one page, reflect on your experience as a researcher. On a second page, explain what you learned during your investigation. On a third page, list the sources that you used.

Community Links

In addition to Brooke's reflection, read one or two other first-person accounts such as "The Story of a Garment Worker" (pp. 205–207) from the work community, "Organizer: Bill Talcott" (pp. 357–361) from the public community, or another selection from a Community Voices section. In what ways do the selections you have read use the first person (*I*) effectively? In what ways are the writers' first-person voices similar or different? How do you account for these similarities or differences? Go beyond the obvious differences in content or structure to examine more subtle differences in tone, word choice, or persona (the writer's character or image as it is presented or revealed to readers in a particular text).

Documented Problem–Solution Essay
FUELING THE REVOLUTION
Matt Woodard, Student Writer

♦

Professor R. James Goldstein assigned his English 1127 class an argumentative essay using sources. The assignment was to identify a problem and then advocate a solution to it. Students were to write as if they were preparing reports for a citizen's group that intended to take the issue to Washington in order to convince an elected representative of the solution's merits. To support the proposed solution, students were to use a minimum of three scholarly resources, all cited using the version of the Modern Language Association (MLA) style then current. Matt Woodard selected immigration as the problem he wanted to tackle in his essay.

Matt Woodard
Dr. Goldstein
Honors English II
8 November 2000

Fueling the Revolution

1   During the past ten years, the United States has experienced an economic revolution. Thanks to new computer technology, which has "been responsible for more than one-third of all economic growth since 1995" (White 1), the United States has experienced "unprecedented economic expansion" (Senate 1). Because of the amazing economic revolution we have undergone in the past few years, many economists have begun using the term New Economy to describe this computer-powered world that we live in today. The New Economy is perhaps the biggest change in the economic workings of the world since the Industrial Revolution. It is in large part powered by the Internet, which has helped to make the New Economy not just prevalent in the United States but a global factor that has made the entire world realize that we are ever more dependent on each other.

2   However, while the United States has had great success not only in creating but also in thriving in this New Economy, its success is threatened by one of the most severe labor shortages in 50 years (White 2). According to a study released in April 2000 by the Information Technology Association of America, 850,000 high-tech jobs are vacant in the United States because no one is qualified to fill them (Masters and Ruthizer 5). This number is up from 350,000 only two years ago (Hoffman 1). This labor shortage will continue to grow because the demand for information technology workers is ever-increasing, yet U.S. schools are simply not turning out enough qualified people to fill the jobs. According to Auren Hoffman, president of BridgePath, Inc., "only about 25,000 computer science majors enter the workforce each year—down 30 percent from the totals of ten years ago" (Hoffman 2). Yet during the same time period, information technology employment has doubled (Jerome 3). As any first-year economics student can tell you, supply is not meeting demand, and we have a serious problem on our hands.

3   Responding to the immense cry for help from information technology firms, Congress passed and President Clinton signed into law a bill that would raise the cap on H-1B visas from 115,000 during 2000 to 195,000 for the next three years (Fact 1). The H-1B visa allows a U.S. company to bring in a foreign worker for up to six years, provided that this worker has some special skill that cannot easily be found here at home. While this type of visa could technically apply to almost any skilled job area, most of these visas are issued to workers who have skills in the information technology sector.

4   The passage of this bill is certainly a step in the right direction. However, these visas are only a temporary fix, and there are still not enough visas to solve the problem. After all, 195,000 visas will not compensate for the 850,000 and growing high-tech job shortage in this country. Also, after six years, these workers are required to go back home. This creates two serious problems. The

first is the fact that we are basically telling these brilliant, creative, and wonderfully productive people, "take all of the skills you have learned here in the past six years, and go back to your native country, our economic competitor, and use them against us." The second problem is that since these workers are only here for six years, most of them try to send as much money back home to their families as possible because most of these workers come from underdeveloped countries such as India and China. So, instead of buying a home here and spending their money in our economy, a large portion of it is sent back to their native countries.

5   Therefore, immigration laws need to be loosened to allow highly skilled foreign workers to enter the U.S. permanently so that they might continue to help fuel this economic revolution. Thus, the H-1B visa program should be abolished and replaced by a green card program with the same restrictions and with the ultimate goal of making the green card holders citizens. In the global market, countries will be forced to compete for scarce high-tech workers in order to survive economically. These highly skilled workers would be much more inclined to come to the United States if we could guarantee them and their immediate families a permanent stay here. These workers would benefit the U.S. economy in several ways. They would increase U.S. productivity, thus creating jobs, not costing Americans jobs, as many critics of this issue claim. They would also give a boost to the economy because they would become economic consumers themselves.

6   In order to stay competitive, the U.S. must move quickly on this issue. According to Susanne Masters, who sits on the board of directors for the National Immigration Forum, "In a global marketplace where skilled employees are in short supply, nations will be forced to compete for them. The U.S. would be foolish to forgo its strategic advantage by unduly restricting the flow of skilled workers to this country" (Masters and Ruthizer 1). Other economic superpowers like Great Britain and Germany are beginning to bring in the best minds from countries such as China, India, and Argentina. Even Japan, which has worked for centuries to keep its population homogeneous, is now considering easing its strict immigration laws in order to remain competitive (Immigration 3). While it managed to become an economic powerhouse only a few short years ago, Japan has lost much of its economic prowess in the New Economy era. Japan's lack of workers skilled in the technology sector along with its aging workforce has ushered in its fall from grace. By 2020, more than one out of every four Japanese will be over 65 (Japan 4). To stabilize its working population, the United Nations estimates that it will need to import over 600,000 workers every year until 2050 (Immigration 7). While the thought of this strikes fear into the heart of every Japanese, it is a reality that they must accept in order to survive economically.

7   The United States is in a similar situation, facing both a high-tech labor shortage and an aging population. If countries like Japan, whose entire culture rests on the idea of keeping foreigners out, are looking outside their borders for workers, then the United States, a country of immigrants, should be ashamed of lagging so far behind. Yet if we could offer these highly skilled immigrants and their families a permanent stay here in the U.S., they would be

much more likely to come here instead of going to other countries. They would help us to stay tops in the economic world instead of using their skills to compete against us.

8   Yet at a time when importing skilled workers seems so key to our economic survival, there are many who would like to slow down and even stop such immigration. Trade and labor unions such as the AFL-CIO and the Institute for Electrical Engineers claim that "skilled immigrants work for lower pay and take jobs away from U.S. citizens" (Hoffman 7). Opponents such as Norman Matloff, professor of computer science at The University of California-Davis, claims that information technology companies "want more [foreign workers] so they can hire cheaper, younger labor. There are many out-of-work, mid-level programmers who've been laid off and who can't get hired because the companies don't want to pay for their experience" (Mottl 8). However, this is simply not the case. Companies certainly aren't hiring immigrants because they are a cheap source of labor. According to Daniel Griswold, associate director of the Center for Trade Policy Studies at the Cato Institute, "companies pay a $10,000 to $15,000 premium to cover the relocation and visa application costs of a skilled immigrant under the H-1B program" (Griswold 12) and do not reduce costs for labor. Clearly, hiring U.S. citizens would avoid such costs (Griswold 12). According to data from the National Academy of Sciences and the National Science Foundation, there is good reason to believe that immigrants with high-tech skills "typically earn slightly more than their native-born counterparts with the same academic credentials and experience" (Griswold 10). Thus, immigrants are not causing Americans to lose jobs because they are working for less pay. The reason that the middle-aged American programmers are not getting jobs is not because companies aren't willing to pay for their experience, but because they simply do not have the necessary, up-to-date computer skills that companies so desperately need. In an economy where there are 850,000 high-tech job shortages, any qualified person should be able to get a job. Yet while organizations such as the AFL-CIO and the Institute for Electrical Engineers question whether there is a shortage at all, numerous studies by the Information Technology Association of America, the Virginia Polytechnic Institute, and several think tanks all seem to verify the shortage. An even better sign of a shortage is the increase in wages for programmers, systems analysts, and other highly skilled workers whose numbers do not meet current demand (Griswold 3).

9   In fact, instead of immigrants taking jobs away from Americans, the exact opposite is actually true. Letting in more highly skilled immigrants would create far more jobs for American workers than the immigrants themselves take up. Auren Hoffman, who also writes for the American Enterprise Institute for Public Policy Research, claims that due to the skilled worker shortage, "American companies are underproducing and under inventing" (Hoffman 1), because they are having to postpone new research projects (Griswold 5). A recent survey of information technology companies indicated that two-thirds of the companies said that their lack of highly skilled workers was a "barrier to their future growth" (Griswold 5) because postponing projects means decreases in research, sales, and profits (Griswold 5). Skilled immigrants increase America's productivity and thus create more jobs. Hoffman writes that T. J.

Rodgers, president and CEO of Cypress Semiconductor, "estimates that his 172 immigrant engineers have created 860 jobs at his company." Also, the increased productivity of Cypress due to immigrant engineers has given the local economy a boost because Cypress has had to "build bigger offices, order more business cards, buy more computers, and use more telephones" (Hoffman 10). By allowing highly skilled immigrants in permanently, they will continue to provide this boost to our economy.

10   Although the AFL-CIO and Institute for Electrical Engineers claim that Americans will lose jobs if more immigrants are allowed in, Americans will actually lose jobs in the long run if we do not. If companies cannot find the talent they need here in the U.S., they "will be forced to set up operations in other countries" (Costlaw 9). According to Terry Costlaw, a writer for the Electronic Engineering Times, "one company boils it down to 'a choice between importing people or exporting jobs'" (Costlaw 2).

11   There are still other possible benefits from allowing high-tech workers to immigrate to the U.S. permanently. By becoming citizens, the high salaries that these workers make would become taxable, thus helping our national government's resources. Also, by being able to stay here permanently, these workers would have the chance to start companies of their own, which would create countless more jobs. According to Hoffman, "Immigrants have founded thousands of successful companies that employ millions of Americans" (Hoffman 9). One such example is Intel's chairman, Andy Grove. Imagine how many more successful companies could be founded if more highly skilled foreign workers were allowed to enter the country on a permanent basis.

12   Many people believe that we could create the same economic results that importing workers would create by simply educating more American workers to do these jobs. However, the large majority of the $1000 per visa fee that companies must pay to the federal government in order to hire foreign workers goes to training U.S. workers and providing scholarships for American students in math, engineering, and computer science (Fact 2). Yet even with scholarships available and the near certainty of a high paying job upon graduation, the number of students majoring in these fields remains relatively low. Also, many companies feel that workers from overseas are much more qualified to do the job because U.S. schools simply aren't preparing students like they should. "Many companies see a vast discrepancy between the high skill levels of most H-1B visa holders and the entry-level skills of most [U.S.] graduates" (Vaas 6). In part, the reason for this skills discrepancy is that many H-1B holders have Ph.Ds, making them far more knowledgeable in their field than their bachelor's degree-holding American counterparts (Vaas 6). Companies cannot afford to wait several years hoping that the numbers of U.S. students will go back up or that those students will be better qualified to fill those jobs. We need more skilled workers now—and if we do not get them, we risk falling behind in this extremely competitive global market.

13   We have seen the benefits that will arise from letting in highly skilled foreign workers. By letting them in permanently, they will continue to be a boost to our thriving economy. Everyone will benefit from the many jobs that these workers will help create, as well as from the tax dollars that they will help to generate. However, if we do not bring these workers in, we are playing Russian

Roulette with our economic future. We were tops in the Old Economy, but can we stay on top in the New Economy? If we do not have enough skilled workers, the answer is almost surely not.

Works Cited

Costlaw, Terry. "Senate Set to Vote This Week on Visa-Cap Bill—High Noon Approaches for H-1B Friends, Foes." Electronic Engineering Times 2 Oct. 2000: 1. Online. Expanded Academic ASAP. 21 Nov. 2000.

"Fact Sheet: American Competitiveness in the Twenty-First Century Act." US Newswire. 17 Oct. 2000. Online. Westlaw. 21 Nov. 2000.

Griswold, Daniel T. "Let High-Tech Workers In!" Journal of Commerce 30 Mar. 1998. Online. Expanded Academic ASAP. 21 Nov. 2000.

Hoffman, Auren. "Don't Starve U.S. Businesses for Skilled Workers." American Enterprise. July-Aug. 1998: 73. Online. Expanded Academic ASAP. 15 Nov. 2000.

"Immigration in Japan—The Door Opens, a Crack." Economist 2 Sept. 2000: 37. Online. Expanded Academic ASAP. 21 Nov. 2000.

"Japan to Allow in Foreign Nurses to Care for Old." British Medical Journal 25 Mar. 2000: 825. Online. Expanded Academic ASAP. 21 Nov. 2000.

Jerome Levy Economics Institute. "Is There a Shortage of Information Technology Workers?" Current Issues SourceFile. CD-ROM. Record: R218-9. 21 Nov. 2000.

Masters, Suzette Brooks, and Ted Ruthizer. "Does the U.S. Need to Import Professional Workers?" USA Today Sept. 2000: 18. Online. Expanded Academic ASAP. 15 Nov. 2000.

Mottl, Judith N. "Firms Lobby for Foreign Labor." Internet Week 9 Mar. 1998: 58. Online. Expanded Academic ASAP. 21 Nov. 2000.

"Senate Votes to Keep Economy Booming; Congress Needs to Pass Other Immigration Measures." US Newswire 4 Oct. 2000. Online. Expanded Academic ASAP. 21 Nov. 2000.

Vaas, Lisa. "Failing Grades." ZDWire 17 Sept. 2000: n. pag. Online. Westlaw. 21 Nov. 2000.

White, Dan. "Employers Will Soon Be Unable to Obtain New H-1B Visas for Foreign High-Tech Workers." National Law Journal 22.25 (2000). Online. Westlaw. 21 Nov. 2000.

Reading Responses

1. What does Matt propose in his essay? Where does he state this proposal?

2. Based on the description of the assignment that precedes Matt's essay, how well do you think he has fulfilled the requirements? In what ways has he shaped his essay to show his primary reader—Professor Goldstein—that he understands the assignment and its purpose?

3. If you were in a peer review group in Matt's composition class, what would you say about his essay? What do you like about the essay? What are its strengths? What changes would you suggest?

Writing Activities

1. An essay that proposes a solution is likely to include specific sections, each accomplishing a task that will help to persuade readers to accept the argument. These parts describe the problem, explain the proposed solution, justify the solution using logical reasons and evidence, acknowledge

other views, and counter possible objections. Working individually or in a small group, outline Matt's argument, paragraph by paragraph, to show how his essay is organized.

2. Write a paragraph that summarizes Matt's proposal and briefly explains the main points that support the proposal.

3. Write your own argumentative essay proposing a solution to a problem. Investigate a specific problem on your campus or in the local community. Address your essay either to those who could implement the solution or to others on campus who might help lobby for the proposal. To learn more about the problem and possible solutions, find and cite pertinent campus or local resources such as library materials; governmental or institutional documents or studies; newspaper articles and editorials; campus handbooks, policies, or other materials; campus, community, or organizational Web sites; interviews with local experts; and observations or other field investigations. Develop and organize your essay so that it accomplishes the typical tasks listed in question 1.

Community Links

Contrast Matt's argument essay proposing a solution with a grant proposal such as "Communicating Common Ground" (pp. 183–187), "Proposal for a Cornell College Living & Learning Group" (pp. 554–559), or the grant proposal for the United States Botanic Garden (pp. 559–565). How does an essay proposing a solution differ from or resemble other proposals?

Research Paper

THE EVOLUTION OF CORAL-ZOOXANTHELLAE SYMBIOSES: IMPLICATIONS OF CORAL BLEACHING

Valerie Gamble, Student Writer

◆

For her biology seminar on evolution, a required course for majors, Valerie wrote a research paper investigating the symbiotic relationship between coral and zooxanthellae, a type of algae. Her broad subject, coral reefs, reflects a special area of interest at her college. Both biology and geology students have traveled with their professors to the Bahamas to study coral reefs, lagoons, and tidal flats; other stu-

dents have analyzed coral samples on campus. One standard expectation of the biology department is that students model their papers after articles in scientific journals. Valerie selected The Quarterly Review of Biology, *a publication directed to general biologists. This journal expects brief, clear articles that readers from fields other than biology can understand. Source citations are expected to follow the style used by the Council of Science Editors, formerly the Council of Biology Editors.*

Valerie Gamble
Cornell College
February 2000
Prof. Marty Condon

Abstract

1   Scleractinian corals and zooxanthellae have been symbiotic partners for 200 million years. This symbiosis is a mutual relationship involving the exchange of nutrients between heterotroph and autotroph. The presence of ahermatypic, or non-symbiotic, coral suggests that corals do not need zooxanthellae to survive. Zooxanthellae are also found as free living dinoflagellates, indicating that they can also survive outside of the symbiotic relationship. Hermatypic, or symbiotic corals, are the only kind found building massive reef frameworks, and this process has been linked to the presence of zooxanthellae. Coral bleaching, the expulsion of zooxanthellae from the symbiotic host coral, is becoming widespread. This stress reaction to increased temperature leaves the corals weak and susceptible to diseases. This paper addresses the history and development of the symbiotic relationship, as well as possible reasons for coral bleaching and the termination of a beneficial symbiotic interaction.

Introduction

2   Scleractinian corals developed into symbiotic and non-symbiotic forms during the Triassic period in geologic history (Stanley and Swart 1995). These two coral types have been successful in different, non-overlapping ecosystems. The symbiotic corals are especially important because they develop large coral reef structures that are home to many species of fish, crustaceans, and plants. Research and observation have shown that the coral-zooxanthellae symbiosis is the main reason for reef building because the non-symbiotic corals do not create large limestone structures (Prothero 1998).

3   This paper addresses the reasons behind the symbiosis by examining coral and algal ecology, the nutrient exchange between them, and the effects of temperature stress on the relationship. The working hypothesis is that coral and zooxanthellae receive mutual benefits from their relationship and that large-scale coral bleaching causes disease susceptibility by weakening the corals. Bleaching may be part of an evolutionary mechanism in corals because it allows for recombination of different strains of algae and species of coral (Buddemeier and Fautin 1993). Further experiments are needed to determine the extent of evolutionary possibilities through symbiotic recombination.

Coral Ecology

4   Scleractinian corals have been extensively studied due to their prominence in tropical reef communities. Two types of scleractinian corals, hermatypic and ahermatypic, evolved in the Mesozoic period and have persisted to the present day. The hermatypic corals are defined by the symbiotic algae always found within their endodermal tissues. These corals have adapted to live only in clear, shallow, nutrient-poor waters (Prothero 1998). The ahermatypic corals do not contain symbiotic algae and are found in colder climates and deep water. The hermatypic corals are reef framework builders worldwide because of their symbiotic relationship with zooxanthellae that allows for increased efficiency through the recycling of carbon, nitrogen, and phosphorus between the heterotroph and the autotroph (Darley 1982).

5   Coral colonies are composed of a thin layer of tissue covering a massive limestone skeleton. The tissue is composed of corallites, clonal polyps formed during asexual reproduction, which are interconnected by gastrovascular channels and nervous systems (Sorokin 1993). These physiological connections unite the polyps into a single animal. Coral colonies are heterotrophic and feed on zooplankton using cilia located on the polyps. Corals do exhibit polytrophism because the polyps can actively hunt moving prey, be sedimentary filter feeders, and utilize products of photosynthesis created by their symbiotic zooxanthellae (Muscatine and Porter 1977). All corals reproduce sexually and asexually (Sorokin 1993) and exhibit either sessile or motile forms at different stages in their development. Planula larvae are the motile products of sexual reproduction used for dispersal of the coral. They become sessile and settle only on hospitable substrate (Schwarz et al. 1999). Once the larvae settle, they reproduce asexually and develop a colony of genetically related polyps.

Zooxanthellae Ecology

6   Zooxanthellae are a group of unicellular dinoflagellates known generally as the genus *Symbodinium* spp. They reproduce through mitotic cell division (Kinzie 1999) and are phototrophic. Water chemistry, temperature, pressure, and light availability affect the different groups of algae, including zooxanthellae, to varying degrees. Marine algae can tolerate the slightly alkaline pH of seawater and, to some extent, seasonal temperature variances. Thirty to thirty-five degrees Celsius is the upper temperature limit for most algae, however (Prescott 1968). Algae are also affected by the amount of light in an environment. Water clarity and depth limit the photosynthetic zone and therefore limit the ecological ranges of various strains of algae in the ocean.

7   Zooxanthellae are often found as symbionts in the endodermal tissue of scleractinian corals and are best known for this association. There are also free-swimming forms of zooxanthellae that can live independently of coral tissue, and when cultured, zooxanthellae have been documented to alternate between the motile and non-motile life forms (Domotor and D'Elia 1986; Muller-Parker and D'Elia 1997). Species of zooxanthellae are hard to distinguish because of their physiological similarities. Current taxonomic analysis supports eight genera of symbiotic dinoflagellates that can be classified in four or five

main orders of the Division Dinophyta (Trench 1997). Earlier genetic studies showed that there were three main groups of zooxanthellae that associated with corals. One of these groups is closely related to the free-living zooxanthellae as well as the other two symbiotic groups (Rowan and Powers 1991).

Symbioses

8 The source of the partner, the establishment, the specificity, and the recognition of certain partners in the relationship define symbioses (Douglas 1994). Symbiotic relationships form either through vertical or horizontal transmission. Vertical transmission is direct passage of the symbiont from the parents to the offspring along with genetic material. Horizontal transmission in a species means that each offspring has to obtain the symbiont from its surrounding environment. Coral polyps usually display horizontal transmission through ingestion. One study demonstrated that coral larvae are typically without symbionts at fertilization but metamorphose and acquire the zooxanthellae, through feeding, from their environment within five days (Schwarz et al. 1999).

9 Symbioses that are mutualistic interactions are often characterized by a higher diversity of host types than symbiont types (Smith 1991). More zooxanthellae and non-specific interaction would result in the formation of a parasitic relationship, but corals and zooxanthellae do not display parasitism. Genetically different species of coral are symbiotic with very closely related strains of zooxanthellae, showing more disparity of form in hosts than in symbionts (Rowan and Powers 1991). Host corals have to adapt to greater environmental differences than their symbionts and therefore show greater diversity in morphology.

10 Mutual symbioses are beneficial for the host and the symbiont. The host animal, in this case the coral polyp, is the ecological environment for the symbiotic zooxanthellae for almost its entire life span (Read 1970). If both organisms function better in isolation than in association, the symbiosis is non-beneficial (Douglas 1994). Williams (1966) stated that symbioses would be expected if both organisms have a higher survival rate in the relationship. The aid provided has to be adapted for by both organisms and somehow add to their chance of passing on genes. In the case of coral and zooxanthellae, the host benefits from the supply of photosynthetic products, and the symbiont receives a relatively safe and ordered environment as well as a supply of nutrients. The coral-zooxanthellae relationship is biotrophic (Douglas 1994), meaning that the host derives nutrients from the living cells of the algae. The coral supplies necessary nutrients for photosynthesis to occur, and the algae utilizes those nutrients to create photosynthetic products that the host coral uses (Douglas 1994).

Coral-Zooxanthellae Interactions

11 The coral-zooxanthellae relationship has been traced, using stable isotopes of C12 and C13, to the beginning of the scleractinian coral record in the Late Triassic (Stanley and Swart 1995). It is difficult to determine an exact forma-

tion time because the zooxanthellae are soft bodied and not preservable in the fossil record. In addition, scleractinians may have originated more than once in geologic history (Romano and Palumbi 1996). Hermatypic coral species invaded an open ecological niche prior to the end-Triassic extinction, benefiting both the coral and the zooxanthellae by giving them space to diversify (Stanley and Swart 1995). Hermatypic corals were also quick to come back and diversify again after the end of the Triassic. The large Triassic radiation and the Jurassic radiation after the Triassic extinction have both been attributed to the novel approach of symbiosis utilized by hermatypic corals (Stanley and Swart 1995).

12 The coral-zooxanthellae relationship forms in most species just after fertilization. Planula larvae ingest zooxanthellae after the formation of feeding mechanisms, and the zooxanthellae appear in larval endodermal tissue within one hour of ingestion (Schwarz et al. 1999). The addition of zooxanthellae may trigger developmental changes in the larvae; symbiotic species have been observed settling earlier than aposymbiotic species (Schwarz et al. 1999). The larvae are able to acquire different strains of zooxanthellae, and it has been demonstrated that adult corals can acquire a different strain of algae than their usual symbiont (Kinzie and Chee 1979). Adult coral can also contain more than one species of zooxanthellae, although certain types reproduce more readily than others do within the coral polyps (Rowan and Knowlton 1995, and Kinzie and Chee 1979).

13 Zooxanthellae produce photosynthate that the host coral can use for nutrition and skeletal framework development. The algae get materials in return from the host such as amino acids and inorganic nitrogen, carbon, and phosphorus (Muller-Parker and D'Elia 1997). It is currently thought that the release of the photosynthate is evoked by a host factor of free amino acids located in the coral polyp (Gates et al. 1995). These amino acids have been documented in controlled experiments to cause the release of the photosynthate from the zooxanthellae and also enhance carbon (Gates et al. 1995). The translocation of reduced organic carbon from the zooxanthellae to the coral increases coral calcification rates and supplies a continual source of carbon for metabolic functions (Muscatine and Porter 1977). The coral-zooxanthellae symbiosis evolved as a response to low nutrient supply in the water (Muller-Parker and D'Elia 1997). The transport of inorganic material to the algae is an exchange for carbon, which increases the rate of production of calcium carbonate in the host coral polyps and gives them nutrients that cannot be gathered from the water.

Evolutionary Implications

14 The symbiosis between corals and zooxanthellae is a mutualistic interaction. The corals receive organic carbon, nitrogen, and phosphorus as products of photosynthesis, and the algae receive a safe, balanced place to live as well as inorganic materials to fuel their metabolism. Calcification of coral using carbon from the algae produces carbonate ions that cause a re-equilibration of the marine bicarbonate-dominated system. This produces carbon dioxide that can be utilized by the photosynthetic algae (Buddemeier 1997). Because both host

and symbiont benefit from the interaction, it has persisted, and the genes controlling zooxanthellae intake and distribution in corals have been selected for. Genes controlling the symbiotic association in zooxanthellae have also been selected. Each organism seeks out the association and its resulting benefits, making it an adaptation that contributes to fitness (Williams 1966).

15   The organismal requirements for both the coral and the zooxanthellae restrict the association to specific depths, salinities, temperatures, and photic zones. Selection of certain combinations of coral and algae is not due to random recombination because the modern groupings of algae and coral have recognizable patterns across species. Community gradients of zooxanthellae have been documented in Caribbean corals and are explainable by differences in irradiance (Rowan et al. 1997). Three distinct groups of zooxanthellae were found at three different depths on the same coral species with little algal community overlap. They were exposed to decreasing amounts of light at depth and differences in temperature, both of which greatly affected the algae population composition (Rowan et al. 1997). Photoadaptation in zooxanthellae also accounts for the dominance of certain types of coral at different depths (Iglesias-Prieto and Trench 1997). The host will live in the most productive region for its symbiont and will become specialized for certain depth, light, and temperature conditions through stabilizing selection (Buddemeier and Fautin 1993).

Bleaching: Global Problem or Adaptive Mechanism

16   The symbiotic relationship is important because of its effect on reef development and health (Prothero 1998). Coral reefs are a major ecological environment present in the modern world, and many different species of fish, invertebrates, and plants rely on the reefs for food and shelter. If the reefs are degraded, those dependent species will not be able to survive unless they can adapt to the new conditions. Today many kinds of diseases also affect the reefs but none of them to the extent of coral bleaching. Bleaching is the termination of the symbiotic relationship through the expulsion of zooxanthellae from the coral polyps as a result of temperature stress (Gates et al. 1992). This weakens the corals, slows their growth, and leaves them more susceptible to bacterial diseases.

17   Bleaching is occurring on a global scale and could drastically change the composition of modern reefs or cause their extinction (Buddemeier and Smith 1999). Corals are a geologically rare phenomenon, but they have appeared over and over again within the past 200 million years. This recurrence shows that, while reefs are delicately balanced and susceptible to thermal perturbations, they are resilient enough to remain viable during large-scale global change (Buddemeier and Smith 1999). Zooxanthellae are also resilient and diverse but are more sensitive to changes in their surrounding environment than their host corals. Thermal stress due to increased water temperatures disrupts photosystem II in zooxanthellae by degrading the D1 protein (Warner et al. 1999), causing photosynthesis to stop. The damaged zooxanthellae are expelled from the coral polyps in endodermal cells, causing a bleaching event (Gates et al. 1992). However, if environmental conditions stabilize, the zooxanthellae re-

cover, and the algae count in the polyps returns to normal (Warner et al. 1999).

18   Coral bleaching can also be examined as an adaptive mechanism if environmental conditions do not stabilize quickly. A long-term study on zooxanthellae showed that population density within coral colonies varied throughout the year and suggested that bleaching events could be part of a longer cycle (Fagoonee et al. 1999). Bleaching affects different areas of some corals because of the variety of symbionts housed in the polyps. The zooxanthellae strain with the most specific light and temperature requirements will bleach first under stress (Rowan et al. 1997). This leaves open space on the coral polyps for a more tolerant symbiont to invade, creating a coral-zooxanthellae interaction stronger and more resistant to stress than the original. Stable zooxanthellae-coral relationships would be selected for, so the bleaching provides a mechanism for recombination if one symbiosis is not effective (Buddemeier and Fautin 1993). Zooxanthellae have one or two specific coral species that they typically join with, but during times of environmental change, that specificity changes as well to increase survival potential (Buddemeier and Fautin 1993).

Conclusions

19   The coral-zooxanthellae symbiosis evolved during the Late Triassic to fill an open ecological niche in the environment: clear, shallow, and nutrient-poor water. Specific corals have evolved to live with one or a few species of zooxanthellae (Rowan et al. 1997) that maximize their metabolic efficiency through a mutualistic exchange. The coral larvae do not acquire zooxanthellae until they develop feeding mechanisms and can ingest the algae from their surrounding environment (Schwarz et al. 1999). This allows for greater flexibility of symbiosis because zooxanthellae suited for the specific environment in which the coral larvae end up settling are ingested.

20   Habitat restriction for hermatypic coral is controlled by the requirements of their symbionts. The algae need varying amounts of light, warmth, and nutrients, making them sensitive to environmental change. Thermal stress causes the expulsion of zooxanthellae, which results in bleaching and weakened corals, but the stress reaction can be seen as an adaptive process because it allows new, possibly more stress resistant combinations of coral and algae to form (Buddemeier and Fautin 1993). Excessive or prolonged temperature increases will cause serious damage to the reef ecosystem, however, because the zooxanthellae will be unable to recover their D1 proteins and become symbionts. This could lead to reef degradation because the hermatypic corals require the zooxanthellae to produce limestone framework structures.

References

Baker AC, Rowan R, Knowlton N. 1997. Symbiosis ecology of two Caribbean Acroporid corals. *Proc 8th Int Coral Reef Symp* 2: 1295–1300.

Buddemeier RW. 1997. Making light work of adaptation. *Nature* 388: 229–30.

Buddemeier RW, Fautin DG, 1993. Coral bleaching as an adaptive mechanism. *Bioscience* 43, 5: 320–326.

Buddemeier RW, Smith S. 1999. Coral adaptation and acclimatization: a most ingenious paradox. *Am Zoologist* 39: 1–9.

Darley WM. 1982. *Algal biology: a physiological approach*. Oxford: Blackwell Scientific. p 111–119.

Domotor SL, D'Elia CF. 1986. Cell-size distributions of zooxanthellae in culture and symbiosis. *Biological Bull* 170: 519–525.

Douglas AE. 1994. *Symbiotic interactions*. Oxford: Oxford Univ Pr. p 56–99.

Fagoonee I, Wilson HB, Hassell MP, Turner JR. 1999. The dynamics of zooxanthellae populations: a long-term study in the field. *Science* 283: 843–845.

Gates RD, Baghdasarian G, Muscatine L. 1992. Temperature stress causes host cell detachment in symbiotic cnidarians: implications for coral bleaching. *Biological Bull* 182: 324–332.

Gates RD, Hoegh-Guldberg O, McFall-Ngai MJ, Bil KY, Muscatine L. 1995. Free amino acids exhibit anthozoan "host factor" activity: they induce the release of photosynthate from symbiotic dinoflagellates in vitro. *Proc Nat Acad Sci* 92: 7430–7434.

Iglesias-Prieto R, Trench RK. 1997. Photoadaptation, photoacclimation, and niche diversification in invertebrate-dinoflagellate symbioses. *Proc 8th Int Coral Reef Symp* 2: 1319–1324.

Kinzie R III. 1999. Sex, symbiosis and coral reef communities. *Am Zoologist* 39: 80–91.

Kinzie RA III, Chee GS. 1979. The effect of different zooxanthellae on the growth of experimentally reinfected hosts. *Biological Bull* 156: 315–327.

Muller-Parker G, D'Elia CF. 1997. Interactions between corals and their symbiotic algae. In: *Life and death of coral reefs*. Ed. Birkeland C. New York: Chapman and Hall. p 96–113.

Muscatine L, Porter JW. 1977. Reef corals: Mutualistic symbioses adapted to nutrient-poor environments. *Bioscience* 27: 454–460.

Prescott GW. 1968. *The algae: a review*. Boston: Houghton Mifflin. p 189–196, and 307–312.

Prothero D. 1998. *Bringing fossils to life*. Boston: WCB/McGraw-Hill. p 223–225.

Read CP. 1970. *Parasitism and symbiology*. New York: Ronald. p 3–18.

Romano SL, Palumbi SR. 1996. Evolution of scleractinian corals inferred from molecular systematics. *Science* 271: 640–642.

Rowan R, Knowlton N. 1995. Intraspecific diversity and ecological zonation in coral-algal symbiosis. *Proc Nat Acad Sci* 92: 2850–2853.

Rowan R, Knowlton N, Baker A, Jara J. 1997. Landscape ecology of algal symbionts creates variation in episodes of coral bleaching. *Nature* 388: 265–269.

Rowan R, Powers D. 1991. A molecular genetic classification of zooxanthellae and the evolution of animal-algal symbioses. *Science* 251: 1348–1351.

Schwarz JA, Krupp DA, Weis VM. 1999. Late larval development and onset of symbiosis in the scleractinian coral *Fungia scutaria*. *Biological Bull* 196: 70–79.

Smith JM. 1991. A Darwinian view of symbiosis. In: *Symbiosis as a source of evolutionary innovation*. Eds. Margulis L, Fester R. Cambridge: MIT Pr. p 26–39.

Sorokin YI. 1993. *Coral reef ecology*. New York: Springer-Verlag. p 296–325.

Stanley GD, Swart, PK. 1995. Evolution of the coral-zooxanthellae symbiosis during the Triassic: a geochemical approach. *Paleobiology* 21(2): 179–199.

Trench RK. 1997. Diversity of symbiotic dinoflagellates and the evolution of micro-algal-invertebrate symbioses. *Proc 8th Int Coral Reef Symp* 2: 1275–1286.

Warner MF, William K, Schmidt GW. 1999. Damage to photosystem II in symbiotic dinoflagellates: A determinant of coral bleaching. *Proc Nat Acad Sci* 96: 8007–8012.

Williams GC. 1966. *Adaptation and natural selection*. Princeton: Princeton Univ Pr. p 246–7.

Reading Responses

1. What is Valerie's main point? Why is research about coral bleaching important?

2. What is the purpose of Valerie's abstract?

3. How does Valerie organize her paper? How does she help readers follow her organization?

Writing Activities

1. Prepare an analytical outline of Valerie's paper, summing up each section in a sentence or two. After you finish your outline, write a paragraph explaining how she organized her paper.
2. Briefly summarize the problem that Valerie explores in her paper: the possible implications of coral bleaching. Write your summary in your own words, and direct it to readers with minimal scientific background.
3. Visit your campus library, and find a well-regarded academic journal in a field that interests you. Examine several recent articles in terms of writing style and clarity, structure and organization, and documentation of sources. Based on these articles, write a brief description of the journal's expectations.

Community Links

Examine another research report from the academic community such as "The Cell Cycle and Cancer" (pp. 105–108) or "Money Management Practices of College Students" (pp. 165–170). Then, examine a report from the work community such as "Young Adults: New Customers/New Foods" (pp. 325–331) or a report from the public community such as "Sex Without Strings, Relationships without Rings" (pp. 518–529). Based on the similarities and differences in these reports, which characteristics seem to be shared by research reports and which seem to be flexible, varying with the community, the aims of the writer, the expectations of specific readers, or the potential applications of the report?

Review of a Book

REVIEW OF *STICKS AND STONES: THE TROUBLESOME SUCCESS OF CHILDREN'S LITERATURE FROM SLOVENLY PETER TO HARRY POTTER* BY JACK ZIPES

◆

This book review was originally published in Adolescence, *a journal for psychologists, sociologists, educators, and others interested in the age group identified in its title. This publication, like many scholarly journals, regularly includes a section ti-*

tled "Book Reviews." *Here, books of professional interest are reviewed to assist readers in keeping up with current research, theory, or other literature pertinent to the profession. In this issue of* Adolescence, *for example, eleven books are reviewed, each in a paragraph. Besides* Sticks and Stones, *these books cover a wide range of topics, as a few of their titles illustrate:* Down to Earth Sociology: Introductory Readings; A Guide to Treatments That Work; Totally Private and Personal: Journaling Ideas for Girls and Young Women; *and* Teen Pregnancy and Parenting: Social and Ethical Issues. *The names of the reviewers are not identified with the reviews.*

ZIPES, Jack. *Sticks and Stones: The Troublesome Success of Children's Literature from Slovenly Peter to Harry Potter.* New York: Routledge, 2001, 213 pp. $24.95 (h).

1   Zipes explores the world of children's literature, and its connection to the socialization of children. He questions whether children have ever really had a literature of their own. He contends that books written for children are, in many ways, "the grown-ups' version"—a story about childhood that adults tell to children, and this can be a problem: even experts do not know what children make of what adults give them. Zipes discusses tales ranging from the grisly nineteenth-century moral lesson of Slovenly Peter (whose fingers get cut off) to the male-dominated Harry Potter series, and argues that books written for children have systematically reflected the values and norms of society, which instead of empowering children conversely curtails their freedom. The indoctrinating of children acts to homogenize them and, in effect, rob childhood of its essence. Zipes also discusses several key issues, including why children are best served neither by the current polemics of the religious right or the radical left and the death of honest criticism and expertise regarding children's literature. Further, he gives clear voice to the forces behind the huge boom in children's book publishing since the 1980s, which has served to form a safe veil of promoting literacy that disguises its own truth, namely that children are seen as commodities and used as pawns to increase parental consumerism.

 Reading Responses

1. What does the reviewer emphasize in this review of *Sticks and Stones*?
2. How objective (unbiased) or subjective (influenced by personal views or judgments) does the reviewer seem to be? What criteria does the reviewer use to evaluate the book?
3. In what ways does this review address likely interests of the readers of *Adolescence*?

Writing Activities

1. This review covers an entire book in one paragraph. Write a brief analysis of the strategies the reviewer uses to keep that paragraph focused and unified so that it is easy for a reader to follow.
2. Imagine that you are the editor of a new publication for college students. You want to include short, helpful reviews of nonfiction books that students might want to read. Using the review of *Sticks and Stones* as an example, write a brief guide for your reviewers explaining how to write a short review.
3. Select an article or essay that you have recently read. Identify a group of people who might also be interested in reading it—your fellow students in a specific class, students majoring in a certain field, the readers of a magazine that you enjoy, people who live in a certain region, or some other group. Write a paragraph-length review directed to the interests of that group of people.

REVIEW OF *WHY WE WATCH: THE ATTRACTIONS OF VIOLENT ENTERTAINMENT*, EDITED BY JEFFREY H. GOLDSTEIN

Gordon W. Russell

◆

This book review appeared in Aggressive Behavior, *a journal "devoted to the experimental and observational analysis of conflict in humans and animals." Instead of supplying short reviews of many publications, this journal carries essay-length reviews, but only one in this issue. In addition, the reviewer is identified.*

Why We Watch: The Attractions of Violent Entertainment, edited by Jeffrey H. Goldstein. New York: Oxford University Press, 1998, 270 pp.

1   When a group conversation turns to questions of media violence, homespun explanations quickly surface. A few are on target; most are not. The social scientist who is present volunteers to enlighten everyone. He or she takes pains to summarize a wealth of research on the consequences of peoples' exposure to violent portrayals whether on television, in video arcades, or at sports venues. Most seem satisfied, but one or two individuals press on. "But why do people watch this stuff?" "Why are we so fascinated with blood and gore?" At this point, cracks begin to appear in the scientist's authoritative demeanor. Of course, the reason is that evidence on this most basic of questions is sketchy, and such theory as exists is largely speculative and untested.

2   Jeffrey Goldstein has made a heroic attempt to draw together what is known about the attraction to violence. To this end, he has assembled a diverse set of eminent scholars, with each expert addressing the question from the perspective of his or her respective discipline. That diversity is reflected throughout the 10 chapters of *Why We Watch*. The fundamental question of why we are drawn to violence is explored in a variety of settings that range from children's toys and literature to religion, media, and sports.

3   The chapters are uniformly well written, informative, and thought provoking. A few examples will convey the tenor of the book. Sports historian Allen Guttmann (chapter 1) traces the appeal for spectators of violence in classical Greece and Rome through the Middle Ages to the present day. The public's seeming appetite for blood sports, e.g., gladiatorial combat, knightly tournaments, and modern-day boxing, emerges as a dominant theme in his historical review. Guttmann offers some tentative explanations, one of which draws attention to the sadomasochistic elements in gladiatorial combat and contemporary bullfighting. He concludes by pointing researchers in the direction of a largely neglected topic in observing that "the triadic association of sports, eros, and violent death has seldom been investigated by serious scholars" (p 26).

4   Goldstein (chapter 3) initially draws an important distinction between aggression and play fighting. In the case of play fighting, there is an absence of any intent to injure. In contrast to the vigorous activity of mock fighting on playgrounds by boys, girls are often seen to stand around chatting. However, if their conversations turn to gossip and attempts to ostracize other girls, then their actions can be equated with aggression. Goldstein observes, "What at first sight appears to be aggressive boys and nonaggressive girls may, in deed and in consequence, be the other way round" (p 54). The differing perceptions of aggressive play by men and women is also examined, as is the historical prevalence of play fighting during wartime. The balance of this chapter considers the merits of the biological/physiological, psychological, and social/cultural reasons advanced to account for youngsters' interest in war toys.

5   Joanne Cantor makes a solid contribution to this volume (chapter 5) in investigating the attraction of children to violent television programming. She draws on the results of two large-scale surveys conducted in Wisconsin involving parents as subjects in one and children in the other. Cantor skillfully integrates the findings with the media literature to answer questions such as the popularity of violent vs. nonviolent programming. Overall, youngsters show a clear preference for family-centered situation comedies. In concluding, Cantor emphasizes the need for researchers to direct their efforts at understanding the attractiveness of nonviolent genres. She notes that even extremely violent programming often portrays affiliative relations among its principals, an element that may also contribute to its popularity.

6   Clark McCauley (chapter 7) examines the reactions of people exposed to media presentations that ostensibly exceed the bounds of what generally might be regarded as entertaining. Bloody footage leaves viewers disgusted, disturbed, and distressed but nonetheless entertained! It is this paradox that McCauley endeavors to resolve in offering a "tentative" resolution.

7   In possibly the strongest chapter in the book (chapter 9), Dolf Zillmann provides an in-depth review and systematic evaluation of the merits of a wide

range of speculative views of the reasons why violence proves to be so attractive to so many. Some of the explanations have merit; others, while intuitively plausible, miss the mark on closer inspection. Yet another set of explanations is untestable and/or simply far-fetched. A sampling of explanations includes a number of catharsis hypotheses, Jungian and Freudian doctrines, evolutionary notions, protective vigilance and fear mastery, among others. The contributors to this volume would in all likelihood find themselves in agreement with Zillmann's concluding remarks regarding violent portrayals: "There is no single quality of violence, nor a single circumstance in the exposure to its depiction, that could adequately explain the apparent attraction of the portrayals in question." In conceding our rudimentary understanding of people's attraction to violence he further notes "there seem to exist a multitude of conditions that are poorly interrelated and, hence, difficult to integrate into a universal theory" (p 209).

8   In a concluding chapter, Goldstein presents a summary of the contributors' explanations for the drawing power of violent fare. He also provides a summary table (p 223) listing the characteristics of individuals most attracted to violent imagery, along with characteristics of violent imagery that increase its appeal to viewers.

9   In the writer's view, *Why We Watch* is a pivotal work that charts a new course for future investigations of violence in the media. Goldstein has addressed head-on a question that previously has been sidestepped or largely ignored. As a result, this work represents a sharp departure from all other books on the subject of media violence. It is the starting point for those who ask why and researchers who would seek to answer the question. This volume has earned a place front and center on the bookshelves of the layperson and social scientist alike.

Reading Responses

1. What does the reviewer emphasize in this review of *Why We Watch*?
2. How objective (unbiased) or subjective (influenced by personal views or judgments) does the reviewer seem to be? What criteria does the reviewer use to evaluate the book?
3. In what ways does this review address the likely interests of the readers of *Aggressive Behavior*?

Writing Activities

1. Summarize Russell's evaluation of the book. State his opinion or judgment in one sentence. Then, briefly explain the main reasons for his opinion.
2. In an essay-length review, a reviewer needs to balance overall description or evaluation with more detailed examples and specifics. Write a brief analysis of the strategies this reviewer uses to accomplish both objectives and to help the reader move between the two levels.

3. Write an essay reviewing a book like *Why We Watch*—a collection of chapters or readings by different authors, all related to a particular topic. You might use a book assigned in another course, a book you've used for a research project, or even this book. (If you have not yet finished reading the whole book, you will need to have read several selections so that you can discuss them in your review.) Write a review like Russell's; explain the overall collection, evaluate it, and discuss several selections that support your point and illustrate notable aspects of the book.

Community Links

Find the area in the library that displays current issues of periodicals. Skim through a few scholarly journals and magazines, looking for book reviews. Compare one or two reviews to each other or to the reviews included here. Consider the approach of each review and the way it addresses its scholarly, general, or special-interest readers.

Abstract

TEMPORAL VARIATION IN BIRD COUNTS WITHIN A HAWAIIAN RAINFOREST*

John C. Simon, Thane K. Pratt, Kim E. Berlin, James R. Kowalsky, Steven G. Fancy, and Jeff S. Hatfield

◆

Many scholarly journals include an abstract before each article. This abstract preceded an article in The Condor: An International Journal of Avian Biology, *published by the Cooper Ornithological Society and distributed to its members. As the journal's title suggests, the* Condor's *readers are international. For each article, the journal includes an abstract in both English and Spanish, under 250 words for a featured article or 150 words for shorter articles. The abstract is supplied by the article's authors who are also asked to supply the Spanish translation if possible. The key words following the abstract are used to index the article under appropriate topics.*

1 We studied monthly and annual variation in density estimates of nine forest bird species along an elevational gradient in an east Maui rainforest. We conducted monthly variable circular-plot counts for 36 consecutive months along transects running downhill from timberline. Density estimates were compared by month, year, and station for all resident bird species with sizeable popula-

---

*Manuscript received 2 July 2001; accepted 18 April 2002.

tions, including four native nectarivores, two native insectivores, a non-native insectivore, and two non-native generalists. We compared densities among three elevational strata and between breeding and nonbreeding seasons. All species showed significant differences in density estimates among months and years. Three native nectarivores had higher density estimates within their breeding season (December–May) and showed decreases during periods of low nectar production following the breeding season. All insectivore and generalist species except one had higher density estimates within their March–August breeding season. Density estimates also varied with elevation for all species and for four species a seasonal shift in population was indicated. Our data show that the best time to conduct counts for native forest birds on Maui is January–February, when birds are breeding or preparing to breed, counts are typically high, variability in density estimates is low, and the likelihood for fair weather is best. Temporal variations in density estimates documented in our study site emphasize the need for consistent, well-researched survey regimens and for caution when drawing conclusions from, or basing management decisions on, survey data.

Key words: bird counts, density estimation, Hawaiian honeycreepers, phenology, rainforest, variable circular-plot.

Variación Temporal en Conteos de Aves en una Selva Lluviosa de Hawai

Estudiamos la variación mensual y anual en estimaciones de la densidad de nueve especies de aves a lo largo de un gradiente altitudinal en una selva lluviosa del este de Maui. Realizamos conteos mensuales en parcelas circulares por un período de 36 meses consecutivos a lo largo de transectas ubicadas desde la línea del bosque hacia abajo. Las estimaciones de densidad fueron comparadas entre meses, años y estaciones considerando todas las especies de aves residentes con poblaciones considerables, incluyendo cuatro nectarívoros nativos, dos insectívoros nativos, un insectívoro no nativo y dos generalistas no nativos. Comparamos densidades entre tres estratos altitudinales y entre las estaciones reproductivas y no reproductivas. Todas las especies mostraron diferencias significativas en las estimaciones de densidad entre meses y años. Tres nectarívoros nativos presentaron estimaciones de densidad mayores durante sus épocas reproductivas (diciembre–mayo) y mostraron disminuciones durante períodos de baja producción de néctar luego de la estación de cría. Excepto una, todas las especies insectívoras y generalistas presentaron mayores estimaciones de densidad durante sus épocas reproductivas (marzo–agosto). Las estimaciones de densidad de todas las especies también variaron con la altitud, y se encontraron cambios estacionales en las poblaciones de cuatro especies. Nuestros datos muestran que el mejor momento para realizar conteos de aves nativas de selva en Maui es enero–febrero, cuando las aves están criando o preparándose para criar, los conteos son típicamente altos, la variabilidad en las estimaciones de densidad es baja y la probabilidad de buen tiempo es más alta. La variación temporal en las estimaciones de densidad documentadas en nuestro sitio de estudio enfatizan la necesidad de regímenes de muestreo consistentes y bien establecidos, y sugiere cautela a la hora de sacar conclusiones para conservación o tomar decisiones de manejo a partir de datos de muestreos.

Reading Responses

1. According to the abstract, what did the authors study? How did they conduct the study? What did they discover?
2. What does the abstract identify as the significance of the authors' study?
3. Based on the abstract and the key words, what do the authors seem to assume about the interests and concerns of the *Condor*'s readers? What strategies do the authors use to address readers and to emphasize issues likely to concern them?

Writing Activities

1. Rewrite a sentence or two of the abstract, including all the information in the original but stating it in your own words. Count the words in your version and in the original. Which is longer? Why? Write a brief report, explaining your sentence experiment and your findings.
2. Select one of the readings in this book that you understand well. Write an abstract for that reading. Keep your abstract brief, but cover all the main points in the reading. Direct your abstract to other students, and make it clear enough that they could understand it without reading the selection it summarizes.
3. Based on your experience with the previous two activities, write out guidelines for writing an effective abstract. Direct your advice to other students.

Community Links

Compare one or two of the abstracts preceding sample articles and reports with one or two of the executive summaries (pp. 156–159 and 297–300). (For lists of alternatives, refer to the Guide to Themes, Topics, and Rhetorical Strategies at the end of the book.) In what ways are these similar or different? How do you account for the similarities or differences?

Executive Summary

In Memoriam: Understanding Teaching as Public Service

David Blacker

◆

TCRecord, *sponsored by Teachers College, Columbia University, publishes scholarly articles about education in online and print versions. Major articles may be thirty pages or even longer, published in a single unit or in a series of sections. They are preceded by abstracts of less than two hundred words. The online version of "In Memoriam: Understanding Teaching as Public Service" began with the abstract. Next came the Executive Summary, summarizing the paper in five paragraphs. Then the article itself followed, about eight pages long in single-spaced, printed text, including twenty notes with source citations.*

1. Like the nig.httime lightning flash that briefly but dazzlingly illuminates the landscape, the deeds of September 11th's public servants clearly reveal something about the nature of public service, something of which we are all too rarely aware. Beneath the mountains of rules and regulations, the paperwork, the bureaucracy, the incessant managerial "reform" schemes, the budgetary wrangling, even the political controversies, there persists a *moral nobility* inherent in public service—in those "job descriptions" and, even more, in the spirit and traditions behind those jobs themselves—that is too easily forgotten. It is easy to forget even for the public servants themselves. Furthermore, that moral lightning flash illuminates very generally how deeply precious and worthwhile—how transcendently beautiful—a life dedicated to public service can be. Such examples can in this regard help provide a moral beacon for public servants such as teachers. The heroism and self-sacrifice of September 11 can, I believe, help call teachers back toward their true moral homes, and away, for example, from the mirage of "professionalism," with all its managerial and technical emphases, all its implied distance from other, supposedly less-credentialed, recipients of public funds such as, indeed, New York City police officers and firefighters. One indirect effect of the tragedy may be to help teachers situate themselves back into a more satisfying and meaningful occupational identity of "public servant." I believe this could be a salutary development for teaching, an indirect and longer-term saving power, if you will. Seeing teaching as more clearly situated alongside other public service occupations may help us take clearer stock of why, in the end, we value teaching itself and how, beneath the distractions of the daily news and the latest experts' "reports," it remains structurally as integral as ever to our cherished democracy. We have had the luxury of our vision being too often obscured in this regard.

2. One of democracy's challenges is to acknowledge its dependency upon certain occupational groups while also regulating and holding them accountable to itself. How can democracy make the institutions in which it has a compelling state interest serve its political needs while allowing those same institutions to pursue their unique extra-political—and in many cases life or death—missions? The stakes are all the higher when one considers how certain occupations function as "keystone species" within what might call the cultural and institutional "ecology" of the democratic state. K–12 public school teaching is one of these democratic "keystone" occupations, though one currently confronting serious questions basic to its moral and occupational identity. Viewing teaching as a central part of a larger democratic ecosystem helps highlight one of the most debilitating features of contemporary teaching at both the level of the classroom and that of educational institutions generally: the degree of the enterprise's artificial isolation

from other relevant interests. Working toward correcting this isolation is a needed and appropriate goal for educational theory. Accordingly, I aim to show here how it is somehow at once daunting yet surprisingly hopeful to perceive, finally, that the teachers are not at all alone in the swirling crosswinds of democratic governance.

3   Though widely used and overused, "public servant" is an identity now somberly ripe for the taking, as it were, for teachers and those engaged in what I'll contend are allied "public service" occupations, namely, police, firefighters, public librarians, nurses, social workers, and EMT/paramedics. These seven occupations (below I'll make the case for why these seven and not others) form an interlocking ring of occupational involvement that lies at the center of our far-flung and ungraspably complicated democracy. Along with the direct exercise of political rights themselves, these occupations and their discretionary ambit constitute the *sine qua non* of any contemporary liberal democratic society able to yield the quality of life necessary to sustain domestic tranquility and citizens' pursuit of happiness. More than sentimentalized "unsung heroes," these public servants are structurally indispensable guarantors of access to the social spheres widely regarded as most basic and, in a general sense, uncompromisingly open to all citizens: security in one's person and property, basic health care and rescue services, K–12 education (if not higher education as well), at least a transitional threshold level of basic life needs like food and shelter, and, perhaps most recently emergent as a basic democratic need in these cyber-times, access to information.

4   It is alongside these gatekeepers of democracy that teaching belongs. Recognizing as much will provide a much solider normative basis—and one simply more rhetorically compelling—than anything professionalization has to offer. One may wish still to employ the term as shorthand to denote behavior proper within the public service occupation in question (as in the admonition, "that is unprofessional!"). But let us not allow a handy colloquialism to obscure that which is truly fundamental and upon which we all depend. To most of us as individuals, throughout most of our lives and in our everyday affairs, the public servants we encounter *are* the democratic state; they are its face and voice, its triumphs and failures, its heroes and villains. The brutal or racist cop, the indifferent nurse, the jaded teacher, and the icy caseworker are in the ensemble graver threats to our democracy than a hundred bin Ladens or a stock market crash. Not only they as individuals but we collectively are responsible for their failures, even as we all rightly share in their successes. More palpably than is the case with either GM or Microsoft, as our public servants go, so goes the nation.

5   By detailing the case for the accuracy of the label "public servant" as applied to teachers and the relevant other groups, this study helps clear the way for further exploration of the moral contours of what I argue are the seven key public service occupations, how they differ from one another and more importantly, along lines indicated by my working hypothesis, what precisely they share. Understanding better how teachers "fit" into the complex institutional

ecology of democracy is bound to be salutary, both for teachers and for our self-understanding as democratic citizens.

Reading Responses

1. According to the Executive Summary, what is Blacker's main point?
2. How does Blacker define the role of the public servant? Why does he see public servants as essential to democracy?
3. What might be the reasoning, especially for online publication, for including an abstract and an executive summary with an article? What might this format suggest about the needs of readers?

Writing Activities

1. How would you summarize the Executive Summary? Write a paragraph-length abstract, using your own words and including Blacker's major points. (Aim for less than two hundred words, the maximum length for other *TCRecord* abstracts of articles.)
2. Based on your experience writing an abstract in activity 1 above, explain how you went about the process of cutting five long paragraphs to one short paragraph.
3. Write an essay responding to Blacker. You may agree, disagree, extend, supplement, illustrate, or otherwise react to his views about teaching.

Community Links

Compare this executive summary with those from the work community (pp. 297–300). What similarities or differences do you see? How do you account for these?

Literature Review

ERIC REVIEW: COMMUNITY COLLEGE STUDENTS: RECENT FINDINGS AND TRENDS

Alyssa N. Bryant

◆

Bryant's article appeared in the quarterly journal Community College Review. *In her literature review, she covers the topics included here as well other topics about community college students: their objectives, characteristics, assessment and placement, success and retention, transfer rates, and postcollege earnings. For each topic, she summarizes current issues and research findings, noting the pertinent "literature"—the articles, books, papers, or other sources that substantiate her points. She then provides an extensive list of references. Her title refers to Educational Resources Information Center* (ERIC), *an extensive database and resource for information about education.*

1 To serve the diverse community college student population, institutions must remain cognizant of student needs when developing policies, programs, and services. Demographic shifts, such as Tidal Wave II, will affect future student populations. Although women, minorities, nontraditional age, and part-time students have swelled enrollments on community college campuses in the past decades, projections indicate that community colleges will witness an influx of traditional-age students into the system.

2 A review of the current state of the community college in relation to students will enable adequate planning for student services and curriculum. In particular, this review presents a discussion of the impact of recent trends on admissions criteria and open access and updates findings on student objectives and characteristics. It also analyzes institutional responses such as assessment, tracking, and retention efforts, and it reports on outcomes such as the transfer function and post-college earnings.

Admissions Standards and the Community College Mission

3 The development of community colleges offered access to higher education that could not be realized in the selective four-year colleges and universities. The two-year college, with its flexibility and open admissions, has provided opportunities for disadvantaged individuals who might otherwise not attend college (Fusch, 1996).

4 Table 1 presents admission criteria used for the selection of students in public two-year institutions.

5 Of all the factors, the high school diploma is the criterion most often considered by institutions for admission, while class standing is the least often considered. Age and test scores are selection factors in nearly 40% of the two-year schools, while more than 60% use "ability to benefit" as admission criteria. Clearly, the table indicates that open admissions continues to be a central function of the community college.

6 However, Phelan (2000) believes that the open door policy of community colleges is "threatening to close" (p. 1) as a result of rising enrollments and declining public interest and investment in higher education. He suggests that the available policy options such as capping enrollments, instituting performance-based funding, and restricting the enrollment of students already hold-

Table 1 Admission Criteria for Selection in Public Two-Year Colleges, 1999–2000

Criteria	Percentage of Institutions Using Criterion for Selection Purposes
High School Diploma	83.7
High School Class Standing	6.4
Admissions Test Scores	39.8
Ability to Benefit	62.3
Age	39.4
Open Admission	62.4

Source: National Center for Education Statistics, 2000, Table 309.

ing degrees have been positive and negative implications for community college access.

Rendón (2000) maintains that community colleges ought to view themselves as unique institutions functioning for the purpose of providing access to a wide range of students. She suggests that the focus of the community college be on educating students and encouraging students to become active and responsible citizens. In a similar vein, Nora (1999) recommends that community colleges advance into the twenty-first century prepared for a diverse student body. She advocates motivating students to pursue higher levels of education, providing opportunities for students to integrate themselves into the college experience, and involving faculty more fully in the preparation and validation of students.

Community colleges are faced with widely varying needs related to their diverse student population. Pulled in many directions, these institutions must find ways to accommodate a broad range of students simultaneously lest the fundamental values of democracy and universal access on begin to fade. [. . .]

Student Success and Retention

Student success is difficult to define in a community college context because students' reasons for enrolling vary widely. Harris (1998) identifies student goal attainment, course retention, success in coursework, fall-to-fall persistence, degree or certificate completion, and placement rate in the workforce as indicators of success. Certainly this broad range of indicators is inclusive of the similarly broad purposes of community college enrollees. Palmer (1998) warns, however, that indicators of student progress (i.e., persistence and retention) are not necessarily indicative of institutional quality. He suggests that the context of the community college be considered when interpreting institutional transfer, persistence, or degree completion rates as, for example, a college serving a poor community faces different challenges than a college in a wealthy suburban area.

10   Napoli and Wortman (1998) indicate that academic and social integration have both direct and indirect effects on persistence in college overall. Students who are integrated have stronger goal and institutional commitments, and these in turn influence persistence. The findings from studies of social integration are fairly consistent. Overall, community college students are less involved on their campus compared to students at four-year institutions, participating less frequently in campus organizations and rarely attending campus-sponsored events (Maxwell, 2000). However, Hagedorn, Maxwell, Rodriguez, Hocevar, and Fillpot (2000) indicate that men participate more frequently in campus activities than do their female peers. Perhaps the lack of social integration is related to the extensiveness of many students' work schedules. Table 3 shows that the vast majority of students (both full-time and part-time enrollees) work at least part-time, with one half of all students working full-time. Even students who are full-time enrollees are heavily engaged in work activities; overall, 75% of them work.

11   Though both male and female students rarely meet with faculty outside of class, interactions with peers occur more often. Typically, peer interactions for students in community colleges revolve around study sessions or discussions about coursework (Maxwell, 2000). Hagedorn et al. (2000) reveal that women especially tend to form study groups with other students and also report having less difficulty meeting and making friends than do male students. Overall, women attain higher levels of informal social integration than men.

12   Residence halls have not usually been considered critical components in community colleges. In fact, for much of the past they have been nearly nonexistent. Currently, only 60 of the nation's 1,050 two-year institutions have on-campus housing. Still, there is a movement, however small at the present, to incorporate residential experiences in community colleges in order to attract and recruit students. Some predict that residence halls will become increasingly common on community college campuses because student demand for

Table 3   Employment Status of Community College Students, 1995–96

Attendance Status	Percentage
Exclusively Full-Time Enrollment	
Not Working	24.7
Working Part-Time	45.1
Working Full-Time	30.3
Exclusively Part-Time Enrollment	
Not Working	13.7
Working Part-Time	31.9
Working Full-Time	54.4
All Students	
Not Working	16.3
Working Part-Time	33.4
Working Full-Time	50.4

Source: National Profile of Community Colleges: Trends and Statistics, 1999, pp. 48.

campus housing is on the rise and because residence halls offer an enrollment incentive for international students, athletes, and individuals from distant locations (Lords, 1999).

Murrell, Denzine, and Murrell (1998), in their study of 14 community colleges with residence halls, found that students felt generally positive about their residential experience and believed that it facilitated their academic pursuits. Students reported that, by eliminating their commute, they were able to spend more time studying. Study groups were also cited as valuable resources, as was proximity to campus facilities such as the library and classrooms. Finally, students reported that fewer family distractions improved concentration on their academic endeavors. By and large, residence halls on community college campuses provide opportunities for students to integrate both academically and socially into campus life. [. . .]

Conclusion

The current literature affirms that, overall, community colleges offer opportunity and access, providing students with social mobility as well as the chance to flourish academically and personally. Community college students are increasingly diverse in both identity and intentions. The institutions that serve them face challenges related to admissions policies, legitimacy within the broader system of higher education, and ever-changing enrollment patterns. The community college engages in a perpetual balancing act between open access and admissions requirements, between traditional and nontraditional students, and between diverse programmatic goals (i.e., transfer vs. nontransfer). The shifts in student composition serve to shape the community college missions and policies, and these in turn have implications for students seeking enrollment in the two-year colleges.

References

Fusch, G.E. (1996). *The community college of the 21st century*. British Columbia: Canada. (ERIC Reproduction Service Document No. ED 417 771)

Hagedorn, L.S., Maxwell, W., Rodriguez, P., Hocevar, D., & Fillpot, J. (2000). Peer and student-faculty relations in community colleges. *Community College Journal of Research and Practice, 24* (7), 587–598.

Harris, B.W. (1998). Looking inward: Building a culture for student success. *Community College Journal of Research and Practice, 22* (4), 401–418.

Lords, E. (1999, November 12). More community colleges are building dormitories. *The Chronicle of Higher Education*.

Maxwell, W.E. (2000). Student peer relations at a community college. *Community College Journal of Research and Practice, 24* (3), 207–217.

Murrell, S.P., Denzine G., & Murrell, P.H. (1998). Community college residence halls: A hidden treasure. *Community College Journal of Research and Practice, 22* (7), 663–674.

Napoli, A.R., & Wortman, P.M. (1998). Psychosocial factors related to retention and early departure of two-year community college students. *Research in Higher Education, 39* (4), 419–455.

National Center for Education Statistics. (1999). *Digest of Education Statistics*. [On-line]. Washington, D.C.: United States Department of Education. Available on the World Wide Web: http://nces.ed.gov/pubs2000/digest99/listoftables.html.

164 The Academic Community

Nora, A. (2000). Reexamining the community college mission. *New Expeditions: Charting the Second Century of Community Colleges. Issues Paper No. 2.* American Association of Community Colleges: Washington, D.C. (ERIC Document Reproduction Service No. ED 438 871)

Palmer, J. (1998). Fostering student retention and success at the community college. [Online]. A Policy Paper. Denver, Colorado: Education Commission of the States, Center for Community College Policy. (ERIC Reproduction Service Document No. ED 439 768). Available: *http://www.communitycollegepolicy.org/html/publications.htm.*

Phelan, D.J. (2000). Enrollment policy and student access at community colleges. A Policy Paper. Denver Colorado: Education Commission of the States, Center for Community College Policy.

Phillippe, K.A., & Patton, M. (1999). *National Profile of Community Colleges: Trends and Statistics*, 3rd Edition. Washington, D.C.: Community College Press, American Association of Community Colleges. (ERIC Reproduction Service Document No. ED 440 671)

Rendón L. (2000). Fulfilling the promise of access and opportunity: Collaborative community colleges for the 21st century. *New Expeditions: Charting the Second Century of Community Colleges. Issues Paper No. 3.* American Association of Community Colleges: Washington, D.C. (ERIC Document Reproduction Service No. ED 440 670)

Reading Responses

1. Why does Bryant review current literature on community colleges? What is her purpose?
2. How does Bryant introduce and conclude her article? How does she present the sources she reviews?
3. What readers does Bryant address? How might they use the information in her literature review?

Writing Activities

1. Examine one of the tables in Bryant's article. Write a paragraph explaining the information in the table.
2. If decision makers on a typical campus acted on the information supplied in Bryant's literature review, what changes might they make? Write an essay speculating about what might happen.
3. Write your own brief review of literature about a specific topic. You may use related materials that you are reading for another class or use several selections from this book. Organize your sources by topic. Following Bryant's model, introduce the topic and then sum up and cite each source.

Community Links

Compare and contrast this literature review, which appears as a full article, with the literature reviews in some student papers or reports from the three communities. (Refer to the table of contents or to the Guide to Themes,

Topics, and Rhetorical Strategies at the back of the book for possible selections to consider.) Based on these readings, in what ways do literature reviews within articles or essays resemble or differ from a literature-review article?

Report of Field Research
MONEY MANAGEMENT PRACTICES OF COLLEGE STUDENTS
Reasie A. Henry, Janice G. Weber, and David Yarbrough

◆

Published in College Student Journal, *this article reports the findings of the authors' investigation into students' ability to manage money. This research report includes conventional sections: an introduction to the problem with a review of the related literature, a description of the research method, a summary of the results or findings, a discussion of the significance of the results, and a conclusion. It ends with several tables, displaying results in graphical form, and a list of references.*

Many college students are living on the edge of financial crisis and many of them do not possess the knowledge needed to manage their money. The purpose of the study was to determine the use of money management practices of Education college students at the University of Louisiana at Lafayette. The sample consisted of 126 Education majors in randomly selected Education courses which were being taught, at each academic level, in the Spring 2000 semester. Subjects were administered a 13-item questionnaire including items concerning demographic data, income, debt, and budgeting practices. Frequency distributions and Pearson Chi-Square were computed. Findings showed that women were more likely to have a budget than men, married students with budgets were more likely to follow them, and those aged 36 to 40 were more likely to follow them most of the time.

1 Many college students are living on the edge of financial crisis and many of them do not possess the knowledge needed to manage their money. While students at the university, they are constantly accumulating debt, through student loans and credit cards. They may not realize how their current debt can negatively affect their future credit rating. Without consistent money management practices, students will find it difficult to reach financial goals (Bowen & Lago, 1997).

2 What does a good money management plan include? According to Musk & Winter (1998), it will include "regular generation of financial statements; budgeting; control of spending; recording income and expenses; and tax, insurance, investment, retirement and estate planning" (p. 1). The difficulty in

creating and using a money management plan is that many students are not familiar with money management practices (Chen & Volpe, 1998). Chen & Volpe (1998) blame the colleges for not providing financial management courses for students. The Youth and Money Survey (1999) found that even though 65% of the students had an opportunity to schedule a money management course, only 21% of them took the course. The amount of financial information a student has usually impacts their ideas and choices regarding finances (Chen & Volpe, 1998). Kendrick (1999) stated that only 44% of students understand the term 'budget'; in fact, only 18% of the general population possesses a basic appreciation of simple money management practices (Elliot, 1997). Another hindrance to students is simply that they are not as capable of coping with actual circumstances involving finances that they will encounter when they are older (Family Values, 1998). One reason is that most of them are in the beginning phase of their "financial life cycle" and a majority of their money is spent rather than invested (Chen & Volpe, 1998, p. 5).

3 Although the primary rationale given by students for obtaining a credit card is to establish a good credit history (Murdy & Rush, 1995), 28% of students carry monthly credit card debt (Youth and Money Survey, 1999). Due to the easy access to credit cards in colleges, approximately 80% of full-time undergraduate students have credit cards with an "average outstanding balance (of) $2,226 and 10% of them have outstanding balances of more than $7,000" (Kendrick, 1999, p. 1).

Method

4 The sample was drawn from randomly selected Education courses, offered at the University of Louisiana at Lafayette, which were being taught, at each academic level, in the Spring 2000 semester. The instrument used was a 13-item questionnaire. It was constructed by the researchers, because our study only required a limited amount of data and some of the other questionnaires either included unnecessary items or contained items inappropriate to our population (education majors). Items contained in the questionnaire included demographic data, such as gender, race, marital status, classification, major, citizenship, and age. The second section dealt with employment status (full- or part-time), number of jobs, and total gross yearly income estimate. The final section required students to describe their budgeting practices, such as whether they had a written budget, how often they followed it, if they had one, and estimate their total debt.

5 The data were collected over a one week period from both undergraduate and graduate education majors registered in randomly selected education classes. Students were administered the questionnaire at the beginning of class and steps were taken to ensure that no one completed more than one questionnaire. All were informed that participation in the study was voluntary and all responses were anonymous.

Results

6 Data analysis was performed for the entire population and also various subcategories. Both frequency distributions and Pearson Chi-Square were computed. Crosstabulations were also performed. There were 106 females, which corresponded to 84% of the sample and only 20 males. A majority of the students were Caucasian (76%), 84% were 30 years old or younger, and 98% were U.S. citizens. The two largest classifications represented were freshman at 26% and graduate students at 21%. Fifty-three percent were elementary education majors, 29% were secondary education majors, and the remaining 12% were comprised of either music, special or vocational education majors. Sixty-nine percent of the students were never married. The results showed that the average student income was almost $16,000, while the average student debt was approximately $13,000. Based on reported yearly income, 44% of the students had more than 31% debt. The researchers wanted to determine if students actually had a written budget and whether they followed it. Of the 42% reported having a budget, 38% did not follow it all the time, and only 4% of them never followed their budget. Also of interest, was whether undergraduates had more debt than graduate students. It was found that only 40% of undergraduates had debt as opposed to 96% of the graduate students. Gender was related to having a budget with women (35%) more likely to have a budget than men (10%) (see Table 1). Age was significantly related to how often students follow their budget, with those students in the 36 to 40-age group (100%) more likely to have a budget and follow it most of the time (see Table 2). Married students with a budget were more likely to follow them, although they followed them only 52% of the time (see Table 3). Fifty-two percent of the graduate students had a budget and followed it (see Table 4). No significance was found between major and total debt, number of jobs and having a budget, classification and total debt, gender and debt, and age and debt.

Discussion

7 Those participants who followed their budgets fairly often were 32% of the sample, while those interviewed in the Youth and Money Survey (1999) were 30%. Though our sample was limited to a specific population and was not as large as the above-mentioned study, our findings were similar to theirs. The statistics seem to imply that students are either not knowledgeable of money management practices or they are not willing to spend the time to manage their money. Even though our students asked students to estimate debt and income, some gave both household and individual estimates of debt and income. Due to this problem, a debt-to-income ratio was not able to give an accurate picture of the students' debt. More research should be performed concerning college students and money management practices. Budgeting was only one aspect of money management, but savings, retirement planning, and investments should also be studied. An accurate picture of their debt-to-income ratio would be something they might want to see and may provide motivation to manage their money better.

Table 1 Gender and Budget

Count Row percent	Yes Completed	No Completed	Missing	Row Total
Male	2	17	1	20
	10.0	85.0	5.0	100.0
Female	36	68	1	105
	34.3	64.8	.9	100.0

Table 2 Age and How often students followed their budget

Count Row Percent Column Percent	No Budget	Always Followed	Mostly Followed	Fairly Often	Sometimes, Rarely, or Never	Row Total
Under 20	27	4	4	1	6	42
	64.3	9.5	9.5	2.4	14.3	100.0
	36.9	44.4	18.1	11.1	50	33.6
21 to 25	30	3	5	3	4	45
	66.7	6.7	11.1	6.7	8.9	100.0
	41.1	33.3	22.7	33.3	33.3	36.0
26 to 30	11	0	5	2	1	19
	57.9	0.0	26.3	10.5	5.3	100.0
	15.1	0.0	22.7	22.2	8.3	15.2
31 to 35	2	1	2	0	0	5
	40	20	40	0.0	0.0	100.0
	2.7	11.1	9.1	0.0	0.0	4.0
36 to 40	0	0	4	0	0	4
	0.0	0.0	100.0	0.0	0.0	100.0
	0.0	0.0	18.2	0.0	0.0	3.2
41 to 60	3	1	2	3	1	10
	30.0	10.0	20.0	30.0	10.0	100.0
	4.1	11.1	9.1	33.3	8.3	8.0
Column Total	73	9	22	9	12	125
	58.4	7.2	17.6	7.2	9.6	100.0
	100.0	100.0	100.0	100.0	100.0	100.0

Conclusion

8 Our data showed that a majority of the students do not have a written budget, that women were more likely to have a budget than men, married students with budgets were more likely to follow their budgets, and those aged 36 to 40 were more likely to follow their budgets most of the time. Based on the findings, it appears that University students are vulnerable to financial crisis.

Table 3 Current Marital Status and How often Students follow their Budget

Count Row Percent Column Percent	No Budget	Always Followed	Mostly Followed	Fairly Often	Sometimes, Rarely, or Never	Row Total
Never Married	56	6	10	5	10	87
	64.4	6.9	11.5	5.7	11.5	100.0
	76.7	66.7	45.5	55.6	83.3	69.6
Married	14	3	9	4	1	31
	45.2	9.7	29.0	12.9	3.2	100.0
	19.2	33.3	40.9	44.4	8.3	24.8
Separated/Divorced	3	0	3	0	1	7
	42.9	0.0	42.9	0.0	14.3	100.0
	4.1	0.0	13.6	0.0	8.3	5.6
Column Total	73	9	22	9	12	125
	58.4	7.2	17.6	7.2	9.6	100.0
	100.0	100.0	100.0	100.0	100.0	100.0

Table 4 Classification and How often Students follow their Budget

Count Row Percent Column Percent	No Budget	Always Followed	Mostly Followed	Fairly Often	Sometimes, Rarely, Never	Row Total
Missing Data						(1)
Freshman	24	0	2	2	5	33
	72.7	0.0	6.1	6.1	15.2	100.0
	33.3	0.0	9.1	22.2	41.7	26.6
Sophomore	11	2	5	3	4	25
	44.0	8.0	20.0	12.0	16.0	100.0
	15.3	22.2	22.7	33.3	33.3	20.2
Junior	11	5	6	0	1	23
	47.8	21.7	26.1	0.0	4.3	100.0
	15.3	55.6	27.3	0.0	8.3	18.5
Senior	14	1	0	1	2	18
	77.8	5.6	0.0	5.6	11.1	100.0
	19.4	11.1	0.0	11.1	16.7	14.5
Graduate Student	12	1	9	3	0	25
	48.0	4.0	36.0	12.0	0.0	100.0
	16.7	11.1	40.9	33.3	0.0	20.2
Column Total	72	9	22	9	12	124
	58.1	7.3	17.7	7.3	9.7	100.0
	100.0	100.0	100.0	100.0	100.0	100.0

References

Bowen, C. F., & Lago, D. J. (1997). Money management in families: A review of the literature with a racial, ethnic, and limited income perspective. *Advancing the Consumer Interest, [Online], 9*(2), p32, 11p. Available: *www.ehostvgw8.epnet.com* [2000, February 25].

Chen, H., & Volpe, R. P. (1998). An analysis of personal financial literacy among college students. *Financial Services Review [Online], 7*(2), p107, 22p. Available: *www.ehostvgw.8epnet.com* [2000, February 10].

Elliot, J. (1997). Young and in debt: A focus on prevention. *Credit World [Online], 85*(4), p35, 3p. Available: *www.proquest.umi.com/pqd-web* [2000, March 31].

Family values. (1998, December). *Kiplinger's Personal Finance Magazine, [Online], 52*, p62, 1/3p. Available: *www.ehostvgw2.epnet.com* [2000, March 21].

Kendrick, E. (1999). Give 'em credit: When is it right for students? *Austin Business Journal. [Online], 19*(25), p26, 3/8p. Available: *www.ehostvgw2.epnet.com* [2000, March 25].

Murdy, S., & Rush, C. (1995). College students & credit cards. *Credit World [Online], 83*(5), p13, 4p. Available: *www.proquest.umi.com/pqd-web* [2000, March 31].

Musk, G., & Winter, M. (1998). Real world financial management tools and practices. *Consumer Interests Annual [Online]*, (44), p19, 6p. Available: *www.ehostvgw.8epnet.com* [2000, February 10].

Youth and money survey. (1999). *American Savings Education Council [Online]*, 16p. Available: *www.asec.org* [2000, April 14].

Reading Responses

1. How did the authors of the article conduct their study?
2. What were the results of the study?
3. How do the authors interpret their results?

Writing Activities

1. Using your own words, summarize the reasons why the authors feel that money management and their study of students' money management practices are important.
2. Select one of the tables in this article. Write a paragraph explaining what you consider the most important information in the table.
3. Write an essay proposing several steps that might help students become better money managers.

Community Links

After reading this academic research report on students' money management practices, turn to two selections from the public community that also discuss money management: "Your Driving Costs 2003: Figuring It Out" from the American Automobile Association (pp. 530–541) and "How to Make a Budget and Stick to It" from Nolo (pp. 543–547). Compare and contrast the purposes, approaches, recommendations, and community expectations of the academic report and one of the public readings.

Report of Laboratory Study

HOW TO TELL A SEA MONSTER: MOLECULAR DISCRIMINATION OF LARGE MARINE ANIMALS OF THE NORTH ATLANTIC

S. M. Carr, H. D. Marshall, K. A. Johnstone,
L. M. Pynn, and G. B. Stenson

◆

This article appeared in The Biological Bulletin, *published by the Marine Biological Laboratory in Woods Hole, Massachusetts. This journal, directed to biologists and general readers, publishes reports on research experiments. "How to Tell a Sea Monster" explains how to determine the species of an unidentified marine animal that might seem to be sea monster. Like other research reports, it includes conventional sections: an introduction, a description of materials and methods, an explanation of results, and a discussion of the findings, in this case combined with conclusions.*

"Either we do know all the varieties of beings which people our planet, or we do not. If we do not know them all—if Nature has still secrets in the deeps for us, nothing is more conformable to reason than to admit the existence of fishes, or cetaceans of other kinds, or even of new species . . . which an accident of some sort has brought at long intervals to the upper level of the ocean."
—*Jules Verne,* Twenty Thousand Leagues Under the Sea, *1870*

Abstract

[1] Remains of large marine animals that wash onshore can be difficult to identify due to decomposition and loss of external body parts, and in consequence may be dubbed "sea monsters." DNA that survives in such carcasses can provide a basis of identification. One such creature washed ashore at St. Bernard's, Fortune Bay, Newfoundland, in August 2001. DNA was extracted from the carcass and enzymatically amplified by the polymerase chain reaction (PCR): the mitochondrial NADH2 DNA sequence was identified as that of a sperm whale (*Physeter catodon*). Amplification and sequencing of cryptozoological DNA with "universal" PCR primers with broad specificity to vertebrate taxa and comparison with species in the GenBank taxonomic database is an effective means of discriminating otherwise unidentifiable large marine creatures.

Introduction*

2   At least since the *Iliad*, the possible occurrence of unusually large, exotic marine creatures has exerted a powerful hold on the human imagination. Professor A. C. Oudemans' 1892 book *The Great Sea Serpent* described more than 200 reports of unknown marine creatures (Ley, 1959). Ellis (1994) gives a contemporary list. Even in the first year of a new century when the complete human genome has become known (International Human Genome Sequencing Consortium, 2001), the possibility that entirely new, previously unknown species may unexpectedly present themselves remains tantalizing. Discovery in the last century of the first coelacanth (*Latimeria*), the "megamouth" shark (*Megachasma*) and, most recently, a second species of coelacanth in the waters off Sulawesi in Indonesia (Holder *et al.*, 1999) keeps us alert to the possibility of "new varieties of beings" in the deeps. Modern methods of phylogenetic systematics, based on detailed morphological and molecular analyses, have made it possible to place such discoveries in their evolutionary context.

3   Morphological analysis of putative new species may be hampered by incomplete or poorly preserved material; in such cases, molecular biology may hold the key to natural history. Enzymatic amplification by the polymerase chain reaction (PCR) (Saiki *et al.*, 1988) of the minute amounts of DNA persisting in ancient or forensic biological material has been shown to be an effective means of individual and species identification (Herrmann and Hummell, 1994). The extra-nuclear mitochondrial (mt) DNA genome has been particularly valuable, as more than a decade of molecular systematic work has provided an extensive database ("GenBank") of molecular "type" sequences for many species of marine sharks, fish, and mammals (Wheeler *et al.*, 2000; Benson *et al.*, 2000). Routine species identification of subfossil material hundreds or thousands of years old (Hofreiter *et al.*, 2001) is possible, as is forensic determination of questioned species in commercial products such as salted or dried fish (S. M. Carr and H. D. Marshall, unpubl. obs.), or processed whale meat (Baker *et al.*, 1996) including that from endangered species (Palumbi and Cipriano, 1998). We report here what appears to be the first successful use of PCR-based recovery of DNA to identify a "sea monster."

4   On 2 August 2001, residents of the community of St. Bernard's, Fortune Bay, on the south coast of the island of Newfoundland, were confronted with an enormous, whitish mass of rotting flesh that had washed up on a local beach overnight. They contacted the Department of Fisheries and Oceans in St. John's, who sent experts to examine the carcass (Fig. 1). The remains were about 5.6 m long and 5.0 m wide. Neither head nor tail was present: the carcass consisted primarily of bleached tissue. The surface was rough and fringed with material initially characterized as "hair," which upon closer inspection appeared to consist of abraded tissue mixed with seaweed and sand. There were seven or eight lobes or slits that extended roughly one-third the length of one

---

*Received 19 September 2001; accepted 13 November 2001.

Figure 1. "Sea monster" discovered at St. Bernard's, Fortune Bay, Newfoundland, 2 August 2001. The maximum length of the carcass is 5.6 m. The transverse cuts were made during dissection. Note the lobes at the right-hand end on the side facing the camera.

side from one end; the last two slits did not extend to the outer margin. No lobes were present on the opposite side, but tissue had evidently been lost from that side. The remainder of the mass tapered slightly. No soft tissue or bones were present; dissection of the side opposite the lobes revealed a small amount of cartilage. The surface layer retained a structure consistent with muscle, but the interior had decomposed to an amorphous mass. Definite identification was impossible due to the state of decomposition and the absence of any remaining external features. The size and general morphology were consistent with either a large shark, such as a basking shark (*Cetorhinus maximus*), or one of the several species of large cetaceans present in Newfoundland waters. The possibility of a giant squid (*Architeuthis dux*) was excluded due to general morphology (Aldrich, 1991).

Materials and Methods

5   Scientists from the Department of Fisheries and Oceans removed a number of pieces of tissue from just under the exterior of the carcass. DNA was extracted in duplicate from four pieces of tissue by a protease-based method

with a QIAamp® DNA Mini Kit (Qiagen, Inc.), according to the manufacturer's instructions.

On the basis of the availability in GenBank of sequences for the mitochondrial (mt) DNA NADH subunit 2 gene (hereinafter NADH2) for a variety of shark (Naylor et al., 1999) and whale species, we performed a series of polymerase chain reaction (PCR) experiments with two forward and reverse primer pairs that amplify a 1103-bp region that includes the complete NADH2 gene as two overlapping regions of 564 and 711 bp, respectively:

p8F: 5' aagctatcgggcccataccc 3' and p8R: 5' tttagtcctcctcagcctcc 3'
p9F: 5' cataatcctactcacatgac 3' and p9R: 5' cttacttagggctttgaagg 3'

PCR reactions were carried out as a two-step procedure designed to enhance amplification of dilute DNA or of DNA with a poor match between template and primer. In this strategy, an initial set of PCR cycles with dilute primers (2.5% of usual concentration) generates a small quantity of amplified template with ends that have an exact match to the primers. A second phase follows, with primers at standard concentration to produce sufficient template for sequence analysis. In the first stage of the procedure, we prepared 25-μl reactions containing 1X PCR reaction buffer and 1 U of *Taq* polymerase (Roche Molecular Biochemicals, Inc.), 10 nM of each primer (Cortec DNA Service Laboratories, Inc.), 100 μM of each deoxynucleoside triphosphate (dNTP; Amersham Pharmacia Biotech), and 2 μl of template DNA. Following an initial incubation at 93 °C for 3 min, samples were taken through 23 cycles, each comprising denaturation at 93 °C for 45 s, annealing at 45 °C for 45 s, a ramp from 45 °C to 55 °C over 45 s, and extension at 72 °C for 1 min. The last cycle was followed by a further extension at 72 °C for 10 min. In the second stage, a second 25-μl reaction volume was added to each reaction tube, containing 1X PCR reaction buffer, 1 U *Taq* polymerase, 800 nM each primer (so as to bring the final concentration of each to 400 nM in a 50-μl volume), and 100 μM of each dNTP. Samples were taken through an additional 45 cycles of PCR, as described above. All thermal manipulations were achieved using the GeneAmp PCR System 9600 (Perkin-Elmer).

PCR product sizes were verified by electrophoresis of 5 μl of the product through 2% agarose in 1X TBE buffer followed by ethidium bromide staining. Excess primer and nucleotides were removed from the PCR products using a QIAquick® PCR Purification Kit (Qiagen, Inc.).

DNA sequencing was accomplished by fluorescent dye-terminator chemistry carried out on an Applied Biosystems 3700 Automated DNA sequencer (Qiagen Genomics Sequencing Service, Qiagen Genomics Inc.) with the same primers that were used for amplification.

Results

No special difficulties were encountered in DNA extraction. Agarose electrophoresis of small portions of the extracted product indicated the presence of high molecular weight DNA in all but one of the tissue samples.

Amplification with the two pairs of NADH2 primers was successful in about one-half of trials, and produced amplification products of the expected size. Inspection of electrophoretic separations indicated clean but weak amplification. Products from three replicate amplifications of each region were pooled for DNA sequencing.

11   A complete NADH2 sequence was obtained by assembly of the overlapping forward and reverse sequences of the two amplified regions. A BLAST search against the complete GenBank database indicated that the composite sequence had a 99.6% (1040 out of 1044 bp) match with the published NADH2 sequence for a sperm whale (*Physeter catodon*) (Árnason et al., 2000: GenBank accession NC002503). The four nucleotide differences included one second codon position C ↔ T transition difference that would be expected to result in a threonine ↔ methionine amino acid difference between the GenBank type and Fortune Bay sequences, respectively. The magnitude of the differences is consistent with expected intraspecific variation. The DNA sequence was submitted to GenBank and assigned the accession number AF414121.

Discussion and Conclusions

12   The Fortune Bay "sea monster" is the carcass of a sperm whale (*Physeter catodon*). Sperm whales are the largest of the toothed whales (Odontoceti), they are not uncommon in the waters off the southern shore of the island of Newfoundland (Leatherwood et al., 1976), and strandings of more or less intact whales are not infrequent (G. B. Stenson, unpubl. data). The carcass appears to be a mass of decomposing muscle tissue that has separated from the vertebral column and ribs. The peripheral lobes, which might be mistaken for a set of chondrichthian gill arches, are consistent with intercostal flesh. The feathery or hairy appearance is apparently abraded tissue. Exact postmortem age of the carcass is impossible to determine, but it is likely to have been in the water a long time.

13   Accounts and pictures in the popular press indicate that carcasses resembling the one found in Fortune Bay have washed up in several oceans of the world; some of these have attracted international media attention. Verrill (1897) initially described a large, whitish carcass that appeared in St. Augustine, Florida, as a new species of giant octopus, though he later withdrew this identification. Original newspaper reports in 1962 of a Tasmanian creature dubbed the "Globster" described it in the following terms: "It was initially covered with fine hair.... There were five or six gill-like hairless slits on each side of the fore part. There were four large hanging lobes in the front, and between the center pair was a smooth, gullet-like orifice. The margin of the hind part had cushion like protuberances... and each of these carried a single row of spines, sharp, and hard, about as thick as a pencil and quill-like ... [It had] a resilient flesh which appeared to be composed of numerous tendon-like threads welded together in a fatty substance...." (quoted in Ellis, 1994). There was no bone. A later scientific investigation reported the carcass as 8 feet long, 3 feet wide, 10 inches thick, and without spines. A 1988 report from

Bermuda described a "Glob," "2 1/2 to 3 feet thick . . . very white and fibrous with five 'arms or legs,' rather like a disfigured star. . . . It had no bones, cartilage, visible openings, or odor. . . ." (quoted in Ellis, 1994). In 1990, another carcass washed ashore in the Hebrides Islands, Scotland: "It had what appeared to be a head at one end, a curved back and seemed to be covered with eaten-away flesh or even a furry skin and was 12 feet long [and] it had all these shapes like fins along its back. . . ." (L. Phitts to S. McLean, Hancock Museum, Newcastle, UK; pers. comm. to S. M. Carr). Definitive species identification of any of these carcasses has been impossible. Pierce *et al.* (1995) concluded on the basis of ultrastructure and amino acid analysis that the Bermuda carcass was the remains of a vertebrate, and that Verrill's "giant octopus" was actually whale blubber.

14   In common with the Fortune Bay carcass, these and other reports (see Ellis, 1994) describe oblong whitish carcasses, several meters in length, bordered at one end with fleshy lobes, fringed with feathery white material resembling hair, and without apparent bone or cartilage. In contrast with other reports, we did not find the surface especially difficult to cut, and close examination revealed the presence of cartilage. We suggest that these and other similar remains are likely of cetacean origin. Given the variation in size of the various carcasses, it would be of interest to know the species diversity among such remains. Dead basking sharks present a somewhat different appearance. Decomposition of beached carcasses is accompanied by erosion of the caudal fin and sloughing of the head, leaving a long bony "tail" and a small chondrocranium "head" (Scott and Scott, 1988). A 1977 discovery in the nets of a Japanese fishing trawler was initially described as a "plesiosaur," but detailed morphological examination strongly suggests chondrichthian origins (Kuban, 1997). In future, discrimination of such carcasses should be possible by the means described here.

15   Because mtDNA is present in high copy number (~1% of total DNA) in vertebrate cells, any particular mitochondrial gene is far more likely to survive postmortem degradation, enzymatic breakdown, and mechanical damage than is any typical single-copy nuclear sequence (Hermann and Hummel, 1994). Here, adventitious "pickling" by prolonged immersion in cold seawater has left enough intact DNA for positive identification. Hofreiter *et al.* (2001) caution that care must be taken to avoid contaminating the minute amounts of DNA present in forensic material with exogenous species: in this case, no (other) sperm whale tissue was present in the laboratory, and appropriate experimental controls were always negative.

16   When anatomical identification is not possible and DNA can be recovered, effective identification of unknown marine creatures begins with PCR amplification with "universal" primers designed to be homologous to gene regions that are evolutionarily conserved across a diversity of taxa (Kocher *et al.*, 1989; Palumbi, 1996). The resultant DNA sequence can then be compared against the complete GenBank database of the National Center for Biotechnology Information (NCBI) [http://www.ncbi.nlm.nih.gov] by means of a BLAST search (Altschul *et al.*, 1997). This involves a simple "cut and paste" submission

of the sequence data over the Internet: an answer is usually obtained within minutes (here, in under 30 seconds). The search returns a set of matches, ranked in order of degree of sequence similarity. In this case, an essentially exact match was obtained, which indicates a positive species identification.

Were a more inexact match to be obtained, phylogenetic analysis would be necessary to ascertain or at least narrow species affinities among the usual suspects. The GenBank taxonomy database currently comprises DNA sequences from more than 50,000 species, of which more than 9600 are vertebrate species, including 110 Elasmobranchii and 80 Cetacea. Reference sequences for the mitochondrial NADH2 gene, the cytochrome *b* gene, or both are available from 3 of the 4 species of sharks and 10 of the 11 species of whales that are found in Atlantic Canadian waters and exceed 6 m in length (Table 1).

Table 1   Large marine animals of the North Atlantic

Name and taxonomy	Max. size (meters)	GenBank accession	
		NADH2	Cyt *b*
Elasmobranchii (sharks)[1]			
thresher shark (*Alopias vulpinus*)	6	U91432	U91442
white shark (*Carcharodon carcharias*)	8	U91426	L08031
basking shark (*Cetorhinus maximus*)	13	U91429	U91439
whale shark (*Rhincodon typus*)[2]	18	—	—
Greenland shark (*Somniosus microcephalus*)	7	—	—
Mysticeti (baleen whales)[3]			
bowhead whale (*Balaena mysticetus*)	20	—	X75588
Minke whale (*Balaenoptera acutorostrata*)	10	X87775	X75753
Sei whale (*Balaenoptera borealis*)	19	—	X75582
blue whale (*Balaenoptera musculus*)	26	NC001601[5]	
finback whale (*Balaenoptera physalus*)	27	NC001321[5]	
beluga (*Delphinapterus leucas*)	6	—	X92531
northern right whale (*Eubalaena glacialis*)	16	—	—
humpback whale (*Megaptera novaeangliae*)	16	—	X75584
Odontoceti (*toothed whales*)[3]			
Atlantic pilot whale (*Globicephala melaena*)	6	—	AF084056
killer whale (*Orcinus orca*)	9	—	X92532
sperm whale (*Physeter catodon*)	21	NC002503[5]	
Cephalopoda (squids & relatives)			
giant squid (*Architeuthis dux*)[4]	18	—	—

[1] Size data from Scott and Scott (1988).
[2] Not known to occur in Canadian Atlantic waters.
[3] Size data from Leatherwood et al. (1976).
[4] Aldrich (1991).
[5] Both sequences contained in the accession for the complete mtDNA genome.

Failure to obtain positive identification through GenBank does not necessarily indicate an unknown species, but may instead indicate a previously recognized species for which genetic data, or data from a particular locus, are as yet unknown. Continuing studies in marine biology and molecular systematics will improve the range and depth of our knowledge of the genetics of these species, and should provide exact tests for future cryptozoological specimens.

Acknowledgments

We thank the people of St. Bernard's for drawing our attention to this interesting specimen; Mr. W. Peney, Mr. H. Whitney, Mr. W. King, and Mr. W. Mayo for their assistance in obtaining specimen material; Mr. Scott Federhen for help with GenBank; Mr. Steve McLean at the Hancock Museum for discussion of the Hebrides carcass; Dr. Sidney K. Pierce for discussion of the Bermuda carcass; Mr. Edward Ormondroyd for his thoughts on sea monsters; and Dr. Christoph Koenig at Qiagen for indulging our e-mails and phone calls. We thank Dr. Pierce, Ms. Dale Parmiter, and two anonymous reviewers for helpful comments on earlier drafts of this manuscript. Ms. Johnstone and Ms. Pynn were supported by the Women in Science and Engineering (WISE) program. This work was performed as part of the Strategic Alliance agreement between the Department of Fisheries and Oceans and Memorial University of Newfoundland, which includes investigation of the genetics and genomics of marine organisms.

Literature Cited

Aldrich, F. A. 1991. Some aspects of the systematics and biology of squid of the genus *Architeuthis* based on a study of specimens from Newfoundland waters. *Bull. Mar. Sci.* **49:** 457–481.

Altschul, S. F., T. L. Madden, A. A. Schäffer, J. Zhang, Z. Zhang, W. Miller, and David J. Lipman. 1997. Gapped BLAST and PSI-BLAST: a new generation of protein database search programs. *Nucleic Acids Res.* **25:** 3389–3402.

Árnason, U., A. Gullberg, S. Gretarsdottir, B. Ursing, and A. Janke. 2000. The mitochondrial genome of the sperm whale and a new molecular reference for estimating eutherian divergence dates. *J. Mol. Evol.* **50:** 569–578.

Baker, C. S., F. Cipriano, and S. R. Palumbi. 1996. Molecular genetic identification of whale and dolphin products from commercial markets in Korea and Japan. *Mol. Ecol.* **5:** 671–685.

Benson, D. A., I. Karsch-Mizrachi, D. J. Lipman, J. Ostell, B. A. Rapp, and D. L. Wheeler. 2000. GenBank. *Nuc. Acids Res.* **28:** 15–18.

Ellis, R. 1994. *Monsters of the Sea.* Knopf, New York.

Hermann, B., and S. Hummel, eds. 1994. *Ancient DNA.* Springer-Verlag, New York.

Hofreiter, M. D., D. Serre, H. N. Poinar, M. Kuch, and S. Pääbo. 2001. Ancient DNA. *Nature Rev. Genetics* **2:** 353–359.

Holder, M. T., M. V. Erdmann, T. P. Wilcox, R. L. Caldwell and D. M. Hillis, 1999. Two living species of coelacanths. *Proc. Nat. Acad. Sci. USA* **96:** 12616–12620.

International Human Genome Sequencing Consortium. 2001. Initial sequencing and analysis of the human genome. *Nature* **409:** 860–921.

Kocher, T. D., W. K. Thomas, A. Meyer, S. V. Edwards, S. Pääbo, F. X. Villablanca, and A. C. Wilson. 1989. Dynamics of mitochondrial DNA evolution in animals: amplification and sequencing with conserved primers. *Proc. Nat. Acad. Sci. USA* **86:** 6196–6200.

Kuban, G. J. 1997. Sea-monster or shark? An analysis of a supposed plesiosaur carcass netted in 1977. *Reports of the National Center for Science Education* **17:** 16–28.

Leatherwood, S., D. K. Caldwell, and H. E. Winn. 1976. Whales, dolphins and porpoises of the Western North Atlantic. A guide to their identification. *NOAA Technical Report* NMFS CIRC-396, 176 pp.

Ley, W. 1959. *Exotic Zoology.* Knopf, New York.

Naylor, G. J. P., A. P. Martin, E. K. Mattison, and W. M. Brown. 1999. Interrelationships of Lamniform sharks: testing phylogenetic hypotheses with sequence data. Pp. 199–218 in *Molecular Systematics of Fishes.* T. D. Kocher and C. A. Stepien, eds. Academic Press, New York.

Palumbi, S. R. 1996. Nucleic acids II: the polymerase chain reaction. Pp. 205–247 in *Molecular Systematics.* D. M. Hillis, C. Moritz, and B. K. Mable, eds. Sinauer, Sunderland, MA.

Palumbi, S. R., and F. Cipriano. 1998. Species identification using genetic tools: the value of nuclear and mitochondrial gene sequences in whale conservation. *J. Hered.* **89:** 459–464.

Pierce, S. K., G. N. Smith, Jr., T. K. Maugel, and E. Clark. 1995. On the Giant Octopus (*Octopus giganteus*) and the Bermuda Blob: homage to A. E. Verrill. *Biol. Bull.* **188:** 219–230.

Saiki, R. K., D. H. Gelfland, S. Stoffel, S. J. Scharf, R. Higuchi, G. T. Horn, K. B. Mullis, and H. A. Ehrlich. 1988. Primer-directed enzymatic amplification of DNA with a thermostable DNA polymerase. *Science* **239:** 487–491.

Scott, W. B., and M. G. Scott. 1988. *Atlantic Fishes of Canada.* Univ. Toronto Press.

Verrill, A. E. 1897. The supposed great Octopus of Florida: certainly not a cephalopod. *Amer. J. Sci.*, 4th series, **3:** 355.

Wheeler, D. L., C. Chappey, A. E. Lash, D. D. Leipe, T. L. Madden, G. D. Schuler, T. A. Tatusova, and B. A. Rapp. 2000. Database resources of the National Center for Biotechnology Information. *Nucleic Acids Res.* **28:** 10–14.

Reading Responses

1. According to the introduction section, what is the importance of this research?
2. Why are the sections "Materials and Methods" and "Results" so technical? Why don't the authors use nontechnical language or simply summarize the information in these parts?
3. According to the section "Discussion and Conclusions," what did the researchers discover about the Fortune Bay "sea monster"?

Writing Activities

1. Briefly explain what problem this research addresses and how the research can help solve the problem.
2. What might a resident of St. Bernard's write about the event that initiated this research? Write the account that you imagine, but stick to the essential facts mentioned in the report.
3. Write an article that would be appropriate for the campus newspaper. In your article, explain what this report means for sea monsters.

Community Links

Consider how research problems present themselves to researchers in various communities and situations. Compare and contrast the situation described in "How to Tell a Sea Monster" with that identified or implied in another report such as Mogelonsky's "Young Adults: New Customers/New Foods" (pp. 325–331) from the work community or Popenoe and Whitehead's "Sex without Strings, Relationships without Rings" (pp. 518–529) from the public community.

Examination and Examination Answers
HITCHCOCK FINAL WITH ANSWERS
Leslie Hankins, Professor
Anderson Muth, Student Writer

◆

The midterm or final examination is a traditional form of academic assessment. It may take the form of an in-class essay, a timed writing, a take-home essay, various types of objective questions, or some combination of questions. The objective final examination included here requires two types of answers, both demonstrating knowledge about the Alfred Hitchcock films the class had studied.

Identification Answers from Question Sheet

Please give the name and date of the film on this sheet and then, on a separate sheet or in a bluebook, briefly (in a sentence or two) outline the significance of the item in the context of the film or Hitchcock's oeuvre as a whole.

1. The exposition of the film is truly remarkable. You open up with the perspiring face of James Stewart; you move on to his leg in a cast, and then, on a nearby table, you see the broken camera, a stack of magazines, and, on the wall, pictures of racing cars as they topple over on the track.
   Rear Window, 1954

2. "GOLDEN CURLS TONIGHT"
   Lodger, 1926

3. "A boy's best friend is his mother."
   Psycho, 1960

4. Kim Novak acts and rehearses and acts . . .
   Vertigo, 1958

5. The experimental expressionist soundtrack mutes most of the dialogue, while from the protagonist's perspective, we hear the word "knife" jump out, shrieking in crescendo.
   Blackmail, 1929

6. Screenplay by Ben Hecht; some designs by Salvador Dali
   Spellbound, 1945

7. Mr. Memory recites his exit lines against the backdrop of a chorus line
   The 39 Steps, 1935

8. Traces of German expressionism in the inky lighting, title cards, and vampire motifs—and the expressionist use of shadows
   Lodger, 1926

9. "Loved her? I hated her!!"
   Rebecca, 1940

10. As Cary Grant plays a redcap, the bird's eye camera allows us a color-coded visual joke.
    North by Northwest, 1959

Significance Answers from Bluebook

1. James Stewart's entire situation (occupation, accident, etc.) is thoroughly explained without the use of dialogue. A well done introduction!

2. This marquee sign at first is menacing when the Avenger is out killing blondes; at the end, it reappears, as does normalcy.

3. This statement is Norman's defense as to why he has no friends. The fact that his mind belongs mainly to mother makes this almost perversely humorous. It's also a bit of foreshadowing of the conclusion that Mother *is* Norman.

4. Novak plays Madeleine but is really Judy and later, as Judy, is forced by Scottie to emulate Madeleine, whom she was playing earlier.

5. The soundtrack is evidence of surrealist film influences on Hitchcock. Since the heroine stabbed her attempted rapist, a knife is on her mind and thus that's the word she dwells on.

6. The Dali dream sequence, chock full of symbolism, is the most notable part of Spellbound (except for the brilliant skiing scene) and lends great depth to the plot.

7. Mr. Memory's death seems meaningless: the show goes on as he dies. He was used by "The 39 Steps" organization, but they ended up killing him.

8. Hitchcock's first real work, being a silent black and white film, relied on other excellent methods of conveying suspense and darkness. Ivor Novello looks like he's straight out of Nosferatu as he creeps about in search of the Avenger, showing how words are unneeded if the visuals are well done.

9. The truth explodes about Mr. De Winter's feelings toward Rebecca, as the new Mrs. De Winter, along with the audience, is finally brought into the light about why her husband is so haunted by his former wife.

10. Cary Grant as a redcap is wearing a red cap. Color connections (such as green in Rear Window) are used by Hitchcock in most of his color films.

Reading Responses

1. What kinds of knowledge does this examination test? Why might a professor want to test these types of knowledge?
2. How does Professor Hankins specify what information students are expected to supply? Identify the key words in her instructions that suggest how she will grade the answers.
3. How might an instructor evaluate Anderson's Significance Answers? Does he follow the directions, supply clear answers, and respond to the questions asked? Which answers seem particularly strong or weak? Why?

Writing Activities

1. Imagine that you have taken the Hitchcock film class. Write a short essay, advising students in the next Hitchcock class about how to study for the objective final.
2. Write an examination for your composition class (or another course that a group of classmates are taking or have taken). Supply clear directions about what the test takers need to do and how you will grade the examination. Trade exams with a classmate, and take each other's tests. Exchange exams again, and read your partner's answers. Conclude by writing a paragraph that briefly evaluates how well your exam worked.
3. Using your own past exams or samples from a group of classmates, conduct a small research study. Examine the questions asked. Work out a useful classification system, identifying common types of questions or types of directions. Write a brief report explaining your findings.

Community Links

Examinations, like most class assignments, are opportunities for assessment. Select a few other texts that have undergone an assessment process. You might examine a grant proposal (assessed by a funding organization), a proposal like that of the Cornell Players Foundation (assessed by the campus office that authorizes living groups), a scholarly paper (assessed by peer reviewers or editors who approve publication), an application (assessed by those who admit or hire), or other comparable examples. Use these examples to help you consider the nature of assessment: how it works in various contexts, how criteria are established, how judgments are made, or how the assessment process improves, or might improve, the quality of the products assessed.

Grant Proposal
COMMUNICATING COMMON GROUND
Kathryn Sorrells

♦

Grant proposals request funding for specific projects from government agencies, nonprofit organizations, or other sponsoring groups. Often the funder circulates a Request for Proposals (RFP) that outlines the organization's goals, requirements, selection criteria, deadlines, and available funds for the projects to be selected. Interested groups submit proposals for their projects, which are then evaluated to determine who will be awarded the grant money. The following grant proposal, posted on the Web, outlines a collaborative project between California State University, Northridge, and a nearby public school, Grant High School.

Communicating Common Ground: A collaborative partnership between the Department of Communication Studies at California State University, Northridge and Grant High School
Grant Proposal Written by: Kathryn Sorrells, Ph.D., Project Director, Department of Communication Studies, CSUN
Submitted by: Department of Communication Studies, CSUN; Center for Community-Service Learning, CSUN; Grant High School, Van Nuys, CA
Initiative Sponsored by: The National Communication Association, Southern Poverty Law Center, American Association for Higher Education, Campus Compact

Introduction

1 This proposal outlines a pilot partnership with the Department of Communication Studies at California State University, Northridge, Grant High School, a San Fernando Valley secondary school, and the Center for Community-Service Learning, CSUN. The primary outcome of this partnership is the articulation of a replicable, nation-wide model that can guide schools

in creating environments where hate and hate speech are not tolerated and where the benefits of a culturally diverse community are actively fostered. Utilizing service learning pedagogy, the partnership seeks to promote collaborative learning opportunities for students, faculty, and related community members in both educational institutions and in the greater San Fernando Valley.

2   A summary of the social and cultural topography of the region provides a context for understanding the intercultural challenges and educational resources of the area. The description that follows underscores the need for cooperative educational initiatives such as *Communicating Common Ground*.

The Community

3   The San Fernando Valley, located approximately 20 miles northwest of Central Los Angeles, is one of the nation's most ethnically diverse communities. With a population of nearly 1.9 million, the Valley is 52% White, 34% Latino, 4% African-American, and 9% Asian Pacific Islander. If the San Fernando Valley were a city, it would be the nation's sixth largest. Children, between the ages of 5 and 19, comprise over 15% of the population.

4   Grant High School, the San Fernando Valley school participating in this inaugural partnership, is one of the most diverse high schools in the Los Angeles Unified School District (LAUSD), with more than 25 ethnic cultures represented among the student body. Students attending school in the Grant High School complex are predominately low-income with 23% coming from families that earn between $25,000 and $34,000, and 54% earning less than $15,000.

5   Last October, a long-standing feud between Latino and Armenian students at Grant High erupted into a lunchtime brawl that involved 200 students and resulted in five arrests, 40 detentions and ten injuries. Grant's principal, Joe Walker told the *Los Angeles Times*, "What it comes down to is a tradition of fighting between the largest ethnic groups on campus." Other LAUSD administrators attribute the tensions, in part, to long-forgotten disputes over earthquake relief drives in the 1980s after quakes struck Mexico and Armenia. Students from each ethnic group claimed the other received more sympathy and relief from the school and community, leading to classroom arguments.

6   A Grant High alumnus wrote a letter to the editor of the *Los Angeles Times* that noted, "The problems between Latino and Armenian students really start at home. One need only speak with the parents to find out where the racial intolerance and ignorance come from."

7   Although Grant High has taken proactive measures including flying banners with words and images confronting stereotypes and promoting diversity and respect, as well as the signing of a "peace treaty" by students, much remains to be done at the school and in the community. The San Fernando Valley is also the location of last summer's shooting tragedy at the North Valley Jewish Community Center. Just last month, a 17-year-old student at another Valley high school was clubbed with a tire iron and fatally stabbed in the heart after he tried to intervene in a fight fueled by ethnic tensions be-

tween Armenian-Americans and Latinos. Six days later, a carload of young men opened fire on seven Armenian-Americans, wounding one. The San Fernando Valley is clearly a community in need of healing and understanding; it is a community that can benefit from the vision, purpose, and collaboration that are integral components of this grant application.

California State University, Northridge

8   CSUN, established in 1956, is one of 22 campuses in the California State University system. With an enrollment of nearly 28,000 students, CSUN is the only four-year institution of higher education committed to responding to the needs of the multicultural community of the San Fernando Valley. CSUN faculty and its student body echo the diversity of its community, with a student population that is 24% Latino, 9% African American and 16% Asian and Pacific Islander. CSUN is a federally designated Minority Serving Institution (MSI) and Hispanic Serving Institution (HSI).

9   The Department of Communication Studies at CSUN is committed to developing students' communication competencies and providing them with opportunities to effectively address the challenges of our multicultural society. Faculty members in the department contribute expertise in a range of knowledge and skill-development areas relevant to the proposal, as well as experience designing and implementing community-service learning projects. Considering the mission of CSUN, the goals of the department, and the diverse student community we serve, the Department of Communication is ideally positioned to serve as a pilot partner in the *Communicating Common Ground* project.

Pilot Partnership Goals

10   The partnership between the Department of Communication Studies at CSUN and Grant High School has three interrelated goals. The central aim of the partnership is to develop a model that can be used in other locations in the U.S. for creating hate-free school environments where the benefits of a culturally diverse community are supported. In the process of developing this model, the partnership serves a second purpose, which is to provide a site for CSUN undergraduate and graduate students, and faculty to engage in community-service-learning projects. The service-learning projects will offer CSUN students the opportunities to actively apply their learning in socially responsible ways. The partnership also enables CSUN students to serve as role models for Grant High School students who may otherwise have little opportunity to interact with mentors who are committed to a university education. The third goal of the pilot partnership is to strengthen relations among educational institutions, pre-K through higher education, and to join forces with the larger metropolitan community of the San Fernando Valley to address critical social issues that challenge our diverse society.

Proposed Model and Activities

11   The first phase of the model is primarily process-oriented and is intended to initiate dialogue within the school community on diversity-related issues. CSUN Communication Studies students, who will be instructed on how to facilitate focus groups on culturally challenging issues, will facilitate the dialogues in a variety of classroom and school community settings. The purpose of focus group sessions is to encourage interest in and ownership of the project within the school community, as well as to identify who (for example, parent leaders along with students, teachers, and administrators) needs to actively participate in the project.

12   The focus group sessions serve the additional purpose of providing information to assess the needs of the specific school community. The second phase of the model entails the development and implementation of learning activities and curricular projects to meet these needs. Possible areas of instruction include basic communication skills, intercultural communication competencies, conflict negotiation skills, activities related to the reduction of hate speech and related incidents, and culture-specific knowledge components (for example, Armenian, Latino/Hispanic and other cultural groups represented in the San Fernando Valley).

13   CSUN students and faculty in a variety of courses including intercultural communication, interpersonal communication, language and symbolic process, debate, performance, and social change, and group communication will work with Grant High School students and teachers to research, develop and facilitate educational programs and learning activities in areas most responsive to the needs of the community. Instructional material from the Southern Poverty Law Center will be used in conjunction with other available resources. Alternative forms of instruction may include the use of interactive drama workshops designed to engage participants in creative problem solving through the creation of scripts and performances.

14   The third phase of the model involves sharing knowledge, skills, and attitudes gained in the pilot partnership project with the broader metropolitan area. Students in participating classes at Grant High School will be expected to continue the community-service-learning component of the project by sharing their learning in local middle, elementary, and/or pre-K schools. These service-learning projects may take the form of teaching lessons, facilitating discussions, and/or presenting theatrical performances. Additionally, CSUN students will be responsible for arranging opportunities for Grant High School students to visit the CSUN campus and learn about student life in a university setting.

Community Links: Grant High School, CSUN, and the San Fernando Valley

15   Currently, Grant High School is involved in several programs that interface with the proposed pilot partnership, including a peer mediation project developed in response to intercultural conflicts at the school and a mentoring proj-

ect. The Department of Educational Psychology at CSUN is already working with Grant High School in the placement of graduate students in counseling roles at the school. Faculty and graduate students from the Department of Educational Psychology will serve as liaisons for the Communication Studies faculty and will assist in implementing the programs during the course of the pilot partnership. In addition, links to area pre-K, elementary, middle, high schools and other San Fernando community organizations will develop through the community-service learning component that Grant High School students are required to organize.

Assessment

16 The pilot partnership project includes assessment of the model developed by the project, as well as evaluation of different programs and constituent groups throughout the process. After completion of the initial phases of the project at Grant High School, the model will be introduced in another area school where assessment from outside evaluators will be conducted. During the development phases, Grant High School students in classes that are partnering with CSUN service learning projects will be given pre and post assessments to evaluate the effectiveness of each class program. Assessment tools and activities will be developed in collaboration with the American Association of Higher Education. Student learning for both Grant High School and CSUN students will be assessed through instruments developed by the Center for Community-Service Learning at CSUN. Additionally, graduate students in the Department of Educational Psychology who function in school counseling roles will assist in developing assessment tools for evaluating the changes in overall school climate as a result of the pilot project.

Timeline

Fall 2000	Develop and implement test case service learning project. Undergraduate students in the COMS 356 Intercultural Communication class will work with 9th and 10th grade geography classes at Grant High School. Initial focus groups will be followed by learning activities. CSUN students will host Grant High School students at the CSUN campus as culminating project.
Spring 2001	Develop and implement service learning projects in additional Communication Studies courses. Coordinate implementation and assessment of projects with graduate students in Department of Educational Psychology, CSUN.
Fall 2001	Continue service learning projects based on input from assessments. Articulate a replicable, nation-wide model to guide schools in creating environments where hate and hate speech are not tolerated and where the benefits of a cultural diverse community are actively fostered.
Spring 2002	Introduce model in additional school community. Assessment conducted by outside evaluators.

Reading Responses

1. Although funding organizations may supply very specific requirements for proposals, the sections in this proposal are fairly standard components. What is the function of each of the eight sections in the proposal? How do these sections support the purpose of the proposal as a whole?
2. Based on the tone and approach of the proposal, how would you characterize the expectations of the readers who will evaluate the proposal and decide whether to fund it?
3. Which arguments in the proposal seem most or least compelling to you? Why?

Writing Activities

1. Imagine that you work for a nonprofit group. Write a letter to the partners that applied for this grant. Congratulate them, clearly explaining why your organization has awarded funding to them.
2. Investigate the demographics or population characteristics of the local community around your campus. Look for facts and statistics like those presented in "The Community," the second section of the CSUN proposal. You might turn to county or school-district data, federal census data available online, local library resources, local newspaper profiles of the community, or Web sites such as http://library.csun.edu/mfinley/zip-stats.html, which explains how to locate resources by zip code. Based on your demographic research, write a description of the community that concentrates on identifying a major community strength, problem, or both. Include selected data that supports your description.
3. Write a portion of your own academic grant application. Propose a worthwhile project (real or imagined) on behalf of a campus organization or partnership. First, write an introduction that identifies your project and the organization or partnership making the application (see CSUN section 1). Next, using the CSUN proposal as a guide, write an additional section that would support your application, such as *one* of the following:
    a. a community description, including facts about the local or campus population and situation, that explains the compelling need for your project (see CSUN, "The Community")
    b. a description of your academic institution and group, establishing your group's credibility and its ability to carry out the project (see CSUN, "California State University, Northridge")
    c. a goals statement (see CSUN, "Pilot Partnership Goals") that explains what you'd like to accomplish
    d. a time line that identifies what your project would do during a set period of time (such as several months, one semester, or one year) (see CSUN, "Timeline")

Community Links

Compare and contrast the CSUN grant proposal from the academic community with one of the other proposals in this book such as those by the Cornell Players Foundation (pp. 555–559), or the National Fund for the United States Botanic Garden (pp. 559–565). Consider the two proposals you select, identifying similar or different purposes, goals, factors, and activities. How might you account for these similarities or differences?

Graduate School Application Essay
STATEMENT OF PURPOSE
Melanie Dedecker, Student Writer

◆

Early in her senior year, Melanie Dedecker compared graduate programs in anthropology, visited their Web sites, and examined application requirements. She developed a list of her accomplishments at Cornell College in Iowa, talked with others about how to organize her applications, and then worked on a general statement of purpose—an essay explaining why she wanted to attend graduate school in anthropology. One version of that essay appears here. As she prepared each specific application, she added particulars about her interest in that program. Melanie was accepted by one of the top graduate programs in anthropology.

1 My passion for Anthropology is a result of my fascination with the mysteries and puzzles of the past. For me, the past is the path to enlightenment, a way to understand our own behavior, our own culture; the past is relevant both to the present and to the future. I now hope to fulfill this passion by pursuing my interests through graduate study and by making Anthropology my career.

2 More specifically, I intend to pursue a concentration in Archaeology because Archaeology provides me with the opportunity to satisfy both my curiosity about the past and my passion for examining human behavior and culture. At the same time, Archaeology is interdisciplinary, incorporating the natural sciences, the social sciences, and the humanities. This interdisciplinary approach not only is necessary to the study of culture but also is satisfying to my interdisciplinary interests, deepening my dedication to Archaeology.

3 Through Cornell College's unique academic system (One Course at a Time), I have pursued my interdisciplinary interests during my undergraduate studies, choosing to major both in Classical Studies and in Archaeology. As a Classical Studies major, I have developed language skills as well as being constantly involved in the study of ancient culture. My extensive study of both Latin and ancient Greek at Cornell College, as well as my immersion in Turkish during my Semester in Turkey (Fall 2002) and my coursework in Japanese throughout high school, has allowed me to develop a platform and

methodology for the rapid and successful acquisition of new languages. These skills will be necessary to pursue my interests in the American Southwest, as I will not only need to learn Spanish, but perhaps also one or more Native American languages.

4   My undergraduate interests in the Ancient Mediterranean have focused on human perception of the world, especially in terms of religion, ideology, and the creation of social identities. In particular, I conducted an independent study during Spring 2002 (junior year) comparing various Greco-Roman mystery cults and the Kachina Cult of the Pueblo Indians. I was interested in two things: defining what exactly a mystery cult is based on structure, ceremonies, and social functions and then, based on these factors, determining whether the Kachina Cult could be considered a mystery cult.

5   As a result of my research, I completed a paper entitled "Defining Mystery Cults: An Examination of Greco-Roman Mystery Cults and the Kachina Cult," which I presented at Cornell College's Student Symposium in April 2002. I learned that mystery cults specifically functioned as agents to create social identity and group unity, albeit among select groups, during periods of intense social stress. Since my presentation, I have become even more interested in this phenomenon, especially in terms of how group identity, specifically gender identity, is created and understood. Through graduate study, I plan to apply these interests to the archaeology of the American Southwest, especially through continued examination of religion and agency.

6   More specifically, I intend to examine the religious ideology of the American Southwest, beginning with the Kachina Cult, in order to understand what effect it had on social structure. The Kachina Cult developed during a period of intense social stress, resulting in a complete reorganization of Pueblo settlement patterns (and the adoption of the new religion). I want to investigate the significant changes in the social organization of these cultures that must have accompanied these dramatic changes. Specific issues include the role of agency, both individual and group oriented, in the appearance and continuation of the Kachina Cult; the effect of the acceptance of the Kachina Cult on social relations, particularly gender relations and roles; and the way the answers to these questions are recorded in the archaeological record, especially because the change in the study of the Pueblo ideology with the appearance of the Kachina Cult involves cognitive aspects of culture.

7   While my studies in Classics have supplied me with the necessary skills for text interpretation and the study of cognitive aspects of culture, I have also developed archaeology skills as an interdepartmental Archaeology major. Although Cornell has a small and culturally oriented Anthropology department, I chose to pursue archaeology on my own and through Cornell's open academic policy. During the summer after my freshman year (2000), I participated in a field school through the University of Nevada at Las Vegas, which focused on both the Geoarchaeology and the Pleistocene Archaeology of the Goshute Valley in northwestern Nevada. Through this experience, I not only developed field skills, including learning how to analyze landscapes, survey, identify sites and artifacts, and plan and physically excavate, but I also became convinced that I wanted to pursue archaeology.

8 As a junior, I worked with the Office of the State Archaeologist (OSA) in Iowa City, Iowa, to design an internship that would introduce me to the non-field techniques and analysis associated with archaeology. During my three-week internship, I participated in various activities ranging from sorting and cataloguing artifacts to assisting a graduate student in the preliminary stylistic identification of pottery shards from a prehistoric Iowa site. I also conducted my own mini-research project using the OSA's comparative lithic collection to try and identify a collection of lithics that had been donated to the Cornell College Geology Department. My favorite part of the internship, however, was working with the Public Archaeologist to organize time capsules from various periods of Iowa prehistory to use as teaching agents for elementary school students.

9 In terms of future career goals, I definitely intend to pursue a research-based career. An incredible amount of information needs to be explored, and I continuously aspire to find and analyze that information. However, I believe that archaeology can make a significant and unique contribution to today's society. Accordingly, I want to work in an environment in which I have the ability to bring archaeology to the public. At the same time, as a result of my personal college experience, I also desire to bring archaeology to small liberal arts schools. My involvement working with other students at Cornell as Anthropology Interest Group president and cataloging the Anthropology collection in the library's government documents also introduced me to the satisfaction that encouraging interest in Anthropology and helping the discipline expand can bring.

10 Of all fields, Anthropology willingly examines all aspects of human culture and therefore allows the most holistic study, understanding, and application of human behavior. My interest in Anthropology is not simply a hobby; it is a passion that I intend to turn into a career I will enjoy. I believe that the university's Anthropology Department offers a wonderful opportunity for me to pursue my research interests successfully. I hope to continue my studies through your program.

Reading Responses

1. What is the main idea that Melanie develops in her essay?
2. What impression of herself does Melanie convey? How does she create this impression?
3. How does Melanie use supporting detail in her essay? Which details do you find most effective?

Writing Activities

1. Imagine that a friend or relative is planning to apply to a graduate program. Write an e-mail message or a letter to this person, offering advice on how to write an application essay that explains why he or she should be admitted.
2. Imagine that you are a member of the admissions committee in the anthropology department to which Melanie applied. Write her a letter of acceptance that explains why her essay persuaded you to admit her.

3. Write an application essay for a semester abroad, an internship, a special academic program, a graduate program, or some other academic opportunity. Use your essay to show why you should be accepted for that opportunity.

Community Links

Read Leo Stoscheck's college application essay (pp. 94–95) and some of the other letters and appeals in this book. In what ways are one or two of them similar to or different from Melanie's statement of purpose? How does each appeal to its readers?

Academic Address

IN PRAISE OF THE RESEARCH UNIVERSITY: REMARKS AT THE BRANDEIS COMMENCEMENT, MAY 1996, SCHOOL OF SCIENCE CEREMONIES

Harry Mairson

◆

Harry Mairson, a professor of computer science at Brandeis, gave this speech in May 1996 at the commencement ceremony for students in the School of Science. Besides congratulating members of the class of 1996, he also reflects on the values and goals of higher education in this address, now posted on the Web.

1   I have been an undergraduate, graduate student, postdoctoral fellow, and faculty member at several universities both in the United States and in Europe. During that time, I've sat through more than my share of commencement speeches. Academic addresses can be longwinded, pompous and boring, and when they were, I would fidget in my seat, doodle in programs, read stuff I'd sneaked in under my gown, dream of standing up and yelling vile oaths, and, more often than not, fantasize about giving an equally stultifying address of my own.

2   *But before I do,* I would like to congratulate and give my best wishes to the class of 1996. You may not realize it, but you did the most difficult, challenging, and honest work of anyone in the university. Really. You learned new things, and made your brains work in new ways. Not everyone at the university is so nobly and gainfully employed.

3   You memorized and learned how to use dozens of complex reactions in organic chemistry—I have nostalgic memories of my freshman roommate, now a physics professor at Columbia, composing obscene doggerels to commit these reactions to memory. You learned about programming algorithms using recursively defined procedures—first you curse, and then you recurse. You learned

how to do mathematical proofs, and how to multiply matrices and compute cross products.

4   Or you didn't learn all these things. Well, you students didn't venture out into this risky unknown, fraught with the danger of showing how ignorant you were precisely when everybody was watching, just out of youth and curiosity. You *have* to—we *make* you—otherwise you can't graduate.

5   This brings me to the first serious thing I want to say today. What do undergraduates get out of the *research* university? Among many things, *you get to be taught by faculty who, in principle, are doing the same thing that you are doing.* How can a faculty member ask an undergraduate to take the risk in learning new things without doing so himself? And since students sometimes fail to learn, faculty have to be willing to run the risk of their own similar failure.

6   Unfortunately, there are many reasons why faculty do not do research, even at a research university. It is not easy to find something new to do—saying something new about Shakespeare takes ingenuity and nerve. There are personal demands on time and energy—a spouse, children—that may not have existed earlier in one's career. There is the politics of the job—hustling grant proposals, editorial and committee work, and the like. There are impediments of turf: like gang warfare, research areas are staked out by colleagues whose wrath you risk inciting upon entering their territory, as you challenge their prominence and threaten their grant support. There are tenured faculty who lose interest in the work, but not in the perquisites, and a university job becomes a prestigious backdrop or financial foundation for other ambitions. There is the seduction of teaching. There is burnout: we are not all, to paraphrase Newton, in the prime of our age for invention.

7   Finally, there is the risk of failure: if you set your sights on something really difficult, you run the risk of screwing up and looking dumb. It is unprofessional, it is shameful, and it hurts: professors are not supposed to look dumb. The anxiety is justifiable. In graduate school, I once cleaned my kitchen floor with a toothbrush rather than face up to my dissertation research. Yet the risk of looking dumb is exactly the risk we ask students to take.

8   Not that all research is scary, and like a good portfolio manager, you learn to control risk. A balance needs to be struck between barely incremental *research* for things that you, or someone else, already found, and the maddening vertigo of trying something so new that you haven't the foggiest idea what to do. But a research life—and an academic life—without risk is not worth the effort, and our language abounds with sayings to that effect: a man's reach should exceed his grasp, or what's a heaven for?

9   As a professor, if you are going to talk the talk, you have got to walk the walk. Research is just like taking classes, except you make up the syllabus yourself, and the answers to even numbered problems aren't in the back of the book. As a teacher, one of my responsibilities is to make students realize that their frustration over not understanding and sometimes failing is our jointly suffered occupational hazard. Furthermore, in confronting this frustration, these students confront the limits of the potential and creativity that define them as educated men and women. This, for me, was the moral of Peter Shaffer's *Amadeus:* for those of us who bear a greater resemblance to Salieri, what can you do with your life that is worthwhile if you are not Mozart?

10   Teachers who actively participate in research careers have a responsibility to communicate the real excitement of intellectual creation and the birth of new ideas. Some people at this university think that we would be better off as a college, without a research function. Arguments have been made—in the **Brandeis Review,** even—that there isn't any interesting or significant research left to be done, but only to throw mud, flowers, or weeds in the crevices of the walls of knowledge. To paraphrase the Sanskritist Richard Gombrich, rarely—mercifully rarely—must I respond to opinions so profoundly orthogonal to my own that truth cannot be reconciled with charity or honesty with politeness. People who don't believe in the research enterprise ought to visit the Museum of Fine Arts in Boston, where there is an exhibit of early man-made flints. Apparently, the flint makers from 60,000 years ago knew almost everything there was to know about sharpness, because 30,000 years later, the flints were only a little sharper! To live a university life as if, similarly, everything of significance has already been thought of, strikes me as—well, Neanderthal.

11   The walls of ignorance still dwarf the walls of knowledge: where else but at a university will they get a reasoned assault? Not all aspects of the assault are monumental and fascinating: a rock climber learns to put one hand in front of another, and so should a researcher. Faculty who so retreat from the research enterprise, whether out of the fear of commitment or the fear of rejection that is inherent in failure, make me recall a bachelor friend of my father's, who used to joke that he remained single because the only woman he ever loved married someone else—the woman in question turned out to be Princess Grace of Monaco.

12   Classroom dissemination of an artificial or virtual conception of research by those who don't do it, rather than the real thing founded on individual experience, reminds me—to speak personally—of the difference between artificial insemination and insemination: one of them is profoundly unsatisfying. Undergraduates too often forget that knowledge is not a bunch of equations and dates and who invaded where when, but rather the consequences of real people and real passions. (Go see the new movie version of *Richard III* if you want to know what I mean.) As a teacher of theoretical computer science, for example, I want students to realize that the theorems they study are not only interesting, and occasionally fun, but also the results of real people who sweated over the ideas as much as they sweated over their first date.

13   The romantic and even sexual allusions I have made are deliberate, because I think research is like that. In the complete commitment to solving a research problem, there is a binding of the heart and soul that is not unlike an infatuation. As I have asked myself in these moments, am I five minutes away from the solution, or five weeks, or five years, or never? Is it not unlike the desperate lover on a date who can only think, are we going to kiss tonight? And to find the sublime answer to our desire!—a mental connection, a union with our other creative and spiritual half. An undergraduate I advised said it well in a fellowship essay: "Money and power are ephemeral, as you can gain them and lose them, but when you prove a theorem, it is yours forever."

14   Now if research is indeed the pursuit of true love, why would anyone want to teach? Let me mention one reason that is most relevant to the pursuit of research. In any research enterprise, you want to develop analytic tools and techniques that get to the heart of the matter, and shuck off the irrelevant and the

merely technical—even the Neanderthals knew that success depended on having the sharpest tools available. In this spirit, the famous Hungarian mathematician Paul Erdos has spoken of a divine book of knowledge that records the most perfect, revealing, elegant proof of every theorem, and suggested that the challenge to every mathematician is to find out what is in that book. Part of my job is to teach that elegance of thought.

15   In the introduction to the famous *Feynman Lectures on Physics*, its editors emphasize the sheer challenge Richard Feynman enjoyed in reformulating complex ideas of physics so that they could be presented to students—the standard by which he measured whether something was really understood. They wrote:

> *Feynman was once asked by a Caltech faculty member to explain why spin 1/2 particles obey Fermi-Dirac statistics. He gauged his audience perfectly and said, "I'll prepare a freshman lecture on it." But a few days later he returned and said, "You know, I couldn't do it. I couldn't reduce it to the freshman level. That means we really don't understand it."*

16   Anyone who thinks that excellence in teaching and excellence in research are mutually exclusive is wrong. If the challenge to do both well is indeed a Gordian knot, remember how Alexander the Great resolved the difficulty—sharp tools.

17   I have tried to describe an ideal synergy between teaching and research, but I haven't described how it impacts the personal relationship between student and teacher. This is the last subject I'd like to comment on today. When I told my Ph.D. advisor that I aspired to be friends with my students, he told me that they would be better off with a dog. At the time, I found his comment to be antisocial and misanthropic. Twelve years later, I think I understand better.

18   Because we are all people, it is inevitable that a human fraternity can grow between faculty and students. But you cannot be friends with your teachers any more than you can be friends with your parents. I once heard a project presentation by a Brandeis undergraduate who concluded with an acknowledgement to his faculty mentor—we don't say "faculty patron" because *patronage* sounds political and bad, while *mentoring* sounds nurturing and good. The student said, "Professor S. was my friend." I could barely keep myself from shouting, "well, then, if he's your friend, why don't you call him Bob, or Chuck, or Dave?" Since when do we call our friends "Professor"? Remember that the organization of a modern university is medieval, right down to the academic regalia worn at commencement. It is hierarchical, with its own version of serfs, knights, barons, and kings. Friendship does not transcend that hierarchy easily.

19   You do not get grades or letters of recommendation from friends, nor do you pay close to $30,000 a year to spend time with them—for that kind of money, you could buy a Mazda Miata, take a wonderful vacation, throw a great party for your friends, and still have a fair pocket of change left over.

20   Going to college may serve all sorts of social functions that, in my mind, have nothing to do with its real goal. It may be a great socializing experience—some years ago, a colleague tried to convince me that the point of college is, most importantly, to get away from home and have "relationships." (Unsocialized as I am, I responded that I thought it was about problem sets.)

In moments of despair, I've worried that college is a modern-day form of papal indulgence or bourgeois nobility for sale, where you pay a small fortune to advance in society and escape its hell. Or that it's a kind of intellectual olestra—that new cooking oil with no calories—which makes you *feel* like you're learning effortlessly, and only later do you find how it has depleted your opportunity.

21   But I truly believe that college is none of these things—college isn't summer camp, Disney, or MTV. It's work—how else are we going to make anything of ourselves? That's why the faculty, and teaching assistants, and labs, and libraries—and equally important, the absence of most all other responsibilities—are there. A professor I had in graduate school once told me, in a personal aphorism, how to do research: find a comfortable chair, a nice pen, inviting paper, a quiet room—now, he said, *think real hard.* The university provided *you* with that quiet room—metaphorically speaking, so forget about the loud stereo next door—where you could do your own very hard thinking. In years ahead, when your kids are yapping at you, or your boss is breathing down your neck, or your company is "restructuring," or your Ph.D. advisor has you chained to a project that helps build his pyramid, but doesn't do much for your learning experience, that quiet room will be a lot harder to find.

22   The relationship between professor and student exists, above all, to do the hard work that we celebrate at Commencement. To replace the difficult and often frustrating labor of learning with *merely* a personal relationship does a great disservice to both parties. A friend of mine, who is a physician, once said that the first responsibility of a doctor is to love your patients. The first responsibility of a professor is to love your students, but that love is not manifested in hugs, or bull sessions, or lunches at the faculty club, or false senses of intellectual success. It's manifested in the clear demonstration of what is known, and in the inspiration to confront the unknown.

23   Because I love jokes, I will conclude with one that is very appropriate for today's celebration. A young college graduate is filling out a job application. When asked to list his strengths, he writes, "I am a hard worker, I am mature, I pick up new things easily, I am self-motivated, I like working with others, I am a good listener, I accept criticism, . . ." and so on and so forth. When asked to list his weaknesses, he only writes, "Well, sometimes I am not all of those things." During your undergraduate years at Brandeis, I hope you got to confront those limits to your abilities. I hope you got to find out that you were "not all of those things." It's inevitable, it's part of being human. How you learn to deal with that inevitability will tell what kind of person you become. Thank you, and congratulations again to all of you.

 Reading Responses

1. Although commencement ceremonies draw many people—parents, other relatives, family friends, university administrators, faculty, and students—Mairson speaks primarily to students. How does he indicate, directly and indirectly, that students are his primary audience? How does he try to engage his student listeners?

2. How does Mairson adjust his word choice and tone to suit the event at which he speaks? Point out specific wording that contributes to Mairson's tone and level of formality.
3. What is Mairson's main point? What are the implications of that point for the students in his audience?

Writing Activities

1. Write a short speech that you'd like to present to a group of people who are "commencing"—moving on to another stage or situation. Consider how the places where they've been will help shape their experiences in the places where they go. You might address those now graduating from your high school or elementary school, those concluding the season for a sport or other activity, those leaving one job for another, those moving from your home town, or others making a comparable shift.
2. Write a summary of Mairson's speech. State his main point and his supporting points in your own words, writing as clearly and succinctly as you can.
3. Using examples and information from Mairson's speech, write an essay that explains what Mairson considers the "real goal" of going to college.

Community Links

Compare or contrast Mairson's academic address to one of the civic addresses in this book such as President Bush's "Address to a Joint Session of Congress and the American People, September 20, 2001" (pp. 433–438) and Martin Luther King, Jr.'s "I Have a Dream" (pp. 439–442). Identify how and why the two speeches are similar or different, using examples from each.

Web Site
ONLINE WRITING LAB (OWL):
HTTP://OWL.ENGLISH.PURDUE.EDU
Purdue University

◆

The Purdue Online Writing Lab (OWL), established in 1993, is one of the most widely admired academic sources for online writing assistance. Many sites for academic writers supply links to this OWL, and many college faculty members recommend it to their students. Its home page, reprinted here, identifies what it offers to writers, in or out of the academic community.

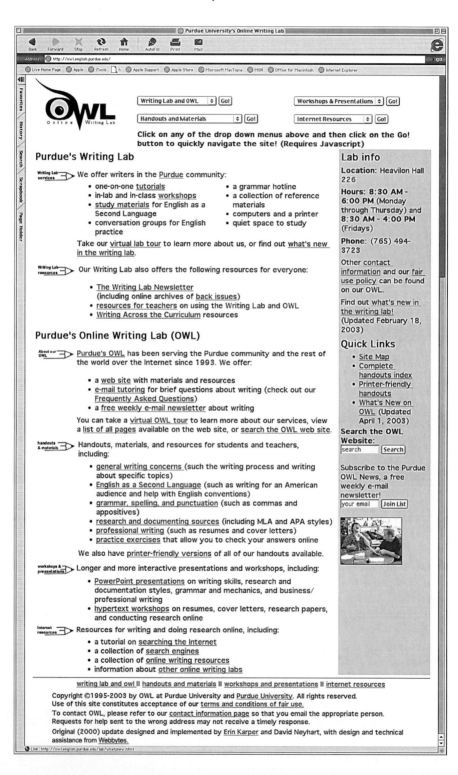

Reading Responses

1. What visitors does the Purdue OWL home page address? What might these visitors want or need to find?
2. How does the design and organization of the home page try to address the probable needs of visitors?
3. Examine carefully the short phrases and sentences used on the home page. What strategies have the site's writers used to make these statements easy to understand? What changes or improvements (if any) would you suggest?

Writing Activities

1. Visit the Purdue OWL online. Write a journal entry or personal account of your "journey" through the site. What did you find that might be useful for you personally? What surprises did you discover?
2. Visit your campus OWL, or follow one of the links supplied at the Purdue site. Write a brief analysis of the goals, organization, and content of that site.
3. Suppose that you are the student representative on a campus committee that will oversee the development of a special Web page for first-year students. Write a paragraph defining what you think this page should do. Then, outline a structure for the topics and links that you'd like the page to include.

Community Links

Compare and contrast the Purdue OWL home page with a work site such as Technical Standards (pp. 347–350) or a public site such as Smoke Free Movies (pp. 566–567) or College Drinking (pp. 568–571). (For this comparison, you may use the print versions in the book or visit the sites on the Web.) Which of the features of the Purdue home page particularly reflect its goals as an academic resource? Which features of the other site reflect its community goals? Which features of both sites are common characteristics of many Web sites?

Part 2

The Work Community

Introduction: Reading and Writing in the Work Community

A. Community Voices
B. Community Perspectives and Issues
C. Community Ethics
D. Texts and Documents from the Work Community

Introduction: Reading and Writing in the Work Community

The work community focuses on an organization's mission, whether it is to sell a product or to provide a service. In this general community, participants request information, provide advice, analyze options, propose alternatives, recommend action, solve problems, and promote the organization and its products or services. They are motivated by loyalty to the organization, confidence in its product or service, or the need for employment and a paycheck. Supervisors and staff communicate among themselves, with others in the organizational hierarchy, and with outside contractors, suppliers, government agencies, professional colleagues, and existing or prospective clients and customers. This community conveys messages about products, services, and internal operations in many ways: through mission statements, policies, guidelines and directions for employees, reports, internal memos, letters exchanged with outsiders, directions for customers, verbal presentations at meetings, and promotional materials in multiple media.

As you enter the work community as an employee or an intern, you listen, read, observe, and meet with others to learn about the values, culture, expectations of employees, hierarchical structures, collaborative work arrangements, and approaches to competition typical of an organization in this community. As you advance within an organization or move elsewhere for greater opportunity, you will become increasingly adept at understanding certain sectors of the workplace—the jobs available, the tasks accomplished, the skills needed, and the types of communication routinely conducted.

Despite the great variety of work environments, most workplace readers expect clear, concise communication. Most employees are busy, especially as they advance within an organization. They expect written materials to concentrate efficiently on the task, problem, or event that triggers communication. Readers respect pertinent information based on solid research and on professional advice from recognized experts and authorities. As they read, they expect to grasp the issue or problem, weigh clear alternatives, and identify what might be done. They often want to get right to the problem and thus appreciate documents organized to summarize or explain major priorities first, followed by additional discussion, substantiating evidence, cost or project analyses, marketing and sales projections, or other supporting material. Despite common concerns with efficiency, the wise allocation of time and money, this community expends both to create strong bonds among valued employees or to gain and retain loyal customers.

Workplace writers strive to satisfy readers' expectations by identifying problems clearly, organizing materials efficiently, and supporting recommendations with pertinent evidence. They show their respect for the company hierarchy and the organizational culture by following expected procedures and using standard forms. They consider the customary concerns of the organization, group, or individual addressed. At the same time, they may seek innovative options—whether developing, promoting, delivering, or maintaining products and services.

Readings in the Work Community

The opening readings for this community introduce its goals, issues, and expectations. Four community voices speak first, introducing both the low and high ends of the workplace, the sweatshops where Liu works, the low-paid jobs Ehrenreich investigates, the entrepreneurial domain of Woody's Chicago-Style hot dog carts, and the corporate world of retail giant Wal-Mart. Next come half a dozen perspectives on the work community. Ulrich makes recommendations about creating community, while Lutz (who turned around Chrysler) advocates attention to detail. Next, Eisenberg explores job trends, and Bolman and Deal offer advice on cultural sleuthing on the job. Then Rifkin presents the new cultural, rather than industrial, capitalism, and Helgesen analyzes how changes in the workplace contribute to the conversion of life and leisure to work. Ethical questions in the workplace concern Zielinski, who examines copyright violations, and Alford, who studies whistle-blowers.

Finally an assortment of workplace texts and documents illustrates how this community efficiently communicates. The section begins with jobs—announcements, résumés, job-hunting advice that opens the door to employment, and an organizational welcome to employees. It turns next to professional resources that help people develop their expertise and stay informed about current issues. Then assorted materials illustrate how organizations communicate, internally and externally, through forms as varied as memos, letters, reviews, and reports. Finally instructions, organizational promotions, advertisements, and Web sites further illustrate workplace outreach to existing or prospective clients and customers.

Community Voices

THE STORY OF A GARMENT WORKER

Lisa Liu, as told to David Bacon

◆

Lisa Liu's story appeared in Dollars & Sense *as part of a special issue devoted to work situations faced by women. David Bacon, a journalist and a former union organizer, explains at the beginning of the article that he originally interviewed Liu for a radio series that delved into sweatshops, factories, or plants with unhealthy environments where workers were forced to accept poor pay and long work days.*

Lisa Liu is a garment worker in Oakland, California. She came to the U.S. from China over a decade ago, but found that while the U.S. had fewer restrictions on workers in some ways, life as a worker was much less secure than she had expected. She became active in efforts to tell other San Francisco-area garment workers about their rights, through an Oakland-based community organization, Asian Immigrant Women Advocates. I interviewed her as part of an in-depth series of radio programs investigating life in sweatshops, in the U.S. and around the world, for KPFA radio.
—David Bacon

1 I'm a seamstress in a factory with twelve other people. We sew children's clothes—shirts and dresses. I've worked in the garment industry here for twelve years, and at the factory where I am now for over a year.

2 In our factory we have to work ten hours a day, six to seven days a week. The contractor doesn't pay us any benefits—no health insurance or vacations. While we get a half-hour for lunch, there are no other paid breaks in our shift.

3 We get paid by the piece, and count up the pieces to see what we make. If we work faster we get paid more. But if the work is difficult and the manufacturer gives the contractor a low price, then what we get drops so low maybe we'll get forty dollars a day. The government says the minimum wage is $5.75, but I don't think that by the piece we can reach $5.75 an hour a lot of the time.

4 When we hurt from the work we often just feel it's because of our age. People don't know that over the years their working posture can cause lots of pain. We just take it for granted, and in any case there's no insurance to pay for anything different. We just wait for the pain to go away.

5 That's why we organize the women together and have them speak out their problems at each of the garment shops. If we stop being silent about these

things, we can demand justice. We can get paid hourly and bring better working conditions to the workers.

6   Our idea is to tell them how to fight for their rights and explain what rights they have. Everyone should know more about the laws. We let them know about the minimum wage and that there should be breaks after four hours of work. We organize classes to teach women that we can be hurt from work. And we've opened up a worker's clinic to provide medical treatment and diagnosis. We do this work with the help of Asian Immigrant Women Advocates here in Chinatown.

7   We can't actually speak to the manufacturers whose clothes we're sewing because they don't come down to the shops to listen to the workers. So when we have a problem it's difficult to bring it to them. Still, we've had campaigns where we got the manufacturer to pay back-wages to the workers after the contractor closed without paying them. We got a hotline then, for workers to complain directly to the manufacturers. That solved some problems. The fire doors in those shops aren't blocked anymore, and the hygiene is better.

8   But it's not easy for women in our situation, and many are scared. Because they only work in the Chinese community, they're afraid their names will become known to the community and the bosses will not hire them. That's why we try to do things together. There's really no other place for us to go. Most of us don't have the training or the skills to work in other industries. We mostly speak just one language, usually Cantonese, and often just the dialect Toishanese.

9   When I first came to the United States I needed a lot of time to work to stabilize myself. So after seven years that's why I'm only now having my first baby. We don't have any health insurance and we have to pay the bill out of our own pockets. Health insurance is very expensive in the United States. We can't afford it. In the garment industry here they do not have health insurance for the workers.

10   Before I came here, my experience in China was that life was very strict. I heard that in America you have a lot of freedom, and I wanted to breathe the air of that freedom. But when I came here I realized the reality was very different from what I had been dreaming, because my idea of freedom was very abstract. I thought that freedom was being able to choose the place where you work. If you don't like one place, you can go work in another. In China you cannot do this. When you get assigned to a post, you have to work at that post.

11   Since I've come to the United States, I feel like I cannot get into the mainstream. There's a gap, like I don't know the background of American history and the laws. And I don't speak English. So I can only live within Chinatown and the Chinese community and feel scared. I cannot find a good job, so I have to work the low-income work. So I learned to compare life here and in China in a different way.

12   Many people say life here is very free. But for us, it's a lot of pressure. You have to pay rent, living costs so much money, you have all kinds of insurance—car insurance, health insurance, life insurance—that you can't afford. With all that kind of pressure, sometimes I feel I cannot breathe.

13   Everywhere you go you just find low pay. All the shops pay by the piece, and they have very strict rules. You can not go to the bathroom unless it's lunch time. Some places they put up a sign that says, "Don't talk while you work." You're not allowed to listen to the radio.

14   Wherever you go, in all the garment factories, the conditions and the prices are almost the same. The boss says, "I cannot raise the price for you and if you complain any more, then just take a break tomorrow—don't come to work." So even though I can go from one job to another, where's the freedom?

Reading Responses

1. Do you think that the factory where Liu works qualifies as a sweatshop? Explain your view.
2. What did Liu expect when she came to the United States? How did reality measure up to her expectations?
3. In what ways is Liu trying to change the working conditions in the garment factories? Based on Bacon's interview, what other changes do you think that she would be likely to favor?

Writing Activities

1. Based on Liu's account, write a paragraph summing up the worst aspect of her job. (First reach a conclusion about which aspect you consider the worst, and then support that conclusion with information from the article.)
2. Write a first-person account of your experience with a difficult job.
3. Interview someone whose job is *not* the one you dream of finding once you complete your degree. The job might have low pay, difficult work, or undesirable conditions. Prepare interview questions in advance, considering what you'd like to learn about the job, the working conditions, the worker's view of the job, and any effort or opportunity to change the conditions or leave the job. Write your interview, weaving together direct quotations (accurately recorded in your notes), paraphrases in your own words, and your own observations.

Community Links

Compare one or two other interviews with Bacon's presentation of Liu's story. You might consider Rose's "Lilia" (pp. 19–21), Terkel's interview with Bill Talcott (pp. 357–361), or another reading that includes an interview. Examine the interviews to discover how they are similar or different, how they bring the person interviewed to life, or how they convey larger issues as well.

EVALUATION
Barbara Ehrenreich

This reading is part of the conclusion of Barbara Ehrenreich's Nickle and Dimed: On (Not) Getting By in America, *an account of her personal exploration of the low-wage workplace. As a journalist, Ehrenreich investigated this end of America's work world just as welfare regulations were changing to move many people from welfare to work. In various parts of the country, she took half a dozen jobs, such as cleaning houses, serving at a restaurant, and caring for residents in a nursing home. During this time, she recorded her work experiences and efforts to earn enough to cover basic living expenses. In this selection, she evaluates the experience and her success.*

1. How did I do as a low-wage worker? If I may begin with a brief round of applause: I didn't do half bad at the work itself, and I claim this as a considerable achievement. You might think that unskilled jobs would be a snap for someone who holds a Ph.D. and whose normal line of work requires learning entirely new things every couple of weeks. Not so. The first thing I discovered is that no job, no matter how lowly, is truly "unskilled." Every one of the six jobs I entered into in the course of this project required concentration, and most demanded that I master new terms, new tools, and new skills—from placing orders on restaurant computers to wielding the backpack vacuum cleaner. None of these things came as easily to me as I would have liked; no one ever said, "Wow, you're fast!" or "Can you believe she just started?" Whatever my accomplishments in the rest of my life, in the low-wage work world I was a person of average ability—capable of learning the job and also capable of screwing up.

2. I did have my moments of glory. There were days at The Maids when I got my own tasks finished fast enough that I was able to lighten the load on others, and I feel good about that. There was my breakthrough at Wal-Mart, where I truly believe that, if I'd been able to keep my mouth shut, I would have progressed in a year or two to a wage of $7.50 or more an hour. And I'll bask for the rest of my life in the memory of that day at the Woodcrest when I fed the locked Alzheimer's ward all by myself, cleaned up afterward, and even managed to extract a few smiles from the vacant faces of my charges in the process.

3. It's not just the work that has to be learned in each situation. Each job presents a self-contained social world, with its own personalities, hierarchy, customs, and standards. Sometimes I was given scraps of sociological data to work with, such as "Watch out for so-and-so, he's a real asshole." More commonly it was left to me to figure out such essentials as who was in charge, who was good to work with, who could take a joke. Here years of travel probably stood me in good stead, although in my normal life I usually enter new situations in some respected, even attention-getting role like "guest lecturer" or "workshop leader." It's a lot harder, I found, to sort out a human microsystem when you're looking up at it from the bottom, and, of course, a lot more necessary to do so.

4   Standards are another tricky issue. To be "good to work with" yourself, you need to be fast and thorough, but not so fast and thorough that you end up making things tougher for everyone else. There was seldom any danger of my raising the bar, but at the Hearthside Annette once upbraided me for freshening up the display desserts: "They'll expect us all to start doing that!" So I desisted, just as I would have slowed down to an arthritic pace in any job, in the event that a manager showed up to do a time-and-motion study. Similarly, at Wal-Mart, a coworker once advised me that, although I had a lot to learn, it was also important not to "know too much," or at least never to reveal one's full abilities to management, because "the more they think you can do, the more they'll use you and abuse you." My mentors in these matters were not lazy; they just understood that there are few or no rewards for heroic performance. The trick lies in figuring out how to budget your energy so there'll be some left over for the next day.

5   And all of these jobs were physically demanding, some of them even damaging if performed month after month. Now, I am an unusually fit person, with years of weight lifting and aerobics behind me, but I learned something that no one ever mentioned in the gym: that a lot of what we experience as strength comes from knowing what to do with weakness. You feel it coming on halfway through a shift or later, and you can interpret it the normal way as a symptom of a kind of low-level illness, curable with immediate rest. Or you can interpret it another way, as a reminder of the hard work you've done so far and hence as evidence of how much you are still capable of doing—in which case the exhaustion becomes a kind of splint, holding you up. Obviously there are limits to this form of self-delusion, and I would have reached mine quickly enough if I'd had to go home from my various jobs to chase toddlers and pick up after a family, as so many women do. But the fact that I survived physically, that in a time period well into my fifties I never collapsed or needed time off to recuperate, is something I am inordinately proud of.

6   Furthermore, I displayed, or usually displayed, all those traits deemed essential to job readiness: punctuality, cleanliness, cheerfulness, obedience. These are the qualities that welfare-to-work job-training programs often seek to inculcate, though I suspect that most welfare recipients already possess them, or would if their child care and transportation problems were solved. I was simply following the rules I had laid down for myself at the beginning of the project and doing the best I could to hold each job. Don't take my word for it: supervisors sometimes told me I was doing well—"fine" or even "great." So all in all, with some demerits for screwups and gold stars for effort, I think it's fair to say that as a worker, a jobholder, I deserve a B or maybe B+.

7   But the real question is not how well I did at work but how well I did at life in general, which includes eating and having a place to stay. The fact that these are two separate questions needs to be underscored right away. In the rhetorical buildup to welfare reform, it was uniformly assumed that a job was the ticket out of poverty and that the only thing holding back welfare recipients was their reluctance to get out and get one. I got one and sometimes more than one, but my track record in the survival department is far less admirable than my performance as a jobholder. On small things I was thrifty enough; no

expenditures on "carousing," flashy clothes, or any of the other indulgences that are often smugly believed to undermine the budgets of the poor. True, the $30 slacks in Key West and the $20 belt in Minneapolis were extravagances; I now know I could have done better at the Salvation Army or even at Wal-Mart. Food, though, I pretty much got down to a science: lots of chopped meat, beans, cheese, and noodles when I had a kitchen to cook in; otherwise, fast food, which I was able to keep down to about $9 a day. But let's look at the record.

8   In Key West, I earned $1,039 in one month and spent $517 on food, gas, toiletries, laundry, phone, and utilities. Rent was the deal breaker. If I had remained in my $500 efficiency, I would have been able to pay the rent and have $22 left over (which is still $78 less than the cash I had in my pocket at the start of the month). This in itself would have been a dicey situation if I had attempted to continue for a few more months, because sooner or later I would have had to spend something on medical and dental care or drugs other than ibuprofen. But my move to the trailer park—for the purpose, you will recall, of taking a second job—made me responsible for $625 a month in rent alone, utilities not included. Here I might have economized by giving up the car and buying a used bike (for about $50) or walking to work. Still, two jobs, or at least a job and a half, would be a necessity, and I had learned that I could not do two physically demanding jobs in the same day, at least not at any acceptable standard of performance.

9   In Portland, Maine, I came closest to achieving a decent fit between income and expenses, but only because I worked seven days a week. Between my two jobs, I was earning approximately $300 a week after taxes and paying $480 a month in rent, or a manageable 40 percent of my earnings. It helped, too, that gas and electricity were included in my rent and that I got two or three free meals each weekend at the nursing home. But I was there at the beginning of the off-season. If I had stayed until June 2000 I would have faced the Blue Haven's summer rent of $390 a week, which would of course have been out of the question. So to survive year-round, I would have had to save enough, in the months between August 1999 and May 2000, to accumulate the first month's rent and deposit on an actual apartment. I think I could have done this—saved $800 to $1,000—at least if no car trouble or illness interfered with my budget. I am not sure, however, that I could have maintained the seven-day-a-week regimen month after month or eluded the kinds of injuries that afflicted my fellow workers in the housecleaning business. [. . .]

10 Something is wrong, very wrong, when a single person in good health, a person who in addition possesses a working car, can barely support herself by the sweat of her brow. You don't need a degree in economics to see that wages are too low and rents too high. [. . .]

11 You would have to read a great many newspapers very carefully, cover to cover, to see the signs of distress. You would find, for example, that in 1999 Massachusetts food pantries reported a 72 percent increase in the demand for their services over the previous year, that Texas food banks were "scrounging" for food, despite donations at or above 1998 levels, as were those in Atlanta.[1] You might learn that in San Diego the Catholic Church could no longer, as of

January 2000, accept homeless families at its shelter, which happens to be the city's largest, because it was already operating at twice its normal capacity.[2] You would come across news of a study showing that the percentage of Wisconsin food-stamp families in "extreme poverty"—defined as less than 50 percent of the federal poverty line—has tripled in the last decade to more than 30 percent.[3] You might discover that, nationwide, America's food banks are experiencing "a torrent of need which [they] cannot meet" and that, according to a survey conducted by the U.S. Conference of Mayors, 67 percent of the adults requesting emergency food aid are people with jobs.[4]

12   One reason nobody bothers to pull all these stories together and announce a widespread state of emergency may be that Americans of the newspaper-reading professional middle class are used to thinking of poverty as a consequence of unemployment. During the heyday of downsizing in the Reagan years, it very often was, and it still is for many inner-city residents who have no way of getting to the proliferating entry-level jobs on urban peripheries. When unemployment causes poverty, we know how to state the problem—typically, "the economy isn't growing fast enough"—and we know what the traditional liberal solution is—"full employment." But when we have full or nearly full employment, when jobs are available to any job seeker who can get to them, then the problem goes deeper and begins to cut into that web of expectations that make up the "social contract." According to a recent poll conducted by Jobs for the Future, a Boston-based employment research firm, 94 percent of Americans agree that "people who work full-time should be able to earn enough to keep their families out of poverty.[5] I grew up hearing over and over, to the point of tedium, that "hard work" was the secret of success: "Work hard and you'll get ahead" or "It's hard work that got us where we are." No one ever said that you could work hard—harder even than you ever thought possible—and still find yourself sinking ever deeper into poverty and debt.

13   When poor single mothers had the option of remaining out of the labor force on welfare, the middle and upper middle class tended to view them with a certain impatience, if not disgust. The welfare poor were excoriated for their laziness, their persistence in reproducing in unfavorable circumstances, their presumed addictions, and above all for their "dependency." Here they were, content to live off "government handouts" instead of seeking "self-sufficiency," like everyone else, through a job. They needed to get their act together, learn how to wind an alarm clock, get out there and get to work. But now that government has largely withdrawn its "handouts," now that the overwhelming majority of the poor are out there toiling in Wal-Mart or Wendy's—well, what are we to think of them? Disapproval and condescension no longer apply, so what outlook makes sense?

14   Guilt, you may be thinking warily. Isn't that what we're supposed to feel? But guilt doesn't go anywhere near far enough; the appropriate emotion is shame—shame at our *own* dependency, in this case, on the underpaid labor of others. When someone works for less pay than she can live on—when, for example, she goes hungry so that you can eat more cheaply and conveniently—then she has made a great sacrifice for you, she has made you a gift of some part of her abilities, her health, and her life. The "working poor," as they are

approvingly termed, are in fact the major philanthropists of our society. They neglect their own children so that the children of others will be cared for; they live in substandard housing so that other homes will be shiny and perfect; they endure privation so that inflation will be low and stock prices high. To be a member of the working poor is to be an anonymous donor, a nameless benefactor, to everyone else. As Gail, one of my restaurant coworkers put it, "you give and you give."

15   Someday, of course—and I will make no predictions as to exactly when—they are bound to tire of getting so little in return and to demand to be paid what they're worth. There'll be a lot of anger when that day comes, and strikes and disruption. But the sky will not fall, and we will all be better off for it in the end.

Notes

1. "Study: More Go Hungry since Welfare Reform," *Boston Herald*, January 21, 2000; "Charity Can't Feed All while Welfare Reforms Implemented," *Houston Chronicle*, January 10, 2000; "Hunger Grows as Food Banks Try to Keep Pace," *Atlanta Journal and Constitution*, November 26, 1999.
2. "Rise in Homeless Families Strains San Diego Aid," *Los Angeles Times*, January 24, 2000.
3. "Hunger Problems Said to Be Getting Worse," *Milwaukee Journal Sentinel*, December 15, 1999.
4. Deborah Leff, the president and CEO of the hunger-relief organization America's Second Harvest, quoted in the *National Journal*, op. cit.; "Hunger Persists in U.S. despite the Good Times," *Detroit News*, June 15, 2000.
5. "A National Survey of American Attitudes toward Low-Wage Workers and Welfare Reform," Jobs for the Future, Boston, May 24, 2000.

Reading Responses

1. How does Ehrenreich answer her own opening question in paragraph 1?
2. What does Ehrenreich consider the real question? How does she answer that one?
3. What different approaches does Ehrenreich use to document her experiences and to provide evidence to support her conclusions?

Writing Activities

1. In your own words, state Ehrenreich's overall conclusion about her experiences. Compare your statement with those of some others in your class. Working together, combine and revise your individual statements to produce a collaborative statement.
2. Identify the criteria for job success that Ehrenreich presents in the first six paragraphs of "Evaluation." Based on Ehrenreich's criteria, write a short essay evaluating your success in your current job or in a past job.

3. Investigate hunger, homelessness, or employment in your local community or region, looking for information to update Ehrenreich's data in paragraph 11. Write a report that presents and interprets your findings. Be sure to cite your sources, which can include this selection from Ehrenreich's book.

Community Links

Assuming that you work during the school year or the summer, use Nolo's "How to Make a Budget and Stick to It" (pp. 543–547) to calculate your income and expenses. Use this information to respond to Ehrenreich's question about managing life. Or, use Nolo's advice to calculate your current status as a working student and to project your anticipated status once you move into the professional job you'd like. Use this comparative information to consider Ehrenreich's questions about work and money.

AND THE WEINER IS . . .

Marty Jones

◆

This story about Coe Meyer and his hot-dog carts first appeared in Westword, *a popular weekly alternative newspaper that circulates in metropolitan Denver. Like many alternative papers,* Westword *covers local issues and events: eateries, entertainment, sports, and cultural activities. In his "Consumed" column, which features Denver's "oddball and unsung dining and drinking assets," Marty Jones describes Meyer, his "Woody's Chicago Style" hot-dog carts, and the delectable hot dogs they bring to the public.*

1   If the folks at the National Hot Dog & Sausage Council had their way, you'd already know that July is National Hot Dog Month and July 24 is National Hot Dog Day.

2   If Coe D. Meyer had his way, *every* day would be a hot-dog day. From his office in Morrison, Meyer is launching a bid to become the country's only nationwide hot-dog vendor. By placing his "Woody's Chicago Style" hot-dog carts at home-improvement centers and on sidewalks across America, he plans to bring the pleasures of frankfurter flesh to the walking hungry.

3   For the people who own and run them, Woody's carts deliver something else: financial independence. "I've got air-traffic controllers, blood technicians, registered nurses, contractors, flight attendants," Meyer says of his franchisees. "We've got twenty stands going in the Seattle area, and we're picking up ex-Boeing executives. They're tired of looking over their shoulders, tired of being laid off.

4   "There are two things people want to own in their life," Meyer continues. "A bar and a hot-dog stand." Meyer had both in 1984, when he owned the B

Lift Pub at Copper Mountain and set up a hot-dog cart to boost the bar's income. The response to his dogs was overwhelming and inspired him to leave the bar business for the weiner wars. Affirms Meyer: "Everybody looks at a guy who is selling hot dogs and thinks, 'Now, there's a guy that's got it made.'"

5   Following this all-beef epiphany, Meyer moved to Hawaii to launch a hot-dog venture on the beaches there. That culture proved less dog-friendly, so by 1990, he shifted from selling hot dogs to selling hot-dog stands. He wangled a contract to set up in the lobbies of Eagle Hardware stores in Hawaii and a few West Coast states; his empire expanded when Lowe's Home Improvement Warehouse bought out Eagle, and he returned to Colorado. Today Meyer has 55 carts in eleven western states, with more states and staff on the way.

6   His office will soon be a training camp for future frankfurter moguls. Training, Meyer says, is the key to his country-conquering concept. Millions of Americans refuse to eat sidewalk hot dogs because so many carts—and their operators—lack curb and culinary appeal. A Woody's cart, on the other hand, is run by a well-groomed, uniformed staffer who "speaks fluent English, can communicate well and make proper change," Meyer says.

7   "In a lot of areas," he adds, "the day of the independent hot-dog guy with the Grateful Dead T-shirt on and a cigarette in one hand is rapidly diminishing, because companies like mine are offering an alternative." That sounds like the corporatization of a quirky American standard—and that's exactly what Meyer's going for. "You don't go to McDonald's because they offer a great hamburger," Meyer says. "You go there because it's safe, it's clean, and you know exactly what you're going to get."

8   A Woody's dog starts with a weiner from Vienna Beef, a legendary brand in Chicago. (The company has been in business for over a hundred years and works under USDA meat stamp number "1.") Loyalty to the Vienna dog, according to Vienna's Chuck Whitesell, stems largely from the fact that it's made of meat from uncastrated bulls. "It's very rich and very dense," he says. "It almost looks purple." That manly meat is blended with tender trimmings from the brisket and belly sections used to make Vienna Beef's pastrami. The combination makes for a dog with balls, one that holds up under cooking and delivers the distinct "snap" that Chicagoans crave. The hot dogs are also naturally smoked over hickory, Whitesell says, instead of being dosed with the smoke flavorings used by Oscar Mayer and Ball Park.

9   For the past four years, Jordan Little has served up Woody's dogs from a permanent cart in the lobby of the Lowe's at 5405 Wadsworth Bypass in Arvada. "Everybody eats hot dogs," Little says. "It's like pizza and sex—even when they're bad, they're still kinda good. And it's something that, when you eat them out, they're better than when you try and cook them at home."

10   His purebred dogs are condiment-heavy creations unlike any homemade dog, franks that showcase the more-is-best philosophy of the Chi-town standard. Each starts with a Vienna on a steamed poppyseed bun that may then be graced with "green" (an iridescent relish that nearly glows), minced white onions, "sport peppers" (pickled serranos), a slab of kosher dill pickle, a wedge of tomato, even a slice of cucumber—"That's called 'draggin' it through the

garden,'" Little says of the toppings process—before finishing things off with yellow mustard. "If you're going for ketchup, don't let me see it," Little warns.

11   The result is doggone good. With each bite, your mouth moves through a mush of bun, a punch of peppers and a tangy blend of relish, pickle and onion. Those thrills meld with mustard before your teeth sink into the salty goodness of the dog itself for a total blue-collar taste sensation. (Some Woody's carts, including Little's, also serve a coriander-laced bratwurst and a cayenne-spiked Fire Dog along with snacks, sodas and coffee.)

12   This is mobile food for the masses. "Hot dogs, chips and perplexing questions answered—that's how I see this job," Little says. "If you're a bit of a philosopher, if you like talking to people, it's a lot of fun. It's like owning a bar without the responsibilities of babysitting the drunks."

13   According to Meyer, an average Woody's cart brings in an average of $150,000 a year; a cart's pre-tax profit is about 50 percent. Operators make "somewhere in the area of $50,000 to $75,000 for running a hot-dog cart," Meyer says. "I've got guys that do a whole lot more." An operator in Colorado Springs, for example, will gross close to $300,000 this year. Cart owners typically pay back their $35,000 to $45,000 initial investment in their first year.

14   Little says his annual sales are in line with Meyer's average, but making those sales requires putting in a lot of hours with little vacation time. Still, the gig brings in enough money that his wife can stay home with their child and tend to his Woody's books. "I'm pulling down decent money," he says. "With a couple years of college, I wasn't going to get a good job, so I had to make my own job. It was nice to find this."

15   And it was nice to be in a position to provide the opportunity, according to Meyer, who's watched dogged determination pay off. "Hot dogs are associated with fun, with good times," he says. "We're doing sausage the way it's supposed to be done.

16   "I've had so much fun watching all these Internet people go up the wire and come back down again," he adds. "But my guys go to work every day and stand there for eight hours, with no air-conditioned rooms or pool tables. They're looking for a way to make the mortgage payment, put in eight hours a day and live happily ever after. And that's pretty much what we offer."

17   That, and dogs with bite.

 Reading Responses

1. What is the purpose of Jones's column? What does Jones assume about his readers' possible interests and concerns?

2. What criteria does Jones use to evaluate the Woody's hot dog? If you were evaluating a hot dog, in what ways would you change or add to Jones's criteria?

3. How does Jones match his language to his topic? How does he use language to engage a reader's interest? Locate some examples of wording that illustrate his strategies.

Writing Activities

1. Write a paragraph summarizing Coe Meyer's philosophy about work and what he thinks people want from their work.

2. Write a brief review of a food sold on or near campus. Be sure that you describe the food so that readers can imagine how it tastes, looks, smells, sounds, and feels. In addition to describing the food, evaluate it using criteria that you convey to a reader. You may direct your review to readers who are potential customers or people interested in a possible business venture or investment. (Reread paragraphs 8–12 for ideas about how to describe and evaluate a food product.)

3. Arrange an interview with someone on campus or in the nearby community who works in a local eatery or dining establishment. Plan the interview questions so that you can find out what you want to know, but be flexible in adjusting to the flow of the conversation. Take notes to keep track of main points and to record direct quotations accurately during your conversation. Write down your own observations and impressions immediately after the interview. Based on your interview, write an article like Jones's, exploring an unusual local establishment.

Community Links

After reading "And the Weiner Is . . . ," compare and contrast it with at least one other selection that incorporates interviews such as Rose's "Lilia" (pp. 19–21) from the academic community, "The Story of a Garment Worker" (pp. 205–207) from the work community, or Terkel's "Organizer: Bill Talcott" (pp. 357–361) from the public community. Consider the strategies used by the interviewers to present their subjects in ways that engage readers and convey a clear main impression of the person interviewed.

RUNNING A SUCCESSFUL COMPANY: TEN RULES THAT WORKED FOR ME

Sam Walton with John Huey

◆

This selection is the next-to-last chapter in Sam Walton: Made in America: My Story *by Sam Walton with John Huey. Here, Walton sums up his principles for business success, the principles he used to build Wal-Mart from a local experiment to a dominant retailer that is both admired for its success and accused of irrevocably changing retail business, especially in smalltown America.*

"One thing you'll notice if you spend very much time talking with Sam about Wal-Mart's success. He's always saying things like 'This was the key to the whole thing,' or 'That was our real secret.' He knows as well as anyone that there wasn't any magic formula. A lot of different things made it work, and in one day's time he may cite all of them as the 'key' or the 'secret.' What's amazing is that for almost fifty years he's managed to focus on all of them at once—all the time. That's his real secret." —David Glass

1. I think we've covered the story of how all my partners and associates and I over the years built Wal-Mart into what it is today. And in the telling, I think we've covered all the principles which resulted in the company's amazing success. A whole lot has changed about the retailing business in the forty-seven years we've been in it—including some of my theories. We've changed our minds about some significant things along the way and adopted some new principles—particularly about the concept of partnership in a corporation. But most of the values and the rules and the techniques we've relied on have stayed the same the whole way. Some of them are such simple commonsense old favorites that they hardly seem worth mentioning.

2. This isn't the first time that I've been asked to come up with a list of rules for success, but it *is* the first time I've actually sat down and done it. I'm glad I did because it's been a revealing exercise for me. The truth is, David Glass is right. I do seem to have a couple of dozen things that I've singled out at one time or another as the "key" to the whole thing. One I don't even have on my list is "work hard." If you don't know that already, or you're not willing to do it, you probably won't be going far enough to need my list anyway. And another I didn't include on the list is the idea of building a team. If you want to build an enterprise of any size at all, it almost goes without saying that you absolutely must create a team of people who work together and give real meaning to that overused word "teamwork." To me, that's more the goal of the whole thing, rather than some way to get there.

3. I believe in always having goals, and always setting them high. I can certainly tell you that the folks at Wal-Mart have always had goals in front of them. In fact, we have sometimes built real scoreboards on the stage at Saturday morning meetings.

4. One more thing. If you're really looking for my advice here, trying to get something serious out of this exercise I put myself through, remember: these rules are not in any way intended to be the Ten Commandments of Business. They are some rules that worked for me. But I always prided myself on breaking everybody else's rules, and I always favored the mavericks who challenged my rules. I may have fought them all the way, but I respected them, and, in the end, I listened to them a lot more closely than I did the pack who always agreed with everything I said. So pay special attention to Rule 10, and if you interpret it in the right spirit—as it applies to you—it could mean simply: Break All the Rules.

5. For what they're worth, here they are. Sam's Rules for Building a Business:

Rule 1: COMMIT to your business. Believe in it more than anybody else. I think I overcame every single one of my personal shortcomings by the sheer passion I brought to my work. I don't know if you're born with this kind of passion, or if you can learn it. But I do know you need it. If you love your work, you'll be out there every day trying to do it the best you possibly can, and pretty soon everybody around will catch the passion from you—like a fever.

Rule 2: SHARE your profits with all your associates, and treat them as partners. In turn, they will treat you as a partner, and together you will all perform beyond your wildest expectations. Remain a corporation and retain control if you like, but behave as a servant leader in a partnership. Encourage your associates to hold a stake in the company. Offer discounted stock, and grant them stock for their retirement. It's the single best thing we ever did.

Rule 3: MOTIVATE your partners. Money and ownership alone aren't enough. Constantly, day by day, think of new and more interesting ways to motivate and challenge your partners. Set high goals, encourage competition, and then keep score. Make bets with outrageous payoffs. If things get stale, cross-pollinate; have managers switch jobs with one another to stay challenged. Keep everybody guessing as to what your next trick is going to be. Don't become too predictable.

Rule 4: COMMUNICATE everything you possibly can to your partners. The more they know, the more they'll understand. The more they understand, the more they'll care. Once they care, there's no stopping them. If you don't trust your associates to know what's going on, they'll know you don't really consider them partners. Information is power, and the gain you get from empowering your associates more than offsets the risk of informing your competitors.

Rule 5: APPRECIATE everything your associates do for the business. A paycheck and a stock option will buy one kind of loyalty. But all of us like to be told how much somebody appreciates what we do for them. We like to hear it often, and especially when we have done something we're really proud of. Nothing else can quite substitute for a few well-chosen, well-timed, sincere words of praise. They're absolutely free—and worth a fortune.

Rule 6: CELEBRATE your successes. Find some humor in your failures. Don't take yourself so seriously. Loosen up, and everybody around you will loosen up. Have fun. Show enthusiasm—always. When all else fails, put on a costume and sing a silly song. Then make everybody else sing with you. Don't do a hula on Wall Street. It's been done. Think up your own stunt. All of this is more important, and more fun, than you think, and it really fools the competition. "Why should we take those cornballs at Wal-Mart seriously?"

Rule 7: LISTEN to everyone in your company. And figure out ways to get them talking. The folks on the front lines—the ones who actually talk to the customer—are the only ones who really know what's going on out there. You'd better find out what they know. This really is what total quality is all about. To push responsibility down in your organization, and to force good ideas to bubble up within it, you *must* listen to what your associates are trying to tell you.

Rule 8: EXCEED your customers' expectations. If you do, they'll come back over and over. Give them what they want—and a little more. Let them know you appreciate them. Make good on all your mistakes, and don't make excuses—apologize. Stand behind everything you do. The two most important words I ever wrote were on that first Wal-Mart sign: "Satisfaction Guaranteed." They're still up there, and they have made all the difference.

Rule 9: CONTROL your expenses better than your competition. This is where you can always find the competitive advantage. For twenty-five years running—long before Wal-Mart was known as the nation's largest retailer—we ranked number one in our industry for the lowest ratio of expenses to sales. You can make a lot of different mistakes and still recover if you run an efficient operation. Or you can be brilliant and still go out of business if you're too inefficient.

Rule 10: SWIM upstream. Go the other way. Ignore the conventional wisdom. If everybody else is doing it one way, there's a good chance you can find your niche by going in exactly the opposite direction. But be prepared for a lot of folks to wave you down and tell you you're headed the wrong way. I guess in all my years, what I heard more often than anything was: a town of less than 50,000 population cannot support a discount store for very long.

6   Those are some pretty ordinary rules, some would say even simplistic. The hard part, the real challenge, is to constantly figure out ways to execute them. You can't just keep doing what works one time, because everything around you is always changing. To succeed, you have to stay out in front of that change.

Reading Responses

1. Why does Walton say that he's not explaining "the Ten Commandments of Business" (paragraph 4)? How does this disclaimer contribute to a reader's image of Walton, and how does it contribute to Walton's message to the reader?
2. What readers does Walton address as he presents his ten rules? What does he seem to assume about their interests, needs, and aspirations?
3. What strategies does Walton use to present his rules? How does he shape his sentences, choose his wording, and convey a distinctive tone? How does his style contribute to his message?

Writing Activities

1. Write a paragraph synthesizing—weaving together—several of Walton's rules that seem to fall into a broader general category.
2. Write an essay analyzing how Walton conveys his persona—the image of himself presented to readers. Support your assertions with examples of his tone, his wording, his illustrations, or other pertinent characteristics.
3. Visit Wal-Mart or another major discount store or retailer. Conduct an observation, watching and taking notes on the way that the store operates and how employees treat customers. Write a report on your findings, explaining what your observations suggest about the principles that guide that particular store.

Community Links

Compare or contrast Walton's advice with one or two other readings that supply advice, such as Vermette's letter (pp. 96–100) from the academic community or Nelson's "A Beginning" (pp. 386–389) from the public community. Consider how each reading presents its advice. Which features of the reading seem to reflect conventions generally accepted by writers who give advice? Which seem to reflect particular expectations, needs, or concerns of readers in their communities?

Community Perspectives and Issues

Six Practices for Creating Communities of Value, Not Proximity

Dave Ulrich

◆

This chapter appeared originally in The Community of the Future, *a collection of essays by many diverse writers. The volume as a whole was edited by Frances Hesselbein, Marshall Goldsmith, Richard Beckhard, and Richard F. Schubert; it was sponsored by the Peter F. Drucker Foundation for Nonprofit Management. Ulrich's chapter appears in Part IV: Creating Communities in Organizations. Ulrich draws examples from his personal experience and from his knowledge of many different organizations as an expert in management and human resources.*

1   Over twenty years ago, as a college freshman, I took the lead in chartering a bus to take a group of students from Brigham Young University in Utah to Kansas City for Christmas. The trip home was uneventful, but on the return trip to Utah, we ran into a snowstorm in Rock Springs, Wyoming. We did not know anyone in Rock Springs, had no extra money, and were not sure how long the snowstorm would close the roads. Almost as a last resort, I looked up the local ecclesiastical leader in Rock Springs who shared our faith, called him, and explained our situation. Within hours all forty of us had housing for the night, food, and support until the roads cleared. We would never again meet the individuals who took care of us then, but we would never forget the lesson of community this experience taught.

2   Rich Teerlink, the chairman of Harley-Davidson, shared with me his experience driving through Ohio with his wife. While eating at a roadside diner, he noticed a Harley outside the restaurant. He claimed that it was not difficult to identify the stereotypical Harley rider in the restaurant—large, tattooed, and tough-looking. Without hesitation, Rich walked over to the miscreant to talk. The rider, aloof at best, did not want to talk to this middle-aged man and his wife. But when Rich started asking about the Harley, the man's interest was piqued. When Rich said that he worked at headquarters (never revealing that he was the chairman), the man began to talk. He proudly showed Rich his Harley, engaged Rich's support for some service requirements and modifications, and invited Rich and his wife to dinner that night at his house. They will likely never meet again, but they were immediately connected as part of a larger community.

3   A large multinational firm that operates in over two hundred countries has always divided the world into areas and regions: North America, Latin America, Asia Pacific, Europe, and so forth. Executives at this firm (and most other firms) believed that these geographic boundaries would provide a structure for sharing information and governing the enterprise. Recently, the firm has begun to recognize that its operations in Chile are more like its operations in Poland and Portugal than Brazil. With global information so easy to share, it now thinks about dividing the markets it serves by market maturation rather than geography. This means that the world might be divided into five or six market segments depending on the maturity of the market in a given country. Information on operations in Chile may just as easily be shared with Poland and Portugal as Argentina and Venezuela.

4   These three stories signify a fundamental shift in thinking about community. Traditionally, a community created boundaries based on proximity. The Mormon pioneers who founded Brigham Young University moved to the Rocky Mountains so that they could live near those who shared their beliefs (and away from those who did not). Companies defined boundaries by geography, with territories, regions, and areas being used to form operating units. Proximity allowed community members to share purpose, monitor process, and govern behavior. Today, boundaries based on values may be more common than boundaries based on geographic proximity. Proximity focuses on what is seen; values focus on what is felt. Proximity assumes the importance of physical presence to share ideas; values create emotional bonds and the ability to share ideas easily across great distances. Communities of the future may be less defined by where we live than by what we believe.

5   Communities bounded and bonded by values are becoming more prevalent because of the ease of information and global distribution systems. Any organization with a dispersed distribution system (for example, McDonald's Corporation, with outlets worldwide) or global operations (for example, the Boeing Company, which sells equipment to Asian countries) must learn to create and operate communities of values, not proximity. This chapter identifies what creates communities of values, with implications for leading these communities.

Creating Communities of Values

6   The following six practices may be used to create communities of values and also build a stronger community overall:

1. Forge a strong and distinct identity.
2. Establish clear rules of inclusion.
3. Share information across boundaries.
4. Create serial reciprocity.
5. Use symbols, myths, and stories to create and sustain values.
6. Manage enough similarity so that the community feels familiar.

Forge a Strong and Distinct Identity

7   In the psychological world, our identity represents how others perceive our career, personality, and behavior. My identity as a professor emerges from how others see my personality and actions as I engage in teaching and writing. In the product and marketing world, identity comes when brands gain symbolic visibility. The Hallmark brand has come to represent quality and "nice people," as evidenced in Hallmark Card's advertising, which encourages us to "turn the card over" and note that any individual carrying a Hallmark bag must be a nice person. Brand identity creates customer equity, so that the customer continues to be loyal to the brand.

8   In the organizational world, identity represents the image of the company as perceived by those inside and outside. An organizational identity may be centered around purpose, values, or some other distinguishing feature of the company. Harley-Davidson has created a strong and distinct identity. Those who relate to and understand the Harley identity immediately become part of the Harley community. Alcoholics Anonymous has created a brand identity with the clear purpose of helping individuals defeat alcoholism through the twelve-step program.

9   Organizations' brand identities operate more on values than proximity. When my teenage daughter wore my leather Harley jacket to high school, she was immediately connected to a group of students she didn't normally hang out with. When I have worn my Harley jacket, people I don't know have stopped to talk with me about Harleys. Alcoholics Anonymous has meetings all over the world. A stranger can walk in, share a story, and immediately be surrounded by others who share similar values. A common identity is forged based on values, not proximity. In the bus story told earlier, the local minister I called shared our values without even knowing who we were except that we were members of a larger community. Because of these shared values, he immediately called others in the congregation to support and help us.

10   Communities of values have clear, strong, and distinct identities that give meaning to members and distinctness to nonmembers.

Establish Clear Rules of Inclusion

11   Communities of values have demarcations that determine what is in and what is out. Rules of inclusion focus on the extent to which an individual shares the purpose of the community as expressed in actions congruent with that purpose. To arrive at rules of inclusion (and exclusion), generic values must be translated into specific behaviors.

12   In the medical profession, a community of values exists in part because doctors share a commitment to the Hippocratic oath. In an emergency, when someone asks, "Is there a doctor present?" those who say yes represent the medical community because of their commitment to service. Licensed physicians make a public commitment to stand by the Hippocratic oath. The licensing process ensures that, before they are licensed, they have both knowledge of medical practices and the values they need to practice medicine. The

American Medical Association has prepared guidelines that censure physicians who violate the Hippocratic oath.

13   Communities of values set expectations for inclusion. Active members might be expected to serve a certain number of hours, receive a prescribed number of hours of coursework per year, have to go through initiation rituals before being included, or behave according to an agreed-upon set of guidelines. Community members who accept these rules of inclusion receive full membership and are able to connect with equally committed members, anywhere, anytime. Members who do not live up to the rules of inclusion may receive only partial membership or may not be accepted over time. By being demanding, the inclusionary process allows members who have been accepted to connect to other members regardless of location.

Share Information Across Boundaries

14   Communities of values share information rapidly across physical boundaries. Information allows ideas generated in one unit to be shared with other units. Most of the large professional service firms have created the position of "director of knowledge transfer," whose primary responsibility is to move information across units. Andersen Consulting leverages technology in moving best practices from one site to another. On completing an assignment, the Andersen consultant is expected to answer some basic questions about the assignment: What was the presenting problem? What were the methods used to deal with the problem? What were the results? What lessons were learned? These answers then merge into an ever-evolving data set that other consultants may draw on for their consulting practice. Andersen has consultants all over the world who are part of its community of values because they share information with each other across boundaries. They are as likely to retrieve information from Europe, Asia, or North America when accessing the Andersen database. The information becomes a carrier of the values of the firm.

15   Under the rubric of "learning," a number of companies have worked to share best-practice information across boundaries. The Coca-Cola Company has hired a number of "directors of learning strategy" whose job is, in part, to share information about organization and management practices from one unit of the firm to another. The U.S. Army has formalized the after-action review in which each critical incident is formally reviewed and the lessons learned are shared with the commander for his or her next similar incident and with others facing similar engagements. AT&T has instituted a best-practice forum where innovative ideas are shared across units.

16   Communities of values also have mechanisms for sharing information about specific issues. For example, in my Rock Springs bus example, the local minister could quickly verify the veracity of our group's story by calling our minister in Kansas City. In a matter of minutes, a leader many miles away could share observations and insights that would help the Rock Springs minister to meet our needs. In our church today, such information sharing often occurs. Recently, one of our Ann Arbor members relocated to Virginia. The local ecclesiastical leader wanted to ask the newly arrived member to accept a

prominent assignment in the congregation. The Ann Arbor minister certified the member's commitment and competence so that the Virginia minister could act with confidence.

17 Communities of values move information, which makes a best practice in one site transferable to another and allows members to draw on the expertise of others to apply it to local conditions.

Create Serial Reciprocity

18 Communities of values have serial reciprocity. Serial reciprocity means that community member A may serve member B and member B will repay the service, not by serving A, but by serving another member (C). Serial reciprocity implies that the inevitable equity required by members to continue to participate in a community may be derived over time, not at any one point in time.

19 In the Rock Springs story, the local minister who served us will not be repaid by us, but we will in turn offer service to others of our community and repay the community, not the individual, over time. His service will be repaid over time as we serve others. To ensure that such reciprocity occurs, the community needs to have a high degree of trust, integrity, and informal sanctions to ensure that members continue to give. In our local church group this fall, about twenty new student families moved in. Resident church members assisted in unloading trucks and getting the new families oriented. Those who received this help will repay the community by helping others who move in, not necessarily those who moved them in.

20 Serial reciprocity requires a strong community of values where fairness is maintained about who gets from and gives to the community. It requires a shift away from a pure transaction model (you get what you give) to more of a trustee model (you will get if you give). Values allow equity or reciprocity to occur over time rather than by proximity, which assumes that transactions must always be in balance.

Use Symbols, Myths, and Stories to Create and Sustain Values

21 Communities of values create and leverage stories and myths. These communities build a legacy that encourages the values to persist over time. At Harley-Davidson, the legacy of "Willie G," a member of the original founding family, rallies employees and customers. Willie rides a Harley, dresses like a Harley rider, and symbolizes the soul of the Harley community. With the Harley myth and story created and perpetuated in this way, the values of the community have meaning to those both inside and outside the community.

22 Stories and myths take a physical form but transcend the day-to-day. The uniforms worn by pilots, doctors, waitresses, and players in a rock band not only define an identity for these communities and create their boundaries; they symbolize the community. A pilot's crisp uniform with bars on the shoulder representing seniority symbolizes the precision of the pilot's work and the experience she or he brings to the job. UPS's plain brown trucks and uniforms symbolize the company's desire to blend in and quietly do its work. When

British Airways changed the British logo on its aircraft to paintings of local cultures, it symbolized its commitment to being a global enterprise.

Stories and myths also occur through traditions. Family traditions around holidays often create unique meanings for those holidays among family members. The rituals embedded in universities, such as graduation ceremonies, symbolize the values of the university and the community it services. Nordstrom's stories of exceptional service are widely shared throughout the Nordstrom community to symbolize and signal what matters most. At the Walt Disney Company, before being hired, a new employee must learn the history of Disney (for example, memorizing the names of the Seven Dwarfs). These stories reinforce values as the glue that holds the community together, even at a distance.

Manage Enough Similarity So That the Community Feels Familiar

Communities of values create predictability through the use of familiar settings. A few years ago, on bike trips with about eight teenage boys, we would enter a new city and ask the boys where they wanted to have lunch. When the city had a McDonald's, the choice was always between McDonald's or a local restaurant. Inevitably, the boys chose McDonald's. Even in very different cities, McDonald's felt familiar. The menu was generally the same, the food tasted much the same, and the boys felt comfortable in familiar surroundings. McDonald's tries to adapt to local conditions, but it wants to maintain its community feeling across all McDonald's restaurants.

U.S. military bases offer the same familiar surroundings. Whether the military base is in Oklahoma, Okinawa, or Oslo, members of the military on the base will find familiar surroundings, post exchanges, housing, recreation facilities, and street layouts. The similarity in the physical settings may allow even the dispersed organization to share common values. A Harley dealer, Nordstrom store, Wal-Mart store, or Hard Rock Café creates community by providing a familiar physical setting that puts both employees and customers at ease.

Leading Communities of Values

Communities based on values, not proximity, are not accidents or flukes. They require planning and diligence to design and maintain them. When this is done well, communities of values become virtuous circles: successive members of the community contribute a little more than the previous members. As such contributions continue, the communities of values increase member commitment, productivity, and the communities' ability to accomplish desired outcomes.

When communities are not based on values, they may dissolve and disband (for example, the Hare Krishna community had great visibility for a short time) or devolve into cults rather than sustained communities. Cults inbreed and learn only from the top; communities of values spread their learning throughout and share knowledge widely. Cults are heavily self-promoting and self-serving; communities' self-interest lies in the service of others. Cults are heavily leader-focused; communities of values share leadership. Cults ban alternative views; communities of values adapt alternative views. Cults define thinking; communities of values define feelings. Cults prescribe solutions; communities of values frame problems. Cults define unity as oneness; communities of values define unity as focused differences. Cults do without knowing why; at their best, communities of values share the why before doing.

28   Leaders create communities of values in a variety of organizational settings. In business organizations like Harley-Davidson, the community feeling among employees and customers shapes identity, motivates employees, and leads to positive business outcomes. In organizations like Alcoholics Anonymous, the community's values give meaning to the association, even across boundaries. In schools like Brigham Young University, a community of values engages and connects individuals from vastly different geographic settings. In public sector organizations like the U.S. Army, the community of values ensures continuity and commitment.

29   The leader's role in creating communities of values begins with shaping a clear identity, defining rules for inclusion, and sharing information. With these aspects in place, the leader then creates stories and myths, builds reciprocity, and ensures consistency across boundaries. In any dispersed organization where units spread across geographic areas, communities of values, more than proximity, will be required to experience success.

30   The outcomes of communities of value include meeting the needs of individuals inside and outside the community in both empirical and empathic ways. As these communities proliferate, people can feel connected and engaged even when not in close proximity.

Reading Responses

1. What overall principle for thinking about communities does Ulrich advocate? Where does he state this central idea? Why doesn't he state it in his first paragraph?
2. Which of Ulrich's many examples seem most effective to you? Explain why you think that they work so well.
3. How does Ulrich expect organizational leaders to use his six principles? Why does he contrast communities with cults? Why does he arrange the principles in the sequence that he uses?

Writing Activities

1. Write a paragraph explaining one of Ulrich's principles in your own words. Exchange paragraphs with other students, making suggestions to help each other revise your explanations.
2. Recount an event or incident—like Ulrich's story of being stranded during the snowstorm—that helps to define community for you. Be certain that you interpret the event for readers and convey its significance, not just what happened.

3. Discuss one of Ulrich's six principles, using your own words to define it and your own examples to explain it and illustrate its applications. You may draw examples from your personal, academic, work, or public experience.

Community Links

Compare and contrast Ulrich's essay with Palmer's "The Quest for Community in Higher Education" (pp. 33–41) or a related reading from the public community such as Covey's "The Ideal Community" (pp. 390–395), Morse's "Five Building Blocks for Successful Communities" (pp. 374–378), or Zobel de Ayala's "Anticipating the Community of the Future" (pp. 405–411). What strategies do these writers use to present their suggestions and observations? For example, how do they use features such as lists, anecdotes, and examples to convey their points? In what ways are their approaches similar or different?

IT'S OKAY TO BE ANAL SOMETIMES
Robert A. Lutz

◆

Guts: The Seven Laws of Business That Made Chrysler the World's Hottest Car Company is Robert Lutz's story of his success transforming Chrysler from a troubled company to a profitable automotive innovator. Lutz identifies seven principles that seem to challenge conventional wisdom, such as "The primary purpose of business is not to make money." (However, further discussion reveals that having a passion for a product or a service is exactly the way to make money.) Lutz then follows his iconoclastic laws with some corollaries, starting with "It's Okay to Be Anal Sometimes," the chapter that this selection begins.

1   Being detail-conscious, being punctual, being fastidious and reasonably well dressed, being punctilious (even so punctilious as to make sure *punctilious* is spelled right), being, in short, a little anal . . . isn't a bad thing. Quite the opposite. In fact, as Martha Stewart likes to say, it's a *good* thing. What of the big picture—doesn't it matter more than details? It matters, but not more. As the saying goes, "Trifles make perfection, and perfection is no trifle."

2   Yet where trifles are concerned, we seem to have lost our capacity for outrage. Sloppiness, carelessness, and thoughtlessness go increasingly unchallenged. You see this slacking off in everything from rudeness on the street to a laid-back "Hey-what's-the-big-deal-it-still-works-doesn't-it?" attitude regarding product defects to my personal pet peeve: typos and misused words in national newspapers and magazines.

3   This insidious drift, far from being trifling, is one of the most fundamental problems now facing the business community and American society. And one

of its foremost causes, I think, is modern human-relations theory—the idea that it's bad form to criticize (even when the criticism is constructive); that it's not smart to make waves (especially not in an era of 360-degree performance evaluations!); and that it's somehow tacky to demand perfection, because, don'tcha know, demanding it just might inconvenience someone. Even more unthinkable, it might dent their self-esteem!

4   I like to think I'm a pretty positive guy. And I also like to think I place a very high value on self-esteem. But by the same token, I don't think that putting feelings ahead of a wholesome regard for workplace performance makes any more sense than putting them ahead of academic performance in the classroom. Why not? Because the self-esteem thus created is, to be blunt, phony and ephemeral. It vanishes the moment the student or the employee hits the real world and can't read a job application or gets laid off because his or her company is no longer competitive.

5   Nobody better understands the importance of performance and of detail than Japanese carmakers. Take Toyota, whose unflinching commitment to excellence shows itself in the fit and finish of the smallest dashboard control knobs. In addition to our Honda study in the late '80s, Chrysler also did a lot of benchmarking of how Toyota ran its business. We particularly looked at the way it had increased profits and cut costs. Toyota had suffered a humiliating brush with bankruptcy in 1949, and it had sworn ever since to eliminating all waste, however small, as one means of maximizing profits. By the time we studied the company in the late '80s, Toyota's cash position was in excess of $10 billion (and is more than $13 billion today), so what they were doing evidently worked!

6   Just how detail-conscious was Toyota? The company's cost-control policy decreed that employees extract every bit of use from everything, even pencils: When a pencil became too short to be held between the fingers, employees were instructed to soften the tip of an old pen with a cigarette lighter, then insert the pencil's stub. The stub then was to be used until there was no longer any of it left to sharpen, even manually.

7   Yours truly caught a fair amount of flak when, emboldened by Toyota's rigor, I urged my colleagues during Chrysler's own humiliating period in the late '80s to be similarly vigilant about cutting out waste. The point I sought to make was that eradicating big, obvious examples of waste would not be enough. If Chrysler were to survive our Crash #2, we'd have to root out waste in every form, however small. Was I being too anal? Decide for yourself. Here are a few examples of what I considered then (and now) to be waste:

9 August 1989
To: Chrysler Motors Officers
From R.A. Lutz
Subject: Avoidance of Waste

8   As I reread the "Toyota-endaka" document [a document about how Japanese automakers were valiantly and rapidly offsetting the effects of a stronger yen] for the third time, it occurred to me more and more that the core

message is: "Cost cannot be reduced as long as waste is tolerated." Only when waste, however minor, is recognized for what it is . . . ([examples of] which, individually, may be small but which, cumulatively, risks our survival) will we be able to make significant progress. . . .

Waste is:

- Needless plaques and in-house commemorative items
- Elaborately produced and framed policies and statements
- New name tags for every event. (I don't know about you, but at any given moment I seem to have a collection of about 50 name tags all saying "Bob Lutz, Chrysler." I suggest executives need only one, which they should be recycling.)
- Late arrival at meetings
- Excessive participants at meetings
- Meetings that run too long
- Elaborate slide presentations for in-house use
- Fat, multitabbed "marketing plans" books
- Back-and-forth memos to either allocate or ward off blame
- Trays and trays of uneaten cookies, Danish, and doughnuts
- Multiple copies of videotapes (when one, circulated, would suffice)
- Missed deadlines
- Lights left on
- Getting photos and certificates framed in-house
- Controlling and explaining variances rather than improving absolutes
- Re-dos
- Anything, anywhere regarded as a neat freebie of working for a big company
- Anything, anywhere not directly tied to the benefit of our customers

9 Too austere? Maybe, but you have to admit it got my point across. And I think I deserve some small credit for *not* suggesting people melt their old pens to accommodate old pencil stubs! Sure enough, Chrysler, through economies not just big but small, did manage to save billions.

10 These suggestions of mine did not exactly endear me to everyone who got them, and before long a memo in reply (part parody, part counterblast) made its way to me through the office grapevine. Here are a few examples of "waste" the unnamed author cited:

- Three brand vice presidents with twelve directors reporting to them
- Any corporate resources used to aid employees practicing helicopter maneuvers on company property [a "shot" at a certain fellow who sometimes flew his chopper to work!]
- $2,000 per night hotel rooms for company presidents in Tokyo, when more modest accommodations are available
- Major corporate reorganizations twice a year every year

11   Regarding the first and last of these: I couldn't have agreed more! In fact, the writer did me a favor by saving me the trouble of having listed them. As for the middle two, these speak to a serious question I mean to tackle later in the book: whether executive privileges do more harm than good. (Not wanting to keep you in suspense, I'll give you a hint: In my upcoming chapter on Leadership, I say hooray for the corporate dining room!) Readers lacking in self-discipline may feel moved to peek at it now. We of sterner stuff, however, will next take on one of the most subtle and pernicious frauds being perpetrated on business today: the forced relaxation of standards of office dress. Yesterday's dictum might have been "dress for success." Today's, apparently, is "dress like a mess!"

Real Creativity versus "Casual Day"

12   A misconception has somehow gained currency that if you neglect to bathe before coming to work, if you dress in a turtleneck sweater, and if your overall deportment suggests you aren't quite sure what day it is, this proves you are a card-carrying creative person, exempt from the rules and standards governing more prosaic employees.

13   What transparent bunk! *Real* creativity has nothing whatsoever to do with such externals. It is the product of courage (an individual's willingness to experiment) and disciplined hard work (his or her determination to keep experimenting until the best solution is found). Yet it's the "turtleneck" conception of creativity, I suspect, that has contributed to the current rage for casual days, dress-down Fridays, or other such exercises in cosmetics. The forced relaxation of standards of dress, so far as I can tell, works but one miracle: It offers new hope to a beleaguered corduroy industry.

14   Let me revise that. It works *two* miracles. The second is that it allows a certain kind of company to create the appearance of doing something about creativity without actually having to come to grips with any of the fundamentals.

15   Let's say an organization is having trouble generating new ideas, that it's embarrassed that it's always last at everything. Senior management either hires a consultant or goes on a retreat (or both), and decides, "We're too rigid; we're too isolated; our employees are afraid of us." Somehow the fix amounts to announcing that henceforth casual wear will be appropriate on certain days at Ajax Corp. so as to provide an environment "free from stress or fear in which every employee feels that he or she can contribute to his or her full ability..." (you provide the rest of this verbiage).

16   Exactly *how* eliminating neckties is supposed to promote original thought is a question that never gets close examination, being taken more or less on faith. I've never found anyone willing to claim that a switch to casual dress made them feel more empowered, freer, or more creative. And my own observation of several decades—of offices both civilian and military—suggests just the opposite is true.

17   Formality of dress—having a "uniform" (literal or figurative)—imbues a group with an extra measure of pride, professionalism, and esprit de corps that

is greater than they would have if they dressed every which way. A uniform—whether fatigues or a coat and tie—signifies the wearer is a member of a team, and that the team has special abilities and a special mission. The act of "dressing for duty" causes a subtle shift in a person's attitude. It focuses the wearer on his task; it signifies that he's about to join a body of peers, who together will do battle with the enemy.

18   Real creativity's first order of business is not the relaxation of standards but the mastery of them; once mastered, they then can be tweaked, flaunted, or otherwise played with. (Isn't that a working description of the creative process?) Being able to think "out of the box" presupposes you were able to think *in* it.

Reading Responses

1. What is Lutz's main point? Where does he state this point?
2. Why does Lutz follow a section on attention to detail with one on creativity? How does Lutz connect these sections and relate their ideas? (In the original chapter, these two sections are followed by others.)
3. What strategies does Lutz use to present his advice? How does he convey his tone, shape his sentences, and choose his wording? How does his style contribute to his message?

Writing Activities

1. Write a response to Lutz's discussion of creativity, especially the relationship between standards or structure and creativity.
2. Write an essay analyzing how Lutz conveys his persona, the image of himself presented to readers. Support your assertions with examples of his tone, his wording, his illustrations, or other pertinent characteristics.
3. Write your own memo about avoidance of waste. You may address it to officers at your current or past workplace, campus administrators, students in your living area or social group, members of your family, or others who would profit from your advice. (See p. 307 for a sample memo that illustrates the usual format.)

Community Links

Compare and contrast "It's Okay to Be Anal Sometimes" with another discussion of creativity such as Katz's "The Pathbreaking, Fractionalized, Uncertain World of Knowledge" (pp. 52–58). What do these discussions suggest about creativity? To what extent do their similarities or differences reflect their communities?

THE COMING JOB BOOM
Daniel Eisenberg

◆

Daniel Eisenberg's article was originally published in Time *but also has appeared in* Marriott Insights, *a periodical distributed to guests at Marriott hotels and other facilities, bringing articles of interest from other publications to business or general readers. Eisenberg's article uses demographics—the study of population statistics—to predict changes in the job market.*

1   At a time when the job market still seems bleak, the outlook for Alex and Cindi Ignatovsky, both 33, could not be much brighter. After trying out a number of different careers, the Aptos, Calif., couple have recently discovered their true callings. Alex, who had been a paralegal and had also done a brief stint as an insurance salesman, has just started working as a juvenile-probation officer, helping kids wend their way through the crowded criminal-justice system. Cindi, who previously was an editor and a graphic designer, is now busy finishing up an intensive, multiyear program to become an acupuncturist. In her view, as she puts it, "there's as much opportunity as I make of it."

2   She's right, about both her and her husband's prospects—but not just because they're passionate and adept at what they do. They have also, as it turns out, each chosen fields—in his case, law enforcement and social services, in hers, health care—that are feeling the first effects of the coming job boom. That's right. Even as thousands of Americans are still getting pink slips, powerful help is on the way. And it has more to do with demographics than economics. The oldest members of the huge baby-boom generation are now 56, and as they start retiring, job candidates with the right skills will be in hot demand. As Mitch Potter of human resources consultant William M. Mercer says, "The dotcom bubble created a false talent crunch. The real one is coming."

3   In certain industries, especially those in which burnout and early retirement are common and demand for services is rising, the crunch has already arrived. As the population ages, hospitals can't find enough nurses or medical technicians. Drugstores are competing to hire pharmacists, bidding some beginners' salaries above $75,000. School districts and universities will need 2.2 million more teachers over the next decade, not to mention administrators and librarians, and are already avidly recruiting. Homeowners can't get their calls returned by skilled contractors, electricians or plumbers. Corporations are scooping up accountants and engineers. For job seekers who have the right skills or are willing to learn them, there are real opportunities in government, construction and technology.

4   To millions of laid-off workers still pounding the pavement, of course, this might seem like wishful thinking. While the economy grew a whopping 5.8% in the first quarter of 2002, the job market usually lags by at least a few months.

Eisenberg, Daniel. "The Coming Job Boom," *Time,* May 6, 2002. © 2002 Time, Inc. Reprinted by permission.

To land a job, record numbers of workers are taking pay cuts or switching industries, according to outplacement firm Challenger, Gray & Christmas; many others are starting their own small businesses. But as hard as it may be to believe, it should not be too long before employees are in the driver's seat. A wave of retirements whose full effect is only starting to be felt will soon ripple through the entire economy. And the savviest workers and employers are already preparing for it.

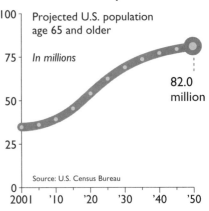

GRAY WAVE

Many boomers are retiring, and their numbers will shoot up after 2010

Projected U.S. population age 65 and older
In millions
82.0 million
Source: U.S. Census Bureau

5   Though the average retirement age is creeping up—and a growing share of Americans, by choice or necessity, are planning to work at least part time well past 65—demographers say there still will not be enough qualified members of the next generation to pick up the slack. So with 76 million baby boomers heading toward retirement over the next three decades and only 46 million Gen Xers waiting in the wings, corporate America is facing a potentially mammoth talent crunch. Certainly, labor-saving technology and immigration may help fill the breach. Still, by 2010 there may be a shortage of 4 million to 6 million workers.

6   Not enough Americans are trained for these jobs. They lack everything from computer literacy and leadership to critical thinking and communication skills. The recent slump, though, may be helping narrow the skills gap in a surprising way. Although generous social-welfare systems in industrialized countries such as Germany and Britain make it easy for the laid off to wait around for a factory to reopen, Americans tend to take the initiative during a downturn, getting educated or trained for a better job and in the process adding to the country's stock of human capital. Applications to graduate programs in everything from law and business to education and engineering are up from last year by 30%–100%. That approach should pay off. Although 1.9 million Americans with a high school diploma or less got the ax from September 2000 to October 2001—a time when the economy was slumping—1.2 million people with college or vocational degrees were hired, according to the Employment Policy Foundation.

7   It isn't just the younger generation that's going back to school, either. Bruce LeBel, 59, a veteran aircraft mechanic who lost his job after Sept. 11, is learning how to service the computer networks that help run more and more factories and power plants. Many of his former colleagues "are afraid to try anything different. They want to stay with a dead horse," he says. "But the only thing that can save me is having a skill that's in demand." To help other job hunters follow LeBel's example, here's a guide to the best job opportunities today—and tomorrow.

A Healthy Prognosis

8   If lately you have had to wait to fill a prescription or get your doctor on the phone, you know why no industry holds more promise than health care.

Caregivers

9   Nurses and pharmacists aren't the only ones being snapped up by hospitals. All across the country, sonogram operators, who make a median salary of $42,000, and radiology technicians are being hired. The people who help patients get back on their feet are also hot properties. Over the next decade, according to the Bureau of Labor Statistics, there will be 255,000 openings for all manner of therapists, including physical and respiratory therapists and speech pathologists.

Drugmakers

10 Firms that dream up wonder drugs are in one of the few industries that have continued to hire in droves. Swiss-based Novartis AG, which has embarked on a major expansion in the U.S., hired more than 1,800 workers last year and plans to keep hiring at a brisk pace. That includes everyone from marketing and manufacturing staff to people in finance, human resources and, of course, research science. This array of jobs pays anywhere from $30,000 to $300,000 a year. Likewise, Abbott Laboratories hopes to fill 5,000 new positions this year, including posts for sales reps who can drive product launches.

Gene Hunters

11 The much hyped biotech industry is finally starting to deliver on its promise, with more small companies shifting from basic research to drug development. That means more jobs, from lab work to medical writing, are in the pipeline as well. Genentech, based in South San Francisco, Calif., is increasing its head count each year by 297, or about 6% annually, hiring everyone from Ph.D.s to community-college grads who can work in manufacturing. Just in the budding field of bioinformatics, in which specialists can make more than $100,000 a year using computers to plow through reams of genetic data, there will be an estimated 20,000 unfilled jobs by 2005. Chemists are also being wooed across industries.

Uncle Sam Wants You

12 Long before Sept. 11 ushered in a new era of respect for government, Washington was poised to enjoy an unlikely job boom. Almost half the Federal Government's 1.8 million workers will be eligible to retire within five years. From the Food and Drug Administration (FDA) and Park Service to the Commerce, Energy and State departments, agencies are bracing for a brain drain, especially at the managerial level. And these aren't your classic paper-pushing jobs—although many of those, as at the busy Social Security Administration, are also going begging.

Law Enforcement

13 Organizations—from the FBI and the CIA to the Coast Guard and the Defense, Justice and State departments—are revving up their recruiting efforts, looking for everyone from computer programmers, budding young diplomats and spooks to lawyers and linguists. The Immigration and Naturalization Service wants to hire thousands of new border-patrol guards and immigration inspectors to process and keep better track of new arrivals to the country; these positions require just a high school diploma and, with overtime, can pay around $40,000 in the first year.

Big Thinkers

14 To help assess the growing tide of innovations that washes across its desks, the Patent and Trademark Office is desperate to find more qualified engineers and intellectual-property lawyers. Other high-end specialists are needed, such as drug reviewers at the FDA; accountants and statisticians at the Labor and Treasury departments, the Internal Revenue Service and the Securities and Exchange Commission; and trade experts at Commerce.

Get Your Hands Dirty

15 In the dotcom mania of the '90s, it was easy to forget that skilled tradespeople can make good money.

Construction

16 A recent industry study showed that at least one-third of St. Louis' 80,000 construction workers are expected to retire in the next five years—a microcosm of the situation nationwide; the industry needs to attract 240,000 new workers each year, from project managers to iron workers, just to compensate for the exodus. The top tradespeople in their fields, such as plumbers, electricians, carpenters, bricklayers, roofers and painters, can make upward of $100,000 a year.

Manufacturing

17 Even in this beleaguered sector, in which many firms have made huge layoffs, companies are having a hard time finding the right people. More than 80% of firms say they face a shortage of qualified machinists, craft workers and technicians, according to a recent survey by the National Association of Manufacturers. That deficit is likely to widen. Although manufacturing will not grow much overall during the next decade, a rapidly aging work force will create more than 2 million job openings—with many positions paying more than $50,000—for welders, tool- and die-makers, line managers and others.

Technicians

18 As machines keep getting more complex, with tiny microprocessors governing their every move, finding enough people to repair and maintain them is becoming harder. Heating and air-conditioning technicians are in high demand. Nationwide there are about 60,000 vacancies for car mechanics, who can earn anywhere from $30,000 to $100,000.

Engineering the Future

19 Despite the layoffs from busted dotcoms, jobs will be abundant in other areas of technology. Computer storage, enterprise software and semiconductors are still growth areas. Analysts expect corporate information-technology spending to stabilize this year and rebound in 2003.

Engineers

20 Over the past 15 years, the number of students graduating with a bachelor's degree in engineering dropped 50%, to 12,400. Companies like Texas Instruments are hiring electrical engineers for product-design, sales and marketing departments. Other engineers—software, mechanical, aerospace, civil and structural—are also hot properties.

Computer Monitors

21 Computer-related jobs will be among the fastest growing in the next decade. Leading the way will be those key employees who help large companies maintain their daunting tangles of technology, from system analysts and support specialists to database administrators.

The Desk Set

22 Thousands of investment bankers, consultants and lawyers have become casualties of the latest round of corporate downsizing. But the long-range picture looks better. As baby boomers scale back their time at the office to concentrate on other activities, from golf to philanthropy, corporate America will be desperate to find qualified managers and executives as well as support staff, from administrative assistants to paralegals.

Finance and Accounting

23 H&R Block has been busy hiring 1,200 financial advisers and marketing staff members as it broadens its tax-preparing business. Financial-services firms continue to look for financial planners and asset managers. Despite their role at Enron and in other corporate scandals this year, accounting and auditing are especially attractive fields, expected to grow nearly 20% in the next decade.

Energy

24 The oil, gas and utility sector is bringing on finance and marketing graduates to help navigate deregulation. Companies such as TXU, Exxon Mobil and Koch Industries are still hiring. A graying work force means the industry also needs to find a new generation of petroleum engineers, geologists and geophysicists.

25 To keep pace in today's fast-moving economy, job hunters must be, above all, flexible. Steve Reyna, 28, who four years ago went to work at TDIndustries, a

The Hot Jobs

SOME OCCUPATIONS WITH THE LARGEST PROJECTED GROWTH, 2000–2010 (Change in number of jobs)

Teachers (K–12)	+711,000
Computer-Software Engineers	+664,000
Registered Nurses	+561,000
Truck Drivers	+561,000
Computer-Support Specialists	+490,000
Accountants and Auditors	+181,000
Marketing and Sales Managers	+168,000
Auto Mechanics	+151,000
Health Therapists	+145,000
Police and Sheriff's Officers	+141,000
Social Workers	+141,000
Engineers	+138,000
Lawyers	+123,000
Electricians	+120,000
Recreation and Fitness Workers	+118,000
Sales Representatives	+118,000

The Cold Jobs

SOME OCCUPATIONS WITH THE LARGEST PROJECTED LOSSES, OR SMALLEST GROWTH, 2000–2010

Farmers and Ranchers	–328,000
Phone-Switchboard Operators	–60,000
Bank Tellers	–59,000
Insurance-Claims Clerks	–58,000
Word Processors/Typists	–57,000
Sewing-Machine Operators	–51,000
Butchers	–13,000
Meter Readers	–13,000
Parts Salespeople	–12,000
Procurement Clerks	–9,000
Movie Projectionists	–3,000
Proofreaders	–2,000
Loggers	–2,000
Funeral Directors	+1,000
Insurance Underwriters	+2,000
Travel Agents	+4,000

Dallas-based mechanical contractor that specializes in air-conditioning and plumbing projects for high-tech companies, knows this better than most. After training as a sheet-metal technician, Reyna moved on to work in the so-called clean rooms of semiconductor companies, learning a little welding and plumbing along the way. Just one of more than 1,300 employees at

TDIndustries who are rigorously cross-trained, Reyna is now ready to work "wherever they need me." If the number crunchers turn out to be right, that could soon mean just about everywhere.

—*With reporting by Cathy Booth Thomas/Dallas, Unmesh Kher/New York, Sean Scully/Los Angeles, Maggie Sieger and Leslie Whitaker/Chicago, Daniel Terdiman/San Francisco, with other bureaus*

Reading Responses

1. How does Eisenberg use population statistics to support his predictions about the job market? In what ways might population shifts change the job market?
2. Find examples in the article of several strategies Eisenberg uses to present and integrate statistics.
3. How does Eisenberg organize his essay? Why would this organization be likely to appeal to readers?

Writing Activities

1. Experiment with text and graphics. Write a paragraph that explains what the "Gray Wave" graph shows. Sketch a graph or table that might be used to present information now explained in the text.
2. Based on the information in the article, write a letter to a friend or relative who is uncertain about what career to pursue. Advise this person about fields that might be interesting and also supply good career possibilities. Be certain to tailor your advice to this person's interests and personality.
3. Write an essay explaining what Eisenberg's projections might mean for a specific type of person—for example, a parent who owns a home, a retiree with health problems, a city engineer who must organize municipal construction projects, a bank teller who was recently laid off, or some other person you invent. Imagine the situation of this person in ten years—what services or products might the person need, and what job might the person want? Then, based on the information in the article, explain what problems or opportunities this person might encounter getting what he or she wants.

Community Links

Compare and contrast Eisenberg's article with Aslanian's "The Community College Pathway" (pp. 59–64) from the academic community. In what ways do these articles differ? What differences may reflect their communities and specific readers? What common views and approaches do they share?

CRACKING THE HIDDEN CODE: BECOMING A CULTURAL SLEUTH

Lee G. Bolman and Terrence E. Deal

◆

In Escape from Cluelessness: A Guide for the Organizationally Challenged, *Lee Bolman and Terrence Deal explain how to crack the secret cultural code in the workplace, offering an alternative to the cynicism or despair many employees feel, especially in large, impersonal organizations. As experts in leadership and organizational systems, the authors supply practical advice to help employees navigate and improve the workplace, tackling issues such as office politics, interpersonal relationships, bureaucracy, and change.*

Ever had a day at the office where nothing seemed to make any sense? Have you and your colleagues ever puzzled about why certain things never change even though they don't work as they're supposed to? Have you ever felt that your coworkers seem to obey some unwritten, secret code, even though no one knows quite why?

1   Workplaces are often weird. Projects are assigned and then forgotten. Status reports are required but never read. Information is collected and then ignored. Meetings go on for hours but nothing gets done. People talk at length without saying anything. Employees wander around in a continual state of puzzlement and discontent. If you look deeper, though, there's sense in the senselessness. Just as fish don't notice water, we don't always see taken-for-granted patterns that govern everyday action. Nor do we see alternatives—things we could do to improve our lot at work.

2   Things get much clearer when you learn to decipher the subtle or hidden cultural clues that abound in any office—artifacts, behavior, language, dress, and ritualized intermissions such as coffee breaks, lunch, and the late afternoon watering hole. Cracking the cultural code reveals the real stuff that lurks just under the surface of everyday life. You understand more, and you can cope better—or know that it's time to leave. As we've noted before, you always have the options to sign up, speak up, sign off, or ship out. It's easier to choose if you know what you're up against.

3   We're all social animals. We crave belongingness and meaning. We depend on the people around us to help us find both. Collectively, we create culture, accepted ways of doing things (see Figure 9-1). We do it through trial and error. In the course of everyday experience, every group and organization gleans lessons about what works and what flops. Over time, we accumulate a history that gradually shapes who we are, what we value, how we think, and how we do things. To reinforce our evolving values and beliefs, we identify human icons—heroes and heroines who embody the best, devils who exemplify the worst. Culture is hard to experience or share in words, so we create rituals and ceremonies—occasions where we bond to one another and share our commitment to something bigger. We also share stories. They're fun, and, more important, they carry valuable lessons. Culture provides the symbolic glue that

"I don't know how it started, either. All I know is that it's part of our corporate culture."

Figure 9-1 The power of culture.
© The New Yorker Collection, 1994, Mick Stevens, from cartoonbank.com. All rights reserved.

holds people and organizations together. In many places, the glue doesn't stick very well. It's more like what you find on the back of a Post-it. But it still helps people learn the ropes, even in a day-to-day life that may look very strange to outsiders.

How do you crack the cultural code at work? Try being a cultural anthropologist for a day. Unless you're an air traffic controller or a brain surgeon, no one is likely to notice that you're taking time to study the natives' folkways rather than focusing strictly on the task at hand.

1. *Study cultural clues.* Open your senses fully and try to take nothing for granted. Notice the architecture—space speaks. Before Hurricane Andrew, Burger King's headquarters in Florida was a feudal kingdom. Expansive executive offices on one floor facing the ocean, everyone else in cramped quarters. After the hurricane devastated the headquarters building, it was rebuilt. In the new building, secretaries and functional people have offices with an ocean view. Executives who travel most of the time occupy small interior offices. The new spatial arrangements reflect a sea change in cultural values. Before, status ruled. Your position in the pecking order determined your perks. Now, space is aligned with what people do. Contribution to overall effectiveness is what counts.

What do you notice about the building in which you work? When you get off the elevator or come off the stairs, what leaps out? How does the place look? How does it smell? What sounds, if any, strike you? Walk around to get the lay of the landscape. Who has the big corner offices? Who gets a tiny cubicle? Notice artifacts. What's on the walls? What do people keep on their desks? Any graffiti in the rest rooms? Check out wastebaskets. What do people toss as opposed to keep?

7. Hang around as people go through their daily doings. Observe meetings. Who arrives late? Who sits where? Who leaves early? How long do meetings last? Do they start on time? Who talks? Who doesn't? Who's listened to or ignored? In one big computer company, meetings always start fifteen minutes late. In the new Continental Airlines, meetings always start on time, to signal the importance of on-time performance. What are the preferred media—flip charts, color slides, computer graphics, or blackboards? In one merger of two companies, a problem became apparent right away. One company relied on multicolored 35mm slides. The other favored simple flip charts. Until they worked it out, meetings were a war zone. Hang out around the water cooler or coffee pot, if one exists. Who shows up at which times? What informal subgroups are apparent? Are subgroups formed around race, gender, position, or function? Do smokers have their own gathering place? As a noted anthropologist tried to pinpoint a company's subcultures, she had trouble figuring out why one subgroup was so cohesive. It turned out they all smoked. Since their office is smoke-free, they gather outside before work, at lunch, and during breaks. This gives them countless opportunities to gab, gossip, and plot.

8. How do people communicate? Face-to-face? E-mail? Memo? What do they say? Listen for pronouns, slang, acronyms, profanity. "I want this done" is very different from "How should we do this?" "This is the way we do things around here" conveys a different attitude than "Shine on and keep your head down." What metaphors are evident in discourse? Sports (slam dunks and goal-line stands)? Military (frontal assaults and sneak attacks)?

9. What do people wear? Do engineers wear regulation costumes—short-sleeve shirts, plastic pocket protectors, and skimpy, nondescript ties? Or are they more often in T-shirts and cutoffs? Do bosses wear standard-issue dark suits? Or aloha shirts? Do women managers dress much like their male counterparts? Or do they favor colors and styles you'd rarely find in a men's department? In the IBM of old, white shirts and dark suits were standard. One recruit showed up in tweed for his first day on the job. His boss asked him where he found the slacks to go with his sport coat. The new hire picked up the signal immediately. In a similar experience, one of us showed up for an evening dinner at a well-known advertising firm wearing a light tan suit. Everyone else was in blue pinstripes. A vice-president highlighted our violation of the dress code by asking, "Where do you get your suits bleached?"

10. What rituals draw people together? Are they held before or after work? At noon over lunch? Does the work itself serve as a ritual as people bond around success or failure? The sign of a ritual is that the same things occur over and over, but with a deeper, more special feeling than mere routine. Rituals typically occur at the day's beginning, end, or midpoint. Notice who attends and who's excluded, and how. What symbols dominate the ritualistic exchange? Coffee and cookies? Wine and cheese? Fancy slides and sophisticated analyses? Each Friday night at Southwest Airline's Love Field Headquarters, employees gather around a barbecue grill. They cook, quaff, chew, and chat, informally mulling over the week's events. Before an operation, surgeons often scrub for a traditional seven minutes, even though modern soaps kill germs in

about thirty seconds. The scrub helps the operating team prepare for the delicate task ahead.

11   What does the culture celebrate? Individual achievement? Collective triumph? Seasonal occasions like holiday parties or summer outings? Corporate anniversaries or individual birthdays? Southwest Airlines celebrates them all, which is one of the reasons that the airline's spirit is so robust and contagious. Do people gather when things get tough? What happens when the inevitable screw-up occurs? One large U.S. retail firm gathers periodically to celebrate its mistakes. The message: We're human and blow it once in a while. But we learn from our errors. When tough decisions are announced, what do people do? Are the downsized honored with a dignified send-off? Are mergers marked with appropriate transition rites? Two large hospitals celebrated their merger with a hilarious video showing the two CEOs being surgically joined at the hip. Do celebrations have sustaining oomph? Or do people just go through the motions?

12   Your own observations will yield thousands of clues to help penetrate fog-shrouded cultural practices. But there's more you can do. Every workplace has a cast of characters who can become your informal guides.

13   2. *Hire guides: priests and storytellers.* There's a cast of characters in every workplace who can be recruited as cultural guides. Locate informal priests or priestesses. Don't look in a big corner office. Priests are more likely to be typing away in a small cubicle, or closeted somewhere in the archives. They're often old-timers who came in with the furniture. The reigning priestess of a California medical center was the head of housekeeping. She could easily cross subcultural boundaries and served as a passionate promoter of the hospital's core mission. One of Anheuser-Busch's priests was an 84-year-old retired brewmaster. He came to work each day and held court. Priests regularly take confessions and are widely respected throughout the organization. They are keepers of history and protectors of tradition. They can tell you how things came to be and instruct you in prevailing cultural mores and norms. Be reverent, pay attention, and you'll find a storehouse of knowledge and wisdom, both ancient and modern. You can also make a friend whose counsel and support could be a big help somewhere down the line.

14   Look too for corporate storytellers; individuals who dramatize everyday exploits and perpetuate corporate lore. Their legendary tales carry grains of truth about important values and taboos. Take storytellers to the local watering hole. Listen to their tales and read between the lines. You'll get important lessons on how to get ahead and what to avoid. You'll hear things you'd almost never find in policy manuals or official publications. Stories make lessons real and memorable. Even though unofficial, the lessons are often right on. The stories will tell you about heroes and heroines—the living logos who exemplify what the organization stands for. Dilbert, for example, is a cultural hero because he exemplifies the pains and frustrations of cubicle life and regularly outwits the boss in the process. In other settings, heroes and heroines represent significant values like hard work, creativity, or courage. There was an employee at 3M many years ago who stubbornly championed the newfangled idea of clear adhesive tape. His boss didn't see any value in it and told him to work on something else. The employee quietly went on working on his tape. He was fired for insubordination,

but came back to work the next day anyway. His embarrassed supervisors put him back on the payroll and asked him just to leave others alone. His idea flowered into Scotch tape—one of 3M's greatest and most enduring product triumphs. That stubborn employee became a cultural icon, an exemplar of the values of creativity and persistence. Years later, his example inspired another stubborn 3Mer to persist in looking for some way to use an adhesive he'd discovered that didn't stick very well. Along came another 3Mer who sang in a church choir. He was looking for bookmarks that wouldn't fall out of hymnals. Of that union was born the Post-it note.

15   On the other hand, you might find that the heroes in your workplace are folks who toe the line and kiss up to the boss. If that's what gets rewarded, but it's not your style, you've learned an important lesson. Maybe you need to find somewhere else to work.

16   3. *Connect with grapevine gossips.* Gossips are always privy to the latest scoop, even things that are supposed to be confidential or hush-hush. Hear them out and you'll often get the best briefing going. Their accuracy isn't perfect, but they're reliable clues about salient issues, concerns, hopes, and fears in your workplace. If you hear a story about how the CEO chewed out a VP in a hotel corridor, the details may be distorted, but you can be pretty sure something big is afoot. Rumors of impending layoffs may be exaggerated, but you'd be wise to prepare for rough seas. Gossip is a two-way street. You have to give in order to receive. Don't be too cautious about divulging a few things yourself. Chances are the truth will be less harmful than what the gossips make up on their own. A few minutes over coffee with your local gossip is often worth more than a multitude of meetings and memos. Information is power. Being up-to-date and in the loop gives you a real advantage over people who rely solely on

---

Frank 'n' Hope: *Girl Scout?*

HOPE: I've been doing some scouting.
FRANK: So now you're a girl scout! You could start a troop and give out merit badges.
HOPE: I might if I thought you'd buy some cookies. But cut the sarcasm and you might learn something.
FRANK: Like what?
HOPE: You know Liz in security?
FRANK: Not very well. Should I?
HOPE: You're missing an opportunity. She sure knows you. There isn't too much she doesn't know.
FRANK: She's been here about ninety years.
HOPE: She talks to people. And they talk to her. When I want the real scoop, I talk to Liz.
FRANK: You'd do about as well talking to my dog.
HOPE: He snarls too much. And Liz has better stories. If you wanna know who's moving ahead, who's topped out and why, Liz is amazing.
FRANK: She say anything about me?

the official channels to keep on top of things. And if there are things you'd like people to be talking about, there's no better place than the grapevine to get the word out. Plant your story with people who are sure to spread the word.

17   4. *Watch for spies.* Finally, be alert to signs of the clandestine intelligence network—the world of spies and counterspies. Most executives have spies, and employees often have a "mole" planted in the boss's corner office. Some organizations even create internal counterespionage units. The secret world of intelligence gathering and espionage isn't necessarily good or bad. It just is. It can work for you or against you. You want to be careful about what you say to anyone who might be a spy. But if you know who the agents are, you can judiciously plant some seeds that might grow nicely for you.

18   5. *Form cabals.* Finally, don't be reluctant to form cabals—groups of like-minded people who join together to launch cultural conspiracies. They share common values and have shared interests in pushing the culture in a certain way. Cabal members may seem to have little in common, yet they share a passion for something intrinsic. Southwest Airlines has an officially sanctioned cabal known as the Culture Committee. It includes representatives from across the company's levels and functions. The only membership requirement is a big heart. Virginia Mason Hospital and Clinic sponsored a similar committee in the 1980s. Its membership included nurses, doctors, technicians, administrators, and staff. The group had a good time planning good times for the hospital. Joining a cabal can supplement your efforts with the collective energy to influence workplace agenda and events.

19   Together, the characters in the informal cultural network can offer you a comprehensive picture of what works below the surface or behind the scenes. Knowing these taken-for-granted traditional ways and unofficial cultural rules provides a welcome escape from cluelessness. The clues are often subtle, but they're always there. They just need to be gathered and arranged in a cohesive pattern. Reading a culture gives you a chance to be better prepared, less stressed, and less often surprised. Equally important, knowing the existential underbelly offers opportunities to shape as well as be shaped by cultural patterns and rules.

Escaping Cluelessness IX: Uncovering Hidden Tribal Ways

- Every group and organization creates cultural ways to make sense and give meaning to life and work.
- Cultural ways and traditions dictate what people wear, how they speak and what they do.
- Understanding culture reduces surprise and stress, increases understanding and confidence.
- Study cultural clues:
    - Enlist guides.
    - Connect to the grapevine.
    - Watch for spies.
    - Form cabals.
- Knowing the existential underbelly lets you shape as well as be shaped by culture.

Reading Responses

1. Why do Bolman and Deal recommend cultural sleuthing? How might it benefit an employee?
2. If you should decide to become a cultural sleuth, what, according to Bolman and Deal, might you want to do?
3. What readers do Bolman and Deal address? What do they seem to assume about readers' problems, concerns, and expectations?

Writing Activities

1. Observe one component of your classroom culture such as the spatial arrangement of the classroom, the traffic flow in the building where you meet, or the dress code that people follow. Explain your findings in a brief report.
2. Using Bolman and Deal's definition of culture in paragraph 3, discuss the "symbolic glue" that holds together a group or organization to which you belong. Consider the history, rituals, icons, or stories of the group. State a thesis that identifies a significant point about the group's culture, and then use examples to explain and illustrate this central idea.
3. Apply Bolman and Deal's first suggestion, "study cultural clues," to your current or former workplace, your college or university, or another organization. Write a report explaining what you have learned about the organization based on your research as a cultural anthropologist.

Community Links

Consider similarities or differences in two or three of the academic, work, or public communities that involve you right now, using Bolman and Deal's advice about cultural observation. For instance, you might contrast their stories, their legendary heroes, or their ceremonies, using examples from each community. Or you might discuss a common cultural feature, illustrating how that feature appears or functions in each community.

THE NEW CULTURE OF CAPITALISM
Jeremy Rifkin

♦

In The Age of Access: The New Culture of Hypercapitalism, Where All of Life Is a Paid-for Experience, *Jeremy Rifkin looks at the changes in capitalism—the transition from an industrial economy based on the production of goods from resources to a new economy based on the production and communication of cultural experience. Rifkin's Chapter 8 examines "cultural capitalism" through changes in the arts, travel, entertainment, recreation, and the marketplace, which is included in the following selection.*

1   The big changes in history, the ones that fundamentally alter how we think and act, have a way of creeping up on society until one day everything we know is suddenly passé and we realize we are in a whole new world. It wasn't until the late nineteenth century, for example, that the British historian Arnold Toynbee coined the term *Industrial Age*, nearly a hundred years after it first arrived on the world scene.[1]

2   Similarly, for the better part of the twentieth century, a new form of capitalism has been slowly gestating and is only now about to overtake industrial capitalism. After hundreds of years of converting physical resources into propertied goods, we are now increasingly transforming cultural resources into paid-for personal experiences and entertainments.

3   In the new age of cultural capitalism, access becomes far more relevant and property far less so in the ordering of commercial life. Property relations are compatible with a world in which the primary task of economic life is the processing, manufacturing, and distribution of physical goods. Inert objects are easily measurable, and because hard goods can be quantified, they're amenable to price. They are solid and therefore exchangeable between parties. They can be possessed by only one party at a time and fit the requisite of exclusivity. They are both autonomous and, for the most part, mobile—with the exception of real estate. They lend themselves to the rather simple notions that underlie property relationships.

4   But in the new cultural economy, the organization of commercial life is not so simple. It is a world of symbols, webs and feedback loops, connectivity and interactivity, in which borders and boundaries become murky and everything that is solid begins to melt.

5   We are entering a new era of digital communications technologies and cultural commerce. In fact, the two together create a powerful new economic paradigm. More and more of our daily lives is already mediated by the new digital channels of human expression. And because communication is the means by which human beings find common meaning and share the world they create, commodifying all forms of digital communications goes hand in hand with commodifying the many relationships that make up the lived experience—the cultural life—of the individual and the community.

6 After thousands of years of existing in a semi-independent realm, occasionally touched by the market but never absorbed by it, culture—shared human experience—is now being drawn into the economic realm, thanks to the hold the new communications technologies are beginning to enjoy over day-to-day life. In a global economy increasingly dominated by a commercial electronic communications grid and every kind of cultural production and commodity, securing access to one's own lived experiences becomes as important as being propertied was in an era dominated by the production of industrial goods.

Communication and Culture

7 Even many of the most ardent supporters of the new communications revolution have yet to fully grasp the close relationship that exists between communications and culture. If culture is, in the words of anthropologist Clifford Geertz, "the webs of significance" human beings spin around themselves, then communications—language, art, music, dance, written text, film, recordings, software—are the tools we human beings use to interpret, reproduce, maintain, and transform these webs of meaning.[2] "To be human," notes media theorist Lee Thayer, "is to be *in* communications in *some* human culture and to be in some human culture is to see and know the world—to communicate—in a way which daily recreates that particular culture."[3] Anthropologist Edward T. Hall reminds us that "communication constitutes the core of culture and indeed of life itself."[4] There is an inseparable link, then, between communications and culture. "Culture communicates," said the late anthropologist Edmund Leach.[5]

8 Information specialists and engineers tend to view communications more narrowly as the transmission of messages. Their focus is on how senders and receivers encode and decode and use channels effectively with the least amount of noise. This process approach to communications, which dates back to the pioneering work of Norbert Wiener and other cyberneticians in the late 1940s and early 1950s, is concerned with how one person uses communication to affect the behavior or state of mind of another person.

9 The anthropological school, in contrast, sees communication as the generation of social meaning through the transmission of texts. Semiotics, a field pioneered by Swiss linguist Ferdinand de Saussure and American philosopher Charles Saunders Pierce, is concerned with how communications establish meaning, reproduce common values, and bind people together in social relationships. Structuralists are interested in how language, myth, and other symbolic systems are used to make sense of shared social experiences.[6] This is the sense in which communications and culture each become an expression of the other.

10 It's no accident, then, that communication and community stem from a common root. Communities exist by sharing common meanings and common forms of communications. While this relationship seems obvious, it's often overlooked in discussions of communications, the implicit assumption being that communication is a phenomenon in and of itself, independent of the so-

cial context it interprets and reproduces. Anthropologists argue that communications cannot be divorced from community and culture. Neither can exist without the other. That being the case, when all forms of communication become commodities, then culture, the stuff of communications, inevitably becomes a commodity as well. And that is what's happening. Culture—the shared experiences that give meaning to human life—is being pulled inexorably into the media marketplace, where it is being revamped along commercial lines. When marketing experts and cyberspace pundits talk about using the new information and communications technologies as relationship tools and preach a commercial gospel based on selling personal experiences, commodifying long-term relationship with customers, and establishing communities of interest, what they have in mind, be it conscious or not, is the commercial enclosure and commodification of the shared cultural commons.

11 Herbert Schiller, professor emeritus of communications at the University of California at San Diego, poignantly observes that "speech, dance, drama, ritual, music, and the visual and plastic arts have been vital, indeed necessary, features of human experience from earliest times." What is different, says Schiller, is "the relentless and successful efforts to separate these elemental expressions of human creativity from their group and community origins for the purpose of *selling them* to those who can pay for them."[7]

12 The evidence is everywhere. The culture industries—a term coined by German sociologists Theodore Adorno and Max Horkheimer in the 1930s—are the fastest growing sector of the global economy. Film, radio, television, the recording industry, global tourism, shopping malls, destination entertainment centers, themed cities, theme parks, fashion, cuisine, professional sports and games, gambling, wellness, and the simulated worlds and virtual realities of cyberspace are the front line commercial fields in an Age of Access.

13 Cultural life, because it is a shared experience between people, always focuses on questions of access and inclusion. One either is a member of a community and culture and therefore enjoys access to its shared networks of meaning and experience, or one is excluded. As more and more of the shared culture deconstructs into fragmented commercial experiences in a network economy, access rights will similarly continue to migrate from the social to the commercial realm. Access will no longer be based on intrinsic criteria—traditions, rights of passage, family and kinship relations, ethnicity, religion, or gender—but rather on affordability in the commercial arena. [. . .]

Mall Culture

14 While travel and tourism is steadily stripping away the cultural landscape, enclosing bits and pieces of it into commodified tourist areas, a similar process is occurring in the public square. For hundreds of years the public square has been regarded as a cultural commons, an open space where people congregate, communicate with one another, share their experiences, and engage in cultural exchanges of various kinds, including festivals, pageants, ceremonies, sports, entertainment, and civic involvement. Although commerce and trade traditionally take place in the public square, the market has always been a derivative

activity. The primary activity has always been the creation and maintenance of social capital, not market capital. It has been the one place open to everyone, rich and poor. There are no gatekeepers or tolls. It is the agreed-upon arena where the culture, in all of its forms, reproduces itself and grows.

15   Now, in less than thirty years, the public square—the meeting ground for culture—has all but disappeared, swallowed up by a radical new concept in human aggregation steeped in commercial relations. After hundreds of years of market activity being peripheral to and a derivative of culture activity, the relationship has been reversed. Today, cultural activities in the public square have been absorbed into enclosed shopping malls and become a commodity for sale. The shopping mall has created a new architecture for human assembly, one immersed in a world of commerce in which culture exists in the form of commodified experiences. In this sense, the shopping mall shares much in common with the modern travel and tourism industry.

16   In fact, the International Council of Shopping Centers even publishes a tourist guide to shopping centers across the United States. It's no wonder. In Alabama, for example, Riverside Galleria is the state's number-one tourist attraction. In Arkansas, the McCane Mall is the state's leading tourist destination. In Illinois, Gurnee Mills is second only to the Lincoln Zoo in tourist visits. Virginia's Potomac Mills draws more tourists than any other site, in a state rich in landmarks and history. The Mall of America in Minneapolis—the largest mall in the United States—attracts more visitors every year than Disney World, Graceland, and the Grand Canyon combined. The U.S. Department of Commerce reports that 85 percent of international visitors listed shopping as their number-one tourist activity while in the United States.[8]

17   Shopping malls are becoming places where one can buy access to lived experiences of every kind. One can attend classes, take in a stage show, drop off a baby at a child-care center, take medical exams, eat, attend an art exhibit or concert, engage in sport, exercise and jog, attend religious services, stay overnight in a hotel, buy conveniences, watch a parade, visit a festival, meet a friend, and congregate with neighbors.

18   The mall culture is a creature of suburban development and the spread of the highway culture. Once confined to American soil, shopping centers now are found in virtually every country in the world. There are more than 43,000 shopping centers—including 1,800 enclosed malls—in the United States.[9] More than half of all retail sales are generated inside these establishments.[10] Even more important, these are the places where most people spend much of their leisure time. By the mid 1980s, American teenagers were spending more time inside shopping malls than anywhere except for home and school.[11] These are the new domains where people live out much of their social life—where they engage one another in discourse or just in passing. Whatever parts of the culture are reproduced are done so largely inside these walls, along the promenades, and under the lit-up atriums and arches.

19   Malls are sophisticated communication mediums designed to reproduce parts of the culture in simulated commercial forms. They rely on all of the most advanced electronic technologies to create an artificial cultural milieu. Carefully choreographed architectural motifs, automated climate-controlled

environments, sophisticated lighting schemes, and computerized surveillance systems all work together to "communicate" a special cultural place, different from the shared cultural spaces that exist on the other side of the mall gates.

20 Of course, the most important difference is that shopping malls are private domains with rules and regulations governing access. While their walkways, benches, and tree-lined open spaces give malls the appearance of being public spheres, they are not. The cultural activity that takes place there is never an end in itself but always instrumental to the central mission, which is the commodification of lived experiences in the form of the purchase of goods and entertainment.

21 The first shopping center in the United States was developed by J. C. Nichols, in Kansas City in 1924. The Country Club Plaza became the prototype for the shopping centers that followed after World War II. With its Mediterranean architecture, tiled fountains, and wrought-iron balconies, it created an attractive fantasylike environment for consumers to browse in.[12]

22 The first enclosed mall—Southdale—was constructed in Edina, a suburb of Minneapolis, in 1956. By controlling the temperature year round, Victor Green, its designer, was able to create a near hermetically sealed simulated environment, a place where people could leave behind the outside world, with its noises, distractions, spontaneous eruptions, and surprises.[13]

23 Today, malls are theatrical spaces, elaborate stages where the drama of consumption is acted out. The developers borrow heavily from Hollywood in the construction of these environments. To begin with, the spaces are planned in a way that encourages visitors to suspend disbelief once inside, as one would in a movie theater. Malls are timeless—there are few or no clocks in malls. The inside ambiance is both exotic and comfortable, with running fountains, small sparkling pools with lily pads floating along the surface, palm trees offering shade from the overhead lights, store façades leading into cavernous interiors stocked with various treasures. Looking down over a second-level railing into the center court of a shopping mall called Greengate, William Kowinski, author of *The Malling of America*, says that he felt as if he were "standing on a balcony looking down on a stage, waiting for the show to begin."[14]

24 Behind the stage, the producers and directors of these elaborate cultural productions have developed a highly sophisticated game plan for ensuring that the theatrical experience leads to sales. Real estate developers, marketing analysts, economists, architects, engineers, space planners, marketing experts, landscape architects, interior designers, and public relations firms work together to create what they call the "retail drama"—the ideal commercial mix of tenants (the talent), stage settings, and performances to guarantee the optimum theatrical experience and maximum sales. The "mix" is the formula used to control which stores are allowed access to the mall. Owners "cast" for the best combination of stores—so many department stores, jewelers, sporting goods stores, video stores, bookstores, restaurants, boutiques, and novelty shops—to create the most appropriate buying environment. The mixes are tailored to the income levels, ethnic compositions, gender, and lifestyles of potential customers. Indexes, like the Value and Life Style (VALS) program created by the Stanford Research Institute, correlate age, income, and family

makeup with data on leisure preferences and cultural backgrounds to anticipate the kinds of shopping experience the customers are likely to want. Shoppers are divided by lifestyle categories. The "achievers" ("hard-working, materialistic, highly educated traditional consumers; shopping leaders for luxury products") are likely to shop at Brooks Brothers, Bloomingdale's, or Neiman Marcus. The "emulators" ("younger, status-conscious, conspicuous consumers") are likely to shop at Ann Taylor or Ralph Lauren. "Sustainers" ("struggling poor") and "belongers" ("middle-class, conservative, conforming shoppers, low to moderate income") tend to be more value oriented and more likely to shop at K-Mart and J. C. Penney.[15]

25   The average American visits a mall every ten days and spends more than one hour and fifteen minutes there. The most commonly mentioned reason for making these weekly pilgrimages is entertainment.[16] "The mall is like three-dimensional television," says Kowinski.[17] Its rush of images and fast-changing façades, endless commercial messages and dramatic settings, are familiar to a generation that grew up with TV. The only difference is that in the mall, the viewer crosses over onto the set and becomes an actor in the unfolding drama. In both mediums, elaborate cultural productions are staged with the goal of entertaining the "audience" or "customers" and, in the process, selling them some form of commodified experience, either a product, service, or memorable event.

26   Malls pride themselves on their unique stage sets. In Scottsdale, Arizona, the Borgata—an open-air mall in the desert—is a scaled-down version of San Gimignano, a quaint, picturesque hill town in Tuscany, Italy. The mall includes a central plaza and tower made of Italian bricks. In Connecticut, Old Mystic Village is a reproduction of a New England main street of the early eighteenth century.

27   The West Edmonton Mall in Canada, the world's biggest shopping mall, is also the largest stage set for cultural productions in the world. Encompassing an area that extends more than 100 football fields, the enclosed structure houses the world's largest indoor amusement park, the world's largest indoor water park, a fleet of submarines, the world's largest indoor golf course, 800 shops, 11 department stores, 110 restaurants, an ice-skating rink, a nondenominational chapel, a 360-room hotel, 13 nightclubs, and 20 movie theaters. Visitors can meander along Parisian boulevards or boogie down New Orleans' Bourbon Street as they make their way from one stage set to another.[18] The internal "grounds" are lush with vegetation, and the ceilings are made from special reflective materials that give the appearance of natural sunshine.[19]

28   The developers of the West Edmonton megamall envisioned bringing the culture of the world into a giant indoor space, where it could be commodified in the form of bits of entertainment to delight and amuse visitors and stimulate the desire to buy. At the opening ceremony, one of the mall's developers, Nader Ghermezion, exclaimed, "What we have done means you don't have to go to New York or Paris or Disneyland or Hawaii. We have it all for you here in one place, in Edmonton, Alberta, Canada!"[20]

29   The West Edmonton mall is a wraparound theater where in any direction one goes, one is surrounded by cultural fragments, performances, and every

kind of entertainment. One can ride a rickshaw; go onboard a full-length replica of the Santa María; pet farm animals in the petting zoo; be photographed with a live lion, tiger, or jaguar; and take part in an "authentic" Mongolian barbecue. Ghermezion sees his commercial venture as a surrogate for—not just a simulation of—culture. The mall, he says, is "to serve as a community, social, entertainment, and recreation center."[21] Except in this private world, culture is bought and access is determined by the mall owners. The architects' and designers' mission, writes Peter Hemingway, was to provide "a sugarcoated dream world where we can shop, play, and experience danger and delight without once stepping outside; where we can change experiences like flipping TV channels . . . where the plastic credit card is the open sesame to every experience."[22]

30   The West Edmonton Mall is on the cutting edge of the vast changes taking place in the global economy as it makes the transition from an industrial- to a cultural-centered capitalism. In the early malls, cultural productions and entertainment were backdrops for selling goods. In the new malls, entertainment and lived experiences are fast becoming the primary commercial activity, and buying goods is becoming, for some at least, more of an accompanying activity.

31   The new malls of the future are called "destination entertainment centers." Giant department stores like Bloomingdale's and Nordstrom are no longer the primary attractions. Instead, IMAX movie theaters, themed nightclubs like the Hard Rock Café and the Rainforest Café, high-tech video amusements, virtual-reality games, and motion-simulator rides are becoming the core commercial business.

32   Sony's new Metreon in San Francisco, which is estimated to have cost upward of $160 million to construct, is a state-of-the-art "urban entertainment destination." The 350,000-square-foot complex houses twelve movie theaters, a 3-D IMAX theater, eight upscale eateries, a games parlor called the "Airtight Garage," and a Sony Play Station where people can order video games at the "computer bar." Other stores showcase Sony electronics, Microsoft software, and the Discovery Channel's line of items. The complex also hosts two major entertainment attractions, "The Way Things Work" and "Where the Wild Things Are." The latter, patterned after Maurice Sendak's children's classic, is a playground the size of a football field, inhabited by giant fanged yellow-eyed monsters hanging from the ceiling and hiding behind various landscapes. Kids pay a seven-dollar admission fee to scamper through caves and tunnels, build their own towers, and yank on ropes and levers that make the monsters jump and dart around. Metreons—the word comes from *Metropolis* and the Greek suffix *eon*, or meeting place—are being readied for Tokyo and Berlin.[23]

33   In an Age of Access, the megamalls and the entertainment destination theme centers are primary gatekeepers to a new commercialized culture. As more and more of people's social encounters and lived experiences take place in these enclosed commercial environments, access to these domains becomes an increasingly important social issue.

34   "Nothing gets in here unless we let it in," warns the manager of the Westmoreland Mall in Greensburg, Pennsylvania.[24] At Tyson Corners in Virginia, notices posted on the entrances read:

Areas in Tyson Corner Center used by the public are not public ways, but are for the use of tenants and the public transacting business with them. Permission to use said areas may be revoked at any time.²⁵

35   The issue of who is to be granted access to malls and under what conditions has become highly charged in both the political arena and the courts. Much of the concern in the United States is centered around First Amendment rights. In the public sphere, every citizen has a constitutional right to congregate, assemble, speak, and petition. But does the Bill of Rights extend to the private megamalls, the new gathering places? Mall owners argue that First Amendment rights end at the front entrance. "I don't mind that people are trying to save the whale," says a manager of a Florida mall, "but I don't want my shoppers stopped to sign petitions."²⁶

36   The United States courts have been wrestling with the issue of political rights versus commercial access for years with ambiguous and often contradictory rulings. In a California case, *Diamond v. Bland*, the court allowed antipollution activists access to a San Bernardino mall, arguing that "in many instances the contemporary shopping center serves as the analog for the town square."²⁷ However, in a later Supreme Court case in 1972 involving antiwar activists distributing literature, the majority of the justices sided with the mall owner, saying that such exercises of freedom of speech and petition are an "unwarranted infringement" of the proprietary interests of the owner.²⁸

37   The late Supreme Court justice Thurgood Marshall is among a minority of judges who worried that the continuing commercial enclosure of the cultural sphere and the public square inside giant megamalls poses a serious danger to basic constitutional safeguards. He warned that in these new domains, "it becomes harder and harder for citizens to find means to communicate with other citizens."²⁹

38   The megamalls and entertainment destination centers, like common-interest developments and tourist spaces, are part of a new competitive environment where success is measured by who has access to cultural production and commodified forms of lived experience and who is left outside the gates. These kinds of access issues are likely to dominate the political agenda in the twenty-first century as society struggles with the question of who is to be included and who is to be excluded from the cultural economy.

Notes

1. Arnold Toynbee, *Lectures on the Industrial Revolution of the 18th Century* (London/New York: Longmans, Green and Co, 1937).
2. Sarah Sanderson King, *Human Communication as a Field of Study* (New York: State University of New York Press, 1989), p. 111.
3. Lee Thayer, *On Communication: Essays in Understanding* (Norwood, NJ: Ablex, 1987), p. 45.
4. Quoted in Warren I. Sussman, *Culture As History: The Transformation of American Society in the Twentieth Century* (New York: Pantheon Books, 1973), p. 252.
5. Ibid.
6. John Fiske, *Introduction to Communication Studies*, 2nd ed. (New York: Routledge, 1990), p. 2.

7. Herbert I. Schiller, *Culture Inc.: The Corporate Takeover of Public Expression* (New York: Oxford University Press, 1989), p. 31.
8. International Council of Shopping Centers, "Shopping Centers Rank High in U.S. Tourist Attractions," *ICSC News*, June 1999, http://www.icsc.org/srch/about/impactofshoppingcenters/shoppingcentersrank.html.
9. International Council of Shopping Centers, "Did You Know That . . ." *ICSC News*, June 1999; http://www.icsc.org/srch/about/impactofshoppingcenters/didyouknow.html.
10. Ibid.
11. William Severini Kowinski, *The Malling of America: An Inside Look at the Great Consumer Paradise* (New York: Morrow, 1985), pp. 349–50.
12. Joan Didion, "On the Mall," in *The White Notebook* (New York: Simon & Schuster, 1979), p. 34.
13. Margaret Crawford, "The World in a Shopping Mall," in Michael Sorkin, ed., *Variations on a Theme Park: The American City and the End of Public Space* (New York: Farrar, Straus and Giroux, 1992), p. 21.
14. Kowinski, *The Malling of America*, p. 62.
15. Crawford, "The World in a Shopping Mall," p. 9.
16. Jennifer Stoffel, "Where America Goes for Entertainment," *New York Times*, August 7, 1988, section 3, p. 11F; Kowinski, *The Malling of America*, p. 71; International Council of Shopping Centers, "Did You Know That . . ."
17. Kowinski, *The Malling of America*, p. 61.
18. Crawford, "The World in a Shopping Mall," p. 3.
19. Tracy C. Davis, "Theatrical Antecedents of the Mall That Ate Downtown," *Journal of Popular Culture* 24, no. 4 (Spring 1991): 4.
20. Crawford, "The World in a Shopping Mall," p. 4.
21. Davis, "Theatrical Antecedents of the Mall That Ate Downtown," pp. 1, 4, 7–9.
22. Ibid., p. 5.
23. Leslie Kaufman, "Sony Builds a Mall, But Don't Call It That," *New York Times*, July 25, 1999, section 3, pp. 1–12.
24. Kowinski, *The Malling of America*, p. 355.
25. Ibid.
26. Ibid.
27. Ibid., p. 356.
28. Ibid.
29. Ibid., p. 357.

Reading Responses

1. How, according to Rifkin, are communication and culture related? Why does he begin the chapter with this explanation?
2. What are the characteristics of "mall culture"? How does Rifkin convey these characteristics to readers?
3. As Rifkin speculates about the future of commerce, what political issues does he expect to arise?

Writing Activities

1. Write a brief explanation of what Rifkin means when he says that "the shopping mall has created a new architecture for human assembly" (paragraph 15).

2. Write an essay that agrees or disagrees with one of Rifkin's assertions or predictions that interests you. For example, given your own experience visiting malls, do you agree that the public square is being redefined? Based on your experience and observations, do you agree that the issue of access will be the major political issue of this century? State your position clearly, and present logical points that support your position. Use evidence from your own experience or other resources to support your views. Be sure to credit your sources appropriately.
3. Write an essay that speculates about how the economy might be different in the upcoming years if this is indeed the era of a major economic shift. Consider what might happen as a result of that shift, how ideas might change, what different choices people might make, or a similar issue.

 Community Links

Compare and contrast "The New Culture of Capitalism" with one or two other readings that examine changes or challenges produced by technology such as Harris's "So Many Numbers—What Do You Do with the Data?" (pp. 109–111) from the academic community, Helgesen's "When Life Itself Becomes Incredibly Complex" (pp. 256–262), or Miller's "Wanted: 'Civic Scientists'" (pp. 362–365) from the public community. In what ways do the readings agree or disagree on the issues and the possible solutions? In what ways might community expectations and the specific concerns of readers influence their views?

WHEN LIFE ITSELF BECOMES INCREDIBLY COMPLEX
Sally Helgesen

◆

Chapter 2 of Thriving in 24/7: Six Strategies for Taming the New World of Work *introduces one of the issues that concerns Sally Helgesen: How do we cope with the exhausting work required not just by work itself, but by the responsibilities of life? To answer this question, Helgesen explores how the same forces that complicate people's work lives are also changing and intensifying their home lives.*

1 Most of us recognize the extent to which our lives are being consumed by work. Agonizing about it has become part of the global conversation. What is less recognized is the extent to which our private lives and even our leisure also require a lot more work these days. Simply meeting the normal responsibilities of adulthood (*forget* having to earn a living) has become something of a

Reprinted with permission of The Free Press, a division of Simon & Schuster Adult Publishing Group, from *Thriving in 24/7: Six Strategies for Training the New World of Work* by Sally Helgesen. Copyright © 2001 by Sally Helgesen.

high-wire act. This is the perplexing reality, even the dirty little secret, of contemporary life: that we are exhausting ourselves not just at work, but also at home.

2   More and more, we find ourselves bringing professional-level skills and tools (PCs, Filofaxes, beepers) into the management of our domestic lives. More and more, we find our personal to-do lists getting the better of us. Arranging a sit-down dinner with the whole family at midweek can involve coordinating five different schedules. Planning a family vacation can be as challenging as holding a meeting of team members from different office locales. Simply trying to see an old friend for coffee can result in a frustrating game of phone tag or a flood of e-mails.

3   And because our private schedules are packed and precarious, ruled by multiple pickups, drop-offs, by children's lessons and personal appointments, we get little relief from the constant pressure. If something unexpected occurs—if the dog gets sick, if the babysitter quits—our precisely choreographed plans can be thrown into disarray. The need to attend to so many details can also distract us from the larger picture. One man related how he and his wife packed up the whole family for a trip, set the house alarms, dropped off the cat and the dog at their respective sitters, drove to the airport, checked six bags, parked in the long-term lot and took a van back, only to discover at the gate that their flight was scheduled for the following day. They had been so caught up with the intricacies of their plans they had forgotten to look at the calendar, or the tickets.

4   We all have similar stories. Why?

5   Our dilemma is that the same forces that have created a more intense and demanding workplace—the breakdown of traditional boundaries, the rapid spread of networked technologies, faster product cycles, higher expectations—are also transforming our lives at home. At the same time, our domestic lives reflect the major trend that dominates the consumer marketplace today: an ever-increasing emphasis on variety and choice. This requires us to make a constant stream of decisions about everything from the ground rules of our marriage to the age at which we have our children to how we exercise. The fact that life at home *and* at work now demands more energy and attention can leave us feeling as if there is no escape.

6   One difficulty (which is in many ways also a blessing) is that ours has become the great "have it your way" society. The incredible range of options we confront enables us to tailor both our activities and our purchases to meet highly specific needs and wants. In my last book, I referred to this as the Starbucks Syndrome of Contemporary Life, for whereas it used to be enough simply to ask for a "coffee to go," we now stand in two different lines to place our order for a "tall double decaf skinny latte with flat foam and a shot and a half of almond syrup"—or whatever highly personalized choice suits our individual taste. The same principle applies to almost every aspect of our lives. There is so much available that we are constantly forced to customize our selections, big and small.

7   Because we have so many options, there are no typical or generic patterns anymore, no "average way of life" we can just slot into without having to give it a lot of thought. At home as well as at work, we find ourselves inventing our

lives as we go along, improvising in an effort to take advantage of the bewildering range of choices that we face. Our situation offers tremendous opportunities for individual fulfillment and self-expression, and keeps the economy humming along. But it also requires that we expend a great deal of energy making what were until recently fairly routine and straightforward decisions. And so we have a richer environment today, but a far more daunting one as well.

8   The convergence of intensity at home and at work requires us to seek new solutions. But before we can identify them, we need a clear understanding of the many ways in which our domestic lives have been transformed over the last two decades. [. . .]

Our Children

9   Raising children is a source of great joy, but the nature of parenting has changed in the last few decades, becoming far more complex and requiring an almost professional level of involvement. Not long ago, kids routinely attended the local school and spent their time afterward riding bikes around the neighborhood, perhaps attending a nearby scouting camp in the summer. Curriculum choices at school were fairly limited, as were extracurricular activities. When the time came for college, teenagers filled out an average of three applications, six pages each.

10 Today, there are specialized schools, charter schools, magnet schools, professional schools, and local schools with special programs—the number and variety of which increase each year. Most require vigorous testing and multiple evaluations before a student is admitted, even to kindergarten. Starting in middle school, children choose from a wide range of courses. During the summer, if families have the means, children attend tennis camps, gymnastics camps, art camps, computer camps, often several in two-week sequences. After school, they take a wide range of lessons. Kids' soccer games—even soccer *practices*—have become major social events, requiring snacks and supporters and transportation.

11 As a result, even young children have schedules: play dates with friends, standing dates with tutors, sessions with private coaches. They may have been diagnosed as being gifted, having ADHD, or being oppositional-defiant, in which case they are seen by counselors and therapists, who may suggest medications that need to be monitored daily. Their applications for college run to scores of pages, and they often apply to as many as twelve schools because gaining entrance has become so competitive. Parents worried about getting their children into college often start marketing them when they are young, creating desirable "packages" or brands: the figure skater, the violin prodigy, the tech whiz, the junior entrepreneur.

12 All this presents many advantages for today's children, offering them a richness of exposure and opportunity that only the most privileged youngsters enjoyed in the past. Still, no one could argue that it has made parenthood any simpler. The emphasis on variety, options, and competition that pervades our lives as adults also characterizes the lives of our children. This requires us to

make a continual investment of time, attention, and high stakes decision-making, along with doing an unprecedented amount of driving and filling out of forms.

13   The sociologist Dolores Hayden has noted that "Americans at the end of the millennium have evolved the most labor-intensive style of parenting ever known to the human race"—a style that is spreading fast to other prosperous parts of the world. That we have adopted this style *at the same time* that many of us are overwhelmed by our work—and in a period when both parents usually work—goes a long way to explaining the pressure we are under.

Our Vehicles

14   Since 1990, there have been more cars registered in the United States than there are licensed drivers, and the disproportion of cars to drivers increases every year. In addition to basic family transport, one of the adults in a two-parent household may have a smaller car that he or she drives, while teenagers who attend different schools (or the same school, but have different after-school activities) are likely to drive their own cars as well. Perhaps the family also has a 4X4 for weekends, a snowmobile for winter sports, or a camper for long vacations. Boat ownership has dramatically increased, up more than 300 percent in the last twenty years, while the number of personal watercraft such as jet skis has gone through the roof. In upscale, though hardly wealthy suburbs, three-car garages are now the norm.

15   More freedom, more independence, more fun, no doubt, but all these vehicles also require a lot more maintenance and record-keeping. In addition, the glut of cars means that we sit in traffic longer: The amount of time we spend in traffic has increased more than 200 percent since 1984. We make more trips to the repair shop, pay a greater number of insurance premiums, spend more time deciding what to buy and shopping for bargains. And of course, most vehicles now come with a daunting range of options for us to choose among—from cold weather packages to global-positioning units—requiring still more decisions, maintenance, and research. [. . .]

Our Stuff

16   Most of us today seek out highly specific items that meet our specialized needs when we shop. We don't dash out and buy a pair of sneakers; we purchase athletic shoes to fit particular activities, such as running, aerobics, cross-training, tennis, and biking. We search out a different bagel flavor to satisfy each member of the family. If we subscribe to a decorating magazine, we select something tailored to our needs—first apartment, contemporary luxury condo, country cottage, restored Victorian, or maybe a magazine entirely devoted to the kitchen or the bath. If we buy sheets, we pay attention to the thread count and whether it will fit our mattress (is it *deep* enough?). Even an item as mundane as dental floss comes in thirty-six varieties!

17   All this customizing and emphasis on choice can be gratifying—it's nice to have our individual needs catered to, to choose from among relaxed, reverse, straight-legged, lean, or classic fit when we buy a pair of Gap jeans. But it also

requires us to spend an enormous amount of time analyzing and procuring even the most basic goods. With multiple products vying for limited shelf space, whatever we ultimately decide on is apt to be out of stock. In addition, the sheer *volume* of goods available requires that they be sold in ever-larger spaces, which means bigger stores with bigger parking lots, often in distant locations. Finally, because so much of what we buy is highly specific, we inevitably end up needing more; this applies to everything from kitchenware to exercise equipment to garden tools and consumer electronics. Small wonder that the American Builders Association reports that the single most desirable feature in a new house these days is a plethora of enormous closets!

18 Several patterns emerge as we consider the various ways in which our domestic lives have grown more demanding.

19 First, we see that the choices that confront us—about how we manage our money and our health, raise our children, select our cars, make our travel plans, purchase basic goods—have become so loaded with options that wading through them requires an incredible amount of concentration, time, and skill. Consumer product and services companies recognize the problem. A study commissioned by Procter & Gamble revealed that *the* major hurdle new products now face in gaining acceptance is that people are overwhelmed by excessive choice. Nevertheless, companies seem powerless to stop the endless proliferation. They fear that if they miss out on a single product variation—triple chocolate chip ice cream with macadamia nuts *and* almonds, mustard with bourbon *and* honey, peppermint-flavored floss, speed dial to reach fifty people, fleece gloves with steering wheel grips—they will leave an unexploited niche that a savvy competitor will rush to fill.

20 Most of us anticipate that things will become easier as we select an ever-larger proportion of our goods and services over the Internet, since part of the problem today is that we are using industrial-era delivery systems (such as big stores) to distribute a postindustrial array of services and products. However, as anyone who has repeatedly had to return items ordered via catalog knows all too well, new methods of procurement present frustrations of their own, requiring us to time our deliveries carefully and to punch in tracking codes on UPS phone trees, thus adding more items to our already crowded list of to-dos and more paperwork to keep track of. In addition, the Internet makes *everything in the world* available to us (at least in theory), a daunting prospect that requires us to become more savvy and to do more research to determine precisely what it is we really want.

21 Second, it becomes apparent that the speed of technology cycles creates new needs even as it satisfies them. If we buy a digital camera, we create a need for new ways of developing and displaying the photos we take. If we buy a digitized audiotape Walkman, we create a need to buy new tapes. And as the price of new technologies plummets, it makes less sense *not* to get the new products, especially when our old products begin to fail and we compare the cost of repair with replacement. In this way, what were formerly considered luxuries have been redefined as needs. How can a color television be a luxury when 93 percent of people in the United States living *below* the poverty line own at least one? As Kevin

Kelly, editor at large for *Wired* magazine, notes, "Each actualization of desire creates a platform for new technologies to create and supply new needs."

22 In other words, *it's endless,* this constant upping of the ante. And it threatens to trap us in an ever-escalating web of decisions about what to buy, where, how, from whom, why, what upgrades to get, when to switch. As with the technologies we use at work, the process is *programmed* to exhaust us by virtue of its speed, its intricacy, and its capacity for change.

23 Whether we choose to regard this situation as wasteful and purposeless, or view it as positive, a proof of vitality and source of job creation, doesn't matter. It's *here,* and it's not going to change. The challenge for each of us is to make satisfying choices and learn to savor what we have rather than simply leaping onto a ceaseless treadmill of endless optimizing.

24 The third pattern that emerges as we examine the reasons our private lives have become so complex is that large numbers of us are living in ways *that only rich people used to live.* Stock portfolios, financial advisers, tennis instructors (for adults and kids), wine tastings, lawn services, different cars for various uses, not to mention five-thousand-square-foot houses: such things used to be indicators of serious wealth. What has happened over the last twenty years is a democratization of what used to be the prerogatives of upper-class life. Few of us, however, have the support systems that used to enable the wealthy to lead complex financial lives, maintain multiple vehicles, and offer children highly specialized activities—the servants, retainers, and professional managers that made their lives go smoothly. We, by contrast, have only ourselves to manage all the work that our daily lives increasingly require.

25 Finally, our lives are more complex simply because we *know* more, have more potential sources of information, and so are inclined to take an activist approach to our problems. If we contract a major illness, for example, we are likely to read books about it, visit medical websites, explore alternative treatments, and join support groups for people who share our experience. In short, we are more likely to become self-taught experts on our problems and to collaborate with the professionals who serve and treat us, instead of simply following their advice.

26 Similarly, if one of our children has trouble learning to read or seems unable to acquire a routine skill, we seek professional guidance, contact other parents whose children face similar challenges, and perhaps band together with them to create an advocacy group to explore new care options. Parental activism, neighborhood activism, environmental activism, patient activism, single-issue activism ranging from Mothers Against Drunk Driving to grassroots efforts aimed at influencing what textbooks are chosen by the local school board: *all* these have become commonplace over the last thirty years. This phenomenon gives us far greater power and control over our individual destinies, and creates more textured and satisfying ways of being in the world. But it also contributes to the professionalizing of our lives and our leisure.

27 Because our private lives have become more demanding at the same time that our work lives have, we may find it difficult to enjoy—or even recognize—the benefits of life in our era. Yet they are many: a lessened dependence upon large

organizations, greater flexibility in how we live and work, easy access to information that was formerly restricted, the crumbling of oppressive hierarchies of control, an end to generic ways of living that gave little scope for personal choice.

28   However, the very freedom we have to make so many choices now lies at the heart of our common dilemma. This brings to mind the old adage about being careful what you wish for. For *choice*—economic, political, social, familial, recreational, reproductive—is the pivot upon which the last few hundred years of history have turned. People have sought choice in every arena. They have campaigned for it, demanded it, fought for it, died for it. They did their job well, with the extraordinary result that choice itself has now become our problem.

29   It may not *feel* as if choice is our problem. We may indeed feel as if we're locked into patterns that now lie beyond our control. But this is usually the result of previous decisions we have made in response to the plethora of choices that we faced: about work, about how we run our households, about our daily schedule.

30   The only way out is to become more conscious about *all* our choices, to be absolutely clear about what we need and what we do not, what serves our true purpose and what is superfluous. We must find ways to pursue elegance and simplicity in all our decisions, aligning them with what lies deepest within us, and adapting them as our needs and interests evolve. We must seek out ways of living and working that allow for greater flow and wholeness, enabling us to take advantage of (or when necessary, resist) what technology has wrought.

Reading Responses

1. According to Helgesen, why has life become so complex?
2. What solution to the growing complexity of home and work life does Helgesen propose? Where does she state that solution?
3. This selection includes three of Helgesen's categories—children, vehicles, and stuff. What strategies does she use to show how complex each category has become and how much work it requires?

Writing Activities

1. In your own words, summarize the four patterns that, according to Helgesen, account for the complication of our lives.
2. Write a personal essay explaining your approaches or solutions to the complexities that turn all aspects of life into work.
3. Select a category—like Helgesen's categories of children, vehicles, and stuff—that is too complicated in your life or the lives of your family or friends. (Helgesen's full chapter also discusses handling financial matters,

managing health care, organizing travel, and arranging basic services such as telephone, cable television, and utilities.) Explain your category by identifying the types of complications that arise and by providing examples.

Community Links

Compare or contrast this selection with another concerned with change and uncertainty such as Katz's "The Pathbreaking, Fractionalized, Uncertain World of Knowledge" (pp. 52–58) from the academic community or King's "I Have a Dream" (pp. 439–442) from the public community. In what ways are the views expressed in the readings similar or different? To what extent do community expectations shape perspectives on change?

Community Ethics

ARE YOU A COPYRIGHT CRIMINAL?
Dave Zielinski

◆

This article, reprinted from Presentations *magazine, discusses intellectual property rights—a writer's (or artist's or other creator's) legal right to control the distribution of an original work. Dave Zielinski explains the responsibility of a presenter to honor copyright law and alerts presenters to the possible consequences of not doing so.*

1 It's getting more tempting to infringe on copyright when creating presentations, thanks to many new scanning and duplicating technologies as well as proliferating Web content. But writers, designers, artists and copyright owners are becoming more aggressive, using new tactics and technologies to enforce their rights. If you don't know the rules, you could end up on the wrong side of a lawsuit.

2 You've seen them at work. Sometimes brazen, sometimes oblivious, they break the law without giving it a second thought. Maybe, without even knowing it, you're one of them.

3 They're copyright claim-jumpers—presenters who slip "Dilbert" cartoons, photographs scanned from magazines, graphics downloaded from the Web, photocopies of trade-journal articles, audio files, video clips or CD music into their presentations or handouts with little or no understanding of how they're trampling on someone else's copyright.

4 Some do it knowingly, assuming their chances of getting nabbed are a small risk for the big payoff of easy access to high-quality prefabricated content. Others are unaware of how their seemingly benign reuse of pre-existing material—articles, pictures, music, songs, scripts or film clips—violates copyright law.

5 Autumn Bell, a training specialist and frequent presenter for the University of New Mexico, says she witnessed her share of copyright abuses in a past life working for a telecommunications company. There, she worked with managers who *ordered* people to copy other companies' training materials to save money. She also saw plenty of lesser violations, such as flagrant photocopying of manuals and books for mass distribution. In six years, Bell says, "Never once did I hear the word *copyright* spoken."

6 Bell believes that many corporate presenters and trainers adopt a "don't ask, don't tell" attitude when it comes to unlawful use of copyrighted material.

"The thinking is, 'As long as I don't know, then I can use ignorance as an excuse,'" she says. "They don't want to learn the nuances of copyright law because they figure as long as they can plead ignorance, they'll be safe."

Cold, Hard Reality

7 It can be easy for busy presenters to give copyright concerns short shrift; after all, there are deadlines to hit and rehearsals to do. And sometimes that article you read last week in *Forbes Magazine* or that photo you downloaded from the Web yesterday fits perfectly into the presentation you're giving—tomorrow. Copyright permission? Who has time? Some token attribution ought to do it, you figure. Surely the copyright owners will welcome the free advertising, right? And what are the chances that they'll even find out?

8 The reality is: Whether the bulk of your presentations are in-house or to external audiences, your odds of being caught violating copyright are improving every day, as are your chances of paying a stiff fine. Statutory damages for infringing on copyright can hit $20,000 per violation, and they can go as high as $100,000 in some circumstances of willful violation—and that's above and beyond the fine for actual damages. Furthermore, commercial copyright violation involving more than 10 copies and a value of more than $2,500 is now a felony in the United States.

9 In one recent case, a corporation paid a seven-figure settlement for its unauthorized photocopying of articles from a trade journal and archiving those copies for internal distribution. With similar violations occurring almost daily in corporate America, and with an increase in piracy on the World Wide Web, licensing organizations, performing-rights societies and other copyright cops have stepped up activity to enforce their rights.

10 The Training Media Association, a watchdog for training-video vendors, offers a $10,000 bounty for reporting illegal copying or unauthorized "public performance" of off-the-shelf training videos. A temporary-employment agency recently paid a six-figure out-of-court fee after one of its employees reported it to the TMA for making illegal copies of four videos (the agency had no license to do so) and sending the copies out for use in its 50 offices.

11 United Media, the distributor of "Dilbert" cartoons, has been asking people to take illegally imported "Dilbert" cartoons off their Web and intranet sites. ASCAP and BMI, two organizations that license the right to play copyrighted music in public settings (including most business-presentation scenarios) have reportedly added large conference centers and hotels to the list of sites they patrol to ensure that those using even small selections of prerecorded music in presentations are properly licensed to do so.

How Prevalent Is Abuse?

12 Is all this talk of copyright abuse overblown? Is the perceived need to protect yourself from prosecution just another anal-retentive legal formality? And aren't the most flagrant abusers a small segment of the presentation community? You'd be surprised at the answers.

13 Although many cases of abuse undoubtedly are small or accidental—busy presenters who in good faith give full attribution but don't seek permission; others who are unaware of public performance rights or who stretch the fair-use doctrine to its limits—interviews and research conducted for this article indicate a serious lack of knowledge about copyright law among frequent presenters. A two-month review of comments posted to listservs frequented by presenters and trainers, for instance, suggests that many people routinely violate copyright law, and that there is a general lack of understanding about what constitutes legal use.

14 Indeed, a 1993 survey by the Training Media Association found that more than 30 percent of videos in survey respondents' corporate libraries were illegal copies, and more than 75 percent of printed training materials in those same libraries were illegally copied. (Survey responses were anonymous.) And TMA director Bob Gehrke says the problem may have worsened in the six years since the study. A typical copyright violator, Gehrke believes, is someone "who thinks he can be a hero by saving his company some money, especially if faced with a tight budget."

A Quick Primer on Copyright Law

15 With so much seemingly gray territory in the area of copyright, how can you make sure you're on the right side of the law? Well, to avoid breaking copyright law you first need to understand it.

16 Under the Copyright Act of 1976, the basis of U.S. copyright law, copyright is automatic when an original work is first "fixed" in a tangible medium of expression. That means material is protected by copyright at the point when it is first printed, captured on film, drawn, or saved to hard drive or disk. (All of the e-mail you write is copyrighted, for instance.)

17 Among original works of authorship cited in copyright statutes are "pictorial, graphic, audiovisual and sound recordings." These are broad categories that include the GIF and JPG image files and WAV audio files commonly found on the Web; U.S. copyright law has proven quite adaptable to new technologies that didn't exist when laws were written. The farsighted statute covers fixed works "now known or later developed."

18 A notice of copyright (as in, "Copyright 1999 John Smith") is no longer necessary to affirm protection. Some presenters believe that if a work doesn't include the copyright notice, they're free to use it without permission. Wrong. If a work was put in "fixed" form, and it has even a minimal amount of originality, it's protected by law, copyright symbol or no.

19 Copyright only applies to original *expression*, however. Ideas and facts cannot be copyrighted, only the original way in which that idea or fact is expressed. Thus the data and facts found on a Web site aren't protected by copyright—but the site creator's unique expression of them is.

20 Copyright owners have five exclusive rights:

1. The right to reproduce the copyrighted work.
2. The right to distribute copies of a copyrighted work to the public.

3. The right to prepare derivative works, or creations based on the original.
4. The right to perform the copyrighted work publicly.
5. The right to display copyrighted work publicly.

21   Abuse any of those rights—that is, photocopy, distribute, customize, publicly perform or display someone else's original work without permission—and you're breaking the law. It's small comfort to know that copyright law is primarily civil law, not criminal law, so if you're caught red-handed, you'll likely get sued, not charged with a crime. Copyright violation might not put you in jail, but it can cost you plenty.

22   Copyright protection now lasts for the lifetime of the author or creator, plus 70 years. Thus if Stephen King writes another book, or 10, this year, and then passes away due to a freak accident on Halloween night, copyright on his books would remain in effect until 2069. After those 70 years, it passes into what's called the "public domain," free to be used by anyone without permission. For example, music by long-dead composers such as Bach or Beethoven can be freely used in presentations. But—here's the catch—an individual *performance* of Beethoven's music by a contemporary group like the New York Philharmonic is a different story. That public performance itself can be copyrighted, and you'd need a special license or permission to play it for anyone other than your friends or family at home—anyone like, say, an audience of sales trainees. So unless you're the one playing the Fifth Symphony on your penny whistle, you'd better contact the orchestra before dropping a piece into your electronic suitcase.

23   Other works in the public domain—those you are free to use without having to worry about copyright—include those created by the U.S. Government. So, for instance, you don't need permission to use screen captures of government Web sites as examples of good or bad design in a class on designing Web pages. But don't assume this applies to foreign countries as well. The government of the United Kingdom, for instance, does claim copyright for its works. So travel with care when reusing governmental works found on the Internet or elsewhere.

24   The "public performance" of copyrighted video or audio is a right unto itself, and requires special permission or a license, regardless of whether you own the video or audio (the CD, for instance). Tom W. Bell, a professor specializing in intellectual property at the Chapman University School of Law in Orange, Calif., says copyright statute largely defines public performance as "showing, playing or displaying the works at a place open to the public, or at any place where a 'substantial' number of persons outside of a normal circle of family and social acquaintances is gathered."

25   What constitutes a "substantial" group? If you're training two or three people in a cubicle and playing a CD as background music, no license is needed, Bell says. But any audience size beyond that is a gray area, and possibly fair game for the copyright police. "You need to trust your gut in most of these cases and use common sense," he says.

26   Also remember this, says Bell: Copyright is violated whether or not you charged money in your reuse or duplication of copyrighted works. In other

words, you'll be liable even if you didn't profit a cent from reuse or copying of a stock photo, cartoon, piece of clip art, illustration or magazine article without permission or a license to do so. And while placing proper attribution on a work is laudable, it doesn't protect you from liability.... For instance, photocopying and reusing this article in a handout, or scanning one of the magazine's photographs, then placing "Reprinted from *Presentations* magazine" on it—without getting permission from the copyright owner, Bill Communications Inc., to do so—won't protect you from prosecution.

Avoiding Copyright Trouble: Permission and Licensing

27   What's the best way to keep the copyright cops from knocking on your door? This is the best rule of thumb: Always assume that any pre-existing work you'd like to use is copyrighted work and that it requires permission from the copyright owner to use or copy.

28   As Brad Templeton, author of the popular "10 Big Myths about copyright explained" Web destination (www.templetons.com/brad/copymyths.html), says, don't rationalize that your use of the material doesn't hurt the copyright owner, or assume that it is a welcome source of free advertising. Ask *them*. "It's up to the owners to decide if they want the free ads or not," Templeton writes. "If they want them, they'll be sure to contact you."

29   What if you want to use only a small fraction of a copyrighted work? The Copyright Act includes a "fair use" exception, granting the ability to use copyrighted material without written permission from the owner.... But, although fair use appears intuitive, grossly liberal interpretations of the clause constitute misuse.

30   In some cases, copyright owners are easy to track down through the contact information listed on their materials. Individual authors or smaller organizations in particular are usually flattered by such requests and willing to negotiate fair terms, often allowing you to reuse their material for free with proper attribution.

31   In other cases, locating and negotiating with copyright holders can be downright frustrating. There's no requirement that they be any easier to find than J.D. Salinger, or that they return your queries before a presentation deadline. Simply identifying true owners can also be tricky. In the case of some trade-journal articles, the true copyright owner may not be the publication but the article's author. The same goes for photos in magazines or stock pictures on the Web; the photographer may still hold the copyright. The copyright owner may also have passed away, leaving rights issues or reuse policies unclear under his or her estate.

It's Up There, So Why Can't I Use It?

32   The Web is a particularly alluring temptress, beckoning with its wide selection of easily accessed content—clip art, fonts, audio files, stock photos—that promise to breathe life into your presentations. If you're vulnerable to the lure, remember this: Just because materials are on an "open" Web site doesn't mean they're in the public domain and free for you to download and reuse or copy.

33   "Too many people still assume that because it's freely accessible on the Web, it's freely available to reuse," says Professor Bell. "The right for you to view something on the Web is different from the right for you to display or perform it on your own site or presentation."

34   To be in the public domain—and free of copyright complications—information on the Web must have been placed there "expressly or deliberately" by the copyright owner himself, most obviously with an accompanying note saying, "I grant this to the public domain." Plenty of copyrighted works have been posted to the Web without authorization of the copyright holder. If you reuse that information without permission, you're breaking copyright law. Lack of knowledge about whether the information you take from the Web has itself been illegally copied or posted is no defense.

35   On his "10 Big Myths" Web page, author Templeton refers to the time the online news service Clarinet paid a fee to publish one of humorist Dave Barry's columns to a large Usenet audience. One person forwarded the column to another mailing list without permission, got caught, and the newspaper chain that employed Dave Barry pulled the column from the Internet.

36   Thus, lifting clip art, fonts, icons, stock photos, WAV sound files or any other content from a Web site for reuse in your handouts or presentation, without written permission or a license to do so, is clear copyright infringement. Bell and other intellectual property attorneys say that the forward-looking language in the copyright statute—"fixed in any tangible medium of expression, now known or later developed"—clearly covers Internet Images and audio file types. GIFs and other graphic image files are akin to "photographs, drawings, logos or other pictorial works" recognized by statute and case law.

37   Purchasing "royalty-free" content is one way around the problem. Here you typically pay a one-time fee for unlimited use (with some restrictions) of music, stock photos, graphics and the like in your presentation materials. Because content-sellers have "bought out" or cleared copyright issues, you don't pay royalties on each use of the material. Organizations offering royalty-free images and music are proliferating on the Web.

38   There are a few caveats, however. Because the Web is a haven for unscrupulous operators, be sure those from whom you are buying images do in fact hold the rights to them and are authorized to resell them. *Playboy* magazine is one business entity that has had problems with people taking images from its Web site, then building their own picture archives and selling access. Some legitimate clip-art vendors have also seen unauthorized Web sites lift and resell their wares. Read the fine print on your license carefully, recommends Woody Johnson of the Copyright Clearance Center in Danvers, Mass. "If your license says you bear all responsibility for use of the images once you've paid a one-time fee—beware," he says. "The seller should bear some responsibility as well."

Tracking Violators—New Tactics

39   Technologies such as "watermarking" software also are making it easier to track down copyright pirates on the Internet. Digital watermarking places a subtle yet visible mark on an image that carries telltale information about its

source. Watermarking can be integrated into Photoshop and other graphics programs to allow creators to save images with embedded copyright information without visibly altering the image. That identifying information is visible to a special reader program when a watermarked image is downloaded and opened. Other programs can then scan the entire Web for watermarks and report unauthorized uses of copyrighted content.

40   A similar concept is used for downloadable CD-quality audio files—and most of those "watermarks" can withstand translation to analog and back to digital form. Experts say vendors may soon stamp audio files for sale on the Web with the name of the buyer, date purchased and additional ID. That way, if the purchaser illegally posted a copy of the audio to his Web site, the copyright holder could trace copies others may have downloaded back to the original buyer.

The New Reality

41   In this environment of increasingly sophisticated tracking mechanisms and heightened sensitivity to copyright issues, it's just common sense for people who use outside materials in their presentations to be aware of potential copyright violations and to take the necessary steps toward compliance. At best, getting caught can be embarrassing. At worst, it could cost you and/or your organization an alarming amount of money—and maybe even your career.

Reading Responses

1. What is the purpose of Zielinski's article?
2. How does Zielinski acknowledge possible assumptions or attitudes of readers? What rationalizations does he counter?
3. How does Zielinski approach the ethical issues involved in violating copyright and ignoring intellectual property rights? In what ways does he appeal to readers or try to motivate them to respect copyright?

Writing Activities

1. Using your own words, write a summary of Zielinski's explanation about how copyright law applies to the Web.
2. Using this article as a source of information, construct a short copyright quiz—about ten basic questions (and answers) about copyright issues that might be important to your colleagues at work or in class or to some of your friends. Design your questions for your specific readers, considering the ways that they are likely to use copyrighted materials. Exchange quizzes with someone else in class, and take each other's quizzes to check for ambiguous questions, unclear wording, or similar problems.
3. Imagine that you are a supervisor at a company that prides itself on collaborative work, including frequent informative and motivational presen-

tations to in-house teams, clients, and prospective clients. You want to be sure that everyone respects the copyright law so that the company does not face any legal issues or public embarrassment. On the other hand, you do not want to damage morale or reduce enthusiasm. Write an advisory memo to your colleagues at work. In your memo, supply advice about best practices for using visual, audio, or textual materials from others. You may limit your memo to a specific matter and offer any necessary support to help employees handle materials appropriately. (See p. 229 and p. 307 for sample memos that illustrate the usual form.)

Community Links

Compare Zielinski's article with Harris's "Anti-Plagiarism Strategies for Research Papers" (pp. 77–86) in the academic community. Look for issues or ethical criteria that are shared as well as specific academic or workplace concerns with the issues.

DON'T JUST DO IT TO SAVE LIVES
C. Fred Alford

In Whistleblowers: Broken Lives and Organizational Power, *Alford reports on his investigation of whistle-blowers, employees who report matters that are morally or ethically ambiguous or that may carry ethical consequences. Chapter 2 opens with Alford's definition of a whistle-blower; the selection from the chapter also presents one of his four profiles of individual whistle-blowers. Alford's primary research interest is the relationship between the whistle-blower and the organization: How do organizations respond to individuals who raise ethical or moral issues? What happens to whistle-blowers, especially if they become scapegoats as a result of the organization's response?*

They wouldn't talk with me about what I said, and they wouldn't talk with me about not talking about it. —A whistleblower

1   Before continuing, it may be helpful to define the whistleblower I am talking about. A common definition, that of Myron Glazer and Penina Glazer (1989, 4) in *The Whistleblowers*, defines the whistleblower as one who (1) acts to prevent harm to others, not him or herself, (2) trying first to rectify the situation within the framework provided by the organization, (3) while possessing evidence that would convince a reasonable person. The harm may be physical, such as the illegal disposal of toxic waste; financial, such as the waste or misuse of taxpayers' money; or legal, the breaking of laws. Often it is all three.

2. Part 2 of Glazer and Glazer's definition cannot possibly be considered a definition, only a piece of advice. Daniel Ellsberg is no less a whistleblower because he did not first go to the chairman of the Joint Chiefs of Staff and ask to release the Pentagon Papers. Neither is part 3 of the definition very useful, though it must be admitted that the law is filled with reasonable men and their standards.

3. Inserted, presumably, to distinguish whistleblower fantasy from intersubjectively shared reality, the reasonable person actually represents the citizen for whom the whistleblower speaks. If the citizen heard both sides, would he find the whistleblower's complaint plausible? Putting it this way might generate a rational standard, but it does not seem a necessary part of the definition itself. An unreasonable whistleblower is still a whistleblower. Like so many, Glazer and Glazer are evidently afraid of the stereotype of the whistleblower as hysterical malcontent, eliminating the possibility in advance by definition. In any case, the key point is the first one.

4. It is admirable, but it is not whistleblowing, to complain of sexual harassment or racial prejudice against oneself.[1] In addition, most would not consider it whistleblowing to complain of an act of sexual harassment against a colleague unless this harassment was part of a pattern that was ignored by management.

5. Some would restrict whistleblowing to issues in which an overriding societal value is at stake, such as health, safety, or fiduciary duty. "Do it to save lives, or don't do it," a policy suggested by one whistleblower, expresses this restriction in its strongest form. But terms like "overriding" may cause more trouble than they are worth, except insofar as they suggest that stupid decisions are not the same as unethical ones.

6. In theory, anyone who speaks out in the name of the public good within the organization is a whistleblower. In practice, the whistleblower is defined by the retaliation he or she receives. Imagine that an employee observes an unethical or illegal act by her boss and reports it to her boss's boss. This is the situation that is most likely to get the employee into trouble. Rarely do employees get fired for reporting the misbehavior of subordinates.

7. Her boss's boss thanks her for the information and corrects the problem. She has performed an act of whistleblowing, but for all practical purposes she is not a whistleblower. She becomes a whistleblower only when she experiences retaliation. If there is no retaliation, she is just a responsible employee doing her job to protect the company's interest. This probably results in overstating the amount of retaliation against whistleblowers. If the whistleblower is defined by the organization's response, then by definition most whistleblowers are retaliated against, and most of them severely.

8. Somewhere between half and two-thirds of the whistleblowers lose their jobs, according to several studies (Miethe 1999, 77–78; Rothschild and Miethe 1996, 15–16; Glazer and Glazer 1989, 206–7). At least one study, however, has found significantly less retaliation (Miceli and Near 1992, 226–27). As might be expected, most of the difference depends on whom and how one counts (Miethe 1999, 73–78).

9. Though I approach whistleblowing differently from the studies to which I refer, the characteristics of the small group of whistleblowers I worked with fit

the statistical profile of the average whistleblower in the literature remarkably closely.[2] I did not intend to find this resemblance. I did not seek whistleblowers who fit the profile, just whistleblowers who would talk about their experiences.

10   Among the whistleblowers I worked with, a little over two-thirds lost their jobs. I found most (but far from all) of the whistleblowers I interviewed through a support and lobbying group for whistleblowers, which may have attracted those who had been punished most severely. The whistleblowers in the group were more likely to be employed by government agencies, however, and it is harder for government than private industry to fire someone for whistleblowing.

11   Seniority and rank offer little protection, as several studies reveal (Devine 1998). On the contrary, many organizations seem most threatened by what they view as defection within the senior ranks and hence are most willing to make an example of the defector. The biggest variable is whether the wrongdoing involved losses to the organization of more than $100,000 and whether the reported conduct was routine. If the answer to both these questions was yes, the whistleblower was most likely to be fired (Rothschild and Miethe 1996, 17). The more systematic the wrongdoing, the greater the reprisal (Miethe 1999, 81).

12   Not only do most whistleblowers get fired, but they rarely get their jobs back. Most never work in the field again. In some tight-knit fields there is an informal blacklist. One whistleblower was fired from her new job in the pharmaceutical industry when she sued a previous employer for wrongful discharge. "[My new boss] said it was unconscionable that anyone working for Personal Products would sue a sister company." (Glazer and Glazer 1989, 95) When all organizations are sisters, the whistleblower has nowhere else to go. That, presumably, is the point.

13   Of the several dozen whistleblowers I have talked with, most lost their houses. Many lost their families. It doesn't happen all at once, but whistleblowers' cases drag on for years, putting a tremendous strain on families. Most whistleblowers will suffer from depression and alcoholism (Clark 1997, 1065; Miethe 1999, 77–78). Miethe (1999, 78) found that half went bankrupt. Most whistleblowers will be unable to retire. A typical fate is for a nuclear engineer to end up selling computers at Radio Shack.

14   These are tremendous shocks to the whistleblower. They are not, I believe, the greatest shock. The greatest shock is what the whistleblower learns about the world as a result—that nothing he or she believed was true. That people can be so deeply shaken by knowledge is not something I had expected to find.

15   One surprising result of these empirical studies of whistleblowing deserves further consideration. One would think that it would make a big difference as to whether retaliation occurred if the whistleblower went first to the newspapers or to the boss. In fact, it makes surprisingly little difference. Miethe (1999, 80) found that it makes only a 10-percent difference. Why would internal whistleblowing, as it is called, be so threatening to the organization that its consequences are virtually the same as for external whistleblowing? People lose not only their jobs but in many cases their careers.[3]

16   In creating the whistleblower, the organization is stating that there is a certain type of person it cannot stand in its midst, not necessarily one who goes outside the organization but one who appears to remember that there is an outside. One whistleblower put it this way: "I decided I needed to go back to work. I interviewed with the state of Texas, the city of Austin, and many industries. . . . But nobody wants to hire former whistleblowers. They are all afraid of what we would do if we were asked to tell the truth about some problem" (Glazer and Glazer 1989, 228).

17   In chapter 1, I defined individuality as the ability to carry on an internal dialogue with oneself about what one is doing, a dialogue authentic enough that it might result in doing something different. I have not yet defined the organization I keep talking about and will not until chapter 6, where its definition will be the leading topic. The key point for now is that whistleblowing is not just an act of speaking out. It is an assertion of individuality, perhaps a more basic assertion, in which we talk with others about what we are doing as we are doing it.

18   It turns out to be surprisingly difficult for whistleblowers to share their internal dialogue with others in the organization. Not only does no one want to listen, but no one wants to talk about not listening. A common comment was the following: "I said I'd do anything [the boss] wanted—keep silent, resign, ask for a transfer. All he had to do was discuss the issue with me. But he wouldn't do it, and he wouldn't talk about not doing it. My insubordination was the only issue."

19   We don't know how important being subordinate is, we don't properly estimate the borders of subservience, until we cross them. Engaging in ethical discourse within the organization is one way to learn these limits quickly, but only in retrospect. At the time there is something crazy-making about the experience, akin to the double bind that was once said to cause schizophrenia. Don't talk about ethical issues, and don't talk about our not talking about ethical issues. In the first case recounted below, Peter James Atherton's supervisors refused to read his report; they would not even allow it to be typed. When it finally emerged, almost two decades later, it was his handwritten version that had been preserved in a little library in Maine.

20   Below are stories of four who spoke out and one who did not but should have. In each story not only would the organization not listen, but it transformed issues of ethics, politics, and policy into a single question, that of insubordination. There is a reason for this. Bauman (1989, 213–15) puts it trenchantly. All social organization, he says,

> consists in subjecting the conduct of its units to either instrumental or procedural criteria of evaluation. More importantly still, it consists in delegalizing all other criteria, and first and foremost such standards as may render behaviour of units resilient to uniformizing pressures and thus autonomous vis-à-vis the collective purpose of the organization (which, from the organizational point of view, makes them unpredictable and potentially de-stabilizing). . . . All social organization consists therefore in neutralizing the disruptive and deregulating impact of moral behavior.[4]

The best way to disrupt moral behavior is not to discuss it and not to discuss not discussing it. Then it doesn't exist. Right?

21   When I say that the organization quells individuality, this is what I mean. Talking about what we are doing is not just talking about process and procedures, how we are going to do it. Talking about what we are doing means talking about how what we do affects others. Talking about what we are doing puts our actions in the larger context of their influence on a world of others. Talking about what we are doing makes these others present, as though they were represented in the discussion. Jürgen Habermas (1984) makes this the mark of communicative rationality, the rationality of the lifeworld, as opposed to the rationality of science and technology, what Bauman calls instrumental or procedural criteria of evaluation.

22   Mine is not a "should" statement; it is an "is" statement. I am not arguing that the organization should care about others outside the organization, only that talking about what one is doing *means* talking about the effects of one's acts on those outside the organization and whether these effects are good or bad, right or wrong.

23   We live in a moral world, not because people are good, or because people always think morally about what they are doing, but because as human beings the categories of right and wrong are part of our natural moral environment.[5] To talk about what one is doing is, in part, to raise these considerations, to make explicit the moral context that is always implicit. To talk about what one is doing means to engage in what Hannah Arendt calls thought, and that is no small deed. For the organizations where these whistleblowers worked, it was too much.

Atherton and the NRC

24   Peter James Atherton is his name, one of the few actual names of whistleblowers used in this book. I use it because he asked me to and because his case is well known. His is not a typical story, but it illustrates much that is. A nuclear engineer and inspector for the Nuclear Regulatory Commission, Atherton became convinced that the electrical cables that would be needed to shut down the Maine Yankee nuclear plant in an emergency were not properly separated. If one failed because of fire, all would fail because they were routed through the same cable tray, as it is called. The plant should be shut down until this and other deficiencies were corrected.

25   Atherton's concerns were not based on fantasy. Just three years earlier, in 1975, some workers used a candle flame to check for air leaks in the containment building that housed the reactor at the Brown's Ferry nuclear plant. The flame touched some insulation, igniting a fire that burned more than two thousand cables and disabled electrical controls at the plant. It took more than three days to shut down the plant's two operating reactors, one of which came close to boiling off its cooling water. Had that happened, a meltdown would have occurred.

26   In the keep 'em glowing climate of the 1970s, plants were rarely shut down for repairs. Atherton's supervisors were aware of his conclusions, and while he

was preparing his report they began preparing a response. Their position was that Atherton was emotionally ill, his report an exaggeration. The NRC would not type up his report, and Atherton began showing a handwritten copy to his colleagues. They refused to read it, and so did his supervisors, or so they said.[6]

27   On the day the NRC met with Maine Yankee officials, Atherton got in his car, drove to downtown Washington, D.C., and carried his report straight to NRC commissioner Victor Gilinsky. When Gilinsky would not shut down Maine Yankee immediately, Atherton went to the top nuclear engineer in the country, President Jimmy Carter. After showing his NRC credentials to the Secret Service agent at the gate, he was admitted to the White House grounds, handcuffed, and sent to St. Elizabeth's Hospital for three days of involuntary psychiatric confinement. He was released and fired.

28   Atherton is in many ways the consummate outsider. Twenty years later he lives in a third-floor room in an aging apartment building in Washington, his room as spartan as a monk's. He sleeps on a mattress on box springs, pulling out a folding metal chair for his guest. Instead of paying rent, he does odd jobs for the owner. He is said to have lived out of his car for a while, but to me he denies it.[7]

29   Although he looks and acts the part of the outsider, the anti-organization man, the anarchic individualist in a corporate world, he did not behave that way on the job. On the contrary, he is proud that he stayed within the chain of command, never going outside. "Jimmy Carter was in the nuclear navy. He was my boss. I never went outside the chain of command, not once. No one ever appreciated that."

30   No one ever will. Atherton is threatening not because he threatened to go outside but because he represents the presence of the outside on the inside: not just the unassimilated individual but the unassimilated citizen. Atherton did not "go public." He spoke for the public in private, bringing the outer world into the inner, transgressing boundaries.

31   Atherton is unassimilated to organizational culture, above all to the idea that one formulates one's position not in response to one's analysis of the situation outside but in response to the situation inside: the expectations of one's superiors, the organizational lay of the land. There are no naive empiricists and positivists in organizational life. Or if there are, they do not last long. One study of whistleblowers found them among the least sensitive to social cues (Jos, Tompkins, and Hays 1989).

A Postscript

32   In 1991, a short-circuit set off a hydrogen gas explosion in the turbine building of the Maine Yankee plant. Supporting beams were bent, and bolts were sheared, splitting pipes that carried hydrogen gas to the plant's generator. Hydrogen fires burned for hours. The plant was shut down for repairs, and anti-nuclear activists in Maine were reinvigorated. One activist found a copy of Atherton's handwritten report in the public documents room in a local library. In addition to the cable separation problem, it described a hydrogen explosion hazard almost identical to the one that had just occurred. No one, in-

cluding Atherton, knows how his report ended up in a little library in Maine. The local paper, the *Lincoln County Weekly*, wrote a story headlined "NRC Knew of Problems 20 Years Ago." Still in question was whether the cables that Atherton cited were the same ones that short-circuited.

33 After an investigation lasting several years, the NRC found additional problems. "The most prevalent one was insufficient separation of safety cables and other wires. Some wires were so close together they might short out" (Weisman 1997). In December 1996, Maine Yankee shut the plant down, pending repair of the separation problem, the same problem Atherton identified nearly twenty years earlier.

34 Maine Yankee has decided that repairs cost too much and has closed the plant for good. The NRC has launched two investigations into the Atherton matter, one on the technical issues he identified, the other by the inspector general on the circumstances of his dismissal. The investigations continue. It is not unusual for a whistleblower's case to drag on this long, now more than twenty years.

35 When I asked Atherton what he thought about the story about him in the *Washington Post Magazine* that laid his personal life bare, he said he spoke to the reporter honestly about his trials in the hope that it might interest him enough to write something about his case. Atherton means the technical details, fire hazards and cable separation. He has learned about using the media, but strictly in the service of his cause. For all his passion, he is strangely distant from his story. Coupled with his black and gray beard, it is what gives him the quality of an Old Testament prophet transported by his cause.

36 Atherton will in all likelihood never get his job back. It is unlikely that he will be compensated in any way for his twenty years in the desert. Yet he has received something that few whistleblowers do, a sort of public vindication. It is what almost every whistleblower seeks. When it comes (and it is rare), it helps, but not as much as one might suppose, certainly not as much as the whistleblower had hoped. He has learned and gone through too much.

Notes
1. Miethe (1999, 58) includes among whistleblowers those who blow the whistle on misconduct directed solely against themselves.
2. The statistical characteristics of the whistleblowers I worked with match almost perfectly the characteristics of whistleblowers in Miethe's (1999) *Whistleblowing at Work*, the most extensive study yet, based on interviews with hundreds of whistleblowers. Miethe also interviewed hundreds who saw abuse but did not blow the whistle, a valuable comparison I occasionally draw on.
3. One reason the number fired for internal whistleblowing is so high is that if you just go to your boss you generally don't acquire privileged status under most laws protecting whistleblowers. For that you have to go outside the organization. If you just go to the boss, it's easier to fire you. Elliston et al. (1985b, 1–15) would restrict whistleblowing to the act of going public. It is not whistleblowing, but something else, more like politics and persuasion within the organization, to go to one's boss's boss. Though this restriction might make sense if the issue were primarily one of clear definition, it would exclude from view that most fascinating observation: there is not much difference between going public and going to the boss's boss as far as retaliation is concerned. In either case one has identified oneself as someone whose loyalties lie elsewhere, and that

is enough. Definitions should serve theory, or at least the interesting observation. For this reason I reject Elliston's distinction, even though his *Whistleblowing Research* contains a remarkably intelligent discussion of problems of definition (1985b, 1–17).

In "Whistleblowing: A Restrictive Definition and Interpretation," Peter Jubb (1999) defines whistleblowing even more narrowly, almost equating it with civil disobedience. Though his definition has the advantage of emphasizing that whistleblowing is a political act, it could obscure the fact that organizations often succeed in turning dissent into an occasion for discipline. That is, the organization prevents whistleblowing from becoming a public act in the first place. This is the topic of chapters 6 and 7.

4. Bauman's book is titled *Modernity and the Holocaust,* but he is writing about every modern organization, not just the ones that made the Holocaust. Indeed, that is the thesis of his book.
5. I don't know how I could prove this statement within the compass of this book. My own perspective is roughly that of Melanie Klein, who argues that love and hate are the basic categories of human experience. As an idealist, Klein (1975) believes we create these experiences out of our hopes and fears (Alford 1989). More recent work in the evolutionary basis of moral psychology seems to support Klein's argument. See especially Frans De Waal (1996), Robert Wright (1994), and James Q. Wilson (1993). That humans see the world in fundamentally moral terms does not, of course, mean that they act morally or that these moral terms correspond to what we would ordinarily think of as "higher" morality. More on this in chapters 4 and 5.
6. Someone must have read it because the NRC rebuts it point by point in an unsigned report of March 3, 1978.
7. Atherton read this case study and says I should tell you that he now sleeps in a bed in a better apartment.

Reading Responses

1. What does Alford mean when he says that "the greatest shock is what the whistleblower learns about the world as a result—that nothing he or she believed was true" (paragraph 14)?
2. What does Alford himself think about the conduct of the whistle-blowers' organizations? At what point does Alford state his view? Why would he wait until this point in the chapter to indicate his position?
3. What does Atherton's story illustrate about whistle-blowing? How does Alford present Atherton's story so that readers can understand and interpret it?

Writing Activities

1. Based on Alford's information, prepare a two-column balance sheet: list the possible rewards of whistle-blowing in one column and the possible costs in another.
2. In your own words, summarize why an organization is nearly as likely to ostracize someone who is an internal whistle-blower (revealing the issue to someone higher up in the organization) as someone who is an external whistle-blower (revealing the issue to someone outside such as a member of an oversight agency or the press).

3. Write your own extended definition of a term that might arise in an ethical issue involving an individual and an organization. Possibilities include *loyalty, authority, insubordination, integrity, honesty,* or *individuality.* As you discuss the term, you may use examples from your experiences or observations of groups or organizations in the work, academic, or public communities.

Community Links

Compare and contrast the selection from Alford's book with other readings on ethical issues. For example, turn to the readings that appear under "C. Community Ethics" for each community (pp. 77–93) for the academic community, pp. 264–279 for the work community, and pp. 412–425 for the public community). Analyze several of these readings, noting their common elements and their differences. Consider whether their differences reflect the expectations of their communities.

Texts and Documents from the Work Community

En el Army, no sólo podrás especializarte en una profesión, también incrementarás la confianza que tienes en ti mismo, el respeto y la auto-disciplina, valores fundamentales para el logro de tus metas y tu desarrollo integral como ser humano.

Recuerda: Todos los valores y habilidades que aprendes en el Army te servirán no sólo hoy, sino toda tu vida.

In the Army, you'll not only become a specialized professional, you'll also gain self confidence, respect and self discipline. Values important to your personal development and to achieving your goals.

Remember: All the values and skills you learn in the Army will serve you, not only today but for a lifetime.

MOS 31L CABLE SYSTEMS INSTALLER-MAINTAINER
Private First Class Jumarixa Toro, Army Reserve.

¡EN EL U.S. ARMY TENDRAS BENEFICIOS UNICOS!

- Una de las más de 200 carreras especializadas
- Entrenamiento garantizado
- Hasta $20,000 como bono de enlistamiento, basado en tus aptitudes
- 30 días de vacaciones ganadas al año
- Servicio médico y dental
- Hasta $50,000 para pagar tus estudios universitarios
- 75 por ciento de apoyo económico para pagar tu universidad
- La oportunidad de viajar a diferentes partes del mundo

DESCUBRE MÁS SOBRE EL ARMY RESERVE.

- Sirve medio tiempo, cerca de casa
- Una de las más de 180 carreras especializadas
- Entrenamiento garantizado
- Hasta $8,000 como bono de enlistamiento, basado en tus aptitudes
- Hasta $20,000 para la universidad
- Hasta 75 por ciento del costo de tus estudios
- Un salario adicional cada mes

YOU WILL FIND UNIQUE BENEFITS IN THE U.S. ARMY!

- One of more than 200 job specialties
- Guaranteed training
- Up to $20,000 enlistment bonus, based on qualifications
- 30 vacation days earned per year
- Medical and dental care
- Up to $50,000 for college
- Up to 75 percent tuition assistance
- The opportunity to travel to different places in the world

FIND OUT MORE ABOUT THE ARMY RESERVE.

- Serve part time, close to home
- One of more than 180 job specialties
- Guaranteed training
- Up to $8,000 enlistment bonus, based on qualifications
- Up to $20,000 for college
- Up to 75 percent tuition assistance
- An additional monthly paycheck

Job Announcement
DISCOVER HOW FAR YOU CAN GO
U.S. Army

◆

The facing page is the inside page of a recruiting brochure promoting one of the job alternatives—over two hundred available—in the U.S. Army. The young woman whose photograph appears on the brochure serves in the reserves and is trained to install and maintain cable systems. Other job categories in the Army include air traffic controllers, construction workers and supervisors, medical personnel, mechanics, police, firefighters, and musicians as well as weapons experts and infantry. The back of the brochure supplies contact information, listing the Army's Web site and toll-free phone number.

Reading Responses

1. What is the purpose of this brochure? What different types of information does it supply?
2. In what ways do the text and layout of the brochure contribute to its overall purpose?
3. What expectations and possible concerns of readers does the brochure address? What expectations of the U.S. Army does the brochure present?

Writing Activities

1. Consider yourself a prospective member of the U.S. Army, trying to decide whether to enlist. Analyze the benefits and the responsibilities suggested by the brochure in terms of your own needs and interests. Write up your analysis in two parts: one for and the other against enlisting.
2. Working with a small group of classmates, gather a collection of job announcements. Check advertisements, company postings, or employment services using the Internet, newspapers, professional publications, or the resources available at your local public library or your campus career center. Work together to analyze your collection. How do the job announcements appeal to prospective applicants? How do they convey the expectations of the employer? Develop either a report of your findings or a guide advising job hunters about job announcements.
3. Identify a job that you would like to hire someone to do in order to simplify your own life. For example, you might want to hire a driver to drop

you off near your classroom (thus avoiding the campus parking lot), a home helper who would manage family meals or chores, a textbook shopper, a dorm room organizer, a personal chef for your living unit, a wake-up caller, or a pet rental service. Write a specific job announcement for this position. Design your announcement to attract and inform applicants.

EDITORIAL INTERNSHIPS
Wilson Quarterly

◆

This Web page announces internships available to both current students and recent college graduates at the Wilson Quarterly, *a well-known publication based at the Woodrow Wilson International Center in Washington, D.C. The announcement describes the job and explains how to apply. These internships are editorial, and interns would work directly with the publication's editor. For those interested in different activities, the page also supplies a link to descriptions of other internships.*

1 The *Wilson Quarterly* offers editorial internships to college students and recent graduates.

2 There are three internship sessions each year: January–May, June–August, and September–December. Interns work full time (40 hours per week), and receive a monthly stipend of $400 ($600/month for fall and spring sessions).

3 Each intern is assigned to one of the *Quarterly*'s editors, and is responsible for researching and fact-checking the articles on which that editor is working. Interns use the Library of Congress, the Wilson Center's library, visit various museums, think tanks, embassies, and government agencies in the Washington area, and perform telephone interviews to gather background information. Interns obtain art for use in the *WQ*, and may write short "sidebars" that appear within the main articles, or contribute to short review sections of the magazine. Some proofreading, newspaper clipping, and general office chores are also part of the interns' duties. Applicants may have any liberal arts major, but excellent writing skills, attention to detail, and the ability to work well under deadline pressure are essential.

4 Interested candidates should send a resume, cover letter, three brief writing samples (500 words each), and a list of three references to:

>James Carman
>Managing Editor
>Wilson Quarterly
>One Woodrow Wilson Plaza
>1300 Pennsylvania Avenue, NW
>Washington, D.C. 20004-3027
>(202) 691-4023

The deadline for the summer internship is **March 15th,** for the fall internship **July 15th,** and for the spring internship **October 15th.** Interested students, however, are encouraged to apply at any time since applications are reviewed and accepted on a rolling admission basis. Please note that we do not accept applications by fax or e-mail.

5   **Other** internships available at the Woodrow Wilson International Center for Scholars.

Reading Responses

1. What would an editorial intern at the *Wilson Quarterly* do?
2. If you wanted to apply for this internship, what information would you try to include in your cover letter? How does this announcement suggest what you might want to include?
3. What does this announcement assume that applicants already know (or can find out) about applying for an internship or a job?

Writing Activities

1. Write a cover letter applying for the position at the *Wilson Quarterly*, showing how your background and experience would make you an excellent intern.
2. Search for other internship announcements on the Web, or visit your campus career office to see what is posted there. Select one announcement that appeals to you. Analyze what the intern would do and what the application requires and assumes of an applicant. Write up your analysis as if you were working at the career center and needed to advise an interested student about this opportunity.
3. Write a cover letter applying for the position that you found and analyzed in activity 2, showing how your background and experience would make you an excellent intern.

Résumé for Job Hunting

◆

A résumé, along with a complementary cover letter, is one of the staple documents expected of a job hunter. These two sample résumés were written by college seniors with different backgrounds and career objectives, both preparing to move from the campus to the workplace. Both writers categorize their experiences and skills, yet each customizes the contents, sequence, and layout of his or her résumé. To locate more sample résumés, visit the career center on your campus, check its Web site, or browse the career center Web sites for other campuses.

MARKETING RÉSUMÉ
Elizabeth Falvo, Student Writer

Elizabeth Falvo
ef@mail.cwru.edu
1200-B East 118th Avenue
Cleveland, OH 44106
(216) 555-5555

Education Case Western Reserve University, Cleveland, OH
B.S., Weatherhead School of Management, May 2003
Major: Marketing Concentration; GPA: 3.24

Work Experience Marketing Consultant, Kozy Kashmir, 10/02-present
- Developed and implemented a comprehensive marketing plan for a start-up company
- Conducted extensive on-site and Internet market research

Teaching/Research Assistant, Economics Department, CWRU, 3/01-10/01
- Offered out-of-class tutoring sessions for students
- Evaluated approximately 100 students
- Organized and ran on-site experiments
- Recorded and organized survey and experiment results

Retail Sales Associate, Hard Rock Cafe, Cleveland, OH, and Niagara Falls, NY, 5/00-present
- Assisted customers with product selection
- Rated consistently as one of the top three salespeople on staff

Related Courses Marketing Communications, Marketing Technology, Marketing Management, E-Marketing, Corporation Finance, Operations Research, Development of MIS, Financial and Managerial Accounting, Econometrics, Organizational Behavior

Activities and Awards Provost's Scholarship, CWRU
Dean's Honor List, Fall 2001
Air Force ROTC Scholarship
Symphonic Winds/Marching Band
Boo at the Zoo Volunteer

Technology Résumé
Brad Roepstorff, Student Writer

Brad Roepstorff
br@mail.cwru.edu

Home Address:
4002 S. Raven Place
Aurora, CO 80013
(303) 555-5555

Campus Address:
1510 Magnolia Street
Cleveland, OH 44106
(216) 555-5555

-OBJECTIVE-
To obtain a full-time position in the technology field using my programming skills and problem-solving abilities.

-EDUCATION-
Case Western Reserve University
B.S., 2003: Major in Computer Science, Minor in Artificial Intelligence
Overall GPA: 3.36, Major GPA: 3.60

-SUMMARY OF QUALIFICATIONS-
Programming: C/C++, Fortran, Perl, MIPS assembly, JavaScript, SQL
Software Suites: Matlab, Mathematica, Visual Studio.Net, Flash MX, 3D Studio Max 4
Operating Systems: Microsoft Windows (all versions), Unix (Solaris, Linux)
Other: Excellent written and verbal abilities, leadership and management experience

-RELATED COURSEWORK-
Artificial Intelligence: Intelligent Systems I & II, Computational Intelligence, Optimization Theory
Computer Graphics: Mathematics of Geometric Design, Computer Graphics
Computing Systems: Operating & Database Systems, Computer Architecture, Systems Programming
Software Theory: Theoretical Computer Science, Software Engineering, Algorithms and Data Structures, Discrete Mathematics
Miscellaneous: Computer Security, Computers in Mechanical Engineering

-SPECIAL PROJECTS-
Optical Character Recognition Using a Backpropagation Neural Network
- Designed and implemented neural network tool in Matlab capable of recognizing handwritten characters with up to 85.8% accuracy
- Analyzed variations in network size and training time; tested previously seen and new images

Hierarchical 3D Model Viewer
- Built model viewer capable of loading and displaying fully articulated multiple-jointed models using OpenGL with Custom SDL (Scene Description Language) for saving object data
- Included user interface that combines mouse and GUI inputs to allow full selection and manipulation of individual sub-objects with fully movable lights and camera

-WORK EXPERIENCE-
Teaching Assistant, CWRU EECS Department — January 2003-Present
Webmaster, CWRU Telephone Services — May-December, 2002
Apprentice Surveyor, Montgomery Phillips, Inc., Land Surveyors — June-August, 2001

-ACTIVITIES-
Phi Kappa Theta Fraternity: President (Spring 2002); IFC (Fall 2002); Brotherhood Chair (Fall 2000)

References available upon request

Reading Responses

1. What is the purpose of a résumé? What reader does a résumé address? What is that reader likely to expect?
2. Generalizing from the selections here, what are typical components of a résumé written by a college student or a recent graduate? Why do you think that Brad and Elizabeth have designed and organized their categories slightly differently?
3. Identify strategies that these writers have used to present information concisely and effectively, such as lists, parallel wording, and the like. In what ways do these strategies help to convey the writers' skills, experiences, and interests?

Writing Activities

1. Prepare a master list of all of your past jobs, skills, activities, and other background experiences. Be sure that you include the pertinent dates, names of contact people, addresses and phone numbers, and other details. Use this master list as a basis for the next two activities, selecting appropriate items from it. (If you continue to add to your master list regularly, it will be an excellent resource when you are ready to graduate and are searching for a professional job.)
2. Identify a particular job or type of job that you would like to have. Write (or revise) your résumé, tailoring it to accompany an application for that job. Select a pattern of organization that highlights your strengths. List pertinent specifics, but limit your résumé to one page.
3. Working with a group of classmates, exchange and critique your résumés. Write out your suggestions from the point of view of a prospective employer.

Community Links

Examine other concise, conventional documents such as memos (pp. 229 and 307), letters (pp. 96–100, 308–319, 471–474, and 512–514), and summaries (pp. 154–159 and 297–300). Using several examples, consider what common characteristics and purposes such texts share with résumés and what characteristics distinguish the various types of documents.

Career Advice

MODEL FORMAT FOR COVER LETTER
(INQUIRY OR APPLICATION)

Jayne Swanson

◆

Career advice is readily available for job hunters or for employees who want to improve their skills. Brochures, leaflets, short articles, and sample documents are accessible online, at libraries, and at your campus career center. Contributed by Jayne Swanson, the director of career services at Cornell College in Mt. Vernon, Iowa, the following selection explains and illustrates how to prepare a basic cover letter. Along with a résumé, the cover letter is an essential component of an effective job search.

(Down far enough so letter is centered on one page)
1   Your personal address
       City, State, Zip Code
       Date of Writing
  2 to 4 spaces
2   Name of recipient
       Title (can also go on line with Name)
       Organization
       Organization's Street Address
       City, State, Zip Code (use state abbreviations: Mt. Vernon, IA 52314)
  1 space
3   Dear Ms./Mr. Blank (always address your letter to a specific person):
  1 space
4   *First paragraph:* Whether you are inquiring about possible openings or applying for one, try to spark the employer's interest with your reasons for wanting to join the organization. Identify the name of the position, field, or general career area about which you are asking or applying. Tell how you found out about the opening or organization as well as why you are interested in that position or field.
  1 space
5   *Body of letter (generally 1 or 2 paragraphs):* Show how your background qualifies you for the job, and use examples that relate your accomplishments, experience, or education to what's required. Always think about the employer's needs, and write about how you can provide the skills, characteristics, or experiences the organization is seeking. This is the

place to "sell" your abilities to potential employers. Think of the specific experiences that taught you those skills and abilities rather than just listing them. Do not just repeat your résumé; instead, emphasize or introduce illustrations and details that will appeal to the employer's interests.

1 space

6   *Last paragraph:* Conclude by offering to provide additional information and to meet with the employer. If you are applying for a specific position, request an interview. If you are inquiring about openings, ask for an opportunity to discuss the company's future needs and your relevant background. Take the active approach, and let the employer know that you will contact him or her by a certain date to discuss the possibility of an interview or check on your status. If you are planning to visit an area where the organization is located, mention the time of your visit. Finally, thank the employer for his or her time and consideration of your application or inquiry.

1 space

    Sincerely,

4 spaces

    (Your handwritten signature here)

    Type your full name
    Enclosure (noting that your résumé is enclosed)

Reading Responses

1. What is the purpose of this model format?
2. Who are the readers addressed by the model format? In what ways does it challenge their assumptions and try to meet their needs?
3. What information does this model format provide about the likely expectations of employers and interviewers? In what ways do these expectations reflect the values of the work community?

Writing Activities

1. Write a "highlights" paragraph about this model format, identifying its most practical or useful advice from your point of view. Begin with a topic sentence that lets your reader know the basis you have used to select the highlights.
2. Visit your campus career center, your public library, or a community job center, in person or online. Identify some of the many sources and types of

career advice available. Based on this investigation, write an analysis of possible reasons why academic institutions, corporations, newspapers, publishers, professional journals, government agencies, or other organizations sponsor or supply career advice for students. What do these reasons suggest about the relationships between the academic and the work communities?
3. Use the model format to help you write a letter of application for a job that would interest you. Follow a standard letter format, and limit your letter to a single page. (If you have also prepared a résumé, be sure to supplement and interpret it rather than repeat it in your letter.)

Community Links

Compare and contrast other texts and documents offering advice with Swanson's "Model Format." For example, turn to Vermette's letter from the academic community (pp. 96–100) or selections from the public community such as "Your Driving Costs 2003" (pp. 530–541) or "How to Make a Budget and Stick to It" (pp. 543–547). For the selections you choose, consider points such as how each presents its advice, appeals to readers, organizes its advice effectively, or uses its design to accomplish its purpose and meet community expectations.

Organizational Welcome to Employees
WELCOME TO THE FAMILY
Olive Garden Italian Restaurant

◆

This selection is part of a booklet used to welcome new employees to the Olive Garden restaurants. The booklet has a colorful cover with a "handwritten" script greeting the new employee. Inside, the text is printed in black with green section headings; Italian cityscapes or small grape clusters, also in green, decorate the page number at the bottom of each page. Besides the sections reprinted here, the brochure also covers employee benefits; payroll procedures, raises, and the pay stub format; procedures for transfers, leaves, and similar matters; guidelines for personal conduct; and workplace issues ranging from disputes to telephone calls. The brochure concludes with the words of two songs that Olive Garden employees sing—the hospitality and the celebration songs—both a memorable part of special dinners at the restaurant.

Welcome...

To the Olive Garden, where *Hospitaliano!* thrives and we hope you will too.

Need a translation? Before long, Hospitaliano! will be part of your daily vocabulary. Hospitaliano! is a feeling we share with our guests and with each other that makes work fun. It's Italian hospitality you will find only at the Olive Garden.

Our restaurants feature tasty food made to order, excellent service, terrific value, and Hospitaliano! in a beautiful garden atmosphere. You, however, are the most important ingredient in our success. You provide each guest with that special Olive Garden experience during every visit.

As a new employee, you will have questions. This book covers the basics, so please take a few minutes to read it. Then cover any questions with your manager.

Please be sure to sign and date the signature page at the end of this booklet, and return it to your orientation manager as soon as possible.

Welcome to the Olive Garden. We're glad you're a part of the team.

Best wishes!

Brad D. Blum

Brad Blum
President

About The Olive Garden

The Olive Garden has its roots in years of market study and consumer research. Findings revealed that guests loved Italian food, but there was no Italian dinner house chain to meet this demand. Additional research showed that consumers would enjoy garden-like surroundings with a warm, family atmosphere. Thus, the Olive Garden was born—with its comfortable interior, fabulous food, friendly service, complimentary refills, and Hospitaliano!

The first Olive Garden opened in Orlando, Florida on December 13, 1982. Within five short years, the restaurant had expanded throughout North America. We are still going strong, opening several new restaurants a year.

In 1995, the Olive Garden and sister company Red Lobster separated from General Mills and became an independent restaurant company, Darden Restaurants. Darden Restaurants, named after William B. Darden, the founder of Red Lobster, is the largest full-service restaurant company in the world.

Hospitaliano!

What is Hospitaliano? It's the foundation of the Olive Garden. Hospitaliano! is best defined as "a passion for 100% guest delight." It means taking pride in doing it right the first time. It's something we share with our guests, our suppliers, and with each other. It's what makes working fun and enjoyable. It's a kind of "Italian hospitality" you'll find only at the Olive Garden.

We practice Hospitaliano! every day, in everything we do, with everyone we serve. We are committed to our guests, to each other, and to our investors. We take pride in all we do, all we have built, and all we will achieve.

Our Vision

Olive Garden is THE choice for Italian. This statement keeps us focused on what's important in our business, and it helps us to do the right thing when making decisions.

Olive Garden is an innovator in the industry, proud of its roots and Italian spirit. We never stop asking more from ourselves to provide 100% guest delight.

We are a family of local restaurants, placing emphasis on consistent, high quality Italian food and personalized service beyond routine. We have an exciting and challenging growth environment which draws enthusiastic people and where diversity is valued.

Our Principles

We have seven principles based on what our employees say they need to get their jobs done and be productive. When we have questions, we look to these principles for guidance and solutions.

- We are committed to open and honest communication, mutual respect and strong teamwork.

- We are clear on each individual's role, accountabilities and key performance measures.
- We do not compromise standards in selection, training and job performance.
  ★ We only hire people with the skills and potential to succeed.
  ★ People advance from training only when they have demonstrated the required competencies.
  ★ Peer interviewing helps us select the right people for the team.
- In the process of making a change, we seek the opinions of those closest to the action, listen and value their ideas.
- Everyone should expect regular, ongoing training opportunities to sharpen and advance their skills.
- When accountabilities are not being met, we act quickly.
  ★ Feedback
  ★ Re-training/Redirection
  ★ Assess results with appropriate consequences
- We will achieve the results and share our successes.

Our Five Policies

We have five policies for ensuring delivery of safe, high quality, delicious food and beverages to our guests. They are simple, yet require you to maintain standards that will be identified throughout your training:

- Hot Food Hot
- Cold Food Cold
- Clean Restrooms
- Money to Our Bank
- Know your Food

These fundamental business principles help us provide Hospitaliano! for our guests. When guests feel good about their experience, they return and that builds our business.

HADU

In addition to Hospitaliano! there is another saying you will come to know at Olive Garden: HADU. You may not wear a green HADU button, but it is still an important part of our attitude.

HADU stands for Honesty, Action, Details, and Urgency.

Honesty means integrity and truthfulness in all circumstances, whether you are dealing with guests, managers, or fellow employees.

Action is doing what needs to be done—now. It means taking responsibility, helping a co-worker, doing your job. It means not waiting for someone else to take action.

Details, our attention to them sets us apart from other restaurants. If you're a server, that means knowing our menu inside and out and sharing your knowledge with guests through suggestive selling. If you're a line cook, it means making sure each dish is perfect every time. Details make the difference between an "okay" dining experience for our guests and an outstanding one.

Urgency means getting the job done when it needs to be done: serving hot food hot, cold food cold, cleaning up spills immediately, and calling for "back-up sticks." Having a sense of urgency encourages you to think quickly and take responsibility.

Equal Opportunity

The Olive Garden is an equal opportunity employer. We provide equal opportunities in employment, training, and promotion regardless of race, color, sex, religion, age, national origin, disability, sexual orientation or status in any group protected by federal, state, or local law. Our primary consideration in the selection of an individual is the person's ability to perform the job.

As part of our commitment to equal employment opportunity, the Olive Garden prohibits acts of harassment, retaliation, or discrimination on the basis of race, color, age, sex, religion, national origin, disability, sexual orientation or status in any group protected by federal, state, or local law. The Olive Garden will not tolerate such unlawful treatment of employees.

Your Opportunity

The lifestyle of the 1990s includes an increasing demand for restaurants. Estimates are that demand for restaurant dining will double within the next 15 to 20 years. The Olive Garden is a direct part of this trend. We have grown from our first restaurant into an international chain, with six geographic divisions in the United States and Canada and corporate headquarters in Orlando, Florida.

Many of our restaurant managers and operations executives started with us as restaurant staff employees. As they learned the business, they decided to make it their career choice. If you are qualified and interested in a restaurant management career, our continued growth can provide that opportunity.

We Are a Team

We're glad you joined Olive Garden, and hope you have fun working here. We're counting on you to help provide our guests with the best Italian food and the finest service. A well-run restaurant depends on teamwork. If all employees don't work together, the restaurant doesn't "work."

Guests are our number one priority and the food and service we provide determines if they'll return. All employees, from the front of the house to the back of the house, uphold our standard of excellent guest service.

Reading Responses

1. What is the purpose of this brochure?
2. In what ways does the brochure express the company culture at the Olive Garden—its ways of defining goals, unifying employees, establishing shared standards, conducting business, and setting expectations for everyone?
3. What tone and approach to new employees does the brochure use? Find wording that illustrates these features. What overall impression does the brochure try to convey to new employees?

Writing Activities

1. Write a sentence explaining what each section of the reading (introduced by a heading) tries to accomplish. Then complete a paragraph by adding introductory and concluding sentences emphasizing the overall impression created by this selection from the brochure. Revise for clarity.
2. Given the approach of the employee brochure, how would you expect the Olive Garden to feel about the guests who dine at the restaurant? Write a short greeting to guests that reflects your sense of the Olive Garden's company values.
3. Based on your work experience, compare or contrast the Olive Garden's orientation for new employees with that of another company where you have worked. Consider similarities and differences in light of the type of business and the general values of the work community.

Community Links

Compare the Olive Garden brochure with the job announcement from the U.S. Army (pp. 280–281) or the appeals to supporters (pp. 447–456) from the public community. Even though these selections have different purposes, consider the strategies that several of them use to convey a clear impression of an organization.

Executive Summary

◆

The Harvard Business Review *is a publication of the Graduate School of Business Administration at Harvard University. Appearing ten times a year, this journal presents articles, case studies, discussions of best practices, book reviews, letters to the editor, and other features. Each issue supplies executive summaries for the articles it includes so that its primary readers—business and corporate managers—can quickly review the month's topics. The abstracts, like the full articles, include reprint numbers so that readers can easily request permission to duplicate an article or order reprints.*

How to Win the Blame Game
David G. Baldwin

Reprint R0107C

1 At some companies, people are all too quick to point fingers, leaving employees more concerned about avoiding blame than about achieving results. Such organizations, ruled by "CYA," have given blame a bum rap.

2 David Baldwin, a former Major League pitcher, says blame can be a powerful and constructive force. It can be an effective teaching tool that helps people avoid repeating their mistakes. When used judiciously—and sparingly—blame can also prod people to put forth their best efforts, while maintaining both their confidence and their focus on goals. Indeed, blame can have a very positive effect when it's done for the right reasons. The key, then, is the way that blame is managed, which can influence how people make decisions and perform their jobs and ultimately affect the culture and character of an organization.

3 In the course of his research on how Major League Baseball managers make decisions, Baldwin became fascinated by the subject of blame—what functions it serves and how it's best managed. His observations led him to identify five rules of blame, which, he says, apply to any organization, whether it's the LA Dodgers, General Motors, or a small start-up. First, know when to blame—and when not to. Second, blame in private and praise in public. Third, realize that the absence of blame can be far worse than its presence. Fourth, manage misguided blame. And fifth, be aware that confidence is the first casualty of blame.

4 Managers who follow these rules will use blame in the most positive and effective ways possible, Baldwin says. Without these rules, blame becomes an ever-more difficult balancing act: Too much erodes people's confidence, while too little hinders them from reaching their full potential.

Get Inside the Lives of Your Customers
Patricia B. Seybold

Reprint R0105E

1 Many companies have become adept at the art of customer relationship management. They've collected mountains of data on preferences and behavior, divided buyers into ever-finer segments, and refined their products, services, and marketing pitches.

2   But all too often those efforts are too narrow—they concentrate only on the points where the customer comes into contact with the company. Few businesses have bothered to look at what the author calls the *customer scenario*—the broad context in which customers select, buy, and use products and services. As a result, consultant Patricia Seybold maintains, they've routinely missed chances to deepen loyalty and expand sales.

3   In this article, the author shows how effective three very different companies have been at using customer scenarios as the centerpiece of their marketing plans. Chip maker National Semiconductor looked beyond the purchasing agents that buy in bulk to find ways to make it easier for engineers to design National's components into their specifications for mobile telephones. Each time they do so, it translates into millions of dollars in orders.

4   By developing a customer scenario that describes how people actually shop for groceries, Tesco learned the importance of decentralizing its Web shopping site and how the extra costs of decentralization could be outweighed by the higher profit margins online customers generate. And Buzzsaw.com used customer scenarios as the basis for its entire business. It has used the Web to create a better way for the dozens of participants in a construction project to share their drawings and manage their projects.

5   Seybold lays out the steps managers can take to develop their own customer scenarios. By thinking broadly about the challenges your customers face, she suggests, you can almost always find ways to make their lives easier—and thus earn their loyalty.

STRATEGY AND THE INTERNET
Michael E. Porter

Reprint R0103D

1   Many of the pioneers of Internet business, both dot-coms and established companies, have competed in ways that violate nearly every precept of good strategy. Rather than focus on profits, they have chased customers indiscriminately through discounting, channel incentives, and advertising. Rather than concentrate on delivering value that earns an attractive price from customers, they have pursued indirect revenues such as advertising and click-through fees. Rather than make trade-offs, they have rushed to offer every conceivable product or service.

2   It did not have to be this way—and it does not have to be in the future. When it comes to reinforcing a distinctive strategy, Michael Porter argues, the Internet provides a better technological platform than previous generations of IT. Gaining competitive advantage does not require a radically new approach to business; it requires building on the proven principles of effective strategy.

3   Porter argues that, contrary to recent thought, the Internet is not disruptive to most existing industries and established companies. It rarely nullifies important sources of competitive advantage in an industry; it often makes them even more valuable. And as all companies embrace Internet technology, the Internet itself will be neutralized as a source of advantage. Robust competitive advantages will arise instead from traditional strengths such as unique products, proprietary content, and distinctive physical activities. Internet technology may be able to fortify those advantages, but it is unlikely to supplant them.

4   Porter debunks such Internet myths as first-mover advantage, the power of virtual companies, and the multiplying rewards of network effects. He disentangles the distorted signals from the marketplace, explains why the Internet complements rather than cannibalizes existing ways of doing business, and outlines strategic imperatives for dot-coms and traditional companies.

Reading Responses

1. What is the purpose of these executive summaries?
2. What information about the article does each summary supply?
3. In what ways are the executive summaries written to appeal to readers? In what ways might the writing style and word choice engage readers?

Writing Activities

1. Select one of the executive summaries, and reduce it further to a single paragraph. Write your summary paragraph in your own words, and concentrate on clearly stating the main point.
2. Write an analysis of one of the executive summaries. Identify the main features of the summary, and explain how these features contribute to the effectiveness of the summary.
3. Select an article or report from this book. (See the table of contents or the Guide to Themes, Topics, and Rhetorical Strategies for possible choices.) Read the selection, and then write an executive summary of it, following the style of the samples from *Harvard Business Review*.

Community Links

Compare and contrast several of the executive summaries and abstracts in this book. (See the Guide to Themes, Topics, and Rhetorical Strategies for examples of each type.) In what ways are these two forms similar or different? In what ways might the differences reflect the expectations of the general community or the specific readers addressed?

Article in Professional Journal
ARE INCENTIVES FOR DRUG ABUSE TREATMENT TOO STRONG?

Mark Simpson

♦

Corrections Today Magazine is published by the American Correctional Association for its members, who are corrections or criminal justice professionals. Mark Simpson's article appeared in an issue devoted to the topic of "drugs, crime, and corrections," his own area of expertise as a regional coordinator for drug abuse programs.

1   Correctional staff who work outside of drug treatment occasionally question if drug abuse incentives are even necessary. Some may argue that the only incentives offenders should have for participating in drug treatment is the opportunity to overcome their addictions and straighten out their lives. They may further argue that any other incentives, e.g., early parole or better prison living conditions, such as preferred housing and enhanced recreational opportunities, only encourage offenders to fake their way through treatment to get the secondary benefits. Incentives, they believe, get in the way of treatment.

2   To some extent, correctional staff who express this opinion have a point. Incentives, if not handled properly, can seriously undermine treatment. On the other hand, without incentives, offenders may not take advantage of the opportunity for treatment in the first place. In a perfect world, incarceration would make offenders realize that their substance abuse has caused them great pain and deprived them of their freedom, and they would gratefully volunteer for drug treatment and devote their full energies toward overcoming their addictions. However, if offenders acted in this manner, they most likely would never be incarcerated to begin with. They would have realized that their substance abuse was causing them unwanted consequences and would have taken the necessary steps to avoid incarceration. However, offenders typically do not think this way and the eventual consequences for their lack of responsibility are arrest and incarceration.

3   To appreciate the importance of drug treatment incentives, one must understand that substance-abusing offenders view drugs in a radically different way than the criminal justice system. For corrections professionals, drug use equals loss of control, personal destruction and possibly death. For offenders, drugs are viewed as the means for obtaining money, power, sex and the relief from overwhelming feelings of shame, guilt and anger. When drug treatment is offered to help offenders, correctional employees believe they are offering them a solution to their problems. However, offenders do not view drug treatment as a solution—drugs and alcohol are their solutions. Drug treatment threatens to remove offenders from the very thing they believe they need for

their survival. When seen from this perspective, it is not surprising that offenders often are reluctant to become involved in drug treatment unless other incentives are provided beyond the opportunity to give up drugs and alcohol.

4   Incentives can provide offenders with the motivation they need to volunteer for drug treatment, even if the initial goal is to gain the incentives rather than to give up drug use or criminal activity. Does it really matter that incentives can induce offenders to volunteer for treatment for what we would regard as the wrong reasons?

5   Interestingly, research consistently indicates that offenders' motivations for entering drug treatment are not as important in treatment outcome as other factors. Major longitudinal studies have found drug treatment effectiveness to be directly related to the length of stay in treatment.[1] Offenders' initial motivation for entering treatment programs is not as important as their ultimate length of stay in treatment. These findings remain consistent regardless of whether their participation in treatment is voluntary or coerced. This point is vital, given the fact that treatment in a correctional environment always involves an element of coercion, even if the offender is not subject to sanctions if he or she does not choose to participate. Incentives can provide the motivation offenders need to volunteer for treatment and remain in treatment long enough to obtain benefits toward reductions in substance abuse and criminal activity.

Effective Incentives

6   To find the most effective incentives, one must understand offenders' motivations. It is a generally accepted truism among addiction treatment specialists that individuals stop growing emotionally when they start to use mind-altering substances. Drugs and alcohol become the coping mechanism for responding to life's stresses. Since offenders typically begin to use alcohol and drugs in their teen-age and preteen years, they lack mature adult coping skills and typically are concerned with satisfying short-term physical desires rather than long-term psychological, social or spiritual needs. They tend to act on short-term emotional reactions rather than long-term rational considerations and are impulsive, prone to anger and unwilling to accept the consequences of their actions. Their relationships with others often are self-serving, constructed solely around satisfying their own short-term desires, and tend to be fleeting and exploitive. Substance-abusing offenders usually do not think critically about their own behavior and prefer to gloss over details of their actions to maintain their perception of themselves as good people who have been wronged by society.[2]

7   Given this psychological constellation, substance-abusing offenders will respond most effectively to incentives that make their immediate lives as comfortable as possible and help them avoid incarceration. Incentives' direct impacts depend on whether the offender is in the community or an institution. Community setting incentives will have the greatest impact if they provide some sort of immediate physical reward, such as food, shelter or avoidance of incarceration. Incentives in an institution will have the greatest impact if they make incarceration more comfortable, for example, preferred housing, greater freedom within the institution or help with getting released.

8   Herein lies the dilemma: Incentives that reward offenders' desires for immediate gratification and avoidance of incarceration also potentially reinforce

the underlying anti-social personality structure that supports offenders' continued criminal activity and drug abuse. This returns us to the question: Can incentives for drug abuse treatment be too strong? In other words, can incentives be so enticing as to obscure the true purpose of treatment, namely, to help substance-abusing offenders overcome their addictions? The answer is yes—potentially. As we have seen, incentives that most powerfully motivate offenders to participate in drug treatment are the same incentives that reinforce offenders' criminal activity and drug use. Criminal justice agencies that use these incentives to entice offenders risk rewarding them for the very same behaviors that brought them into the criminal justice system.

9   Staff who provide drug abuse treatment to offenders are faced with a special challenge due to the dilemma posed by incentives. At the beginning of their treatment, offenders are more interested in the incentives rather than the treatment itself. Activities such as talking with a counselor, divulging personal information in treatment groups, completing reading and workbook assignments, and discussing the hurt they have caused themselves and their victims are viewed as irritants that must be tolerated in order to achieve the promised rewards. As drug treatment staff begin to confront offenders about their problematic attitudes and behaviors, offenders' natural instinct is to hide their criminality and "play the game" of engaging in treatment. They try to tell staff what they want to hear to avoid betraying their lack of commitment to treatment and risk being expelled from the program. Passive offenders comply with staff directives and do only the minimum to remain in the program. Power-oriented offenders attempt to intimidate staff and other participants so that they do not have to confront their anti-social behavior.

10 All the while, offenders view the incentives as entitlements and not rewards for achievement of program goals. Offenders often responded with anger, and on occasion, rage when they are threatened with denial of incentives. If staff do not recognize and confront the offenders' underlying problems and behaviors that prevent them from genuinely engaging in the treatment process, staff can unwittingly reinforce offenders' core beliefs that they deserve whatever they want, whenever they want it, through whatever means they can achieve it. By reinforcing rather than confronting offenders' behavior, bad treatment can be more harmful to society than no treatment at all.

Bureau of Prisons

11 The difficulties posed by incentives can be illustrated by the Federal Bureau of Prisons' (BOP) experience with implementing a drug treatment strategy. In 1988, BOP undertook an ambitious initiative designed to provide drug treatment services to all substance-abusing offenders who requested such services.[3] As a part of this strategy, BOP created intensive, long-term residential programs for offenders who had severe addictive disorders requiring intensive treatment. From the beginning, the idea of incentives were favored prominently in discussions concerning program development. The federal system previously abandoned parole. As a consequence, no mechanism existed within the sentencing structure to provide the incentive for treatment that concerned most inmates, namely early release. In its place, drug treatment staff devised incentives that allowed inmates who participated in treatment to improve their

living conditions within the institution. While these incentives encouraged inmates to volunteer for treatment, the volunteer rate remained low.

12   In 1994, Congress responded by passing a law allowing nonviolent offenders who successfully completed a BOP residential drug abuse treatment program to earn up to 12 months off of their sentences. Virtually overnight, the task of the drug treatment staff shifted from identifying and motivating inmates to volunteer for treatment, to sorting out (and keeping out) inmates who did not qualify for treatment. BOP developed criteria to help staff carry out this task. Inmates used the internal administrative remedy process to challenge every decision that disqualified them from treatment—and from early release consideration—siphoning staff time and energy from the program. Paperwork required to document program-related staff decisions and early release eligibility also increased dramatically. It is interesting to note that inmates rarely challenged the actual structure or content of the treatment programs. They only challenged decisions that impacted the one thing about which they truly cared—early release.

13   Decisions concerning inmates' eligibility for residential treatment were not the only aspect that was challenged. Congress specified that only nonviolent offenders could be eligible for early release. Inmates challenged BOP's implementation of this aspect of the law in various circuit and district courts, with varying success. These court decisions forced BOP to implement policy inconsistently, depending on inmates' geographic locations and the institutions housing the residential program. Finally, in January 2001, the U.S. Supreme Court issued an opinion supporting BOP's implementation of the law authorizing early release, thus allowing the bureau to apply the same criteria for early release to all federal inmates. While the Supreme Court decision effectively ended legal challenges to this aspect of the law governing early release, inmates continue to use BOP's internal administrative remedy process to challenge decisions concerning their eligibility for residential treatment and early release. They rarely use this process to challenge other aspects of the program.

Conflict Resolution

14   Incentives are an invaluable tool for encouraging substance-abusing offenders to seek drug treatment. However, incentives that have the potential to more strongly motivate inmates to seek treatment also have the potential to motivate inmates to use the treatment disingenuously. How can this conflict be resolved?

15   Simply stated, drug treatment staff's tasks are to help offenders shift their focus from treatment's short-term incentives to its long-term benefits, and to genuinely and sincerely engage in the treatment process. This is not easy since most offenders have short-term perspectives, immature coping skills and a general distrust of criminal justice personnel. They resist taking responsibility for their problems, preferring to place blame on others and social institutions that they feel have victimized them. Drug treatment staff, as an extension of the criminal justice system, can be viewed by inmates as another set of victimizers who seek to deprive them of the treatment incentives to which they believe they are entitled.

16   Despite the enormous challenge posed by substance-abusing offenders, research consistently indicates that when drug treatment with criminal justice clients is conducted correctly, it can successfully reduce relapse into drug abuse and criminal recidivism.[4] Andrews[5] and Gendreau[6] identify "principles of effective intervention" that are associated with successful correctional treatment programs. The principles are summarized as follows:

- Treatment should be intensive, long-term (three to nine months), behavioral in nature and focus on the high-risk offender.
- Behavioral strategies should be enforced in a firm but fair manner by qualified staff.
- Treatment should target the antisocial attitudes, values and beliefs supportive of criminal behavior, negative peer associations and substance abuse.
- Treatment providers should be responsive to offenders' learning styles and personalities.
- Treatment providers should relate to offenders in interpersonally sensitive and constructive ways and should be trained and supervised appropriately. Treatment should provide a pro-social environment that reinforces positive behavior and disrupts negative peer influences.
- Treatment should provide relapse prevention in the community.
- Linkage and referral to community services should be provided for institution-based programs.

17   BOP followed these principles closely to formulate its current drug abuse treatment strategy, and it is regarded as vital to the current program's successful operation.

Conclusion

18   While strong incentives can motivate substance-abusing offenders to seek treatment where they otherwise might not, incentives also have the potential to reinforce offenders' anti-social attitudes, values and beliefs that support their continued drug use and criminal activity. Offenders who are allowed to manipulate a program and are granted an incentive without genuinely engaging in the treatment process can leave the program with the increased sense they are unique individuals who can enjoy the benefits of society without having to share in the responsibilities. In this regard, ineffective treatment can be more destructive to society than no treatment at all. On the other hand, well-organized treatment programs with appropriately trained staff can help offenders abandon their anti-social attitudes, values and beliefs, and develop more mature skills for coping with the stresses of life without drugs and alcohol. Strong incentives can powerfully motivate resistant offenders to voluntarily enter the treatment program door. Strong treatment can restore them so that they are worthy of stepping through the door back into society.

Notes

1. Gregrich, John. 1992. Management of the drug-abusing offender. In *Drug abuse treatment in prisons and jails,* eds. Carl G. Leukefeld and Frank M. Tims, 211–231. Rockville, Md.: National Institute on Drug Abuse.

306 The Work Community

2. Lykken, David T. 1995. *The anti-social personalities.* Hillsdale, N.J.: Lawrence Erlbaum Associates Inc. Walters, Glenn D. 1990. *The criminal lifestyle: Patterns of serious criminal conduct,* Newbury Park, Calif.: Sage.
3. Murray, Donald W. 1996. Drug abuse treatment programs in the Federal Bureau of Prisons: Initiatives for the 1990s. In *Drug abuse treatment in prisons and jails,* eds. Carl G. Leukefeld and Frank M. Tims, 62–83. Rockville, Md.: National Institute on Drug Abuse.
4. National Institute on Drug Abuse. 1999. *Principles of drug addiction treatment: A research-based guide.* Washington, D.C.: U.S. Government Printing Office. Peters, Roger H. and Marc L. Steinberg. 2000. Substance abuse treatment services in U.S. prisons. In *Drugs and prisons,* eds. D. Shewan and J. Davies, 89–116. London: Harwood Academic Publishers.
5. Andrews, D.A., I. Zinger, R.D. Hoge, J. Bonta, P. Gendreau and F.T. Cullen. 1990. Does correctional treatment work? A clinically relevant and psychologically informed metaanalysis. *Criminology,* (28):97–104.
6. Gendreau, Paul. 1996. The principles of effective intervention with offenders. In *Choosing correctional options that work,* ed. A. Harland, 117–130. Thousand Oaks, Calif.: Sage.

Reading Responses

1. What question does Simpson investigate? What conclusion about it does he reach?
2. In what ways does Simpson present information so that his readers will find it pertinent and useful?
3. What are Simpson's recommendations? How might readers apply these suggestions?

Writing Activities

1. Write a summary of Simpson's main point, explaining it in your own words.
2. Briefly explain how Simpson uses questions to help readers follow his discussion.
3. Write an essay about the problem of using incentives in circumstances other than corrections. For example, you might consider grading, child-rearing, marketing bonuses, or another situation. Consider, as Simpson does, how incentives are useful and when incentives undermine the desired outcomes. Supply your own recommendations. Address people who are involved in the situation you select and who would be likely to take your analysis and your recommendations seriously.

Community Links

Compare and contrast Simpson's workplace article with an article from an academic journal such as that by States (pp. 112–118), Meyer (pp. 119–125), Small and Kimbrough-Melton (pp. 126–132), or Bryant (pp. 159–164). Both appear in specialized journals for professionals, yet they take different approaches to their topics and their readers. Examine their differences, looking, for example, at how they present a problem, suggest solutions, report research, or appeal to readers.

Memorandum
MEMO TO CU-DENVER COMMUNITY
Georgia Lesh-Laurie

◆

This memo, written by the chancellor at the University of Colorado at Denver, was sent to faculty and staff. It appeals for contributions to the Colorado Combined Campaign, a consolidated system for contributing to individual nonprofit groups or to clusters of groups based on region or orientation. These contributions are easily arranged as monthly payroll deductions using the pledge form that follows this memo. Notice the memo's conventional format, widely used for internal organizational communications.

University of Colorado at Denver

Chancellor's Office
CU-Denver Bldg., Suite 750
Campus Box 168, P.O. Box 173364
Denver, Colorado 80217-3364
Phone: 303-556-2843
Fax: 303-556-2164

MEMORANDUM

TO: CU-Denver Community
FROM: Georgia Lesh-Laurie *Georgia*
SUBJECT: Colorado Combined Campaign
DATE: 3 October 2002

1 A year ago when I wrote a similar memo about the Colorado Combined Campaign (CCC), we were still reeling from the tragedy of September 11. Fortunately, no other devastating event has occurred to force our attention to it and to the needs of others. However, as an urban university, we at CU-Denver are already aware of the many problems and concerns that face citizens of the state of Colorado and society as a whole. We are also in a position to experience the benefits when we get involved in seeking solutions to those problems.

2 Once again CU-Denver is focusing its attention on the CCC during the month of October. The CCC is a great way to get involved in alleviating the suffering of others. Please pay attention when your CCC area coordinator approaches you with a pledge form and information about this year's campaign. Giving to the CCC is an easy and effective way to make a difference.

3 Thank you for making a difference!

Reading Responses

1. How does the memo format prepare a reader for the communication in the memo?
2. Given the conventional brevity of the memo, how does Lesh-Laurie focus and organize her paragraphs? What is the function of each paragraph? How does each one contribute to the overall purpose of the memo?
3. In what ways does Lesh-Laurie appeal to readers to contribute to this campaign?

Writing Activities

1. Write a brief description of the advantages of the memo format for internal communications.
2. Write the memo that might have followed Lesh-Laurie's memo, thanking contributors and commending university employees for their generosity.
3. Write a memo about a topic of interest to you. Follow the conventional format. Use focused paragraphs to keep your message brief.

Community Links

Compare and contrast this memo or Lutz's memo (pp. 229–230) with one of the letters in this book. (See the Guide to Themes, Topics, and Rhetorical Strategies for possibilities.) Consider similarities and differences between a memo, typically used for internal communication, and a letter, typically used for external communication. Use features of the memo and letter you select to illustrate your analysis.

Letter
HOLIDAY GREETINGS
Bill Marriott

◆

Bill Marriott, also known as J. W. Marriott, Jr., is the chairman of the board and the chief executive officer of Marriott International. Marriott hotels, motels, suites, and resorts around the world welcome guests with many types of accommodations. The company rewards frequent guests with special amenities, discounts at selected facilities, credits toward free stays, and similar offers. In addition to regular newsletters, members of the Marriott guest program also received this holiday card.

Holiday Greetings from
J.W. Marriott, Jr.

At Marriott, we think of ourselves as a global family dedicated to helping people. It is our purpose to welcome you and make you feel comfortable when you are away from home. This time-honored tradition of hospitality is why my father and mother started Marriott almost 75 years ago and will continue to be our guiding light well into the future. Nothing will pull us off course, or change our "spirit to serve."

During this important time of the year, we wish you and your family a renewed sense of joy and peace. Thank you for being our guest. Thank you for being our friend. Thank you for being there when it mattered most.

Best personal regards,

Bill Marriott

Dear Customer

J. Katherine Brown-Rowe

◆

This annual first-of-the-year letter from the president of Grassmaster Lawncare, Inc., reminds homeowners to renew their lawn service. The letter reports on program improvements and offers a pre-payment discount. A renewal form is also enclosed so that customers can simply check a box or two and mail back the form. The letter's friendly tone and informal style reflect the owners' direct contact with customers, discussing lawn problems or supplying advice during service calls.

GRASSMASTER LAWNCARE, INC.

January 1, 2001

Dear Customer,

1. We know it's hard to believe but your lawn will be waking up in just a couple of months. We hope you had a joyous holiday season and would like to wish you and your family a Happy and Prosperous New Year.

2. We are extremely pleased with the results of our new **Advanced** program. Last year with record breaking temperatures we saw less heat stress, reduced weed growth and in many lawns reduced water usage. The best thing about the **Advanced** program is that it's an all-in-one program. There is no need for aeration or soil conditioner because it is all included. As with all things new, we are adjusting our product based on customer input, microbiological reports from samples taken last year and advice from our team of agronomists. Our new Custom Blended mixture will offer better and longer greening of the grass along with a more diversified biological component.

3. There are 3 ways to renew this year. Return the enclosed renewal sheet, call us at 303-932-8853 or email us at info@livinglawns.com. We are again offering a 4-, 6-, or 8-coupon payment plan to assist our customers. There are no additional fees to use this plan and this will allow smaller payments over a longer period of time. To take advantage of this offer, check the appropriate box on the renewal form, call 303-932-8853, or email us at info@livinglawns.com. Please note that the email address grssmstr@aol.com is no longer valid.

4. Penetrometer readings (which measure the compactness of the soil) taken last year indicate aerations are not needed with continued use of the **Advanced** program. If you want aeration please specify spring and/or fall. **If you order aeration, please let us know if you have any cables, invisible fences, etc. that are shallowly buried.**

5. As always, you may prepay by February 15, 2001 and receive a 10% discount or prepay by March 15, 2001 and receive a 5% discount off your total bill. Do not

feel obligated to pay in advance. This is an option offered for your savings and convenience only. We realize that circumstances change, so if you wish to discontinue or change service, please call and let us know.

6   Customer referrals have always been important to us. Because of this we will continue the Good Neighbor Program. For every person you refer and that signs up for service, you will receive a **$25.00** discount on your next service (or a $25.00 refund for prepaids)! This is our way of saying thank you for your support.

7   Thank you for your past patronage. We look forward to helping you in the care of your lawn this year.

Sincerely,
Kate
J. Katherine Brown-Rowe
President

8   PS Winter watering is essential. The roots of your lawn need moisture to survive. Watering should be every 3–4 weeks by either Mother Nature or you. Southern and windy exposures need extra care. If you have any questions please call or e-mail us at info@livinglawns.com or visit our website at www.livinglawns.com and email from there.

8549 So. Allison St. • Littleton, CO 80128-6201 (303) 932-8853

President's Message, February 11, 2000
Stephen E. Gibson

◆

The Newport Tiger Fund is a mutual fund that invests in Southeast Asia. This upbeat letter to shareholders, part of the December 31, 1999, annual report, announces good news—a one-year return of 73.14% for Class A shareholders during 1999. It also analyzes the factors that contributed to such a dramatic return while cautioning investors about uncertain regional trends. The letter is followed by required performance information about returns and a review of the fund's year.

Dear Shareholder:

The 12-month period ended December 31, 1999 was very good for investors in Southeast Asia, as the region experienced a strong economic recovery in concert with a worldwide economic rebound. The economies in the region benefited from a level of renewal and improved management. In Hong Kong and China, the private sector has shown unprecedented growth, driven by an entrepreneurial boom in the high technology and telecommunications sectors. These industries are benefiting from surging use of the Internet by both businesses and consumers around the world. Singapore's banking industry continued to thrive, and Taiwan's world-class semiconductor sector emerged from a major earthquake in very good shape. In short, a wide range of factors in the region and worldwide converged to produce what we believe is a solid foundation for future prosperity.

Although we are encouraged by these developments, it is important to note that the region is still in the early stages of recovery from the devastating impact of recession in 1997 and 1998. Much of the growth has been driven by exports — particularly to the U.S. — and internally generated growth is just beginning to appear. Nevertheless, we are very pleased with the progress that we saw throughout the region in 1999.

Newport Tiger Fund continued to benefit from the positive economic trends that occurred during the year, outperforming the average return of its Lipper peer group.[1] The following report will provide you with more specific information about your Fund's performance and the strategies used during the period. As always, we thank you for choosing Newport Tiger Fund and for giving us the opportunity to serve your investment needs.

Sincerely,

Stephen E. Gibson
President
February 11, 2000

[1] Lipper, Inc., a widely respected data provider for the industry, calculates an average total return for mutual funds with similar investment objectives as the Fund. The average total return calculated for funds in the Lipper Pacific Ex-Japan Funds category was 73.21% for the 12 months ended December 31, 1999. The Fund's Class A shares ranked in the second quartile for one year (ranked 38 out of 84 funds) and in the second quartile for three years (ranked 28 out of 70 funds). Rankings do not include any sales charges. Performance for different share classes will vary with fees associated with each class. Past performance cannot guarantee future results.

Because market and economic conditions change, there can be no assurance that the trends described in this report will continue or come to pass.

| Not FDIC Insured | May Lose Value | No Bank Guarantee |

Performance Information

Performance of a $10,000 investment in Newport Tiger Fund Class A shares 12/31/89 – 12/31/99

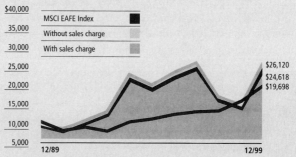

The Morgan Stanley Capital International (MSCI) EAFE (GDP) Index is an unmanaged index that tracks the performance of equity securities of developed countries outside North America, including Hong Kong and Singapore. Unlike mutual funds, indexes are not investments and do not incur fees or expenses. It is not possible to invest directly in an index.

Average Annual Total Returns as of 12/31/1999

Share Class	A		B		C		T		Z	
Inception	4/1/95		4/1/95		4/1/95		5/31/89		5/31/89	
	w/o sales charge	with sales charge	w/o sales charge	with sales charge	w/o sales charge	with sales charge	w/o sales charge	with sales charge	w/o sales charge	
1 year	73.14%	63.18%	71.82%	66.82%	71.85%	70.85%	73.49%	63.51%	73.68%	
5 years	5.34	4.09	4.56	4.22	4.58	4.58	5.55	4.30	5.52	
10 years	10.08	9.43	9.67	9.67	9.68	9.68	10.19	9.54	10.17	

Past performance cannot predict future investment results. Returns and value of an investment will vary, resulting in a gain or loss on sale. All results shown assume reinvestment of distributions. The "with sales charge" returns include the maximum 5.75% charge for Class A and T shares and the maximum contingent deferred sales charges (CDSC) of 5% for one year and 2% for five years for Class B shares and 1% for one year for Class C shares. Performance for different share classes will vary based on differences in sales charges and fees associated with each class.

Performance results reflect any voluntary waivers or reimbursement of Fund expenses by the Advisor or its affiliates. Absent these waivers or reimbursement arrangements, performance results would have been lower.

The Fund was originally introduced on 5/31/89 and became Colonial Newport Tiger Fund on 4/1/95 when Class A, B, and D (since designated as C) shares were offered. As of 4/30/98, the Fund was renamed Newport Tiger Fund. Please see the Fund's prospectus for additional details. Class A, B, and C share performance information includes returns of the Fund's Class T shares for periods prior to the inception dates of those classes. These Class T share returns are not restated to reflect any expense differential (e.g., Rule 12b-1 fees) between Class T shares and the Class A, B, and C shares. Had the expense differential been reflected, the returns for periods prior to the inception date of the Class A, B and C shares would have been lower.

President's Message, February 12, 2001
Stephen E. Gibson

◆

This letter introduces the annual report for the Liberty Newport Tiger Fund for 2000. During this year, Class A shares lost 15.81%. The letter reports that bad news to shareholders. As in the preceding letter that reported a dramatic gain, the president explains market conditions that account for the return.

President's Message

Dear Shareholder:

Recovery from the economic crisis of 1997-98 continued throughout Asia in 2000. The growth rates for the economies of the Tiger countries were strong. In 1999, we pointed out that rising interest rates, an overvalued stock market, and a slowing economy in the U.S. might affect the region. Our expectation was that Asian markets would first react negatively to these situations and then recover when investors refocused on the region's strong domestic growth. Unfortunately, outside of China, regional growth expectations have been cut due to stalled restructuring efforts, political ineffectiveness, and the sharp slowdown in U.S. technology spending. Asian stock prices did not decouple from the declining U.S. market.

Supported by China's broadening domestic and export growth, Hong Kong's economy provided the best return in 2000. Although the market did not provide a positive return, it performed better on a relative basis than the rest of the region. The Morgan Stanley Capital International (MSCI) EAFE (GDP) Index posted a return of negative 15.53% for the 12-month period that ended on December 31, 2000. For the same period the Fund posted a return of negative 15.81%.

The stock markets of Thailand, Indonesia, the Philippines, Malaysia and India gave back much of the previous year's gains. In addition, the worsening global outlook in the technology and telecommunications sectors hit South Korea and Taiwan hard. Both countries are heavily dependent on technology exports. Your Fund's managers continue to seek the best quality companies, which they believe are positioned for long-term sustainable growth within the region.

In the following pages portfolio co-managers Tim Tuttle and Chris Legallet discuss their strategy and the economic and market factors that have affected Fund performance. Thank you for choosing to invest in the Liberty Newport Tiger Fund and for giving us the opportunity to serve your investment needs.

Sincerely,

Stephen E. Gibson
President
February 12, 2001

Performance Highlights (as of 12/31/00)

Net asset value per share

Class A	$11.34
Class B	$11.05
Class C	$11.07
Class T	$11.38
Class Z	$11.35

Past performance cannot predict future results. Returns and value of an investment will vary, resulting in a gain or a loss on sale. All results shown assume reinvestment of distributions.

Not FDIC Insured	May Lose Value
	No Bank Guarantee

Because economic and market conditions change frequently, there can be no assurance that the trends described in this report will continue or come to pass.

Performance Information

Value of a $10,000 Investment in Liberty Newport Tiger Fund 12/31/90 – 12/31/00

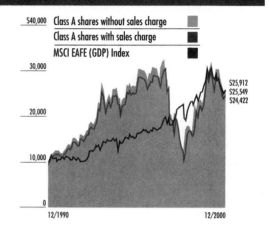

Performance of a $10,000 investment in all shares from 12/31/90 – 12/31/00

	Without sales charge	With sales charge
Class A	$25,912	$24,422
Class B	$24,775	$24,775
Class C	$24,803	$24,803
Class T	$26,246	$24,737
Class Z	$26,178	N/A

The Morgan Stanley Capital International (MSCI) EAFE (GDP) Index is an unmanaged index that tracks the performance of equity securities of developed countries outside North America, including Hong Kong and Singapore. Unlike mutual funds, indexes are not an investment and do not incur fees or expenses. It is not possible to invest directly in an index.

Average Annual Total Returns as of 12/31/00

Share Class Inception Date	A 4/1/95		B 4/1/95		C 4/1/95		T 5/31/89		Z 5/31/89
	Without sales charge	With sales charge	Without sales charge	With sales charge	Without sales charge	With sales charge	Without sales charge	With sales charge	Without sales charge
1 year	(15.81)%	(20.65)%	(16.48)%	(20.65)%	(16.45)%	(17.29)%	(15.58)%	(20.43)%	(15.68)%
5 years	(1.25)%	(2.41)%	(1.99)%	(2.38)%	(2.00)%	(2.00)%	(1.00)%	(2.17)%	(1.05)%
10 years	9.99%	9.34%	9.50%	9.50%	9.51%	9.51%	10.13%	9.48%	10.10%

Past performance cannot predict future investment results. Returns and value of an investment will vary, resulting in a gain or loss on sale.

All results shown assume reinvestment of distributions. The "With sales charge" returns include the maximum 5.75% charge for Class A and T shares and the contingent deferred sales charge (CDSC) maximum charge of 5% for one year and 2% for five years for Class B shares and 1% for one year for Class C shares. Performance for different share classes will vary based on differences in sales charges and fees associated with each share.

Performance results reflect any voluntary waivers or reimbursement of Fund expenses by the Advisor or its affiliates. Absent these waivers or reimbursement arrangements, performance results would have been lower.

The Fund was originally introduced on May 31, 1989 and became Colonial Newport Tiger Fund on April 1, 1995 when Class A, B, and D (since designated C) shares were offered. On April 30, 1998, the Fund was renamed Newport Tiger Fund. The Fund was again renamed on July 14, 2000 to Liberty Newport Tiger Fund. Please see the Fund's prospectus for additional details. Class A, B and C share performance information includes returns of the Fund's Class T shares for periods prior to the inception dates of those classes. These Class T share returns are not restated to reflect any expense differential (e.g., Rule 12b-1 fees) between Class T shares and the Class A, B, and C shares. Had the expense differential been reflected, the returns for the periods prior to the inception date of the Class A, B and C shares would have been lower.

Reading Responses

1. What is the purpose of each of the preceding letters?
2. How does each letter address the expectations and concerns of its readers?
3. How does each letter use its style, tone, and word choice to convey information, to present the writer's persona or image, and to build a relationship with readers?

Writing Activities

1. Although the letters in this section are very different from each other, all reflect the values of the work community. Write an essay discussing and illustrating ways that the letters meet expectations of the work community.
2. Select a pair of letters—for example, the two Newport Tiger letters to shareholders or the two messages to customers. Write an essay comparing and contrasting the pair in terms of purpose, structure, formality, style, tone, or other pertinent issues.
3. Write your own letter, following a business letter format and paying careful attention to wording. Present the message of your choice, and take account of the expectations of a specific reader. For example, you might write to your apartment manager or the student housing office to explain a maintenance problem and request its solution. You might write to the bus company, commending an employee or complaining about the absence of a reliable schedule. You might write a letter for a social group, reminding members to pay their dues—and perhaps to make an extra contribution.

Community Links

Compare and contrast several letters. (See the Guide to Themes, Topics, and Rhetorical Strategies for a list of options.) Pay special attention to the persona or image of the writer and the interests or concerns attributed to the reader. Use several letters to explore similarities, differences, and variations in the presentation of writer and reader.

Review of an Artifact
STEEL BELVEDERE
Michael Webb

♦

The Architectural Review *regularly describes buildings and structures that illustrate the particular theme of the month's issue. "Steel Belvedere" describes the Student Centre at the College of Design in Pasadena, California. In accord with the issue's theme—learning—this article was one of ten reviews of buildings at* schools, universities, and research facilities around the world. Because this British publication is directed to architects and designers, the text of each article is accompanied by photographs, diagrams, and plans that show the innovative or notable features of each project.

Student Centre, Pasadena, California, USA; Architect, Hodgetts & Fung

1   Over the past 26 years, the varied activities of Pasadena's Art Center College of Design have been confined within Craig Ellwood's black steel box, an acclaimed exercise in Miesian minimalism that is, regrettably, sealed off from an idyllic site and a generally benign climate. (Neil Jackson's recent book on Ellwood credits the design to his associate, Jim Tyler.) Richard Koshalek, the new president, intends to burst out of the box with an ambitious plan to expand the campus and move the Center's public education programmes and exhibitions to a former power station on the south edge of Pasadena. Gehry Partners have begun to design a spiral library and have also developed a master plan that includes classroom buildings by Alvaro Siza. As a first step in this programme of growth, Koshalek—who has become the godfather of adventurous architecture in LA, working behind the scenes on a succession of important projects—invited Craig Hodgetts and Ming Fung to design a new building for the students.

2   'We wanted to build a greater sense of community among the 13 different disciplines of the college,' says Koshalek, 'and the students expressed a desire to have greater interaction and a place to gather. I see Craig and Ming as heirs to the legacy of Charles and Ray Eames and I was sure they would have a lively dialogue with the users.'

3   Fifty of the 1500 students participated in a charrette, developing a programme for an outdoor space where they could hang out, display images and videos, organize events and even smoke without feeling like pariahs. The architects picked the site, on the steep slope between the main parking lot and the college, creating a way station on a route already defined by concrete steps

Figure 1
Pavilion in the landscape marks a new phase in the college's evolution.

Figure 2
Approach to the pavilion. Skewed geometry and robust materiality combine to give it a tough presence.

and a wheelchair ramp. Their choice was validated by Gehry's plan, which makes this the hub of the expanded campus, conveniently accessible to all the buildings. A first design proved too costly to build. The second is tough, rational and permeable: a galvanized steel canopy that provides shelter from summer sun and winter rain but is open to the breezes, framing views of mountains and rolling hills and the city in the valley far below.

4   Muscular and scintillating, with a skewed geometry that provides a constantly shifting profile, the pavilion plays off the Ellwood like a David Smith sculpture beside a Donald Judd. From below, it appears as a truncated wedge that broadens and flares out in response to the contours of the site, and is cantilevered off three slender columns. From the parking lot it appears as a slash of silver glimpsed through the trees. A sliding entrance opens to an upper-level sitting area, with a built-in refreshment kiosk, lavatory, and gallery with plywood display walls. Steps lead down past concrete bleachers to an open space that could serve as a stage and a side terrace with vending machines.

5   Inspired by the college's focus on industrial design, the architects have created an interactive building that is full of kinetic elements. A door pivots to shut off the gallery. A trapezoidal window can be hand-cranked down and to one side to protect the sitting area from wind or rain. The kiosk is concealed behind a steel casing with a projecting counterweight that allows it to pivot open diagonally at a touch (Hodgetts likens it to a Lamborghini). The lining of the casing is painted a searing orange, signalling to the eye when it is open and enlivening the grey and silver palette of the pavilion. There is a built-in wall bench and moveable steel and concrete tables, but the interior is intended to be a tabula rasa—a deliberate challenge to its inventive and lively users.

6   As a structure, it reveals all. Every element—steel tubes and I-beams, corrugated roof and cladding, cement-board storage compartments and partitions—is separately articulated, as are the industrial up-lights and sprinklers. A steel plate is bolted to one side of the bleachers to serve as a balustrade.

Figure 3
The inside/outside space is conceived as an armature for various activities.

Figure 4
Flashes of vivid colour animate the industrial palette of grey and silver. Detailing is legibly articulated.

Three tubes branch from a cantilevered I-beam like an acrobat on a high wire to support the roof at the west corner.

7   In contrast to the firm's UCLA Towell Library (AR June 1993) which was inspired by a circus tent and was designed to be lightweight and transportable (it will soon enjoy a second life as the school of architecture at Cal Poly), the new pavilion is massive, rooted, and should prove happily maintenance-free.

Figure 5
Craig Ellwood's Miesian black box broods in the distance.

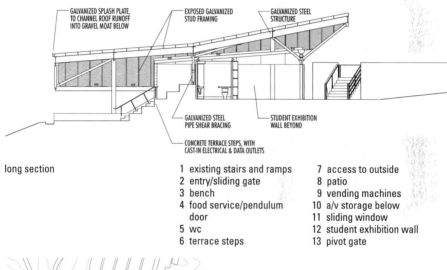

long section

1 existing stairs and ramps
2 entry/sliding gate
3 bench
4 food service/pendulum door
5 wc
6 terrace steps
7 access to outside
8 patio
9 vending machines
10 a/v storage below
11 sliding window
12 student exhibition wall
13 pivot gate

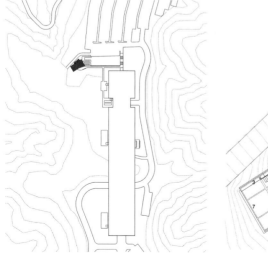
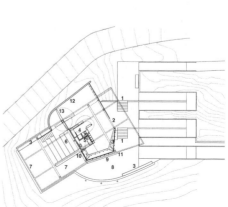

Reading Responses

1. What does the title of this article mean? (If *belvedere* is an unfamiliar word, look it up in a dictionary.) In what ways is this an appropriate title, given the orientation of the publication, the interests of its readers, and the building that is the article's topic?
2. What criteria does Webb use to evaluate this building? How does he indicate his criteria to readers? What does he assume about the interests and knowledge of his readers?
3. Although this article is accompanied by photographs and diagrams, how does Webb also convey visual information in his text? Identify several examples of visual information that you find striking.

Writing Activities

1. If you have never read architectural descriptions, you may find that Webb uses quite a few unfamiliar words. Working with a group of other students, identify the words in his article that you do not know. Divide the list so that each student looks up several words and writes a clear definition relevant to an architectural context, using his or her own words. Compile these definitions in a collaborative glossary, a list of specialized or technical words and meanings.
2. Using the glossary developed in activity 1 or your own notes on the definitions of any unfamiliar terms, reread Webb's article. Consider whether your understanding of his explanations and descriptions has changed. Write an analysis of the value or effect of his word choices, using examples from "Steel Belvedere."
3. Write your own review of a building or structure on or near campus. Visit the site to observe it, and take notes on its features. If you wish, interview people associated with its design, construction, or routine use. In your review, concentrate on a main impression or theme conveyed by the building or structure. Use specific, concrete details to convey this focus. If you use comments from people you have interviewed, quote or paraphrase accurately, and credit your sources.

Community Links

Expand your attention to the varied functions of visual elements that accompany written text, such as "Steel Belvedere." Compare several examples, and consider how each visual functions on its own, relates to the text, appeals to readers, and addresses community expectations. Look, for example, at selections such as these: Web sites ("Online Writing Lab," pp. 197–199; the Technical Standards home page, pp. 347–349; "Smoke Free Movies," pp. 566–567; "College Drinking: Changing the Culture," pp. 568–571), project reports (pp. 332–336), instructions (pp. 337–340), advertisements (pp. 343–346), newsletters (pp. 475–478), or promotions (pp. 341–342 and 548–551).

Industry Report

YOUNG ADULTS: NEW CUSTOMERS/NEW FOODS
Marcia Mogelonsky

◆

In Everybody Eats: Supermarket Consumers in the 1990s, *Marcia Mogelonsky reports on the grocery business. She directs her book to readers within the food industry to alert them to what shoppers want to find in the supermarket. Her chapters discuss shoppers of different ages, racial or ethnic groups, or regions of the country. Mogelonsky's book is published by American Demographics Books, which features many books on demographics or population statistics. For* American Demographics *magazine, she has regularly written a column on grocery shopping trends. The selection here is the beginning of Chapter 4. The rest of the chapter considers the shopping habits of young adults who fit specific subcategories such as married, single with children, budget-conscious, hurried shoppers, nutrition conscious, or environmentally conscious.*

1   "What's wrong with the young people of today?" That age-old lament has described adults between the ages of 18 and 30 for more generations than anyone could have thought possible. But marketers are beginning to realize that the young people of today become the middle-aged consumers of tomorrow. Instead of complaining about them, it is time to take a closer look at where young adults are now, and where they will be in ten or fifteen years.

2   Today's young adults were raised by working parents. They are used to fending for themselves. Both young men and women have been preparing their own snacks, lunches, and even dinners since they were teens, or even younger. They are able to find their way around a kitchen—at least on the well-worn route between the fridge and the microwave. They are also able to shop for groceries by themselves, and by the time they are in their late teens and early twenties, many young people are making informed food choices for themselves or for a whole family.

3   But most young people are also setting out on their own for the first time—whether to college or to the job market. In many ways, they are left to their own devices. No longer shopping from a list prepared by Mom, a young supermarket consumer must make his or her own choices. And marketers know that capturing the loyalty of this emerging market can pay off in shopping loyalty for years to come.

4   The American Management Association reports that 65 percent of the average company's business comes from current satisfied customers. Getting the substantial population of young Americans interested in a product when they are in their 20s spells at least 40 or 50 more years of customer loyalty. That's a worthy investment.

5   "Even in a slowly growing market, some new consumers enter while others leave. The characteristics of these emergent customers vary by product category," explains David W. Stewart, the Robert E. Brooker professor of marketing at the University of Southern California in Los Angeles. According to Stewart, one of the two most important groups for a wide range of consumer products is young people.

6   In order to attract young people, and to build up brand equity with them, Stewart suggests advertising to create awareness of a product, and to build brand image. Advertisements should create a sense of identity with the product and reinforce trial and preference.

7   But building brand loyalty among young consumers may take a little extra effort. Young consumers can be a fickle bunch. They are into new music, new movies, new technologies. And they are on the lookout for new tastes and new food trends—from Pacific Rim to Mediterr-Asian fusion, some young people will try just about anything.

8   Just about anything . . . but only as long as it's the latest fad, and only as long as it's not too expensive. Separating a fad from a trend is a difficult distinction to make, and it is one that benefits best from hindsight. Usually fads have distinctly shorter shelf lives than trends. Fads can also be "subsets" of trends. Nintendo is a trend, while a specific game like Super Mario Brothers is a fad, and marketers must be quick on their feet to distinguish between the two.

9   While young adults will experiment with food, they may not appear to be as adventuresome as middle-aged consumers. The reason for that may be a matter of money, not taste buds. In a recent Roper Starch survey, 30- to 59-year-olds were more likely to have tried such exotic foods as truffles, venison, or caviar than younger people. But the survey did not include low-budget fun foods like bubble gum, jelly beans, or fancy chocolate-bar confections.

10 And even though there are young adults who will try chocolate-covered jalapeños, there are those who are still caught in the "giant soda and burger" slump—for these young people, nutritional eating and adventuresome forays into the new foods department of the supermarket takes a back seat to junk-food feeding.

11 Some supermarketers are attracting this type of loyalist by providing fast-food-type counters in the food store, with submarine sandwiches, pizzas, and salads to go. Others have actually joined the fast-food giants in a profitable partnership by turning over part of their stores to take-out giants such as Pizza Hut, Taco Bell, and Subway.

12 Regardless of how healthy young adults want to be, they have not given up the snacking habits that began while they were children. But their snack habits are more adventuresome than those of their parents and grandparents. Young adults will eat such novelties as blue corn chips and pink beet chips. They will

crunch their way through the rainforest or drink a path through glaciers, all for a taste of something new.

13   In order to finance their trendsetting ways, young people must, of course, be gainfully employed. And that is one of the greatest challenges facing the post-boom generation. In an economy recovering from a recession, and with a top-heavy line of overqualified boomers taking a shrinking number of white-collar and manufacturing jobs, younger generations are facing a rough time.

14   Targeting young shoppers in the food store is not always easy. Sometimes the fads change faster than the products marketed in their wake. Still, there are certain fixed young-adult attributes and habits. Fitness and sports are enduring interests. Marketers have found that capitalizing on this aspect of youth can be profitable. Today's young adults' concerns with ecology and the environment should also be longlasting. And supermarkets that prove themselves to be as eco-wise as their customers can expect a certain loyalty.

15   Young people today want to be noticed in their own right, not merely as being the generation that followed the boomers. And marketers must remember that while this group doesn't come close to their parents in size, it does comprise more than 40 million shoppers. William Dunn, author of *The Baby Bust: A Generation Come of Age,* points out that if today's young adults were a country, they would be ranked at number 24—just ahead of South Korea, and fully one-and-one-half times larger than the population of Canada.

16   And although there has not been a lot of growth among the young consumer crowd, the number of adults under age 30 will begin to grow again as the baby busters are replaced by the baby boomlet. The baby-boomlet generation will begin to assume the position of household heads by the year 2005, at which point the demographic roller coaster will be set for another spin.

Young Spenders

17   When considering the spending patterns of young people, a number of factors come into play. First of all, young shoppers—like all other demographic groups—are not a homogeneous collection of spenders. Some are married; some are parents. And some are married parents, with one, two, or even more children. Still others are college students who live and eat on campus (or in off-campus restaurants) for more than half the year.

18   During the college-vacation months, students may live at home, where they may or may not be expected to pay their share of the weekly food expenses. Or they may spend the summers away from home, working at internships or jobs in college towns or large cities. Some may shop for food and pay for it with their own money; others may do the shopping, but their parents foot the bill.

19   During the 1991 recession, the U.S. jobless rate stood at 6.7 percent, but the rate for 16- to 19-year-olds was 18.6 percent. And for 20- to 24-year-olds, it was 10.8 percent, according to the Bureau of Labor Statistics. The figure dropped to 6.0 percent for workers aged 25 to 34. In 1993, the unemployment rate dropped to 6.8 percent overall. It was 19 percent for job seekers aged 16 to 19 and 10.5 percent for 20- to 24-year-olds. The rate for workers aged

Young Adults on the Move

Forty-six percent of young adults between the ages of 18 and 24 switched primary grocery stores between January of 1993 and January of 1994. That's because young adults are a wandering group. People in their early 20s are the most mobile Americans, according to the Bureau of the Census. Fully 35 percent changed their address between 1985 and 1991. Compare this with 17 percent of Americans in general and 5 percent of people aged 65 and older who did so, and it becomes clear that young adults do not like to sit still.

Young adults move for a number of reasons. They go off to college; they go back home; they leave again to find a job; they go back home again; they leave the nest again to marry or for another job opportunity; and so on.

How can a retailer win a young adult's loyalty and keep it? It depends partly on the young person and partly on the retailer. If a young person moves from one home to another in the same town, chances are he or she will remain loyal to the same food store, especially if the store is near the town's greatest young people's asset—their parents. If a young person moves far away from the parental home, whether it is in the same town or in a different locale altogether, a chain store may have a better chance of keeping him or her loyal. Name recognition is big among young adults—just look at their clothing, emblazoned with brand names. A familiar store name will draw them in just as a familiar beer name draws them to a new neighborhood bar.

If a young person moves to an area in which the food stores do not bear the familiar logos of their hometown markets, there are still things that can be done to draw them in. Some food stores in younger areas have become known as social gathering places—even the stores' audio systems are attuned to young adults' musical tastes instead of golden oldies. In order to attract shoppers, other stores offer sales on youth-preferred products, like frozen pizzas and snack foods.

While young adults are mobile on the grand scale—moving from city to city—they are not always as mobile in their day-to-day lives. Big-city young adults often live without cars; they rely instead on public transportation and pedal power to get around. These young adults, driven either by economics or ecology, would be more likely to be loyal to a food store within walking distance of their apartments or to stores that offer home delivery.

When choosing a primary food store, young adults have a number of criteria. Stores that are conveniently located, with competitive prices and a sense of environmental responsibility, are in a good position to attract and keep the lion's share of their local market.

Young Adults

The number of young adults aged 20 to 34 is expected to decrease in the 1990s.

(number of persons aged 20 to 24 and 25 to 34, 1980, 1990, and 2000, in thousands)

age	1980	1990	2000
20 to 24	21,319	19,132	17,947
25 to 34	37,082	43,161	38,237

Source: Bureau of the Census

25 to 44 was 6.1 percent. Finding a full-time, well-paying job gets harder and harder for young adults.

20   With unemployment looming, many young adults today are either delaying their flight from the family nest or returning to it. College students may continue to live at home when school is not in session, and with the high cost of college educations, many young people are opting to live at home while attending two-year schools or community college. And the tough work of finding a permanent job has driven many college graduates back home. The economic realities of such a move are felt not only in the shopping patterns of the twenty-somethings who continue to depend on parents for food and shelter, but also for their parents, who are feeding a lot more hungry mouths than they may have planned on in their pre-retirement years. But as the economy continues to improve, young people will once again venture forth. They will have more money to spend, and they will be looking for more ways to spend it.

21   Household size does play a part in accounting for the difference in spending between young adults and the middle-aged. In 1992 there was an average of 3.2 people in a household or "consumer unit"* headed by someone aged 35 to 44, according to the Consumer Expenditure Survey (CE). There were 2.8 when the householder was aged 25 to 34, and only 1.9 when the householder was under age 25.

22   But young adults spend less than other Americans even on a per-capita basis. Annual per capita expenditures on food at home for households headed by someone under age 25 were $758, according to the 1992 CE. The per capita expenditure for households aged 25 to 34 was $888. For Americans in general, the annual per capita food bill was $1,057.

23   Consumer units headed by adults under the age of 25 spend consistently less on food than any other group, but they do not lag too far behind in some staples. Per-capita spending on canned fish like tuna for these young consumers was about $36.50, compared with a national per capita expenditure of $37.00. But spending on roast beef, a considerably more expensive item, was about one-quarter of the national average among young householders. And while these young people spend about the same on pork chops (about $12.80 annually) as the average American, they spend less than half as much on ham ($9.51 annually).

---

* The Bureau of Labor Statistics' consumer units are not exactly comparable to households as defined by the Bureau of the Census.

The Young Market Basket

Young adult consumers spend less than average on most food items, with the exception of 25- to 34-year-olds' spending on ground beef.

(average annual household expenditures for selected grocery products, by age, 1992)

product	all households	under 25	25 to 34
Fresh fruit	$127.39	$62.64	$102.52
Milk and cream	133.81	84.37	131.53
Fresh vegetables	126.58	66.68	114.25
Poultry	123.10	72.71	114.23
Ground beef	86.66	54.10	88.56
Bread	76.28	39.20	70.90
Potato chips/nuts/snacks	75.64	49.79	72.70
Nonprescription drugs	74.51	36.35	48.84
Toilet paper/tissues	56.62	21.22	47.07
Coffee	38.95	15.08	27.99

Source: Bureau of Labor Statistics, 1992 Consumer Expenditure Survey

24   But convenience foods and sodas are a young person's essentials. Per capita spending on miscellaneous canned and packaged foods—products other than soups, such as canned stews, spaghetti, and other meals—is actually lower among adults under the age of 25 than other groups, as is per capita spending on carbonated beverages other than cola. And young households spend less per capita than the national average on cake, eggs, frozen meals, and cola. But they still don't eat their vegetables or fruit, spending only about two-thirds the national average.

25   They do spend money on baby food, though. Households headed by people under age 25 spend $30.17 per year on food for babies and infants, compared with $47.77 for consumers aged 25 to 34. Paying for baby food must stretch the budget for young single parents, many of whom have only one source of income.

26   Households headed by someone aged 25 to 34 spend more per capita on almost all food products than younger adults do. But their per capita spending is in line with the national average for almost all products. These young adults spend slightly more than the national average on frozen meals, and canned and packaged prepared foods other than soup. They spend more on fruits and vegetables than do people under age 25, but they still lag behind the national averages in both of these "healthy choice" categories.

27   Americans in general spent more on foods such as frozen dinners, baby foods, condiments, snack foods, and soup in 1991 than they did in 1986. Spending on these items increased 28 percent in that five-year interval. And young adults rely on these convenience products more than older adults, who make things from scratch.

References

Ambry, Margaret. *The Official Guide to Household Spending.* Ithaca, New York: New Strategist Publications, 1993.

American Demographics. *American Spending.* Desk Reference Series, No. 5, 1993.

Brouillette Research, Inc. *The Service Advantage: How Customers Evaluate Service in Their Supermarkets.* Cincinnati, Ohio, 1991.

———. *How to Win and Influence Shoppers, 1992.* Cincinnati, Ohio, 1992.

Carson, Patrick, and Julia Moulden. *Green Is Gold: Business Talking to Business about the Environmental Revolution.* Toronto, ON: HarperCollins Inc., 1991.

Crispell, Diane. "Movers of Tomorrow," *American Demographics,* June 1993, 59.

Dunn, William. *The Baby Bust: A Generation Comes of Age.* Ithaca, NY: American Demographics Books, 1993.

"Food Spending by Female-Headed Households: Review of Previous Research," *Family Economics Review,* 6:1 (1993), 32–34.

Food Marketing Institute. *Trends in the United States: Consumer Attitudes and the Supermarket, 1992.* Washington, D.C.: Food Marketing Institute, 1992.

Giles, Jeff. "The Myth of Generation X," *Newsweek,* June 6, 1994, 62–72.

"Green Consumerism in the Supermarket." *Green MarketAlert,* September 1992, 7–8.

Herbig, Paul, William Koehler, and Ken Day. "Marketing to the Baby Bust Generation," *Journal of Consumer Marketing,* 10:1 (1993), 4–9.

Lino, Mark. "Income and Expenditure of Families with a Baby," *Family Economics Review,* 4:3 (1991), 9–15.

——— and Geraldine Ray. "Young Husband-Wife Households with Children," *Family Economics Review,* 5:1 (1992), 9–16.

Lutz, Steven M., James R. Blaylock, and David M. Smallwood. "Household Characteristics Affect Food Choices," *Food Review,* May–August 1993, 12–18.

Mitchell, Susan. "How to Talk to Young Adults," *American Demographics,* April 1993, 50–54.

Price, Charlene. "Fast Food Chains Penetrate New Markets," *Food Review,* January–April 1993, 8–12.

Slaughter, Ed. *Prevention Magazine and the Food Marketing Institute Survey of Public Concern Regarding Good Nutrition.* (Princeton, N.J., March 1992).

Snack Food Association. *Consumer Snacking Behavior Report.* Alexandria, VA: Snack Food Association, 1992.

"Special Report: The Future of Households," *American Demographics,* December 1993, 27–40.

"Supermarkets Strut Their Stuff," *Green MarketAlert,* November 1990, 3–4.

Reading Responses

1. Which of Mogelonsky's many observations about young adults as food shoppers intrigues you the most? Why?

2. How has Mogelonsky used demographic data—population statistics—in this chapter? How has she integrated this data with her general assertions and other detailed information?

3. In what ways does Mogelonsky consider her primary readers, those involved in the food industry? Note examples of topics—such as brand loyalty—that appeal to the interests of those readers.

Writing Activities

1. Based on Mogelonsky's data, write your own advice to young adults recommending better or less expensive food options, healthier choices, or small but valuable lifestyle changes.
2. Write a report for your fellow beef ranchers, carrot farmers, banana growers, or other food producers. Explain the implications of Mogelonsky's information for your industry. Suggest ways that you and your fellow food producers might develop a larger share of the young adult market.
3. Consider Mogelonsky's description of the preferences of young adults. Write an essay proposing new products, updated packaging, or other possible ways of meeting their preferences.

Community Links

Compare and contrast Mogelonsky's industry report with Popenoe and Whitehead's report (pp. 518–529) to the public community. In what ways are they similar or different? What expectations of workplace or public documents may shape these reports? What differences in specific audience or possible applications may account for their differences?

Project Report and Public Information

INTRODUCTION TO T-REX CONSTRUCTION PHOTOS TRAFFIC UPDATES

T-REX Transportation Expansion Project

◆

Like the mighty dinosaur, T-REX (Transportation Expansion Project) lumbered into the Denver metropolitan region, coordinating highway improvements and light rail expansion in one mighty engineering project. The T-REX Web site also unifies information about the project—the design, public safety issues in the extensive construction zone, traffic reports, environmental issues, the project schedule, and other related topics of concern to both the T-REX team and the public.

Introduction to TREX

By 2006, in the southeast metro Denver area, you'll have light rail transit and numerous highway improvements to make your travel easier.

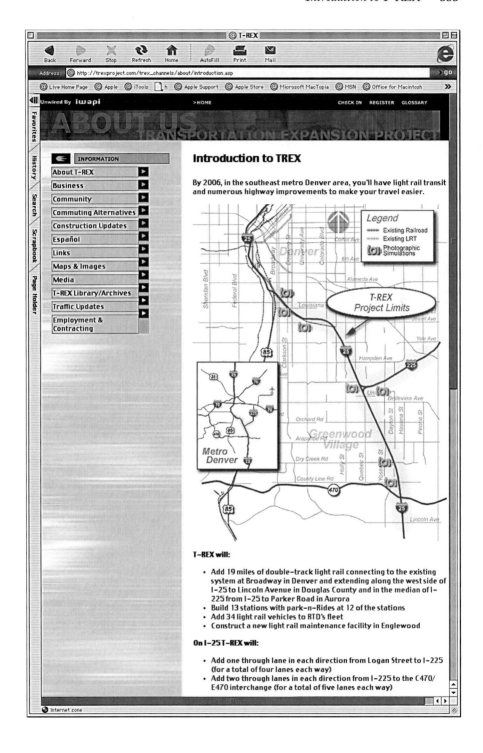

T-REX will:

- Add 19 miles of double-track light rail connecting to the existing system at Broadway in Denver and extending along the west side of I-25 to Lincoln Avenue in Douglas County and in the median of I-225 from I-25 to Parker Road in Aurora
- Build 13 stations with park-n-Rides at 12 of the stations
- Add 34 light rail vehicles to RTD's fleet
- Construct a new light rail maintenance facility in Englewood

On I-25 T-REX will:

- Add one through lane in each direction from Logan Street to I-225 (for a total of four lanes each way)
- Add two through lanes in each direction from I-225 to the C470/E470 interchange (for a total of five lanes each way)

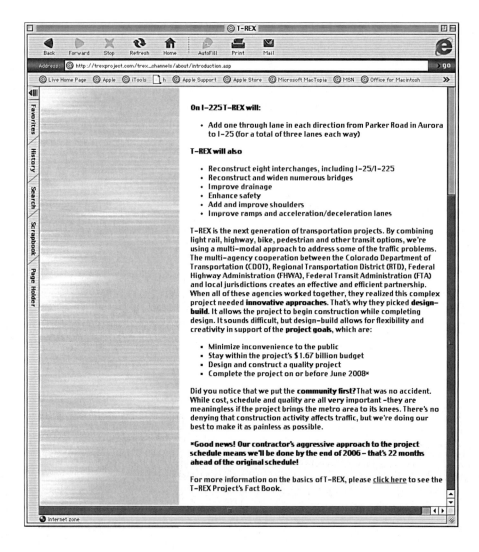

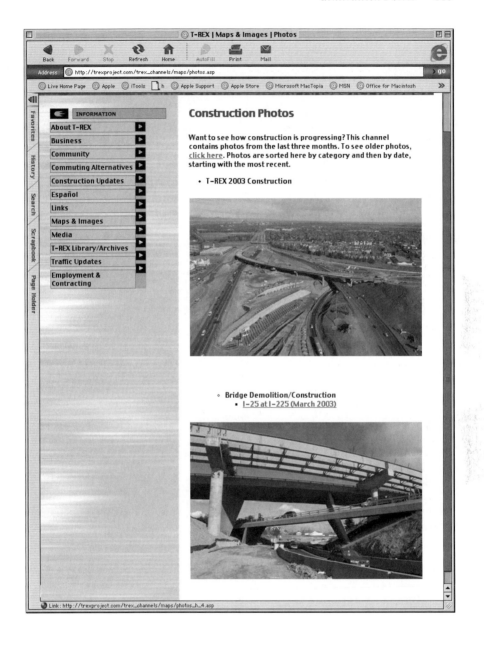

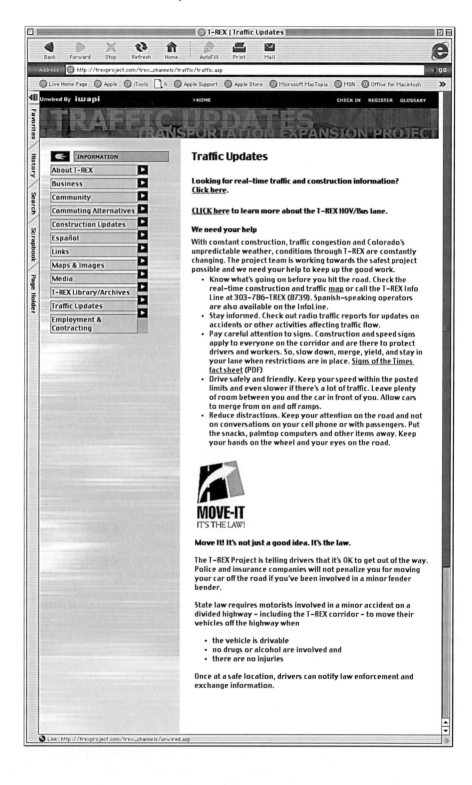

Reading Responses

1. What major transportation changes will the T-REX project accomplish?
2. What public goals does T-REX support?
3. What is the purpose of the traffic updates and the "Move It" campaign? Why is this information included on the Web site? Who are the readers that this page addresses?

Writing Activities

1. Analyze the variety of information supplied in these selections from the T-REX Web site. Write an essay considering what information the site provides and how it appeals to readers.
2. Consider the T-REX map and photographs. Write an essay considering how these visual materials present information to readers and supplement the written text.
3. In what ways does the World Wide Web change opportunities for information and interaction about projects like T-REX? Using the T-REX site as an example, discuss the potential of the Web to alter communication between the work and public communities.

Community Links

Compare and contrast the T-REX project with "Communicating Common Ground" (pp. 183–187) in the academic community or one of the Web sites (pp. 566–571) in the public community. Consider both differences and similarities, including how each provides public information.

Instructions
LaserJet Toner Cartridge Recycling Program
Hewlett-Packard

◆

The following pages come from a leaflet that accompanies Hewlett-Packard LaserJet Toner Cartridges. When customers open the carton containing a new printer cartridge, these instructions encourage them to recycle the old cartridge as they install the new one. The carton includes directions for installing a new cartridge, returning an old one, and using a pre-paid shipping label so that cartridge recycling costs a customer nothing more than a few minutes of time.

Hewlett-Packard LaserJet Toner Cartridge Recycle Program Information and Instruction Guide

LaserJet Toner Cartridge Recycling Program

Recycling made simple!
Recyclage simplifié!
¡Es fácil reciclar!
回收利用轻而易举。

LaserJet Toner Cartridge Recycling Program

HP Planet Partners™ LaserJet Toner Cartridge Recycling Program (applicable for HP LaserJet color and black & white consumables)

- In keeping with Hewlett-Packard's long-established commitment to balancing company progress and efficiency with good corporate citizenship, we offer HP Planet Partners LaserJet Toner Cartridge Recycling Program. Your participation is essential!
- To continue the program's realization, we've made it easier than ever for you to become part of the solution along with us. The impact your contribution will have on this worthwhile partnership is considerable.
- For example, since 1990, with increased consumer input, we were able to divert over 18 million pounds of material from landfills by recycling every toner cartridge received. Returned HP cartridges are converted into raw materials to be used in the manufacture of everyday products.
- From design to manufacture to packaging and recycling, we're meeting critical environmental goals. And we're determined to go right on improving our performance, too. Here's how you can help us achieve this objective:
- We appreciate your efforts in supporting the HP Planet Partners LaserJet Toner Cartridge Recycling Program. Working together, we will form an active union to assure the world's invaluable resources are conserved.

United States and Puerto Rico Program

Large Volume Returns
For an environmentally responsible returns process for large quantities of used toner cartridges, please use the HP Large Volume Returns Program for shipments of eight or more pieces. Please call 1-800-340-2445 for more information. HP will provide the appropriate packaging and pickup services free of charge for large volumes of returned HP cartridges.

Small Volume Returns
- Place used toner cartridge into the bag containing your new HP toner cartridge.
- Securely place the toner cartridge into the box which came with your replacement toner cartridge or a suitable container. (The box and internal packaging materials will be recycled). We encourage you to send multiple cartridges with each UPS (United Parcel Service) label as a way to further help our environment.
- Up to eight (8) cartridges can be bundled securely with tape or placed in a single large carton.
- Apply the pre-paid, pre-addressed UPS shipping label which is found in every new HP toner cartridge box to the package.

IMPORTANT:
Please do not use the HP Planet Partners LaserJet Toner Cartridge Recycling Program for defective cartridges. Defective cartridges which are still under warranty as described in the HP Toner Cartridge Warranty Statement should be exchanged with an authorized dealer or service center. Used toner cartridges which are inadvertently sent to the HP Planet Partners LaserJet Toner Cartridge Recycling Program can not be returned.

- When your cartridges are of no further use, just follow the simple directions detailed in this brochure. You'll find several return options from which to choose, from a Small Volume Returns Program for returning up to eight cartridges to a Large Volume Returns Program for up to 180 cartridges per container.
- By partnering together, we can convert the plastic components from thousands of returned cartridges into useful products where plastics are needed.

To Ship the Package:
- Give the package to the UPS driver for pickup when you receive your next delivery. (Requested UPS pickup will be charged normal pickup rates.)

OR

- Drop off the package at your nearest UPS service center. For the location of your nearest UPS center, please call 1-800-PICKUPS or see http://www.UPS.com

OR

- Take the package to your local MBE (Mail Boxes Etc.) center. You may also take unpacked toner cartridges to MBE where they will collect and package the cartridges for shipment. For the location of your nearest MBE center, please call 1-800-789-4MBE or see http://www.MBE.com

Please call 1-800-340-2445 for replacement UPS labels.

For residents of Alaska and Hawaii
Do not use the UPS label. Please call 1-800-340-2445 for information and instructions. The US Postal Service provides no-cost cartridge return transportation services under an arrangement with HP for Alaska and Hawaii.

For further information about the HP Planet Partners LaserJet Toner Cartridge Recycling Program, please call 1-800-340-2445 or visit our Website at http://www.hp.com/go/ljsupplies

Material Safety Data Sheets can be obtained by calling the HP Fax Retrieval Service at 1-800-231-9300.

Hewlett-Packard has toner cartridge recycling programs throughout the world. If a program for your country is not described in this guide, please contact a local HP sales office for more information.

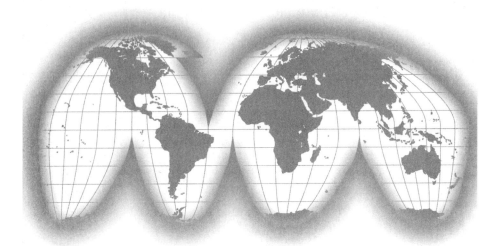

Please Recycle
Nous Recommandons Le Recyclage
Por Favor, Recicle
请回收利用

Printed on recycled paper

LaserJet Toner Cartridge Recycling Program

P/N 5010-6392 ED01   PRINTED IN JAPAN/IMPRIME AU JAPON PUB.W-ZM-015-V1e-0700F107

Reading Responses

1. Both the front and back pages of the Hewlett-Packard leaflet show the earth. What is the message carried by these visuals? What other aspects of these two pages reinforce that message?
2. The inside of the leaflet describes the recycling program and gives directions for returning the cartridges. (The English version is included here; directions are also supplied for consumers who speak French, Spanish, and Asian languages.) How does this part of the leaflet use multiple methods of presenting and highlighting information?
3. In what ways does this leaflet appeal to readers and guide them? What strategies have the leaflet writers and designers used to ensure clear communication?

Writing Activities

1. Write a description of the Hewlett-Packard recycling program, aimed not at supplying directions, but at persuading the students at your school or the office staff at your company to participate.
2. Write an essay analyzing the multiple ways that the leaflet addresses its readers in order to communicate clearly and simply.
3. Write clear directions for another recycling procedure. Be sure to explain each step in sequence. If appropriate, include visuals as well.

Community Links

Consider the Hewlett-Packard instructions in relation to Cullis-Suzuki's appeal in "The Young Can't Wait" (pp. 355–356). Analyze how each document takes its own approach to solving a common problem.

Organizational Promotion
ROMEO AND J L ET
United Illuminating Company

◆

The following page appeared in the program for the Long Wharf Theatre in New Haven, Connecticut, along with other promotional pieces, advertisements, and lists of sponsors supporting the theater's productions. The United Illuminating Company is a utility company that distributes electricity to over 300,000 customers in the New Haven region. As part of its community orientation, it supports various regional cultural organizations.

ROMEO AND J L ET

It's hard to imagine the arts without u.i.
That's why we're proud to support them every chance we get. www.uinet.com

Reading Responses

1. What is the purpose of this promotional page? In what ways does it appeal to the values of both the work and public communities?
2. In what ways is this page tailored to its readers? What does it assume about the likely interests and expectations of those readers?
3. Would this page be more effective if it added visual material to its brief text? Why or why not?

Writing Activities

1. Write an explanation of this promotional piece's appeal to readers.
2. Look through other programs for cultural, civic, or sports events. Analyze how the promotional pages are designed to appeal to readers who attend or support a specific type of event. Write up your conclusions, considering what strategies make a promotional piece effective.
3. Design your own promotional piece for the sponsor of an event or organization in the public community. As you promote this sponsor, carefully consider who your readers will be and what they might expect and value.

Community Links

Compare and contrast other methods of advertisement or promotion included in this book with the United Illuminating selection. In what ways do the examples you select illustrate different ways of approaching and influencing readers? In what ways do they use similar methods?

Advertisement

DEDICATED, FOCUSED, AND DIVERSIFIED

Glenbrook Life, Allstate Financial Group

◆

The following advertisements appeared over some months, each inside the front cover of an issue of the ABA Banking Journal. *Others in the series included "Protected," featuring a German shepherd and announcing an annuity product, and "Pedigreed," featuring an elegant Afghan show dog and announcing Glenbrook Life's merger with Allstate. All of the advertisements were directed to the journal's readers—banking and financial professionals—and offered workplace insurance products.*

344 The Work Community

Dedicated is the way our clients describe us. Because we focus entirely on your financial institution. Your needs. Your working style. Providing you flexible annuity and life insurance solutions. And with the strength of Allstate behind us, why would you want anyone else on your side?

Call 1.866.361.5815 and start a new relationship.

GLENBROOK LIFE
A Member of Allstate Financial Group

©2001 Allstate Insurance Company. Glenbrook Life and Annuity Company is a wholly owned subsidiary and its policy obligations are reinsured by Allstate Life Insurance Company, Northbrook, IL.

Focused is the way we do business. Giving you our undivided attention. Building strong one-on-one relationships. Bringing you our financial expertise with annuity and life insurance solutions. All with the strength of Allstate behind us.

Call 1.866.361.5815 and get things started.

GLENBROOK LIFE
A Member of Allstate Financial Group

© 2001 Allstate Insurance Company. Glenbrook Life and Annuity Company is a wholly owned subsidiary and its policy obligations are reinsured by Allstate Life Insurance Company, Northbrook, IL.

Diversified is what makes our new breed of variable annuity and life insurance solutions indispensable. Introducing the Glenbrook Provider Series—five highly adaptable products with top-selling fund families and the latest features, from competitive costs to extra credit to no surrender charges. And each has cafeteria-style option packages.

Call 1.866.361.5815 and talk to Ralph Schmidt or Rob Shore to expand your options.

GLENBROOK LIFE
A Member of Allstate Financial Group

©2001 Allstate Insurance Company. Products issued by Glenbrook Life and Annuity Company, an indirect subsidiary of Allstate Insurance Company, Northbrook, IL. Products underwritten by ALFS, Inc. Prospectus available from Glenbrook Life. 04/01

Reading Responses

1. How do the key words and the photographs in the advertisements work together? What messages do they convey to readers?
2. What does the brief text in each advertisement convey?
3. How do these advertisements specifically appeal to the readers of the *ABA Banking Journal*? In what ways do they generally appeal to the likely values of many readers in the work community?

Writing Activities

1. Write an explanation of the multiple ways that these three advertisements appeal to readers.
2. Write an analysis of the written text included in one of the advertisements. What makes the text effective—what strategies have the writers used, and how does the text appeal to readers?
3. Design your own advertisement associating a particular animal with a value that will appeal to your readers. Begin by deciding what you want to advertise and which readers you want to address. You might want to design another advertisement that an insurance company would want to use, or you might decide to advertise your own virtues, the values of a particular group or organization, or an imaginary product.

Community Links

Compare and contrast other methods of advertisement or promotion included in this book with the three Glenbrook Life advertisements. In what ways do the examples you select illustrate different ways of approaching and influencing readers? In what ways do they use similar methods?

Web Site

WWW.TECSTANDARDS.COM
Technical Standards, Inc.

◆

The Technical Standards Web site introduces a company that offers documentation services—designing and preparing clear manuals, brochures, and other materials. Here, the home page, site map, and contact information page illustrate the principles that the company also applies in its professional work.

348 The Work Community

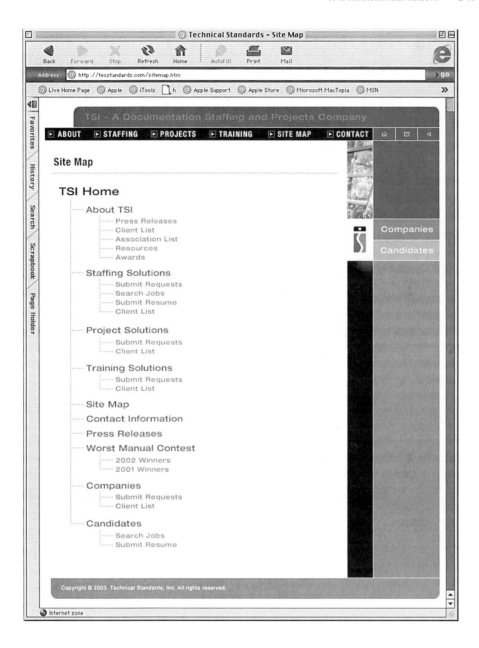

 Reading Responses

1. What do you consider the most striking aspect of the home page or the site map? How does the page create that effect?
2. In what ways are these pages designed to establish the company's credibility and expertise doing its work—designing documents?
3. How are these pages designed with readers in mind? What are the likely needs and interests of visitors to this site?

Writing Activities

1. Write a paragraph identifying the main impression conveyed by one of the pages and describing how the components of the page create that impression.
2. Write a paragraph analyzing and explaining the impact of the site's visual design on readers.
3. Visit the site and click on the contest to identify the "worst manual." Using those manuals and the Technical Standards site itself, develop a list of criteria or factors that can contribute to a well-designed document. Write a report explaining your criteria to people who wish to learn more about effective document design.

Community Links

Compare and contrast Web sites from different communities. (See the Guide to Themes, Topics, and Rhetorical Strategies for a list of the Web sites in this book.) Consider how each combines written text with visual features to illustrate or apply principles that help to establish its credibility within its community and for its specific readers.

Part 3

The Public Community

Introduction: Reading and Writing in the Public Community

A. Community Voices
B. Community Perspectives and Issues
C. Community Ethics
D. Texts and Documents from the Public Community

Introduction: Reading and Writing in the Public Community

The public community focuses on values—issues and interests that passionately engage people who hold widely varied viewpoints. In this broad community, participants read and write, negotiate and debate. They are motivated by their zeal for a cause, a pressing problem or need, an important activity, or a compelling interest. Participants in the public community may be civic advocates who promote better government, more parks, or stronger citizens' rights. They may be passionate partisans, supporting their political party, their snowboarding club, their children's school, or their group's annual fund-raiser. They may be indignant defenders of the wetlands, abandoned animals, children with leukemia, or others who are threatened, embattled, or downtrodden. They may be generous contributors to worthy organizations with religious, cultural, educational, health, or environmental missions. Individually or collectively, they may appeal to their fellow citizens, lobby officials, publicize little-known facts, present local or regional research findings, cite respected authorities, write to newspapers, send a check, circulate petitions, call out the vote, or stage rallies.

Whether you enter the public community as a concerned citizen, a passionate activist, or a political aspirant, you exercise your right to speak and write, to participate in democratic processes, to join a civic exchange, or to take sides on an issue. As you gain experience in the civic or public arena, you may expand your reading and writing in order to become better informed, to understand or challenge other views with increased self-assurance, or to convey information that more effectively persuades or motivates others. The public community may tolerate enthusiasm—even flamboyance—far greater than that acceptable at work or school. Even so, most people expect even passionate advocates to respect others who hold different views—and have the same right to participate and advocate. Values are at stake, but many civic decisions balance competing interests, using shared concerns to shape viable compromise.

Public writers often must address the expectations of a wide range of readers. They need to motivate supporters and advocate shared views clearly. They may want to appeal to potential supporters, forging alliances through shared values. They expect to champion the actions and solutions that will achieve their goals, often by persuading decision makers that their views are sound and their proposals viable. To do so, participants in the public community tend to focus on their own views or positions, respectfully acknowledging rather than emotionally attacking other positions. In addition, they gather pertinent evidence to support their views and persuade others of the importance of the issue or the seriousness of the problem. Most importantly, they articulate clear objectives—identifying needed changes, marshaling specific support, proposing solutions, and promoting specific actions. In short, they typically want to act, to move, and to create change.

Readings in the Public Community

Readings in four sections introduce values and concerns of civic and nonprofit groups, partisan activists, and earnest citizens. Four voices—Cullis-Suzuki, Talcott, Miller, and Moyers—express the passion, fervor, intensity, and commitment typical of the public community. Six other writers take different perspectives on the nature of the public arena, beginning with Morse, who identifies characteristics of communities that succeed. Hutton and Phillips define the nonprofit organization, Nelson specifies ways that readers can contribute to change, and Covey portrays the ideal community. Varied issues engage this community: for Jamieson, political processes, and for Zobel de Ayala, the definition of community within this country and in the global community beyond national boundaries. Two thoughtful considerations conclude the introduction to the public community: Pratkanis and Aronson examine the power of propaganda while Gomes explores the moral values and calls that might inspire this generation of young adults.

Finally, a collection of texts and documents illustrates how the passion and intensity of the public community may take shape in written form. The section opens with formal civic documents—the Declaration of Independence, the Treaty Initiative to Share and Protect the Global Water Commons, President Bush's address on September 20, 2001, and King's "I Have a Dream." Next, several clusters of documents illustrate calls to action, appeals to supporters, appeals to voters, letters to officials, and newsletters. Others illustrate communication and exchange through arguments, debates, and position papers. An editorial, letters to the editor, and an opinion piece all rely on the newspaper as a forum for public exchange. Finally, reports, advice, promotional brochures and flyers, proposals, and Web sites complete the exchange of public information and opinion.

Community Voices

THE YOUNG CAN'T WAIT
Severn Cullis-Suzuki

This selection, originally a "Viewpoint" column, appeared in Time *magazine as part of a special report called "How to Save the Earth." When Severn Cullis-Suzuki wrote the column, she was a 22-year-old Yale graduate with a major in biology. She had attended—and addressed—her first environmental conference ten years earlier when she went to the Rio Earth Summit.*

1. When you are little, it's not hard to believe you can change the world. I remember my enthusiasm when, at the age of 12, I addressed the delegates at the Rio Earth Summit. "I am only a child," I told them. "Yet I know that if all the money spent on war was spent on ending poverty and finding environmental answers, what a wonderful place this would be. In school you teach us not to fight with others, to work things out, to respect others, to clean up our mess, not to hurt other creatures, to share, not be greedy. Then why do you go out and do the things you tell us not to do? You grownups say you love us, but I challenge you, please, to make your actions reflect your words."

2. I spoke for six minutes and received a standing ovation. Some of the delegates even cried. I thought that maybe I had reached some of them, that my speech might actually spur action. Now, a decade from Rio, after I've sat through many more conferences, I'm not sure what has been accomplished. My confidence in the people in power and in the power of an individual's voice to reach them has been deeply shaken.

3. Sure, I've seen some improvements since Rio. In my home city of Vancouver, most people put out their recycling boxes. The organic grocery and café on Fourth Avenue is flourishing. Bikes are popular, and there are a few gas-electric hybrid cars gliding around. But as this new century begins, my twenty-something generation is becoming increasingly disconnected from the natural world. We buy our drinking water in bottles. We eat genetically modified organisms. We drive the biggest cars ever. At the same time, we are a generation aware of the world—of poverty and social imbalance, the loss of biodiversity, climate change and the consequences of globalization—but many of us feel we have inherited problems too great to do anything about.

Source: Cullis-Suzuki, Severn. "The Young Can't Wait," *Time,* August 26, 2002. © 2002 Time, Inc. Reprinted by permission.

4   When I was little, the world was simple. But as a young adult, I'm learning that as we have to make choices—education, career, lifestyle—life gets more and more complicated. We are beginning to feel pressure to produce and be successful. We are learning a shortsighted way of looking at the future, focusing on four-year government terms and quarterly business reports. We are taught that economic growth is progress, but we aren't taught how to pursue a happy, healthy or sustainable way of living. And we are learning that what we wanted for our future when we were 12 was idealistic and naive.

5   Today I'm no longer a child, but I'm worried about what kind of environment my children will grow up in. In Johannesburg the delegates will discuss the adoption and implementation of documents by governments. Yes, important stuff. But they did that at Rio. What this meeting must really be about is responsibility—not only government responsibility but personal responsibility. We are not cleaning up our own mess. We are not facing up to the price of our lifestyles. In Canada we know we are wiping out the salmon of the West Coast, just as we wiped out cod from the East Coast, but we continue overfishing. We keep driving our SUVs in the city, even though we are starting to feel the effects of climate change—a direct result of burning too much fossil fuel.

6   Real environmental change depends on us. We can't wait for our leaders. We have to focus on what our own responsibilities are and how we can make the change happen.

7   Before graduating from college last spring I worked with the Yale Student Environmental Coalition to draft a pledge for young people to sign. Called the Recognition of Responsibility, the pledge is a commitment from our generation to be accountable and a challenge to our elders to help us achieve this goal and to lead by example. It includes a list of ways to live more sustainably—simple but fundamental things like reducing household garbage, consuming less, not relying on cars so much, eating locally grown food, carrying a reusable cup and, most important, getting out into nature. (For the full text, go to *www.skyfishproject.org*.) Three friends and I will take the Recognition of Responsibility to Johannesburg, where we will meet with South African students and then present the pledge to the World Summit as a demonstration of personal commitment.

8   But in the 10 years since Rio, I have learned that addressing our leaders is not enough. As Gandhi said many years ago, "We must become the change we want to see." I know change is possible, because I am changing, still figuring out what I think. I am still deciding how to live my life. The challenges are great, but if we accept individual responsibility and make sustainable choices, we will rise to the challenges, and we will become part of the positive tide of change.

Reading Responses

1. What does Cullis-Suzuki advocate? What does she want readers to do?
2. How does Cullis-Suzuki use the past, the present, and the future to structure her column and lead readers to her conclusion?

3. Which readers does Cullis-Suzuki appeal to most strongly? How does she try to establish connections with them?

Writing Activities

1. Summarize the contrasts between past and present in Cullis-Suzuki's article.
2. What would you add to the Recognition of Responsibility? Write several paragraphs explaining specific lifestyle changes that you think most people could make that might contribute to "a happy, healthy or sustainable way of living" (paragraph 4).
3. Write your own Viewpoint column. Identify an issue or an area where you believe that change is needed, acknowledge other views or partial progress, present your reasons using explanation and supporting evidence to show why you believe that change is necessary, and propose the solution or specific change that you advocate.

Community Links

After reading Cullis-Suzuki's article, read one or two other argumentative selections such as Small and Kimbrough-Melton's "Rethinking Justice" (pp. 126–132) from the academic community, Simpson's "Are Incentives for Drug Abuse Treatment Too Strong?" (pp. 301–306) from the work community, or Barlow and Clarke's "The Standpoint" (pp. 479–489), Kerry and Bond's exchange on fuel economy (pp. 495–503), or the American Civil Liberties Union's "Briefing Paper: Hate Speech on Campus" (pp. 504–509), all from the public community. First consider what common approaches are shared by the arguments you select. Which of these approaches seem to be basic features of arguments regardless of community? Then consider how the arguments differ. In what ways might the community or the specific readers account for these differences?

ORGANIZER: BILL TALCOTT
Studs Terkel

◆

Studs Terkel went straight to the authorities—the ordinary people who work—for his 1972 book Working: People Talk About What They Do All Day and How They Feel About What They Do. *For three years, Terkel tracked down interesting people to interview and included well over a hundred of them in the final volume. In this selection, Bill Talcott tells Terkel—and Terkel's readers—about his life as an organizer. Talcott describes his background using abbreviations common at the time: NCO (noncommissioned officer, selected from enlistees), SNCC (Student Nonviolent Coordinating Committee, called "Snick"), and OEO (Office of Economic Opportunity, which sponsored programs to reduce poverty through education, employment, and community action).*

1. My work is trying to change this country. This is the job I've chosen. When people ask me, "Why are you doing this?" it's like asking what kind of sickness you got. I don't feel sick. I think this country is sick. The daily injustices just gnaw on me a little harder than they do on other people.

2. I try to bring people together who are being put down by the system, left out. You try to build an organization that will give them power to make the changes. Everybody's at the bottom of the barrel at this point. Ten years ago one could say the poor people suffered and the middle class got by. That's not true any more.

3. My father was a truckdriver with a sixth-grade education. My uncle was an Annapolis graduate. My father was inarticulate and worked all his life with his hands. My uncle worked all his life with his mouth and used his hands only to cut coupons. My father's problem was that he was powerless. My uncle's problem was that he was powerless, although he thought he was strong. Clipping coupons, he was always on the fringe of power, but never really had it. If he tried to take part in the management of the companies whose coupons he was clipping, he got clipped. Both these guys died very unhappy, dissatisfied with their lives.

4. Power has been captured by a few people. A very small top and a very big bottom. You don't see much in-between. Who do people on the bottom think are the powerful people? College professors and management types, the local managers of big corporations like General Motors. What kind of power do these guys really have? They have the kind of power Eichmann claimed for himself. They have the power to do bad and not question what they're told to do.

5. I am more bothered by the ghetto child who is bitten by rats than I am by a middle-class kid who can't find anything to do but put down women and take dope and play his life away. But each one is wasted.

> I came into consciousness during the fifties, when Joe McCarthy was running around. Like many people my age—I'm now thirty-seven—I was aware something was terribly wrong. I floundered around for two years in college, was disappointed, and enlisted in the army. I was NCO for my company. During a discussion, I said if I was a black guy, I would refuse to serve. I ended up being sent to division headquarters and locked up in a room for two years, so I wouldn't be able to talk to anybody.
>
> At San Francisco State, I got involved with the farm workers movement. I would give speeches on a box in front of the Commons. Then I'd go out and fight jocks behind the gym for an hour and a half. (Laughs.) In '64, I resigned as student body president and went to Mississippi to work for SNCC. I spent three years working in the black community in San Francisco.

At that point, I figured it was time for me to work with whites. My father was from South Carolina. We had a terrible time when I visited—violent arguments. But I was family. I learned from that experience you had to build a base with white people on the fringe of the South. Hopefully you'd build an alliance between blacks and whites.

6   I came to East Kentucky with OEO. I got canned in a year. Their idea was the same as Daley's. You use the OEO to build an organization to support the right candidates. I didn't see that as my work. My job was to build an organization of put-down people, who can *control* the candidates once they're elected.

7   I put together a fairly solid organization of Appalachian people in Pike County. It's a single industry area, coal. You either work for the coal company or you don't work. Sixty percent of its people live on incomes lower than the government's guidelines for rural areas.

8   I was brought in to teach other organizers how to do it. I spent my first three months at it. I decided these middle-class kids from Harvard and Columbia were too busy telling everybody else what they should be doing. The only thing to do was to organize the local people.

9   When I got fired, there were enough people to support me on one hundred dollars a month and room and board. They dug down in their pockets and they'd bring food and they'd take care of me like I was a cousin. They felt responsible for me, but they didn't see me as one of them. I'm not an Appalachian, I'm a San Franciscan. I'm not a coal miner, I'm an organizer. If they're gonna save themselves, they're gonna have to do it themselves. I have some skills that can help them. I did this work for three years.

10 The word organizer has been romanticized. You get the vision of a mystical being doing magical things. An organizer is a guy who brings in new members. I don't feel I've had a good day unless I've talked with at least one new person. We have a meeting, make space for new people to come in. The organizer sits next to the new guy, so everybody has to take the new guy as an equal. You do that a couple of times and the guy's got strength enough to become part of the group.

11 You must listen to them and tell them again and again they are important, that they have the stuff to do the job. They don't have to shuck themselves about not being good enough, not worthy. Most people were raised to think they are not worthy. School is a process of taking beautiful kids who are filled with life and beating them into happy slavery. That's as true of a twenty-five-thousand-dollar-a-year executive as it is for the poorest.

12 You don't find allies on the basis of the brotherhood of man. People are tied into their immediate problems. They have a difficult time worrying about other people's. Our society is so structured that everybody is supposed to be selfish as hell and screw the other guy. Christian brotherhood is enlightened self-interest. Most sins committed on poor people are by people who've come to help them.

13 I came as a stranger but I came with credentials. There are people who know and trust me, who say so to the others. So what I'm saying is verifiable. It's possible to win, to take an outfit like Bethlehem Steel and lick 'em. Most

people in their guts don't really believe it. Gee, it's great when all of a sudden they realize it's possible. They become alive.

14   Nobody believed PCCA[1] could stop Bethlehem from strip mining. Ten miles away was a hillside being stripped. Ten miles away is like ten million light years away. What they wanted was a park, a place for their kids. Bethlehem said, "Go to hell. You're just a bunch of crummy Appalachians. We're not gonna give you a damn thing." If I could get that park for them, they would believe it's possible to do other things.

15   They really needed a victory. They had lost over and over again, day after day. So I got together twenty, thirty people I saw as leaders. I said, "Let's get that park." They said, "We can't." I said, "We can. If we let all the big wheels around the country know—the National Council of Churches and everybody start calling up, writing, and hounding Bethlehem, they'll have to give us the park." That's exactly what happened. Bethlehem thought: This is getting to be a pain in the ass. We'll give 'em the park and they'll shut up about strip mining. We haven't shut up on strip mining, but we got the park. Four thousand people from Pike County drove up and watched those bulldozers grading down that park. It was an incredible victory.

16   Twenty or thirty people realized we could win. Four thousand people understood there was a victory. They didn't know how it happened, but a few of 'em got curious. The twenty or thirty are now in their own communities trying to turn people on.

17   We're trying to link up people in other parts of the state—Lexington, Louisville, Covington, Bowling Green—and their local issues and, hopefully, binding them together in some kind of larger thing.

18   When you start talking to middle-class people in Lexington, the words are different, but it's the same script. It's like talking to a poor person in Pike County or Mississippi. The schools are bad. Okay, they're bad for different reasons—but the schools are bad.

19   The middle class is fighting powerlessness too. Middle-class women, who are in the Lexington fight, are more alienated than lower-class women. The poor woman knows she's essential for the family. The middle-class woman thinks, If I die tomorrow, the old man can hire himself a maid to do everything I do. The white-collar guy is scared he may be replaced by the computer. The schoolteacher is asked not to teach but to baby-sit. God help you if you teach. The minister is trapped by the congregation that's out of touch with him. He spends his life violating the credo that led him into the ministry. The policeman has no relationship to the people he's supposed to protect. So he oppresses. The fireman who wants to fight fires ends up fighting a war.

20   People become afraid of each other. They're convinced there's not a damn thing they can do. I think we have it inside us to change things. We need the courage. It's a scary thing. Because we've been told from the time we were born that what we have inside us is bad and useless. What's true is what we have inside us is good and useful.

> In Mississippi, our group got the first black guy elected in a hundred years. In San Francisco, our organization licked the development agency there. We tied up two hundred million dollars of its money for two

years, until the bastards finally came to an agreement with the community people. The guy I started with was an alcoholic pimp in the black ghetto. He is now a Presbyterian minister and very highly respected.

21   I work all the way from two in the morning until two the next morning seven days a week. (Laughs.) I'm not a martyr. I'm one of the few people I know who was lucky in life to find out what he really wanted to do. I'm just havin' a ball, the time of my life. I feel sorry for all these people I run across all the time who aren't doing what they want to do. Their lives are hell. I think everybody ought to quit their job and do what they want to do. You've got one life. You've got, say, sixty-five years. How on earth can you blow forty-five years of that doing something you hate?

22   I have a wife and three children. I've managed to support them for six years doing this kind of work. We don't live fat. I have enough money to buy books and records. The kids have as good an education as anybody in this country. Their range of friends runs from millionaires in San Francisco to black prostitutes in Lexington. They're comfortable with all these people. My kids know the name of the game: living your life up to the end.

23   All human recorded history is about five thousand years old. How many people in all that time have made an overwhelming difference? Twenty? Thirty? Most of us spend our lives trying to achieve some things. But we're not going to make an overwhelming difference. We do the best we can. That's enough.

24   The problem with history is that it's written by college professors about great men. That's not what history is. History's a hell of a lot of little people getting together and deciding they want a better life for themselves and their kids.

25   I have a goal. I want to end my life in a home for the aged that's run by the state—organizing people to fight 'em because they're not running it right. (Laughs.)

Note
1. Pike County Citizens' Association.

Reading Responses

1. What is an organizer? What does an organizer do?
2. Why did Talcott become an organizer?
3. What are the challenges an organizer has to overcome? How does Talcott manage to achieve his victories?

Writing Activities

1. Make a list of the organizing projects that Talcott recalls. Read over your list, and write a paragraph describing what the list reveals about Talcott's efforts or about relationships among the projects.

2. If you have been involved in a civic project or event, write an account of your experience. Explain your purpose (what you set out to achieve), your activities, and your accomplishments, interpreting them all for readers.
3. Interview someone who is an activist or who works in the public community—for a nonprofit organization, for a civic group, or for a cause. Before the interview, plan questions that will help you discover what this person does, why he or she has been drawn to the job, and how success is measured and achieved. Take notes during the interview; immediately afterwards, record your own comments and observations as well. Write up your essay, weaving together accurate direct quotations from the person you interviewed, summaries or paraphrases of the person's words, and your own interpretation or commentary to help bring this person to life for readers.

Community Links

Along with Bill Talcott's interview, consider several other first-person accounts such as Malcolm X's "Prison Studies" (pp. 16–18) and hooks's "Keeping Close to Home" (pp. 22–31) from the academic community, Liu's "The Story of a Garment Worker" (pp. 205–207) or Walton's "Running a Successful Company" (pp. 216–219) from the work community, and Cullis-Suzuki's "The Young Can't Wait" (pp. 355–356) also from the public community. (For other suggestions, turn to the Guide to Themes, Topics, and Rhetorical Strategies.) How would the accounts that you consider be different if they were told in the third person (*he* or *she*) rather than the first (*I*)? What does the first person add, and what are its limits? How might the writing situation and the community affect a writer's decision to use first person?

WANTED: "CIVIC SCIENTISTS" TO EDUCATE THE PUBLIC, PRESS AND POLICY MAKERS

Katharine S. Miller

◆

This article appeared in the Stanford Report, *a campus paper distributed to faculty and staff at Stanford University and mailed to off-campus subscribers. Available in print or online, this publication includes campus news, calendar events, reports on campus meetings such as Faculty Senate, opinion pieces, and information about people on campus. Katharine Miller, the article's author, was an intern with the* Stanford Report, *specializing in science news.*

Fewer than one-third of all Americans understand the term "DNA."

Fewer than 15 percent understand the term "molecule."

Only about 50 percent know that humans didn't live at the time of the dinosaurs.
—*Science & Engineering Indicators 2000,* published by the National Science Foundation

1 To reduce scientific illiteracy, scientists need to write and teach about science whenever and however they can, be connected to the news media and advise policy makers when an important scientific question arises, say two Stanford faculty members.

2 Michael Riordan, a particle physicist, spoke as part of a Feb. 16 panel called "Cultivating the Civic Scientist" at the annual meeting of the American Association for the Advancement of Science. Microbiologist Lucy Shapiro was scheduled to appear on that panel as well but, at the last minute, was unable to attend. She spoke in a recent interview.

3 Scientists need to speak out, Shapiro said, because without scientific understanding, people fear things they don't understand, the press legitimizes erroneous pseudoscience and the government promulgates wrongheaded and dangerous public policies.

4 According to Riordan, "A civic scientist is one who is willing to engage in a dialogue about the nature of science, the future of science and its potential impacts on society. The highest expression of the term 'civic scientist' refers to a scientist who disinterestedly makes his expertise available to further the welfare of the country."

5 On issues from missile defense to antibiotic resistance and breast cancer policies, the government needs the advice that only scientists can provide. Riordan and Shapiro both fulfill that civic obligation, but also educate the public through their writing and speaking.

6 "People are hungry to hear this stuff," Shapiro said, referring to the public's appetite for clear explanations of science. "Newspeople consistently underestimate the curiosity of a typical TV audience and their tolerance for learning something." About 15 years ago, Shapiro decided she had to do something about it. "I lecture whenever I can because I'm a clear speaker," Shapiro said. "Not everyone can do it, but those who can should."

7 Riordan agrees that the popular press isn't capable of covering the more difficult science. That's one reason he has written four popular books, with a fifth on the way. "The more complex stories may have to be written by scientists themselves," he said.

The Civic Physicist

8 Riordan was part of the team that discovered the so-called "top" quark at Stanford's Linear Accelerator Center (SLAC) in the early 1970s. But his career has taken a different path in the last 15 to 20 years: He writes books for the general public about science, the history of science and science policy.

9. He also gets calls from the press on a regular basis and often is quoted in newspapers and magazines. His own stories for the *New York Times* and *New Scientist* and *Science* magazines have covered such topics as the discovery of neutrinos, the search for the Higgs boson and the need for an American quark-busting machine.

10. During his career, Riordan has worked closely with a number of people he considers great civic scientists. He points to SLAC's Wolfgang Panofsky and Sidney Drell, whose contributions to nuclear arms control are widely known.

11. Riordan himself helped formulate the American Physical Society's recently published official position on the technical viability of a national missile defense system, urging the United States not to deploy such a system unless it is proven effective against anticipated countermeasures.

12. But Riordan says scientists don't have to be bigshots to play important roles in public life. "To become a scientist involved in policy, you must spend time on committees getting to know the policy issues and the policy makers," he said. Federal agencies like the Environmental Protection Agency, the Nuclear Regulatory Commission and the State Department all need science advisers.

13. Scientists also play an important role in civic life when they interact with the press. Unfortunately, Riordan said, many scientists are leery of the press. "They see that the press doesn't always get things right and it leaves out complexities and qualifiers scientists feel are necessary to explain their work."

14. Nevertheless, scientists have to overcome their fears and distrusts and learn to tell the public, through the news media, why it's important to do what they do, he said: "The press is the conduit to a large and influential audience."

The Civic Biologist

15. Lucy Shapiro, the Virginia and D. K. Ludwig Professor in the departments of Developmental Biology and Genetics, is a laboratory scientist, first and foremost. But about 15 years ago she decided she could also be a civic scientist. It's hard to do both in early stages of a scientific career, she said. When she was an assistant and then associate professor, she was too busy getting grants, running a lab and starting a family.

16. "But there comes a time in your career when you can do more," Shapiro said. She could have written a textbook or started a company, but making science accessible to the public was the best fit for Shapiro's strength: public speaking.

17. "I'm just a run-of-the-mill scientist trying to make people less frightened about technology," she said. "To make intelligent decisions, there's no substitute for real information."

18. The talks she gives to the public often reach only a few people, but on occasion she speaks to policy makers. At one point, Shapiro was invited to the White House along with several other scientists to speak to President Clinton and his Cabinet about the risks biologically altered pathogens pose to national security and the food supply.

19. After several hours of scripted presentation, the Cabinet members were getting sleepy. When she stood up to speak, Shapiro went off-script.

20 "Do you know what genetic engineering is?" she asked.
21 "Why don't you tell us," Clinton said.
22 As she spoke, Clinton shooed away aides, who were peeved because Shapiro had made him late for other appointments.
23 So Shapiro taught the Cabinet members that genetic engineering goes on in nature all the time: Bacteria can pick up genetic material from other bacteria and add it to their own, all without human intervention. In fact, she said, nature added a toxin gene to the *E. coli* that made killers out of Jack in the Box hamburgers in 1993. And it is nature that encourages the evolution of bacteria into antibiotic-resistant forms. The lesson: We have more to fear from nature than from international terrorists.
24 During a videotaped talk to the National Academy of Sciences (NAS), Shapiro delivered the same message. The tape is one of the most commonly requested in the NAS collection.
25 Before she began speaking to the public, Shapiro "worked very hard to do it right." Early on, she practiced her speeches on her physicist husband, who had to stop her "every two seconds to ask what a word meant." She eventually learned that she need not use complicated lingo to get the information across.
26 Though her research involves bacteria, Shapiro also speaks about other scientific subjects. A few years ago she decided to address people's fears about breast cancer. She made it her business to learn everything she could about breast cancer, and she started speaking to groups of women about it. "This is what is real," she told the women. "Only 5 percent of breast cancer is inherited."
27 And in the early '90s, she reached out to educate even larger audiences about science and scientists. Along with other board members from the Scientists' Institute for Public Information, she met with John Lithgow and other prominent Hollywood figures. "We told them to stop presenting images of mad scientists and to make them human," she said. "It didn't work, but we tried."

Reading Responses

1. What event probably triggered the preparation of this article?
2. What is a civic scientist? What should one do? Why do Riordan and Shapiro promote the role of the civic scientist?
3. In what ways has Miller shaped her story to appeal to her original readers at Stanford?

Writing Activities

1. Write a paragraph summarizing the contributions of a civic scientist.
2. How might Miller's article have been different if she had written it for a student newspaper, a daily general-interest newspaper, a business-oriented newspaper, or a monthly professional newspaper? Rewrite a brief

section of her article to appeal to the readers of a different newspaper. (Be sure to identify the newspaper and its orientation.)

3. Write a profile of a person who would be a good civic representative of his or her specialty. Describe the person, adding quotations or details from an interview if possible, and explain why or how this civic role would be useful or beneficial.

Community Links

Compare and contrast Miller's profiles of Riordan and Shapiro with one or two profiles in other readings. (See the Guide to Themes, Topics, and Rhetorical Strategies.) How is each profile shaped for its community and specific readers?

JOURNALISM & DEMOCRACY: ON THE IMPORTANCE OF BEING A "PUBLIC NUISANCE"

Bill Moyers

◆

Published in The Nation, *this article by Bill Moyers was based on a speech that he had presented a few weeks earlier to the National Press Club. On that occasion, celebrating his thirty years in television journalism, he talked about his passion for his work. He also reminded his listeners (and later his readers) of the importance of journalism for democracy.*

1   Hi. My name is Bill, and I'm a recovering Unimpeachable Source. I understand "Unimpeachable Source" is now an oxymoron in Washington, as in "McCain Republican" or "Democratic Party." But once upon a time in a far away place—Washington in the 1960s—I was one. Deep Backgrounders and Unattributable Tips were my drugs of choice. Just go to Austin and listen to me on those tapes LBJ secretly recorded. That's the sound of a young man getting high . . . without inhaling. I swore off thirty-four years ago last month, and I'm here to tell you, it hasn't been easy to stay clean. I can't even watch *The West Wing* without breaking into a sweat. A C-SPAN briefing by Ari Fleischer pushes me right to the edge. But I know one shot—just one—and I could wind up like my friend David Gergen, in and out of revolving doors and needing to go on *The NewsHour* for a fix between Presidents.

2   But I'm not here to talk about my time in the White House. I haven't talked much about it at all, though I do plan to write about it someday soon. During the past three and a half decades, I have learned that the job of trying to tell the truth about people whose job it is to hide the truth is almost as complicated and difficult as trying to hide it in the first place. Unless you're willing

to fight and refight the same battles until you go blue in the face, to drive the people you work with nuts going over every last detail to make certain you've got it right, and then to take hit after unfair hit accusing you of having a "bias," or these days even a point of view, there's no use even in trying. You have to love it, and I do.

3   I always have. Journalism is what I wanted to do since I was a kid. Fifty years ago, on my 16th birthday, I went to work at the *Marshall News Messenger*. The daily newspaper in a small Texas town seemed like the best place in the world to be a cub reporter. It was small enough to navigate but big enough to keep me busy, happy and learning something new every day. I was lucky. Some of the old-timers were out sick or on vacation and I got assigned to cover the Housewives' Rebellion. Fifteen women in Marshall refused to pay the new Social Security withholding tax for their domestic workers. The rebels argued that Social Security was unconstitutional, that imposing it was taxation without representation, and that—here's my favorite part—"requiring us to collect [the tax] is no different from requiring us to collect the garbage." They hired themselves a lawyer—Martin Dies, the ex-Congressman best known (or worst known) for his work as head of the House Committee on Un-American Activities in the 1930s and 1940s. Eventually the women wound up paying the tax—while holding their noses. The stories I wrote for the *News Messenger* were picked up and moved on the Associated Press wire. And I was hooked.

4   Two years later, as a sophomore in college, I decided I wanted to become a political journalist and figured experience in Washington would show me the ropes. I wrote a man I had never met, a United States senator named Lyndon Johnson, and asked him for a summer job. Lucky again, I got it. And at summer's end LBJ and Lady Bird offered me a job on their television station in Austin for $100 a week. Looking back on all that followed—seminary, the Peace Corps, the White House, *Newsday*, PBS, CBS and PBS again—I often think of what Joseph Lelyveld, the executive editor of the *New York Times*, told some aspiring young journalists. "You can never know how a life in journalism will turn out," he said.

5   It took me awhile after the White House to learn that what's important in journalism is not how close you are to power but how close you are to reality. Journalism took me there: to famine in Africa, war in Central America, into the complex world of inner-city families in Newark and to working-class families in Milwaukee struggling to survive the good times. My life in journalism has been a continuing course in adult education. From colleagues—from producers like Sherry Jones—I keep learning about journalism as storytelling. Sherry and I have been collaborating off and on for a quarter of a century, from the time we did the very first documentary ever about political action committees. I can still see the final scene in that film—yard after yard of computer printout listing campaign contributions unfurled like toilet paper stretching all the way across the Capitol grounds.

6   That one infuriated just about everyone, including friends of public television. PBS took the heat and didn't melt. When Sherry and I reported the truth

behind the news of the Iran/*contra* scandal for a *Frontline* documentary called "High Crimes and Misdemeanors," the right-wing Taliban in town went running to their ayatollahs in Congress, who decried the fact that public television was committing—horrors—journalism. The Clinton White House didn't like it a bit, either, when Sherry and I reported on Washington's Other Scandal, about the Democrats' unbridled and illegal fundraising of 1996.

7 If PBS didn't flinch, neither did my corporate underwriter for ten years now, Mutual of America Life Insurance Company. Before Mutual of America I had lost at least three corporate underwriters, who were happy as long as we didn't make anyone else unhappy. Losing your underwriting will keep the yellow light of caution flickering in a journalist's unconscious. I found myself—and I could kick myself for this—not even proposing controversial subjects to potential underwriters because I had told myself, convinced myself: "Nah, not a chance!" Then Mutual of America came along and the yellow light flickers no more. This confluence of good fortune and good colleagues has made it possible for us to do programs that the networks dare not contemplate.

8 Commercial television has changed since the days when I was hired as chief correspondent for CBS Reports, the documentary unit. A big part of the problem is ratings. It's not easy, as John Dewey said, to interest the public in the public interest. In fact, I'd say that apart from all the technology, the biggest change in my thirty years in broadcasting has been the shift of content from news about government to consumer-driven information and celebrity features. The Project for Excellence in Journalism conducted a study of the front pages of the *New York Times* and the *Los Angeles Times*, the nightly news programs of ABC, CBS and NBC, and *Time* and *Newsweek*. They found that from 1977 to 1997 the number of stories about government dropped from one in three to one in five, while the number of stories about celebrities rose from one in every fifty stories to one in every fourteen.

9 Does it matter? Well, as we learned in the 1960s but seem to have forgotten, government is about who wins and who loses in the vast bazaar of democracy. Government can send us to war, pick our pockets, slap us in jail, run a highway through our garden, look the other way as polluters do their dirty work, take care of the people who are already well cared for at the expense of those who can't afford lawyers, lobbyists or time to be vigilant. It matters who's pulling the strings. It also matters who defines the news and decides what to cover. It matters whether we're over at the Puffy Combs trial, checking out what Jennifer Lopez was wearing the night she ditched him, or whether we're on the Hill, seeing who's writing the new bankruptcy law, or overturning workplace safety rules, or buying back standards for allowable levels of arsenic in our drinking water.

10 I need to declare a bias here. It's true that I worked for two Democratic Presidents, John Kennedy and Lyndon Johnson. But I did so more for reasons of opportunity than ideology. My worldview was really shaped by Theodore Roosevelt, who got it right about power in America. Roosevelt thought the central fact of his era was that economic power had become so centralized and dominant it could chew up democracy and spit it out. The power of corporations, he

said, had to be balanced in the interest of the general public. Otherwise, America would undergo a class war, the rich would win it, and we wouldn't recognize our country anymore. Shades of déjà vu. Big money and big business, corporations and commerce, are again the undisputed overlords of politics and government. The White House, the Congress and, increasingly, the judiciary reflect their interests. We appear to have a government run by remote control from the US Chamber of Commerce, the National Association of Manufacturers and the American Petroleum Institute. To hell with everyone else.

11   What's the role of journalism in all this? The founders of our nation were pretty explicit on this point. The First Amendment is the first for a reason. It's needed to keep our leaders honest and to arm the powerless with the information they need to protect themselves against the tyranny of the powerful, whether that tyranny is political or commercial. At least that's my bias. A college student once asked the journalist Richard Reeves to define "real news." He answered: "The news you and I need to keep our freedoms." Senator John McCain echoed this in an interview I did with him a couple of years ago for a documentary called "Free Speech for Sale." It was about the Telecommunications Act of 1996, when some of America's most powerful corporations were picking the taxpayers' pocket of $70 billion. That's the estimated value of the digital spectrum that Congress was giving away to the big media giants.

12   Senator McCain said on the Senate floor during the debate, referring to the major media, "You will not see this story on any television or hear it on any radio broadcast because it directly affects them." And, in our interview, he added, "The average American does not know what digital spectrum is. They just don't know. But here in Washington their assets that they own were being given away, and the coverage was minuscule." Sure enough, the Telecommunications Act was introduced around May of 1995 and was finally passed in early February of 1996. During those nine months, the three major network news shows aired a sum total of only nineteen minutes on the legislation, and none of the nineteen minutes included a single mention of debate over whether the broadcasters should pay for use of the digital spectrum.

13   The Founders didn't count on the rise of mega-media. They didn't count on huge private corporations that would own not only the means of journalism but also vast swaths of the territory that journalism should be covering. According to a recent study done by the Pew Research Center for the People and the Press for the *Columbia Journalism Review,* more than a quarter of journalists polled said they had avoided pursuing some newsworthy stories that might conflict with the financial interests of their news organizations or advertisers. And many thought that complexity or lack of audience appeal causes newsworthy stories not to be pursued in the first place.

14   I don't mean to suggest there was a Gold Age of journalism. I told you earlier about covering the Housewives' Rebellion in Marshall, Texas, fifty years ago. What I didn't tell you is that it was the white housewives who made news with their boycotts of Social Security, not the domestic workers themselves. They were black; I wasn't sent to interview them, and it didn't occur to me that I should have. Marshall was 50 percent black, 50 percent white, and the

official view of reality was that only white people made news. I could kick myself for the half-blindness that has afflicted me through the years—from the times at the White House when I admonished journalists for going beyond the official view of reality in Vietnam to the times I have let the flickering yellow light turn red in my own mind on worthy journalistic projects.

15   I'm sure that growing up a Southerner and serving in the White House turned me into a fanatic—at least into a public nuisance—about what journalism should be doing in our democracy. In the South the truth about slavery was driven from our pulpits, our newsrooms and our classrooms, and it took the Civil War to bring the truth home. Then the truth about Jim Crow was censored, too, and it took another hundred years to produce the justice that should have followed Appomattox. In the White House we circled the wagons, grew intolerant of news that didn't comfort us and, if we could have, we would have declared illegal the sting of the bee. So I sympathize with my friends in commercial broadcasting who don't cover the ocean they're swimming in. But I don't envy them. Having all those resources—without the freedom to use them to do the kinds of stories that are begging to be done—seems to me more a curse than a blessing. It reminds me of Bruce Springsteen's great line, "It's like eating caviar and dirt."

16   But I am not here to hold myself up as some sort of beacon. I've made my own compromises and benefited from the special circumstances of my own good luck. But the fact that I have been so lucky shows that it can be done. All that is required is for journalists to act like journalists, and their sponsors—public or private—to back them up when the going gets a little rough. Because when you are dealing with powerful interests, be they in government or private industry, and bringing to light what has been hidden, the going does—inevitably—get a little rough.

17   Let me give you a couple of examples of what I mean—why the battle is never-ending: Some years ago my colleague Marty Koughan was looking into the subject of pesticides and food when he learned about a National Academy of Sciences study in progress on the effects of pesticide residuals on children. With David Fanning of *Frontline* as an ally, we set about a documentary. Four to six weeks before we were finished the industry somehow purloined a copy of our rough script—we still aren't certain how—and mounted a sophisticated and expensive campaign to discredit the documentary before it aired. They flooded television reviewers and the editorial pages of newspapers with propaganda. A *Washington Post* columnist took a dig at the broadcast on the morning of the day it aired—without even having seen it—and later admitted to me that the dig had been supplied to him by a top lobbyist in town. Some station managers were so unnerved that they protested the documentary with letters that had been prepared by industry. Several station managers later apologized to me for having been suckered.

18   Here's what most perplexed us: Eight days before the broadcast, the American Cancer Society—a fine organization that in no way figured in our story—sent to its 3,000 local chapters a "critique" of the unfinished documen-

tary claiming, wrongly, that it exaggerated the dangers of pesticides in food. We were puzzled: Why was the American Cancer Society taking the unusual step of criticizing a documentary that it hadn't seen, that hadn't aired and that didn't claim what the society alleged? An enterprising reporter in town named Sheila Kaplan later looked into this question for *Legal Times*, which headlined her story: "Porter/Novelli Plays All Sides." It turns out that the Porter/Novelli public relations firm, which has worked for several chemical companies, also did pro bono work for the American Cancer Society. Kaplan found that the firm was able to cash in some of the goodwill from that pro bono work to persuade the compliant communications staff at the society to distribute some harsh talking points about the documentary that had been supplied by, but not attributed to, Porter/Novelli.

19   Others used the society's good name to discredit the documentary, including the right-wing polemicist Reed Irvine. His screed against what he called "Junk Science on PBS" called on Congress to pull the plug on public broadcasting. PBS stood firm. The report aired, the journalism held up (in contrast to the disinformation about it) and the National Academy of Sciences was liberated to release the study that the industry had tried to cripple.

20   But there's always the next round. PBS broadcast our documentary on "Trade Secrets." It's a two-hour investigative special based on the chemical industry's own archives, on documents that make clear, in the industry's own words, what the industry didn't tell us about toxic chemicals, why they didn't tell us and why we still don't know what we have the right to know. These internal industry documents are a fact. They exist. They are not a matter of opinion or point of view. They state what the industry knew, when they knew it and what they decided to do.

21   The public policy implications of our broadcast are profound. We live today under a regulatory system designed by the industry itself. The truth is, if the public, media, independent scientists and government regulators had known what the industry knew about the health risks of its products—when the industry knew it—America's laws and regulations governing chemical manufacturing would be far more protective of human health than they are today. But the industry didn't want us to know. That's the message of the documents. That's the story.

22   The spokesman for the American Chemistry Council assured me that contrary to rumors, the chemical industry was not pressuring stations to reject the broadcast. I believed him; the controversy would only have increased the audience. But I wasn't sure for a while. The first person to contact us from the industry was a public relations firm here in Washington noted for hiring private detectives and former CIA, FBI and drug enforcement officers to do investigations for corporations. One of the founders of the company is on record as saying that sometimes corporations need to resort to unconventional resources, and some of those resources "include using deceit." No wonder Sherry and I kept looking over our shoulders. To complicate things, the single biggest recipient of campaign contributions from the chemical industry over the past

twenty years in the House has been the very member of Congress whose committee has responsibility for public broadcasting's appropriations. Now you know why we don't take public funds for reports like this!

23   For all the pressures, America, nonetheless, is a utopia for journalists. In many parts of the world assassins have learned that they can kill reporters with impunity; journalists are hunted down and murdered because of their reporting. Thirty-four in Colombia alone over the past decade. And here? Well, Don Hewitt of *60 Minutes* said to me recently that "the 1990s were a terrible time for journalism in this country but a wonderful time for journalists; we're living like [GE CEO] Jack Welch." Perhaps that's why we aren't asking tough questions of Jack Welch.

24   I don't want to claim too much for our craft, but I don't want to claim too little, either. The late Martha Gellhorn spent half a century observing war and politicians and journalists, too. By the end she had lost her faith that journalism could, by itself, change the world. But she had found a different sort of comfort. For journalists, she said, "victory and defeat are both passing moments. There is no end; there are only means. Journalism is a means, and I now think that the act of keeping the record straight is valuable in itself. Serious, careful, honest journalism is essential, not because it is a guiding light but because it is a form of honorable behavior, involving the reporter and the reader." And, one hopes, the viewer, too.

Endnote

Editors' Postscript: This article is adapted from Moyers's [2001] speech to the National Press Club on March 22, hosted by PBS to observe his thirtieth year as a broadcast journalist. The chemical industry's trade association did attempt to discredit the March 26 documentary, "Trade Secrets" (see "The *Times* v. Moyers," April 16), accusing Moyers and Jones of "journalistic malpractice" for inviting industry participation only during the last half-hour of the broadcast. Moyers replied that investigative journalism is not a collaboration between the journalist and the subject.

Reading Responses

1. Why does Moyers believe that journalism is so important for democracy? Where does he state this view?
2. How has news coverage shifted in recent years? What might be the consequences of that shift?
3. What pressures do journalists face? What are some of the possible consequences of these pressures?

Writing Activities

1. Explain in your own words the importance of being a public nuisance.
2. Write a brief analysis of the significance of several of the news stories that Moyers uses as examples.

3. Write an essay considering Moyers's closing quotation from Martha Gellhorn, defending the value of journalism as "a form of honorable behavior, involving the reporter and the reader" (paragraph 24).

Community Links

Consider Moyers's article, originally a speech, in relation to other speeches such as Mairson's commencement remarks (pp. 192–196) from the academic community, President Bush's address on September 20, 2001 (pp. 433–438), King's "I Have a Dream" speech (pp. 439–442), or the Kerry–Bond debate (pp. 495–503), all from the public community. Using several of these as examples, identify some ways in which speeches may differ from other written texts, especially in their approaches and appeals to readers.

Community Perspectives and Issues

FIVE BUILDING BLOCKS FOR SUCCESSFUL COMMUNITIES

Suzanne W. Morse

This selection is an essay from The Community of the Future, *edited by Frances Hesselbein, Marshall Goldsmith, Richard Beckhard, and Richard F. Schubert and sponsored by the Peter F. Drucker Foundation for Nonprofit Management. From her vantage point as a nonprofit director and former academic administrator, Morse outlines her building blocks—keys to strong, successful communities.*

1 A few years ago, while attending a midnight church service, I witnessed a lesson about community building that has stayed with me. During the finale of one of the most majestic songs of the season, there was a momentary break in the chorus, at which time a small but clear voice rang out, "E-I-E-I-O." The parents' mortification notwithstanding, the innocence of the child spoke volumes about inclusion and contributing what you know. Community building is a little like that. Despite the mounds of data and the mountains of reports, people most often act on what they know. The problem comes when the circumstances of that knowledge are unfamiliar or, in psychological terms, community cognitive dissonance occurs. The confusion comes when what we know doesn't work anymore and when the interrelationships of the issues before us require that we take different approaches and include different people. The challenge for the twenty-first-century community is to be realistic about changing circumstances and challenges, innovative about the responses, and bold about the action that is needed.

2 The term *community* has taken on a new meaning in the last several decades. No longer is it defined by geographic boundaries or ethnic background, as in "the Litchfield community" or "the Puerto Rican community." Rather, the evolution of community seems to be settling on two new nexuses: the community of *interests* and the community of *relationships*. When Alexis de Tocqueville visited the United States in the nineteenth century, he was impressed by the associational life of Americans but also by the common interests that bound them together, caused them to talk over the back fence on issues of mutual concern, and challenged them to think about community in terms of the common good. Then, as now, the future belongs to those who will have the processes, the public will, and the systems to work together. We know that boundaries, from city limit signs to fire districts, are no longer applicable or even practical. Our lives are entangled and interrelated so that suburbs are

extensions of central cities, rural areas meet metropolitan areas in close proximity, and small towns abut other small towns. Illustrations of overlap and interdependence come day after day and issue after issue. Try as we may, we cannot separate ourselves from each other. There are no gates high enough or walls thick enough.

3   Identifying our common interests and broadening our relationships will be the defining elements of twenty-first-century communities. Those who can develop thriving positive relations in, among, and beyond their boundaries will be the most successful economically, socially, and civically. Places that hold on to narrow definitions of community not only will suffer declines in population but will be impoverished by their lack of inclusion. As we examine communities around the world that have prospered and grown, certain elements in the way they define community provide keys to their success. Generally, these communities think more strategically and are less reactive. But more than that, they operate on a set of principles about community life that can be ascribed to and followed.

4   The framework for successful communities for the next century and beyond will have five key elements: mechanisms for deciding, organization of community work, accessible community life, creation of broad avenues for civic leadership, and action for the next generation. Each will independently cut across agencies, governments, and neighborhoods. Collectively, the five will interrelate in a synergistic way so that (1) communities consider long-term results, not just short-term expediency; (2) communities affirm that all citizens are critical to the overall success of the community and none are forgotten; and (3) communities recognize that stability and sustainability occur only when the vast majority of citizens have a stake in and contribute to the community. These five key success elements are not targeted to issues, but rather to outcomes. They provide the foundation for the way a community organizes itself and cares for all its people.

Mechanisms for Deciding

5   The successful community of the future will be one that has, by a process of dialogue and deliberation, discovered for itself the basic elements required to find common ground. This process will be like a version of the Greek *polis*, where people talk about the issues and strategies that affect their common futures. Perhaps the most important revelation about community for the late twentieth century is the interrelationship of issues and the systems that support them. Citizens and policymakers know that if solutions are to be found to society's most intractable problems, new ways of talking, deciding, and moving to action must be discovered. Whether the technique is based on technology, town meetings, or neighborhood discussion groups, the function of deciding together is critical for communities now and in the future.

6   The vehicles are less essential than the outcomes. The growing literature on social capital makes it clear that involving people in the decisions that affect their lives is not only good civic business but a critical way to build trust, relationships, and networks among citizens. The purpose of civic dialogue is to

move discussion from what "I" think to what "we" think. In this process of implementing collective ways to decide will be a growth and a stabilization of mediating or convening institutions in every community. These institutions will be charged with finding ways and opportunities to convene and to disseminate the community's business. The design, location, and structure of these convening institutions will be critical to the possibilities for community decision making.

Organization of Community Work

7 The potential of strong communities lies in their ability to design and implement systems at all levels and in all sectors that are less about form and more about the work to be done. The organization of the communities of the twenty-first century will look less like a pyramid and more like a series of interrelated circles. From local government to social systems, we will hardly recognize the community from its earlier forms. Social systems will focus on development and sufficiency, not prevention or subsidy. Local governments will be more like regional communities, relying on economies of scale, interrelationships of goods and services, and decentralized decision making to create engines in all sectors that produce goods and commodities, not just provide service delivery and infrastructure repairs. The structural changes in the way a community organizes its work will rely on its ability to be clear about its "big-picture" hopes and dreams and will depend on a series of large and small shifts in the design of its current systems. As Peter Senge explains in *The Fifth Discipline*, "Systems thinking shows that small, well-focused actions can sometimes produce significant enduring improvements, if they're in the right place" (pp. 63–64). Sustainable community change will depend on how people in these systems define and do their jobs from day to day, the expectations of the public, and the priorities about our common lives that we set together.

Accessible Community Life

8 The future stability and success of communities will depend on their creation of a community life that is accessible to everyone. All too often the conversation about access has stayed within the parameters of open meetings, transportation, and fair entrée. However, the access of the future has more to do with connecting people than it does with access to services or transportation. Communities must find ways to connect neighborhoods and the people within them not only to each other but also to the larger civic life. No longer is it acceptable for children who live in urban areas not to have seen a park or lake across town, for parents not to know about educational opportunities for their children, or for new citizens not to know about rights, responsibilities, and services. Successful civic experiments in the new century will give much attention and direction to finding avenues for engaging people in the complete life of a community. Transportation can help, but what is more important is an attitude about access. It is not a question of making something available to everyone, such as the art museum and public library; rather, it is having a strategy for ensuring access and use.

9   Accessibility will also mean inclusion. Successful communities will have both a place and a large enough space for the diverse races, beliefs, and ideas that make up our society. This access and inclusion goes far beyond acceptance to practices like dual translation, literacy and language programs, balanced media coverage, and a whole range of proactive measures that include rather than exclude—or, worse, ignore.

Creation of More Avenues for Leadership

10   Successful communities, even those with long traditions of organized community leadership, will continue to broaden the circles of leadership to create a system for the community that is neither centralized nor decentralized, but rather *polycentric*. The polycentric view of community leadership assumes that there are many centers of leadership that interrelate. No longer will all decisions be made "downtown" by a few people. Rather, the new system will operate on the premise that while action must ultimately be taken, appropriate vehicles for making decisions will exist on different levels, guided by a common vision held by the community. This notion of vision and polycentric leadership might play itself out in this way. A critical part of the vision for the community is quality, public education. The polycentric model looks at that vision and finds avenues for the community's many constituencies to work together on the most appropriate ways to contribute to that goal. No longer does responsibility rest with one group or one board. The tasks of deciding and acting are assumed by a wide range of people.

11   The solutions for society's ills and the promises of its opportunities, whether social, economic, or human, will not be created by a government-sponsored program, an outside intervention, or any single brand of political leadership. The severity of the problems and the enormous challenge of the opportunities in communities have forced citizens to ask themselves, What will work? and What can we do? These questions will be answered as channels and vehicles for civic leadership are expanded to allow civic work to be approached collaboratively through multiple efforts and multiple leaders.

Action for the Next Generation

12   Successful communities think as much about tomorrow as they do about today. The expediency of quick fixes and easy answers is bypassed to consider systematic causes and permanent solutions. These communities think more about development and less about deficits; they think in terms of all, not the few; and they know without question that the issues and opportunities facing them are interrelated. Yet with these caveats, they are able to act. They express this action for the next generation by creating and enforcing programs that protect the environment; by supporting school levies and bond issues; by investing in public transportation, public parks, and public recreation; by building health and safety nets for children; and, finally, by ensuring economic stability for all. Strong communities understand the importance of the prevention of pathologies, both social and physical, and structure their social service and health systems to support good health for everyone in the community.

13   In addition to physical and social health, communities that work will have economic health as a primary focus. The broad divisions of wealth and income will be not only acknowledged but addressed through work and educational programs, as well as through support systems like affordable housing, transportation, and child care, which are as important to performing and keeping a job as the skills themselves.

14   Critical to the actions of the next generation is a commitment to all children and all people. This point is no better illustrated than by a greeting used by Masai warriors in Africa: "How are the children?" The traditional response is, "*All* the children are well." Successful communities understand the power of this statement and take action to make it true.

Conclusion

15   These five building blocks for sustainable, working communities rest ultimately in the song we know. Decades of research and practice have shown us that the strongest communities build on assets, think strategically about the future and the issues that inform and shape it, create opportunities for citizens to connect and find areas of common interest, value the richness of diversity, and, ultimately, take action. None of this will be done quickly or easily. Rather, the road to building stronger communities will begin when communities design themselves and their processes for success and inclusion by relying on the tried-and-true songs while reaching to compose new ways of working together.

Reading Responses

1. How does Morse define *community*? What challenges does she believe that communities now face?
2. What are Morse's five building blocks? What, in Morse's view, can these building blocks help communities accomplish?
3. Why does Morse open her essay with the story of the child singing at church?

Writing Activities

1. Write an essay responding to Morse's definition of a successful community. You might want to propose another essential building block, expand or qualify one of her building blocks, provide examples of possible applications, or adapt her building blocks to the college campus.
2. If you are aware of an effective local or campus activity, consider how it implements one or several of Morse's building blocks. Explain how the activity operates, including whatever information a reader would need to understand how it helps to build community.
3. Write a persuasive essay, advocating the implementation of a change or an activity that you believe would strengthen your local or campus commu-

nity. Direct your essay to college students who might be apathetic, uninvolved, or doubtful of the benefits of your proposal. As persuasively as possible, explain what you advocate and how it would benefit readers.

Community Links

Compare and contrast Morse's "Five Building Blocks for Successful Communities" with Palmer's "The Quest for Community in Higher Education" (pp. 33–41) from the academic community, Ulrich's "Six Practices for Creating Communities of Value, Not Proximity" (pp. 221–227) from the work community, or one of the related readings from the public community such as Covey's "The Ideal Community" (pp. 390–395) or Zobel de Ayala's "Anticipating the Community of the Future" (pp. 405–411). Synthesize several of these readings, weaving together their definitions of community, as you develop your own definition.

TUNING IN TO THE WORLD OF NONPROFIT ORGANIZATIONS

Stan Hutton and Frances Phillips

◆

This reading is a selection from Nonprofit Kit for Dummies, *one of the popular "For Dummies" series noted for its straightforward explanations of all sorts of activities and topics. According to the authors, this book was written for people who are curious about or already involved with a nonprofit organization—perhaps organizing, directing, working for, contributing to, or sitting on the board of one. Hutton and Phillips draw on their own extensive experience with nonprofits, doing what they describe as engaging and challenging work that also implements their values. Much of their advice about fundraising or managing a nonprofit is designed to help readers improve their own organizations. Chapter 1, however, begins with the basics—what are nonprofit organizations, and what do they do? The answers to these questions help to define a major type of institution in the public community.*

1   It's morning in America. The radio alarm clicks on in your rural hometown. After tuning in to the weather, news, and livestock reports, you finish the kitchen chores while listening to an interview with a poet teaching at the small college in town. You hurry your two young kids away from *Sesame Street* and into the minivan for the regular a.m. run to the co-op preschool next to the volunteer fire station. Seeing the station reminds you to unload the bag of canned goods you bought for the county food drive. You drop the bag at the firehouse door and go take on the day.

Source: From *Nonprofit Kit for Dummies* by Stan Hutton and Frances Phillips. Copyright © 2001 by Wiley Publishing Inc. All rights reserved. Reproduced here by permission of the publisher. For Dummies is a registered trademark of Wiley Publishing, Inc.

2   It's morning in America. The radio alarm clicks on in your big-city hometown. After tuning in to the weather and stock market reports, you finish the kitchen chores while listening to a symphony recorded at the nearby concert hall. You drag your teenagers out of bed before leaving the apartment, reminding them that you'll pick them up tonight at the youth center. You hurry down the street to the subway, grab a newspaper, and notice that the city's largest hospital has a headline—a staff physician is getting results with a startling new treatment. You read about it on the train as you head to work.

3   Both of these mornings are filled with nonprofit organizations. The small town offers public radio and television, *Sesame Street*, a private college, a volunteer-run preschool, and a community food bank. The city scene includes public radio, a symphony orchestra, a youth club, and a hospital. Behind those layers of nonprofit organizations is another layer: the small press publisher and distributor of the poet's latest book, the medical school where the physician was educated, the economic think tank that analyzes stocks and commodities, and the agency providing emergency preparedness training to volunteer firefighters.

4   The nonprofit sector is not a distinct place, not some plaza or district that you'll come upon suddenly as you weave your way through your day. It's more like a thread of a common color that's laced throughout the economy and our lives. You'll find it and its influence no matter where you are—from the wilderness to the metropolis.

So, What's a Nonprofit Organization?

5   People hear the term *nonprofit organization* and picture Mother Hubbard's cupboard, as in awfully bare or zero bank balance. In fact, some nonprofit organizations turn very tidy profits on their operations, and that's good, because cash flow keeps an enterprise humming, whether it's a for-profit business or not.

6   The main financial difference between a for-profit and a not-for-profit enterprise is what happens to the profit. In a for-profit company like Ford or Microsoft or Disney or your favorite fast-food establishment, profits are paid to the owners, including shareholders. But a nonprofit can't do that. Any profit remaining after the bills are paid has to be plowed back into the organization's service program. So profit can't be distributed to individuals, such as the organization's board of directors, who are volunteers in every sense of the word.

7   What about shareholders—do nonprofits have any shareholders to pay off? Not in terms of a monetary payoff, like a stock dividend. But in a broad, service sense, nonprofits do have "shareholders." They are the people who benefit from the nonprofit's activities, like the people who tune in to public radio and TV or receive free food through the county food program.

8   Understanding the nonprofit sector is easier if you understand the characteristics of nonprofit organizations. They are

- Private (separate from government)
- Organizations (privately incorporated)
- Self-governing (controlling their own activities)

- Voluntary (overseen—at least in part—by volunteers and benefiting from the work and contributions of volunteers)
- Not distributing profits to their owners (nonprofits have no owners, but are overseen by volunteer board members)
- For public benefit (serving a public purpose and contributing to the public good)

9   What's sometimes confusing is that organizations doing the same kind of work as nonprofits may be *for*-profit organizations. For example, the majority of radio and television stations are profit-making enterprises. So are most publishing establishments. Some theaters and concert halls are nonprofit, and some are for-profit. And then you have an entirely different kind of organization—*government*-run schools, youth agencies, colleges, and medical facilities. They're not part of the nonprofit sector.

10 Neither is that charming little store on the corner where you pick up bread and milk. It may contribute to your family's welfare, but if it was created to earn a profit for the owners, it's not a nonprofit organization—even if it's losing money! Its status depends on its intent, how it's organized, and whether it includes volunteers.

Introducing the One and Only 501 (c)(3)

11 When we use the term *nonprofit organization* in this book, for the most part, we're talking about an organization that the Internal Revenue Service has classified as a 501(c)(3). If that term is new to you, add it to your vocabulary with pride. In no time, "five-oh-one-see-three" will roll off your tongue as if you're a nonprofit expert. There *are* other kinds of nonprofit organizations, formed to benefit their members, to influence legislation, or to fulfill other purposes. They receive exemption from federal income taxes and sometimes relief from property taxes at the local level. (Chapter 2 discusses these organizations in greater detail.)

12 Nonprofit organizations classified as 501(c)(3) receive extra privileges under the law. They are, with minor exceptions, the only group of tax-exempt organizations that can receive tax-deductible contributions from individuals and organizations.

13 Being a nonprofit organization does not mean that an entity is exempt from paying all taxes. Nonprofit organizations pay employment taxes just like for-profit businesses do. In some states, but not all, nonprofits are exempt from paying sales tax, so be sure that you're familiar with your local laws.

14 Charitable organizations have to be careful about *lobbying*—stating their positions on specific legislation to legislators and supporting or opposing candidates running for election. It's okay for them to let the public know how a piece of legislation might affect the cause their organization supports, but it becomes lobbying when they ask supporters to contact their legislators about it. Lobbying is not completely forbidden, but 501(c)(3) organizations have to report on their IRS tax forms how much they spend on the activity. They must demonstrate that no substantial part of their revenues went to lobbying.

15   A close relative of the 501(c)(3)—a kind of nonprofit cousin—is the 501(c)(4), or social welfare organization. A 501(c)(4) is not restricted from lobbying and may engage in some political campaign activity, but it may not receive tax-deductible contributions. [. . .]

16   You might say that the nonprofit sector is the part of a nation's economy that's composed of all these public-serving nonprofit organizations and defined by tax codes. But the sector is more elusive than that. Nonprofit voluntary groups were formed in the United States in colonial times, before they were sanctioned by or benefiting from any kind of formal, legal status. In fact, one reason that the sector is so varied and vibrant in the United States is that ways of providing assistance to those in need were needed in the colonies before the government was formed or mature. And nonprofit activities continue to crop up informally all over the world when an idea or need arises.

17   Some complain that the nonprofit sector is made up of a lot of old-fashioned do-gooders or a bunch of liberals, that it benefits only the poor, and that only the rich volunteer. But none of these generalizations is true: The sector reaches beyond political and religious affiliations, and its influence is felt throughout all classes in society.

A sector by any other name

Not everyone thinks that *nonprofit sector* is the best term. That's because there's an array of organizations with different kinds of nonprofit status. Some of these organizations are formed to benefit their members—like fraternities and labor unions—and do not share a broad public-serving intent. Alternative terms that may be used include the following:

- Voluntary sector: This term emphasizes the presence of volunteer board members and the significance of voluntary contributions and services to the work of 501(c)(3)–type organizations. In this definition, it's not the organizations alone that represent the meaning of *nonprofit*, but the vast web of their supporters who participate as volunteers and donors.
- Independent sector: This term emphasizes the public-serving mission of these organizations and their volunteers and their independence from government. (Independent Sector is also the name of a nonprofit organization that sponsors research, publications, and public programs about the sector. You can find it at *www.indepsec.org*.)
- Charitable sector: This term emphasizes the donations these organizations receive from individuals and institutions.
- Third sector: This term emphasizes the organization's important role alongside government and the for-profit business economy.

We're going to use the term *nonprofit* sector throughout this book, but we want you to understand its limitations and be familiar with other commonly used terms.

Sometimes it's easiest to remember what a nonprofit *is* by recognizing what it *isn't:*

- It isn't a government agency with a mandate to serve all citizens with equity and the ability to collect taxes to implement programs.
- It isn't a for-profit business whose purpose is to return profits to its owners by creating and selling products or services.

Getting Inspired

18 The nonprofit sector is exciting and inspiring. It encourages individuals with ideas about solving social problems or enhancing arts, culture, the environment, or education to act on those ideas. It creates a viable place within our society and economy for worthy activities that have little chance of commercial success. We think that it combines the best of the business world with the best of government, bringing together creativity, zeal, and problem solving from the business side with a call to public service from the government side.

19 We also find volunteerism inspiring. Everyone has heard stories of tightly knit communities where neighbors gather to rebuild a barn. That spirit of pitching in to help is the best part of the essence of a community in which values and ideas are shared.

20 Many people live in communities that contain people from a wide variety of backgrounds. The nonprofit sector provides an array of institutions in which all people can come together, with both those who resemble them and others who are unlike them, to work toward the common good. Volunteerism enables everyone to pitch in to rebuild "the barn" in a wide variety of contexts.

21 Some compare the role of the nonprofit sector to the ancient practice of maintaining a *commons*—an area of land between farms and villages that was shared and maintained by and for the benefit of an entire community. The commons was a place to turn when one needed a passageway, one's own fields were overgrazed, or one's house burned.

22 So the nonprofit sector provides common ground for creative, sometimes small-scale, often labor-intensive, and yet innovative approaches to solving problems and enhancing quality of life.

Bigger than a Breadbox

23 The nonprofit sector is larger than many people realize. Here are some facts and figures from the National Center on Charitable Statistics about U.S. nonprofits' size and scope in 1999:

- Their annual budgets combined total more than $700 billion.
- They contribute 8 percent to the country's gross domestic product, or GDP. That percentage has been growing since the 1960s, when they represented 3.6 percent of the GDP.

- They employ 10.2 million people as full-time or part-time workers, and their employees represent 11 percent of the entire workforce of the United States.
- In the United States, 93 million people volunteer 20.3 billion hours in total time helping nonprofits. The value of that contributed time and effort is more than $200 billion.
- Many nonprofit organizations are very small—only one-third have annual revenues of $25,000 or more.

24 One distinctive feature of the nonprofit sector is its dependency on contributions. We devote many pages of this book—most of Part III—to advice about getting contributions.

25 Gifts from individuals of money, goods, services, and property make up the largest portion of that voluntary support. This is also the oldest part of the voluntary tradition in the United States and goes back to colonial times. Since the late 19th century, private philanthropic foundations have emerged as another major source of support, and in the 20th century—particularly after World War II—the federal government and corporations became important income sources. Many nonprofits also sell some kind of service, and a trend in the sector shows earned income becoming a larger portion of total revenues.

26 Tables 1–1 and 1–2 give you a quick picture of nonprofit revenue sources. Over the past 30 years, private contributions (18.9 percent) have come to represent a smaller portion of overall revenue for nonprofits as the portions derived from government (31.7 percent) and revenues from service fees (38.6 percent) have increased.

Table 1–1   Nonprofit Funding in the United States: 1996

Source of Income	Percentage of Total Income
Dues, fees, and charges	38.6%
Government	31.7%
Private contributions	18.9%
Other revenues	10.8%

Source: America's Nonprofit Sector in Brief

Table 1–2   Sources of Private Contributions: 1999

Source of Income	Amount of Total Giving	Percentage of Total Giving
Individuals	$143.71 billion	75.6%
Foundations	$19.81 billion	10.4%
Bequests	$15.61 billion	8.2%
Corporations	$11.02 billion	5.8%
Total	$[190.15] billion	100%

Source: America's Nonprofit Sector in Brief

27 Among private, nongovernmental sources of support (the 18.9 percent item in Table 1–1), gifts from living individuals—as opposed to bequests from people who have died—have always represented the largest portion of total giving, but philanthropic giving by foundations and corporations has been growing. Table 1–2 outlines sources of private contributions in 1999.

Reading Responses

1. What strategies do the authors use to define a nonprofit organization?
2. What needs and concerns of readers might Hutton and Phillips hope to address through their various definitions of nonprofits?
3. What are the functions of Tables 1–1 and 1–2? What do they tell readers? How might readers apply this information?

Writing Activities

1. In your own words, write a brief definition of a nonprofit organization. Instead of addressing a prospective nonprofit organizer or director, address a volunteer—someone who is willing to get involved but wants to know what kind of organization he or she will be helping out.
2. Suppose that you have volunteered to help a local nonprofit group currently planning its first fund-raising effort. This new organization wants to build a strong community base, not just get one big grant. Using the information in Tables 1–1 and 1–2, write a proposal explaining your general fund-raising recommendations to the group. What people should the group members contact? What should they seek—contributions, dues, purchases, volunteers, or other types of support? Where might they find the support that they want? (Feel free to identify the group's mission and add any appropriate details about its community.)
3. Write a guide for new students on your campus, introducing some of the nonprofit organizations involved with students or campus life at your school. (You may need to do some research about the organizations that are involved on campus, offer specific services to students, sponsor service-learning projects, or encourage student volunteers or interns. If you cannot locate many organizations, write a report that identifies the nonprofit organizations that you wish were active on your campus.)

Community Links

Compare and contrast Hutton and Phillips's methods of defining with those used in other readings. Select one or two other readings that supply substantial definitions. (See the Guide to Themes, Topics, and Rhetorical Strategies.) Consider the various methods of definition used in these readings. In what ways do particular forms of definition appeal to readers' needs or expectations?

A Beginning
Jill Nelson

◆

Jill Nelson is the author of Straight, No Chaser: How I Became a Grown-Up Black Woman. *In the book's introduction, Nelson explains that she wrote the book to connect with other black women—to create change through common bonds. She sees one culture dying and another emerging. Not surprisingly, she finds that such change may create uncertainty, tension, blame, and anger—and the opportunity for black women to speak up and advance the coming transformation. The selection here, "A Beginning," is the final chapter in her book.*

1. I used to hate the day when report cards came, not because my grades were low but because even when I got A's and B's, in the space for comments my teachers would inevitably write, "Jill is not living up to her potential." In a weird way, I wanted to be either without potential or a kid who got all C's and next to them the teacher scrawled, "Good work!" It is not until I am grown that I understand this classmate does not exist, that if there is one thing we all share it is the potential to do better, reach more distant goals. Even knowing this, old habits die hard.

2. It is only recently that I have been able to admit to myself that even though I never liked dolls and have known for a very long time that for the most part I exist outside the culture, some secret part of me still thought I had a shot at being Barbie. Not literally. I'm long past coveting hair, or skinniness, or rock-hard perky breasts, and I never wanted to be white. Still, I thought it was possible to be independent, outspoken, and adversarial most of the time, and then when it was convenient switch over into being none of these things, become a pretty, silent airhead, spiffily dressed, strolling hand in hand with my Afro Ken. Now I know that this is not possible, that once on the road to self-definition, voice, and visibility, there are detours, but no turning back, no way to pretend I do not know, feel, and see myself and what is around me. This is the price I pay for no longer feeling alone, or invisible, or crazy. I still have occasional pungent moments of wanting to tune out, front myself off, moments of Barbie yearning. The good news is that as time goes on these moments are fewer.

3. What is constantly on my mind is how I learn more about what it does, can, and should mean to be a grown-up black woman, not just for myself, but for my sisters, brothers, and everyone else. I am convinced that black women can and must be a powerful voice in the local, national, and international dialogue, that we are a crucial part of transforming the culture into one that is safe for all of us. Once we know what the problems and challenges are, the question is how most effectively to take action.

4. The work that we have to do is both internal and external. What bothers me about many of the self-help, spiritual uplift, know thyself, meditation books on the market, books that are extremely successful and marketed specifically to women, is that more often than not they suggest that the work to be

done is solely or largely internal, as if the problems that confront women are primarily self-created. Too often, the subtext of these books is "Get yourself together and everything will be all right." Nothing could be further from the truth. You can read spiritual adages, meditate, and work on yourself twenty-two hours a day, but during those two hours when you have to go outside and interact with others you will inevitably be bombarded by the values and violence of the society in which we live. It's crucial to be clear that the work is both internal and external. The challenge is to get ourselves together and simultaneously engage in external activism. The time that we spend overtly engaged in the internal work of knowing and improving ourselves serves to fuel and drive our engagement with the external world of community, work, and the nation. At the same time, the external work we do tests, expands, and puts into action the things we learn and believe.

5   Most important is that as black women we get actively involved, both with ourselves and the world outside ourselves, declare ourselves important players. What follows are some suggestions for how to get started that work for me. If you don't relate to them, cool. Create your own. The thing not to do is nothing. That's the same as erasing yourself.

6   1. Schedule time to spend with yourself. In this way you declare yourself important, place yourself at the center. If you don't, why should anyone else? I exercise an hour a day. That hour swimming, running, or lifting weights is a meditative time for me. I spend it thinking about everything and nothing, but every day I feel smarter, calmer, and clearer. This isn't a workout book, and I'm not pushing exercise. It doesn't matter what you do. Meditate, sit in your favorite chair, pray, take a walk, listen to music, as long as you make time for yourself.

7   2. Learn how to look at culture critically. We're all raised to be cultural consumers and absorb what's around us passively, like sponges. This makes many black women feel inadequate, enraged, or crazy. Make the effort to see independent films, read history, criticism, nonfiction, and get information from outside mainstream media. The proliferation of black women's book clubs, in which groups of women meet regularly—usually in someone's apartment with a potluck dinner—to discuss books they've read, is another good route. So are lectures and seminars in schools, churches, and community-based organizations that are usually free, open to the public, and encourage discussion.

8   Understand that the personal is political, the political personal. When you watch television, flip through a magazine, see a movie or an art exhibit, don't fool yourself that you're simply being passively entertained. Ask yourself questions. Some of mine are: How were black women and black people portrayed? What was presented as "normal" and what as "abnormal"? What was the political agenda? Do I feel dissed and assaulted or challenged and affirmed by the work? Talk back to those who portray us negatively. Don't take misrepresentation passively.

9   3. Make time to spend with a group of black women where you talk about yourselves, and not in terms of anyone else. Think about how much time women spend talking about men, or children, or the job, and how little we talk

about ourselves and each other, who we are and who we'd like to be. The first step to sisterhood and forming a collective identity as black women is to talk honestly about and amongst ourselves.

4. Learn about feminism. We've all been manipulated and scared off by the word, but get over it. The simple definition of feminism is the theory of the political, economic, and social equality of the sexes. Period. Hard to argue with that. If you have a problem with the word, find another one. The important thing is to believe and act in ways that support your right to equality. Read the work of black women writers on the subject.

5. Get involved in your local community. We've become so alienated from each other that we have lost the basis of what community is, individuals interacting with each other for the betterment of all. I know we're all busy as hell, but on the real side we manage to find time to run our mouths on the telephone, stare at bad television, or be depressed, time that could be better spent building community. The knowledge that you are powerful and can effect change grows out of involvement with your community. Volunteer at a community-based organization, religious institution, or community center. Join the food co-op, tutor students, coach sports, help the elderly, organize your neighbors for street beautification, crime watch, plant a community garden.

6. Speak. Or at least nod. One of the nicest things about the 1960s and early 1970s was that black people made eye contact, said good morning, spoke to one another. Nowadays, meeting someone's eye is seen as a threat. Speaking is a way of acknowledging all of our visibility. It serves to reaffirm our connection as women, men, a people, and humans. That connection is what community is about. Speak to white folks. They need it, too. Home training, as we all know, comes through black women.

7. Think about politics from a self-interested perspective. Then do something. Bad as the political scene is, it's dangerous denial to pretend it doesn't affect all of our lives. From the current move by Christian fundamentalists to take over local school boards across America, to the control of the House and Senate by the right, to the increasingly backward decisions of the Supreme Court, to the national increase of violence against women, we're all affected. Whatever your party or personal politics, whether you participate in elections or your agenda is the establishment of an independent black homeland, do something. If you don't, you're not cool, a superior jaded intellectual, or in the vanguard, you're a victim.

8. Ask for, and offer, help. Forget the super-black-woman-who-can-do-everything-including-squat-in-the-field-birth-a-baby-and-keep-on-pickin'-dat-cotton stereotype. Knowing you need help and asking for it is the first step in solving problems. So is recognizing that other women need support and offering it. Assistance can range from something as simple as taking a friend's children for a day before she has a niggerbitchfit on them, to volunteering for a local candidate, to going on the Internet to ask a nation of wired black women for support and counsel, to asking a friend to refer you to a therapist. Reach out instead of doing what we usually do when we need help, which is to deny it and do even more until we go into crisis and collapse.

9. Don't compare yourself out. Don't look around for sisters you can feel superior to, then use them to make yourself feel better and justify remaining

exactly where you are. Women in search of visibility, voice, and a place at the table are linked, whatever our age, class, physical attributes, job, color, or geographical location. We need to remember this and approach each other with love, acceptance, and active support. This is an important step in creating a collective consciousness.

16   10. Recognize, understand, and put your rage to use. Take that negative, internalized niggerbitchfit and use it to work toward positive internal and external change. Imagine how powerful we would be, what we could accomplish, if black women across the country were communicating and organizing. Reach out to black women where you find them.

17   Sisters! Come out, come out! Wherever you are.

Reading Responses

1. What is Nelson's purpose as a writer? What does she want to achieve?
2. How does Nelson relate internal and external change? Why are both so important to her?
3. How does Nelson appeal to her specific readers? How does she acknowledge their likely assumptions and possible responses? How does she try to counter their possible reservations?

Writing Activities

1. In your journal, in a computer file, or in your notebook, write your response as a reader to Nelson's chapter.
2. Write an explanation of the title of this selection. Consider why Nelson calls her last chapter "A Beginning."
3. Write your own list of suggestions for active involvement. Direct your list to the specific interests of a group that you define—people of a certain age, with a particular cultural or ethnic background, at the same stage in life, in the same social group, on the same team, in the same dorm, at the same crowded store, or in the same parking line before eight o'clock classes. Carefully consider the assumptions, possible responses, and possible reservations of the members of this group. Address these considerations as you identify and explain your suggestions about what members of this group might do to improve a common situation.

Community Links

Compare or contrast Nelson's chapter with other selections that advocate and advise such as Vermette's letter to his son (pp. 96–100) from the academic community, Walton's "Ten Rules That Worked for Me" (pp. 216–219) from the work community, or another selection from the public community. Using the readings that you select as examples, consider either how writers can motivate readers or how readers can absorb and apply advice from writers. Either way, examine the expectations of both writers and readers.

THE IDEAL COMMUNITY
Stephen R. Covey

◆

Sponsored by the Peter F. Drucker Foundation for Nonprofit Management, The Community of the Future *is a collection of essays edited by Frances Hesselbein, Marshall Goldsmith, Richard Beckhard, and Richard F. Schubert. This selection is written by Stephen Covey, the well-known author of* The Seven Habits of Highly Effective People *and* The Seven Habits of Highly Effective Families. *Here, he turns his attention to the human need for connections to others, for an ideal community.*

1   In real estate, the key to success is location, location, location. In the world at large, the key is connections, connections, connections. The survival and success of every enterprise will be based upon stakeholder relationships—on human and electronic connections to a much broader community.

Creating Connections

2   Every leader is trying to create a type of Camelot, an ideal community—ideal, at least, in light of its reason for being—meaning that the organization is ideally structured, staffed, positioned, managed, and operated relative to its mission. Of course, we never quite achieve the ideal, but within our circles of influence—our own families, teams, companies, agencies, and communities—we can achieve an approximation of the ideal. And in most societies, even highly competitive markets, approximations are "good enough." Our success is rarely measured by an absolute standard of perfection; rather, it is judged relative to the competition and to other options available to our customers. In truth, most of us—individually and collectively—are only as good as we have to be to compete or cope comfortably.

3   This much I know: we will move further faster toward our ideal community if we start making connections with the causes and resources that are already aligned with our personal mission. Why? In a world so "fragmented and segmented," as Peter Senge says, into teams, causes, countries, and companies, the key to success becomes connections, both within one's own community and, through meaningful outreach, into broader communities.

4   So, what's a person to do? Here are a few options to consider.

Source: Covey, Stephen R. "The Ideal Community." Reprinted with permission by Franklin Covey Co. All rights reserved.

Join a Cause

5   Now, I must confess, I'm not what you would call a "joiner" of every cause that comes along. But I recently joined the Points of Light Foundation, a bipartisan effort to make a difference in our country and communities. One of the inspirational founders of this organization was George Romney, former automobile executive and governor of Michigan. President Bill Clinton hosted its recent "presidential summit" along with the four living former U.S. presidents, President Reagan being represented by his wife, Nancy. Colin Powell is the chairperson.

6   A few months before he died, Romney held a meeting wherein he expressed his disgust with certain church and educational institutions for not stepping up to the plate in training their membership and students to get more involved in solving the social problems of this country. He thought that churches, generally, are doing a better job than universities in this regard; in fact, he felt that many universities are abdicating their social responsibility. He was passionate. And at the end of the meeting, he turned to me as if passing a baton and said, "Stephen, you've got to help carry on this work." That's why I joined the Points of Light Foundation. But it's also why you should join, or otherwise pledge to start, some "points of light" cause to make a difference in your community of choice.

Be a Volunteer

7   Every person has a chance to be influential and make a difference in the world by being a volunteer. You can start small, on a local level. But you can greatly magnify your influence if you have or join an organization, or if you work from the top by getting the president to promote the ethic: "Everybody is a volunteer in this organization. Everyone has some stewardship or personal responsibility to improve our community."

8   Because of media attention and many other factors, people often get a distorted image of the depth and breadth of social problems and perceive these problems as the dominant force of our society. In truth, the dominant force of our society is the *goodness* in the overwhelming majority of the people. Our country does more volunteer work than any country in the world, by far. We are volunteering. But we need to step up our pace, to lengthen our stride, and to look for ways to leverage our influence—not with the motive of becoming "rich and famous," but to benefit and bless many others more effectively.

Tithe Your Time

9   One good way to lengthen your stride and leverage yourself is to tithe your time in community service. I'm trying to live this simple principle of tithing my time—and what a difference it has made in my life, in my family, in our company, and in our stakeholder communities. I consider a tenth of my time as a minimum contribution. A tenth is an equal measure for every member. Once the practice becomes a norm in the culture, every person in the community will have a sense of stewardship and look for ways to reach out in solving our social problems. I also learned from George Romney that social problems lead to

economic problems, political problems, and health problems, and they can best be dealt with through individual volunteerism. Business is not well equipped to deal with them. Neither is government; in fact, well-intended government programs often make the situation worse. Only the nonprofit sector and the so-called third domain are well equipped to deal with social problems.

10   Some seventy-five years ago, John Fletcher Moulton, a noted English judge, talked about the three domains of human action. The first is the domain of law, where our actions are prescribed by laws binding upon us; the second is the domain of free choice, those areas where we enjoy complete freedom or personal preference; and, in between, Lord Moulton identified the domain of "obedience to the unenforceable." While this domain may include moral duty, social responsibility, and proper behavior, it extends beyond them to cover "all cases of doing right where no one can make you do it but yourself." It's the domain in which individuals, out of their own minds and hearts, volunteer to carry on some cause.

11   I suggest that in strong communities, all members have a very real sense of stewardship and practice the principle of tithing their time as a minimum contribution. All community members receive the call to volunteer service, based on what *they* sense the need to be. The service need not be mandated, dictated, generalized, or federalized.

Adopt a Cause

12 Many worthwhile causes are like children who need a good home. In effect, they are "up for adoption." You might adopt some good cause as part of your individual and family mission statement. You can leverage yourself further in this cause by involving your friends and family and by making a core contribution in one or more of four areas: living (the economic area), loving (the emotional and social area), learning (the mental and intellectual area), and leaving a legacy (the spiritual area).

13   For example, I recently attended a conference for high school principals. The secretary of education spoke just before I did, and at the end of his speech he pleaded with the forty-five hundred principals in attendance to build connections and relationships with businesses in the private sector. Soon after, I attended the international conference of the Young Presidents Organization (YPO) in Argentina. There the plea given to YPO members and corporate executives was "Adopt schools and school systems." One presenter recommended not adopting schools at risk, but adopting the best schools to create model learning environments.

14   I find it interesting that leaders in both the public and private sectors are pleading with their members to make connections and build relationships with each other. They know, from experience, the value of cross-community bridge building.

Meld Theory and Application

15 The research done by one YPO presenter shows that America is ahead in education from the point of view of preparing people for more education, but not for life. In preparing people for application, we're in the middle, behind both

Europe and Asia. Part of the problem is the pattern of arrogance in American education—the attitude that "we don't get involved in application because we're into theory."

16 Of course, all application is based on theory, and so the ability to apply what you learn is really a superior level of intelligence. The few fields where North America still leads the world include medicine, dentistry, engineering, and executive development programs, only because in those fields we care so much about application. But in all other areas, applied science is not highly valued, and so we're falling further and further behind. Thus, the plea at the YPO conference was "Adopt schools so that you can help students to see the application of what they're learning and so that there is a connection between the theory and the practice."

Common Elements of the Ideal Community

17 What are some elements of the ideal community? If you embrace the Thomas Jefferson notion of the "practical idealist," you won't be guilty of King Arthur's mistake of having more vision and idealism than practical application. If you have practical idealism, you will have a sense of how to get from here to there, from where you are in current reality to where you can imagine yourself to be at some point in the future.

18 What are some elements of the ideal community of the future? I suggest that four apply equally to any ideal community.

19 1. *One standard: principle-centered goodness.* People seek to live in righteousness, to live by principles with respect for law and order. There is shared trust because of trustworthiness. It's a community of open doors and few locks. Honesty is prized; lying, cheating, and stealing are punished. People willingly adhere to natural laws and correct principles, knowing that lasting solutions to the very real social problems we face will be based on the principles of a shared vision and a synergistic approach.

20 2. *One heart: vision and direction.* People in this community place great value on being of one heart—on true obedience, not conformity. They recognize their interdependency. They know that business carries an enormous burden in modern society and that if the social environment is not conducive to business, the economy will suffer. They know that social problems don't stop at the employment door: problems of the community carry over into business. Members acknowledge the interdependency not only between business and the community but also between the profit and nonprofit sectors. They use the key to success—connections, connections, connections—to build infrastructure in every area of our society, including government, business, industry, education, and nonprofit entities. They realize that each segment of society has to achieve a certain level of independence before it can reach out and become interdependent; the private victory precedes the public victory.

21 3. *One mind: purpose, mission, and unity, not uniformity; oneness, not sameness.* There is a community mission statement. Everyone is involved in developing it over a period of time, so that an ethic and a norm grow around it. It says, "In this community, we care about each other, and so our approach to

problem solving is synergistic, not adversarial. We have forums for open communication, dialogue, and synergy." People value differences, even see them as strengths. They seek first to understand, sincerely, without an intent to manipulate others for personal gain or to close a sale.

22   4. *Economic equality: no poor among them.* The principle is that *healthy, wealthy communities help sick, poor communities.* At a Fortune 500 conference held in San Francisco, the topic for the morning session was "How are you going to stay at the top of your craft so you are there in five years?" Participants were divided into two groups and asked to address the question. In one group, someone accidentally started talking about what his company was doing to help the community. He reported that they couldn't hire people who were literate. Job applicants didn't know how to read. They didn't know how to solve problems. When he opened up this topic, the whole focus of the conference shifted, because there was so much energy behind it; it was so compelling that it eclipsed the other topic.

23   Some of the sponsors of the conference later observed that they had never seen so much human energy released at a business conference. These were very caring executives, not greedy capitalists who were trying to squeeze the community and kill the goose that lays their golden eggs. They cared about the goose—the environment, the children, safety on the streets. They well understood how social problems are deepening to the point where they may discombobulate our society. That's what they cared about. All they wanted to talk about was what they were doing in their communities.

Working Examples

24 No community is perfect; therefore, no model is perfect, but many serve as work-in-progress examples of the community of the future. Let me briefly mention four here that merit attention.

Mauritius

25 There are few communities in which the entire population is involved in a massive interdependent and significant effort. One is Mauritius, a tiny island nation off the east coast of Africa, where the norm for the 1.3 million people who live there is to work together to take care of the children. Everyone takes responsibility for these children. The community works to improve training for people in marketable skills, so there is no unemployment or homelessness. They have no poor, no crime, no unemployment. They have 100 percent employment and 98 percent literacy, which puts them ahead of the top fifteen industrial nations. The nation includes people from five distinct cultures—people who value differences so highly that they even celebrate one another's religious holidays. They are a Third World, poor country, trying to move into the First World. But socially, they are way ahead of us. The police officers don't even carry guns. Their deeply integrated interdependence reflects their values of order, harmony, cooperation, synergy, and respect for all people, particularly children.

The Oneida Indian Nation

26 This sovereign nation that surrounds Green Bay, Wisconsin, has engaged in a project of individual and community transformation through a principle-centered revitalization program. The Oneida are distinguished by their progressive use of revenues to reconnect the community to native traditions and principles. For example, the tribe allotted sixteen million dollars to construct an elementary school in the shape of a turtle; it is an impressive monument to the tribe's determination to reintegrate traditional values into tribal life. The turtle figure is found prominently in the Oneida creation myth and is an icon or symbol in Native American tradition. Many classrooms are devoted to teaching the Oneida language and culture. Their motto is "Seven habits for seven generations." They could not be accused of thinking only of the short term.

Kauai, Hawaii

27 Kauai launched a principle-centered community program to build its economy, families, and community. The program began when twenty-five local facilitators from a cross-section of the community were trained and then, in turn, each trained 120 local residents. The process will take about two years. At the end of that time, at least three thousand people should be practicing the principle-centered approach. Mayor Maryanne Kusaka stated, "It's no good if government does a great job at managing internal affairs; in fact, it's counterproductive if we hit stone walls in the community. We need to have everyone committed to the same way of life to improve the quality of life."

Columbus, Indiana

28 In an age of malaise, cynicism, and whiners, Columbus, Indiana, became the first U.S. community to adopt a principle-centered development program. More than three thousand of the thirty-five thousand residents received training. Reportedly, people are happier and more positive at work and at home. They set more goals and take responsibility for their actions and for communicating more effectively. One citizen, Anne Courtney, notes, "What is common sense is not necessarily common practice. I know what I want to do and I try to live consistent with that vision, but in the past I'd often fall off the wagon. Now, because of the discipline, when I'm dealing with the moment of truth, I stop and think, 'What is the right thing to do?' I know I've done a lot more apologizing." The program helps people to get a better sense of who they are, to strip away the titles and facades, and to interact more easily and honestly with others. In some cases, there have been dramatic changes.

29   I'm convinced that any person with some vision, passion, and purpose can cause important community improvements, but that those who occupy leadership positions can be major forces for good if they exercise some initiative along the lines of a compelling shared vision or mission.

30   Trust me. Your community and my community will be the communities of the future. It's only a matter of time. So the only questions are these: What kinds of communities will they be? and What can you and I do to make a positive difference in bringing about the vision of the ideal?

Reading Responses

1. Why, according to Covey, are connections to a community important? Why should people invest their energies in building community?
2. What does Covey suggest that individuals might do?
3. Why does Covey follow these suggestions for individuals with a description of the characteristics of an ideal community and with four examples? How does he expect these three sections to fit together? How might he expect the three to affect a reader?

Writing Activities

1. Select one of Covey's suggestions for individuals. Explain this point persuasively for an audience of other students or another specific audience that you define. Use explanations and examples that would appeal to their interests, address their needs, and counter their possible reservations.
2. Write an essay responding to Covey's definition of the ideal community. You might want to propose another characteristic based on your own values, qualify one of his elements, supply examples of possible applications, or adapt his elements to the college campus. You also might want to disagree with the values that underlie his four elements. If so, propose your own definition of an ideal community.
3. If you are aware of an effective community effort or participate in a local or campus organization, describe it as Covey describes his four examples. Your example does not need to be as broadly based as Covey's examples, but you will need to explain the purpose of the effort, identify the activities involved, illustrate its progress or successes, and add any other information that a reader would need to understand why you think that this effort or group makes a positive contribution.

Community Links

Compare and contrast the recommendations in Covey's essay with those in Palmer's "The Quest for Community in Higher Education" (pp. 33–41) from the academic community, Ulrich's "Six Practices for Creating Communities of Value, Not Proximity" (pp. 221–227) from the work community, or one of the related readings from the public community such as Morse's "Five Building Blocks for Successful Communities" (pp. 374–379) or Zobel de Ayala's "Anticipating the Community of the Future" (pp. 405–411). Synthesize several of these readings, weaving together their common points, but also account for differences that reflect community expectations or individual perspectives.

PREFACE TO *EVERYTHING YOU THINK YOU KNOW ABOUT POLITICS... AND WHY YOU'RE WRONG*

Kathleen Hall Jamieson

♦

In her preface to Everything You Think You Know About Politics . . . And Why You're Wrong, *Kathleen Jamieson introduces her topic—political campaigns. Through her research, sponsored by the Annenberg School for Communication of the University of Pennsylvania, she investigated this question: "What does the public know about politics, and how does it know it?" This book reports her findings, often as surprising challenges to common preconceptions about politics and campaigns, and invites readers to learn more.*

Preface

1 November 30, 1999. The face on the screen is that of George W. Bush, Republican, governor of Texas, son of a former president, and presidential aspirant. On the issue of U.S. trade policy, the Texas Republican says, "China will find in America a confident and willing trade partner." He adds, "Trade freely with China, and time is on our side." Arizona Senator John McCain appears next. Same issue. "I don't believe in walls," he notes. "If I were president, I would negotiate a free trade agreement with almost any country willing to negotiate with us."

2 There is, however, dissent in the ranks of the Republican contenders for president. Former Reagan administration official Gary Bauer, who opposes China's entry into the World Trade Organization (WTO), declares, "My party needs to listen to Main Street, not to Wall Street on this issue." Businessman Steve Forbes agrees. "No more turning a blind eye to Chinese spies in our nuclear labs," he says, "no more keeping silent about Chinese slave labor camps."

3 And what of the former Republican contender who is now seeking the spot at the head of the Reform Party ticket, Pat Buchanan? His position too is clear and concise. "Global economy must call into existence a global government, and globalism is at war with patriotism," he intones. These six statements, averaging sixteen and a half words and 6.83 seconds each, digest the substance of the agreement between Bush and McCain and the crux of the disagreement between those two and Bauer and Forbes on the issue of China's admission to the WTO. Taken together, the statements profile with dispatch the stands of the Republican contenders.

4 CNN's Brooks Jackson weaves the soundbites into a narrative that includes context and skillful paraphrase of related candidate beliefs. From him we learn that Al Gore is "for fast-track negotiating theory, for China's entry into the World Trade Organization . . . And the same for Bill Bradley. Here he is at the signing of NAFTA." Note the efficiency of Jackson's closing sentence: "So,

unless there's a huge upset, the next president of the U.S. will be a strong free trader, just like the incumbent."

The candidates' positions are as clear here as in their extended answers to questions about trade in the first townhall forums of the primary season. Note, for example, George W. Bush's answer December 7, 1999, in the Arizona townhall to a question from Gary Bauer asking why he had embraced the Clinton-Gore policy of giving China most-favored-nation status and membership in the World Trade Organization?

> BUSH: I appreciate that, but you know how to insult a guy by saying [I] follow the policies of Clinton-Gore. I don't. They believe in what's called a strategic partnership. I believe in redefining the relationship to one of competitor. But I believe competitors can find common ground. I think it's in our nation's best interests to open up Chinese markets to Arizona farm products, to Iowa farm products, to high-tech manufactured goods. It's in our best interests to sell to the Chinese. It's also in our best interests to make sure that the entrepreneurial class in China flourishes. I think we make China an enemy, they'll end up being an enemy. I think if we trade with China, and trade with the entrepreneurial class, and give people a breath of freedom, give them a taste of freedom, I think you'll be amazed, Gary, at how soon democracy will come. And so, I also believe . . . China ought to be in the World Trade Organization. I also believe that Taiwan ought to be in the World Trade Organization. But let me make this clear to you and to the Chinese. I will enforce the Taiwan relations law if I'm the president. If the Chinese get aggressive with the Taiwanese, we'll help them defend themselves.
>
> BAUER: Governor, we would have never made the argument that you just made if we were talking about Nazi Germany. Is there no atrocity that you can think of, the labor camps doubling in their slave labor, a bigger crackdown, more priests disappearing in the middle of the night, is there anything that would tell you to put trade on the back burner?
>
> BUSH: Gary, I agree with you that forced abortion is abhorrent. And I agree with you when leaders try to snuff out religion. But I think if we turn our back on China and isolate China, things will get worse. Imagine if the Internet took hold in China. Imagine how freedom would spread. In my earlier answer, I said our greatest export to the world has been, is, and always will be the incredible freedom we understand in America. And that's why it's important for us to trade with China to encourage the growth of an entrepreneurial class. It gets that taste of freedom, it gets that breath of freedom, in the marketplace.

Taken together, the soundbites from the two candidates and their townhall answers paint a more complete picture of their positions than either response alone. There is obvious merit in paying attention to both. But if time is of the essence, Jackson's report can serve as a telegraphic substitute for the townhall exchange. The reason is simple. Whereas candidates take time to get to the point, Jackson has cut to the chase. In boiling their positions down to essentials, he has confirmed that soundbites can be substantive, that there is nothing inherently vacuous about brief candidate statements, and that his investment in finding these core statements has made it possible for us to learn in less than three minutes what otherwise would have taken an hour and a half. Soundbites can be superficial or substantive. Substantive soundbites are the stuff of which the best news stories are made.

7   If that is the case, why is the brevity of candidate statements in news taken as prima facie evidence that the discourse of democracy has decayed? What accounts for the casual assumption that a soundbite is by definition superficial?

8   My theory goes like this. Someone created a neutral word to describe the selection of a brief section of a candidate's speech for a newscast. Soundbite. Someone else—someone who had forgotten that "I love you," "Will you marry me?" "It's a healthy baby girl," "I will go to Korea," "Ask not what your country can do for you," and "We have nothing to fear but fear itself" meet the definition of soundbite—appropriated the word to describe a superficial, crafted candidate statement designed to be excerpted into news. If asked to use the word in a sentence, a student might now write, "That's a great soundbite, but where's the substance?" "Soundbite" came to function as a synonym for superficial.

9   Other phrases, such as "negative ad" or "negative campaign," have been so variously defined as to be meaningless. Like a soundbite, a negative campaign is presumed to be bad for democracy. This is an instance of what rhetorical critic Kenneth Burke meant when he noted that language does our thinking for us. The thinking done by soundbite and negative campaigning leads reformers to call for longer soundbites, unmindful that length and substance are not synonyms, and for less negativity, apparently unaware that without attack we would lack the information needed to differentiate the candidates. I have been as guilty of this as others.

10 Misapplied concepts are not the only problem. Listen to the pundits during a campaign and you will hear suspect assumptions treated as dogma. They include such "truisms" as attack is bad for the public; attack drives voters from the polls; debates are boring; there is nothing to be learned from paying attention to debates; and politicians break most of their campaign promises. If such notions are the scaffolding on which the indictment of the discourse of politics is built, the structure is shaky.

11 It is often difficult to know whether a book is worth reading, particularly a book whose title is an unabashed provocation. How, after all, do I know what you know about politics? And even if I could read your mind, your mail, your magazines, and your ballot, by what breach of strategic sense would I want to announce to the world (or to you) that you are wrong?

12 Of course, I don't know that you personally are wrong. What I do know is that many of the students in my classes, friends in the neighborhood, and reporters on the phone make assumptions about the way U.S. politics works that just don't check out against the record as I see it.

13 You may be the exception. To save you the trouble of reading a book that tells you what you already know, I've concocted a quiz. No time limit. Open book. No penalty for consulting with the political junkies in your life. Before you begin, however, a caution. Read the questions from the assumption that they are claims about what happens most of the time. There are exceptions. I will note them in the book. Read the questions armed with a sense of irony.

After all, the conflict I am trying to set up between what you think you know and what the data reveal is employing a norm that I will later argue should accompany and not replace one that values consensus. In the same vein, reducing complex questions to true or false answers and you to being wrong with the implication that I am right is as simplistic as some of the assumptions I am challenging. You might say that I am using conflict, simplified narratives, and manipulative devices just as news and ads do—to entice you into watching and reading. You'd be right about that.

Here's the quiz.

1. In 1992, the phrase "the economy, stupid" and not the communication surrounding the campaign deserves full credit for the election of Bill Clinton.

    A. True B. False

2. Most presidents make a strong effort to keep most of their campaign promises.

    A. True B. False

3. Over a third of the typical general-election speech by a major-party presidential candidate is devoted to attacking the other party's nominee.

    A. True B. False

4. General-election presidential political ads spend more than half of their air time attacking.

    A. True B. False

5. When candidates make statements in speeches, they usually expect us to take them at their word and so provide no supporting evidence.

    A. True B. False

6. Most candidate ads lie most of the time.

    A. True B. False

7. The quality of presidential general-election campaigns has steadily worsened over the years.

    A. True B. False

8. Campaign discourse in speeches and debates has become steadily more negative over the years.

    A. True B. False

9. Reporters pretty accurately represent the content and level of attack in their stories about candidate speeches.

    A. True B. False

10. Voters make a distinction between attack that is accurate and attack that is inaccurate, between attack that is personal and attack that is issue based, and between attack that is histrionic and attack that is stated in a neutral fashion.
    A. True   B. False

11. Voters prefer ads that contrast the records of the candidates to ads that simply attack.
    A. True   B. False

12. There isn't very much useful information in campaigns; it's all mainly hype.
    A. True   B. False

13. Attack turns off voters. The high level of attack in the general-election presidential campaign of 1996 was a main reason that voter turnout was down.
    A. True   B. False

14. Attack benefits the sponsor and hurts the person attacked.
    A. True   B. False

15. Political advertising turns off voters and they stay away from the polls as a result.
    A. True   B. False

16. There is no useful information for voters in reporting about campaign strategy and tactics.
    A. True   B. False

17. Women know less than men about politics.
    A. True   B. False

18. The *New York Times* gave Dole less coverage in 1996 than Clinton.
    A. True   B. False

19. The person who is ahead in the polls gets more strategic coverage than the underdog.
    A. True   B. False

20. Reporters are right when they say there isn't much that can be learned from watching debates.
    A. True   B. False

For the correct answers, see the next page.

Answers

1. In 1992, the phrase "the economy, stupid" and not the communication surrounding the campaign deserves full credit for the election of Bill Clinton.

    False

2. Most presidents make a strong effort to keep most of their campaign promises.

    True

3. Over a third of the typical general-election speech by a major-party presidential candidate is devoted to attacking the other party's nominee.

    False

4. General-election presidential political ads spend more than half of their air time attacking.

    False

5. When candidates make statements in speeches, they usually expect us to take them at their word and so provide no supporting evidence.

    False

6. Most candidate ads lie most of the time.

    False

7. The quality of presidential general-election campaigns has steadily worsened over the years.

    False

8. Campaign discourse in speeches, ads, and debates has become steadily more negative over the years.

    False

9. Reporters pretty accurately represent the content and level of attack in their stories about candidate speeches.

    False

10. Voters make a distinction between attack that is accurate and attack that is inaccurate, between attack that is personal and attack that is is-

sue based, and between attack that is histrionic and attack that is stated in a neutral fashion.

True

11. Voters prefer ads that contrast the records of the candidates to ads that simply attack.

    True

12. There isn't very much useful information in campaigns; it's all mainly hype.

    False

13. Attack turns off voters. The high level of attack in the general-election presidential campaign of 1996 was a main reason that voter turnout was down.

    False

14. Attack benefits the sponsor and hurts the person attacked.

    False

15. Political advertising turns off voters and they stay away from the polls as a result.

    False

16. There is no useful information for voters in reporting about campaign strategy and tactics.

    False

17. Women know less than men about politics.

    True and False

18. The *New York Times* gave Dole less coverage in 1996 than Clinton.

    False

19. The person who is ahead in the polls gets more strategic coverage than the underdog.

    False

20. Reporters are right when they say there isn't much that can be learned from watching debates.

    False

Scoring:
18–20 correct—Top of the class. Exceptional.
16–18 correct—Not bad.
14–16 correct—Still above average.
12–14 correct—Approaching the danger zone.
10–12 correct—You could almost reach this level by sheer chance.
0–10 correct—You have the instincts of some working pundits.

If your answers differ from mine and you are growling that you know you are right and I'm wrong, I invite you to read on. [Here Jamieson encourages readers to continue reading her book.]

Reading Responses

1. Take Jamieson's quiz. Individually or in a group, check your answers. Which answers surprise you?
2. What is Jamieson's central idea? Where does she state that idea?
3. What is the point of Jamieson's opening examples? Why does she begin with them?

Writing Activities

1. In your own words, write a summary of Jamieson's central point.
2. The purpose of Jamieson's book is to show readers that their ideas are wrong. How does Jamieson manage to tell readers that they don't know what they think they do without provoking them into tossing the book aside? Write an essay explaining her strategies for delivering challenging information to readers and for keeping readers engaged despite the challenge to their beliefs. Use examples from the selection to illustrate your points about her methods.
3. Write your own short quiz for your classmates, either to educate them or to overcome their preconceptions about something. Select a topic about which you are knowledgeable but your classmates may not be. Word your questions carefully so that they are clear, and also write the answers. Exchange quizzes with your classmates, and discover how much everyone learns.

Community Links

Based on this introduction to Jamieson's research, consider the effectiveness of some specific campaign materials. Analyze a sample from "Appeal to Voters" (pp. 457–471) in light of her findings, or examine some material from a current campaign in your home or campus community.

ANTICIPATING THE COMMUNITY OF THE FUTURE

Jaime A. Zobel de Ayala II

◆

This essay was originally published as the final chapter in The Community of the Future, *edited by Frances Hesselbein, Marshall Goldsmith, Richard Beckhard, and Richard F. Schubert. This essay collection was sponsored by the Peter F. Drucker Foundation for Nonprofit Management. In his concluding essay, Jaime Zobel de Ayala, active in civic and business organizations in the Philippines, extends consideration of community to global dimensions as he anticipates the future.*

1   In his studies of group behavior and his community-building workshops, the psychiatrist M. Scott Peck, writing in *World Waiting to Be Born*, reports that human individuals on the way to social coherence evolve through four stages, which he calls *pseudo-community, chaos, emptiness,* and *community.* In the final stage, after transcending false community, individual differences, prejudices, and fixed expectations, the group becomes a true community. Then, says Peck, a spirit of peace pervades the room. There is more silence, yet more of worth gets said. The people work together with an exquisite sense of timing like a finely tuned orchestra—making decisions, planning, negotiating, acting—often with phenomenal efficiency and effectiveness.

2   I see the communities of the future taking on the qualities of Peck's laboratory community, high technology and globalism notwithstanding. Whether we are speaking of community as a neighborhood, a church group, a college, a professional association, a civic club, a nongovernment organization (NGO), or even a corporate organization, people will continue to gather as groups. They will cohere even more intimately and closely than they do today. Community members will be governed by a deeper sense of group culture and personal responsibility. And they will venture into undertakings that redound not only to the benefit of the group but also to that of the larger society.

3   My optimism might seem strange considering that we hear and read much today about the breakdown of community in contemporary society. From the developed to the developing world, many are the laments about the weakening and collapse of communities of obligation and commitment. People mourn the decline of families, neighborhoods, villages, churches, civic clubs, and other groups that once gave men and women a sense of belonging and of being needed. It is also paradoxical that at a time when the world is narrowing into one global economy and the borders between nation-states are becoming porous, I am anticipating a surge of communitarian feeling among citizens around the world. To many, after all, globalization looks more like a threat, rather than a boon, to human community. The idea of a world community seems more metaphoric than real.

4   These trends, indeed, seem to point to the uprooting of people from traditional ways of living. But I will argue that the natural desire of human beings to commune in relatively homogenous groupings will flourish in the new

millennium, though perhaps not exactly in the forms we see now. Already, new and promising signs of community building are abroad in the world. In many countries, people are striving to rediscover the sense of living and working together. *Inclusion* and *participation* are words we increasingly hear these days.

Communal Trends

5   The telltale signs are still random and far from settled. But they already remind me that community has not become a thing of the past. Among these signs are:

- The surge of voluntarism that has made nonprofit institutions and organizations a vital sector in many countries
- The rise of local communities in the developing world to a new level of empowerment and purpose
- The resurgence of family values and civility in place of the old fixation on individualism and personal lifestyles
- The new concern over responsibilities compared to a selfish obsession with individual rights
- The growing interest of corporate culture in norms, values, and social responsibility
- The devolution of many tasks from big governments and institutions to the private sector, citizens' groups, and even families
- The growing prominence of issues that have little to do with power or the creation of wealth and everything to do with the quality of life on the planet, such as the care of the environment
- The revival of religious feeling amid the secular world of the marketplace

6   Around these activities and concerns, old and new forms of community have been rising in import in recent years. Although the world remains demarcated into separate nations, regions, cultures, and civilizations, there are commonalities of feeling and action in all the hemispheres. When Peter Drucker observes that nonprofit institutions in America are now a third sector, along with business and government, he could say as much about what is happening in the developing world. The old hierarchies of government and religion are giving way to smaller units for public service and worship. Echoing General Colin Powell's volunteer movement in America, citizen-led efforts in countries like Bangladesh and the Philippines help poor communities to organize and help themselves. If, as I expect, the twenty-first century will usher in a more bountiful world economy and higher standards of living, the impetus to civility and community should also gather momentum. Advances in science and technology—current and forthcoming—will abet, not deter, this natural human longing.

7   The enduring changes brought by the twentieth century should have taught us by now to regard history as process, rather than simple cause and effect. Realities emerge out of a continuing process of transformation, and not just because people wish to make them so. Other factors come into play, some-

times in unexpected ways, to produce the outcomes. So I see the community of the future as evolving from and through the major forces shaping our lives today. Three of these forces are: (1) information technology and the knowledge society, (2) the emergence of poor nations and a bigger middle class in the global economy, and (3) the growing democratization of the world.

Knowledge Communities

8 Information technology (IT) is the single biggest shaper of contemporary society, and it will no doubt abide as a powerful catalyst of change in the future. At first glance, IT looks like a tool that transforms individuals into couch potatoes before their computers, removing them from the need to relate to their fellow human beings. There are enough monstrosities on the Internet for us to seriously worry about alienation and anomie arising from this technological breakthrough. This should not cloud, however, the fact that this powerful technology can serve as a tool for breaking down barriers between people, for breaking up massive government and corporate bureaucracies, and for enabling men and women to bond together.

9 Knowledge, let us not forget, is one of the most powerful glues for human fellowship and sharing. This is because communication is its essence. And communication fosters the sense of community. Already, we can see IT transforming the organization of work and the workplace. Work is being organized today into ever smaller and more autonomous work units. Workers can take part in the new economy without leaving their homes and their neighborhoods. Networking has become an important way for us to build linkages to others.

10 In an even deeper way, the knowledge society is bringing individuals toward a greater sense of common experience. One of the oldest forms of human community is the community of science and scholarship that transcends nations. This community has always been united by an insatiable curiosity and thirst for knowledge. It has an interdependence among its members, who are all doing their own small part but collectively enriching the tree of knowledge. In the new knowledge society, IT has dramatically speeded up and enhanced the process of sharing knowledge. All societies, rich and poor alike, can now take part in the flow of information and knowledge. Indeed, the absorption, cataloging, analysis, and dissemination of knowledge has become an industry in its own right. Thus, as the new technologies of communications and computers get ever more sophisticated, so will knowledge communities flower around the world.

Development of the Third World

11 The same sense of interdependence is evident in the global economy today. Globalization has served as a powerful force for enabling poor nations to develop and even catch up with the advanced countries. Developing nations are setting the pace for global expansion. The creation of wealth is no longer the exclusive domain of a "rich nations club."

12   The globalization of markets, of course, has provoked much apprehension about its corrosive impact on community life everywhere. As one analyst has noted, markets may be good servants but they are bad masters. Just as science earlier displaced religion as the engine driving human hopes and aspirations, today economics appears to be taking over from science. Most people, it is feared, see themselves no longer as neighbors, friends, or even citizens, but as consumers. Economic efficiency and cost-effectiveness could become the custodians of the future.

13   As a business executive, I can appreciate the concern. But the fear of a robotic, consumerist future seems to me apocalyptic and exaggerated. Globalization does not destroy the faith by which free and civilized people live. Indeed, I would suggest that this powerful force could confer fresh and exciting opportunities for human community. Just as companies forge strategic partnerships to produce new products for the world markets, so globalization can induce peoples to relate to one another in new and more meaningful ways.

14   Notice how the constant experience of seeing foreigners traffic daily through one's neighborhood is banishing the old estrangement of people of different colors. More than the formal pacts of governments, the conduct of business on a transnational scale is creating opportunities for people to bond. Some may scoff at this as just the experience of consuming the same products and having the same lifestyle. But I don't think it is as trite as that. We can also view this phenomenon as the creation of networks that transcend time and space and that allow people to communicate and interact with one another. Recent experience in the Third World is especially instructive as to how the engineering of development can foster the sense of community. The so-called Asian economic miracle has not descended from the top down; it has risen from the bottom up. Along with the thousands of small and medium-scale enterprises that underpin growth, local communities, NGOs, and citizens' organizations have become a dynamic part of the process of change. People, not governments, have made the miracle happen.

15   The role of community action will not recede as countries like the Philippines participate more actively in the global economy. The emergence of a bigger and stronger middle class does not kill the community spirit. As we have seen in many countries, increases in income and higher living standards lead people to seek greater well-being and a better quality of life that is not purely monetary. They want more than just food on their table or a roof over their head. They demand better services from their government and in their public life. They want to get more from their leisure and free time. They want an environment that is cleaner and less destructive of nature, one that they can leave as a legacy to their children. All this inevitably leads to their banding together to create more meaning in their lives and to gain a greater say in the institutions that rule over them. The hierarchies of government, religion, and other social institutions are yielding down the line to smaller groups wherein members can innovate and experiment without the burdens of bureaucracy and rigid doctrines.

16   No doubt, the global economy has created—and will continue to create in the future—large organized systems that circumscribe our lives today and that

may weaken our older forms of community. But in response to this, people are creating and will create the smaller subsystems, to use John Gardner's term, through which they can experience greater fellowship. The challenge is to infuse in the new communities some of the values we have cherished in our traditional communities.

Citizenship and Community

17   In a world where more peoples and nations can take part in the banquet of development, individuals can forge a stronger sense of civil society and community. Democracy and markets go together. Economic liberation naturally leads to greater democratization. We see vivid proof of this in South Korea and Taiwan. The rise of their economies and the expansion of their middle class seeded the flowering of democracy in their societies. Democratic participation in turn has brought about a political order that resembles democracy as it is known in the Western world.

18   The sequence of change is fairly simple to follow. In order to enforce their demands for a better quality of life, the rising middle classes need democratic government to govern them and their society. They need the freedom to be and to do within the limits of civilized society. They thus need an accountable but limited government. In a word, they need citizenship in a free society.

19   If this merely connoted a citizenship that claims rights for the individual and leaves responsibilities to government, I would not be too sanguine about the prospects for democratization to enhance human community. But we can see where the future is tending in the growing belief that citizens of democracies must meet responsibilities and obligations to society in addition to enjoying rights and privileges. The communitarian agenda of enabling people to take greater control over their lives and to contribute to the common good is again alive and flourishing.

20   All this has great meaning for Asia today, where traditionally the primacy of society has always reigned over the claims of the individual. Democracy frees the Asian for citizenship, but this need not—and I believe will not—lead to the kind of extreme individualism so prevalent in Western society. I would suggest that in the current debate between Western values that foster individualism and Asian values that prize social cohesion, community could provide the middle ground for mutual understanding. We can find the balance between individual freedom and the common good.

21   In the republican tradition, as developed first in ancient times, association and the creation of common interests was seen as the whole basis for society. The essence of citizenship was direct involvement in the process through which people banded together and agreed on the rules that would govern them. A good political system gave them a shared interest in seeking what was best for all.

22   The meeting of the old and the new is exemplified by what is happening in the Philippines today. As a people, we have a long tradition of community, at the local if not the national level. Local traditions such as *bayanihan* (cooperation), *pakikipagkapwa-tao* (fellowship), and *pakikisama* (working together) are

in the national grain. Beyond family ties, which are very strong, Filipinos have historically always banded together to provide for mutual support and understanding. Onto this tradition have been grafted the forms of community of a new time. NGOs, people's organizations, and civic organizations have mushroomed all over the country in the democratic space created by the 1986 revolution of Corazon Aquino, during which "People Power" became the rallying cry and force for change.

23   These organizations have become a powerful force in the shaping of our national life, enshrined in our constitution and consulted by government for all major issues. They are networked by sector or issue, such as women's rights, children and youth, environment, population, livelihood, poverty alleviation, and the like. There are also multisectoral local and national networks, such as the Association of Foundations and the Coalition of Development NGOs. And Philippine business supports these communities through various funding programs.

24   My sense of these developments in our country is that they are powered by a deep concern by citizens that major national problems cannot be solved by economic growth alone or by government alone. We must all be involved in problem solving, especially in rooting out mass poverty in our country. Looking to the future, then, I see citizenship and community growing side by side in our country. Democracy will grow new shoots in our midst, not by following the course of selfish individualism that has scarred Western societies, but by marrying Asian values of social trust with the democratic idea of personal responsibility.

Different Nations, Different Trends

25   When I look at the great variety of cultures and societies in the world we live in that are moving through different stages of development, I cannot foresee the community of the future as the same in all climes and places. Community, like politics, is local. Local conditions will shape the communities of tomorrow. In *Birth of a New World: An Open Moment in International Leadership*, Harlan Cleveland has observed that because of the new economy, modern civilization is built less and less around communities of place and more and more around communities of people. This expresses one major trend in the West today. It does not necessarily apply to developing societies like our own, where the communities of place are still very strong in spite of our linkage to the global economy and the Internet.

26   These differences aside, I believe that we are entering a new century full of opportunities for the human impulse to community. Troubled by the breakdown of the sense of family and community and civil society, humankind will strive hard to restore and strengthen the bonds that will enable people to live and prosper together.

27   I see the communities of the future as:

   1. No less intimate and cohesive than traditional communities, because citizens will use their civic space to be more engaged in their local

communities where they live and work and where their efforts can have more meaning and impact
2. More voluntaristic and altruistic, because people will join together, no longer along the lines of ideology or class, but for causes that advance the public weal

28   This is an optimistic view of the future. But I'm a great believer in change for the better, not for the worse. The world will continue to change in rapid and unexpected ways. But human beings will continue to form communities that excite their sense of obligation and commitment. They will prefer to belong rather than secede.

Reading Responses

1. According to Zobel de Ayala, what three major forces will help shape global community?
2. How does Zobel de Ayala envision the communities of the future? Why does he think that communities will continue to thrive?
3. Have you observed evidence of any of Zobel de Ayala's signs of increasing community?

Writing Activities

1. Write a summary of one of the three forces Zobel de Ayala identifies.
2. Select one of Zobel de Ayala's communal trends (paragraph 5). Write an essay that supports or challenges the existence of these trends using concrete examples from your experience, observation, or research.
3. Write a personal response to Zobel de Ayala's discussion of knowledge communities. Based on your experiences with electronic resources, especially the Web, reflect on the effects of the expansion of knowledge.

Community Links

Compare and contrast Zobel de Ayala's essay on global community with another essay on community such as that by Palmer (pp. 33–41), Ulrich (pp. 221–227), Morse (pp. 374–378), or Covey (pp. 390–395). What are their points of agreement or disagreement? What points do they view from different perspectives? Synthesize the essays, weaving them together and integrating them into your own discussion about the need for community or its development.

Community Ethics

OUR AGE OF PROPAGANDA
Anthony R. Pratkanis and Elliot Aronson

◆

In Age of Propaganda: The Everyday Use and Abuse of Persuasion, *Anthony Pratkanis and Elliot Aronson, two social psychologists, examine the difference between propaganda and persuasion. They raise questions about the pressures of persuasion today, suggesting the consequences of not understanding and using persuasion wisely. The selection here is part of the first chapter of the book.*

In the early 1990s, seventeen-year-old Demetrick James Walker was sentenced to life in prison for killing a sixteen-year-old. The reason for the slaying: Demetrick so badly wanted a pair of $125 Nike Air Jordans like the ones he had seen on TV that he put a .22-caliber pistol to the head of Johnny Bates, pulled the trigger, and walked off with a new pair of high-tops. During the trial, Houston prosecutor Mark Vinson placed some of the blame on the images created by advertising. Said Vinson, "It's bad when we create an image of luxury about athletic gear that it forces people to kill over it."[1]

The 1990 North Carolina U.S. Senate race was one of the most heated—and expensive—political contests in recent years. Going into the last weeks of the campaign, the black Democratic challenger, Harvey Gantt, held a slight lead in the polls over the white Republican incumbent, Jesse Helms. Eight days before the election, Helms broadcast an ad dubbed "White Hands." The spot, created by political consultant Alex Castellanos, showed a pair of white hands crumpling a letter of rejection. The voice-over: "You needed that job, but they had to give it to a minority because of racial quotas. Is that really fair?" Although Gantt was on record as opposed to quotas, the spot appears to have had its intended effect: Helms squeaked through and by a slim margin was reelected to the Senate, supported by a huge majority in white precincts. The tactic worked so well that Helms did it again in his 1996 rematch with Gantt; this time Helms accused Gantt of being the recipient of preferential treatment in the awarding of contracts.[2] In the 2000 U.S. presidential election, Alex Castellanos again achieved notoriety when he produced a 30-second ad for the Republican National Committee. This ad contained the word RATS subliminally flashed across the television screen.

Some years ago, CBS aired the film *Cry Rape*. Essentially, the story made it clear that a rape victim who chooses to press charges against her attacker runs the risk of undergoing an ordeal that may be as harrowing as the rape itself. In this case the rapist, exuding boyish innocence, presented a convincing argument to the effect that he had been seduced by the woman. During the next few weeks, there was a sharp decrease in the number of rapes reported by victims to the police—apparently because victims, taking their cue from the television movie, feared the police would not believe them.

In October 1982, when seven people in the Chicago area died after taking Tylenol headache capsules laced with cyanide, the event was widely publicized by the national news media. Indeed, for several days it was difficult to turn on the TV or radio, or pick up a newspaper, without encountering the Tylenol poisonings. The effects of this prominent coverage were immediate: Similar poisonings were reported in cities across the country, involving the contamination of mouthwash, eyedrops, nasal spray, soda pop, even hot dogs. Dramatically billed as "copycat poisonings," these incidents, in turn, received widespread media attention. The public reaction spiralled: Many people panicked, seeking medical aid for burns and poisonings when they suffered from no more than common sore throats and stomachaches. False alarms outnumbered actual cases of product tampering by 7 to 1.

1 What do Demetrick James Walker, the voters of North Carolina, rape victims, and, indeed, anyone who has ever watched television or read a newspaper or magazine have in common? Every time we turn on the radio or television, every time we open a book, magazine, or newspaper, someone is trying to educate us, to convince us to buy a product, to persuade us to vote for a candidate or to subscribe to some version of what is right, true, or beautiful. This aim is most obvious in advertising: Manufacturers of nearly identical products (aspirins, for example, or toothpastes, or detergents, or political candidates) spend vast amounts of money to persuade us to buy the product in their package. Influence need not be so blatant—the impact of television news shows and programs such as *Cry Rape*, for instance, extends far beyond their most obvious effects as documentaries or dramatizations. This influence can be very subtle indeed, even unintentional. As the response to the movie about rape aptly illustrates, even when communicators are not directly attempting to sell us something, they can succeed in influencing the way we look at the world and the way we respond to important events in our lives. The purpose of this book is to look at the nature of persuasion in our everyday life—to understand how it influences our behavior, how we can protect ourselves from unwanted propaganda, and how we can ultimately come to use persuasion wisely.

A Glut of Influence

2 The primary vehicle for many persuasive appeals is the mass media. The statistics on the pervasiveness of the mass media are startling.[3] Communications is a $400-billion-plus industry with $206 billion spent on mass communications, that is, communications produced and distributed in identical form to people in different locations. In the United States, there are 1,449 television

stations and four major networks, 10,379 radio stations, 1,509 daily newspapers and 7,047 weekly newspapers, more than 17,000 magazines and newsletters, and nine major film studios. Americans have ample opportunity to consume mass media messages, and consume they do. Each year the typical American watches 1,550 hours of TV, listens to 1,160 hours of radio on one of 530 million radio sets, and spends 180 hours reading 94 pounds of newspapers and 110 hours reading magazines. Each year an American has the opportunity to read more than 50,000 new books in print. More than half of our waking hours are spent with the mass media.

3   If you watch thirty hours of TV per week (as does the typical American), you will view roughly 38,000 commercials per year. The average prime-time hour of TV contains more than 11 minutes of advertising. That works out to more than 100 TV ads per day. You are likely to hear or see another 100 to 300 ads per day through the other mass media of radio, newspapers, and magazines.

4   And the advertising glut does not stop there. More than 100 million orders will be placed after home viewers watch continuous advertising on networks such as QVC and the Home Shopping Network—resulting in sales of more than $2.5 billion. This year you will receive, on average, 252 pieces of direct-mail advertising (a $144.5-billion industry and still growing) and about fifty phone calls from telemarketers, who contact 7 million persons a day. Americans purchase $600 billion worth of goods and services over the phone each year. Today advertisers are developing new ways of delivering their message using the Internet and World Wide Web. Each day more than 257 million Internet users worldwide check more than 11.1 million available Web sites featuring a range of information, propaganda, and, of course, merchandise for sale. Each year, American businesses spend $150 billion to hire more than 6.4 million sales agents. Approximately one in every twelve American families has a member working in sales. This force of millions attempts to persuade others to purchase everything from cars to shoes to small and large appliances, to contribute vast sums to needy charities, to enlist in the military, or to enroll in a specific college.

5   If you walk down just about any city street in America, you will encounter countless billboards, posters, bumper stickers, and bus and cab displays, each with a separate advertising appeal. Your kitchen cupboard is probably full of product packages and labels, each containing at least one sales message. It seems that no place is free of advertising. Go to the racetrack and you will see 200-mile-an-hour race cars carry advertising worth $75 million per year. Go to a tennis tournament, a jazz festival, or a golf match and you will find corporate sponsors, such as the makers of Virginia Slims, Kool, and Doral cigarettes. Go to a movie and you will find that marketers have paid a handsome sum (roughly $50 million per year) to have your favorite stars use their products in the film. Even 007's famous martini dictum, "shaken, not stirred," is not sacred, as James Bond orders a "Smirnoff Black, neat" in *Goldeneye* thanks to a pricey product-placement fee paid to the movie's producers. Look at just about anyone in America and you will see human bodies turned into walking bill-

boards with brand names appearing on T-shirts and ballcaps, not to mention the ubiquitous designer labels.

6   On any given day, Americans are exposed to 18 billion magazine and newspaper ads, 2.6 million radio commercials, 300,000 TV commercials, 500,000 billboards, and 40 million pieces of direct mail. With 6% of the world's population, the United States consumes 57% of the world's advertising. Manufacturers spend more than $165 billion a year on advertising and more than $115 billion a year on product promotions (coupons, free samples, rebates, premiums, and the like). This corresponds to spending 2.2% of the U.S. gross national product on advertising (compared to 0.95% in Japan and 0.9% in Germany), or more than $1,000 per year per American—a sum larger than the yearly income of a typical citizen of a third world nation.

7   But persuasion is not just the specialty of advertisers and marketers. The U.S. government spends more than $400 million per year to employ more than 8,000 workers to create propaganda favorable to the United States. The result: ninety films per year, twelve magazines in twenty-two languages, and 800 hours of Voice of America programming in thirty-seven languages with an estimated audience of 75 million listeners—all describing the virtues of the American way.

8   Persuasion shows up in almost every walk of life. Nearly every major politician hires media consultants and political pundits to provide advice on how to persuade the public and how to get elected (and then how to stay elected). For example, in the 2000 U.S. presidential election, George W. Bush raised more than $184 million to support his campaign, with Al Gore collecting more than $133 million in his bid for the White House. Once elected, the typical U.S. president is likely to spend millions of dollars to hire personal pollsters and political consultants in an attempt to keep those positive approval ratings.

9   Virtually every major business and special-interest group has hired a lobbyist to take its concerns to Congress or to state and local governments. Today, such political action committees serve as a primary source of funds for most political campaigns. Is it any wonder that Congress is loath to instigate serious curbs on major lobbyists such as the NRA, AARP, or AMA? In nearly every community, activists try to persuade their fellow citizens on important policy issues.

10 The workplace, too, has always been fertile ground for office politics and persuasion. One study estimates that general managers spend upwards of 80% of their time in verbal communication—most of it with the intent of cajoling and persuading their fellow employees. With the advent of the photocopying machine, a whole new medium for office persuasion was invented—the photocopied memo. The Pentagon alone copies an average of 350,000 pages a day, the equivalent of 1,000 novels. Sunday may be a day of rest, but not from persuasion, as an army of preachers takes to the pulpits to convince us of the true moral course of action. They also take to the airwaves, with 14% of all radio stations airing programs extolling the virtues of Christianity.

11 And should you need assistance in preparing your persuasive message, millions stand ready in the wings to help (for a fee). Today there are 675,000

lawyers actively arguing and persuading in courts of law—and in the courts of public opinion when their high-profile clients so require. More than 300 companies (at billings of $130 million per year) provide "image consulting"—advice on how to make your personal image more appealing. Public relations firms can be hired to deal with any public opinion problem. There are more than 500 major marketing research and opinion-polling firms ready to find out what Americans think about any conceivable issue. These firms query more than 72 million Americans a year. The top 100 marketing research firms alone have combined revenues of more than $5 billion.

12 Every day we are bombarded with one persuasive communication after another. These appeals persuade not through the give-and-take of argument and debate but through the manipulation of symbols and of our most basic human emotions. For better or worse, ours is an age of propaganda. [...]

The Distinction Between Propaganda and Persuasion

13 The forms of persuasion that have come to dominate our twentieth-century lifestyle are much different from those seen in any other age of persuasion, certainly much different from those experienced by colonial Americans. For this reason, we use the term *propaganda* to refer to the techniques of mass persuasion that have come to characterize our postindustrial society. The word *propaganda* is of relatively recent origin. Its first documented use occurred in 1622, when Pope Gregory XV established the Sacra Congregatio de Propaganda Fide. At the time, in the wake of the Protestant Reformation, the Roman Catholic Church was engaged in mostly unsuccessful holy wars to reestablish the faith by force of arms. Realizing that this was a losing effort, Pope Gregory established the papal propaganda office as a means of coordinating efforts to bring men and women to the "voluntary" acceptance of church doctrines. The word *propaganda* thus took on a negative connotation in Protestant countries but a positive one (similar to that of *education* or *preaching*) in Catholic areas.

14 The term *propaganda* did not see widespread use until the beginning of the twentieth century, when it was used to describe the persuasion tactics employed during World War I and those later used by totalitarian regimes. *Propaganda* was originally defined as the dissemination of biased ideas and opinions, often through the use of lies and deception. However, as scholars began to study the topic in more detail, many came to realize that propaganda was not the sole property of "evil" and totalitarian regimes and that it often consists of more than just clever deceptions. The word *propaganda* has since evolved to mean mass "suggestion" or "influence" through the manipulation of symbols and the psychology of the individual. Propaganda involves the dextrous use of images, slogans, and symbols that play on our prejudices and emotions; it is the communication of a point of view with the ultimate goal of having the recipient of the appeal come to "voluntarily" accept this position as if it were his or her own.[4] [...]

15 The eloquent rhetoric of ancient Greek and Roman, as well as colonial American, is a far cry from the typical communication of today, with its em-

phasis on the use of simple slogans and images. Increasingly, the goal of modern propaganda is not to inform and enlighten but rather to move the masses toward a desired position or point of view. The persuasion landscape of today differs vastly from those of the past in some very important ways.

16 We live in a message-dense environment. The advertisers Al Ries and Jack Trout call ours an "overcommunicated" society.[5] The average American will see or hear more than 7 million advertisements in his or her lifetime. In contrast, the average pious Puritan attending church once a week in seventeenth-century New England would hear about 3,000 sermons in a lifetime. This message-dense environment places a burden on both the communicator and the recipient of a message intended to persuade. The communicator must design a message that will not only be appealing but will also attract special notice in this cluttered environment. On the other hand, the recipient is so deluged by messages that it becomes difficult to devote the mental energy necessary to make sense of many of the important issues of the day.

17 Our age of propaganda differs in another way as well. Puritan sermons could last as long as two hours. Roman orators of the second century took courses to improve their memory so that they could remember all that they had to say. Early American patriots spent the entire summer of 1787 debating the U.S. Constitution and then produced, for the newspapers of the day, eighty-five articles totaling nearly 600 pages in its defense. Today, a televised political advertisement typically runs for thirty seconds or less. Magazine ads often consist of little more than a picture and a phrase. News of the day comes in short "soundbites" and "news snippets." For example, 70% of all local TV news stories are a minute or less in length. As the columnist George Will once put it, if Lincoln were to issue the Emancipation Proclamation today, he would probably say: "Read my lips. No more slavery." Our age of persuasion is populated with short, catchy, and often visually oriented messages. Although such persuasive images are frequently successful in capturing our attention in the message-dense environment, they substitute slogans and images for well-reasoned arguments and can turn complex issues into vulgar black-and-white caricatures of reason.

18 Persuasion in modern times is also much more immediate. The Puritan would wait all week for a sermon and months for news from England. Since the launch of *Telstar 1* in July 1962, any event happening almost anywhere in the world can be covered immediately. For example, despite efforts by the Chinese government to the contrary, CNN's coverage of the Tian'anmen Square massacre consisted of journalists telephoning detailed reports of the violence as well as play-by-play descriptions of government action and student reaction, which were then quickly broadcast to an eagerly waiting but stunned world. In a similar vein, a week before the Allied bombing of Iraq in 1991, Tariq Aziz, foreign minister of Iraq, claimed to understand American politics because he got his news from CNN. Over 1 billion people in 108 nations tuned in to CNN to watch its live and on-line coverage of the Persian Gulf war. After the nation was entertained by O. J. Simpson's slow-speed chase, CNN, E!, Court TV, and others offered continuous coverage and immediate "analysis" of the trial. More than 150 million Americans watched the delivery

of the verdict on TV. Such intense coverage was repeated again only a short time later—but this time it was the president of the United States, Bill Clinton, on trial for lying about his affair with a young intern.

19   In the 2000 U.S. presidential election, this itch for immediacy created a bizarre situation in which the news media first claimed that Al Gore had won in the state of Florida (before some polls even closed in the state) and then later in the same evening stated that the vote in Florida was too close to call and then finally reported that George W. Bush had won the state. This news prompted Gore to telephone Bush conceding the election. However, before announcing his concession to the nation, Gore found out that the election was once again too close to call and retracted his statement. The news media's rush to call the election and then recall it sent the candidates and the nation on an emotional roller coaster, creating confusion and anger on all sides.

20   And the immediacy of today's persuasion is getting even more immediate. As just one indicator: The first TV movie about the 1978 mass suicide in Jonestown took 513 days to produce; only 34 days elapsed between the fire at the Branch Davidian compound in Waco, Texas, and the first TV movie about it. The result is timely information—but often, perhaps, too timely. Whereas the Puritan could spend all week mulling over the implications of last Sunday's sermon, today's TV viewer and magazine reader has little time to think about one persuasive image before another one quickly takes its place: The trees are replacing the forest.

21   Perhaps the major difference between our own and past eras is the way in which we instruct our citizens about persuasion. If you were a citizen of a Greek city-state in the third century B.C., your education would include four years of rhetoric designed to teach you how to understand persuasive arguments and to construct your own. Should you miss your lessons, a Sophist could be hired to provide further instruction. Roman students of the first century took courses in persuasion from perhaps the greatest professor of rhetoric of all times, Quintilian, whose textbook on the subject was used for almost 1,000 years. Students at Harvard College in seventeenth-century America also had many opportunities to learn about persuasion. Every Friday afternoon for four years, the students would study how to argue; at least once a month they were required to demonstrate what they had learned by taking a stand, defending it, and attacking the views of others.

22   These cultures, unlike our own, considered an understanding of persuasion to be an essential skill needed by every citizen in order to participate fully in the affairs of state. The teaching of persuasion was a basic component of their education. In contrast, few Americans have taken a formal course on social influence. "Pop" books on the subject typically present exaggerated warnings of the dire consequences of persuasion and the mass media or simplistic "how-to-get-ahead" instructions. Although we are bombarded daily with persuasive messages, we have little opportunity to learn about the techniques of persuasion and to understand how they work. Sadly, such a state of affairs can lead to a sense of alienation and cynicism, as many Americans become bewildered by the basic decision-making processes of their society.

References

1. Colford, S. W. (1990, March 19). Athlete endorsers fouled by slayings. *Advertising Age*, p. 64.
2. Barrett, L. T. (1990, November 19). Race-baiting wins again. *Time*, p. 43.
3. Statistics are from recent issues of *American Demographics* and *Brill's Content*. Bogart, L. (1995). *Commercial culture*. New York: Oxford University Press; Jacobson, M. F., & Mazur, L. A. (1995). *Marketing madness*. Boulder, CO: Westview; Ries, A., & Trout, J. (1981). *Positioning: The battle for your mind*. New York: Warner; Aaker, D. A., & Myers, J. G. (1987). *Advertising management*. Englewood Cliffs, NJ: Prentice Hall. For a description of the mass media, see Pratkanis, A. R. (1997). The social psychology of mass communications: An American perspective. In D. F. Halpern & A. Voiskounsky (Eds.), *States of mind: American and post-Soviet perspectives on contemporary issues in psychology* (pp. 126–159). New York: Oxford University Press.
4. For a discussion of the nature of propaganda and persuasion in a democracy, see Pratkanis, A. R., & Turner, M. E. (1996). Persuasion and democracy: Strategies for increasing deliberative participation and enacting social change. *Journal of Social Issues*, 52, 187–205; Sproule, J. M. (1994). *Channels of propaganda*. Bloomington, IN: EDINFO; Sproule, J. M. (1997). *Propaganda and democracy: The American experience of media and mass persuasion*. New York: Cambridge University Press.
5. Ries & Trout (1981), see note 3.

Reading Responses

1. Why do the authors begin this selection (and their book) with the opening series of examples?
2. In the section "A Glut of Influence," how do the authors use statistics and details to support their point?
3. According to the authors, how does the communication of today differ from that of the past?

Writing Activities

1. Using your own words, explain *propaganda* and *persuasion*, clarifying how they differ.
2. Write an essay about the pervasiveness of persuasion. State a clear thesis about persuasion or propaganda today. Then supply your own examples to substantiate your thesis.
3. Write an essay about the ethical issues posed by persuasion.

Community Links

Turn to section C, "Community Ethics," for each of the other communities to locate more readings about ethical issues. Select one or two of these readings to compare and contrast with "Our Age of Propaganda." Use these readings as resources as you consider how to identify ethical issues, how to translate abstract discussions of ethics into practical applications, or a similar topic.

A More Excellent Way
Peter J. Gomes

◆

Peter Gomes is the minister of The Memorial Church at Harvard University. This reading comes from his recent book, The Good Life: Truths That Last in Times of Need, *which wrestles with the problem of applying beliefs and values in day-to-day life. The selection here, part of Chapter 1, uses a commencement story to establish the quest for those truths that last.*

> But earnestly desire the higher gifts. And I will show you a still more excellent way.   —1 Corinthians 12:31

1   Harvard Yard is never more grand than it is on Commencement Day. Beneath its shading elms, thirty thousand proud parents, friends, and pumped-up, soon-to-be graduates sit in the glow of unmitigated mutual self-congratulation. On the platform in front of the towering portico of the University's Memorial Church, dedicated to the Harvard dead of America's twentieth-century wars, sit the great and the good, which includes faculty from all over the world, resplendent in academic regalia; candidates for honorary degrees and the University's most favored guests of the day; and the vaguely familiar faces of those who actually run the place, the members of the governing boards, the deans, and the administrators. Harvard Commencement is arguably America's oldest continuing public ceremony, doing business since 1642 in essentially the same form.

2   In June 2001, in the midst of this heady mix of pomp and circumstance, the undergraduate speaker, Seth Moulton,[1] rose and, doffing his cap, making his ceremonial bow to the president, and squaring his feet at the microphone, began his five-minute oration. Unlike most American colleges, Harvard does not have to endure a major address at the time it gives out its degrees, and thus the only speeches are those given by three students, one speech of which is in Latin and thus mercifully inaccessible to all but the seniors and faculty who have been provided a translation. Our young orator could be expected to touch upon the usual pieties: students helping one another through the trials of college life, the sense of joy and relief at going out into the "real world," and the greatness of Harvard and, by implication, its newest graduates. It became clear early on, however, that this young orator was not proposing to rest content with the conventional wisdom of Commencement Day.

3   After invoking a litany of Harvard greats: John Adams and John Quincy Adams, Theodore Roosevelt and Franklin Delano Roosevelt, W. E. B. Du Bois, Helen Keller, and John Fitzgerald Kennedy, he asked what they all had in common, and then answered his own question. "Dead," he said. "They are all dead. The University now belongs to us, as do the times. What will we do with them?" Earlier generations had been summoned from the Commencement platform to lives of conflict and responsibility. The grandparents of many seniors—the much-celebrated "Greatest Generation"—had grown up in the

Great Depression and responded to the demands of World War II and Korea. The parents of many present on this day had found themselves engaged in the war in or about Vietnam, and for many others of that era there had been struggles for civil rights and women's rights and the peace movement. Our orator essentially asked his classmates: What will be our call to greatness, our summons to nobility? In this season of endless prosperity and self-interest, is there anything that will require the best of what we have to offer? Is there any cause great or good enough to provoke goodness and greatness in us?

4 As with much discourse, the questions were better than the answers, and our young speaker received a polite but not enthusiastic response to his eloquence. The alumni magazine, in fact, took so little notice of the speech that neither it nor the speaker was mentioned in its major news and feature accounts of Commencement. The question of a call to nobility, however, touched a nerve among many of the young present that morning.

5 My own observation had long been that students were becoming increasingly restive about the moral dimension of their education. Certainly they appreciated the opportunity provided by study at a great university, and most of them had done reasonably well at their tasks and had had some fun into the bargain. Nearly all of them had interesting futures upon which to embark as soon as they left Cambridge, which included going on to graduate and professional schools, taking up foreign fellowships and travel or coveted entry-level positions with New York consultancy or financial houses, or even a little unprogrammed R and R; as one student pointed out to me, "My parents have had me on this college track since I was in day care, and now, after twenty-two years, I'd like a little time to myself."

6 Noble thoughts would appear to be far away from the minds of this indulged and indulgent generation, yet many conversations over recent years have told me otherwise. More and more students are asking questions about the moral use of their lives and their education, and about their value, when value questions about education used to be rigorously utilitarian. "How much is my degree worth," the students used to ask, "and how much will it get me of this world's goods?" It is not because of the intrinsic intellectual merit of the field of economics that most undergraduates have chosen to major in that subject over the past decade. The primacy of economics, the so-called dismal science, is acute everywhere, and particularly so at Harvard, where the last three Commencement speakers have included such economic superstars as Amartya Sen, Alan Greenspan, and Robert Rubin and where the new president, Lawrence H. Summers, who served briefly as Secretary of the Treasury in the Clinton administration, is an economist by profession. The value questions now, however, which were once tied to potential net worth, increasingly have to do with matters of moral value, public and private virtue, and a sense of a fit vocation for making a good life and not just a good living.

7 Our student orator that Commencement Day was my student and is now my friend, and over the course of his college career we had many conversations about the large questions of value, virtue, worth, and vocation and what, if anything, his college education had to do with any of them. He and many of his classmates had recognized a disconnect between the ideas and moments of

which they had heard and read in their studies and the sense of what they might be called upon to do in life beyond simply satisfying a set of course requirements.

8   Except for the occasional deferential nod to the notion of public service, American higher education in the last decades of the twentieth century has seemed to go out of its way to avoid any kind of moral claims upon the minds, hearts, and lives of its young constituents. It almost seems as though, with the death of the concept *in loco parentis* and the demise of parietal rules and dress codes, any claims for public good on behalf of the highly educated young were considered, if at all, either in the baccalaureate sermon or in the Commencement address, where they were offered too late to do much harm or to be of much good. In 1701, for instance, Yale was founded to fit the best and the brightest for "service in church and state," which fairly well summed up eighteenth-century Connecticut's public sector; and nearly every other American college since has stored among its founding documents a notion having to do with the noble civic and virtuous ends for the public good toward which the educational product of the institution was directed. [. . .]

9   Seth Moulton entitled his Commencement oration "Achieving Greatness," and it delivered not the usual invitation to go out and make a success of oneself. Describing the Western world of most of his listening contemporaries as "dominated by contentment and threatened by mediocrity," he invited his classmates to become the kind of people who are "bold and courageous . . . who are willing to take extraordinary steps to an uncertain future." Then, as if in contemplation of some summons to an as yet unidentified difficult challenge on some future day, he cited a favorite aphorism: "When you're damned if you do and damned if you don't; always do." Within three short months, and before the start of the next academic year, that challenge would present itself on the morning of September 11, 2001.

After the Fall

10 In the *Boston Globe* of Monday, September 10, 2001, in a column entitled "Don't Sell Teens Short—They Are the Future," Lily Rayman-Read, a senior at Lexington High School in that historic Massachusetts town famous for the opening skirmishes of the American Revolution, described her summer job as part of a Boston inner-city garden project:

> Garden Futures is an organization that connects people in different communities and neighborhoods by cultivating and developing a garden, and through these community gardens many bonds are formed, and a sense of community is strengthened. . . . By meeting so many different people, I learned a great deal about the significance of diversity for gardens and for people.

11 She also learned a greater lesson that she wished to share. Acknowledging that "teenagers have a reputation for apathy and not caring about the world around us," Lily went on to note: "The truth is, we do care; we often just don't know what to do or how to make a difference." I doubt very much that young Lily

had read Howe and Strauss's new book, *Millennials Rising: The Next Great Generation,* or that she could have anticipated the calamitous events that within twenty-four hours of the appearance of her article in the newspaper would destabilize her world forever, but in the final paragraph of her article, which was prominently sited on the op-ed page, she wrote:

> Thanks to my experiences throughout the summer, I realize that all teenagers have the power to make a difference for ourselves and for our communities. If people gave us the chance to help out, I think the world would be surprised at just how committed teens can be in improving the world around us, because we are, after all, the future.

12 Lily's homily was lost in the terror of the next day and the epidemic of anxiety that has since been stylized simply as "9/11," but in her appeal to allow the realization of the potential goodness and greatness of her much-maligned generation, she has placed herself and her peers in the face of the greatest challenge to face our nation since the Civil War, the last time American blood was spilled on American soil.

13 The question for each rising generation since World War II has always been this: In the absence of a crisis, would the young know one when they saw one, and would they be capable of rising to meet it, indulged and diverted as they had been for nearly all of their young lives? The story is yet to be told about the young's capacity to respond to the events of September 11, but it certainly seems as if they have been in preparation for a long while for such a claim on their sense of identity and purpose. The Seths, the Lilys, and the thousands described as the "next great generation" seem to have anticipated the character-forming sense of crisis as a moment of moral opportunity, a proving ground for what the Bible calls, in St. Paul's words, "a more excellent way." In the aftermath of September 11 we have seen the young willingly respond to the call of their country for both military and social service. We have seen heroic youthful volunteer efforts in light of the horrific needs at Ground Zero. We have seen a revival of youthful patriotism, not simply of the flag-waving "U.S.A., U.S.A." sporting events sort, but of a desire to—in the famous and at once antique phrase of John F. Kennedy's inaugural address—"Ask not what your country can do for you; ask what you can do for your country." This youthful new patriotism, as I will call it, manifests itself within the new realities of our pluralistic culture and world.

14 Among the many urgent concerns I heard in the College Yard on the afternoon of September 11 was the desire for the well-being of Muslim students, and especially of those from Arab lands. In the Christian prayer groups that sprang into action within hours of the terrible news from New York, prayers for "our Muslim brothers and sisters" were uttered with a sincerity and passion that described the new patriotism as American, Christian, and compassionate. In many places, including at Harvard, young Jews, Christians, and Muslims gathered together by instinct for prayer and encouragement.

15 While I do not know this, I cannot imagine that on Sunday afternoon, December 7, 1941, many prayers were offered for our Japanese brothers and sisters. What I do know is that when The Reverend Charles Joy, minister of

the First Parish Church in Portland, Maine, declared in a sermon preached just as we entered World War I, in April 1917, "If I remain your minister, prayers shall ascend for Germany and America alike," on the very next day he was burned in effigy on the iron railings in front of his church.[2]

16   Somehow, and often with little help from their elders, our young people, particularly in our schools, colleges, and universities, have begun to discover those truths that last in times of need. Unbeknownst to much of the profit-driven mavens of a corrosively materialistic popular culture that preys on the susceptibilities and anxieties of youth, these very same youth, shrewd critics of that culture and of those who run it, have been on a search for greatness, for goodness, and even for nobility, that "more excellent way" of which St. Paul speaks. They have been looking for that time, their time, in which to transform and be transformed. That time, I suggest, has now come, and the truths for making the most of that time will always expose the lies.

Notes

1. Seth Wilbur Moulton, '01, was chosen to give the undergraduate English "part" by the Standing Committee on Commencement Parts, a faculty body with responsibility for the selection of three student speakers to address the gathering at the morning exercises of Harvard Commencement. A University-wide competition is held in early spring, when the final three students are chosen; the "parts" are memorized, and the students deliver them in great style before an audience of some thirty thousand people, thus carrying on a tradition that began in 1642 with the first Harvard Commencement. Moulton has since enrolled in the Officer Corps of the United States Marines. A native of Marblehead, Massachusetts, he is also a graduate of Phillips Academy, Andover, Massachusetts.
2. *Down East: The Magazine of Maine* (December 2001): 81.

Reading Responses

1. Why doesn't Gomes begin with Seth Moulton's questions in paragraph 1? Why does he hold those questions until paragraph 3?
2. The section "After the Fall" concludes the first chapter. What does this heading mean?
3. Why does Gomes begin by talking about commencement and end by discussing September 11? How does he lead a reader along his path?

Writing Activities

1. Write an essay that discusses and illustrates the ways that Gomes uses contrasts.
2. In your own words, summarize Gomes's answer to Moulton's question (paragraph 3). Explain what Gomes believes that this generation of college students will do with the times that are theirs.
3. Write an addition to Gomes's chapter, a section that illustrates from your observation or experience the capacity of the current generation of students to rise to the challenge of a crisis.

Community Links

Compare and contrast this selection by Gomes with another reading that calls on readers to meet a challenge. For example, you might turn to one of the civic addresses such as Bush's address following September 11 (pp. 433–438) or King's "I Have a Dream" (pp. 439–442), to Katz's "The Pathbreaking, Fractionalized, Uncertain World of Knowledge" (pp. 52–58) or Mairson's commencement address (pp. 192–196) from the academic community, or to Ehrenreich's "Evaluation" (pp. 208–212) from the work community.

Texts and Documents from the Public Community

Civic Declaration

THE DECLARATION OF INDEPENDENCE*

Thomas Jefferson

◆

Part of a committee appointed by the Second Continental Congress, Thomas Jefferson drafted the Declaration of Independence in June 1776. Other members of the committee, Benjamin Franklin and John Adams, made small revisions. The Continental Congress made further changes, passed a resolution of independence on July 2, and then approved the declaration on July 4. The document remains an essential statement of the principles that underlie the nation to which it gave rise.

IN CONGRESS, JULY 4, 1776

The unanimous Declaration of the thirteen united States of America

1 WHEN in the Course of human events, it becomes necessary for one people to dissolve the political bands which have connected them with another, and to assume among the powers of the earth, the separate and equal station to which the Laws of Nature and of Nature's God entitle them, a decent respect to the opinions of mankind requires that they should declare the causes which impel them to the separation.

2 We hold these truths to be self-evident, that all men are created equal, that they are endowed by their Creator with certain unalienable Rights, that among these are Life, Liberty and the pursuit of Happiness. That to secure these rights, Governments are instituted among Men, deriving their just powers from the consent of the governed,—That whenever any Form of Government becomes destructive of these ends, it is the Right of the People to alter or to abolish it, and to institute new Government, laying its foundation on such principles and organizing its powers in such form, as to them shall

---

*The text of the Declaration of Independence follows that at pages xxxix-xli, Volume I, the 1988 Edition of the United States Code. Inconsistencies of style present in the source texts are reproduced here.

seem most likely to effect their Safety and Happiness. Prudence, indeed, will dictate that Governments long established should not be changed for light and transient causes; and accordingly all experience hath shewn, that mankind are more disposed to suffer, while evils are sufferable, than to right themselves by abolishing the forms to which they are accustomed. But when a long train of abuses and usurpations, pursuing invariably the same Object evinces a design to reduce them under absolute Despotism, it is their right, it is their duty, to throw off such Government, and to provide new Guards for their future security.—Such has been the patient sufferance of these Colonies; and such is now the necessity which constrains them to alter their former Systems of Government. The history of the present King of Great Britain is a history of repeated injuries and usurpations, all having in direct object the establishment of an absolute Tyranny over these States. To prove this, let Facts be submitted to a candid world.

3   He has refused his Assent to Laws, the most wholesome and necessary for the public good.

4   He has forbidden his Governors to pass Laws of immediate and pressing importance, unless suspended in their operation till his Assent should be obtained; and when so suspended, he has utterly neglected to attend to them.

5   He has refused to pass other Laws for the accommodation of large districts of people, unless those people would relinquish the right of Representation in the Legislature, a right inestimable to them and formidable to tyrants only.

6   He has called together legislative bodies at places unusual, uncomfortable, and distant from the depository of their public Records, for the sole purpose of fatiguing them into compliance with his measures.

7   He has dissolved Representative Houses repeatedly, for opposing with manly firmness his invasions on the rights of the people.

8   He has refused for a long time, after such dissolutions, to cause others to be elected; whereby the Legislative powers, incapable of Annihilation, have returned to the People at large for their exercise; the State remaining in the mean time exposed to all the dangers of invasion from without, and convulsions within.

9   He has endeavoured to prevent the population of these States; for that purpose obstructing the Laws for Naturalization of Foreigners; refusing to pass others to encourage their migrations hither, and raising the conditions of new Appropriations of Lands.

10   He has obstructed the Administration of Justice, by refusing his Assent to Laws for establishing Judiciary powers.

11   He has made Judges dependent on his Will alone, for the tenure of their offices, and the amount and payment of their salaries.

12   He has erected a multitude of New Offices, and sent hither swarms of Officers to harass our people, and eat out their substance.

13   He has kept among us, in times of peace, Standing Armies without the Consent of our legislatures.

14   He has affected to render the Military independent of and superior to the Civil Power.

15   He has combined with others to subject us to a jurisdiction foreign to our constitution, and unacknowledged by our laws; giving his Assent to their acts of pretended Legislation:

    For quartering large bodies of armed troops among us:

    For protecting them, by a mock Trial, from punishment for any Murders which they should commit on the Inhabitants of these States: For cutting off our Trade with all parts of the world:

    For imposing Taxes on us without our Consent:

    For depriving us in many cases, of the benefits of Trial by Jury:

    For transporting us beyond Seas to be tried for pretended offenses:

    For abolishing the free System of English Laws in a neighbouring Province, establishing therein an Arbitrary government, and enlarging its Boundaries so as to render it at once an example and fit instrument for introducing the same absolute rule into these Colonies:

    For taking away our Charters, abolishing our most valuable Laws, and altering fundamentally the Forms of our Governments:

    For suspending our own Legislatures, and declaring themselves invested with power to legislate for us in all cases whatsoever.

16   He has abdicated Government here, by declaring us out of his Protection and waging War against us.

17   He has plundered our seas, ravaged our Coasts, burnt our towns, and destroyed the lives of our people.

18   He is at this time transporting large Armies of foreign Mercenaries to compleat the works of death, desolation and tyranny, already begun with circumstances of Cruelty & perfidy scarcely paralleled in the most barbarous ages, and totally unworthy the Head of a civilized nation.

19   He has constrained our fellow Citizens taken Captive on the high Seas to bear Arms against their Country, to become the executioners of their friends and Brethren, or to fall themselves by their Hands.

20   He has excited domestic insurrections amongst us, and has endeavoured to bring on the inhabitants of our frontiers, the merciless Indian Savages, whose known rule of warfare, is an undistinguished destruction of all ages, sexes and conditions.

21   In every stage of these Oppressions We have Petitioned for Redress in the most humble terms: Our repeated Petitions have been answered only by repeated injury. A Prince, whose character is thus marked by every act which may define a Tyrant, is unfit to be the ruler of a free people.

22   Nor have We been wanting in attentions to our Brittish brethren We have warned them from time to time of attempts by their legislature to extend an unwarrantable jurisdiction over us. We have reminded them of the circumstances of our emigration and settlement here. We have appealed to their native justice and magnanimity, and we have conjured them by the ties of our common kindred to disavow these usurpations which, would inevitably interrupt our connections and correspondence. They too have been deaf to the voice of justice and of consanguinity. We must, therefore, acquiesce in the necessity, which denounces our Separation, and hold them, as we hold the rest of mankind, Enemies in War, in Peace Friends.

23   We, THEREFORE, the Representatives of the UNITED STATES OF AMERICA, in General Congress, Assembled, appealing to the Supreme Judge of the

world for the rectitude of our intentions, do, in the Name, and by Authority of the good People of these Colonies, solemnly publish and declare, That these United Colonies are, and of Right ought to be FREE AND INDEPENDENT STATES; that they are Absolved from all Allegiance to the British Crown, and that all political connection between them and the State of Great Britain, is and ought to be totally dissolved; and that as Free and Independent States, they have full Power to levy War, conclude Peace, contract Alliances, establish Commerce, and to do all other Acts and Things which Independent States may of right do. And for the support of this Declaration, with a firm reliance on the protection of divine Providence, we mutually pledge to each other our Lives, our Fortunes and our sacred Honor.

JOHN HANCOCK

New Hampshire

JOSIAH BARTLETT,
WM. WHIPPLE,
MATTHEW THORNTON.

Massachusetts Bay

SAML. ADAMS,
JOHN ADAMS,
ROBT. TREAT PAINE,
ELBRIDGE GERRY.

Rhode Island

STEP. HOPKINS,
WILLIAM ELLERY.

Connecticut

ROGER SHERMAN,
SAM'EL HUNTINGTON,
WM. WILLIAMS,
OLIVER WOLCOTT.

New York

WM. FLOYD,
PHIL. LIVINGSTON,
FRANS. LEWIS,
LEWIS MORRIS.

New Jersey

RICHD. STOCKTON,
JNO. WITHERSPOON,
FRAS. HOPKINSON,
JOHN HART,
ABRA. CLARK.

Pennsylvania

ROBT. MORRIS,
BENJAMIN RUSH,
BENJA. FRANKLIN
JOHN MORTON,
GEO. CLYMER,
JAS. SMITH,
GEO. TAYLOR,
JAMES WILSON,
GEO. ROSS.

Delaware

Caesar Rodney, Tho. M'Kean.
Geo. Read,

Maryland

Samuel Chase, Charles
Wm. Paca, Carroll of
Thos. Stone, Carrollton.

Virginia

George Wythe, Thos.
Richard Henry Lee Nelson, Jr.,
Th. Jefferson, Francis
Benja. Harrison, Lightfoot
Lee,
Carter
Braxton.

North Carolina

Wm. Hooper, John Penn.
Joseph Hewes,

South Carolina

Thos. Heyward, Thomas
Junr., Lynch,
Edward Junr.,
Rutledge, Arthur
Middleton.

Georgia

Button Gwinnett, Geo.
Lyman Hall, Walton.

 Reading Responses

1. What is the purpose of the Declaration of Independence? Where is this purpose stated?
2. In what ways does Jefferson justify the decision of the Continental Congress to declare independence?
3. What readers does Jefferson address? In what ways does he acknowledge possible expectations of readers?

Writing Activities

1. Paraphrase the first two paragraphs of the Declaration of Independence by restating its ideas in your own words.
2. Make a brief outline of the main sections of the Declaration. Write a paragraph explaining how Jefferson organized the argument in the document.
3. Write your own declaration of independence from whatever tyranny oppresses you. Follow the general structure used by Jefferson.

Community Links

Compare and contrast the Declaration of Independence with one or two other arguments in this book. For example, you might consider Lee's "The Case Against College" (pp. 73–75) or Mairson's "In Praise of the Research University" (pp. 192–196) from the academic community, Simpson's "Are Incentives for Drug Abuse Treatment Too Strong?" (pp. 301–306) from the work community, or Cullis-Suzuki's "The Young Can't Wait" (pp. 355–356), also from the public community.

THE TREATY INITIATIVE TO SHARE AND PROTECT THE GLOBAL WATER COMMONS

Maude Barlow and Jeremy Rifkin

◆

This Treaty Initiative was approved on July 8, 2001, at Water for People and Nature, an international summit held in Vancouver. It precedes the first section of Blue Gold: The Fight to Save the Corporate Theft of the World's Water *by Maude Barlow and Tony Clarke. This book outlines a global water crisis and challenges the sale of water resources, privatizing the control of water and treating it as a market commodity rather than protecting it as a resource to be shared by all. The Treaty Initiative asserts the principles and values of the movement to protect an essential global resource: fresh water.*

1   We proclaim these truths to be universal and indivisible:

That the intrinsic value of the Earth's fresh water precedes its utility and commercial value, and therefore must be respected and safeguarded by all political, commercial, and social institutions,

That the Earth's fresh water belongs to the Earth and all species, and therefore must not be treated as a private commodity to be bought, sold, and traded for profit,

That the global fresh water supply is a shared legacy, a public trust, and a fundamental human right, and therefore, a collective responsibility,

And,

Whereas, the world's finite supply of available fresh water is being polluted, diverted, and depleted so quickly that millions of people and species are now deprived of water for life and,

Whereas governments around the world have failed to protect their precious fresh water legacies,

Therefore, the nations of the world declare the Earth's fresh water supply to be a global commons, to be protected and nurtured by all peoples, communities, and governments of all levels and further declare that fresh water will not be allowed to be privatized, commodified, traded, or exported for commercial purposes and must immediately be exempted from all existing and future international and bilateral trade and investment agreements.

The parties to this treaty—to include signatory nation-states and Indigenous peoples—further agree to administer the Earth's fresh water supply as a trust. The signatories acknowledge the sovereign right and responsibility of every nation and homeland to oversee the fresh water resources within their borders and determine how they are managed and shared. Governments all over the world must take immediate action to declare that the waters in their territories are a public good and enact strong regulatory structures to protect them. However, because the world's fresh water supply is a global commons, it cannot be sold by any institution, government, individual, or corporation for profit.

Reading Responses

1. What basic principles does the Treaty Initiative proclaim? In what ways does it say that these principles have been violated?
2. What does the Treaty Initiative declare? What steps does it advocate?
3. What wording signals the structure and progression of the argument in the Treaty Initiative?

Writing Activities

1. Make a brief outline of the main sections of the Treaty Initiative. Write a paragraph explaining how Barlow and Rifkin organize the argument in the document.
2. How might the Treaty Initiative be implemented? Write an essay proposing possible next steps, relying on the implications of the Treaty Initiative or your own ideas based on your existing knowledge or research about water issues. (For more information on this issue, see also "The Standpoint," pp. 479–489.)
3. Write an initiative for the protection or preservation of something that you value. Follow the structure used by Barlow and Rifkin.

Community Links

Compare and contrast the Declaration of Independence (pp. 426–430) and the Treaty Initiative, considering similarities and differences in structure, assumptions, values, logical grounds, or other points that engage your attention.

Civic Address

ADDRESS TO A JOINT SESSION OF CONGRESS AND THE AMERICAN PEOPLE, SEPTEMBER 20, 2001

President George W. Bush

◆

On September 20, 2001, President George W. Bush addressed the Congress and the nation about the events nine days before—the attacks on the World Trade Center and the Pentagon on September 11. His speech lasted forty-one minutes and was frequently interrupted by applause.

1 THE PRESIDENT: Mr. Speaker, Mr. President Pro Tempore, members of Congress, and fellow Americans:

2 In the normal course of events, Presidents come to this chamber to report on the state of the Union. Tonight, no such report is needed. It has already been delivered by the American people.

3 We have seen it in the courage of passengers, who rushed terrorists to save others on the ground—passengers like an exceptional man named Todd Beamer. And would you please help me to welcome his wife, Lisa Beamer, here tonight.

4 We have seen the state of our Union in the endurance of rescuers, working past exhaustion. We have seen the unfurling of flags, the lighting of candles, the giving of blood, the saying of prayers—in English, Hebrew, and Arabic. We have seen the decency of a loving and giving people who have made the grief of strangers their own.

5 My fellow citizens, for the last nine days, the entire world has seen for itself the state of our Union—and it is strong.

6 Tonight we are a country awakened to danger and called to defend freedom. Our grief has turned to anger, and anger to resolution. Whether we bring our enemies to justice, or bring justice to our enemies, justice will be done.

7 I thank the Congress for its leadership at such an important time. All of America was touched on the evening of the tragedy to see Republicans and

Democrats joined together on the steps of this Capitol, singing "God Bless America." And you did more than sing; you acted, by delivering $40 billion to rebuild our communities and meet the needs of our military.

8   Speaker Hastert, Minority Leader Gephardt, Majority Leader Daschle and Senator Lott, I thank you for your friendship, for your leadership and for your service to our country.

9   And on behalf of the American people, I thank the world for its outpouring of support. America will never forget the sounds of our National Anthem playing at Buckingham Palace, on the streets of Paris, and at Berlin's Brandenburg Gate.

10   We will not forget South Korean children gathering to pray outside our embassy in Seoul, or the prayers of sympathy offered at a mosque in Cairo. We will not forget moments of silence and days of mourning in Australia and Africa and Latin America.

11   Nor will we forget the citizens of 80 other nations who died with our own: dozens of Pakistanis; more than 130 Israelis; more than 250 citizens of India; men and women from El Salvador, Iran, Mexico and Japan; and hundreds of British citizens. America has no truer friend than Great Britain. Once again, we are joined together in a great cause—so honored the British Prime Minister has crossed an ocean to show his unity of purpose with America. Thank you for coming, friend.

12   On September the 11th, enemies of freedom committed an act of war against our country. Americans have known wars—but for the past 136 years, they have been wars on foreign soil, except for one Sunday in 1941. Americans have known the casualties of war—but not at the center of a great city on a peaceful morning. Americans have known surprise attacks—but never before on thousands of civilians. All of this was brought upon us in a single day—and night fell on a different world, a world where freedom itself is under attack.

13   Americans have many questions tonight. Americans are asking: Who attacked our country? The evidence we have gathered all points to a collection of loosely affiliated terrorist organizations known as al Qaeda. They are the same murderers indicted for bombing American embassies in Tanzania and Kenya, and responsible for bombing the USS Cole.

14   Al Qaeda is to terror what the mafia is to crime. But its goal is not making money; its goal is remaking the world—and imposing its radical beliefs on people everywhere.

15   The terrorists practice a fringe form of Islamic extremism that has been rejected by Muslim scholars and the vast majority of Muslim clerics—a fringe movement that perverts the peaceful teachings of Islam. The terrorists' directive commands them to kill Christians and Jews, to kill all Americans, and make no distinction among military and civilians, including women and children.

16   This group and its leader—a person named Osama bin Laden—are linked to many other organizations in different countries, including the Egyptian Islamic Jihad and the Islamic Movement of Uzbekistan. There are thousands of these terrorists in more than 60 countries. They are recruited from their own

nations and neighborhoods and brought to camps in places like Afghanistan, where they are trained in the tactics of terror. They are sent back to their homes or sent to hide in countries around the world to plot evil and destruction.

17 The leadership of al Qaeda has great influence in Afghanistan and supports the Taliban regime in controlling most of that country. In Afghanistan, we see al Qaeda's vision for the world.

18 Afghanistan's people have been brutalized—many are starving and many have fled. Women are not allowed to attend school. You can be jailed for owning a television. Religion can be practiced only as their leaders dictate. A man can be jailed in Afghanistan if his beard is not long enough.

19 The United States respects the people of Afghanistan—after all, we are currently its largest source of humanitarian aid—but we condemn the Taliban regime. It is not only repressing its own people, it is threatening people everywhere by sponsoring and sheltering and supplying terrorists. By aiding and abetting murder, the Taliban regime is committing murder.

20 And tonight, the United States of America makes the following demands on the Taliban: Deliver to United States authorities all the leaders of al Qaeda who hide in your land. Release all foreign nationals, including American citizens, you have unjustly imprisoned. Protect foreign journalists, diplomats and aid workers in your country. Close immediately and permanently every terrorist training camp in Afghanistan, and hand over every terrorist, and every person in their support structure, to appropriate authorities. Give the United States full access to terrorist training camps, so we can make sure they are no longer operating.

21 These demands are not open to negotiation or discussion. The Taliban must act, and act immediately. They will hand over the terrorists, or they will share in their fate.

22 I also want to speak tonight directly to Muslims throughout the world. We respect your faith. It's practiced freely by many millions of Americans, and by millions more in countries that America counts as friends. Its teachings are good and peaceful, and those who commit evil in the name of Allah blaspheme the name of Allah. The terrorists are traitors to their own faith, trying, in effect, to hijack Islam itself. The enemy of America is not our many Muslim friends; it is not our many Arab friends. Our enemy is a radical network of terrorists, and every government that supports them.

23 Our war on terror begins with al Qaeda, but it does not end there. It will not end until every terrorist group of global reach has been found, stopped and defeated.

24 Americans are asking, why do they hate us? They hate what we see right here in this chamber—a democratically elected government. Their leaders are self-appointed. They hate our freedoms—our freedom of religion, our freedom of speech, our freedom to vote and assemble and disagree with each other.

25 They want to overthrow existing governments in many Muslim countries, such as Egypt, Saudi Arabia, and Jordan. They want to drive Israel out of the Middle East. They want to drive Christians and Jews out of vast regions of Asia and Africa.

26 These terrorists kill not merely to end lives, but to disrupt and end a way of life. With every atrocity, they hope that America grows fearful, retreating from the world and forsaking our friends. They stand against us, because we stand in their way.

27 We are not deceived by their pretenses to piety. We have seen their kind before. They are the heirs of all the murderous ideologies of the 20th century. By sacrificing human life to serve their radical visions—by abandoning every value except the will to power—they follow in the path of fascism, and Nazism, and totalitarianism. And they will follow that path all the way, to where it ends: in history's unmarked grave of discarded lies.

28 Americans are asking: How will we fight and win this war? We will direct every resource at our command—every means of diplomacy, every tool of intelligence, every instrument of law enforcement, every financial influence, and every necessary weapon of war—to the disruption and to the defeat of the global terror network.

29 This war will not be like the war against Iraq a decade ago, with a decisive liberation of territory and a swift conclusion. It will not look like the air war above Kosovo two years ago, where no ground troops were used and not a single American was lost in combat.

30 Our response involves far more than instant retaliation and isolated strikes. Americans should not expect one battle, but a lengthy campaign, unlike any other we have ever seen. It may include dramatic strikes, visible on TV, and covert operations, secret even in success. We will starve terrorists of funding, turn them one against another, drive them from place to place, until there is no refuge or no rest. And we will pursue nations that provide aid or safe haven to terrorism. Every nation, in every region, now has a decision to make. Either you are with us, or you are with the terrorists. From this day forward, any nation that continues to harbor or support terrorism will be regarded by the United States as a hostile regime.

31 Our nation has been put on notice: We are not immune from attack. We will take defensive measures against terrorism to protect Americans. Today, dozens of federal departments and agencies, as well as state and local governments, have responsibilities affecting homeland security. These efforts must be coordinated at the highest level. So tonight I announce the creation of a Cabinet-level position reporting directly to me—the Office of Homeland Security.

32 And tonight I also announce a distinguished American to lead this effort, to strengthen American security: a military veteran, an effective governor, a true patriot, a trusted friend—Pennsylvania's Tom Ridge. He will lead, oversee and coordinate a comprehensive national strategy to safeguard our country against terrorism, and respond to any attacks that may come.

33 These measures are essential. But the only way to defeat terrorism as a threat to our way of life is to stop it, eliminate it, and destroy it where it grows.

34 Many will be involved in this effort, from FBI agents to intelligence operatives to the reservists we have called to active duty. All deserve our thanks, and all have our prayers. And tonight, a few miles from the damaged Pentagon, I

have a message for our military: Be ready. I've called the Armed Forces to alert, and there is a reason. The hour is coming when America will act, and you will make us proud.

35   This is not, however, just America's fight. And what is at stake is not just America's freedom. This is the world's fight. This is civilization's fight. This is the fight of all who believe in progress and pluralism, tolerance and freedom.

36   We ask every nation to join us. We will ask, and we will need, the help of police forces, intelligence services, and banking systems around the world. The United States is grateful that many nations and many international organizations have already responded—with sympathy and with support. Nations from Latin America, to Asia, to Africa, to Europe, to the Islamic world. Perhaps the NATO Charter reflects best the attitude of the world: An attack on one is an attack on all.

37   The civilized world is rallying to America's side. They understand that if this terror goes unpunished, their own cities, their own citizens may be next. Terror, unanswered, can not only bring down buildings, it can threaten the stability of legitimate governments. And you know what—we're not going to allow it.

38   Americans are asking: What is expected of us? I ask you to live your lives, and hug your children. I know many citizens have fears tonight, and I ask you to be calm and resolute, even in the face of a continuing threat.

39   I ask you to uphold the values of America, and remember why so many have come here. We are in a fight for our principles, and our first responsibility is to live by them. No one should be singled out for unfair treatment or unkind words because of their ethnic background or religious faith.

40   I ask you to continue to support the victims of this tragedy with your contributions. Those who want to give can go to a central source of information, libertyunites.org, to find the names of groups providing direct help in New York, Pennsylvania, and Virginia.

41   The thousands of FBI agents who are now at work in this investigation may need your cooperation, and I ask you to give it.

42   I ask for your patience, with the delays and inconveniences that may accompany tighter security; and for your patience in what will be a long struggle.

43   I ask your continued participation and confidence in the American economy. Terrorists attacked a symbol of American prosperity. They did not touch its source. America is successful because of the hard work, and creativity, and enterprise of our people. These were the true strengths of our economy before September 11th, and they are our strengths today.

44   And, finally, please continue praying for the victims of terror and their families, for those in uniform, and for our great country. Prayer has comforted us in sorrow, and will help strengthen us for the journey ahead.

45   Tonight I thank my fellow Americans for what you have already done and for what you will. [L]adies and gentlemen of the Congress, I thank you, their representatives, for what you have already done and for what we will do together.

46   Tonight, we face new and sudden national challenges. We will come together to improve air safety, to dramatically expand the number of air marshals on domestic flights, and take new measures to prevent hijacking. We will come

together to promote stability and keep our airlines flying, with direct assistance during this emergency.

47   We will come together to give law enforcement the additional tools it needs to track down terror here at home. We will come together to strengthen our intelligence capabilities to know the plans of terrorists before they act, and find them before they strike.

48   We will come together to take active steps that strengthen America's economy, and put our people back to work.

49   Tonight we welcome two leaders who embody the extraordinary spirit of all New Yorkers: Governor George Pataki, and Mayor Rudolph Giuliani. As a symbol of America's resolve, my administration will work with Congress, and these two leaders, to show the world that we will rebuild New York City.

50   After all that has just passed—all the lives taken, and all the possibilities and hopes that died with them—it is natural to wonder if America's future is one of fear. Some speak of an age of terror. I know there are struggles ahead, and dangers to face. But this country will define our times, not be defined by them. As long as the United States of America is determined and strong, this will not be an age of terror; this will be an age of liberty, here and across the world.

51   Great harm has been done to us. We have suffered great loss. And in our grief and anger we have found our mission and our moment. Freedom and fear are at war. The advance of human freedom—the great achievement of our time, and the great hope of every time—now depends on us. Our nation—this generation—will lift a dark threat of violence from our people and our future. We will rally the world to this cause by our efforts, by our courage. We will not tire, we will not falter, and we will not fail.

52   It is my hope that in the months and years ahead, life will return almost to normal. We'll go back to our lives and routines, and that is good. Even grief recedes with time and grace. But our resolve must not pass. Each of us will remember what happened that day, and to whom it happened. We'll remember the moment the news came—where we were and what we were doing. Some will remember an image of a fire, or a story of rescue. Some will carry memories of a face and a voice gone forever.

53   And I will carry this: It is the police shield of a man named George Howard, who died at the World Trade Center trying to save others. It was given to me by his mom, Arlene, as a proud memorial to her son. This is my reminder of lives that ended, and a task that does not end.

54   I will not forget this wound to our country or those who inflicted it. I will not yield; I will not rest; I will not relent in waging this struggle for freedom and security for the American people.

55   The course of this conflict is not known, yet its outcome is certain. Freedom and fear, justice and cruelty, have always been at war, and we know that God is not neutral between them.

56   Fellow citizens, we'll meet violence with patient justice—assured of the rightness of our cause, and confident of the victories to come. In all that lies before us, may God grant us wisdom, and may He watch over the United States of America.

57   Thank you.

Reading Responses

1. What is the purpose of this speech? Why does the president wait until paragraph 12 to identify September 11 explicitly?
2. The phrase "Americans are asking" is repeated several times. How is it used to introduce major sections of the speech? How do the words *asking* and *ask* help unify the speech?
3. In what ways does the president acknowledge his audience—those present in the Capitol and those watching and listening all around the country and the world?

Writing Activities

1. Make an outline of the main sections of the speech. Write a paragraph briefly analyzing how the speech is organized.
2. Examine the use of repeated words and expressions in the speech. Write an essay about how this feature of the speech contributes to its effectiveness. Use specific examples from the speech to illustrate and support your points.
3. Write the speech you would like to give, inspiring others in the face of some specific adversity or challenge.

Community Links

Compare and contrast President Bush's Address with some other efforts to encourage and inspire. Look, for example, at readings such as Vermette's letter to his son (pp. 96–100) from the academic community, Lesh-Laurie's memo (p. 307) from the work community, Gomes's "A More Excellent Way" (pp. 420–424) from the public community, or a similar reading. Based on two or three of these readings, what are some common methods of encouraging and inspiring readers? Or consider differences such as these: In what ways does a presidential address differ from other texts with similar goals? In what ways does a speech differ from other written texts?

I Have a Dream
Martin Luther King, Jr.

♦

On the afternoon of August 28, 1963, Martin Luther King, Jr., spoke to several hundred thousand people before the Lincoln Memorial in Washington, D.C. This massive crowd, black and white, had gathered in support of civil rights, marching on Washington on the centennial of the Emancipation Proclamation. An even larger audience watched the event on television. A powerful and eloquent orator, King delivered on that occasion what many consider his finest speech: "I Have a Dream."

1. I am happy to join with you today in what will go down in history as the greatest demonstration for freedom in the history of our nation.

2. Fivescore years ago, a great American, in whose symbolic shadow we stand today, signed the Emancipation Proclamation. This momentous decree came as a great beacon light of hope to millions of Negro slaves who had been seared in the flames of withering injustice. It came as a joyous daybreak to end the long night of their captivity.

3. But one hundred years later, the Negro still is not free; one hundred years later, the life of the Negro is still sadly crippled by the manacles of segregation and the chains of discrimination; one hundred years later, the Negro lives on a lonely island of poverty in the midst of a vast ocean of material prosperity; one hundred years later, the Negro is still languished in the corners of American society and finds himself in exile in his own land.

4. So we've come here today to dramatize a shameful condition. In a sense we've come to our nation's capital to cash a check. When the architects of our republic wrote the magnificent words of the Constitution and the Declaration of Independence, they were signing a promissory note to which every American was to fall heir. This note was the promise that all men, yes, black men as well as white men, would be guaranteed the unalienable rights of life, liberty, and the pursuit of happiness.

5. It is obvious today that America has defaulted on this promissory note in so far as her citizens of color are concerned. Instead of honoring this sacred obligation, America has given the Negro people a bad check; a check which has come back marked "insufficient funds." We refuse to believe that there are insufficient funds in the great vaults of opportunity of this nation. And so we've come to cash this check, a check that will give us upon demand the riches of freedom and the security of justice.

6. We have also come to this hallowed spot to remind America of the fierce urgency of now. This is no time to engage in the luxury of cooling off or to take the tranquilizing drug of gradualism. Now is the time to make real the promises of democracy; now is the time to rise from the dark and desolate valley of segregation to the sunlit path of racial justice; now is the time to lift our nation from the quicksands of racial injustice to the solid rock of brotherhood; now is the time to make justice a reality for all God's children. It would be fatal for the nation to overlook the urgency of the moment. This sweltering summer of the Negro's legitimate discontent will not pass until there is an invigorating autumn of freedom and equality.

7. Nineteen sixty-three is not an end, but a beginning. And those who hope that the Negro needed to blow off steam and will now be content, will have a rude awakening if the nation returns to business as usual.

8. There will be neither rest nor tranquility in America until the Negro is granted his citizenship rights. The whirlwinds of revolt will continue to shake the foundations of our nation until the bright day of justice emerges.

9. But there is something that I must say to my people who stand on the warm threshold which leads into the palace of justice. In the process of gaining our rightful place we must not be guilty of wrongful deeds.

10. Let us not seek to satisfy our thirst for freedom by drinking from the cup of bitterness and hatred. We must forever conduct our struggle on the high plane of dignity and discipline. We must not allow our creative protest to degenerate into physical violence. Again and again we must rise to the majestic heights of meeting physical force with soul force.

11. The marvelous new militancy which has engulfed the Negro community must not lead us to a distrust of all white people, for many of our white brothers, as evidenced by their presence here today, have come to realize that their destiny is tied up with our destiny and they have come to realize that their freedom is inextricably bound to our freedom. This offense we share mounted to storm the battlements of injustice must be carried forth by a biracial army. We cannot walk alone.

12. And as we walk, we must make the pledge that we shall always march ahead. We cannot turn back. There are those who are asking the devotees of civil rights, "When will you be satisfied?" We can never be satisfied as long as the Negro is the victim of the unspeakable horrors of police brutality.

13. We can never be satisfied as long as our bodies, heavy with fatigue of travel, cannot gain lodging in the motels of the highways and the hotels of the cities. We cannot be satisfied as long as the Negro's basic mobility is from a smaller ghetto to a larger one.

14. We can never be satisfied as long as our children are stripped of their selfhood and robbed of their dignity by signs stating "for whites only." We cannot be satisfied as long as a Negro in Mississippi cannot vote and a Negro in New York believes he has nothing for which to vote. No, we are not satisfied, and we will not be satisfied until justice rolls down like waters and righteousness like a mighty stream.

15. I am not unmindful that some of you have come here out of excessive trials and tribulation. Some of you have come fresh from narrow jail cells. Some of you have come from areas where your quest for freedom left you battered by the storms of persecution and staggered by the winds of police brutality. You have been the veterans of creative suffering. Continue to work with the faith that unearned suffering is redemptive.

16. Go back to Mississippi; go back to Alabama; go back to South Carolina; go back to Georgia; go back to Louisiana; go back to the slums and ghettos of the northern cities, knowing that somehow this situation can, and will be changed. Let us not wallow in the valley of despair.

17. So I say to you, my friends, that even though we must face the difficulties of today and tomorrow, I still have a dream. It is a dream deeply rooted in the American dream that one day this nation will rise up and live out the true meaning of its creed—we hold these truths to be self-evident, that all men are created equal.

18. I have a dream that one day on the red hills of Georgia, sons of former slaves and sons of former slave-owners will be able to sit down together at the table of brotherhood.

19 I have a dream that one day, even the state of Mississippi, a state sweltering with the heat of injustice, sweltering with the heat of oppression, will be transformed into an oasis of freedom and justice.

20 I have a dream my four little children will one day live in a nation where they will not be judged by the color of their skin but by content of their character. I have a dream today!

21 I have a dream that one day, down in Alabama, with its vicious racists, with its governor having his lips dripping with the words of interposition and nullification, that one day, right there in Alabama, little black boys and black girls will be able to join hands with little white boys and white girls as sisters and brothers. I have a dream today!

22 I have a dream that one day every valley shall be exalted, every hill and mountain shall be made low, the rough places shall be made plain, and the crooked places shall be made straight and the glory of the Lord will be revealed and all flesh shall see it together.

23 This is our hope. This is the faith that I go back to the South with.

24 With this faith we will be able to hear out of the mountain of despair a stone of hope. With this faith we will be able to transform the jangling discords of our nation into a beautiful symphony of brotherhood.

25 With this faith we will be able to work together, to pray together, to struggle together, to go to jail together, to stand up for freedom together, knowing that we will be free one day. This will be the day when all of God's children will be able to sing with new meaning—"my country 'tis of thee; sweet land of liberty; of thee I sing; land where my fathers died, land of the pilgrim's pride; from every mountain side, let freedom ring"—and if America is to be a great nation, this must become true.

26 So let freedom ring from the prodigious hilltops of New Hampshire.

27 Let freedom ring from the mighty mountains of New York.

28 Let freedom ring from the heightening Alleghenies of Pennsylvania.

29 Let freedom ring from the snow-capped Rockies of Colorado.

30 Let freedom ring from the curvaceous slopes of California.

31 But not only that.

32 Let freedom ring from Stone Mountain of Georgia.

33 Let freedom ring from Lookout Mountain of Tennessee.

34 Let freedom ring from every hill and molehill of Mississippi, from every mountainside, let freedom ring.

35 And when we allow freedom to ring, when we let it ring from every village and hamlet, from every state and city, we will be able to speed up that day when all of God's children—black men and white men, Jews and Gentiles, Catholics and Protestants—will be able to join hands and to sing in the words of the old Negro spiritual, "Free at last, free at last; thank God Almighty, we are free at last."

 Reading Responses

1. What was the purpose of the march on Washington and King's speech?

2. How does King identify the injustices that ignored or denied civil rights?
3. How does King identify areas in which the American dream remains unrealized? How does the speech define the American dream?

Writing Activities

1. Make an outline of the main sections of the speech. Write a paragraph briefly analyzing how the speech is organized.
2. Examine the use of repeated words and expressions in the speech. Write an essay about how this feature of the speech contributes to its effectiveness. Use specific examples from the speech to illustrate and support your points.
3. Write a response to King's speech, testifying to its power, questioning its lasting relevance, exploring its vision of the American dream, or responding in some other way. Be sure to state your general points clearly and support them with specifics.

Community Links

Compare and contrast King's "I Have a Dream" speech with President Bush's Address (pp. 433–438). What strategies does each use to speak to the moment and to history?

Call to Action
WHY YOU NEED TO VOTE
Christie Brinkley

◆

Christie Brinkley, well known as a supermodel, wrote this letter for the "On My Mind" column in Cosmopolitan *magazine. In it she describes how she became active in civic issues, eventually attending the Democratic National Convention in 2000 that nominated Al Gore as the party's presidential candidate. In addition to recounting her experiences, Brinkley calls readers to action, encouraging them to cast a vote in the presidential election in November 2000.*

1   My modeling career has taken me all over the world, but no matter how many fascinating and exotic places I've visited, I have always felt fortunate to call America my home.

2   That was never more true than during the past year, when I made two trips to the war-torn Balkans—one with the USO and the other as part of the Secretary of Defense's Christmas tour to entertain our troops. After seeing firsthand the indescribable destruction of war, I returned home determined to become more involved in the future of my own country. It wasn't enough to be a grateful citizen: I had to be an active one.

3   One battle that I've been fighting hits particularly close to home. Where I live, on the east end of Long Island, we are graced with many miles of gorgeous shoreline, charming towns, and pristine farms. Unfortunately, we are also in close proximity to several old nuclear reactors that may be contaminating our air and water with low-level radioactive emissions.

4   I tried to contact the appropriate authorities, but that got me nowhere. So I joined the board of directors of the STAR (Standing for Truth About Radiation) Foundation, a group of concerned citizens determined to stop the leakage. It wasn't easy, but we managed to raise public awareness of the problem, along with money for our cause. We finally won the cooperation of Energy Secretary Bill Richardson, who recently shut down one of the old reactors. In the process, I discovered that the best way to fight for change is to support the politicians who will champion your beliefs.

5   So when the Democratic National Committee invited me to run as a delegate, I jumped at the chance. It was an opportunity to campaign for Al Gore—a dedicated environmentalist. He also advocates stronger gun control and defends abortion rights so that women can choose what happens to their own bodies. His views on education and health care are also parallel to mine, and, well, I just happen to believe that he has the depth, character, and experience to stand up to the people and organizations that threaten our country's future.

6   But don't just take my word for it. Before you decide which candidate to support, read as much as you can about each of them. Check their voting records, and see how closely their beliefs match yours. As my 14-year-old daughter, Alexa, says, "When you cast your ballot, you're really voting for yourself." Don't think *Which candidate do I want to support?* Instead, think *Which candidate do I want to support me for the next four years?*

7   But whatever you decide, be absolutely sure to cast your vote—and be an active participant in the most crucial decision we'll have to make in this decade.

Reading Responses

1. At what point in the column does Brinkley state her call to action? Why does she choose this point to state?
2. Why does Brinkley recall her visits to the Balkans, her involvement with STAR, and her trip to the Democratic Convention? How do these recollections contribute to her call to action?

3. How does Brinkley reverse standard appeals to vote? Why does she do this?

Writing Activities

1. Write a short essay exploring how Brinkley uses appeals to the reader's self-interest in her column.
2. Recount an incident or event that motivated you to take some kind of action, such as supporting a cause, working on a committee, joining an issue-oriented group, or attending a political gathering. Briefly explain the event or tell the story, showing how it led up to your more active involvement.
3. Write your own opinion column, urging readers to take some sort of action.

Community Links

Compare this column with other opinion pieces in this book such as Lee's "The Case Against College" (pp. 73–75) from the academic community or Rhodes's "Think You Can Teach? Pass This Test" (pp. 515–517), also from the public community. How are the opinion pieces you select alike or different? How do you account for the similarities and differences?

DEAR FRIEND

Donna Dees-Thomases

◆

On Mother's Day in May 2000, women (and men) across the country gathered, marched, and spoke in support of gun control as part of the Million Mom March. Donna Dees-Thomases organized this event in Washington, D.C., with simultaneous events in Chicago, Denver, Los Angeles, and elsewhere. She was motivated to do so after watching the television coverage of a shooting at a daycamp the previous August. Similar moments of violence were recalled during the Million Mom March itself, including the shootings at Columbine High School, which had taken place slightly more than a year earlier just outside of Denver. The Million Mom March, like marches and gatherings to support many causes, was publicized through newspaper advertisements, local broadcast and print news stories, the networks of local groups with similar interests and values, and a Web site where Dees-Thomases posted her call to action.

MILLION MOM MARCH
P.O. Box 762, Washington, D.C. 20044-0762, (888) 989-MOMS

Dear Friend:

1   On August 10th, I had a wake-up call. I was watching news about the Granada Hills day camp shooting. The images of terrified children being led in a line from the carnage that had just taken place inside were too much to bear. They looked bewildered, confused and scared to death.

2   I couldn't stop thinking of those kids mainly because I was just too afraid to think of the other ones—the children shot and clinging to life. Those kids are about the same age as my own two. I felt ashamed. Ashamed because I've sat back while others battle the gun lobby to protect our children.

3   One week later, I applied for a permit to march on the Mall in Washington, D.C., nine months later. As a mother, I know what can be created in this amount of time.

4   Please join the hundreds of mothers already involved to recruit mothers and others of all ages, races, religions, and political parties to mobilize for the "Million Mom March" on Mothers' Day, May 14th, 2000. With thousands of mothers and others on the National Mall, we will put Congress on notice that common sense gun policy—specifically licensing and registration—is the will of the people.

5   For too long we have ignored the gun violence epidemic because it was always in somebody else's backyard. We cannot afford to ignore it any longer. Our children's lives are far too precious.

6   Thank you, fellow mother, for wanting to help.

Donna Dees-Thomases
Just One of a Million

Reading Responses

1. Why do you think that Dees-Thomases begins her letter with her memory of the Granada Hills shootings rather than with details about the time and location of the march?
2. In what ways does her letter appeal to readers and try to motivate them?
3. Dees-Thomases might have circulated her call to action in many ways, but she chose to post a letter on the Web. Why might she have chosen to use the letter form and to post it on a Web site?

Writing Activities

1. List the reasons for joining the march that are stated and implied in the letter. Compare your list with those of others in your class. Do you all agree about the reasons stated? Do you also agree about the reasons implied?

2. Based on this letter, write a brief definition of a call to action.
3. Write your own letter calling people to action. (Write about an actual upcoming event or an invented one that you wish would happen.) Organize your letter as Dees-Thomases organizes hers.

Community Links

Compare and contrast this letter with others in this book. For example, consider Vermette's letter to his son (pp. 96–100) from the academic community, the letters (pp. 308–318) from the work community, or the appeals to supporters from the public community (pp. 447–456). Consider what makes a letter effective and how effective letters succeed in establishing a compelling connection with a reader.

Appeal to Supporters
SAFE Colorado:
Sane Alternatives to the Firearms Epidemic

John Head and Arnie Grossman

◆

Sent by SAFE (Sane Alternatives to the Firearms Epidemic) Colorado, this letter was addressed to people who had signed a petition to place a gun-show loophole initiative on the Colorado ballot. This issue intensified in Colorado following the shootings at Columbine High School because weapons involved in that tragedy had been purchased at a gun show. This letter reminds supporters of that event as it appeals to them for financial contributions.

SAFE Colorado
Sane Alternatives to the Firearms Epidemic
P. O. Box 461152, Denver, CO 80246
Telephone: 303-563-7233/FAX: 303-308-1887
Website: www.safecolorado.org
E-mail: info@safecolorado.org

October 25, 2000

Dear _____ ,

1 There are two parts to every initiative campaign—getting on the ballot and getting a majority of voters to vote "Yes."

2 Thanks to you and 110,000 Colorado voters like you, our effort to close the gun show loophole is on the ballot as Amendment 22.

3 Now we need your help again, this time with money to persuade Coloradans to vote for Amendment 22. We do not think the National Rifle Association will let us win by default. Despite a recent poll showing 85% support for Amendment 22, the NRA tends to lie in wait and then flood the media with attack ads. In 1997 they defeated an initiative like ours in Washington state that began the campaign with 75% voter support. The NRA spent nearly $3.5 million late in the campaign and defeated the initiative by a 3-1 margin.

4 The NRA is a formidable adversary. It relies upon the generous financial support of its members to mount well-financed campaigns opposing reasonable gun regulation. Our aim is to match that level of dedication and support. You helped us begin by signing the petitions for Amendment 22. Now we ask for your financial support as well.

5 We suggest a contribution of $25 or more, although any amount will be welcome. We ask you to make a contribution now, use the enclosed envelope and mail it today. Or, you can contribute via our Web site at www.safecolorado.org. If we in the Columbine State can pass a reasonable gun control initiative closing the gun show loophole this year, it will ensure that the tragedy at Columbine High will not have been in vain.

Sincerely yours,

John Head *Arnie Grossman*
John Head, Co-President   Arnie Grossman, Co-President

Contributions to SAFE Colorado are not tax deductible.

Honorary Chairmen: Richard D. Lamm, Democrat, Former Governor; John A. Love, Republican, Former Governor. *Board of Directors:* Mary Estil Buchanan, Republican, Former Secretary of State; Steven Foster, Democrat, Rabbi, Temple Emanuel; Arnold Grossman, Democrat, Political Consultant; John Head, Republican, Lawyer; J.D. MacFarlane, Democrat, Former Attorney General; David A. Sprecace, Republican, Lawyer.

Reading Responses

1. What do you think that the SAFE Colorado organization hoped to accomplish in this letter?
2. In what ways does the letter use specific details and statistics as part of its appeal?
3. How does the SAFE Colorado letter appeal to readers and try to motivate them?

Writing Activities

1. Outline the structure of this letter, paragraph by paragraph. Write a concise explanation of the way the letter weaves together its many threads—gratitude, voter information, political background, and a financial appeal.
2. Write a short essay analyzing the strategies that this letter uses to motivate readers.
3. Write your own letter of appeal, seeking a contribution to an actual organization that you support or an invented organization that you would like to support.

Community Links

Compare and contrast this letter with the Million Mom March letter (pp. 445–446). Consider how each one tries to establish a connection with a reader and motivate the reader to respond to the letter.

BECOME A NATIONAL SPONSOR
National Rifle Association Foundation

◆

The Web site for the National Rifle Association (NRA) includes volunteer and contribution forms, advice about contacting legislators and the media, and many resources about the second amendment and gun laws. The NRA Foundation page included here appeals to supporters to become national sponsors of the Friends of NRA.

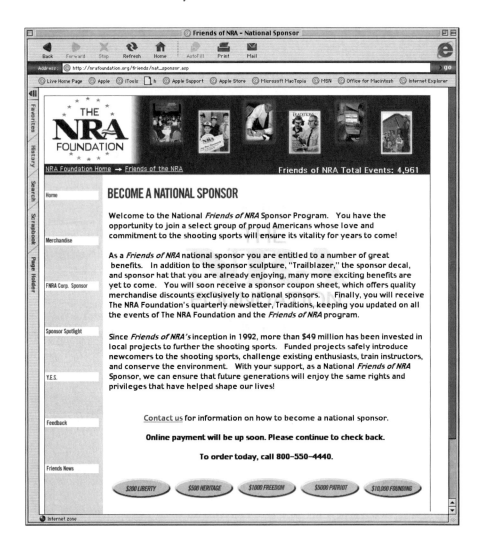

Reading Responses

1. What do you think that the NRA Foundation hopes to accomplish through this Web page?
2. What will the contributions of national sponsors support?
3. How does the national sponsor page appeal to readers and try to motivate them?

Writing Activities

1. Write a paragraph explaining how the Web features such as the buttons and visuals contribute to the purpose of the letter.

2. Write a short essay analyzing the strategies that this appeal uses to motivate supporters.
3. Write your own letter of appeal, seeking a contribution to an actual organization that you support or an invented organization that you would like to support.

Community Links

Compare and contrast this Web appeal to supporters with other Web sites that promote an organization or urge support for one side of an issue. Look, for example, at the Technical Standards site (pp. 347–349) from the work community or others from the public community such as the Rice for Peace (pp. 471–472), Smoke Free Movies (pp. 566–567), or College Drinking (pp. 568–571) sites. In what ways are the examples you select similar or different? In what ways do they capitalize on features available on the Web?

DEAR OHIO STATE GRADUATE
Susan L. Huntington

◆

This letter from the Vice Provost and Dean of the Graduate School at The Ohio State University appeals to graduates for contributions. Whether addressed to former students by year of graduation, major, or prior contribution level, such letters are familiar communications to the graduates of many institutions.

August 2002

Dear Ohio State Graduate:

1   Recently, The Ohio State University articulated an Academic Plan to help guide us to becoming a premier academic institution. The Graduate School is working hard on two fronts to help the university achieve the goals of the Academic Plan. First, we are accelerating our efforts to recruit the best possible students and, second, we are implementing an aggressive plan to enhance the graduate experience of every student in our programs. This letter is to inform you of some of our activities and to ask for your support.

2   To help recruit top Ohio and other U.S. students, the Graduate School has:

- Implemented a campus visitation program for our strongest prospective U.S. graduate students to meet our faculty and students, and see our facilities.

- Improved our fellowship program to create incentives for student recruitment.

To help improve the quality of the experience our students receive, the Graduate School:

- In partnership with the Council of Graduate Students, has conducted an extensive study that forms the basis of our plan to improve the quality of graduate student life on campus.
- Has created new funding opportunities to support students' growth through internships, participation in training programs, and other professional development activities.
- Sponsors a travel program to help graduate students present their work at professional meetings, thus providing visibility for our students *and* our programs.

3   Substantial funds are needed, so I hope you will consider making a gift to the Graduate School. Every dollar we raise will help bring Ohio State closer to its goal. Whether you make a major gift or a contribution of $25, $50, or $100, you can have a significant impact on the life of a graduate student.

4   If Ohio State is to reach our ambitious academic goals, we must have the support of our alumni. As the reputation and quality of the university improves, the value of the degree that you earned at Ohio State also increases. Your contribution will be well spent and well used. Thank you for your generosity.

Sincerely,

Susan L. Huntington

Susan L. Huntington
Vice Provost and Dean

250 University Hall • 230 North Oral Mall • Columbus, OH 43210-1366 • (614) 292-6031

Reading Responses

1. Why, according to the letter, was Ohio State seeking contributions at that time?
2. Which activities are highlighted in this letter? How might these programs appeal to prospective contributors?
3. In what ways is the letter tailored to its recipients? How does it appeal to the self-interest of graduates?

Writing Activities

1. Write a few sentences in your own words summarizing the reasons why the university is requesting support.

2. Write two paragraphs, one describing the persona or image that the vice provost projects and the other explaining the effectiveness of that persona in achieving the objectives of the appeal. Consider tone, word choice, diction level, degree of formality, or other features that help to create a writer's persona.
3. Write a letter addressed to graduates of your college or university, appealing for contributions to the academic program that you have entered or plan to enter.

 Community Links

Compare or contrast the writer's persona in this letter with the persona created by the writer in one or two other letters such as Vermette's letter to his son (pp. 96–100) from the academic community or the welcome letter to new employees that begins the Olive Garden brochure (pp. 289–296) or the Grassmaster "Dear Customer" letter (pp. 311–312), both from the work community. Consider how each writer's persona is conveyed and how the persona contributes to the letter's effectiveness.

DEAR SUBSCRIBER
Richard Whittaker

◆

Richard Whittaker is the editor—and founder—of works + conversations, *a small and beautifully produced magazine dedicated to the arts. This letter is his renewal request to subscribers, but, like the magazine, the letter goes much further than a typical renewal notice. Instead of simply prodding readers to send a check, he reminds them of the value of the publication and entices them to renew by mentioning an upcoming interview. Their renewals support this publication through SRCA, the Society for the ReCognition of Art.*

Dear Subscriber,

1 Your subscription expires with this issue.

2 I hope you'll renew your subscription and continue your much appreciated support of this unusual magazine which takes so long to produce.

3 Although our prices have gone up with the new issue (to $20/3 or $26/3 sent by first class mail) you can renew your subscription at a special rate of $15 for 3 issues. Or if you'd like the magazine sent by first class mail, your rate would be $20/3 issues.

4 While *works + conversations* looks more or less like other established magazines, I believe that is largely a matter of crafty disguise. Producing the magazine at the level we do is not easy. Our per-issue cost is about $6000.00 which

goes toward printing and mailing costs mostly. With fewer than 600 subscribers—as of this writing—the economics of it would be impossible for anyone expecting just to break even. How do we do it? By paying ourselves nothing and kicking in the extra out of our own pockets. It isn't easy to find such an enterprise in our culture and, in fact, I'm aware of no other magazine that is quite like ours.

5 Perhaps it should not be surprising that I think of each issue of *works + conversations* more as a work of art itself than as a business product. Being short on both money and exposure seems to be a condition typical of art and artists, but fortunately they are not the definitive aspects.

6 We've already begun work on #5. That issue will be anchored by an interview with the visionary architect, Paolo Soleri and I'm comfortable making a guarantee that future issues will continue to be full of interesting material.

7 In the event you'd like to support us at a higher level you can renew at the higher rate, or consider making a gift subscription. *works + conversations* makes a special gift for the right person. We will extend our $15 rate to gift subscriptions. But just your renewal is a real encouragement and will be very much appreciated. Please make out your check to "SRCA" and send it with your name and address. For gift subscriptions we send a note to the new subscriber with the name of the gift giver and send you a note of confirmation that the subscription is in force.

Thank you,
Richard Whittaker, editor

works + conversations   P.O. Box 5008   Berkeley CA 94705   510-653-1146   rwhit@jps.net

Reading Responses

1. What is the purpose of Whittaker's letter?
2. How does his letter use its style, tone, word choice, and selection of information to build a relationship with readers?
3. In what ways is his letter tailored to its recipients? How does it appeal to the interests of subscribers?

Writing Activities

1. Write a few sentences in your own words summarizing the reasons why Whittaker urges subscribers to renew or contribute additional support.

2. Write two paragraphs, one describing the persona or image that Whittaker projects and the other explaining the effectiveness of that persona in achieving the objectives of the appeal. Consider tone, word choice, diction level, degree of formality, or other features that help to create a writer's persona.
3. Write your own letter, appealing to your readers to subscribe to or support your publication or event (real or imagined). Persuasively describe your publication or event—whether cultural, artistic, athletic, or charitable—taking into account the expectations of your readers.

Community Links

Compare and contrast Whittaker's letter with another appeal to supporters from the public community (pp. 447–456) or a call to action (pp. 443–446) or with a workplace letter (pp. 308–319). Use several letters to explore similarities, differences, and variations in the ways the writers appeal to readers, taking into account community differences.

INVITATION TO THE 8TH ANNUAL REPUBLICAN SENATORIAL REGAIN THE MAJORITY DINNER

Republican Presidential Roundtable

◆

This invitation introduced a packet of materials offering membership on the Republican Presidential Roundtable to the recipient, characterized as a business or community leader, in return for a generous contribution. The inside panels of the invitation outline upcoming spring activities of the roundtable, the agenda for the fall meeting preceding the dinner, and recommendations for Washington hotel and tour arrangements (at the recipient's expense). Additional materials in the same mailing included letters from Vice President Cheney and Senator Bill Frist, both emphasizing the importance of the midterm election fast approaching in November 2002, as well as a membership reply form.

On behalf of the

Republican Senate Leadership

you are cordially invited
to attend

THE **8**TH ANNUAL
REPUBLICAN SENATORIAL
Regain the Majority
DINNER

**WITH SPECIAL GUEST
PRESIDENT GEORGE W. BUSH**

Wednesday, September 25, 2002
6:00 pm Reception
7:00 pm Dinner

The National Building Museum
401 F Street, Northwest
Washington, District of Columbia

RSVP

by September 6, 2002
800.877.6776

Reading Responses

1. What is the purpose of this invitation to a political dinner? How might its effectiveness be measured?
2. In what ways does this invitation appeal to recipients?
3. In what ways does the layout of the invitation contribute to its effectiveness?

Writing Activities

1. Write a critique of the design of this invitation, identifying its strengths and noting any suggestions that might increase its effectiveness.
2. Briefly annotate each section of the text in the invitation, noting which chunks are visually emphasized, which are most succinct, which have more embellishment, or which have other notable features. Write a brief analysis of the contributions of the text to the invitation as a whole.
3. Design an invitation to a special fund-raising event, using wording, layout, and other components to increase its effectiveness.

Community Links

Compare or contrast this invitation with Marriott's "Holiday Greetings" (pp. 308–310). Consider how effectively each communication combines written words with visual design and to what extent each is tailored to meet the expectations of its broad community or to suit its particular occasion.

Appeal to Voters
CITY OF CENTENNIAL: YES
Centennial Supporters

◆

The following political "doorhanger" was designed to slip onto the doorknob at a home as volunteers walked house to house leaving election materials. It urges voters to approve the incorporation of a new city—Centennial. It also introduces the economics of annexation, a primary campaign issue. To some, cities adjacent to the proposed city of Centennial seemed to be annexing unincorporated commercial areas (whose taxes would add to the coffers of the annexing city) while not annexing residential areas (whose tax contributions would be offset by their need for city services). Some residents in the proposed city of Centennial feared that these annexation procedures would leave their neighborhoods without an adequate tax base to pay for needed services through the county. As a result, an activist group proposed the city of Centennial, which, if approved by voters, would eliminate further annexations by other cities.

CENTENNIAL

After 224 years, it's still true...
Government of the people, by the people and for the people
is better than
taxation without representation

VOTE FOR INCORPORATION

The election is this Tuesday
September 12
7:00 a.m. until 7:00 p.m.

Check out the back to find out where your polling place is

With Centennial	Without Centennial
Over 100,000 people are included with commercial property in a balanced community	Mostly commercial property is annexed to benefit Greenwood Village and other cities, with few people included and split neighborhoods
Sales taxes are used in our community and are determined by Centennial Citizens	Greenwood (3%) and Aurora (3.75%) sales taxes and head taxes are imposed on surrounding commercial property with millions of our dollars going to annexing cities
Property taxes stabilize or go down	Property taxes go up or services go down
We elect a City Council and Mayor from our own community to represent our interests	We depend on one individual to represent us on the Arapahoe County Board of Commissioners
Our City Council controls planning and zoning issues	County Commissioners, representing the entire County, including cities like GV and Aurora, make planning and zoning decisions in our area
Clout - We have economic and political viability	Weakness - We have few political or economic tools to get things done
Inclusion	Exclusion
Community	Division and disarray
Centennial Citizen	**Second Class Citizen**

☑ yes CITY OF CENTENNIAL

FRONT

Who's Supporting Centennial...

The Denver Rocky Mountain News
The Denver Post
Centennial Town Journal
Centennial Citizen

South Metro Denver Chamber of Commerce;
   Brian Vogt, President, and Bob Lee, Chairman
ACCORD - Arapahoe County coalition of 54
   homeowners associations; Randy Pye, President
South Suburban Park and Recreation District Board of Directors

Arapahoe County Commissioner John Brackney
Arapahoe County Commissioner Marie Mackenzie
Arapahoe County Commissioner Steve Ward
Arapahoe County Sheriff Pat Sullivan
Arapahoe County Assessor Ed Bosier
Arapahoe County Treasurer Bernie Ciazza

State Senator Tom Blickensderfer
State Senator John Andrews
State Representative Nancy Spence
State Representative Gary McPherson
State Representative Joe Stengel

Cunningham Firefighters Association
Fraternal Order of Police, Lodge 31
Arapahoe County Undersheriff Grayson Robinson
Former Arapahoe County Commissioner Tom Eggert
Former State Representative Paul Schauer

Plus thousands of your neighbors
and local business people!

Join us election night for a
Centennial Celebration!
6:30 p.m.
Embassy Suites Denver South
10250 East Costilla Avenue
Take Arapahoe Road a mile or so east of I-25 to
Costilla Avenue. Go south. You can't miss it!

If you received an absentee ballot and have not yet returned it, you cannot turn it in at the polling place. It must be returned to the Clerk and Recorder's Office by 7:00 p.m. September 12. Use the following locations: 5334 S. Prince St. (Prince and Santa Fe) OR the Motor Vehicle SE Branch, 12600 E. Arapahoe Rd., Bldg. C, Suite B (SW corner of Arapahoe Road and Revere).

Your polling place is:

Indian Ridge Elementary
16501 E. Progress Dr.
Take S. Buckley Rd. south from
Smoky Hill Rd. Go west on E. Progress Dr.

BACK

A New City?
City of Greenwood Village

◆

This political brochure opens to reveal information for voters on three panels, inside and out. Mailed to voters by the city of Greenwood Village, it urges a "no" vote on Centennial. It addresses economic and other issues while defending Greenwood Village's interest in this issue. Not surprisingly, the views of Greenwood Village on the annexation issue differ from those of the other side.

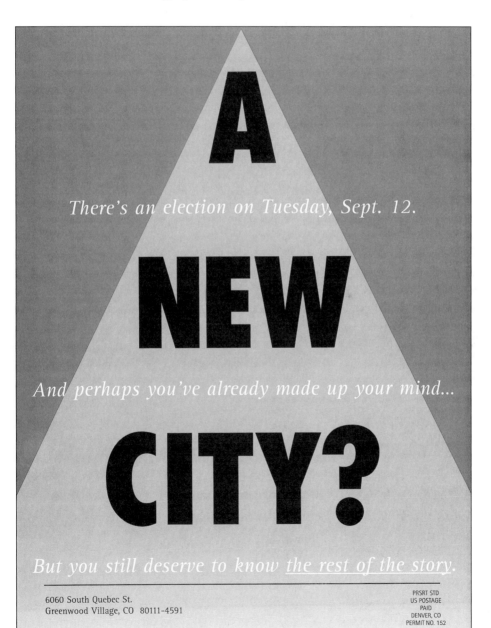

SEPARATE THE FACTS FROM

FICTION:	FACT:
"Very few people are included in the mostly commercial annexations planned by Greenwood Village." (Source: "Centennial: It's Our City" by Arapahoe Citizens for Self-Determination)	Actually, Greenwood Village's proposed annexations would encompass about 10,000 people, all of whom would become Greenwood Village residents and receive city services. That's hardly "very few people." In fact, about 85% percent of the lots proposed for annexation by Greenwood are residential—not commercial. For example, the Greenwood Village annexations don't encompass some of the area's major commercial centers such as Inverness and other large business parks. The annexations also don't include large shopping centers like Park Meadows or Southglenn Mall. (In contrast, Centennial City would encompass commercial areas including Southglenn Mall, substantially raising the mall's previously low sales tax and thus eliminating what Southglenn feels is one of its competitive advantages.)
"If Greenwood Village is able to annex taxes will go up." (Source: Pro-Centennial City flyer by Arapahoe Citizens for Self-Determination)	The areas that Greenwood Village's sales tax would affect are small compared to the areas that would be faced with the proposed city of Centennial's sales tax. Furthermore, Arapahoe County will continue to collect the same amount of taxes from the annexed areas as the unincorporated areas. The Arapahoe County Attorney stated in a letter that the County incurred no loss in property tax revenues as a result of Greenwood Village's past annexations. Under the Greenwood Village annexations, the revenue from a special Sheriff's Department tax would decline. However, there would also be a decrease in the Sheriff's Department's responsibilities and expenses. Arapahoe County's own report indicates that the incorporation of Centennial City would have a much larger negative impact on County revenues and employees than Greenwood Village's annexations.
"Is a 1.5 cent sales tax adequate to operate the City of Centennial? Yes." (Source: Pro-Centennial web site by Arapahoe Citizens for Self-Determination)	First, it's worth clarifying that this would be 1.5 percent <u>extra</u> sales tax over and above the current sales tax you pay. Yet an analysis by BBC Research & Consulting concluded: "Centennial will need more than a 1.5 cent sales tax. Of the 34 cities and towns in the Denver Metropolitan Area, more than 80 percent have sales tax rates of 3.0 percent or above." Centennial backers say that "when Centennial is incorporated, citizens will set their own taxes." (Source: "Centennial: It's Our City" by Arapahoe Citizens for Self-Determination). But these same Centennial City promoters have set the election on incorporation well over a year before they plan on bringing the question of taxes before voters. (For whatever reason, they decided against letting residents vote on the question of incorporation and taxes together this November.) Therefore, when you vote on incorporation, there's no way to know exactly how much taxes will be proposed later. If voters approve incorporation but not the subsequent taxes, residents of the proposed Centennial City could be facing a real problem.

THE FICTION

FICTION:
"Added tax revenue (from Greenwood Village annexations) will be used to further fund projects and services in Greenwood Village."

(Source: Centennial Update)

FACT:
Greenwood Village's proposed annexations are based on three objectives:
1) Ensuring quality development in response to explosive regional growth.
2) Funding regional transportation solutions. (In a written agreement with the City of Aurora and Arapahoe County, Greenwood Village commits to regional road improvements—many of which are outside Greenwood Village. The annexations would give Greenwood Village jurisdiction over some of these roads and the ability to contribute toward funding these projects.)
3) Furthering Greenwood Village's effective opposition to commercial service (both passenger and cargo) at Centennial Airport.

All of these goals have value to the entire region. Greenwood Village also has taken a leading role on water and air quality issues in our region, including preserving Cherry Creek Reservoir water quality.

FICTION:
The proposed Centennial City will oppose scheduled passenger service at Centennial Airport.

FACT:
Maybe—maybe not. Centennial City has not yet been formed so no one can predict whether Centennial City's government would oppose or support scheduled passenger service at Centennial Airport. *Some Centennial City supporters say they oppose scheduled passenger service, but at least one key Centennial City supporter has fought for scheduled airline service in the past.*

Meanwhile, Greenwood Village's formal opposition to scheduled passenger service and increased cargo activities has long been on record.

FICTION:
Centennial City's proposed incorporation is about "self determination".

(Source: Centennial City fundraising letter by Arapahoe Citizens for Self-Determination)

FACT:
In fact, the incorporation of Centennial City would interfere with the right of self-determination for many Arapahoe County residents. Greenwood Village's proposed annexations were initiated when residents of unincorporated Arapahoe County submitted petitions asking that their neighborhoods be made part of the Village. These first petitions came well before Centennial City was proposed. Yet the incorporation of Centennial City would prevent these residents from ever getting a chance to vote on joining Greenwood Village.

Last year, Greenwood Village spent about $400,000 fighting expanded passenger or cargo service at Centennial Airport. Year after year, Greenwood Village has taken the lead on this issue, even though increased aircraft noise impacts the entire area.

Let's Set the Record Straight

Greenwood Village's proposed annexations would encompass 10,000 residents of unincorporated Arapahoe County—not just a "few" as claimed by Centennial City promoters.

None of us live in a vacuum. We are separate communities but, in many ways, we're tied together. Therefore, we must not just coexist but also collaborate if we are all to prosper. It's not enough to be against Greenwood Village; our area deserves positive agendas and real solutions to our regional problems.

get the facts

IF YOU'VE WITNESSED THE PRO-CENTENNIAL CITY INCORPORATION CAMPAIGN, YOU'VE PROBABLY HEARD A LOT ABOUT US.

In fact, you may have heard more about us than about the new city that's being proposed.

So before you vote...

even if you've already

made up your mind...

we encourage you to

take a few minutes to

get all the facts and

consider the other

side of the story.

We're Greenwood Village—though, during this campaign, you might have heard us called some other things.

For example, we've been compared to the British fighting against independence in the Revolutionary War. (In case you were wondering, Centennial backers compare themselves to Paul Revere and the original Patriots.)

That's certainly powerful imagery. Unfortunately, it doesn't have much to do with the realities of running a successful modern city in the Denver suburbs and dealing with the complex issues of traffic... growth... and providing services.

You might have heard that a vote for the proposed Centennial City will "send Greenwood Village a message." Actually, a vote for Centennial City won't change a thing inside Greenwood Village.

We're not the ones who will live in the new city— you are.

That's why we thought you'd want the facts about the proposed Centennial City so that you'd be able to make an informed decision.

This is not about throwing boxes of tea overboard or firing muskets at Redcoats— no matter how glamorous such statements might sound.

Rather, this is about preserving and enhancing the quality of life that first attracted all of us to this wonderful slice of Colorado. And it's about doing so in a planned, thoughtful, responsible and tax-sensitive manner.

We're not the ones who will live in the new city—you are.

Why does Greenwood Village care so much about Centennial City?

You probably know that Greenwood Village over the past couple of years has taken a strong stand against the incorporation of the proposed Centennial City.

And this mailing makes our position clear.

Let us take a moment to explain why we care so much about what happens outside of our existing city limits.

The proposed Centennial City incorporation matters to the entire Southeast Metro region. Whether we live in Greenwood Village or unincorporated Arapahoe County, we share the same roads, views and enviable quality of life.

But we also face many of the same challenges, from growth to traffic to efforts to expand Centennial Airport.

The incorporation of Centennial City could have a huge impact on you and these issues—and we're concerned that it may not be a positive impact.

If residents vote to incorporate Centennial City, Greenwood Village will cooperate with our new neighbor as much as possible.

Greenwood Village and other neighboring governments also would expect a newly incorporated Centennial City, which would become Colorado's sixth largest city, to meet its obligations and responsibilities to the region.

Those obligations would include millions of dollars for Southeast Corridor Light Rail and regional road improvements.

By incorporating, Centennial City would prevent Greenwood Village's annexations and thus prevent the Village, for example, from funding regional transportation improvements outside of our current boundaries. Centennial City should have its own plan for addressing regional traffic congestion if it's going to block Greenwood Village and others from taking positive steps.

We need positive agendas and real solutions to our regional problems.

This mailing was produced and paid for by:

City of Greenwood Village
6060 South Quebec Street
Greenwood Village, CO 80111-4591

For more information about any of these issues, contact Greenwood Village Annexation Task Force Chair Doug Morris at 303-486-5745

Reading Responses

1. Compare and contrast the information provided on the two pieces of Centennial literature. What were the issues in this campaign?
2. In what ways does each piece of literature appeal to voters?
3. How do the design, layout, and visual presentation of each piece contribute to its message to voters?

Writing Activities

1. Select a topic about which both pieces of literature comment. Write a paragraph or several paragraphs comparing and contrasting the two views on the issue.
2. If possible, gather some campaign literature from both sides of a current regional, local, or campus issue. Write an essay comparing and contrasting the literature of the two sides in terms of issues, tone, appeals to voters, or other points of comparison.
3. Select an issue that concerns you. (It need not be an actual ballot issue.) Design a piece of campaign literature that persuades others to agree with your view.

Community Links

Compare and contrast the Centennial campaign literature with other materials that are politically oriented such as the calls to action (pp. 443–446), appeals to supporters (pp. 447–456), or letters to officials (pp. 471–474). For the selections you choose, consider how each appeals to readers or presents its position.

ANNOUNCEMENT REMARKS
Senator Wayne Allard

◆

In January 2002, Senator Wayne Allard announced his intention to seek reelection to the United States Senate. His announcement was posted on his campaign Web site.

1 I am here today to announce that I am running for reelection to the U.S. Senate.

2 I want to continue to make a difference for Colorado and our nation as we move forward in one of the most challenging periods in our history.

3 During my campaign for the U.S. Senate 5 years ago, I made just one promise—that I would work hard to make a difference for the people of Colorado.

4   With a year still left in this term, I'm proud that the record shows a promise already fulfilled.

- I've worked hard to hold a town meeting in each of Colorado's counties each year. And I look forward to holding 64 town meetings this year with the addition of Broomfield County.
- I've worked hard to earn a voting attendance record of more than 99% while holding hundreds of town meetings in Colorado.
- I've worked hard to be frugal with taxpayer dollars by returning unspent money from my office account to the Treasury because I think elected officials need to practice what we preach. Since serving in Congress I've returned over $2.4 million to the taxpayers.
- And I've worked hard for real change, fighting to make a difference on the issues that really matter; a stronger national security, more tax cuts, a balanced federal budget, greater local input and control on important public policy issues, a better education for our kids, and protecting our special Colorado quality of life.

5   So I'm proud that the record shows we have made a difference, a big difference, on the things Coloradans really care about. But this campaign is about the future. As we move forward I want to continue to make a difference.

6   It's a different time, with new challenges requiring new solutions, with new problems requiring smarter answers.

7   It's a time that demands a Congress that is more practical and less political as we continue to rebuild our nation's security and restore our economic prosperity.

8   As we face the future, I want to draw on my experience as U.S. Senator, a Congressman, a Colorado State Senator, a small businessman, and a veterinarian, to continue to be a catalyst for change—for a better Colorado and a better America.

9   Since the tragic terrorist acts of September 11th America's challenge has never been greater.

10 Admiral "Bull" Halsey, once said, "There are no great people in this world, only great challenges which ordinary people rise to meet."

11 On that day of disaster last September, ordinary Americans became heroes for the ages.

12 On that day ordinary people in countries around the world, some barely friendly to America, became our allies.

13 And following that tragic day, the ordinary men and women who serve in the United States Congress became agents of change. They quickly moved our nation to the bipartisan footing necessary for our President to pursue war against terrorism around the world. And they acted to begin immediate repair of the damage to our families and our jobs here at home.

14 Today, we can be proud of how ordinary people have risen to the challenge. We can be proud of what we have accomplished together. But there is still much to be done.

15 We must secure America.

16   Prior to September 11th, there was too little constructive debate in Congress about our national security systems. Weapons programs, military training and our intelligence services were too often seen, by too many, as just budgets to be cut. But now the Congressional debate about rebuilding our national security is becoming more sharply focused. It is no longer a subject of casual debate in the United States Congress. It's a very serious set of issues, many with deep Colorado roots. And there is still much to be done. As a member of the Armed Services Committee I will continue to lead the charge.

17   We must restore our economic prosperity.

18   The economic slide that began more than a year ago, accelerated after September 11th. But, you know, our economy is like the weather in Colorado. If you don't like it today, just stick around because it will change. And most economists now agree, change is underway. Depending on whose crystal ball you look at we may be in the upswing already or it may come later this year.

19   But one thing is certain. As we rebuild our nation's security we will see our surpluses continue to melt away. And once again the advocates of deficit spending will rise up in congress.

20   I won't be standing with them. I'll be fighting to restore our surpluses.

21   More federal spending is not the answer for today's economic slowdown. Holding down our tax burden is. That's why I'll be pushing for tax cuts that leave more money in the taxpayer's pockets and stimulate job growth.

22   We must protect social security and Medicare.

23   Our nation needs to face up to our health care needs by dealing with the problem of uninsured Americans and the cost and availability of health care.

24   There is much to be done. One major change I'll be fighting for is making health insurance tax deductible for individuals and small businesses.

25   We must provide a better education for all our kids.

26   President Bush's landmark education proposal, the "Leave No Child Behind" bill, passed Congress with huge bipartisan support. I was proud to vote for this bill because it points the way to a better partnership between the federal government and state and local government when it comes to education in America.

27   More money and more flexible decision-making with fewer mandates are provided to local schools. At the same time more serious accountability for results is demanded.

28   We must improve our special quality of life.

29   I want to do more than just protect our quality of life.

30   I want to improve our quality of life.

31   That's why I've worked closely with Coloradans and local governments to preserve our open space and protect our environment.

32   Colorado will, forever, be a better place because, working together, we created the Great Sand Dunes National Park, the Spanish Peaks Wilderness Area, the Rocky Flats Wild Life Refuge and provided for the restoration of the endangered fish species in the Colorado River Basin.

33   Colorado will, forever, be a safer place because working together we accelerated the clean up of Rocky Flats nuclear waste. A south Denver community will forever be safer because, working together, we forced the federal bureau-

cracy to finally remove the hazardous waste buried at the Shattuck Superfund site.

34   Colorado, and the nation, will move closer to energy independence because, working together, we have maintained funding for the critical mission of the National Energy Lab in Golden.

35   Our new national security and economic strategies will depend, in part, on energy conservation technologies and new ideas that are being developed right here in Colorado's backyard. As a founder, and now Co Chair of the U.S. Senate Renewable Energy Caucus, I will continue to push for even more progress.

36   As I launch my reelection campaign I am mindful that there are two kinds of people, those who just talk, and those who work to get things done. There are show horses, and there are workhorses.

37   As a longtime veterinarian I know the difference!

38   That's why I've been a workhorse for Colorado as your Senator. And that's why I will be a workhorse as a candidate for reelection.

39   I want to continue to make a difference for Colorado.

STRICKLAND ANNOUNCES CANDIDACY FOR U.S. SENATE

Tom Strickland

Tom Strickland opposed Wayne Allard for the Senate seat in a heated rematch of their contest six years earlier. His announcement, made in August 2001, also was posted on his campaign Web site.

1   Thank you for coming. I am honored to be here in Pueblo to announce my candidacy for the United States Senate from Colorado.

2   This will be a different kind of campaign, one focused squarely on the future, on what I believe we must do to make it a bright one for every Colorado family who works hard, plays by the rules and respects their neighbors and their environment.

3   Six years ago I started a similar journey. I was honored to receive my party's nomination but unfortunately fell short in the general election. I learned a lot from that experience, and from my defeat.

4   But life works in ways we can't predict, or sometimes fully appreciate until later. Had I not lost that campaign, I never would have become U.S. Attorney—which has been the most important job of my life.

5   I was sworn into that position on April 20, 1999—the day after the Columbine tragedy. Like all Coloradans, our family was devastated by this senseless violence. I'm sure your family's conversations about this tragedy were similar to our family's—what has gone wrong when we can't provide a safe environment at our children's schools. Our daughter Lauren was a senior at East High School at the time, and I'll never forget when she told us that the one place she had felt completely safe before the shootings was her school library.

6   Based on that experience, I vowed to use the tools provided me as U.S. Attorney to help make our neighborhoods safer, our environment cleaner, our criminal justice system fairer and more responsive.

7   And I'm proud to say that during my term as U.S. Attorney, prosecutions were up 20%. I took on and beat drug traffickers, white-collar criminals and consumer rip-off artists.

8   But after Columbine the biggest priority was to try to break the cycle of gun violence.

9   As U.S. Attorney, I supported efforts to close the gun show loophole, and I also launched Colorado Project Exile to toughen enforcement of our existing gun laws.

10   We were able to find rare consensus for Colorado Project Exile. Wayne LaPierre from the NRA joined with James Brady from Handgun Control, Inc.; Democrats joined with Republicans, and state law enforcement joined with federal law enforcement. The message is simple: gun crime means hard time. Over a 24-month period the number of defendants charged with gun crimes in the U.S. Attorney's office nearly tripled.

11   I loved the job. I'd still be there if I could. I hope I left the office somewhat better for my time there—I know I'm better for the experience. One of the lessons I learned as U.S. Attorney is that problems can only be addressed when partisanship gives way to progress, and when we worry less about who gets the credit and more about what's in the community's best interest. The victims of crime aren't Democrats or Republicans. They are men and women and, unfortunately, children who deserve justice, not politics.

12   I grew up in a family that believed in the American Dream. The values of hard work and self-improvement come from one grandfather who was a sharecropper and another who spent 39 years as a switchman for the Sante Fe Railroad. My father saw a college education as his way out from the life his father led in the fields, and struggled for eight years during the depression to earn an engineering degree. My lot wasn't so daunting, though I spent summers on an oilrig then at two-a-day practices as I worked my way through college on a football scholarship. Later, I worked my way through law school.

13   Since then, first and foremost, I've tried my best to be a good husband and father. I've worked hard to provide for my family, but also to put something back into the community. I'm proud of the success I had as a lawyer. I believe I was a strong and effective advocate for my clients, but that's not all I did, and that was not all I was about. Like many Coloradans, I spent hours volunteering nights and weekends.

14   As Chairman of the Colorado Transportation Commission I helped lead the effort for mass transit and better highways.

15   As a member of the board of the Colorado Children's Campaign I was part of their ongoing advocacy for Colorado's children.

16   I worked for campaign finance reform as a Colorado Common Cause board member.

17   My concern for preserving Colorado's special beauty led me to join the Great Outdoors Colorado Campaign to restore misdirected lottery dollars back to parks, open space and wildlife, and I served on the first GOCO Board.

18   And at a time not so long ago when our economy was weak and jobs were scarce, I worked as a member of the board of the Denver Chamber of Commerce to help attract jobs and economic development.

19   These experiences in business and civic affairs taught me that government can't solve all our problems, and that business and community leadership matters.

20   If I am fortunate enough to become the Democratic nominee, I am going to ask for people's support based on strong principles and values, not just Party labels.

21   I believe there are critical battles being fought every day in the United States Senate—battles that deserve common sense solutions, not partisan bickering—battles that will determine the future of this country and affect the lives of every person in this state.

22   Independence and bipartisanship are more than just words for me; I've always tried to approach issues with my values firm but with a willingness to work across party or other lines to solve problems—on the GOCO Board, Transportation Commission, as U.S. Attorney.

23   We need more people in office who put the interests of the public ahead of partisan politics. John McCain demonstrates that kind of independence when he teams up with Democrats on campaign finance reform, a patient's bill of rights, and closing the gun show loophole. Joe Lieberman does that when he raises questions about the entertainment industry's impact on our children. I want to offer this kind of independent voice as a United States Senator.

24   Not everyone will agree with my views on every issue—but I won't shy away from them. I will be active and vocal in every debate, and Coloradans will always know where I stand.

25   The issues in this campaign are important because they fit into a broader vision of the world our children and grandchildren inherit from us.

26   This is a time to tackle the challenge of protecting our natural beauty while allowing growth that makes sense. It's a time to limit the influence of special interests in our politics and limit the intrusion of government and corporations into our privacy. It's a time to help families who are struggling to educate their children for the challenges of a competitive world and to help seniors battling the high costs of prescription drugs. It's a time to work with farmers and ranchers who are struggling to preserve their future. It's a time to protect a woman's right to choose and a time to protect every citizen from crime and drugs. And, with Washington spending money it doesn't have to the point where the Medicare trust fund has already been raided this year, it is a time for an honest budget policy before we spend ourselves back into deficits and recession.

27   In the comings weeks and months I'll travel around Colorado. I'll seek the wisdom and counsel of good citizens through the state. I'll go visit them where they live and work and play—I won't ask them to come to me. Along the way I'll offer positions on a range of important issues that will spell out my views.

28   And, finally I'll do my best to set a tone for this campaign that moves past the politics of cynicism. I challenge my opponent to join with me in giving Colorado voters a different kind of campaign, one that focuses on issues, not personal attacks. We can elevate the tone of this campaign, and bring people back into the process who have been turned off by years of negative campaign-

ing. The focus should be upon who can be the most effective advocate for Colorado, and who will do the most to make Colorado a better place to live.

29   As we look to Colorado's future, we have great cause for optimism. No state is better poised to prosper in the new economy—we have the best business climate, a highly educated and skilled work force and an unparalleled quality of life. We are all proud that the lyrics to "America the Beautiful" were inspired by our mountains. Yet we know that we benefit from the stewardship of those who came before us. We must do our best to provide leadership to match our mountains. I would be honored to try to provide such leadership as Colorado's next United States Senator.

Reading Responses

1. What qualifications and interests does each candidate emphasize about himself?
2. How does each candidate present himself? What values, concerns, and personality emerge for each?
3. How does each candidate appeal to voters?

Writing Activities

1. Write an essay comparing and contrasting the candidates in terms of issues.
2. Write an essay comparing and contrasting the two candidates' presentations in terms of character, personality, and values in their speeches.
3. Write an announcement speech, running for whatever office appeals to you.

Community Links

Compare and contrast these announcements with other speeches in the book. Look, for example, at Mairson's commencement speech (pp. 192–196), President Bush's Address (pp. 433–438), King's "I Have a Dream" (pp. 439–442) or Kerry and Bond (pp. 495–503). For the speeches you choose, consider which characteristics seem to be typical of speeches in general and which seem to be typical of political or other types of speeches.

Letter to Officials
DEAR PRESIDENT BUSH
Rice for Peace

◆

In January 2003, the Rice for Peace Web site proposed to visitors that they send a message to President Bush: a letter opposing war with Iraq along with a small amount of rice. The site provided a sample letter that Rice for Peace participants could send if they did not wish to compose their own letters. The site's home page explains the symbolism of the rice packet and provides a link to the sample letter.

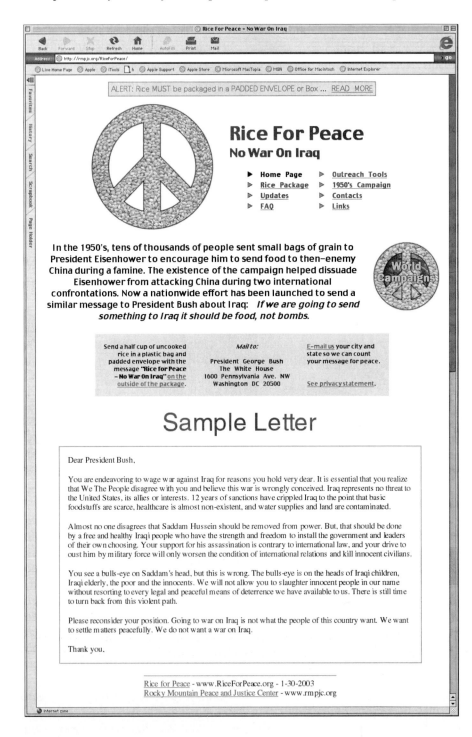

Reading Responses

1. What is the purpose of sending the small bag of rice to President Bush?
2. What reasons does the letter supply for opposing war with Iraq? In what ways does it try to persuade the president to pay attention to alternate views?
3. How do the visual elements on the Web site reinforce the proposed communication with the president?

Writing Activities

1. Consider the Rice for Peace home page. Write an explanation of the ways that it appeals to readers to join the letter-writing campaign.
2. Analyze the letter to the president, noting the points of agreement and disagreement it raises and the request it makes of the president. Write an analysis of its approach to its reader.
3. Write your own letter to a public official. Present your views on a current issue, and try to persuade the official to respect your opinion if not to agree with you.

Community Links

Consider how the letter to the president compares or contrasts with other types of writing that present a position. For example, turn to Lee's "The Case Against College" (pp. 73–75) from the academic community, Simpson's "Are Incentives for Drug Abuse Treatment Too Strong?" (pp. 301–306) from the work community, or Cullis-Suzuki's "The Young Can't Wait" (pp. 355–356) also from the public community. For each reading that you select, consider its purpose, readers, reasoning, appeals, community expectations, or other pertinent characteristics.

DEAR DENVER PUBLIC LIBRARY CUSTOMER
Rick Ashton

♦

This postage-paid mailer, available on counters at the library, welcomes comments and suggestions from visitors to the Denver Public Library. The City Librarian himself invites replies.

474 The Public Community

AGENCY _____

Dear Denver Public Library Customer:

How are we doing? Meeting your needs is our most important goal. Your concerns and comments mean a lot to us. If we're not meeting your needs, please let us know. If we are doing our job well, we'd like to hear that also. Thank you for sharing your ideas and suggestions with us.

Rick J. Ashton

Rick Ashton, City Librarian

Dear Rick:

Date _____

_____
_____
_____
_____
_____
_____
_____
_____
_____
_____
_____
_____
_____
_____
_____
_____
_____
_____
_____
_____
_____
_____
_____
_____
_____
_____
_____
_____

Name _____
Address _____

Zip _____ Phone _____

THE DENVER PUBLIC LIBRARY

Reading Responses

1. What is the purpose of Rick Ashton's message at the top of the reply form?
2. Why does the reply form begin with "Dear Rick" rather than another greeting?
3. On the reverse side of the form, one flap inquires about courteous treatment, success finding material, and any other comments. Lines for responses follow these three questions. Why do you think that these questions were not written on the full response page?

Writing Activities

1. Analyze and explain what this reply form might suggest about the values and concerns of the library and the city librarian.
2. Write your own comments to the head of your local or campus library.
3. Prepare a response form for another situation—for customers at work, for visitors to an organization that regularly interacts with the public, for citizens using government services, for students dropping by a campus office or facility, or for some other group of people in contact with an organization. Write the introduction to the form considering those likely to fill it out.

Community Links

Consider how representatives of organizations present themselves and their groups to other people. Compare and contrast this form with the homepage for Purdue's OWL (pp. 197–199), Lesh-Laurie's memo (p. 307), one of the workplace letters (pp. 308–318), Huntington's "Dear Ohio State Graduate" (pp. 451–452), Whittaker's "Dear Subscriber" (pp. 453–454), or a similar selection. For the readings that you select, consider the persona or image that the writers project, the image and values attributed to the organizations, and the methods used to convey these impressions.

Newsletter

NEWSLETTER

Greenwood Village, Colorado

◆

This is the cover of the June issue of the newsletter published monthly by Greenwood Village for its residents. Inside, the newsletter carries greetings from the mayor, questions submitted by the public with answers from the Village, announcements of community meetings and programs, brief updates on topics of local interest, a sum-

mary of city council actions, tentative agendas for future council meetings, and descriptions of upcoming events. The newsletter, mostly printed on slick paper, uses tinted articles, vivid and varied colors, photographs, images such as logos and maps, and other visual features.

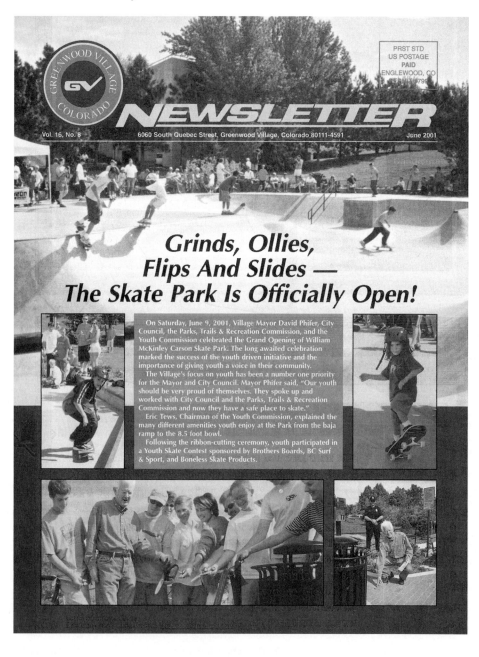

MESSAGE FROM CHRIS, CSR TODAY
Christine M. Ladisch

♦

CSR Today *is a newsletter published for students, graduates, and friends of the Consumer Sciences and Retailing (CSR) department at Purdue University. Inside, this newsletter includes photographs and news about faculty and staff, achievements and professional activities of members of the department, descriptions of student groups, notable student activities, brief feature stories about the successes of graduates, a commencement feature, key dates, and a reply form for news from the reader. The newsletter cover carries the following greeting from Christine Ladisch, the CSR department head. Her message, directly below the* CSR Today *masthead, is accompanied by her photograph.*

Message from Chris

1 Greetings from the faculty and staff of the Department of Consumer Sciences and Retailing. As I conclude my first year as Head of the department, I look back on our accomplishments with pride and I look forward to the next academic year with enthusiasm and optimism. This newsletter, the first of many so that we can keep in touch, will tell you why.

2 We continue to grow in enrollment. There are over 600 undergraduate CSR students! Most of the current growth is in our two newest majors, selling and sales management and small business. This year the apparel design and technology program almost doubled in size. We have worked hard to retain quality programs during this growth. The average SAT score for incoming freshmen is at an all-time high. This was the first year of our core curriculum which includes a freshman-only course that focuses on study skills, Purdue resources, CSR programs, and future career opportunities. Students rave about our hiring a full-time in-house academic advisor in order to provide immediate access to counseling and registration assistance. Several faculty have received national recognition for research that has made a difference in the quality of our lives. We will feature more about their work in the next issue of this newsletter.

3 The students of today are in some ways more demanding than I was at their age. They expect state-of-the-art, high technology teaching techniques and facilities. They look at career options before they have taken their first freshman course. Many plan to include a study abroad experience in their academic program. Our ability to meet these expectations and the challenges that go with them is greatly enhanced by your help. We welcome you into our classrooms to share your experiences and successes. Your financial generosity helps provide scholarships and support for some of the special projects and

student opportunities that are described in this newsletter. We thank you for remembering us and believing in what we do.

Sincerely,

Christine M. Ladisch
Department Head

Reading Responses

1. How does the cover for each newsletter suggest what readers will find in the rest of the newsletter? How does each represent its organization?
2. In what ways does each newsletter appeal to its readers?
3. How does the text on the cover contribute to the overall impression conveyed by each newsletter?

Writing Activities

1. Write a comparison and contrast of the approaches of the two covers.
2. Write two paragraphs, one for each cover, explaining the ways in which each is designed to appeal to the newsletter's readers and address their expectations.
3. Sketch the visuals and draft the text for a cover that might be appropriate for a newsletter for an organization that you know well. Describe the organization, the likely readers of the newsletter, and the impression that you would like the newsletter to convey.

Community Links

Compare and contrast the Greenwood Village newsletter cover with at least one other selection that balances text with visual components, such as the Web sites from all three communities (pp. 197–199, 347–349, and 566–571), a brochure such as "Your Driving Costs 2003" (pp. 530–541), or other similar material in the book. For the samples that you select, consider how the visual components support the overall impression of the publication and meet the expectations of the community and specific readers.

Civic Argument

THE STANDPOINT: HOW COMMON PRINCIPLES AND GOALS CAN SAVE THE WORLD'S WATER

Maude Barlow and Tony Clarke

◆

Blue Gold: The Fight to Save the Corporate Theft of the World's Water, by Maude Barlow and Tony Clarke, *outlines the global water crisis, explains the political situation, and advocates protecting water rights rather than selling them. This reading, part of Chapter 9, takes and explains a stand on water, outlining ten principles that should guide its protection. The rest of the chapter discusses stewardship, equality, universality, and peace, all in relation to water.*

1 University of Toronto Professor Emerita Ursula Franklin says that the most important social movements in history are grounded by the presence of a "standpoint." A standpoint, explains Dr. Franklin, is an ethical framework that informs one's purpose and one's work. "Where you stand and where you look tell you what is in the foreground, what is in the background, what is big and what is small." A standpoint brings a sense of priority, a sense of proportion, and a sense of obligation. Having the courage to find a place to stand, and if necessary, fight for what you believe, is required before any person or movement can effect real social change. The tragedy of most modern governments, says Franklin, is that they have embraced economic globalization, which denies the standpoint of community or environmental stewardship in favor of the sole standpoint of profit. For governments and corporations, the profit is big and in the foreground, and the care for people, Nature, and democratic principles has vanished. If the world's water is to be saved for future generations, millions of the world's citizens will have to take a stand based on a set of principles and ethical considerations directly opposed to the predominant standpoint of the global economy.

2 At the dawn of the millennium, the world is poised to make crucial, perhaps irrevocable, decisions about water. Individuals, countries, and corporations all over the globe are still polluting the very water that gives them life. Treatment systems are nonexistent or pushed to the limit in the poorer countries, and even in the wealthier nations, hormones and deadly chemicals are found in local water supplies. Some polluters keep pouring poisons into water systems even when confronted with evidence of the damage they have created, but the harm done to water to date has been largely unintentional and reactive—a combination of benign neglect, ignorance, greed, too many demands on a limited resource, careless pollution, and reckless diversion. On the whole,

the human race has taken water for granted and massively misjudged the capacity of the earth's water systems to recover from our carelessness. Although we must now answer to the great harm we have caused, it is probably fair to say that no one set out to create a global water shortage or to deliberately destroy the world's water supply.

Crossroads

3 However, lack of malice is no longer a good enough excuse. We know too much. We know how careless environmental practices such as clearcutting and toxic dumping are destroying waterways. We understand the connection between energy-hungry industrial and personal practices and the global warming which is destroying aquatic habitat. There is mounting evidence that we are depleting aquifers at a totally unsustainable rate but we keep on mining groundwater supplies because we won't stop polluting surface water. And we know that our irrigation practices are not only leading to desertification of land, but destroying water tables as well.

4 Yet societies all over the world, or at least their governments and private sector leaders, have bought into tenets of economic globalization based on a model of unlimited growth and the allure of unchecked consumerism. We continue to create conditions that force small farmers to abandon their land and head for overcrowded cities. We implement global trade policies that reward ecologically unsustainable production methods of goods and food. We favor governments that generate low consumer prices by cutting back on domestic regulation of agriculture, food production, chemical use, and industrial dumping. In fact, almost everything we do in modern industrialized society is guaranteed to deepen the global fresh water crisis. Huge transnational corporations are operating under the umbrella of trade regimes like the North American Free Trade Agreement, which make governments roll back environmental legislation for fear of reprisals at trade tribunals. Meanwhile, corporations pay minimal taxes or hide their profits in tax havens, thus diminishing potential government revenue that could have paid for water infrastructure improvements, sanitation services, and safe water practices. Our leaders have entrusted our lives to those driven solely by the profit imperative.

5 And now, as we have seen, transnational corporations, backed by international trade and financial institutions like the International Monetary Fund and the World Bank are moving in to profit directly from the global fresh water crisis. If we allow these private sector companies to take control of the world's water supplies, we will lose the capacity to save the world's water. We will be allowing the emergence of a water elite that will determine water use based on its own interests. Instead, we should be working to help people and communities around the world take responsibility for a shared resource and treat it in ways that will ensure a water-secure future for their descendants.

6 The move to commodify depleting global water supplies is wrong—ethically, environmentally, and socially. It ensures that decisions regarding the allocation of water center almost exclusively on commercial, not environmental or social, considerations. Corporate shareholders seek maximum profit, not sus-

tainability or equal access. Privatization means that the management of water resources is based on principles of scarcity and profit maximization rather than long-term sustainability. Corporations are dependent on increased consumption to generate profits and are therefore much more likely to invest in the use of chemical technology, desalination, and water diversion than in conservation.

7   And the trend to commodify what has been a public service makes it much more difficult for citizens to allocate and manage their own water sources. The concentration of power in the hands of a single corporation and the inability of governments to reclaim management of water services once a private water supplier has been contracted allows corporations to reduce the democratic power of citizens. And as transnational water companies lobby to reduce environmental regulations and deregulate water standards, they gain undue influence over government policies.

8   In spite of the obvious dangers it presents, the commodification of the world's fresh water is advancing at an alarming rate. Decision making over this precious resource appears to have fallen into a relatively small number of hands—bureaucrats at the World Bank and the UN, a cadre of professional water experts who advise them, government aid agencies, trade economists, and powerful water corporations with a personal stake in the outcome. This small but powerful group has determined that the debate is over; "everyone" supports the privatization of water, it asserts. This, of course, is patently untrue. The citizens of the world have not been consulted or even informed of this development. In fact, as outlined in Chapter 8, evidence is mounting that when citizens are given the choice about the control of their water, they opt for public, local, and transparent control.

9   What seems clear is that governments are not going to take the lead in this debate; instead, citizens will be forced to create the political arguments that will keep the world's water in the public "commons" for all time. To do so, general agreement must be reached about the fundamental principles needed to ensure a water-secure future for the world—and to come to agreement on these principles, five ethical questions about water must be addressed, questions concerning the commons, stewardship, equality, universality, and peace.

The Water Commons

10   The antidote to the commodification of water is its decommodification. Water must be declared and understood for all time to be common property. In a world where everything is being privatized, citizens must establish clear perimeters around those areas that are sacred to life or necessary for social and economic justice. Equal access to water is absolutely central to both life and justice.

11   As Indian physicist and activist Vandana Shiva points out, commonly owned water is not destroyed—as long as its use is controlled by conservationist rules. In fact, the only strategy for conserving water that has proved successful in time of scarcity is the renewal and rejuvenation of common property rights so that patterns of use are governed by Nature's limits of renewability and the social limits of water equity. Those who hold water in common must

set rules as to its use because a few individuals within a group could take more than their fair share if there were no disincentives. "Privatizing water through property rights will not reverse this degradation," says Shiva, "it will accelerate it. It will unleash water wars by pitting person against person, region against region, the rural areas against privileged and rich urban centers and the poor against the rich."

12   International water crusader Riccardo Petrella explains that it is an essential feature of the market that one should be able to choose among several goods of the same or a different nature, using for that choice such criteria as price and quality. The argument for commodifying water is the same argument used for the commodification of widgets: the marketplace is the optimum model for the most efficient allocation of material and natural resources, as well as the distribution of wealth. That is, each country will produce what it does best, and all will compete in the open marketplace. Hence, wealthy countries market technology, ideas, and telecommunications, while poor countries, with cheap labor, export goods made under poor conditions. Countries that are wealthy in natural resources like oil or water also "compete," selling these "products" in the global marketplace. According to this argument, government standards and subsidies for export are merely impediments to "efficient" competition in an open market.

13   However, to have access to water is not a matter of choice or of efficient accumulation of wealth; it is a matter of life and death. Water is not something to be bought and sold for profit like a pair of shoes or a pizza. It's true that water-bottling companies are marketing their "goods" just like hats or gloves or cars, presenting them in an amazing array of "options." But all of this is an illusion, of course. In addition, water is too precious a resource to be processed and distributed according to profit principles, which unleash a juggernaut of ever-accelerating consumption and ever-expanding markets. All bottled water comes from the same finite source. Supplies cannot be infinitely increased to serve continually burgeoning markets. There is no source of life comparable to water within the ecosystem, apart from soil and air. Water is unique, of limited supply, irreplaceable, and necessary for all life. The very fact that it cannot be replaced with anything else makes water a basic asset that cannot be subordinated to the principles of the marketplace. Thus, says Petrella, water is essential to the functioning of society as a whole and is therefore a social asset and a common good basic to any human community.

14   Vandana Shiva adds that water markets will not guarantee water availability to all, but will only guarantee access to the economically powerful while excluding the poor and the marginalized. As we become slaves to the whimsical dynamics of the deregulated "free" market, the commons is being destroyed and the weaker sections of society are being denied their right of access to a resource that is essential to their health and life.

15   This tragic outcome is completely unnecessary. Instead of commodifying water even further, we need to recover it by treating it as part of the commons and by strengthening community participation in water management—according to conservationist principles. Activist groups in South Africa have pointed out that when water is treated as part of the commons—a right to

which all individuals are entitled—it is supplied to more people, on a more equitable basis, than if it was subjected to the dynamics unleashed by the profit motive. This means that more people have better health and therefore have greater ability to contribute to the common good. This generates economic activity. At the same time, the resource is conserved because the profit motive has not driven suppliers to produce more and more until their water sources dry up. This enhances the health of the earth and helps maintain the balance of its ecological processes. And when the planet is healthy, it can better support responsible, sustainable economic activity, thus enhancing the prosperity of its citizens. In other words, the water commons not only recognizes the right of the individual to water for life, but also promotes the common good. As Petrella argues, this is why every society must collectively cover the costs of providing basic access to water for all. It is a basic human obligation and it makes long-term ecological and economic sense. [...]

Ten Principles

16 To save our diminishing water resources and stave off further conflict, all levels of government and communities around the world need to begin working together, as they have done in the past to rebuild communities in the aftermath of war. But to embark on this mission, we must soon come to agreement on a set of guiding principles and values. We have outlined ten here, as a starting point for dialogue and action that will lead to renewal.

1. Water belongs to the earth and to all species.
2. Water should be left where it is whenever possible.
3. Water must be conserved for all time.
4. Polluted water must be reclaimed.
5. Water is best protected in natural watersheds.
6. Water is a public trust, to be guarded by all levels of government.
7. Access to an adequate supply of clean water is a basic human right.
8. The best advocates for water are local communities and citizens.
9. The public must participate as an equal partner with government to protect water.
10. Economic globalization policies are not water-sustainable.

1. Water belongs to the earth and to all species.

17 Without water, humans and other beings would die and the earth's systems would shut down. Unfortunately, however, modern society has lost its reverence for water's sacred place in the cycle of life as well as its centrality in the realm of the spirit, and this loss of reverence for water has allowed humans to abuse it. Over time, we have come to believe that humans are at the center of the universe, not Nature, and decision makers have forgotten to take into account the fact that water belongs to the earth, to all species, and to future generations. They have shunted these stakeholders aside and failed to consider their interests. For all our brilliance and accomplishment, we are a species of

animal who needs water for the same reasons as other species. Unlike other species, however, only humans have the power to destroy the ecosystems upon which all depend, and that is the destructive path on which we have embarked. Only by redefining our relationship to water and recognizing its essential and sacred place in Nature can we begin to rectify the wrongs we have done. Only by considering the full impacts of our decisions on the ecosystem can we ever hope to replenish depleted water systems and to protect those that are still unharmed.

2. *Water should be left where it is whenever possible.*

18 Nature put water where it belongs. Tampering with Nature by removing vast amounts of water from watersheds has the potential to destroy that ecosystem and systems far beyond it. The large-scale removal of water from lakes, rivers, and streams has disastrous impacts on the land surrounding them and on the coastal environments where rivers eventually empty into the sea. Diversion and destruction of healthy bodies of water also destroys the local economy of Indigenous peoples and others who depend on them for their livelihoods.

19 While there may be an obligation to share water (and food) in times of crisis, it is not a desirable long-term solution. When one country or region becomes dependent on another for its water supplies, it is in a precarious position. Modern transportation and technology have also blinded many of us to the fact that importing water from long distances is neither cost-effective nor secure. If the full environmental costs of dam building, water diversion, and tanker transport were taken into account, we would see that the globalized trade in water makes no sense. By importing this basic need, a relationship of dependency would be established that is good for neither side. Instead, we need to learn the nature of water's limits and to live within them, looking at our own regions, communities, and homes for ways to meet our needs, while respecting water's place in Nature. Then, in times of emergency, watersheds and groundwater sources will be in better condition and available to temporarily help those who are far away.

3. *Water must be conserved for all time.*

20 Each generation must ensure that the abundance and quality of water is not diminished as a result of its activities. This will mean radically changing our habits, particularly concerning water conservation. People living in the wealthy countries of the world must change their patterns of water consumption, especially those in water-rich bioregions. If we do not change these habits, any reluctance to share our water—even for sound environmental and ethical reasons—will rightly be called into question.

21 If we change these patterns, we may maintain sustainable groundwater supplies, ensuring that extractions do not exceed recharge. In addition, some water destined for cities and agribusiness will have to be restored to Nature and small and medium-sized farming operations. Government subsidies of wasteful corporate practices and industrial farming must therefore end. By refusing to subsidize such abusive water use and by rewarding water conserva-

tion, governments will send out the message that water is not abundant and cannot be wasted.

22 Large tracts of aquatic systems must also be set aside for preservation, and governments must agree on a global target. Planned major dams and river diversions must be put on hold while better solutions are found, and some existing river diversions need to be reoriented back to their natural seasonal flow. Governments everywhere need to put priority on improving aging and broken water-delivery infrastructure. Huge amounts of water are lost every year because of leakage, and aging pipes can carry disease-bearing organisms.

4. Polluted water must be reclaimed.

23 The human race has collectively polluted the world's water supply and must collectively take responsibility for restoring it. Water scarcity and pollution are caused by economic values that encourage the overconsumption and inefficient use of water, which are already depleting aquifers and will eventually put our health and lives at risk. A resolution to reclaim polluted water is an act of self-preservation. Our survival, and the survival of all species, depends on restoring naturally functioning ecosystems.

24 Governments at all levels and communities in every country must clean up polluted water systems and stop the unthinking and rampant destruction of wetlands and watersheds. More rigorous laws must be passed and enforced to control water pollution from agriculture, municipal discharge, and industrial contaminants—the leading causes of water degradation. Governments must regain control over transnational mining and forestry operations, whose unchecked practices continue to cause untold damage to water systems.

25 Furthermore, the water crisis cannot be viewed in isolation from other major environmental issues such as clearcutting of forests and human-induced climate change. The destruction of waterways due to clearcutting severely harms fish habitat. Climate change will cause (and is already causing) more extreme weather conditions: floods will be higher, storms will be more severe, and droughts will be more persistent—the pressure on existing fresh water supplies will be magnified. To restore so much damaged water, countries will have to make international commitments to dramatically reduce human impacts on climate.

5. Water is best protected in natural watersheds.

26 The future of a water-secure world is based on the need to live within naturally formed "bioregions," or watersheds. The surface and groundwater conditions in these watersheds act as a set of parameters that govern virtually all of life in that region, including flora and fauna, which are related to the area's hydrological conditions. Living within the ecological constraints of a region is called bioregionalism, and watersheds are an excellent starting point for establishing bioregional practices.

27 Another advantage of thinking in watershed terms is that water flow does not respect nation-state borders. Watershed management is therefore one way

to break the gridlock among international, national, local, and tribal governments that has plagued water policy around the world for so long. Thinking in terms of watersheds, not political or bureaucratic boundaries, will lead to more collaborative protection and decision making.

6. Water is a public trust, to be guarded by all levels of government.

28 Because water, like air, belongs to the earth and to all species, no one has the right to appropriate it or profit from it at someone else's expense. It is a public trust that must be protected by all levels of government and by communities everywhere. This means that water should not be privatized, commodified, traded, or exported in bulk for commercial purposes. To ensure that this rampant commercialization does not take place, governments all over the world must take immediate action to declare that the waters in their territories are a public good and to enact legislation to protect them. Water should also be exempted from all existing and future international and bilateral trade and investment agreements, and governments must ban the commercial trade in large-scale water projects.

29 While it is true that governments have failed badly in protecting their water heritage, it is only through democratically controlled institutions that this situation can be rectified. If water becomes clearly established as a commodity to be controlled by the private sector, decisions about water will be made solely on a for-profit basis, and individual citizens will have no say as to how the resource will be used.

30 Each level of government must protect its water trust. At the municipal level, urban centers should no longer divert water resources from rural areas to service their own needs. At the municipal and regional levels, watershed cooperation should be carried out to protect larger river and lake systems. National and international legislation should apply the rule of law to transnational corporations and end abusive corporate practices. Governments should tax the private sector adequately to pay for infrastructure repair. And all levels of jurisdiction should work together to set targets for global aquatic wilderness preserves.

7. Access to an adequate supply of clean water is a basic human right.

31 Every person in the world has a right to clean water and healthy sanitation systems no matter where they live. This right is best protected by keeping water and sewage services in the public sector, regulating the protection of water supplies, and promoting the efficient use of water. This is the only way to preserve adequate supplies of clean water for people in water-scarce regions.

32 It is also vital to remember that Indigenous peoples have special inherent rights to their traditional territories, including water. These rights stem from their use and possession of the land and water in their territories and their ancient social and legal systems. The inalienable right of self-determination of Indigenous peoples must be recognized and codified by all governments, and water sovereignty is fundamental to the protection of those rights.

33 In addition, governments everywhere must implement a "local sources first" policy to protect the basic rights of all citizens to fresh water. Legislation

that requires all countries, communities, and bioregions to protect local sources of water and seek alternative local sources before looking to other areas will go a long way to halting the environmentally destructive practice of moving water from one watershed basin to another. "Local sources first" must be accompanied by a principle of "local people and local, small-scale farmers first." Agribusiness and industry, particularly large transnational corporations, must fit into a "local-first" policy or be shut down.

34   This does not mean that water should be "free" or that everyone can help themselves to limitless quantities. However, a policy of water pricing that guarantees an essential amount of water to every human would help conserve water and preserve the rights of all to have access to it. Water pricing and "green taxes" (which raise government revenues while discouraging pollution and resource consumption) should place a heavier burden on agribusiness and industry than on private citizens, and funds collected from these sources should be used to provide basic water supplies for all.

8. *The best advocates for water are local communities and citizens.*

35 Local stewardship, not private business, expensive technology, or even government, is the best protector of water security. Only local citizens can understand the overall cumulative effect of privatization, pollution, and water removal and diversion on their own community. Only local citizens know the effect of job loss or loss of nearby farms when water sources are taken over by big business or diverted for far-away uses. Local citizens and communities are the frontline "keepers" of the rivers, lakes, and underground water systems upon which their lives and livelihoods rest. They need to be given the political power to exercise that stewardship effectively.

36   Reclamation projects that work are often inspired by environmental organizations and involve all levels of government and sometimes private donations. But in order to be affordable, sustainable, and equitable, the solutions to water stress and water scarcity must be locally inspired and community-based. If they are not guided by the common sense and lived experience of the local community, they will not be sustained.

37   In water-scarce regions, traditional Indigenous practices, such as local water sharing and rain catchment systems that have been abandoned for new technology, are already being revisited with some urgency. In some areas, local people have assumed complete responsibility for water distribution facilities and established funds to which water users must contribute. The funds are then used to provide water to all in the community. Techniques like this should be applied in other water-scarce regions of the world.

9. *The public must participate as an equal partner with government to protect water.*

38 A fundamental principle for a water-secure future is that the public must be consulted and engaged as an equal partner with governments in establishing water policy. For too long, governments and international economic institutions such as the World Bank, the OECD, and trade bureaucrats have been driven by corporate interests. Even in the rare instances that they are given a

seat at the table, nongovernmental organizations (NGOs) and environmental groups are typically ignored. Corporations that heavily fund political campaigns are often given contracts for water resources—and too frequently, corporate lobby groups actually draft the wording of agreements and treaties that governments then adopt. This practice has created a crisis of legitimacy for governments everywhere.

Processes must be established whereby citizens, workers, and environmental representatives are treated as equal partners in the determination of water policy and recognized as the true inheritors and guardians of that irreplaceable resource.

10. Economic globalization policies are not water-sustainable.

The values of unlimited growth and ever-increasing international trade inherent in economic globalization are incompatible with the search for solutions to water scarcity. Designed to reward the strongest and most ruthless, economic globalization locks out the forces of local democracy so desperately needed for a water-secure future. If we accept the principle that to protect water we must attempt to live within our watersheds, the practice of viewing the world as one seamless consumer market must be abandoned.

Economic globalization undermines local communities by allowing for easy mobility of capital and the theft of local resources. In addition, liberalized trade and investment enables some countries to live beyond their ecological and water resource means while others abuse their limited water sources to grow crops for export. In wealthy countries, cities, agribusiness, and industries are mushrooming on deserts. A water-sustainable society would denounce these practices.

Global sustainability can be reached only if we seek greater regional self-sufficiency, not less. Building our economies on local watershed systems is the only way to integrate sound environmental policies with peoples' productive capacities and to protect our water at the same time.

Although world water supplies are dwindling and transnational corporations are working hard to reap substantial profits from that scarce supply, it is not too late to turn the situation around. Universal and equitable access to water is possible. The water commons can be saved from those who are already invading, to use it for their own profit. Private citizens do not have to stand by and watch as bottling companies move into their area, drain aquifers, fill their own pockets, and then depart. They don't have to put up with the privatization of water services. The people most affected by water-guzzling private interests can take matters into their own hands and prevent the destruction of their watersheds and the takeover of water delivery systems. Governments, so far, have not taken the lead to protect the water on which their constituents' lives depend. So it will be up to nongovernmental organizations and citizens' groups to change the way water is obtained and distributed and to protect this life-giving resource for coming generations.

Notes

Although we disagreed with most of the contributions in the collection, we read the arguments for water privatization in the 2000 World Bank book, *The*

Political Economy of Water Pricing Reforms, published by Oxford University Press and edited by Ariel Dinar. On the other hand, we did make extensive use of arguments put forward by Public Services International and its publications, such as the 2001 *Water in Public Hands,* written by David Hall. *World Water Watch: The Magazine of the Freshwater Environment* (now unfortunately no longer published) was also a source of many of the arguments, for and against privatization. Eric Gutierrez of the Institute for Popular Democracy in the Philippines provided insight in a paper he wrote for a September 1999 conference of the U.K. NGO WaterAid, called "Boiling Point: Water Security in the 21st Century."

Philip Lee of the *Ottawa Citizen* provided a useful series on the solutions to water in late August 2001. Patrick Bond of the University of Witwatersrand in Johannesburg wrote an excellent paper in the summer of 2001 called "Valuing Water beyond 'Just Price It': Costs and Benefits for Basic Human and Environmental Needs." And we wish to give special thanks to colleague Dr. Vandana Shiva of the Research Foundation for Science, Technology and Ecology in New Delhi for many books and publications on the commons. Particularly, we cite her July 1999 paper, "The Politics of Water: Water as Commons or Water as Private Property."

Reading Responses

1. What is a standpoint? What does it do?
2. What is the central issue as Barlow and Clarke define it?
3. How might the ten principles that they propose help to build cooperation and consensus around water issues?

Writing Activities

1. In your own words, write a summary of the central issue in the water debate.
2. Select one of the ten principles. Explain it in your own words, adding any pertinent examples that help to clarify or illustrate it.
3. Write several principles that you think would help to resolve another important issue. Select an issue about which you are knowledgeable or do enough research about the issue to understand the central conflicts.

Community Links

Consider this reading in relation to another reading that is also concerned with values, understanding, and their application to practical issues. Consider, for instance, Donald's "Learning, Understanding, and Meaning" (pp. 43–51) and Tannen's "The Roots of Debate in Education and the Hope of Dialogue" (pp. 65–72) from the academic community, the ethics readings for each community, or another reading that you select. Consider how each reading establishes its values, justifies the need for change, and derives working principles.

Civic Debate

FUEL ECONOMY OVERVIEW: EVOLUTION OF THE CURRENT POLICY

PRO & CON: SHOULD CONGRESS SET HIGHER MPG REQUIREMENTS FOR CARS AND LIGHT TRUCKS?

Senator John Kerry, Massachusetts

Senator Christopher S. Bond, Missouri

◆

Congressional Digest *is an independent publication featuring controversial topics in ten issues each year. "Americans and Their Cars" is the theme of the issue from which the next three readings come. First, "Fuel Economy Overview" introduces the issue and the legislative background. Next, two senators debate the issue, one arguing pro and the other con.*

1 The Arab embargo of 1973–1974 and the tripling in the price of crude oil brought into sharp focus the fuel inefficiency of U.S. automobiles. New car fleet fuel economy had declined from 14.8 miles per gallon (mpg) in model year (MY) 1967 to 12.9 mpg in 1974. In the search for ways to reduce dependence on imported oil, automobiles were an obvious target.

Energy Policy and Conservation Act

2 The Energy Policy and Conservation Act (EPCA) established corporate average fuel economy (CAFE) standards for passenger cars for model years 1978–1980 and 1985 and thereafter. The CAFE standards called for essentially a doubling in new car fleet fuel economy, establishing a standard of 18 mpg in MY 1978 and rising to 27.5 by MY 1985. (Interim standards for model years 1981–1984 were announced by the Secretary of Transportation in

---

From the Library of Congress, Congressional Research Service reports Automobile and Light Truck Fuel Economy: Is CAFE Up to Standards? *and* Global Climate Change: The Kyoto Protocol.

June of 1977.) EPCA also established fuel economy standards for light-duty trucks, beginning at 17.2 mpg in MY 1979, and currently 20.7 mpg.

3   Compliance with the standards is measured by calculating a sales-weighted mean of the fuel economies of a given manufacturer's product line, with domestically produced and imported vehicles measured separately. As originally enacted, the penalty for noncompliance was $5 for every 0.1 mpg below the standard, multiplied by the number of cars in the manufacturer's new car fleet for that year. Civil penalties collected from 1983 to 1995 have totaled over $400 million.

4   When oil prices rose sharply in the early 1980s, smaller cars were selling well, and it was expected that manufacturers would have no difficulty complying with the standards. However, oil prices had declined by 1985. Sales of smaller cars tapered as consumers began to place less value on fuel economy and gasoline cost as an input in the overall costs of vehicle ownership. In response to petitions from manufacturers facing stiff civil penalties for noncompliance, the National Highway Traffic Safety Administration (NHTSA) relaxed the standard for model years 1986–1989, but it was restored to 27.5 in MY 1991.

CAFE Standards

The Energy Policy and Conservation Act of 1975 required passenger car and light-truck manufacturers to meet CAFE standards. The CAFE standards are applied on a fleet-wide basis for each manufacturer; i.e., the fuel economy ratings for a manufacturer's entire line of passenger cars must average at least 27.5 mpg for the manufacturer to comply with the standard.

If a manufacturer does not meet the standard, it is liable for a civil penalty of $5 for each 0.1 mpg its fleet falls below the standard, multiplied by the number of vehicles it produces. For example, if a manufacturer produces 2 million cars in a particular model year, and its CAFE falls 0.5 mpg below the standard, it would be liable for a civil penalty of $50 million.

Manufacturers earn "credits" for exceeding CAFE standards. These credits can be used to offset fuel economy shortfalls in the three previous and/or three subsequent model years.

Two vehicle fleets are defined for CAFE purposes: Vehicles with 75 percent or more U.S./Canadian content are considered to be "domestics"; vehicles with less than 75 percent U.S./Canadian content are considered to be "imports." If a manufacturer has both domestic and import fleets, each fleet must comply separately with the CAFE standard.

Therefore, there could be an incentive for a manufacturer to raise or lower U.S./Canadian content in order to "move" a vehicle from one fleet to the other in order to meet the standard for both fleets.

Source: U.S. Department of Commerce, International Trade Administration

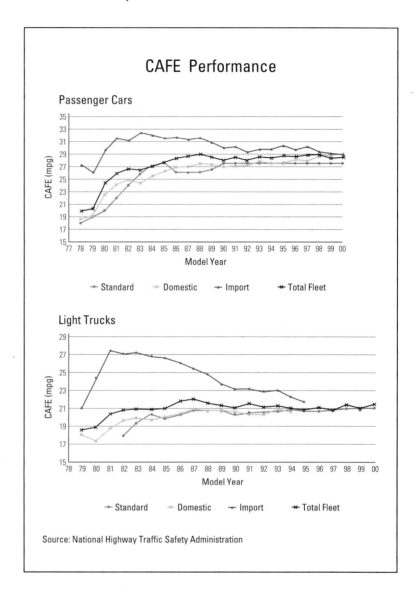

5   The Persian Gulf War in 1990 caused a brief spike in oil prices, but it also demonstrated that it was unlikely that the United States or many of the oil-producing nations would tolerate a prolonged disruption in international petroleum commerce. As a consequence, U.S. dependence upon imported petroleum, from a policy perspective, was considered less of a vulnerability. It was also becoming apparent that reducing U.S. dependence on imported oil would be extremely difficult without imposing a large price increase on gasoline, or restricting consumer choice in passenger vehicles.

6   Many argued that the impacts of such actions upon the economy or the automotive industry would be unacceptable. Meanwhile, gasoline consumption,

which fell to 6.5 million barrels per day (mbd) in 1982, averaged nearly 8.4 mbd in 1999, and was peaking at 8.6–8.8 during the summer of 2000 despite the surge in prices.

7   There were highly controversial attempts to significantly raise the CAFE standards on passenger cars in the early 1990s. One proposal included in omnibus energy legislation was so controversial that it contributed to the Senate's inability in 1991 to bring the bill up for debate on the floor.

8   NHTSA typically established truck CAFE standards 18 months prior to the beginning of each model year, as the Environmental Protection Agency allows. However, such a narrow window permitted NHTSA to little more than ratify manufacturers' projections for the model year in question. In April 1994, the agency proposed to abandon this practice and issued an Advance Notice of Proposed Rulemaking inviting comment on the level of standards that might be established for trucks for MY1998–MY2006.

9   The following year, however, after a change in congressional leadership, Congress included language in the Fiscal Year (FY) 1996 Department of Transportation (DOT) Appropriations to prohibit expenditures for any rulemaking that would make any adjustment to the CAFE standards. Identical language was included in the appropriations and spending bills for FY 1997–2000. It was also in the FY 2001 DOT Appropriations approved by the House Committee on Appropriations, May 16, 2000, and approved by the House, May 19, 2000.

Refocusing on Fuel Economy

10   Recent developments have focused fresh attention on the CAFE standards and fuel economy in general. The sharp increase in crude oil and gasoline prices that began in 1999 has brought into higher relief the continuing loss of market share of passenger cars to the larger, multipurpose sport utility vehicles (SUVs) that are subject to the less stringent light-truck fuel economy standard.

11   A 1996 study conducted for the Department of Transportation found that consumers valued the larger vehicles for their versatility and roominess and the availability of four-wheel drive. The increasing market share of these vehicles, combined with their lower average fuel economy, has contributed to a lowering in overall average fuel economy since the mid-1980s.

12   Other pressures have had less to do with energy security and more to do with environmental objectives. The Kyoto Agreement would have required the United States to achieve a 7 percent reduction in 1990 levels of carbon dioxide emissions, which implied a significant reduction in gasoline consumption, among other elements.

13   Preferring to forestall any State or Federal regulation, General Motors, Ford, Chrysler, and Toyota announced on February 4, 1998, that they would produce cars in MY 1999 with engine and catalytic converter technologies that would achieve lower emissions.

14   In early 1998, the California Air Resources Board voted to reclassify SUVs as passenger cars and hold those vehicles to California emissions standards.

Ford Motor announced in late July 2000 that it would improve the fuel economy of its SUV model line by 25 percent over a five-year period. Other manufacturers echoed similar intentions.

Kyoto Protocol

15   Negotiations on the Kyoto Protocol to the United Nations Framework on Convention on Climate Change were completed December 11, 1997, committing the industrialized nations to specified legally binding reductions in emissions of six "greenhouse gases." The United States signed the protocol on November 12, 1998. The treaty would commit the United States to a target of reducing greenhouse gases by 7 percent below 1990 levels during a "commitment period" between 2008 and 2012.

16   Major decisions on finalizing the operational rules of the Kyoto Protocol were expected at the sixth Conference of the Parties (COP-6) in The Hague, Netherlands, in November 2000. The COP-6 negotiations collapsed when the United States and the European Union failed to reach agreement on key issues. Talks were suspended until a resumed COP-6 meeting, termed "COP-6-bis," in Bonn, Germany, in July 2001.

17   In late March 2001, the Bush Administration indicated it considered the Kyoto Protocol "dead" in terms of U.S. policy, and announced a cabinet-level review of climate policy. In mid-June, President Bush outlined his preferred approach and confirmed U.S. rejection of the Kyoto Protocol. He indicated that the United States would remain engaged in the international negotiation process, with positions favoring strengthened scientific research and voluntary measures and market mechanisms.

18   At COP-6-bis, the United States remained on the sidelines. To the surprise of many, negotiators reached agreement on most of the outstanding political issues. At the following COP-7 meeting in Marrakech, Morocco, in October–November 2001, most remaining operational decisions were completed. The parties announced their intention to seek enough ratifications to bring the protocol into force by a self-imposed deadline of the World Summit on Sustainable Development, scheduled for August–September in Johannesburg, South Africa.

19   On February 14, 2002, President Bush announced his own plan to reduce emissions. The Administration's Clear Skies Initiative is designed to cut powerplant emissions of the three worst air pollutants—nitrogen oxides, sulfur dioxide, and mercury—by 70 percent. A new global climate change policy includes a strategy to cut greenhouse gas intensity by 18 percent over the next 10 years as well as further climate change research.

Pro
Honorable John Kerry

United States Senator, Massachusetts, Democrat

Senator Kerry was first elected to the U.S. Senate in 1984. He served as Lieutenant Governor of Massachusetts from 1982 to 1984. He is Chairman of the Small Business and Entrepreneurship Committee and a member of the Commerce, Science, and Transportation Committee, the Judiciary Committee, and the Foreign Relations Committee. He also chairs the Senate Hispanic Task Force and the Steering and Coordination Committee of the Senate Democratic Leadership. The following is from the March 12, 2002, Senate floor debate on amendments to S. 517, the National Laboratories Improvement Act.

1   I have listened with great interest to the comments now of a number of my colleagues—each of those who are the sponsors of the Bond-Levin amendment—and I have really listened with interest because the debate that I think the Senate deserves to have right now is one based on the truth, based on the facts, based on science, and based on history. I have heard some of the most remarkable Alice-in-Wonderland comments in the last few minutes that I find it hard to believe we are really talking about the same thing.

2   Senator [Christopher S.] Bond [MO-R] suggested that if we don't accept their amendment, people are going to actually be driven into getting into golf carts—a string of golf carts—which is not a very efficient way for a family to be transported. I heard another comment that we don't want to push people into imported vehicles. Well, of course, we don't.

3   I just listened to a very appropriate and distinguished speech about workers in this country. I remember with great pride that moment in 1971 when Leonard Woodcock introduced me to the United Auto Workers, and I was inducted as a lifetime member. I don't know anybody who runs for office in this country on a getting-rid-of-jobs platform. I don't know anybody who comes to the floor of the Senate suggesting, knowingly—and I hope not negligently and inadvertently—that a plan they are submitting is going to render Americans jobless.

4   I am here to defend the workers in Detroit, and in other parts of this country, just as much as anybody else. When I hear the notion invoked about who goes to fight our wars and who comes back as veterans and these are the people who work there—I know those people, and you bet I want them to keep working. I believe they can keep working. There is nothing that suggests that somebody in Detroit cannot make a better car than the Japanese. There is nothing to suggest that a Detroit worker, or one in any other part of the country, can't make a better and more efficient car than the Germans. American workers are the best workers, the most productive workers in the world. Those workers are handicapped by choices made by management.

5   The worker does not decide what the model is going to be. The worker does not decide which car is going to be manufactured and what the changeover date will be. They report every day and go to the floor. They punch

in and make the cars that the designers and the executives give them to make, and they do it well.

6   I proudly drive one of those minivans. I drive a Chrysler minivan. I think it is a terrific car. It is my second one, and I hope to get another one down the road.

7   There is nothing in the CAFE [corporate average fuel economy] standard that makes me believe I will not be able to drive a minivan at any time in the future. Nothing.

8   I point out this editorial in *Automotive News:*

> Let's get real. It's time for automakers to deal forthrightly with fuel economy issues. These are not the 1970s or 1980s or even the 1990s. To deny or refuse to admit that there is technology that can reduce fuel consumption significantly is ludicrous. The industry's credibility is at stake.

9   Let me emphasize, this is *Automotive News* writing that the industry's credibility is at stake. I urge my colleagues not to be intimidated by these hollow threats.

10   I do not know how many millions of dollars have been spent in the last weeks on television advertising to farmers that you cannot farm in a compact car. Really? I mean, what a phenomenal concept. People believe that? CAFE standards do not even apply to tractors. They do not even apply to heavy trucks now. And if we do our will in the Senate, they probably will not apply to pickup trucks. What are we talking about here?

11   We heard a threat about safety. We heard a reading from the National Academy of Sciences [NAS] about safety. That was page 28 of the National Academy of Sciences. Let me read page 70 from the National Academy of Sciences. It says as follows: "It is technically feasible and potentially economical to improve fuel economy without reducing vehicle weight or size and, therefore, without significantly affecting the safety of motor vehicle travel."

12   Those workers in Detroit and elsewhere, about whom we all care, can build the cars of the future. They can build a more efficient vehicle. They can build the hybrid electric SUVs [sport utility vehicles] with all the room and all the power one would want and twice the mileage if Detroit will choose to ask them to do so.

13   That is what this debate is about. It is about the future for our country in national security, on environmental issues such as global warming, and even it is about whether or not we intend to be competitive with the Japanese and Germans because, as I will show, the Japanese and Germans are building vehicles that Americans want and increasingly they are growing the marketplace in the United States.

14   Toyota and Honda are moving plants to the United States. The same pattern can be shown for other automakers. Now they are making something like 600,000 vehicles in the United States. What kind of vehicles are they selling in the United States, even though the Big Three [Ford, Chrysler, and General

Motors] continue to dominate the market? You have to look at trends. You have to look at the direction in which you are moving.

15   This debate is not just about this moment in time. It has a history and we have to balance the choices we face today against the history of where we have traveled. Motor vehicle miles in the personal automobile vehicle are at the lowest level in 20 years. We are going backwards in fuel efficiency.

16   My colleagues say: We do not need to have a dictate from Congress. We are going to get there because the automobile industry is going to get there without a mandate.

17   Let me show the record for the last years. From 1988 until the year 2001, of all the new technologies that were developed by the American automobile industry, 53 percent of those new technologies went into horsepower; 18 percent went into acceleration; 19 percent went into weight; minus 8 percent went into fuel efficiency.

18   We now have cars on the road that can go 140 miles an hour, even though the speed limit is 65, 70, 80 permissibly in some places. One can only go so fast between stoplights in many cities. Minus 8 percent on fuel efficiency. I like driving a big car, too. I am just like any other American.

19   Indeed, for a number of years, all of us have been forced to think in the defensive way that has been referred to. You see another big car on the road, you get a little intimidated and say: Gee, if I am going to protect my kids, I am going to have a big car on the road, too.

20   In fact, what has happened in the last years, according to the National Academy of Sciences, is that the Toyotas and the Honda Civics went from weighing about 1,800 pounds up to 2,600 pounds. The Honda Civic grew in weight, and indeed some of the other big SUVs grew also. It is true if a Honda Civic hits a big SUV, your chances of doing well in the Honda Civic are not as great. I understand that.

21   The older National Academy of Sciences study did not include airbags. It did not include the new standards of restraints. It also did not include what we have in our bill, which are rollover standards, because the biggest single problem for Americans in terms of SUVs is rolling over and being crushed because we have no standard for the roof and for the roll capacity of the car. So the fact is these cars can be made efficient and safe at the same time. They are trying to scare people with this safety standard. I heard one of my colleagues say we have to do this based on science. Well, it is based on science. It is not arbitrary. This is not a figure picked out of the sky, as one of my colleagues has said. This is a figure that is less than many scientific analyses say we can achieve.

22   The current fleet average is about 25 miles per gallon. If we cannot go 7 miles per gallon in 13 years, what can we do? That is the vote. This is a vote whether or not we want no standard at all and you turn it over to NHTSA [National Highway Traffic Safety Administration], which has a long reputation of being managed by administrations and by outside interests and not being able to set the standard. It is not even staffed efficiently enough today to be able to do it. The NAS is in fact better staffed and has had more background research than they have done in years, because on the other side of the aisle in 1995 [House] Speaker [Newt] Gingrich [GA-R] and the Republicans

brought a complete prohibition on the ability of the EPA [Environmental Protection Agency] to even analyze what might be the benefits of raising the standards.

23   That tells you a huge story. It says what you have is an ongoing process by which the industry is fighting against whichever forum might be the least friendly to it. When Congress might do something, they say go to NHTSA if the administration has a handle on NHTSA. When NHTSA might do something, if they are in control of Congress they say go to Congress; Congress ought to do it.

24   In 1989 and 1990, they specifically said, we really think NHTSA is the proper place to do this. Then lo and behold, the Republicans controlled the House and the Senate in 1995 and Andrew Card, then representing the automobile manufacturers, said, oh, no, we do not think NHTSA is the right place, contrary to what they had said for the last few years. They said, we had better go to Congress.

25   What we see today is an effort to congressionally implement the same kind of forum shopping for the least standard possible for the least environmental effort possible.

26   Let me point to some of the comments of the industry as we analyze where we are trying to go. In the last three weeks, this is what the industry has said publicly: "Make no mistake, the Senate proposals would eliminate SUVs, minivans, and pickup trucks. If these proposals pass, the only place you will see a light truck is in a museum."

27   What they said in 1975 was:

> If this proposal becomes law and we do not achieve a significant technological breakthrough to improve mileage, the largest car the industry will be selling in any volume at all will probably be smaller, lighter, and less powerful than today's compact Chevy Nova, and only a small percentage of all models being produced could be that size.

28   That was the threat in 1975. That was General Motors. Let me read what Chrysler had to say:

> In effect, this bill would outlaw a number of engine lines and car models, including most full-size sedans and station wagons. It would restrict the industry to producing subcompact-size cars, or even smaller ones, within five years, even though the Nation does not have the tooling capacity or capital resources to make such a change so quickly.

29   Did that happen? Did any of this happen?

30   Then Ford said: "Many of the temporary standards are unreasonable, arbitrary...."

31   "Arbitrary." That is a word we have heard again—and technically unfeasible. If we cannot meet them when they are published, we will have to close down.

32 The fact is, the industry flourished. The industry met the standards, and more people were employed. The industry actually turned around and became competitive.

33 We are trying to save jobs in America by making an industry that is so reluctant to embrace change live up to a standard that will make their automobiles competitive. In fact, the National Academy of Sciences says the cost of doing this is saved to the consumer in the gasoline savings over the lifetime of a car. The gasoline savings will save the differential in cost, in addition to which we are prepared to provide a tax credit to people who buy the efficient cars.

34 So we can make up the difference of cost to Detroit. We can make up the difference of cost largely to the consumer if that is what we want to do. This is not a zero sum game of jobs or national security, protecting the environment, reducing our dependence on oil, and being more efficient, and reducing, incidentally, extraordinary costs to our citizens of the air quality that they breathe.

35 I might add, if we were to do what we are seeking to do, we would cut global warming pollution by 176 metric tons by the year 2025. There is no other effort in the United States of America that is as significantly capable of adding now to the Clean Air Act efforts already in effect than to try to join the world in being responsible about global warming.

36 That is part of what this vote is about.

37 The scare tactics being used by the industry today are absolutely no different than the scare tactics they used 25 years ago, when there was a completely opposite outcome from what they predicted. Every scientific input and analysis shows you can create net jobs at no net cost to the consumer with no loss of safety. That is the finding of the National Academy of Sciences.

38 Let me read a statement from the two important automobile safety groups in America, the Public Citizen and Center for Automobile Safety, which are both supporting a CAFE standard.

39 This is what they say:

> The auto industry is using an outdated, inaccurate, and hypocritical argument about safety to try to derail stronger corporate average fuel economy standards. Public Citizen and the Center for Auto Safety have long been two of the strongest voices calling for safer vehicles in the United States. We do not believe that stricter fuel economy standards must cost lives, and we know that a strong fuel economy bill can save lives by changing the nature of America's vehicle fleet.

40 How does it change the nature of America's vehicle fleet? Very simply: It reverses this trend where all the technology goes into horsepower and acceleration for cars that already go twice the speed limit—and puts some of it into weight and fuel efficiency so you actually reduce the largest weight and size. You do not have to give up any capacity within a car. A minivan will stay a minivan. It will still take soccer moms to soccer games. It can still be filled up with whatever the legal number of kids is, and dogs, and all of the paraphernalia of sports.

41 But guess what? It will get to the soccer game costing less money. It will get to the soccer game in a way that repays the cost of the car over the lifetime and may even create greater savings, and savings when our standards for rollover and safety are adopted.

42 This is the most bogus argument I have ever heard in my life.

43 The history of this issue proves it is. In 1972, 1973, and 1990, each time, the auto industry has said: We cannot do this.

44 They said it about seatbelts. They said it about laminated windshields. They have said it about every single requirement, each time Congress has agreed we ought to try to do these things. Yet once the CAFE standards were implemented, all three companies met and exceeded the standards.

45 I can imagine the pressure you are under from those same companies and others as you consider raising the standards. But as you embark on this process, I strongly urge you to recall our experiences in developing the first set of CAFE standards. You should feel confident that the automobile manufacturers do have the ability to achieve and, in fact, surpass whatever standards you set.

Con
Honorable Christopher S. Bond

United States Senator, Missouri, Republican

Senator Bond was first elected to the U.S. Senate in 1986. He was Missouri Assistant Attorney General from 1969 to 1970, Missouri Auditor from 1970 to 1972, and Missouri Governor from 1972 to 1976 and 1980 to 1984. He is the Ranking Minority Member of the Small Business and Entrepreneurship Committee and a member of the following committees: Appropriations; Budget; Environment and Public Works; and Health, Education, Labor, and Pensions. The following is from the March 12, 2002, Senate floor debate on amendments to S. 517, the National Laboratories Improvement Act.

1 There are many important issues in an energy bill, but what happens to our automobile economy, what happens to the workers, what happens to the people who buy them, what happens to the people on the highways should be a very important consideration.

2 I think when you talk about energy and fuel economy standards, the impact on jobs and safety needs to be at the top of anyone's list. That is why I am pleased to join my colleague from Michigan, Senator [Carl D.] Levin [D], in crafting a commonsense amendment to the energy bill that will increase passenger car and light truck efficiency while protecting jobs, highway safety, and consumer choice.

3 Before we get into the details of the amendment, let me just take a moment to review the state of our economy.

4 A few weeks ago, I was disappointed that the Senate had stalled out on an economic stimulus package. We have been in a recession for months, and although there are signs of a recovery, there are still many Americans without jobs. Of course, as you know, we did pass a smaller bill to increase the time of

payment for unemployment compensation that did have a portion of the stimulus package in it. Now, what would be the link between higher fuel economy standards and economic recovery and stimulus and jobs? I will tell you.

5   The only way for car companies to meet the unrealistic numbers in the underlying amendment is to cut back significantly on making the light trucks, the minivans, and the SUVs [sport utility vehicles] that the American consumers want, that the people of my State and the people of the other States want—to carry their children around safely and conveniently, to do their business. If they have jobs in one of the trades, they need minivans and compartment trucks and others to carry their goods. If they are farmers, they need pickup trucks to take care of their livestock and to haul equipment and feed.

6   I know some in this Chamber believe our fellow Americans cannot be trusted to make the right choice when purchasing a vehicle. But when it comes down to choosing between the consumer and the government as to who is best to make a choice, I will side with the consumer every time.

7   I don't pretend to know what is best for each of the 15 million Americans who will be purchasing a new vehicle this year and the ones next year or in the years after. Those who want higher government CAFE [corporate average fuel economy] or miles-per-gallon standards always claim to have the best interests of the consumer in mind and always promise that the last thing they want to do is hurt the car manufacturers. Well, they have missed the mark by a mile with language that ended up in the bill before us today.

8   Proponents portray this CAFE provision, authored by Senator [John] Kerry [MA-D] and others, as reasonable and necessary. I have other words in mind to describe it. It is antisafety, anticonsumer, and antijob.

9   I also have the numbers to consider during this debate. How about 6.6 million? That is the number of Americans employed in direct or spin-off jobs related to the automotive industry. In fact, every State in America is an auto State. We all know that Michigan, Indiana, Missouri, and Ohio are big manufacturing States. But even smaller States such as Nebraska, New Hampshire, and Delaware have suppliers and other industries where success and business profitability are directly related to the large car assembly plants in the Nation.

10 I prefer to listen to those who are actually engaged in the business of making cars, of designing cars, servicing cars, selling cars and trucks. They tell me one consistent message: The CAFE provision is a job killer, a threat to the safety of our friends and families, and a mandated market that eliminates consumer choice. For those who say, too bad, we must force Detroit to build more fuel-efficient cars and trucks, do you know that under CAFE it doesn't matter what the companies manufacture and build? It is calculated based on what the consumer buys.

11 There are over 50 of these high-economy models in the showrooms across America today. But guess what? They represent less than 2 percent of total sales. Americans don't want them. You can lead a horse to water; you can't make him drink. You can lead the American consumer to a whole range of fancy, lightweight, long-distance automobiles, but you can't make them buy them.

12   Meanwhile, consumers from families, soccer moms, farmers, people with teenagers, people with soccer teams, they want the minivans. A constituent of mine, Laura Baxendale in Ballwin, Missouri, asked: "Senator, our minivan is used to transport two soccer teams, equipment and seven players, how would this be possible in a smaller vehicle?"

13   I have to tell Ms. Baxendale, the bad news is they would have to have a string of golf carts. You can see the golf carts going down the highway to soccer practice, maybe two kids in each golf cart. It is not a very safe or efficient way to transport.

14   Here is a quote from Jeffrey Byrne, of Byrne Farm in Chesterfield, Missouri: "As a farmer I do not purchase pickup trucks because of their fuel economy, I purchase them for their practicality." He buys them because he needs them. He is taking care of his livestock. Did you ever try to put a load of hay in the back of a golf cart? It doesn't make a very big delivery vehicle.

15   Under the new CAFE numbers, the production of these popular vehicles would need to be curtailed. I don't want to tell a mom and dad in my home State they can't get the SUV they want because Congress decided that would be a bad choice. I don't think that is a sound way to set public policy.

16   After hearing from assembly line workers, farmers, auto dealers, and others directly impacted by government CAFE standards, I fully believe the appropriate fuel economy standards are best decided by experts within the Department of Transportation who have the technology and the scientific know-how to determine what is feasible to help lead us down the path towards the most efficient, economical, and environmentally friendly standards, rather than by politicians choosing some political number out of the air. We could get in a bidding war, but we are bidding on something we know nothing about—how efficient can engines be made.

17   Under the Levin-Bond amendment, the experts at the National Highway Traffic Safety Administration [NHTSA] are directed to refer to sound science in promulgating an appropriate and feasible increase. Think of that. This would be historic, if this body said we are going to use sound science on a technological issue before us.

18   Senator Levin and I believe the time has come. This amendment will strengthen the regulatory process to ensure that the miles-per-gallon or CAFE levels are accurate and reflect the needs of consumers, the technology development, without undo consequences for safety and jobs.

19   Ultimately, I do believe science, not politics, should drive the deliberations on the CAFE or miles-per-gallon standards. I would be most interested to see what hard data and solid science our colleagues who have pushed for this 35-mile-an-hour CAFE standard say justifies it, the standard in the bill. I am waiting to see what scientist thinks there is a technology to meet it. I don't believe I would hold my breath because I don't think it exists.

20   This is, unfortunately, a political number pulled out of thin air. Even worse, it is a number that could have deadly consequences for American drivers and passengers. I have read the 2001 National Academy of Sciences [NAS] report on the CAFE standard. Let me share with you a key finding about safety and higher standards.

21 This is a report in *USA Today*. It says: "The fatality statistics show that 46,000 people have died because of a 1970s-era push for greater fuel efficiency that has led to smaller cars."

22 The National Academy of Sciences says: "In summary, the majority of that committee finds that the downsizing and weight reduction that occurred in the late 1970s and early 1980s most likely produced between 1,300 and 2,600 crash fatalities and 13,000 to 26,000 serious injuries in 1993."

23 They estimate that 2,000 people were killed in 1993. I fear that has been replicated every year since. It goes on to say: "If an increase in fuel economy is effected by a system that encourages either downweighting or the production and sale of more small cars, some additional traffic fatalities would be expected."

24 That National Academy of Sciences report offers all of us clear guidance and expert scientific analysis as we debate fuel economy levels. I would also point out that the NAS panel was extremely careful to caution its readers that its fuel economy targets were not recommended CAFE goals because they did not weigh considerations such as employment, affordability, and safety.

25 Opponents of our amendment may question how effective the experts at NHTSA will be in leading the new fuel economy standards. Some might prefer that Congress set a political number as we find in the current energy bill.

26 Our amendment takes an approach that, rather than politics and guesswork, hard science and technological feasibility should be the prime consideration in the development of any new CAFE standards.

27 It is vitally important that we strike the people-killing, jobs-killing, market-killing, CAFE or miles-per-gallon provisions because they would only hurt the consumer and do very little for fuel economy. Let's save jobs and save American lives by voting yes on the Levin-Bond amendment.

Reading Responses

1. What is the issue presented here?
2. What are the major pro arguments presented by Kerry? How does Kerry shape his presentation of the pro side of the issue?
3. What are the major con arguments presented by Bond? How does Bond shape his presentation of the con side of the issue?

Writing Activities

1. Prepare a two-column list or an outline identifying major pro arguments on one side and major con arguments on the other.
2. Summarize in your own words the main arguments of each senator.
3. Enter this debate yourself by writing your own pro or con statement. Be sure that any quotations you include are accurate and any sources you use are credited.

Community Links

Compare and contrast the statements by Kerry and Bond. Then take another approach after looking at "Your Driving Costs 2003" (pp. 530–541). Evaluate the pro and con statements in terms of their possible applications to you as a car driver.

Position Paper

BRIEFING PAPER: HATE SPEECH ON CAMPUS

American Civil Liberties Union

◆

The American Civil Liberties Union (ACLU) prepares briefing papers on many potentially difficult or complex issues. This briefing paper from the ACLU Web site includes an introduction to the issue followed by a series of questions that raise common preconceptions or alternate views. Its discussion of hate speech begins not with the biases of the speaker, the target of the speech, or the responses of others on campus, but with the First Amendment, which guarantees the freedom of speech.

In recent years, a rise in verbal abuse and violence directed at people of color, lesbians and gay men, and other historically persecuted groups has plagued the United States. Among the settings of these expressions of intolerance are college and university campuses, where bias incidents have occurred sporadically since the mid-1980s. Outrage, indignation and demands for change have greeted such incidents—understandably, given the lack of racial and social diversity among students, faculty and administrators on most campuses.

1 Many universities, under pressure to respond to the concerns of those who are the objects of hate, have adopted codes or policies prohibiting speech that offends any group based on race, gender, ethnicity, religion or sexual orientation.

2 That's the wrong response, well-meaning or not. The First Amendment to the United States Constitution protects speech no matter how offensive its content. Speech codes adopted by government-financed state colleges and universities amount to government censorship, in violation of the Constitution. And the ACLU believes that all campuses should adhere to First Amendment principles because academic freedom is a bedrock of education in a free society.

3 How much we value the right of free speech is put to its severest test when the speaker is someone we disagree with most. Speech that deeply offends our morality or is hostile to our way of life warrants the same constitutional protection as other speech because the right of free speech is indivisible: When one of us is denied this right, all of us are denied. Since its founding in 1920,

the ACLU has fought for the free expression of all ideas, popular or unpopular. That's the constitutional mandate.

Where racist, sexist and homophobic speech is concerned, the ACLU believes that more speech—not less—is the best revenge. This is particularly true at universities, whose mission is to facilitate learning through open debate and study, and to enlighten. Speech codes are not the way to go on campuses, where all views are entitled to be heard, explored, supported or refuted. Besides, when hate is out in the open, people can see the problem. Then they can organize effectively to counter bad attitudes, possibly change them, and forge solidarity against the forces of intolerance.

College administrators may find speech codes attractive as a quick fix, but as one critic put it: "Verbal purity is not social change." Codes that punish bigoted speech treat only the symptom: The problem itself is bigotry. The ACLU believes that instead of opting for gestures that only appear to cure the disease, universities have to do the hard work of recruitment to increase faculty and student diversity, counseling to raise awareness about bigotry and its history, and changing curricula to institutionalize more inclusive approaches to all subject matter.

Questions

Q: I just can't understand why the ACLU defends free speech for racists, sexists, homophobes and other bigots. Why tolerate the promotion of intolerance?

A: Free speech rights are indivisible. Restricting the speech of one group or individual jeopardizes everyone's rights because the same laws or regulations used to silence bigots can be used to silence you. Conversely, laws that defend free speech for bigots can be used to defend the rights of civil rights workers, anti-war protesters, lesbian and gay activists and others fighting for justice. For example, in the 1949 case of Terminiello v. Chicago, the ACLU successfully defended an ex-Catholic priest who had delivered a racist and anti-semitic speech. The precedent set in that case became the basis for the ACLU's successful defense of civil rights demonstrators in the 1960s and '70s.

The indivisibility principle was also illustrated in the case of Neo-Nazis whose right to march in Skokie, Illinois in 1979 was successfully defended by the ACLU. At the time, then ACLU Executive Director Aryeh Neier, whose relatives died in Hitler's concentration camps during World War II, commented: "Keeping a few Nazis off the streets of Skokie will serve Jews poorly if it means that the freedoms to speak, publish or assemble any place in the United States are thereby weakened."

Q: I have the impression that the ACLU spends more time and money defending the rights of bigots than supporting the victims of bigotry!!??

10 A: Not so. Only a handful of the several thousand cases litigated by the national ACLU and its affiliates every year involves offensive speech. Most of the litigation, advocacy and public education work we do preserves or advances the constitutional rights of ordinary people. But it's important to understand that the fraction of our work that does involve people who've engaged in bigoted and hurtful speech is very important:

> Defending First Amendment rights for the enemies of civil liberties and civil rights means defending it for you and me.

11 **Q: Aren't some kinds of communication not protected under the First Amendment, like "fighting words?"**

12 A: The U.S. Supreme Court did rule in 1942, in a case called *Chaplinsky v. New Hampshire,* that intimidating speech directed at a specific individual in a face-to-face confrontation amounts to "fighting words," and that the person engaging in such speech can be punished if "by their very utterance [the words] inflict injury or tend to incite an immediate breach of the peace." Say, a white student stops a black student on campus and utters a racial slur. In that one-on-one confrontation, which could easily come to blows, the offending student could be disciplined under the "fighting words" doctrine for racial harassment.

13 Over the past 50 years, however, the Court hasn't found the "fighting words" doctrine applicable in any of the hate speech cases that have come before it, since the incidents involved didn't meet the narrow criteria stated above. Ignoring that history, the folks who advocate campus speech codes try to stretch the doctrine's application to fit words or symbols that cause discomfort, offense or emotional pain.

14 **Q: What about nonverbal symbols, like swastikas and burning crosses—are they constitutionally protected?**

15 A: Symbols of hate are constitutionally protected if they're worn or displayed before a general audience in a public place—say, in a march or at a rally in a public park. But the First Amendment doesn't protect the use of nonverbal symbols to encroach upon, or desecrate, private property, such as burning a cross on someone's lawn or spray-painting a swastika on the wall of a synagogue or dorm.

16 In its 1992 decision in *R.A.V. v. St. Paul,* the Supreme Court struck down as unconstitutional a city ordinance that prohibited cross-burnings based on their symbolism, which the ordinance said makes many people feel "anger, alarm or resentment." Instead of prosecuting the cross-burner for the content of his act, the city government could have rightfully tried him under criminal trespass and/or harassment laws.

17 The Supreme Court has ruled that symbolic expression, whether swastikas, burning crosses or, for that matter, peace signs, is protected by the First Amendment because it's "closely akin to 'pure speech.'" That phrase comes from a landmark 1969 decision in which the Court held that public school students could wear black armbands in school to protest the Vietnam War. And in another landmark ruling, in 1989, the Court upheld the right of an individual to burn the American flag in public as a symbolic expression of disagreement with government policies.

18 **Q: Aren't speech codes on college campuses an effective way to combat bias against people of color, women and gays?**

19 A: Historically, defamation laws or codes have proven ineffective at best and counter-productive at worst. For one thing, depending on how they're interpreted and enforced, they can actually work against the interests of the people they were ostensibly created to protect. Why? Because the ultimate power to decide what speech is offensive and to whom rests with the authorities—the government or a college administration—not with those who are the alleged victims of hate speech.

20 In Great Britain, for example, a Racial Relations Act was adopted in 1965 to outlaw racist defamation. But throughout its existence, the Act has largely been used to persecute activists of color, trade unionists and antinuclear protesters, while the racists—often white members of Parliament—have gone unpunished.

21 Similarly, under a speech code in effect at the University of Michigan for 18 months, white students in 20 cases charged black students with offensive speech. One of the cases resulted in the punishment of a black student for using the term "white trash" in conversation with a white student. The code was struck down as unconstitutional in 1989 and, to date, the ACLU has brought successful legal challenges against speech codes at the Universities of Connecticut, Michigan and Wisconsin.

22 These examples demonstrate that speech codes don't really serve the interests of persecuted groups. The First Amendment does. As one African American educator observed: "I have always felt as a minority person that we have to protect the rights of all because if we infringe on the rights of any persons, we'll be next."

23 **Q: But don't speech codes send a strong message to campus bigots, telling them their views are unacceptable?**

24 A: Bigoted speech is symptomatic of a huge problem in our country; it is not the problem itself. Everybody, when they come to college, brings with them the values, biases and assumptions they learned while growing up in

society, so it's unrealistic to think that punishing speech is going to rid campuses of the attitudes that gave rise to the speech in the first place. Banning bigoted speech won't end bigotry, even if it might chill some of the crudest expressions. The mindset that produced the speech lives on and may even reassert itself in more virulent forms.

25 Speech codes, by simply deterring students from saying out loud what they will continue to think in private, merely drive biases underground where they can't be addressed. In 1990, when Brown University expelled a student for shouting racist epithets one night on the campus, the institution accomplished nothing in the way of exposing the bankruptcy of racist ideas.

26 **Q: Does the ACLU make a distinction between speech and conduct?**

27 A: Yes. The ACLU believes that hate speech stops being just speech and becomes conduct when it targets a particular individual, and when it forms a pattern of behavior that interferes with a student's ability to exercise his or her right to participate fully in the life of the university.

28 The ACLU isn't opposed to regulations that penalize acts of violence, harassment or intimidation, and invasions of privacy. On the contrary, we believe that kind of conduct should be punished. Furthermore, the ACLU recognizes that the mere presence of speech as one element in an act of violence, harassment, intimidation or privacy invasion doesn't immunize that act from punishment. For example, threatening, bias-inspired phone calls to a student's dorm room, or white students shouting racist epithets at a woman of color as they follow her across campus—these are clearly punishable acts.

29 Several universities have initiated policies that both support free speech and counter discriminatory conduct. Arizona State, for example, formed a "Campus Environment Team" that acts as an education, information and referral service. The team of specially trained faculty, students and administrators works to foster an environment in which discriminatory harassment is less likely to occur, while also safeguarding academic freedom and freedom of speech.

30 **Q: Well, given that speech codes are a threat to the First Amendment, and given the importance of equal opportunity in education, what type of campus policy on hate speech would the ACLU support?**

31 A: The ACLU believes that the best way to combat hate speech on campus is through an educational approach that includes counter-speech, workshops on bigotry and its role in American and world history, and real—not superficial—institutional change.

32   Universities are obligated to create an environment that fosters tolerance and mutual respect among members of the campus community, an environment in which all students can exercise their right to participate fully in campus life without being discriminated against. Campus administrators on the highest level should, therefore,

- speak out loudly and clearly against expressions of racist, sexist, homophobic and other bias, and react promptly and firmly to acts of discriminatory harassment;
- create forums and workshops to raise awareness and promote dialogue on issues of race, sex and sexual orientation;
- intensify their efforts to recruit members of racial minorities on student, faculty and administrative levels;
- and reform their institutions' curricula to reflect the diversity of peoples and cultures that have contributed to human knowledge and society, in the United States and throughout the world.

33   ACLU Executive Director Ira Glasser stated, in a speech at the City College of New York: "There is no clash between the constitutional right of free speech and equality. Both are crucial to society. Universities ought to stop restricting speech and start teaching."

Reading Responses

1. What is the ACLU's position on hate speech? What are your reactions to that position?
2. What does the ACLU propose as a campus policy instead of prohibiting free speech?
3. Given that some readers may not agree with the ACLU approach to this issue, in what ways does this briefing paper address the expectations and concerns of readers?

Writing Activities

1. Summarize in your own words the ACLU position on the First Amendment.
2. Write a response to the ACLU proposal for a campus hate-speech policy. Evaluate the proposal, identifying what you do or do not consider useful. Add your own suggestions as well, bearing in mind the First Amendment.
3. Write your own position paper, following the ACLU organization with an opening introduction followed by a series of questions and answers.

Community Links

Consider in what respects the briefing paper on hate speech defends the core values of the academic community but challenges some academic practices. (For readings that present perspectives on the academic community, turn to pp. 33–76.)

Editorial
THE ER NIGHTMARE
Denver Post

◆

The following editorial from the "Perspective" section of the Denver Post *tackles an issue common in many communities—crowded emergency rooms that cannot accept the number of patients who need treatment. This discussion specifies Denver's problems but also expands the discussion from local particulars to general points, applicable across the country. The editorial is written by members of the* Post's *editorial board, but individual writers are not identified. Instead, all are listed at the bottom of the editorial column, right after a note that identifies the editorial column as the only place where the paper expresses its opinion.*

1   Imagine you've had a heart attack. You're in an ambulance rushing toward the nearest emergency room. Suddenly, the driver gets a radio call: Sorry, but that emergency room is full, you'll have to divert to another hospital. As the ambulance heads for the next hospital, the radio crackles again: That hospital is "on divert," too. When every minute counts, your ambulance spends nearly an hour trying to find an ER that's still accepting patients.

2   This nightmare is real. At times, 12 of Denver's 15 emergency rooms are so overcrowded that they can't take any more patients. Ambulances must bypass hospital after hospital because all the ERs in between are full.

3   Overall, ER visits in metro Denver are up 19 percent in five years, but some increases have been exponential. For example, when it was built in 1989, the ER at Littleton Adventist Hospital was designed to handle 10,000 patients annually. Last year, it saw 50,000.

4   Simply put, metro Denver's emergency rooms are in critical condition—as are ERs nationwide. But the ER crisis is like the canary in the mine warning of greater danger, America's Hydra-headed health-care mess is finally rearing to its full height. No longer is the issue just escalating insurance premiums. Now the very quality of care is at risk, too. The same factors ailing the ERs threaten the entire health-care system.

5   There aren't enough ERs. In fact, as metro Denver's population soared in the last five years, the number of hospital beds fell. When ER doctors want to admit patients, there often isn't any place to send them, so they languish in hallways or take up space in the jam-packed ERs.

6   There's also a shortage of exam beds, so patients who aren't in life-and-death danger face horrible delays. The average metro-area ER wait is *eight hours.*

7   Too, there's an alarming shortage of qualified ER staffers, particularly nurses. The professionals who remain are under increasing pressure to handle more patients, exacerbating on-the-job burnout and escalating the risk of medical mistakes.

8   Meantime, Colorado has shunned its responsibility toward the mentally ill, so psychiatric patients needlessly wind up in the ERs, which are ill-suited to help them.

9   ERs are expensive places to seek treatment, yet the very people least able to afford any medical care have nowhere else to go. Our health-care system has all but closed its doors to the medically indigent, those Americans who don't have insurance but who don't qualify for public assistance. The only places that legally *must* care for them are emergency rooms. Any system that forces the least able consumers to buy the most expensive service is wildly out of whack.

10 Our society must solve the wider problems, especially how to extend health coverage to all Americans. Otherwise, the ER nightmare will just be the prologue to a much larger crisis in American medical care.

Reading Responses

1. What is the opinion of the *Post*?
2. What reasons for the emergency room crisis do the editors of the *Post* identify?
3. How does the editorial integrate statistics and details while avoiding excessive detail?

Writing Activities

1. Develop a list of reasons why the Denver emergency rooms are overcrowded.
2. Write a paragraph summarizing the national problems involved in the issue.
3. Imagine that you are the editor of a local newspaper. Write an editorial about a local topic that concerns you.

Community Links

Look for other sample editorials in the local or regional newspaper and in the campus newspaper. Consider how the editorials from each paper express the concerns and values of the community involved.

Letter to the Editor

◆

These four letters to the editor, published over several weeks in the Denver Post *or the* Rocky Mountain News, *express a variety of perspectives on current issues. Each letter was signed with the writer's name and city. In addition, the newspaper identified Anthony Fabian's credentials as president of the Colorado State Shooting Association, a post relevant to the topic of his letter. Many newspapers accept letters to the editor submitted by community members who wish to address issues or reply to news stories, editorials, other letters, or opinion columns. Most newspapers limit their length; for the* Post, *the maximum length is 200 words. Most newspapers also reserve the right to edit letters before publication and require full contact information from the writer, even though all of that information is not published with the letter.*

IRONY IN THE MORNING

Sandra S. McRae

Re: "Bombing not the way to peace; Hundreds of teens skip classes to protest," March 6 news story.

1   I love irony. What a generous helping I had with my breakfast this morning as I read about the high-school students suspended for walking out of school on March 5 to protest the rush to war against Iraq. Is this not Civics 101, coming to life right out of the textbooks? Since when is hands-on learning "show(ing) disrespect for your school," as one assistant principal put it? Or something to be condemned in favor of note-taking or answering multiple-choice questions? When was the last time you changed something by taking notes or filling out a multiple-choice questionnaire? A couple of years ago, we learned that even if the questionnaire is a ballot, it doesn't always make the intended difference.

2   I praise those students for their courage to stand up for their beliefs, which is the backbone of the American spirit. Let us not forget that they are also the future of our nation. Whether you agree with their politics or not, you have to admire their guts (and if you don't agree with their politics, make your own sign and hit the streets).

3   What more could an educator hope for than a student's desire to learn by doing? We should rejoice that the youth of America care about their country

and their future. How sad that grown-ups are so hung up on their pride that they can't see it.

4   Who are the real teachers here? My money's on the kids.

GRATEFUL TO *NEWS* FOR GOOD NEWS ON TEENS
Linda Doran

1   I just wanted to thank the *News* for printing a front-page article on Feb. 10 that gave recognition to teens who are making *good* choices. The teen rally, "962:Pure," held in Colorado Springs, focused on the importance of sexual abstinence. During a time when we are bombarded with news regarding the negative behavior of youth, it is encouraging to be reminded that there are thousands of teenagers who are making positive decisions.

2   With teen pregnancies, AIDS and other STDs a growing concern, it is exciting to see young people willing to take a stand against promiscuity. This generation can make a difference and it is important for us to acknowledge the steps they are taking to change a behavior that has become too readily accepted as the norm.

3   As adults we need to encourage, support and applaud these teens for their willingness to publicly recognize abstinence as the best choice for themselves and our society.

ORANGE YOU FEELING THREATENED?
Sarah Davidon

1   In lieu of the color-coded alerts for threats to our national security, perhaps a more appropriate system would be to color-code the threat level to our civil liberties—the two levels of threat seem to be keeping pace with each other. Maybe instead of DEFCON levels, we could institute CIVCON levels, a report on civil-liberties conditions. With the emergence of the Domestic Security Enhancement Act, our current CIVCON level would be a 2, or perhaps even a 1, and our color-coded civil-liberty threat level would, at the very minimum, keep its current "orange" status.

2   In addition to denying Americans reasonable access to information about current threats to their communities and health, the Domestic Security Enhancement Act would allow revocation of U.S. citizenship for "terrorist" activities such as donating to a nonprofit organization or minor vandalism. What a terrible betrayal of trust, liberties and the Constitution of the United States of America.

A Tax, Not a Fee
Anthony J. Fabian

Re: "Let users pay for gun checks," March 6 editorial.

1   It is not surprising to see The Post endorse a proposed $10 charge to Colorado gun buyers to fund the Colorado Bureau of Investigations' Instacheck system, but why don't you call the charge what it is: a tax. What else should one call a mandatory confiscation of an individual's money in order to pay for a government program or service?

2   It is unconscionable, not to mention unconstitutional, to require a citizen to pay for the exercise of a fundamental individual right. It has long been evident that a government cannot charge a citizen a poll tax to exercise his or her franchise. Why does The Post think it is proper for a citizen to pay the government in order to lawfully purchase a firearm?

3   Colorado is not a user-fee state. Services such as law enforcement, fire control and education are funded by *all* taxpayers, not just those who use the services. If the government deems CBI background checks are a necessary prerequisite for firearms purchases, then the government must pay for those checks.

4   Otherwise, no matter what one may like to call it, a charge for checks is simply a new tax on gun owners.

Reading Responses

1. What issues do the letters discuss? What points of view do they express?
2. What kinds of supporting evidence or information do the various letters supply?
3. To what extent do the letters seem to take account of readers' likely concerns or possible views?

Writing Activities

1. Consider whether any of these four letters to the editor share assumptions, opinions, views, types of evidence, or other characteristics. Write an explanation of your conclusions.
2. Write your own letter to the editor in response to a news story, another letter, an editorial, or an opinion column. (Include a copy of that item when you hand in your letter.)
3. Write your own letter to the editor, alerting newspaper readers to an issue that they may not have considered or fully understood.

Community Links

Consider the letters to the editor in relation to other letters such as Vermette's letter to his son (p. 96–100), the letters from the work community (pp. 308–318), or the letters that appeal to supporters from the public community (pp. 447–456). Using several selections as illustrations, compare and contrast different types or examples of letters.

Opinion Piece

THINK YOU CAN TEACH? PASS THIS TEST

Lynn K. Rhodes

◆

When she wrote this opinion piece, Lynn Rhodes was an associate dean at the University of Colorado at Denver and the director of the teacher education program. In those roles, she frequently met people who assumed that teaching was as simple as walking into a classroom and winging it. Even a recent editorial in the newspaper had advocated letting anyone with a college degree teach without any further preparation. Her answers to such notions were published in the "Speakout" section of the Rocky Mountain News.

1   In the recent editorials about education, one of the claims made was that all those with college degrees should be able to teach in the state of Colorado without teacher preparation. The following questions constitute a brief self-assessment for people with college degrees who want to determine if they are ready to teach in public schools. Before you dismiss my question as not applicable because you won't teach "children like that," ask your local school district how their population is changing.

2   University of Colorado at Denver's School of Education prepares those who have previously earned college degrees in a content area for licensure in about a year's time. The topics represented by the test below are some of what we teach in collaboration with educators in our 12 partner schools. We need to ask why we want a college graduate without the knowledge and skills suggested by the test below to teach our own children as well as at-risk children during their first year of teaching.

3   Although I'm sure Gov. Bill Owens and John Elway would make excellent teachers, if they are going to be my son/daughter's teachers, I'd like them to know and be able to do what is implied by the test below before they assume teaching responsibilities for a $23,000 per year salary. Here is the test.

1. The state of Colorado has adopted a standards-based approach in instruction and assessment. Those who want to be elementary teachers: Do you know what the state standards are in the areas of reading, writing, math, science, geography, civics, history, and the arts and do you know how to assess children's performance in relation to those standards?

    Those who want to be secondary teachers: Do you know what the state standards are in your content area and how to assess students' performance? And then are you ready to persevere in your teaching if some of your students don't meet the standards?
2. Lack of knowledge about laws does not excuse you in a court of law. Do you know what laws you will need to abide by in the classroom and school?
3. Those who want to be elementary teachers: The state of Colorado requires that K-3 teachers implement the Literacy Act. Do you know what to do as a teacher so that you meet the demands of the Literacy Act? Those who want to be secondary teachers: Your classroom will include students who cannot read the textbook at all or easily. How will you support these students' learning of your content area and concurrently, improve their reading skills?
4. You have seen the low CSAP writing scores in the newspaper and you know that businesses are complaining that their employees can't write well. What will you do at the elementary or secondary level to improve your students' writing? (This is not just a responsibility for English teachers!) If you don't know what CSAP is, you failed this question.
5. Non-English speaking students will be in your classroom. How would you help these students learn to read and write, and learn mathematical, social studies and science concepts while learning English?
6. All students do not learn like you do or like your own children do. How would you help a student whose learning style or needs are very unlike your own or whose learning development is not at a normal pace?
7. Students with various disabilities will be in your classroom and they will need accommodations and/or support services to achieve content standards. What resources are available to you and how will you plan and organize your teaching so that they learn?
8. Children from all walks of life will be in your classroom. Do you have the knowledge and skills to work with children and their families from cultures and socioeconomic groups other than your own?
9. Your classroom will include students who do not share your values or who are not as well-behaved as your own. How will you discipline these children so that they become good citizens and work hard to learn?
10. Schools are in the process of significant reform. Do you know enough about how schools work and what teachers value so that you can enter

into that reform process and be able to contribute to it in positive and significant ways?

4   If the test itself doesn't convince you of the worth of teacher preparation prior to teaching, we recommend that you substitute for a teacher for a week and then think about having to be accountable for those students' learning for an entire year while concurrently trying to develop the knowledge and skills suggested by the test.

Reading Responses

1. What is Rhodes's central point about teaching?
2. How many of her questions could you answer? (For non-Coloradans, CSAP is the Colorado Student Achievement Profile; every year or few years, many states routinely administer comparable achievement tests in reading, math, and sometimes other subjects.)
3. Aside from identifying the high expectations of teachers defined by the state and required by classroom needs, Rhodes also points out the dedication that teaching requires. How does she suggest this point?

Writing Activities

1. Some of Rhodes's questions have to do with state requirements for teachers; others have to do with the needs of students. Write a paragraph or two explaining the issues that have to do with the needs of students.
2. Select one of Rhodes's questions about the differences in children. Based on your long experience with schools, how do you think that a skillful teacher should handle the issue? Explain your performance standard, using definitions, examples, anecdotes, logical reasons, or other evidence that seems appropriate.
3. Write a profile of a teacher you know who would pass Rhodes's test with flying colors. In your profile, concentrate on creating a powerful impression or image of the person. Use examples, quotations (favorite expressions from memory or current comments from an interview, if possible), observations, and brief incidents to convey this person's qualities as a teacher.

Community Links

Compare the quiz in "Think You Can Teach?" with the quiz following Jamieson's "Preface" (pp. 397–404) and with an academic examination (pp. 180–182). Consider how the purposes of these tests differ and how the "quiz" can be adapted to different community expectations.

Report

SEX WITHOUT STRINGS, RELATIONSHIPS WITHOUT RINGS: TODAY'S YOUNG SINGLES TALK ABOUT MATING AND DATING

David Popenoe and Barbara Dafoe Whitehead

◆

This reading reports the ongoing research, from 1960 on, of The National Marriage Project, based at Rutgers University and funded by Rutgers and nonprofit organizations. Every year or two the project updates its findings about marriage in reports such as "The State of Our Unions 2000." This report included "Sex without Strings" as a special report, and both were available at the project's Web site.

Key Findings

1 The young men and women in this study expect their future marriages to last a lifetime and to fulfill their deepest emotional and spiritual needs. Yet they are involved in a mating culture that may make it more difficult to achieve this lofty goal. Today's singles mating culture is not oriented to marriage, as the mating culture was in the past. Instead, based on the reports of these singles, it is best described as a low-commitment culture of "sex without strings, relationship without rings."

2 The women participants are more pessimistic than the men about their chances of finding a suitable marriage mate. Women in their late twenties are more pessimistic about men and their chances for marriage than women in their early twenties.

3 Both women and men favor living together as a way of gathering vital information about a partner's character, fidelity and compatibility. However, the women in this study are more wary of low-commitment cohabiting relationships than the men.

4 About half of the women in this study say that they consider unwed motherhood an "option," if they are unable to find the right man to marry.

5 Although the empirical evidence suggests that marriage creates important economic benefits, especially for less well-educated young adults, these non-college men and women see marriage as a form of economic exposure and risk, largely due to the prevalence of divorce.

6 Although highly critical of divorce, these young adults are pessimistic about the likelihood of changes in the law or the culture. They look to educa-

tion as the principal means for increasing their chances of marital success. They would like to learn how to communicate more effectively and how to resolve conflict in relationships.

The Neglected Noncollege Majority

7 About a year ago, as part of its Next Generation Program, the National Marriage Project began a study of mating and dating among not-yet-married heterosexual men and women in their twenties. Surprisingly, given the popular interest in young singles and their love lives, there has been little recent research on this topic. Except for studies of cohabitation and dating violence, social science research has generally neglected investigations of contemporary patterns of mating and mate selection among today's young singles.

8 Moreover, what we do know about the not-yet-married young tends to come from studies of college students and four-year college graduates. Almost entirely overlooked in the research are noncollege singles in their twenties. Yet noncollege men and women (those who do not currently attend or hold degrees from four-year colleges) represent a clear majority of young adults in their twenties, and their mating choices will play a crucial role in determining future trends in cohabitation, marriage and divorce. Also, noncollege men and women represent a population that, in the past, has relied on marriage as a way of getting ahead economically. So the mating and marrying behavior of today's noncollege young adults is likely to have important future economic consequences as well.

9 To begin to address this research deficit, we set out to conduct a small qualitative study of noncollege young adults in their twenties, as a first step toward a larger and statistically representative survey. Our purpose was to gather descriptions of the contemporary dating scene from noncollege men and women and to explore the reasoning behind their views on mate selection, cohabitation and future marriage. We convened ten focus groups of not-yet-married heterosexual men and women, ages of 21 through 29, in five major metropolitan areas: Northern New Jersey, Atlanta, Dallas, Chicago, and Los Angeles. In each area, we divided men and women into separate groups. Participants came from a variety of religious and ethnic backgrounds, generally representative of their geographic area.

10 Most of the men and women in this study have some education beyond high school but do not currently attend four-year colleges or hold four-year college degrees. Most are working full-time in service, sales and technical jobs. The men and the women have similar incomes, with most falling into the $10–30,000 range. None has ever married. Except for one young man, no participant reports ever having had a child.

11 This report highlights several key findings in this study. These findings are impressionistic and should not be taken as a statistically representative description of attitudes among the population of noncollege young adults. However, what we learned from this initial study may offer valuable leads for further research into mating and dating patterns among this important but neglected group.

High Aspirations, Low Expectations for Successful Marriage

12 The young men and women in this study aspire to marriage and expect their marriages to last a lifetime. Even in the face of the combined impact of the divorce revolution, sex revolution, and the feminist revolution, they express their deep desire for a happy and lasting marriage. Nor have these young people cynically rejected the ideal of love and friendship in marriage. If anything, they've raised this standard to a higher level. Young men and women today want to marry a best friend and "soul mate" who will share and understand their most intimate feelings, needs and desires.

13 However, despite the strongly held aspiration for marriage and the ideal of a lifelong soul mate, young people, and especially young women, are not confident that they will achieve this goal. Their lack of confidence may be justified. The evidence gathered in this study suggests that the singles mating culture may pose obstacles to reaching the goal of soul-mate marriage.

Getting Ahead Before Getting Wed

14 These twentysomething noncollege men and women are not single-mindedly bent on looking for someone to marry. (See [later in the original posting] "Social Indicators: Marriage.") They are working to get ahead on their own. For many, this is not easy. Most of the men and women in this study describe their economic status as "getting by." In order to get ahead, they have to pay off debts, get more education or find a better job.

15 Putting financial independence ahead of marriage is not new for young men. Traditionally, men have had to prove to themselves and to others that they were able to make a living, or at least had the education or training to make a good living, before they could take on the responsibilities of supporting a family.

16 For women, however, and especially for less well-educated women, the goal of achieving individual financial and residential independence before marriage is relatively new. In this study, we found that women are just as committed as men to making it on their own and getting a place of their own before marriage. Indeed, compared to their male peers, these noncollege women are even more fiercely determined "to take care of myself." They cite the high rate of divorce, their past experience of failed relationships, and their desire to avoid the same mistakes their mothers made, as reasons why they are intent on independence. For African-American women, the determination to "do for yourself" is especially strong. As one young African-American woman put it: "We have to take care of ourselves, we have to go back to college, we have to do what we have to do, because our men are strung out on drugs, they're not finishing college, so we are stepping up and taking the initiative."

17 Moreover, these single women say, they are taking their cues from single men who "expect us to take care of ourselves." "Women fought for the right to work, so now men expect you to work," one woman remarks. And that view is

borne out by the men in this study. One of the most frequently cited qualities men say they seek in a girlfriend is "independence."

Where Did Love Go?

18 The mating culture for today's twentysomethings is not oriented to marriage, as it has been in times past, nor is it dedicated to romantic love. Based on the reports of these noncollege singles, it is perhaps best described as a culture of sex without strings and relationships without rings.

19 The men and women in these focus groups rarely volunteer the word "love" or use the phrase "falling in love." Instead of "love," they talk about "sex" and "relationships." This double language reflects the two separate spheres of unwed coupling.

20 Sex is for fun. It is one of the taken-for-granted freedoms and pleasures of being young and single. Both men and women regard casual sex as an expected part of the dating scene. Only a few take a moralistic stand against it. Both men and women also agree that casual sex is no-strings-attached sex. It requires no commitments beyond the sexual encounter itself, no ethical obligation beyond mutual consent. When men and women hook up for sex, they say, it's assumed that one's partner is likely to lie about past sexual history. Accordingly, the conventional wisdom is: "Trust no one." Indeed, these men and women see lying, cheating, and dumping as unremarkable behavior in casual sexual hookups.

21 Compared to casual sex, relationships require greater investments of time and effort. If you are "in a relationship," say these young adults, you are expected to spend time together and to go out as a couple. You have to know what pleases your partner, do "the little things," and act with concern for his or her interests. For example, a young man "in a relationship" says his girlfriend shows she cares for him "financially and emotionally" when she suggests a candlelight dinner at home rather than an expensive dinner out. Being "in a relationship" also requires higher ethical standards than casual sex. Trust, honesty and sexual fidelity are expected. If you depart from these standards, these young people say, you jeopardize the relationship.

He Lies, She Lies: The Rules of Sexual Engagement

22 For the young singles in this study, sex isn't entirely carefree. The threat of HIV/AIDS looms large over the dating scene. Everyone is scared of AIDS. However, although both men and women fear AIDS, they do not take equal responsibility for protecting against it. These young women say that they are the ones who must take the initiative and responsibility for "protection." If we don't insist, they say, the guys won't voluntarily use a condom. The men seem to agree that the responsibility for "protection" belongs to women. Moreover, although both men and women "talk the talk" about using condoms, at least a few admitted that this might be less than accurate description of their real behavior. "You know none of us follow these rules," one young man says, after lis-

tening to other men's testimonies of regular condom use. A woman in another group acknowledges: "When you're drunk, you'll let him do anything."

23   These working singles say they are most likely to go to clubs to socialize with similar-aged peers. However, both men and women see the club scene as a place for drinking, fun and casual sexual hookups rather than for finding a serious love interest. Men especially say they go to clubs for easy sex and when they get it, they have no more responsibility to the woman. As one young man explains: "You've already had your fun." The men have contempt for the women they meet at a club. "You don't go to a club to find a wife," one young man says. Another puts it bluntly: "Club girls are trash." Women have similarly low opinions of the club scene and the men they find there. The men lie, they say, and they're only looking for sex.

24   In seeking a relationship, these young men and women say, you should look for a partner through church, friends or school. Work sometimes offers opportunities for finding a mate, but both men and women express reservations about workplace relationships. "If you have a fight," one participant says, "you still have to see each other the next day."

25   Getting into a relationship usually means postponing sex until you get to know each other, according to both men and women in this study. As one young man explains: "When I met the woman I thought I would spend the rest of my life with, we didn't have sex for a month and a half . . . we went out to dinner, the movies, clubs—all the stuff a guy is supposed to do, pamper the woman and all that. I wanted to find out about her."

26   However, according to some of the men, sex isn't put off for very long. They say that sex on the third date (or after a couple of weeks of meeting) is typical for a more serious relationship. "If you wait too long," says one, "they think you're not interested."

27   A relationship also differs from a sexual hookup in the accepted standards for "using protection." A relationship carries the expectation, or at least the hope, of mutual sexual fidelity. Therefore, before getting seriously involved, these young adults say, a couple gets tested for HIV/AIDS. One woman says she knew her boyfriend was interested in a serious relationship when he spontaneously called up the testing laboratory and handed her the phone to hear his test results. Once a couple can prove to each other that they have recently tested negative, they can be less vigilant about using condoms. "Once we're tested, I can go bareback," one young man says.

Getting to Know You: Cohabitation, or the "24/7" Relationship

28   Another popular form of "being in a relationship" is cohabitation. Indeed, cohabitation is replacing marriage as the first living together union for today's young adults. (See "Social Indicators: Unmarried Cohabitation.") Moreover, surveys indicate, a majority of young people think it is a good idea to live together before marriage. The participants in our study fit this profile. Slightly less than half of the men and women in this study are currently cohabiting or have cohabited in the past. No one expresses blanket disapproval of cohabita-

tion, and most of our participants see it in a favorable light. Indeed, almost all the men agree with the view that you should not marry a woman until you have lived with her first.

29   The men and women in this study offer several reasons for cohabiting relationships. First, they hope to find out more about the habits, character, and fidelity of a partner. These young men and women reject traditional courtship as a way of finding out about a person's character. They see dating as a "game," full of artifice and role-playing, while living together is more natural, honest and revealing. Accordingly, they believe that the only way to truly know your partner is to see him or her "24/7," that is, twenty-four hours a day, seven days a week. "If his head is on your pillow," says one woman, "you know he's being faithful."

30   Second, they want to test compatibility, possibly for future marriage. Young adults view marriage principally as an emotional and spiritual union, and this vision of marriage has set new standards of fitness for marriage. A prospective marriage partner's fitness used to be evaluated, at least in part, by certain objective characteristics and behavior, such as having a good reputation in the community or going to church every Sunday. Today, the measure of marital fitness is far more subjective and individualistic. A couple must connect at a deep emotional and spiritual level, and each person's emotional needs are as unique as a fingerprint. This more subjective and individualistic standard puts the propensity to cohabit in a broader context. Since a relationship, and especially marriage, is idealized as a soul-mate union, then, the reasoning goes, there must be extensive round-the-clock testing to evaluate the emotional fitness and capacities of a mate for this special kind of intimate friendship.

31   According to these men and women, cohabitation also allows more careful scrutiny of a domestic partner over time. Many of these young men and women believe that a partner cannot be trusted to stay the same. "I know people who've gotten married and they didn't know what that person was like when you woke up in the morning," says one young man. "You can think you know someone but there's a lot of stuff you find out when you live together," a young woman remarks.

32   Third, these young men and women say they live together as a way of avoiding the risks of divorce or being "trapped in an unhappy marriage." Here, they are very much influenced by their parents' failed or unhappy marriages; as one young woman says, "my mother is on her third marriage. If she had lived with them before she married, then she would not have had so many divorces."

33   Other reasons for living together include losing a lease, saving money on rent, building a nest egg for the purchase of a house, working on personal "issues" before deciding to marry; and, in one person's opinion, "having the last adventure." And for some, living together may simply provide a way to mark time, until another partner or a new adventure comes along.

34   However, despite their general approval of cohabitation, the women in this study are much more likely than the men to express reservations about living together as a way to nudge a less committed partner toward marriage. At least one woman expresses the view that cohabiting women should not have to deliver the ultimatum "marry me or move out" in order to exact a proposal of marriage. Most agree with the young woman who says "if you want to get

married in the long run, you should wait until you get that ring if that is what you are going for." Also, women are more likely than men to be critical of a long-term, uncommitted cohabiting relationship. "It can go on indefinitely. A lot of people will say we'll see how it goes and one year turns into five years and you see people on Ricki Lake with five kids and there's still not commitment." A few women believe that men get lazy and over dependent in cohabiting partnerships. "Men get too comfortable letting their girlfriend take care of them," notes one. Another comments: "I worked two jobs, he didn't work any." For all these reasons, women think that some cohabiting partnerships can be a "waste of time." Still, the women say that living together can be positive if you know what you want to get out of it.

35   A substantial number of these young women have already lived with and broken up with a cohabiting partner. Although most agree that breaking up is hard and often painful, they believe that it provides valuable life lessons. Living together is a learning experience, according to these young women. It helps you make a better choice for the future.

Optimistic Men, Pessimistic Women

36   Men and women enter their twenties with nearly identical goals. Their first priority is to achieve independence by getting a decent job and a place of their own. Like men, women in their early twenties are in no rush to marry. "People live a lot longer today," one woman explains as the reason for putting off marriage, while another adds: "People change a lot from 20 to 30." However, by the second half of their twenties, men's and women's timetables for marriage begin to diverge. Men are content to continue the pattern established in their early twenties. They are not yet ready to make commitments and to settle down. Many are still trying to establish themselves in decent jobs. And they are reluctant to give up the freedom of single life. At the same time, these men remain optimistic that they will be able to find the right woman when they are ready to marry.

37   On the other hand, single women approaching their late twenties become more serious about the search for a marriage partner. They've gained confidence in their capacity to "make it on their own," and they are ready to think about marriage. However, many say the "men aren't there," they're "not on the same page," or they're less mature. The more they advance into their twenties, the more disenchanted these young women seem to become about the pool of prospective mates and the likelihood of finding a husband.

A marital readiness gap?

38   One possible reason for women's pessimism is that they may be reaching a stage of readiness for marriage before their male peers. In this study, men and women are similarly matched in education, income and occupation as well as age. However, the women in these groups appear more "together" than the men—more confident, articulate, responsible and mature. They also exhibit a higher degree of goal-oriented job behavior. They have clear and generally realistic plans for moving up the career ladder. Many have plans to finish or ex-

tend schooling; for example, one young woman who works as a Licensed Practical Nurse is going back to school part-time to get her RN. Others are contemplating plans, or taking first steps, toward starting businesses in fields allied to their current job. (At the conclusion of one focus group, several women exchanged business cards.)

39 The men in this study, on the other hand, are less able to articulate clear goals. And, when articulated, their goals are often unserious, unfocused or unrealistic. For example, when asked what they hope to accomplish in the short-term, some men say their goals are "get out of bed in the morning," "own an island," "hit the lottery," or "train for the marathon."

40 Of course, there is nothing new in a male/female gap in readiness for marriage. As the age differences between a groom and bride at first marriage have narrowed to little more than two years and as peer marriage has become a social norm, there is often a noticeable disparity between a twentysomething woman's level of maturity and that of her twentysomething mate. What may be new today for these noncollege men and women is not the "marital readiness gap" itself, but the incentives for men to marry when similar-aged women are ready. Today, as compared to earlier times, there are almost no pressures on young men in their twenties to get married in order to meet women's desires, expectations, or timetable.

"The emotional baggage problem"

41 Another reason for women's greater pessimism may be the experience of prolonged exposure to the singles mating culture. This mating culture is oriented to men's appetites and interests, according to the young women in this study. Indeed, at least a few women observe that their sex lives are following a male script. "I'm turning into a man in some respects," one woman says. "I can go out there and dog them the way they do to me." More commonly, noncollege women complain bitterly about a harsh new double standard: men expect them to be submissive *and* strong, faithful *and* independent, while "he's doing what he wants to do." Perhaps because of the prevalence of casual sex, the women in this study have a low opinion of men's fidelity and trustworthiness. Moreover, they say, although men expect them to be independent, the men are hardly exemplars of independence themselves. They are often unfocused, unmotivated, and still live at home "with Mom." Overall, noncollege men are most likely of all young men and women in their twenties to live with parents.

42 A prolonged period of sexually active singlehood also exposes young women to the risks of multiple failed relationships and breakups. Because most young people have first sexual intercourse at younger ages than in the past, they are increasingly unlikely to marry, or even enter a long-term relationship, with their first sexual partner. This often means multiple sexual relationships and breakups before entry into marriage. The prevalence of cohabitation compounds the risks of breakup, since, by recent estimates, only about one-sixth of cohabiting relationships last three years, and only one-tenth last five years or more.

43 Since breaking up is a painful and distressing experience for young lovers, it is desirable for such breakups to be relatively few and far between in the

course of seeking a mate. However, today, a young single woman may experience several breakups during her late teens and twenties, and these breakups seem to have a cumulative negative impact on subsequent relationships. The women in this study say they feel burned, angry, betrayed when they are dumped. They say they are more mistrustful of the next guy who comes along. Moreover, the experience of multiple breakups can lead to a global mistrust and antagonism toward men. Women say they become more suspicious and wary of all men over time. And finally, for some women, mistrust of men has to do with the example set by their mothers. As one woman explains: "I've lived with my mother bouncing from man to man to man, living with all the guys she's with . . . I'm having a terrible time with trusting . . ."

44   Young women become more pessimistic about men and their chances for marriage as they advance through their twenties. For this reason, some say they are willing to contemplate forming a family without a husband if they reach their thirties and are unable to find a suitable mate. The young noncollege women in this study, and increasingly all younger women today, see single motherhood as a distinct possibility and socially acceptable "option," though not ideal. These single women, and some of the men as well, point to women family members who have raised children "on their own" as evidence that it is something that others do, and therefore, that can be done.

45   According to the young men in this study, a single mother with a child is a "big turnoff" and likely to be rejected as a potential marriage partner. Therefore, single motherhood may further diminish the chances for finding a husband.

Soul-Mate Marriages vs. Being Married

46 Despite doubts and difficulties, young men and women have not given up on the ideal of finding a soul mate to marry. On the contrary, they are dedicated to the goal of finding a lifelong best friend and kindred spirit. However, their ideals of soul-mate marriage contrast sharply with personal experience—as well as the popular culture's portrait—of married people. Both media images and real-life models of marriage tend to be more negative than positive. Many in this study have grown up with unhappily married or divorced parents. They know exactly what a bad marriage is, but they are less sure of what a good marriage looks like. Some can only describe a good marriage as "the opposite of my parents." Moreover, a number of study participants say they receive no advice or mainly negative advice about marriage from their parents and relatives.

47   In addition, although young men and women idealize marriage, they see the experience of *being married* as hard and difficult. "Marriage is a full-time job. Period. It's work," says a young man. For many participants in this study, the idea of married life as hard work suffers in comparison to the idea of the single life as freedom and fun. Young men, especially, see their twenties as a time to "drink, go to school, have fun, buy things." Thus, soul-mate marriage and "marriage as hard work" coexist in the minds of some of these study participants. Though very different, both conceptions of marriage are daunting. Perhaps this is one reason why these young men in their twenties are happy to stay single for a time.

Haunted by Fears of Divorce

48 The noncollege men and women in this study are deeply influenced by the experience of growing up in a high divorce society. (See [in original] "Social Indicators: Divorce.") As noted previously, they cite the risk of divorce as a key reason for cohabiting before marriage or as an alternative to marriage.

49 Fear of divorce has also dramatically eroded their confidence in the permanence of marriage and thus of marriage's value as an economic stepping stone. Although study after study demonstrates the economic benefits of marriage, especially for the less well-educated, these noncollege men and women generally reject the idea that marriage is a principal way to get ahead economically. On the contrary, they tend to see marriage as exposing them to economic risk and possibly jeopardizing their hard won individual independence.

50 The men say that marriage puts them at risk because a wife can divorce at will and "take you for all you've got." The women are even more likely than the men to see marriage as economically risky. Some say that any woman who trusts in a man and marriage for economic security is a fool, given the high rate of divorce and the evidence of many women's economic freefall after divorce.

51 Possibly because young adults enter marriage later, often with some individual financial assets, both the men and women in the study are more fearful of the economic consequences of post-divorce property settlements than they are of no-fault grounds that make divorce so easy. Indeed, these noncollege young adults do not favor changing the no-fault divorce laws, nor do they believe that parents who do not "get along" should stay together for the sake of the children. Their tolerance of divorce involving children seems contradictory at first, given many of these young adults' childhood experience of divorce and their determination to avoid it in their future lives. However, the belief that parents who don't get along should divorce is consistent with their idea of marriage as an intensely emotional relationship between a man and a woman. Most do not see marriage as an institution designed to hold a mother and father together in a family household. (See [later in original posting] "Social Indicators: Loss of Child-Centeredness.")

Will Today's Twentysomethings "Save" Marriage?

52 Some social commentators believe that today's young adults will reject divorce, nonmarital childbearing and other trends that contribute to the weakening of marriage. They point out that a culture shift may be occurring among the young, in reaction to high levels of family instability. On the other hand, most social demographers predict a continuation of the current trends. They argue that these trends are persistent and pervasive across advanced western societies and therefore unlikely to change. Who's right?

53 Since today's young adults are putting off entry into marriage until later ages, it is obviously too soon to tell. As our study of noncollege twentysomethings suggests, some evidence indicates a deepening of the current marriage-weakening trends. A longer period of singlehood before marriage, combined with a youthful mating culture oriented to sex and low-commitment relation-

ships, may make it more difficult for young men and women to find suitable marriage mates. Women's growing pessimism about men and marriage, combined with their increasing willingness to contemplate single motherhood as an acceptable option to marriage, may lead more young women to choose single motherhood if they cannot find a suitable husband. High levels of cohabitation and acceptance of cohabitation among young adults are also likely to contribute to the further weakening and deinstitutionalization of marriage. And many young men and women, including those in this study, exhibit a more individualistic orientation to future marriage, with an emphasis on self-investment and protecting oneself against relationship failure. This "hedge-your-bets" approach to marriage may weaken the sense of mutual dedication and commitment that is an important component of successful marriage.

54 However, there are some hopeful signs. The trend toward later age at first marriage may contribute to lower levels of divorce in the future. Also, young adults' persistent aspiration for marriage and their desire to avoid divorce may lead to a greater commitment to address and repair problems in marriage before they become insurmountable. Many of the participants in our study say they favor marriage preparation and education as a way to prevent divorce as well as unhappy marriages. They say they would like to develop skills that might help them resolve problems that arise in marriage.

55 Such help is increasingly available. Churches in more than a hundred communities have joined together to establish a common set of premarital counseling standards and practices for engaged couples. Two states, Arizona and Louisiana, have passed covenant marriage laws, designed for couples who want the choice of entering marriages with stronger legal and counseling supports than are currently available in standard marriage. A few states—Oklahoma, Utah and Arkansas—are launching broad-based initiatives aimed at reducing the divorce and nonmarital birth rates. Florida has passed a law requiring marriage education for high school students. A number of schools across the country are integrating relationships and marriage skills education into sex education and family life curricula.

Changing the Mating Culture?

56 Yet, as our study suggests, it may prove difficult to strengthen marriage unless today's mating culture can somehow be changed. There obviously is a large gap between the aspiration for successful marriage and the pathways available for getting there. Are there ways to encourage a mating culture more oriented to successful mate selection? Is it possible to move today's mating culture away from breakup and failure and toward commitment and marriage?

57 Clearly, this is not a task that lends itself to social engineering. Any positive shift in contemporary patterns of mating and dating is likely to come about as the result of broad-based changes in cultural attitudes about sexual behavior and marriage. At the same time, such changes are possible. Unlike technological change, cultural shifts are more open to modification by concerted social movements, as we have seen in areas of race, women's roles, gay rights, and environmental issues over recent decades. Characteristically, attitu-

dinal changes in these areas began among a small, dedicated and often radical counterculture and then spread to the mainstream in more moderate and diffuse forms.

58 Our study suggests two possible avenues for positive change of the mating culture. One is broad-based public education about the factors that may hinder mating success. The noncollege young in this study are ignorant or misinformed about the likely effects of some common contemporary mating practices. For example, they believe that living together before marriage increases the chances for having a happy marriage, although no evidence exists to support this belief, and some evidence suggests that cohabiting before marriage increases the likelihood of divorce. Some believe that multiple failed cohabiting relationships lead to better future mate selection, though no evidence exists to support this idea. Others believe that the way to avoid divorce is to seek relationships having only limited commitment.

59 A second and potentially more important avenue for changing the mating culture rests with parents. Contrary to the popular notion that the media is chiefly responsible for young people's attitudes about mating and marriage, available evidence strongly suggests that young people get many of their ideas and models of marriage from parents and the parental generation. The noncollege men and women in our study consistently mentioned family influences as the source of both hopes and fears about future marriage. Yet, according to the participants in our study, many parents have had almost nothing good to say about marriage, and often say nothing at all. Much of this negativism may be due to the parental generation's own marital problems and failures.

60 Whatever their personal disappointments, parents do have a huge stake, both economic and emotional, in the success of their children's future marriages. Very few parents look forward to their adult child's first divorce, or eagerly await a grandchild's first custody hearing. If mothers and fathers, as well as grandparents, realized how much their attitudes mattered, they might take it upon themselves to begin talking to children early on about what to look for in a marriage mate and what it takes to have a good marriage. At minimum, parents might consider investing as much time and attention to helping their children think wisely about marriage as they now devote to helping their children think carefully about education and career.

Reading Responses

1. What group did Popenoe and Whitehead study? How did they conduct their research?
2. What are their major findings?
3. Which findings seem surprising and which would you have expected?

Writing Activities

1. Write one or two summary sentences, briefly stating in your own words the point of one section in the reading. (Use the headings to define the

sections.) Repeat this process for several sections. With a small group, review your sentences, and make suggestions for revisions. If your group's sentences cover all of the sections, work collaboratively to revise and combine the sentences to form an overall summary.

2. Describe some contrasts that the study reveals—for example, expectations that don't match reality, conflicting priorities, goals and ideals unlikely to be achieved through current circumstances, and so forth. Examine one or several of these contrasts, and write an explanation of the conflicts involved.

3. Using your own observations or a small set of interviews or surveys of current college students, investigate one of Popenoe and Whitehead's points. According to your limited research, in what ways do current college students resemble or differ from the population studied in "Sex without Strings"? Discuss your findings in a brief report.

Community Links

Compare and contrast the National Marriage Project report with other reports about similar age groups such as Henry, Weber, and Yarbrough's "Money Management Practices of College Students" (pp. 165–170) from the academic community or Mogelonsky's "Young Adults: New Customers/New Foods" (pp. 325–331) from the work community. Select at least two of these reports, synthesizing what they suggest about the values and interpersonal relationships of the young adults studied.

Public Advice

YOUR DRIVING COSTS 2003: FIGURING IT OUT

American Automobile Association

◆

This study of driving costs, published every year since 1950, is sponsored by the American Automobile Association (AAA), a nonprofit corporation that provides educational information for the public as well as travel and automotive services for members. The brochure is designed to help drivers figure out their current expenses and compare those costs with national averages for various vehicles and various levels of car usage. The booklet opens with national averages—costs per mile to drive three different types of cars and a composite average for several annual mileage levels. Next, the brochure leads a reader through the calculations necessary to discover his or her yearly costs per mile. Several tables show how these costs were calculated for the vehicles used for the national averages and for several additional vehicles (an SUV and a van). The booklet concludes with some tips on travel costs and on business reimbursements for driving expenses.

How Much Does it Cost to Drive?

Following are national average per-mile costs and the composite national average for three different cars:

National Average Costs Per Mile

	miles per year		
	10,000	15,000	20,000
2003 Chevrolet Cavalier LS 4-cyl. (2.2-liter) 4-door sedan	55.3 cents	44.5 cents	40.3 cents
2003 Ford Taurus SEL Deluxe 6-cyl. (3.0-liter) 4-door sedan	62.1 cents	51.2 cents	46.3 cents
2003 Mercury Grand Marquis LS 8-cyl. (4.6-liter) 4-door sedan	75.2 cents	59.4 cents	53.1 cents
composite national average	**64.2 cents**	**51.7 cents**	**46.6 cents**

Detailed driving costs can be found on pages 6 and 7. Driving costs for a 2003 Chevrolet TrailBlazer LS and a 2003 Dodge Caravan SE are listed on Page 8. While not part of the composite national average, information on these two vehicles is included to help car buyers estimate operating costs for these two vehicle types only.

What's Covered

AAA's analysis covers vehicles equipped with standard and optional accessories including automatic transmission, air conditioning, power steering, power disc brakes, AM/FM stereo, driver- and passenger-side air bags, antilock brakes, cruise control, tilt steering wheel, tinted glass, emission equipment and rear-window defogger.

All figures reflect the average cost of operating a vehicle primarily under stop-and-go driving conditions.

Fuel costs are based on a fourth quarter 2002 average price of $1.461 per gallon of regular unleaded gasoline, weighted 20 percent full-serve and 80 percent self-serve.

Insurance figures are based on personal use of vehicles driven less than 10 miles to or from work, with no young drivers.

Normal depreciation costs are based on the vehicle's trade-in value at the end of four years or 60,000 miles. For vehicles driven 10,000 miles per year, depreciation is based on six years or 60,000 miles.

Figuring Your Costs

Operating Costs

Gas, oil, maintenance and tire expenditures are operating costs related to the number of miles you drive.

Ownership Costs

Taxes, depreciation, finance charges, registration, insurance and license fees are ownership costs. These costs are incurred regardless of how often you drive your vehicle.

Keeping Track

To determine vehicle costs accurately, keep personal records on the following:

Gas and oil. Begin with a full tank of gasoline and write down the current odometer reading. Each time you buy gasoline, note the number of gallons, how much you pay and the odometer reading. These figures can then be used to calculate average miles per gallon and cost of gas per mile, as follows:

Gas Cost Per Mile

gallons	cost	odometer
beginning		8,850
9.3	$13.59	9,062
9.5	$13.88	9,280
7.6	$11.10	9,456
26.4	$38.57	9,456 - 8,850
		miles driven = 606

miles per gallon: 606 ÷ 26.4 = 23 mpg
gas cost per mile: $38.57 ÷ 606 = 6.4 cents

Figure oil consumption the same way. Remember to add the cost of every oil change.

Maintenance and tires. Jot down what you spend for routine maintenance, repairs and tires.

Insurance. Total the premiums of property damage and liability, comprehensive and collision policies that directly relate to your vehicle's operation.

License, registration fees and property or use taxes. Record these as once-a-year costs. Don't include sales or excise taxes paid — they are part of the vehicle's purchase price.

Depreciation. To calculate depreciation — the difference between what you pay for your vehicle and what you sell it for — subtract the projected trade-in value from its purchase price. Divide the difference by the number of years you plan to keep the vehicle.

Finance charges. Note interest charges if you borrowed money to buy the vehicle.

Annual Cost Per Mile

costs		yearly totals
operating costs		
gas and oil per mile		
total miles driven	x	
total gas and oil	=	
maintenance	+	
tires	+	
total operating costs	+ =	
ownership costs		
depreciation		
insurance	+	
taxes	+	
license and registration	+	
finance charges	+	
total ownership costs	+ =	
other costs		
(washes, accessories, etc.)	+	
total driving costs	=	
total miles driven	÷	
cost per mile	=	

Driving Costs

	2003 Chevrolet Cavalier LS 4-cyl. (2.2-liter) 4-door sedan	2003 Ford Taurus SEL Deluxe 6-cyl. (3.0-liter) 4-door sedan	2003 Mercury Grand Marquis LS 8-cyl. (4.6-liter) 4-door sedan	Average
Operating Costs	per mile	per mile	per mile	per mile
gas and oil	6.1 cents	7.1 cents	8.3 cents	7.2 cents
maintenance	3.9 cents	4.1 cents	4.3 cents	4.1 cents
tires	1.5 cents	1.8 cents	2.2 cents	1.8 cents
cost per mile	11.5 cents	13.0 cents	14.8 cents	13.1 cents
Ownership Costs	per year	per year	per year	per year
comprehensive insurance ($250 deductible)	$238	$191	$180	$203
collision insurance ($500 deductible)	$445	$386	$372	$401
bodily injury and property damage ($100,000, $300,000, $50,000)	$498	$498	$498	$498
license, registration, taxes	$167	$206	$242	$205
depreciation (15,000 miles annually)	$3,051	$3,693	$4,470	$3,738
finance charge (20% down; loan @ 7.5%/4 yrs.)	$554	$751	$927	$744
cost per year	$4,953	$5,725	$6,689	$5,789
cost per day	$13.57	$15.68	$18.33	$15.86
added depreciation costs (per 1,000 miles over 15,000 miles annually)	$161	$188	$195	$181

Total Cost Per Mile

15,000 total miles per year	per year	per year	per year	per year
cost per mile x 15,000 miles	$1,725	$1,950	$2,220	$1,965
cost per day x 365 days ***	$4,953	$5,723	$6,690	$5,789
total cost per year	$6,678	$7,673	$8,910	$7,754
total cost per mile *	44.5 cents	51.2 cents	59.4 cents	51.7 cents
20,000 total miles per year	per year	per year	per year	per year
cost per mile x 20,000 miles	$2,300	$2,600	$2,960	$2,620
cost per day x 365 days ***	$4,953	$5,723	$6,690	$5,789
depreciation cost x 5 **	$805	$940	$975	$905
total cost per year	$8,058	$9,263	$10,625	$9,314
total cost per mile*	40.3 cents	46.3 cents	53.1 cents	46.6 cents
10,000 total miles per year	per year	per year	per year	per year
cost per mile x 10,000 miles	$1,080	$1,220	$1,390	$1,230
cost per day x 365 days ****	$4,449	$4,993	$6,132	$5,190
total cost per year	$5,529	$6,213	$7,522	$6,420
total cost per mile *	55.3 cents	62.1 cents	75.2 cents	64.2 cents

* total cost per year ÷ total miles per year
** excess mileage over 15,000 miles annually (in thousands)
*** ownership costs based on a 4-year/60,000-mile retention cycle
**** ownership costs based on a 6-year/60,000-mile retention cycle

	2003 Chevrolet TrailBlazer LS 6-cyl. (4.3-liter) 2WD 4-door sport utility	2003 Dodge Caravan SE 6-cyl. (3.0-liter) passenger van
Operating Costs	per mile	per mile
gas and oil	7.9 cents	7.1 cents
maintenance	4.1 cents	3.9 cents
tires	1.5 cents	1.6 cents
cost per mile	**13.5 cents**	**12.6 cents**
Ownership Costs	per year	per year
comprehensive insurance ($250 deductible)	$159	$130
collision insurance ($500 deductible)	$402	$354
bodily injury and property damage ($100,000, $300,000, $50,000)	$389	$389
license, registration, taxes	$289	$259
depreciation (15,000 miles annually)	$4,286	$3,772
finance charge (20% down; loan @ 7.5%/4 yrs.)	$867	$755
cost per year	**$6,392**	**$5,659**
cost per day	**$17.51**	**$15.50**
added depreciation costs (per 1,000 miles over 15,000 miles annually)	**$173**	**$171**

Total Cost Per Mile

15,000 miles a year	per year	per year
cost per mile x 15,000 miles	$2,025	$1,890
cost per day x 365 days ***	$6,391	$5,658
total cost per year	**$8,416**	**$7,548**
total cost per mile *	**56.1 cents**	**50.3 cents**
20,000 miles a year	per year	per year
cost per mile x 20,000 miles	$2,700	$2,520
cost per day x 365 days ***	$6,391	$5,658
depreciation cost x 5 **	$865	$855
total cost per year	**$9,956**	**$9,033**
total cost per mile *	**49.8 cents**	**45.2 cents**
10,000 miles a year	per year	per year
cost per mile x 10,000 miles	$1,350	$1,260
cost per day x 365 days ****	$5,194	$4,709
total cost per year	**$6,544**	**$5,969**
total cost per mile *	**65.4 cents**	**59.7 cents**

* ** *** **** see pages 6 and 7

Vacation Planning

AAA's suggested budget for a family of four — two adults and two children — is at least $244 per day for lodging and meals, plus $13.10 per 100 miles for gas, oil, tires and maintenance with the car averaging 23 miles per gallon.

Lodging

The average cost for lodging is $132 per night, based on rates charged by approved accommodations listed in AAA TourBook® guides. This rate includes an extra-person charge for children. However, if children are within an age limit set by management — usually up to 14 — there may not be an extra charge.

Vacation spending depends on a family's preferences and means, but costs also vary by area. Expect higher lodging rates in large metropolitan areas and at resorts in season.

To save on lodging, it's best to make advance reservations. If that's not possible, plan to arrive early for a wider selection of accommodations.

Meals

For a family of four, AAA suggests budgeting at least $112 a day for meals, not including tips or beverages.

Meal costs can be reduced by eating the main meal at midday to take advantage of lower lunch prices at restaurants. Many restaurants offer children's menus and "early bird" dinner specials at reduced prices.

Additional Costs

In addition to lodging, food and driving costs, you should budget for admission fees, road and bridge tolls, recreation and shopping. If you don't carry credit cards, include an emergency fund in your vacation budget. For added security, AAA suggests carrying travelers cheques. AAA members can obtain fee-free travelers cheques and other types of travel money such as prepaid VISA gift cards through any AAA office.

Business Travel

Although some firms continue to provide vehicles to full-time business travelers, a growing number of employees use their own vehicles for company business.

Companies use three primary methods to reimburse employees for business use of personal vehicles.

Getting Reimbursed

Flat mileage allowance. Many companies provide a flat allowance per mile, plus allowances for charges such as tolls and parking. This system minimizes bookkeeping but can result in overpayment or underpayment when compared to actual driving costs.

Fixed periodic reimbursement. Some companies provide a flat dollar reimbursement per day, week or month to cover business use of a personal vehicle. This, too, may result in overpayment or underpayment when compared to actual driving costs.

Combined fixed and mileage rate. Many companies realize that some automobile costs relate to miles driven (fuel, oil, tires and maintenance) and some to ownership (insurance, taxes, interest and depreciation). These companies provide a periodic fixed rate to cover ownership costs and a per-mile rate to cover business miles reported.

The per-mile rates listed in this pamphlet represent the national average of owning and operating a vehicle for a year. Because employees who use their own vehicles for company business also use their vehicles for personal driving, reimbursement should not amount to 100 percent of the total costs.

Sources

AAA

AAA is a federation of motor clubs serving 46 million members in the United States and Canada through more than 1,100 offices.

Founded in 1902, AAA is a not-for-profit, fully taxpaying corporation. Its purpose is twofold: to give members a full range of automotive and travel-related services and to promote the interests of motorists and travelers through legislative and educational activities.

AAA has published *Your Driving Costs* since 1950. That year, driving a car 10,000 miles annually cost 9 cents a mile, and gasoline sold for 27 cents per gallon.

AAA's national office is located at 1000 AAA Drive, Heathrow, FL 32746-5063, telephone: (407) 444-7000. Local AAA clubs are listed in telephone directories under "AAA" and can be found on the Internet at www.aaa.com.

Information on AAA's public service and consumer advocacy activities can be found at www.aaapublicaffairs.com.

Runzheimer International

Runzheimer International is a management consulting firm that specializes in travel and living costs.

Founded in 1933, the firm serves more than 2,000 businesses and government agencies worldwide. The Runzheimer Plan of Automobile Standard Costs forms the basis for the reimbursement of car expenses to 260,000 client employees.

Organizations that operate fleets of 10 or more vehicles can contact Runzheimer directly to learn about individual schedules. Firms with fewer than 10 vehicles may find the national averages in this brochure helpful.

Runzheimer International is located at Runzheimer Park, Rochester, WI 53167, telephone: (262) 971-2200.

AAA Association Communication
1000 AAA Drive
Heathrow, FL 32746-5063
www.aaa.com

AAA acknowledges Runzheimer International
for help in preparing the automotive costs
presented in this booklet.

Contents may be reprinted in part or
in their entirety with attribution.

©AAA 2003   Stock 2717   Printed in USA

Reading Responses

1. What is the overall average national cost for driving during 2003?
2. Look at the costs for the three specific cars used for the national averages. How did the costs for these cars differ? Which cost most and least for operating costs, insurance, finance charges on a car loan, and so forth? Were you surprised by any of the costs calculated by AAA? If so, which ones?
3. In what ways is the AAA brochure designed to meet the needs of readers?

Writing Activities

1. Using the total cost per year from the table on driving costs, calculate a total average cost per day to drive one or several of the cars studied. Conduct some research in your community to find out the average cost per day of transit alternatives (bus, subway, train, or light-rail, for example). Write a report presenting your findings.
2. Write a proposal for alternating drivers, sharing rides, car pooling, or using other methods of reducing driving costs for individual drivers. Use the AAA figures as supporting evidence for your proposal. Be sure to quote and present data accurately from this—or any—source and to cite the source in accord with the expected conventions.
3. Use the brochure to calculate your current driving costs. Write a summary of what you find: your expenses, your costs in relation to national averages, and your own conclusions.

Community Links

Consider the AAA booklet alongside Henry, Weber, and Yarbrough's "Money Management Practices of College Students" (pp. 165–170) from the academic community. Based on your experiences reading and using the AAA brochure and on your personal experiences as a consumer, propose some ways to improve the ability of students to manage their transportation expenses.

How to Make a Budget and Stick to It

Nolo: Law for All

The Nolo: Law for All Web site provides a great variety of practical and legal advice. Topics include the snags of daily life—traffic tickets, barking dogs, landlord–tenant misunderstandings—as well as many more complex legal matters. Nolo's advice on making a budget is a practical alternative to the legal problems that too much debt can cause.

A Realistic Budget Is Your Best Weapon Against Overspending

1   If you want to keep your spending under control, it's essential that you make a budget. A budget allows you to get a handle on the flow of your money—how much is coming in and where it goes out. With that information in hand, you can make intelligent choices about how to spend.

Keep Track of Your Daily Expenses

2   The first step in making a realistic budget is figuring out where your money goes. To keep track, you should make an expense record. You may be tempted to turn to a computer program, such as Intuit's Quicken, to keep track of your expenses. That may seem like an easy way to approach the task, but most of these programs have a significant shortcoming—you don't record your cash outlays. Computer programs have you analyze your expenses paid primarily by check or credit card, and overlook the most obvious source of payment—cash.

3   Rather than relying on a computer program, you can keep track of your expenses in an extremely low-tech but comprehensive way: with some paper and a pen. Here's how:

1. Take out eight sheets of paper. You will use one sheet per week, meaning you will record your expenses for two months. By doing this, you'll avoid creating a budget based on a week or a month of unusually high or low expenses.
2. Select a Sunday to begin recording your expenses.
3. Record that Sunday's date in the blank at the top of one sheet of paper.
4. Carry that sheet with you at all times.
5. Record every expense you pay for by cash or cash equivalent—check, ATM or debit card or automatic bank withdrawal. Don't record credit card charges, as your goal is to get a picture of where your cash goes. When you make a payment on a credit card bill, however, list the items paid for.
6. At the end of the week, put away the sheet and take out another. Go back to Step 3.

7. At the end of the eight weeks, list seasonal, annual, semi-annual or quarterly expenses you incur but did not pay during your two-month recording period. The most common are property taxes, car registration, magazine subscriptions, tax preparation fees, insurance payments, and seasonal expenses such as summer camp fees or holiday gifts.

Total Up Your Income

4 Your expenditures account for only half of the picture. You also need to add up your monthly income.

5 On a blank sheet of paper, list the jobs for which you receive a salary or wages. Then, list all self-employment for which you receive income, including farm income and sales commissions. Finally, list other sources of income, such as the following:

- bonus pay
- dividends and interest
- alimony or child support
- pension or retirement income
- public assistance

6 Next to each source of income, list the net (after deductions) amount you receive each pay period. If you don't receive the same amount each period, average the last 12.

7 Next to each net amount, enter the period covered by the payment—such as weekly, twice monthly (24 times a year), every other week (26 times a year), monthly, quarterly or annually.

8 Finally, multiply or divide the pay period into the net amount to determine the monthly amount. For example, if you are paid twice a month, multiply the net amount by two. If you are paid every other week, multiply the amount by 26 (for the annual amount) and divide by 12. (The shortcut is to multiply by 2.167.)

9 When you are done, total up all the amounts. This is your total average monthly income.

Make Your Budget

10 After you've kept track of your expenses and income for a couple of months, you're ready to create a budget. Your twin goals in making a budget are to control your impulses to overspend and to help you start saving money. Follow these steps:

1. On a blank piece of paper, write down categories into which your expenses fall. (See the chart below [pp. 546–547] for suggested categories.) Also, total up your two months' (or estimated seasonal, annual, semi-annual or quarterly) expenses for the categories you create.

2. Starting on a second piece of paper, list your categories of expenses down the left side of the page. Use as many sheets as you need to list all categories. These are your budget sheets.
3. On the sheets containing your list of categories, make 13 columns. Label the first one "projected" and the remaining 12 with the months of the year. Unless today is the first of the month, start with next month.
4. Using your total actual expenses for the two months you tracked and your estimated seasonal, annual, semi-annual or quarterly expenses, project your monthly expenses for the categories you've listed. To find your projected monthly expenses, divide your actual two months' expenses by two, divide your total seasonal or annual expenses by 12, divide your semi-annual expenses by six and divide your quarterly expenses by four. After you've divided up your seasonal or annual expenses, you might want to include only the major expenses—such as quarterly loan payments or tax bills—in your monthly budget projections. Just make a note of when smaller expenses, such as magazine subscriptions, are due so you can adjust your budget for that month. These temporary adjustments make more sense than trying to save $1.23 each month so you can pay for your magazine subscription once a year.
5. Enter your projected monthly expenses into the "projected" column of your budget sheets.
6. Add up all projected monthly expenses and enter the total into a "Total Expenses" category at the bottom of the projected column.
7. Enter your projected monthly income below your total projected expenses.
8. Figure out the difference.

11   If your expenses exceed your income, you will have to cut expenses or increase your income. One way to do this is to make more money—but let's assume that you are not likely to get a substantial raise, find a new (higher-paying) job, take on a second job or make significant money by selling assets. This means you must decrease your expenses without depriving yourself of items or services you truly need. Review your expenses with an eye toward reducing. Rather than looking to cut out categories completely, look for categories you can comfortably reduce slightly. For example, let's say you need to cut $175 from your budget. You had also planned on spending $75 a month to eat out dinner, but are willing to decrease that to $25, thereby saving $50. Keep looking for categories in which you can make similar, small adjustments.

Staying on Track

12   Don't think of your budget as etched in stone. If you do, and you spend more on an item than you've budgeted, you'll only find yourself frustrated. Use your budget as a guide. If you constantly overspend in an area, you need to change the projected amount for that category—without berating yourself.

Keep in mind that a budget is designed to help you recognize what you can afford; it's not just an exercise in filling in the "correct" numbers. Check your figures periodically to keep an eye on how you're doing. If you never have enough money to make ends meet—you're using credit cards and not paying the balance in full each month—it's time to adjust some more.

13   If you continually come up short, you may need to consider some larger changes. For example, you might sell your newer car for an older used car to free yourself from car payments. As you make adjustments to your budget, give careful thought to your priorities. Everyone has different ideas about what luxury is, and different feelings about what they're willing to give up and what they just can't live without. Think about what you value, and be honest with yourself.

14   You may have to sacrifice some things that feel important to you, but don't expect to stick to your budget if you've taken away funds for almost everything beyond food, shelter and bills for your mundane necessities. Try making a list of things you feel you can't live without, and whittle your other expenses down to accommodate them. For example, you may decide to give up most of your magazine and newspaper subscriptions because you know you'd go nuts if you couldn't go to the movies once a week. If you make room for at least some of the things you love most, you're much more likely to succeed at your plan.

Categories of Expenses

Using a blank piece of paper, make a list of categories into which your expenses fall. You'll need these categories to complete your budget. The following categories are suggestions to help you create your own list.

Home	Self Care	Wearing Apparel	Food
rent/mortgage	toiletries &	clothing &	groceries
property taxes	cosmetics	accessories	breakfast out
insurance (renter's	haircuts	laundry, dry	lunch out
or homeowner's)	massage	cleaning &	dinner out
homeowner's	health club	mending	coffee/tea snacks
association dues	membership		
maintenance &	donations		
repairs	Healthcare		
telephone	insurance		
gas & electric	doctors		
water & sewer	dentist		
cable TV	eyecare		
garbage	medications		
household supplies	vitamins		
housewares			
furniture &			
appliances			
cleaning yard or			
pool care			

Transportation	Entertainment	Dependent Care	Pet Care
insurance	music	care	vet
registration	movies &	clothing	grooming
gasoline	video rentals	allowance	food, toys &
maintenance &	concerts, theater &	school expenses	supplies
repairs	ballet	toys &	
road service	museums	entertainment	
club	sporting events		
car wash	hobbies & lessons		
parking & tolls	club dues or		
public transit	membership		
& cabs	film		
parking tickets	development		
	books, magazines		
	& newspapers		
	software		
	online services		

Education	Travel	Personal Business	
tuition or loan	gifts & cards	supplies	**Taxes**
payments	holidays	photocopying	**Insurance**
books & supplies	birthdays &	postage	**Savings &**
	anniversaries	bank & credit card	**Investments**
	weddings &	fees	
	showers	interest payments	
		lawyer	
		accountant	

Reading Responses

1. What are the major steps that Nolo explains for developing a budget?
2. Nolo provides categories of expenses for people in general. Are there other categories that college students might need to add? Which categories might be most critical for college students to monitor?
3. In what ways has Nolo tried to anticipate the needs of readers who track expenses and develop a realistic budget? How does this page address readers?

Writing Activities

1. Write a brief analysis of the way that Nolo presents advice. Consider how the writer addresses readers, how the steps in the budget process are stated, how extra advice is incorporated, or other features that you notice.

2. Use Nolo's advice to figure out your expenses and your income. Create a preliminary budget. (You can refine this version later if you continue to follow Nolo's advice.) Using your calculations, write an analysis of your spending patterns and propose a realistic plan for meeting your financial goals.
3. Write your own advice, explaining how to carry out some other activity that helps to manage finances or other household activities. Explain each step clearly, supplying directions that a reader could easily follow.

Community Links

Consider Nolo's budget advice, AAA's "Your Driving Costs 2003" (pp. 530–541), Mogelonsky's "Young Adults: New Customers/New Foods" (pp. 325–331) from the work community, and Henry, Weber, and Yarbrough's "Money Management Practices of College Students" (pp. 165–170) from the academic community. Based on your personal experiences as a consumer, the information in the readings, and your calculations using the AAA brochure and Nolo's budget directions, consider what guidelines might help people manage money more effectively or learn how to anticipate the ebb and flow of cash. Tailor these guidelines for a specific group, approaching this group from the perspective of the public community rather than the research-oriented academic community.

Promotional Brochure
ARTISTIC LICENSE
College of Arts and Media, University of Colorado at Denver

◆

This selection presents several panels from a brochure developed by the College of Arts and Media. The brochure announces the dates and times of cultural and theater performances for the year, including an enticing description for each event. It also includes a ticket order form and a map to help the general public find parking and the appropriate campus buildings. The three panels from the brochure included here show how it establishes and carries through a theme in both words and visuals.

Artistic License

EXERCISE YOUR ARTISTIC LICENSE.
BUY TICKETS NOW.

To order tickets, please choose one of the following options:

- **Call the King Center ticket line at 303-556-2296.**
- **Click on the King Center Box Office website; www.kennethkingcenter.org**
- **Order tickets by mail. Send order form below with your payment (checks payable to AHEC) to CAM EVENTS, College of Arts and Media Campus Box 166, P.O. Box 173364 Denver, CO 80217-3364**
- **Or, purchase tickets at the door prior to each event.**

For regular program updates by email, available by request, please send your email address to CAMevents@storm.cudenver.edu. We respect your privacy, and will not give your email address to any commercial entity.

COLLEGE OF ARTS & MEDIA

PLEASE REMEMBER THESE POLICIES

- We accept major credit cards, personal checks and cash.
- Unless noted on your ticket, all seating is general admission on a first-come, first-seated basis.
- Everyone must have a ticket, including children and infants.
- All programs and events are subject to change. Please call the Events Line at 303-556-2296 for the most current information.
- The Kenneth King Center is ADA compliant, offering reserved parking spaces for patrons with disabilities in each of the Auraria campus parking lots, seating areas for patrons using wheelchairs, and accessible restrooms. Call 303-556-4652 at least one week before a performance to make special arrangements because of a disability, including sound enhancement equipment or signing (American Sign Language).
- A limited number of free parking spaces are available in Lot H on the Auraria campus (see map). Mention the performance you will be attending to the booth attendant.
- CU-Denver's College of Arts & Media offers numerous ticket discount programs, often in partnership with other organizations, to ensure that its programs are affordable and experienced by the broadest possible spectrum of patrons. These offers may include subscription, group and faculty/staff/student discounts. Discounts are not available for all events.
- We offer refunds only in the event of an event cancellation.
- Please arrive on time. Latecomers will be seated only during the first suitable break in the show.
- As a courtesy to fellow attendees, turn off cell phones and pagers before entering the performance venue.

TICKET PRICING FOR ALL PERFORMANCES, UNLESS OTHERWISE NOTED:
$10 *General Admission* • $7 *Seniors/Non CU-Denver Students* • $5 *CU-Denver Students*

BRANDISH YOUR ARTISTIC LICENSE
TO SEE, HEAR, FEEL, EXPERIENCE, ART, MUSIC, THEATRE, FILM, LIFE!

Break out of the regimented, hum-drum, rule-filled and regular. You now are the lucky holder of an official University of Colorado at Denver College of Arts & Media Artistic License.

This license entitles you to order tickets and immerse yourself in the joy to be found throughout the year at our cultural events.

Our thrill comes from teaching students the very best arts performance and giving them the chance to shine in their own productions. Join in the joy, as some of the nation's best teachers and aspiring student artists stimulate your mind and emotions.

BUT WAIT, THERE'S MORE.

On these pages you'll find a season full of intriguing events. But we just couldn't fit everything into this program guide. So please check out our latest and greatest offerings in any of these ways:

- **303.556.2296**
- request email updates at: **camevents@storm.cudenver.edu**

NOTE: All events will be held at the Kenneth King Academic and Performing Arts Center, 855 Lawrence Way, on the Auraria Campus in downtown Denver.

Reading Responses

1. What is the purpose of this brochure?
2. In what ways does the brochure try to provide information that meets the expectations of readers? How does it address them? What strategies does it use to engage their interest?
3. How is the brochure's theme carried through these three panels?

Writing Activities

1. Analyze how word choice contributes to the effectiveness of this brochure. Write an analysis that specifies your general conclusions and supports them with examples from the three panels.
2. Contrast the presentation of the information about orders and the list of policies (on the second panel) with the presentation of information on the other two panels. Write an analysis of these differences, using specific examples to illustrate your general conclusions about why and how the panels differ.
3. Sketch the visuals and draft the text for a few panels of your own brochure promoting a campus, civic, or workplace organization. Use a theme to unify the panels you prepare, and tailor the information to your community and your specific readers.

Community Links

Examine several of the brochures, newsletters, and similar visual materials in this book. Compare and contrast their approaches, considering how they try to meet community expectations.

Flyer

CHANGE LIVES ... INCLUDING YOUR OWN

AmeriCorps/VISTA

◆

This bright orange page encourages readers to sign up for a year with VISTA, helping low-income families to get high-quality care for their young children. Like many flyers, this one was placed in a convenient public location with lots of copies handy for interested people to pick up.

AMERICORPS *VISTA

Change Lives......
Including Your Own

Spend a year improving child care for low-income families in Colorado

Catholic Charities needs motivated individuals to:
- Sustain a volunteer program
- Raise funds to support child care and Head Start
- Increase awareness about the need for high-quality early childhood education

VISTA members commit to one year of Full-time service and receive:
- $4,725 education award
- $730 monthly living stipend
- Health insurance
- Child care, if eligible
- Experience of a life time

Interested?
Call Kristin Bieri at
303-308-1420 ext. 120 or
email CCAmCorps@aol.com

Reading Responses

1. Because a flyer often consists of only one page, it needs to be efficiently designed. What are the essentials covered in this flyer?
2. In what ways does the flyer try to appeal to likely or possible interests of readers?
3. How is the information on the flyer organized? What sequence is used? How does the organization of information contribute to its effectiveness?

 Writing Activities

1. Write a critique of the flyer, identifying its strong points and noting any possible improvements that would increase its effectiveness.
2. Based on the information included in the flyer, write a brief description or profile of the type of person it appears to seek.
3. Write your own flyer—recruiting for a group you belong to, announcing an event, or promoting an activity. Carefully analyze exactly what information readers will need to sign up, join, or attend. Then supply this information concisely and effectively.

 Community Links

Compare this flyer with several of the letters, the longer brochures, or similar materials in this book. Compare and contrast their approaches, considering how they try to meet community expectations.

Proposal
LIVING & LEARNING PROGRAM
Cornell College

◆

Each year Cornell College in Mt. Vernon, Iowa, considers proposals from students for the Living & Learning program, as described in the Residence Life Handbook on the campus Web site.

1 The Living & Learning Program provides students with an opportunity to link service, academic or career interests to their living environment. The goal is for students to gain a more holistic education through practicing experien-

tial learning and connecting issues and activities between the classroom, residence hall and real world; greater depth and breadth to their service interests; increased understanding of issues that are important to their peers; refined leadership skills such as goal-setting, working effectively as a team and project management; and the intrinsic rewards of serving others, being involved in the community and making a positive impact.

2   The Living & Learning Program requires a separate application and screening process. Living & Learning communities must reapply each year. Each community determines its own membership. The Living & Learning Program is contingent upon optimizing space; therefore, the Residence Life Office reserves the right to fill the space in a Living & Learning area via the housing process if the community cannot maintain its membership to fill spaces allocated in the halls.

PROPOSAL FOR A CORNELL COLLEGE LIVING & LEARNING GROUP

Anderson Muth, Peter Strutt, Drew Ahrold,
Joe Seabloom, Brian Fenoglio, and Ben Merrill,
Student Writers

◆

A group of students with strong interests in music proposed the Cornell Players Foundation as a Living & Learning community. Their proposal, including the sections required by the college, was submitted, evaluated, and approved.

1   1. The name of our group is, tentatively, the Cornell Players Foundation.
2   2. The purpose of our group is to function as a musical organization representing aspects of music not currently supported by the college. Our basic activities will include the following:
- Provide an open music house for playing at all hours (opportunity not available in dorms)
- Provide available equipment and so on for interested students
- Provide an open jam atmosphere on Sunday nights for anyone interested
- Maintain an extensive music library (of personal CDs, records, etc.)
- Maintain a collection of tablature and music
- Encourage free-form music (non-traditional)
- Establish an open music room, decorated and set up with an elevated stage, posters, lighting, and a sound system in the basement
- Offer music lessons of mastered instruments to interested students

Through these efforts we hope to provide a welcoming, nurturing environment for all musicians (and those who wish to become musicians), such that everyone can experience individual growth while the group gains valuable experience as well.

3A. The main service that we will provide is an open musical atmosphere, one which will be promoted through a Web site and through other venues that anyone is welcome to participate in and take advantage of. This includes not just members of the Cornell Players Foundation, but also any interested people in or out of the Cornell College community. Inviting known area musicians to join us is certainly an available and pursuable option. In addition, the mass of instruments and equipment which will be contained in our music room, combined with the musical education opportunities we aim to provide, will enable interested parties to engage in learning of new instruments and musical styles. Our Sunday night jams will be promoted, on and off campus, in order to encourage a wide array of interested musicians to join us in creating a new musical sound, one which will be recorded for later distribution and promotional purposes.

3B. Timeline:
August/September
- Set up music room
- Build stage
- Install lights/sound system
- Decorate
- Set up instruments, equipment, etc.
- Establish recording system (computer-based or soundboard-based)
- Set up tarp draining system above room to avoid potentially costly flood damage
- Establish a Web site
- Promote through the Web site and through conventional channels (radio ads, etc.)

September → December, January → May: Sunday night jams
Fall & Spring
- Cut an album of live material
- Acquire more instruments and equipment, individually and collectively
- Play elsewhere as a collective (Iowa City, Cedar Rapids)
- Run speakers throughout entire house for true surround sound
- Perform publicly for the community

3C. The success of our goals will be evaluated by the following criteria:
- Status and quality of recording
- Improved individual musicianship
- New instruments, styles, etc., learned
- Improved jam cohesiveness
- Others attracted to community
- Enjoyment of being involved in a successful musical venture

3D. While the members of the Cornell Players Foundation will inevitably benefit the most, it is hoped that outside persons will also gain from interaction with our group. Some possible areas of benefit include the following:
- Members of group experience significant musical or personal growth
- Anyone who comes and plays learns, gains experience, and enjoys the music
- Recording enables later listening and preservation
- A fresh new musical sound comes from the basement of 10th Ave.

7   4. My name is Anderson Muth, and I believe I have a lot to contribute to this Living & Learning group. I have an extensive musical background, including piano, cello, and guitar training, as well as numerous hours spent with my turntables and vinyl collection. I have taken piano, cello, and guitar lessons, played in junior high, high school, and collegiate orchestras (including traveling to Europe last year), and I even was involved in church choir during high school. Now, I primarily DJ and am beginning to relearn the guitar. I also am the Music Director at KRNL, the campus radio station, which deals with the introduction, play, charting, and promotion of new music to the college radio scene.

8   From this group I hope to advance my own personal musicianship, further my guitar playing skills and DJ mixing skills, as well as learn how to play or use both skills in a group atmosphere (something I am completely foreign to). I'm also interested in learning more of the production and recording end of the music industry, and I see this as a great opportunity to do these things. Also, I'm excited to live in a community focused on furthering musical growth since music and sound play an integral part in my life. I think my leadership capabilities, my musical talents, my inventiveness, and my desire to make this a reality (I did organize all this, after all) make me a valuable asset to the group.

9   My name is Peter Strutt, and I have many things to contribute to the group. I play guitar, bass, trombone, and piano. I have taken 10 years of piano lessons, 7 of trombone, and have been playing guitar for 6 years. I sing classically in Concert Choir and Chamber Singers here at Cornell. I take voice lessons and am fully able to pass along what I have learned to others. I have given voice lessons to friends for years. I own 2 guitars, an amplifier, a trombone, and a keyboard. I also have an intense passion for learning and exploring new music, such that I always have something new for me and others to play, listen to, or sing.

10   My name is Drew Ahrold, and I feel that I may not only contribute much to this group, but that I can also learn much from this experience. By contributing to this collective of personas, I would run our music library and keep it in order. I would also be able to assist in the set-up of different sound systems. I have two years experience doing both of these from my high school radio station, KDPS 88.1 FM in Des Moines. From this group I hope to learn to play guitar, something that was never really open to me. This would allow me to accomplish that musical goal and gain a musical talent. I really hope that I can help this group succeed.

11   My name is Joe Seabloom, and I believe that I could contribute much to this group. I have played bass for over seven years and guitar for two. My experience with both of these instruments, combined with several years of music theory training, would allow me to teach others much about music. From this group I hope to learn more about many musical topics and gain experience working with other musicians. I intend to be a very active member in the development of this group.

12   Hi. My name is Brian Fenoglio, and I am very interested in being in the music appreciation Living & Learning group at the 10th Ave. apartments next year. I feel that I could greatly benefit from this, as the entire Cornell community could. I currently play trombone in Cornell's Jazz Ensemble and have some knowledge of both the piano and electric bass. I've taken piano/organ lessons from when I was in grade school (probably second grade) until I graduated from high school. I plan on purchasing a keyboard this summer, and it would be wonderful if I could easily play with others without having to haul equipment all over. Also, I feel my experience can help others learn of various styles of music. I hope to learn a lot myself; my main goal is to become fairly decent at playing the guitar. Furthermore, I have applied for the job of General Manager at KRNL, a position which I feel I have an excellent chance of getting; this will aid in our goal of using the resources of the radio station (i.e. its broadcasting ability) to further the reaches of our own musical experience. Thank you very much for your time and consideration.

13   My name is Ben Merrill. I am planning on being a part of a musically oriented Living & Learning community. In order for this community to succeed, others outside the community must know about it. I plan to design and maintain a Web site to accomplish this. This site would provide, in addition to advertising, a source of information related to the musical community. There are many possibilities created by using technology in other areas as well.

14   The faculty contact for our group is Karen Brown. The role she will play within the Cornell Players Foundation is an advisory role, helping us properly augment our advertising, assisting in our planned ties with KRNL, the campus radio station (for equipment and promotional purposes), and helping our Living & Learning group run smoothly. Monthly meetings should be sufficient, as once our group has initially established itself, most of our concentration will be on our true focus: the music. Contact will be maintained throughout the year quite easily, since at least two members of our group are Philosophy majors, so we regularly see Karen anyway. In addition, e-mail communication can be easily employed if issues arise. Karen will obviously be welcome at any of our events, and we certainly encourage her to participate musically, whether that will be playing at one of our sessions or taking advantage of the lessons we will make available.

15   6. There is only one place (in all honesty) that we are interested in living, and that is the 10th Avenue Apartments. The North Side would be our first selection since it is in better overall condition and it floods less frequently. Thus, the South Side would be our second choice. The reason for our desire to live at 10th Ave. is so that we can take advantage of its basement, a rather unique spatial feature when compared to all other available campus housing. The basement is rather mandatory for setting up our music room (and storing our mass of equipment) since it is unrealistic to try and implement this project in a traditional dorm setting.

Reading Responses

1. What theme unifies this proposal?
2. What is the topic of each of the six sections required in the proposal?
3. How did the proposal writers keep in mind the expectations of their most important readers—the people who would rate the proposal and decide whether to approve it?

Writing Activities

1. Write a critique of the proposal, identifying its strong points and noting any possible improvements that would increase its effectiveness.
2. How do you suppose this Living & Learning group would be received by other students on campus? Write an analysis of the strategies used by the writers to make a convincing case for their possible contributions to campus life.
3. Write your own proposal for a Living & Learning group that you invent or for some program available on your campus. Follow any actual guidelines for a campus program, or follow the format used by the Cornell Players Foundation.

Community Links

Compare and contrast this Living & Learning proposal with other proposals for funded projects such as the CSUN proposal (pp. 183–187) from the academic community or the proposal of the National Fund for the United States Botanic Garden (pp. 559–565), also from the public community. Consider how the Living & Learning proposal resembles and differs from more formal funding proposals and how each proposal addresses the expectations of its community and its specific readers.

Grant Proposal
GRANT PROPOSAL
The National Fund for the United States Botanic Garden

◆

Although the United States Botanic Garden is the country's oldest, operating since 1820, it continues to plan for the future. This proposal seeks funding for a National

Garden that would be located on the mall near the Capitol building in Washington, D.C. Posted on the Web, the proposal outlines the vision for this restful and educational addition to Capitol Hill.

A. Organizational Information

NAME:
THE NATIONAL FUND FOR THE
UNITED STATES BOTANIC GARDEN
245 FIRST ST., SW
WASHINGTON, DC 20024-3201

CONTACT:
ROBERT L. HANSEN, EXECUTIVE DIRECTOR

PHONE: 202-226-4083
FAX: 202-225-7910
EMAIL: bhansen@aoc.gov

1. The National Fund

The National Fund for the United States Botanic Garden (The National Fund) is a not-for-profit organization established by the office of the Architect of the Capitol (AOC) for the sole purpose of and the primary means for raising private funds to design and construct the National Garden at the United States Botanic Garden (USBG). The AOC, under the supervision of the Congressional Joint Committee on the Library, has been authorized by law (public law 100-458) to design, construct, and maintain the National Garden. No money for the design and construction of the National Garden has been appropriated by the U.S. Congress.

The mission of The National Fund is to raise private money to design and construct the National Garden at the USBG. The National Fund supports the USBG's efforts to bring the interdependence of plants, people and the environment to the forefront. This partnership between the public USBG and the private National Fund is designed to help develop new environmentally sensitive programs and to enhance the existing environmental and horticultural educational programs of the USBG through the design and construction of the National Garden. Once all construction funds are raised the National Fund will establish an endowment fund, the interest from which will fund educational programs for the USBG.

All funds raised by the National Fund are used solely for the support of the USBG.

2. The United States Botanic Garden

The United States Botanic Garden was established for the purpose of growing and exhibiting significant plants of horticultural and botanical interest to educate the public. It is the goal of the USBG to illustrate the diversity of America's flora by growing and exhibiting a wide range of exotic and native plants. The emphasis of the plant collections is on rare, threatened or endangered plants, economic plants, medicinal plants, plants of historical significance, plants with educational value, and plants with aesthetic value for exhibition. The USBG is committed to the conservation of the plant world through collections, displays, and educational programs. The USBG is the oldest continuously operating public garden in the USA.

3. The National Garden

The National Garden at the USBG will be a center for environmental education. As an integral part of the USBG, the National Garden will serve three main purposes: a) to educate the public by supporting the USBG's efforts to emphasize people's vital relationship to plants and the environment; b) to educate the public by supporting the USBG's efforts to emphasize people's role in the conservation of plants and the environment; and c) to enrich the quality of life of all ages in the local community. The National Garden will promote energy and water conservation, highlight renewable energy resources, and define the role that gardens play in society. The National Garden will be the USBG's living classroom.

4. Programs and Services

The USBG programs in the National Garden will instruct visitors on how to become effective stewards of the land and the environment. Situated near the U.S. Capitol and the Smithsonian Institution, this site will be ideal for hands-on experiences to teach young people about the natural world and instill in them a sense of responsibility for the land. It is the last vacant lot on the Mall. The National Garden will offer children, their parents and grandparents an opportunity to become more sensitive to the delicacy of the world around them and their role in its preservation. For seniors, it means a place where they can learn and a place that will welcome their active volunteer involvement. All visitors will be inspired from a stroll through the National Garden as well as from scheduled programs for special interests. The National Garden at the USBG will be designed to be accessible to the handicapped. The target audience will include school groups, senior citizen groups, tourists, scientists, researchers and garden clubs. With more than a million annual visitors of all ages, programs will be designed to be age appropriate with content to convey the vital relationship between plants, people and the environment and the critical need for their mutual conservation and preservation. All USBG programs are open to the public without discrimination of race, color or creed. Some programs will carry a fee to cover expenses.

5. **Major Affiliations**
Because of the National Fund's unique mission to support the USBG by raising private funds for the design and construction of the National Garden, the National Fund is not affiliated or partnered with other nonprofit organizations.

6. **Physical Plant**
The National Fund does not have a physical plant. The Conservatory, greenhouses and administrative space of the USBG are operated and maintained by the AOC. The U.S. Congress recently appropriated $33.5 million so the AOC could completely renovate the USBG Conservatory. This project will be accomplished independently of the construction of the National Garden. As stated earlier, the U.S. Congress did not appropriate any money for the National Garden. It was always Congress' intent for the National Fund to raise private money for that purpose.

7. **Board of Trustees**
The Board of Trustees of the National Fund is made up of a bipartisan group of patriotic Americans that was formed in 1992. In 1998 Mrs. Teresa Heinz was elected Chairman. A full listing of all Board members and their affiliation is available on this web site *(Log-in required. Please contact bhansen@aoc.gov for access.).*

8. **Charitable Status**
The National Fund is a charitable organization. Contributions to the National Fund (EIN #52-1722096) have been determined to be exempt from Federal income tax under Section 501(c) (3) of the Internal Revenue Code. The Fund is incorporated in the District of Columbia, and is tax exempt.

B. Detailed Project Information

1. **Project Description**
The National Garden will be an integral part of the USBG located on Capitol Hill in Washington, DC. The National Garden will feature an Environmental Learning Center (ELC), a Water Garden honoring America's First Ladies, a Rose Garden exhibiting many varieties of our national flower, a Showcase Garden, a Butterfly Garden and a Lawn Terrace. The National Garden's classrooms will be both indoors and outdoors. The ELC, located on the West End of the site, will provide

state-of-the-art indoor facilities including a classroom, a library and a multipurpose lecture hall to optimize the educational experience for visitors of all ages. The outdoor gardens will occupy more than three acres. The National Garden will be designed to educate the American public and all visitors (young and old) about the great diversity of Native American plants and their importance to the environment and ultimately the combined interdependence of plants and the environment with people. Once built, the National Garden will be maintained with appropriated funds administered by the AOC.

The ELC will add a new dimension to the public educational programming available for use by the USBG thus making the programs more accessible to the general public.

The existing Conservatory sits on another three-acre plot of land. By doubling the size of the USBG with the three-acre National Garden site the USBG's ability to showcase the diversity of Native American plants will be greatly enhanced.

2. Architectural Plans

A nationwide competition was held to obtain design concepts for the National Garden. There were three winners. EDAW, the nationally renowned landscape architectural firm, is the landscape design contractor.

3. Project Cost Estimates

The following project cost estimates were prepared under the supervision of EDAW:

Mobilization & Demobilization	$ 900,000
Site Preparation	$ 1,150,000
Civil	$ 1,500,000
Structural	$ 4,500,000
Utilities	$ 1,000,000
Plant Materials	$ 750,000
Contingency - 15%	$ 1,200,000
Soft Costs	$ 2,200,000
Escalation	$ 1,000,000
	$14,200,000
10 years of administrative & fund raising costs	$ 3,000,000
TOTAL	**$17,200,000**

4. Regulatory Approvals

This project is sponsored by the U.S. Government, the Architect of Capitol (AOC), and all approvals are in place.

5. Effect of the National Garden on the Operation of the USBG

The USBG reports to and receives its government appropriations through the AOC. The USBG staff will be increased by five people to coincide with the opening of the National Garden to handle the new National Garden's maintenance and operation. These increases are included in the fiscal 2004 operating budget for the USBG/AOC. Operational budget increases are estimated to be $750,000.

C. Fund Raising and Grant Application Information

1. Track Record

A listing of the major donors ($100,000 and above) may be found on this web site. The initial fund raising efforts for the National Garden began in 1991. This is the only fund raising project undertaken by the National Fund.

2. Dollar Goals

Corporate:	$9,000,000
Individual:	$2,000,000
Foundation:	$7,000,000

3. Seven Largest Gifts

U.S. Mint (Commemorative Coin Sales)	$3,200,000
John H. & Teresa Heinz, III Foundation	$1,000,000
Ames True Temper	$1,000,000
HGTV	$1,000,000
Lowes Home Improvement	$1,000,000
Scott's Company	$1,000,000
Allbritton Foundation	$ 820,000

4. Future Fund Raising Progress Expected

Future corporate and foundation contributions are expected to establish a $10,000,000 endowment fund. The interest earned will fund educational programs at the USBG.

5. After Effects

The three most important things that will happen when the National Garden is completed are: (a) increased attendance and therefore increased exposure to the programs and services of the USBG as well as the establishment of a large active volunteer and docent program, (b) increased participation in the public programs offered by the USBG, and (c) the establishment of a national endowment fund, the interest from which will fund future educational programs at the USBG and the National Garden.

6. Naming Opportunity
If a grant is approved, the National Fund would be delighted to discuss such an opportunity with your designee. Usually $100,000 or more is needed for a naming opportunity. All naming opportunities are subject to approval of the Architect of the Capitol.

D. Attachments (Available upon request)

If any of these attachments are required please email our office at bhansen@aoc.gov and they will be sent by overnight mail.

- 2000 Audited Financial Statement—also available on this site.
- 2000 990 Forms—also available directly from the IRS.
- IRS Ruling Letter—also available on this site.

Reading Responses

1. Although funding organizations may define specific requirements for proposals, the sections in this proposal supply standard information. What is the function of each section in the proposal? How do these sections support the purpose of the proposal as a whole?
2. Which points in the proposal seem most or least compelling to you? Why?
3. How did the proposal writers keep in mind the expectations of their most important readers—the people who would rate the proposal and decide whether to approve it?

Writing Activities

1. Write a summary in your own words of the mission of the National Fund for the United States Botanic Garden.
2. Write a summary of the proposed benefits of the National Garden to the public.
3. Write a section of your own grant application. Propose a worthwhile project (real or imagined) on behalf of a campus or civic organization.

Community Links

Compare and contrast this proposal with the CSUN proposal (pp. 183–187) from the academic community. Consider how the two proposals resemble and differ from each other. How does each address the expectations of its community and its specific readers?

Web Site

WWW.SMOKEFREEMOVIES.UCSF.EDU

Smoke Free Movies

◆

The Smoke Free Movies Web site is dedicated to challenging the presence of tobacco in movies. These pages from the site—the home page on the right and "The Problem" below—illustrate its hard-hitting, investigative approach to an issue many people may never have considered.

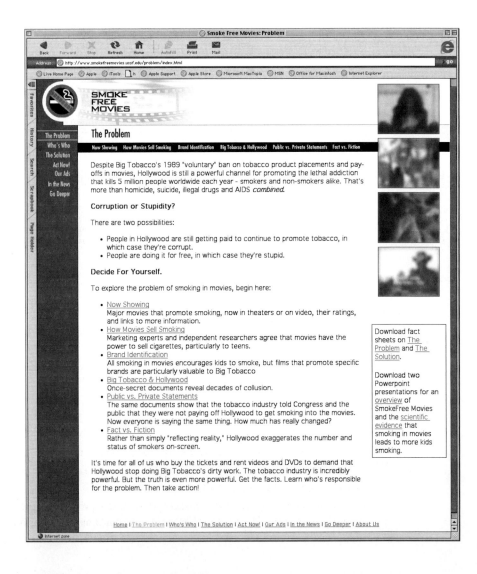

www.smokefreemovies.ucsf.edu **567**

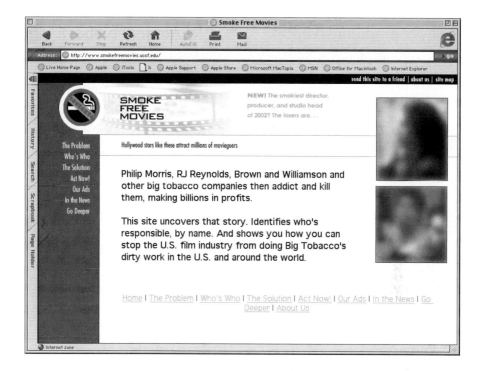

 Reading Responses

1. How does the Smoke Free Movies site appeal to visitors? What might they expect to find?
2. How does the design and organization of the pages try to accomplish the site's purposes?
3. Examine carefully the headings and links used on the sample pages from the site. What strategies does the site use to engage the attention of readers and persuade them to its point of view?

 Writing Activities

1. Visit the Smoke Free Movies site. Write a journal entry or personal account of your reactions to the site's strong partisan position.
2. Write an analysis of some of the strategies that the site uses to persuade visitors to recognize and accept its point of view.
3. Design a draft Web page of your own that passionately presents an issue. Select your issue carefully, and consider how to educate and engage visitors about the issue to which you dedicate your site.

Community Links

Compare and contrast the Smoke Free Movies site with the Purdue OWL home page (pp. 197–199) from the academic community, the Technical Standards site (pp. 347–349) from the work community, or another public site such as College Drinking (pp. 568–571). (For this comparison, you may use the print versions in the book or visit the Web sites.) Which of the features of the Smoke Free Movies site particularly reflect its goals as an issue-oriented advocate? Which features of the other site reflect its community goals? Which features of both sites are common characteristics of many Web sites?

WWW.COLLEGEDRINKINGPREVENTION.GOV

College Drinking: Changing the Culture

◆

This Web site wants to accomplish what its title suggests: change the drinking culture on college campuses. Its approach, however, is to begin with "the facts," one of the pages included here. On the Web, the "facts" are followed by some hard-hitting "FAQs" that answer common questions about drinking with current advice, medical information, and research studies.

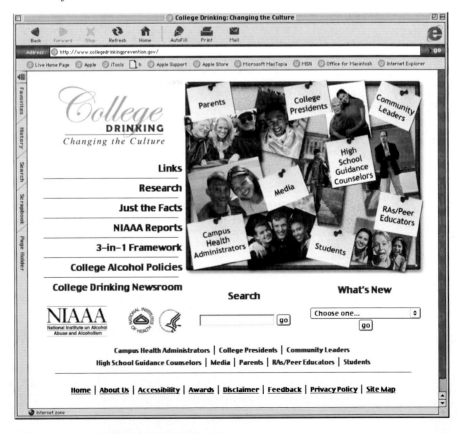

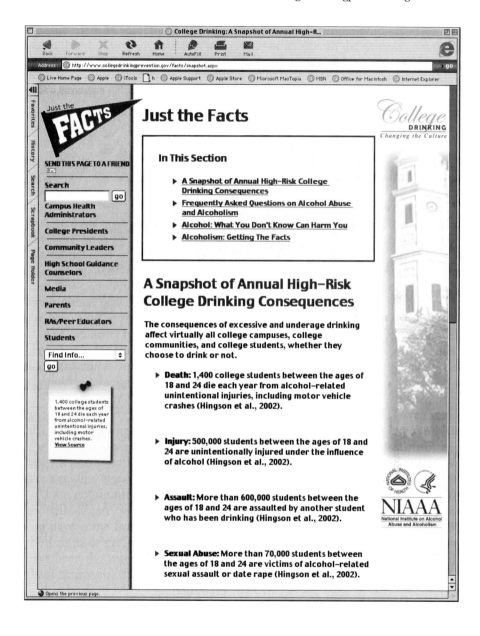

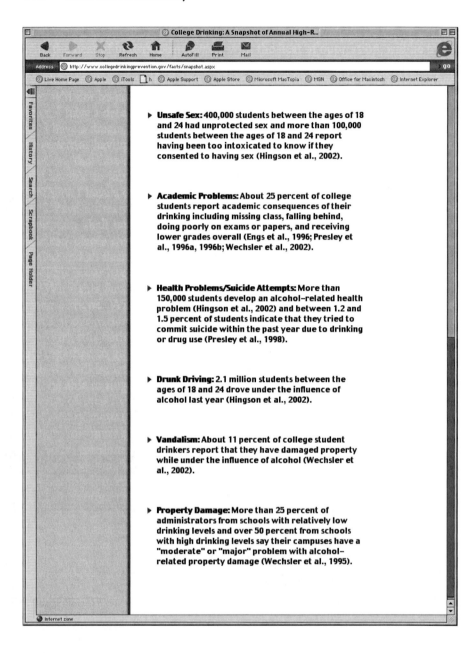

▶ **Unsafe Sex:** 400,000 students between the ages of 18 and 24 had unprotected sex and more than 100,000 students between the ages of 18 and 24 report having been too intoxicated to know if they consented to having sex (Hingson et al., 2002).

▶ **Academic Problems:** About 25 percent of college students report academic consequences of their drinking including missing class, falling behind, doing poorly on exams or papers, and receiving lower grades overall (Engs et al., 1996; Presley et al., 1996a, 1996b; Wechsler et al., 2002).

▶ **Health Problems/Suicide Attempts:** More than 150,000 students develop an alcohol-related health problem (Hingson et al., 2002) and between 1.2 and 1.5 percent of students indicate that they tried to commit suicide within the past year due to drinking or drug use (Presley et al., 1998).

▶ **Drunk Driving:** 2.1 million students between the ages of 18 and 24 drove under the influence of alcohol last year (Hingson et al., 2002).

▶ **Vandalism:** About 11 percent of college student drinkers report that they have damaged property while under the influence of alcohol (Wechsler et al., 2002).

▶ **Property Damage:** More than 25 percent of administrators from schools with relatively low drinking levels and over 50 percent from schools with high drinking levels say their campuses have a "moderate" or "major" problem with alcohol-related property damage (Wechsler et al., 1995).

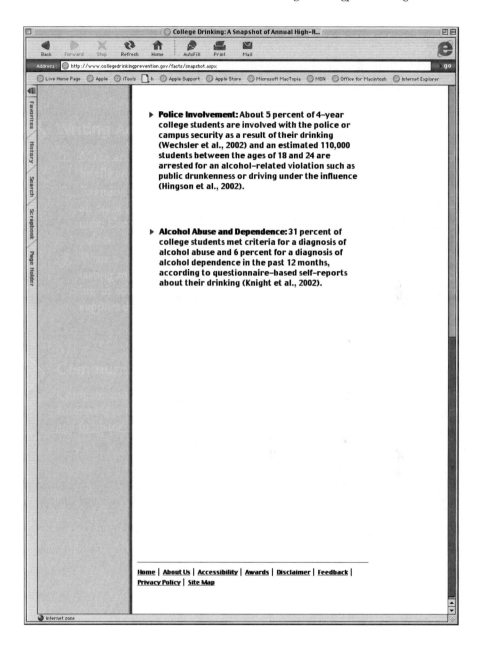
- **Police Involvement:** About 5 percent of 4-year college students are involved with the police or campus security as a result of their drinking (Wechsler et al., 2002) and an estimated 110,000 students between the ages of 18 and 24 are arrested for an alcohol-related violation such as public drunkenness or driving under the influence (Hingson et al., 2002).

- **Alcohol Abuse and Dependence:** 31 percent of college students met criteria for a diagnosis of alcohol abuse and 6 percent for a diagnosis of alcohol dependence in the past 12 months, according to questionnaire-based self-reports about their drinking (Knight et al., 2002).

Reading Responses

1. How does the College Drinking Web site appeal to visitors? What might visitors expect to find?
2. How do the design and organization of the pages try to accomplish the site's purposes?
3. Examine carefully the headings and links used on the sample pages from the site. What strategies does the site use to engage the attention of readers and persuade them to spend some time investigating its resources?

Writing Activities

1. Visit the College Drinking site. Write a journal entry or personal account of your reactions to the site's approach to the alcohol issue.
2. Write an analysis of some of the strategies that the site uses to persuade visitors to become better educated about the possible consequences of drinking.
3. Design a draft Web page of your own that aims to educate viewers about an issue that might have serious consequences for them. Select your issue carefully, and consider how to educate and engage the visitors to your site.

Community Links

Compare and contrast the College Drinking site with the Purdue OWL home page (pp. 197–199) from the academic community, the Technical Standards site (pp. 347–349) from the work community, or Smoke Free Movies (pp. 566–567), also from the public community. (For this comparison, you may use the print versions in the book or visit the sites on the Web.) Which of the features of the College Drinking site particularly reflect its goals as a change agent? Which features of the other site reflect its community goals? Which features of both sites are common characteristics of many Web sites?

Guide to Themes, Topics, and Rhetorical Strategies

This selective guide is designed to help you find related readings and varied illustrations of particular features. Readings are identified by authors' last names and short titles.

Abstracts, see also Executive Summaries
Carr et al.: How to Tell a Sea Monster, 171
Gamble: Evolution of Coral-Zooxanthellae Symbioses, 141
Henry et al.: Money Management Practices, 165
Meyer: Humor as a Double-Edged Sword, 119
Morgan and Korschgen: Ethics of Faculty Behavior, 88
Simon et al.: Temporal Variation in Bird Counts, 154
Small and Kimbrough-Melton: Rethinking Justice, 126

Advertisements and Promotions
AmeriCorps/VISTA: Change Lives, 552
College of Arts and Media: Artistic License, 548
Glenbrook Life: Dedicated, Focused, and Diversified, 343
Technical Standards, 347
United Illuminating Company: Romeo and J l et, 341

Advice
AAA: Your Driving Costs 2003, 530
Bolman and Deal: Cracking the Hidden Code, 240
Covey: The Ideal Community, 390
Lutz: It's Okay to Be Anal, 228
Nelson: A Beginning, 386
Nolo: How to Make a Budget, 543
T-REX: Traffic Updates, 332
Vermette: Improving Understanding, 96
Walton: Running a Successful Company, 216

Applications
Dedecker: Statement of Purpose, 189
Stoscheck: Application Essay, 94

Arguments
ACLU: Briefing Paper, 504
Barlow and Clarke: The Standpoint, 479
Barlow and Rifkin: Treaty Initiative, 431
Cullis-Suzuki: The Young Can't Wait, 355
Jefferson: Declaration of Independence, 426
Kerry and Bond: Pro & Con, 495
Lee: Case Against College, 73
Mairson: In Praise of the Research University, 192
Simpson: Are Incentives for Drug Abuse Treatment Too Strong?, 301
Tannen: Roots of Debate, 65

Brochures
AAA: Your Driving Costs 2003, 530
College of Arts and Media: Artistic License, 548
Greenwood Village: A New City?, 459
Olive Garden: Welcome to the Family, 289
U.S. Army: Discover How Far You Can Go, 280

Cars
AAA: Your Driving Costs 2003, 530
Fuel Economy Overview, 490
Helgesen: When Life Itself, 256
Kerry and Bond: Pro & Con, 495

Cause and Effect
College Drinking, 568
Ehrenreich: Evaluation, 208
Gamble: Evolution of Coral-Zooxanthellae Symbioses, 141
Popenoe and Whitehead: Sex without Strings, 518
Woodard: Fueling the Revolution, 135

Children, see also Families
Dees-Thomases: Dear Friend, 445
Dickens: Nothing but Facts, 11

Greenwood Village: Newsletter, 475
Helgesen: When Life Itself, 256
Review of *Sticks and Stones*, 149
Rose: Lilia, 19

Class Differences
Ehrenreich: Evaluation, 208
hooks: Keeping Close to Home, 22
Rose: Lilia, 19

Classification
Donald: Learning, Understanding, and Meaning, 43
Purdue University: OWL, 197
Vermette: Improving Understanding, 96

Comparison and Contrast
Donald: Learning, Understanding, and Meaning, 43
hooks: Keeping Close to Home, 22
Popenoe and Whitehead: Sex without Strings, 518
States: Troping through Proverbia, 112

Community Definitions
Covey: The Ideal Community, 390
Gomes: A More Excellent Way, 420
Morse: Five Building Blocks, 374
Palmer: Quest for Community in Higher Education, 33
Rifkin: New Culture of Capitalism, 247
Ulrich: Six Practices, 221
Zobel de Ayala: Anticipating the Community of the Future, 405

Community Colleges
Aslanian: Community College Pathway, 59
Bryant: ERIC Review: Community College Students, 159

Consumer Culture
Helgesen: When Life Itself, 256
Review of *Sticks and Stones*, 149
Rifkin: New Culture of Capitalism, 247

Definitions of Terms
Alford: Don't Just Do It to Save Lives, 271
Blacker: In Memoriam, 156
Covey: The Ideal Community, 390
Dickens: Nothing but Facts, 11
Donald: Learning, Understanding, and Meaning, 43
Harris: Anti-Plagiarism Strategies, 77
Hutton and Phillips: Tuning In, 379

Meyer: Humor as a Double-Edged Sword, 119
Miller: Wanted: "Civic Scientists," 362
Morse: Five Building Blocks, 374
Palmer: Quest for Community in Higher Education, 33
Peet: Logos, 101
Pratkanis and Aronson: Our Age of Propaganda, 412
Rifkin: New Culture of Capitalism, 247
States: Troping through Proverbia, 112
Tannen: Roots of Debate, 65
Zielinski: Are You a Copyright Criminal?, 264

Description
Dickens: Nothing but Facts, 11
Jones: And the Weiner Is . . . , 213
Rose: Lilia, 19
Stoscheck: Application Essay, 94

Educational Approaches
Dickens: Nothing but Facts, 11
Donald: Learning, Understanding, and Meaning, 43
Gomes: A More Excellent Way, 420
Harris: Anti-Plagiarism Strategies, 77
Lee: Case Against College, 73
Mairson: In Praise of the Research University, 192
Malcolm X: Prison Studies, 16
McRae: Irony in the Morning, 512
Palmer: Quest for Community in Higher Education, 33
Rhodes: Think You Can Teach?, 515
Tannen: Roots of Debate, 65
Vermette: Improving Understanding, 96

Environment
Barlow and Clarke: The Standpoint, 479
Barlow and Rifkin: Treaty Initiative, 431
Brinkley: Why You Need to Vote, 443
Cullis-Suzuki: The Young Can't Wait, 355
Fuel Economy Overview, 490
Gamble: Evolution of Coral-Zooxanthellae Symbioses, 141
Kerry and Bond: Pro & Con, 495
National Fund: Grant Proposal, 559
Stoscheck: Application Essay, 94

Ethics
Alford: Don't Just Do It to Save Lives, 271
Gomes: A More Excellent Way, 420
Harris: Anti-Plagiarism Strategies, 77

Morgan and Korschgen: Ethics of Faculty
  Behavior, 87
Moyers: Journalism & Democracy, 366
Pratkanis and Aronson: Our Age of
  Propaganda, 412
Zielinski: Are You a Copyright
  Criminal?, 264

Examples (Brief and Extended)
Aslanian: Community College Pathway, 59
Bolman and Deal: Cracking the Hidden
  Code, 240
Covey: The Ideal Community, 390
Dedecker: Statement of Purpose, 189
Gomes: A More Excellent Way, 420
Harris: So Many Numbers, 109
Katz: Pathbreaking, Fractionalized, Uncertain
  World of Knowledge, 52
Lee: Case Against College, 73
Lutz: It's Okay to Be Anal, 228
Miller: Wanted: "Civic Scientists," 362
Mogelonsky: Young Adults: New Customers/
  New Foods, 325
Moyers: Journalism & Democracy, 366
Nelson: A Beginning, 386
Palmer: Quest for Community in Higher
  Education, 33
Pratkanis and Aronson: Our Age of
  Propaganda, 412
States: Troping through Proverbia, 112
Ulrich: Six Practices, 221

Executive Summaries, see also Abstracts
Baldwin: How to Win, 298
Blacker: In Memoriam, 156
Porter: Strategy and the Internet, 299
Seybold: Get Inside, 298

Families, see also Children
hooks: Keeping Close to Home, 22
Popenoe and Whitehead: Sex without
  Strings, 518
Small and Kimbrough-Melton: Rethinking
  Justice, 126
Vermette: Improving Understanding, 96

First-Person Accounts
Cullis-Suzuki: The Young Can't Wait, 355
Dedecker: Statement of Purpose, 189
Ehrenreich: Evaluation, 208
hooks: Keeping Close to Home, 22
Kush: Researching Bedlam, 133
Liu: Story of a Garment Worker, 205

Mairson: In Praise of the Research
  University, 192
Malcolm X: Prison Studies, 16
Moyers: Journalism & Democracy, 366
Nelson: A Beginning, 386
Rose: Lilia, 19
Stoscheck: Application Essay, 94
Terkel: Organizer: Bill Talcott, 357
Vermette: Improving Understanding, 96
Walton: Running a Successful Company, 216

Grant Proposals
National Fund: Grant Proposal, 559
Sorrells: Communicating Common
  Ground, 183

Headings and Subheadings
Carr et al.: How to Tell a Sea Monster, 171
Eisenberg: Coming Job Boom, 233
Gamble: Evolution of Coral-Zooxanthellae
  Symbioses, 141
Harris: Anti-Plagiarism Strategies, 77
Henry et al.: Money Management
  Practices, 165
Meyer: Humor as a Double-Edged
  Sword, 119
Morgan and Korschgen: Ethics of Faculty
  Behavior, 87
National Fund: Grant Proposal, 559
Palmer: Quest for Community in Higher
  Education, 33
Small and Kimbrough-Melton: Rethinking
  Justice, 126
Sorrells: Communicating Common
  Ground, 183
Ulrich: Six Practices, 221

Interviews
Jones: And the Weiner Is . . . , 213
Liu: Story of a Garment Worker, 205
Miller: Wanted: "Civic Scientists," 362
Rose: Lilia, 19
Terkel: Organizer: Bill Talcott, 357

Jobs and Employment
Aslanian: Community College Pathway, 59
Ehrenreich: Evaluation, 208
Eisenberg: Coming Job Boom, 233
Falvo: Marketing Résumé, 284
Jones: And the Weiner Is . . . , 213
Liu: Story of a Garment Worker, 205
Miller: Wanted: "Civic Scientists," 362
Olive Garden: Welcome to the Family, 289

Roepstorff: Technology Résumé, 285
Swanson: Model Format for Cover
  Letter, 287
Terkel: Organizer: Bill Talcott, 357
U.S. Army: Discover How Far You Can
  Go, 280
Wilson Quarterly: Editorial Internships, 282
Woodard: Fueling the Revolution, 135

Language and Communication
ACLU: Briefing Paper, 504
Jamieson: Preface, 397
Malcolm X: Prison Studies, 16
Meyer: Humor as a Double-Edged
  Sword, 119
Pratkanis and Aronson: Our Age of
  Propaganda, 412
Rifkin: New Culture of Capitalism, 247
Sorrells: Communicating Common
  Ground, 183
States: Troping through Proverbia, 112

Letters
Ashton: Dear Denver Public Library
  Customer, 473
Brown-Rowe: Dear Customer, 311
Dees-Thomases: Dear Friend, 445
Gibson: President's Message, Feb. 11,
  2000, 312
Gibson: President's Message, Feb. 12,
  2001, 316
Head and Grossman: SAFE Colorado, 447
Huntington: Dear Ohio State Graduate, 451
Ladisch: Message from Chris, 477
Marriott: Holiday Greetings, 308
Olive Garden: Welcome to the Family, 291
Republican Presidential Roundtable:
  Invitation, 455
Rice for Peace: Dear President Bush, 471
Swanson: Model Format for Cover
  Letter, 287
Vermette: Improving Understanding, 96
Whittaker: Dear Subscriber, 453

Memos
Lesh-Laurie: Memo, 307
Lutz: It's Okay to Be Anal, 229

Money Management
AAA: Your Driving Costs 2003, 530
Ehrenreich: Evaluation, 208
Henry et al.: Money Management
  Practices, 165

Mogelonsky: Young Adults: New Customers/
  New Foods, 325
Nolo: How to Make a Budget, 543

Partisan Views
ACLU: Briefing Paper, 504
Allard: Announcement Remarks, 465
Centennial Supporters: City of Centennial:
  Yes, 457
Davidon: Orange You Feeling
  Threatened?, 513
Dees-Thomases: Dear Friend, 445
Denver Post: The ER Nightmare, 510
Doran: Grateful to *News*, 513
Fabian: A Tax, Not a Fee, 514
Greenwood Village: A New City?, 459
Head and Grossman: SAFE Colorado, 447
Kerry and Bond: Pro & Con, 495
McRae: Irony in the Morning, 512
National Rifle Association: Become a
  National Sponsor, 419
Rice for Peace: Dear President Bush, 471
Smoke Free Movies, 566
Strickland: Strickland Announces, 468

Photographs, see also Visuals
AAA: Your Driving Costs 2003, 530
Carr et al.: How to Tell a Sea Monster, 171
Glenbrook Life: Dedicated, Focused, and
  Diversified, 343
Greenwood Village: Newsletter, 475
T-REX, 332
U.S. Army: Discover How Far You Can
  Go, 280
Webb: Steel Belvedere, 319

Politics, see also Partisan Views
Brinkley: Why You Need to Vote, 443
Jamieson: Preface, 397
Moyers: Journalism & Democracy, 366
Republican Presidential Roundtable:
  Invitation, 455

Problem and Solution
Carr et al.: How to Tell a Sea Monster, 171
Ehrenreich: Evaluation, 208
Harris: So Many Numbers, 109
Helgesen: When Life Itself, 256
Woodard: Fueling the Revolution, 135

Process Directions and Explanations
AAA: Your Driving Costs 2003, 530
Carr et al.: How to Tell a Sea Monster, 171

Gamble: Evolution of Coral-Zooxanthellae
   Symbioses, 141
Hewlett-Packard: LaserJet Toner Cartridge
   Recycling Program, 337
Nolo: How to Make a Budget, 543
Tang: Cell Cycle and Cancer, 105

Profiles, see also Interviews
Jones: And the Weiner Is . . . , 213
Miller: Wanted: "Civic Scientists," 362
Terkel: Organizer: Bill Talcott, 357

Proposals
Muth et al.: Proposal, 555
National Fund: Grant Proposal, 559
Sorrells: Communicating Common
   Ground, 183

References or Works Cited Lists
Alford: Don't Just Do It to Save Lives, 271
Aslanian: Community College Pathway, 59
Bryant: ERIC Review: Community College
   Students, 159
Carr et al.: How to Tell a Sea Monster, 171
Ehrenreich: Evaluation, 208
Gamble: Evolution of Coral-Zooxanthellae
   Symbioses, 141
Gomes: A More Excellent Way, 420
Henry et al.: Money Management
   Practices, 165
Meyer: Humor as a Double-Edged
   Sword, 119
Mogelonsky: Young Adults: New Customers/
   New Foods, 325
Morgan and Korschgen: Ethics of Faculty
   Behavior, 87
Palmer: Quest for Community in Higher
   Education, 33
Peet: Logos, 101
Pratkanis and Aronson: Our Age of
   Propaganda, 412
Rifkin: New Culture of Capitalism, 247
Simpson: Are Incentives for Drug Abuse
   Treatment Too Strong?, 301
Small and Kimbrough-Melton: Rethinking
   Justice, 126
Tang: Cell Cycle and Cancer, 105
Tannen: Roots of Debate, 65
Woodard: Fueling the Revolution, 135

Research Reports and Studies
Bryant: ERIC Review: Community College
   Students, 159

Carr et al.: How to Tell a Sea Monster, 171
Fuel Economy Overview, 490
Gamble: Evolution of Coral-Zooxanthellae
   Symbioses, 141
Henry et al.: Money Management
   Practices, 165
Kush: Researching Bedlam, 133
Meyer: Humor as a Double-Edged
   Sword, 119
Mogelonsky: Young Adults: New Customers/
   New Foods, 325
Morgan and Korschgen: Ethics of Faculty
   Behavior, 87
Popenoe and Whitehead: Sex without
   Strings, 518
Simpson: Are Incentives for Drug Abuse
   Treatment Too Strong?, 301
Tang: Cell Cycle and Cancer, 105
Woodard: Fueling the Revolution, 135

Reviews
Review of *Sticks and Stones*, 149
Russell: Review of *Why We Watch*, 149
Webb: Steel Belvedere, 319

Speeches
Allard: Announcement Remarks, 465
Bush: Address, September 20, 2001, 433
Kerry and Bond: Pro & Con, 495
King: I Have a Dream, 439
Mairson: In Praise of the Research
   University, 192
Strickland: Strickland Announces, 468

Substance Abuse
College Drinking, 568
Simpson: Are Incentives for Drug Abuse
   Treatment Too Strong?, 301

**Summaries, see Abstracts and Executive
Summaries**

Tests and Quizzes
Hankins and Muth: Hitchcock Final, 180
Jamieson: Preface, 397
Rhodes: Think You Can Teach?, 515

Violence and Gun Control
Dees-Thomases: Dear Friend, 445
Fabian: A Tax, Not a Fee, 514
Head and Grossman: SAFE Colorado, 447
National Rifle Association: Become a
   National Sponsor, 419
Russell: Review of *Why We Watch*, 149
Strickland: Strickland Announces, 468

Visuals
AAA: Your Driving Costs 2003, 530
AmeriCorps/VISTA: Change Lives, 552
Bolman and Deal: Cracking the Hidden Code, 240
Bryant: ERIC Review: Community College Students, 159
Carr et al.: How to Tell a Sea Monster, 171
Centennial Supporters: City of Centennial: Yes, 457
College Drinking, 568
College of Arts and Media: Artistic License, 548
Donald: Learning, Understanding, and Meaning, 43
Eisenberg: Coming Job Boom, 233
Fuel Economy Overview, 490
Gibson: President's Message, Feb. 11, 2000, 312
Gibson: President's Message, Feb. 12, 2001, 316
Glenbrook Life: Dedicated, Focused, and Diversified, 343
Greenwood Village: A New City?, 459
Greenwood Village: Newsletter, 475
Henry et al.: Money Management Practices, 165
Hewlett-Packard: LaserJet Toner Cartridge Recycling Program, 337
Mogelonsky: Young Adults: New Customers/New Foods, 325
Morgan and Korschgen: Ethics of Faculty Behavior, 87
National Rifle Association, 449
Purdue University: OWL, 197
Rice for Peace: Dear President Bush, 471
Smoke Free Movies, 566
Technical Standards, 347
T-REX, 332
United Illuminating Company: Romeo and J l et, 341
U.S. Army: Discover How Far You Can Go, 280
Webb: Steel Belvedere, 319

Web Sites
College Drinking, 568
National Rifle Association, 449
Purdue University: OWL, 197
Rice for Peace, 471
Smoke Free Movies, 566
Technical Standards, 347
T-REX, 332

Credits

AAA Brochure is reproduced courtesy of AAA Association Communication, Heathrow, FL. © AAA 2003.

Adolescence Book Review of Jack Zipe's *Sticks and Stones, Adolescence*, 37:146, Summer 2002, by permission of Libra Publishers.

Alford, Fred C. From *Whistleblowers: Broken Lives and Organizational Power.* Copyright © 2001 by Cornell University. Used by permission of Cornell University Press.

Allard, Wayne. Web pages featuring Senator Wayne Allard's "Announcement Remarks," January 7, 2002, are reprinted by permission of the Chief of Staff, Office of Wayne Allard, U.S. Senator, Colorado.

American Civil Liberties Union (ACLU) Briefing Paper Number 16 (1996), "Hate Speech on Campus." http://www.aclu.org. Reprinted with permission.

Americorps/VISTA flyer is reprinted by permission of Catholic Charities, Denver, CO.

"Artistic License." Creative direction, design, and production for the brochure was handled by Barking Otter Design and Capistrano Creative, and reproduced with permission. Also by permission of the University of Colorado at Denver, College of Arts & Media.

Aslanian, Carol. "The Community College Pathway for Underprepared Students," *The College Board Review*, 196. Copyright © 2002 by the College Entrance Examination Board. All rights reserved. Reprinted with permission. www.collegeboard.com.

Bacon, David. "The Story of a Garment Worker" by Lisa Liu, as told to David Bacon, *Dollars and Sense*, 231, September/October 2000. Reprinted by permission of the author.

Barlow, Maude and Tony Clarke. Excerpts from "The Standpoint." from *Blue Gold: The Fight to Stop Corporate Theft of the World's Water.* Copyright © 2002 by Maude Barlow and Tony Clarke. Reprinted by permission of The New Press.

Barlow, Maude and Jeremy Rifkin. "Treaty Initiative" from *Blue Gold: The Fight to Stop the Corporate Theft of the World's Water.* Copyright © 2002 by Maude Barlow and Tony Clarke. Reprinted by permission of The New Press.

Blacker, David. "In Memoriam: Understanding Teaching as a Public Service," *Teachers College Record*, 2002 Special Edition, 8/12/02. http://www.tcrecord.org. Reprinted by permission of Blackwell Publishing Ltd.

Bolman, Lee G. and Terrence E. Deal. From *Escape from Cluelessness: A Guide for the Organizationally Challenged.* Copyright © 2000 by Lee G. Bolman and Terrence E. Deal. Reproduced with permission of American Management Association / AMACOM (B) in format Textbook via Copyright Clearance Center.

Bond, Christopher S. "Higher MPG and Light Trucks?" From the March 12, 2002 Senate floor debate. "Pro & Con," *Congressional Digest*, May 2002.

Brinkley, Christie. "Why You Need to Vote," *Cosmopolitan*, November 2000. Reprinted by permission of Christie Brinkley.

Bryant, Alyssa N., from ERIC Review: "Community College Students: Recent Findings and Trends," *Community College Review*, 29: 3, Winter 2001. Reprinted by permission.

Bush, George W. Address to a Joint Session of Congress and the American People, September 20, 2001.

Carr, S.M., H.D. Marshall, K.A. Johnstone, L.M. Pynn, and G.B. Stenson. "How to Tell a Sea Monster: Molecular Discrimination of Large Marine Animals of the North Atlantic," *The Biological Bulletin*, 202:1, February 2002, 1–5. Reprinted by permission of The Biological Bulletin and Steven M. Carr.

"Centennial: Vote For Incorporation." Reproduced by permission of Mayor Randy Pye, Centennial, CO.

"City of Greenwood Village: A New City?" Reproduced with permission of the City of Greenwood Village, CO.

"College Drinking: Changing the Culture." From the National Institute on Alcohol Abuse and Alcoholism (NIAAA) found at www.collegedrinkingprevention.gov.

CSR Today (2001) Newsletter, "Letter from Chris," written by Christine M. Ladisch. Reprinted with permission from the editor of CSR Today, Department of Consumer Sciences and Retailing, Purdue University.

Davidon, Sarah. Letter to the Editor, "Orange You Feeling Threatened," *The Denver Post* (Open Forum), March 9, 2003. Reprinted by permission of the author.

Dees-Thomasas, Donna. "Million Mom March" letter is reprinted by permission of The Brady Campaign, Washington, DC.

The Denver Public Library letter is reprinted with permission of the Denver Public Library, Denver, CO.

Dickens, Charles. "What Is a Horse?" from *Hard Times*, 1854.

Donald, Janet. From *Learning to Think: Disciplinary Perspectives*. Copyright © 2002 by John Wiley & Sons, Inc. This material is used by permission of John Wiley & Sons, Inc.

Doran, Linda. Letter to the Editor, "Grateful to *News* for Good News on Teens," *The Rocky Mountain News*, (Opinion), February 23, 2003. Reprinted by permission of the author.

Ehrenreich, Barbara. Excerpt from "Evaluation" from *Nickel and Dimed* by Barbara Ehrenreich. Copyright © 2001 by Barbara Ehrenreich. Reprinted by permission of Henry Holt and Company, LLC.

"The ER Nightmare" is from the editorial section of *The Denver Post*, September 2, 2001. Reprinted by permission of The Denver Post.

Fabian, Anthony J. Letter to the Editor, "A Tax, Not a Fee," *The Denver Post*, March 16, 2003. Reprinted by permission of the author.

"Fuel Economy Overview: Evolution of the Current Policy," *Congressional Digest*, May 2002, from *The Library of Congress, Congressional Research Service Reports* "Automobile and Light Truck Fuel Economy: Is CAFE Up to Standards?" and "Global Climate Change: The Kyoto Protocol."

Gomes, Peter. Excerpt from "A More Excellent Way," pp. 14–18, 26–29 from *The Good Life: Truths That Last in Times of Need* by Dr. Peter Gomes. Copyright © 2002 by Peter J. Gomes. Reprinted by permission of HarperCollins Publishers, Inc.

Grassmaster Lawncare, Inc. "Dear Customer" letter dated January 1, 2001 is reprinted with the permission of Grassmaster Lawncare, Inc.

Greenwood Village, Colorado Newsletter, 16:8. June 2001. Reproduced with permission of the City of Greenwood Village, CO.

Harris, Margaret. "So Many Numbers—What Do You Do with the Data?" This article originally appeared in the *Journal of Young Investigators*, 5:9, June 2002. Reprinted with permission of the author and Journal of Young Investigators, http:///www.jyi.org.

Harris, Robert. "Anti-Plagiarism Strategies for Research Papers," *VirtualSalt*, October 19, 2001, http://www.virtualsalt.com. Reprinted by permission of Robert Harris.

Harvard Business Review, Executive Summary of David G. Baldwin's "How to Win the Blame Game," *Harvard Business Review*, July 2001.

Harvard Business Review, Executive Summary of Patricia B. Seybold's "Get Inside the Lives of Your Customers," *Harvard Business Review*, May 2001.

Harvard Business Review, Executive Summary of Michael E. Porter's "Strategy and the Internet," *Harvard Business Review*, March 2001.

Henry, Reasie, Janice Weber, and David Yarbrough, "Money Management Practices of College Students," *College Student Journal*, 35:2, Summer 2001. Reprinted by permission.

Hewlett-Packard Laser Jet Toner Cartridge Recycle Program Information and Instruction Guide. Courtesy, Hewlett-Packard Company. Hewlett-Packard Company makes no warranty as to the accuracy or completeness of the foregoing material and hereby disclaims any responsibility therefore. Reprinted by permission.

hooks, bell. "Keeping Close to Home: Class and Education" from *Talking Back: Thinking Feminist, Thinking Black*. Copyright © 1989 by Gloria Watkins. Reprinted by permission of South End Press.

Huntington, Susan L., vice provost and dean. Letter from the Graduate School at Ohio State University, August 2002. Reprinted with permission of Susan L. Huntington.

Jamieson, Kathleen Hall. From *Everything You Think You Know About Politics . . . And Why You're Wrong* by Kathleen Hall Jamieson. Copyright © 2000 by Kathleen Hall Jamieson. Reprinted by permission of Basic Books, a member of Perseus Books, L.L.C.

Jefferson, Thomas. "The Declaration of Independence," 1776.
Jones, Marty. "And the Weiner Is . . . " from *Westword*, July 18–24, 2002. Reprinted by permission of the author.
Katz, Stanley N., "The Pathbreaking, Fractionalized, Uncertain World of Knowledge," *The Chronicle of Higher Education (The Chronicle Review)*, September 20, 2002. Reprinted by permission of the author.
Kerry, John. "Should Congress Set Requirements for Cars?" from the March 12, 2002 Senate floor debate, as appeared in "Pro & Con," *Congressional Digest*, May 2002.
King, Martin Luther, Jr. "I Have A Dream." Reprinted by arrangement with the Estate of Martin Luther King Jr., c/o Writers House as agent for the proprietor, New York, NY. Copyright 1963 Dr. Martin Luther King Jr., copyright renewed 1991 Coretta Scott King.
Lee, Linda. "The Case Against College," *Family Circle*, June 12, 2001. Reprinted by permission of *Family Circle* magazine.
Lesh-Laurie, Georgia. Memorandum from the Chancellor's Office to the CU-Denver Community, October 3, 2002. Reprinted by permission of Georgia Lesh-Laurie, Chancellor, University of Colorado at Denver.
Liberty Funds. Material and photos from "Newport Tiger Fund Annual Report, 1999" and "Liberty Newport Tiger Fund Annual Report, 2000." Reprinted by permission of Liberty Funds Distributor, Inc., Boston, MA.
Lutz, Robert A. From "It's OK to Be Anal Sometimes" from *Guts: The Seven Laws of Business That Made Chrysler the World's Hottest Car Company*. Copyright © 1998 by Robert A. Lutz. This material is used by permission of John Wiley & Sons, Inc.
Mairson, Harry. "In Praise of the Research University." From remarks at the Brandeis Commencement, May 1996, School of Science Ceremonies. By permission of Harry Mairson.
Malcolm X. From *The Autobiography of Malcolm X* by Malcolm X and Alex Haley. Copyright © 1964 by Alex Haley and Malcolm X. Copyright © 1965 by Alex Haley and Betty Shabazz. Used by permission of Random House, Inc.
Marriott, J.W., Jr. "Holiday Greetings" letter from Bill Marriott. Reprinted by permission of Marriott International Headquarters, Washington, DC.
McRae, Sandra. Letter to the Editor, "Irony in the Morning," *The Denver Post* (Open Forum), March 12, 2003. Reprinted by permission of the author.
Meyer, John C. "Humor as a Double-Edged Sword," *Communication Theory* 10:3, August 2000, pp. 310–315, 329–330. Reprinted by permission of Oxford University Press and the author.
Miller, Katherine S. "Wanted: 'Civic Scientists' to Educate the Public, Press and Policy Makers," *Stanford Report*, February 20, 2001. By permission of Stanford Report News Service.
Mogelonsky, Marcia. From *Everybody Eats*. Copyright © 1995, American Demographics Books. Reprinted by permission of Primedia.
Morgan, Betsy Levonian and Ann J. Korschgen, "The Ethics of Faculty Behavior: Students' and Professors' Views," *College Student Journal*, 35: 3, Fall 2001. Reprinted by permission.
Morse, Suzanne W. "Five Building Blocks for Successful Companies" from *The Community of the Future*, Frances Hesselbein et al., eds. Copyright © 1998 the Peter Drucker Foundation for Nonprofit Management. This material is used by permission of John Wiley & Sons, Inc.
Moyers, Bill. "Journalism and Democracy: On the Importance of Being a Public Nuisance." Reprinted with permission from the May 7, 2001 issue of *The Nation*.
The National Fund for the United States Botanic Garden "Grant Proposal" from www.nationalgarden.org is reprinted with permission.
National Rifle Association. "Become a National Sponsor" web page from http://www.nrafoundation.org/friends/nat_sponsor.asp is reprinted with permission from the National Rifle Association of America.
Nelson, Jill. "A Beginning" from *Straight, No Chaser* by Jill Nelson. Copyright © 1997 by Jill Nelson. Used by permission of G.P. Putnam's Sons, a division of Penguin Group (USA) Inc.
Nolo.com: Law for All. "How to Make a Budget and Stick to It." Reprinted with permission from the publisher, Nolo. Copyright © 2003, http://www.nolo.com.
Olive Garden Italian Restaurant. Material from the Olive Garden "Welcome to the Family" brochure is reprinted with permission.

Palmer, Parker J. Afterword: "The Quest for Community in Higher Education." From *Creating Campus Community* by William M. McDonald. Copyright © 2002 John Wiley & Sons. This material is used by permission of John Wiley & Sons, Inc.

Popenoe, David and Barbara Dafoe Whitehead. "Sex Without Strings, Relationships Without Rings" from *State of Our Unions: The Social Health of Marriage in America, 2000*. Copyright © 2000 by the National Marriage Project at Rutgers University, New Brunswick, NJ. Reprinted by permission.

Pratkanis, Anthony R. and Elliot Aronson. Excerpt from "Our Age of Propaganda" from *Age of Propaganda: The Everyday Use and Abuse of Persuasion,* revised edition by Anthony R. Pratkanis and Elliot Aronson. Copyright © 2001, 1992 by W.H. Freeman and Company. Reprinted by permission of Henry Holt and Company, LLC.

Princeton Project 55, Inc. Excerpts from the 1995 paper, "Princeton University in the 21st Century: Paths to More Effective Undergraduate Education," as appears in Parker Palmer's work, is reprinted by permission of Princeton Project 55, Inc. www.project55.org.

Purdue University Web site, "Online Writing Lab (OWL)," http://owl.english.purdue.edu. Reprinted by permission of the Purdue Research Foundation, Office of Technology Commercialization.

Republican Senate Leadership, invitation to the Eighth Annual Republican Senatorial *Regain the Majority* Dinner, 2002. Reprinted by permission of the National Republican Senatorial Committee.

Rhodes, Lynn K. "Think You Can Teach? Pass This Test," a Speakout column published in the *Denver Rocky Mountain News*, February 1, 1999, p. 13A. Reprinted with permission of the Rocky Mountain News.

"Rice for Peace" Web pages reprinted by permission of the Rocky Mountain Peace and Justice Center, http://rmpjc.org/riceforpeace.

Rifkin, Jeremy. "The New Culture of Capitalism" from *The Age of Access* by Jeremy Rifkin. Copyright © 2000 by Jeremy Rifkin. Used by permission of Jeremy P. Tarcher, an imprint of Penguin Group (USA) Inc.

Russell, Gordon W. Book review of *Why We Watch* from *Aggressive Behavior*, 27:4, 2001. Copyright © 2001 Wiley-Liss, Inc. This material is used by permission of Wiley-Liss, Inc., a subsidiary of John Wiley & Sons, Inc.

"SAFE Colorado" contribution letter dated October 25, 2000, is reprinted by permission of John Head, co-president of SAFE Colorado.

Simon, John C., et al. Abstract in English and Spanish, 'Temporal Variation in Bird Counts within a Hawaiian Rainforest," *The Condor*, 104:3, August 2002. © 2002 the Cooper Ornithological Society. Reprinted by permission of the editor of *The Condor*.

Simpson, Mark. "Are Incentives for Drug Abuse Treatment Too Strong?" from *Corrections Today*, August 2002. Reprinted with permission of the American Correctional Association, Lanham, MD.

Small, Mark A. and Robin Kimbrough-Melton. "Rethinking Justice" from *Behavioral Sciences and the Law*, 20: 4 (2002). Copyright © 2002 John Wiley & Sons, Ltd. Reproduced by permission of John Wiley & Sons Limited.

"Smoke Free Movies" Web pages from http://www.smokefreemovies.ucsf.edu reprinted with permission of Professor Stanton A. Glantz, University of California at San Francisco.

Sorrells, Kathryn. Grant proposal, "Communicating Common Ground" found at http://www.csun.edu/~dlk60325/proposal.html
Reprinted by permission of Kathryn Sorrells., Ph.D., Department of Communication Studies, California State University at Northridge.

States, Bert O., "Troping Through Proverbia." Reprinted with permission from *The American Scholar*, 70:3, Summer 2001. Copyright © 2001 by Bert O. States.

Stoscheck, Leo. "College Application Essays 3—Education in the Outdoors of Rural New York State Taught Many Lessons." © Copyright NPR ® 2001. The text of a news commentary by NPR's Leo Stoscheck was originally broadcast on National Public Radio's "All Things Considered" on March 28, 2001 and is used with the permission of National Public Radio, Inc. Any unauthorized duplication is strictly prohibited.

Strickland, Tom. "Strickland Announces Candidacy for U. S. Senate" from the *Strickland for Colorado* Web site. Reprinted by permission of Tom Strickland.
T-REX Transportation Expansion Project. Web pages from T-REX Project Design Web site reprinted by permission of T-REX Project, Centennial, CO.
Tang, Man (Cristina). "The Cell Cycle and Cancer." This article originally appeared in the *Journal of Young Investigators*, 5:8, May 2002. JYI is the premier online journal of undergraduate scientific research and science writing. Reprinted by permission of the author and JYI, http://www.jyi.org.
Tannen, Deborah. From *The Argument Culture* by Deborah Tannen. Copyright © 1997 by Deborah Tannen. Used by permission of Random House, Inc.
Technical Standards, Inc. Web pages from http://www.tecstandards.com. Reprinted by permission of Technical Standards, Inc.
Terkel, Studs. "Organizer: Bill Talcott." Copyright © 1997 *Working: People Talk About What They Do All Day and How They Feel About What They Do* by Studs Terkel. Reprinted by permission of the New Press.
Ulrich, Dave. "Six Practices for Creating Communities of Value, Not Proximity," from *The Community of the Future*, Frances Hesselbein et al., eds. Copyright © 1998 the Peter F. Drucker Foundation for Nonprofit Management. This material is used by permission of John Wiley & Sons, Inc.
The United Illuminating Company advertisement, "Romeo and J Let," appeared in The Long Wharf Theatre program (2002–2003 season). Reprinted by permission of the United Illuminating Company, New Haven, CT.
"Discover How Far You Can Go," U.S. Army recruiting brochure. Army materials courtesy of the U.S. Government. Reprinted by permission.
Vermette, Paul J. "Improving Understanding and Increasing Grades: 4 Tips for Fall Freshman at Columbus Day, an Open Letter to My Son at College," *College Student Journal*, 34:4, December 2000. Reprinted by permission.
Walton, Sam. From *Sam Walton: Made in America*. Copyright © 1992 by the Estate of Samuel Moore Walton. Used by permission of Doubleday, a division of Random House, Inc.
Webb, Michael. "Student Centre, Pasadena, California, USA," from *Architectural Review*, May 2002. Reprinted courtesy of the Architectural Review and by permission of the author.
Whittaker, Richard. Letter to subscribers of *works+ conversations* is reprinted by permission of the editor, Richard Whittaker.
"Wilson Quarterly Internships" from the Woodrow Wilson International Center for Scholars Web site is reprinted by permission of the managing editor of *The Wilson Quarterly*. http://wwics.si.edu/outreach/wq/wqintern.htm.
Zielinski, David. "Are You a Copyright Criminal?" from *Presentations*, June 1999. Copyright © 1999 by VNU Business Publications USA. Reproduced with permission of VNU Business Publications USA in the format textbook via Copyright Clearance Center.
Zobel de Ayala II, Jaime A. "Anticipating the Community of the Future" from *The Community of the Future*, Frances Hesselbein et al., eds. Copyright © 1998 the Peter F. Drucker Foundation for Nonprofit Management. This material is used by permission of John Wiley & Sons, Inc.

Photo Credits

Page **173**: Dr. Gary Stenson/Dept. of Fisheries and Oceans & St. John's Evening Telegram; **241**: © The New Yorker Collection 1994 Mick Stevens from cartoonbank.com. All Rights Reserved; **320**: Marvin Rand/Marvin Rand Associates; **321**: Marvin Rand/Marvin Rand Associates; **322B**: Marvin Rand/Marvin Rand Associates; **322T**: Marvin Rand/Marvin Rand Associates; **323BL**: Hodgetts & Fung Design Associates; **323BR**: Hodgetts & Fung Design Associates; **323C**: Hodgetts & Fung Design Associates; **323T**: Marvin Rand/Marvin Rand Associates; **344**: Glenbrook Life, Allstate Financial Group; **345**: Glenbrook Life, Allstate Financial Group; **346**: Glenbrook Life, Allstate Financial Group; **456**: The National Republican Senatorial Committee (NRSC); **531**: Reprinted with permission American Automobile Association; **532**: Reprinted with permission American Automobile Association; **533**: Reprinted with permission American Automobile Association; **534**: Reprinted with permission American Automobile Association; **535:** Reprinted with permission American Automobile Association; **536:** Reprinted with permission American Automobile Association; **537:** Reprinted with permission American Automobile Association; **538:** Reprinted with permission American Automobile Association; **539:** Reprinted with permission American Automobile Association; **540:** Reprinted with permission American Automobile Association; **541:** Reprinted with permission American Automobile Association

Index of Authors and Titles

This index lists titles of readings, authors, and major sponsoring groups. See also the Guide to Themes, Topics, and Rhetorical Strategies.

Address to a Joint Session of Congress and the American People, September 20, 2001, 433
Ahrold, Drew, 555
Alford, C. Fred, 271
Allard, Wayne, 465
American Automobile Association, 530
American Civil Liberties Union, 504
AmeriCorps, 552
"And the Weiner Is . . . ," 213
"Announcement Remarks," 465
"Anticipating the Community of the Future," 405
"Anti-Plagiarism Strategies for Research Papers," 77
"Application Essay," 94
"Are Incentives for Drug Abuse Treatment Too Strong?," 301
"Are You a Copyright Criminal?" 264
Aronson, Elliott, 412
"Artistic License," 548
Ashton, Rick, 473
Aslanian, Carol, 59
Ayala, Jaime A. Zobel de, II, 405

Bacon, David, 205
Baldwin, David G., 298
Barlow, Maude, 431, 479
"Become a National Sponsor," 449
"A Beginning," 386
Berlin, Kim E., 154
Blacker, David, 156
Bolman, Lee G., 240
Bond, Christopher S., 495
Brandeis University, 192
"Briefing Paper: Hate Speech on Campus," 504
Brinkley, Christie, 443
Brown-Rowe, J. Katherine, 311
Bryant, Alyssa N., 159
Bush, President George W., 433

California State University, Northridge, 183
Carr, S. M., et al., 171
"The Case Against College," 73
"The Cell Cycle and Cancer," 105
Centennial Supporters, 457
"Change Lives . . . Including Your Own," 552
"City of Centennial: Yes," 457

City of Greenwood Village, 459, 475
Clarke, Tony, 479
College Drinking: Changing the Culture, 568
College of Arts and Media, University of Colorado at Denver, 548
"The Coming Job Boom," 233
"Communicating Common Ground," 183
"The Community College Pathway for Underprepared Students," 59
Cornell College, 180, 287, 554, 555
Covey, Stephen R., 390
"Cracking the Hidden Code: Becoming a Cultural Sleuth," 240
CSR, 477
Cullis-Suzuki, Severn, 355

Davidon, Sarah, 513
Deal, Terrence E., 240
"Dear Customer," 311
"Dear Denver Public Library Customer," 473
"Dear Friend," 445
"Dear Ohio State Graduate," 451
"Dear President Bush," 471
"Dear Subscriber," 453
The Declaration of Independence, 426
Dedecker, Melanie, 189
"Dedicated," 344
Dees-Thomases, Donna, 445
Denver Post, 510
Dickens, Charles, 11
"Discover How Far You Can Go," 280
"Diversified," 346
Donald, Janet, 43
"Don't Just Do It to Save Lives," 271
Doran, Linda, 513

"Editorial Internships," 282
Ehrenreich, Barbara, 208
Eisenberg, Daniel, 233
"ERIC Review: Community College Students: Recent Findings and Trends," 159
"The ER Nightmare," 510
"The Ethics of Faculty Behavior: Students' and Professors' Views," 87
"Evaluation," 208
Everything You Think You Know About Politics . . . And Why You're Wrong, Preface, 397

585

"The Evolution of Coral-Zooxanthellae Symbioses: Implications of Coral Bleaching," 141
"Evolution of the Current Policy," 490

Fabian, Anthony J., 514
Falvo, Elizabeth, 284
Fancy, Steven G., 154
Fenoglio, Brian, 555
"Five Building Blocks for Successful Communities," 374
"Focused," 345
Fuel Economy Overview, 490
"Fueling the Revolution," 135

Gamble, Valerie, 141
"Get Inside the Lives of Your Customers," 298
Glenbrook Life, Allstate Financial Group, 343
Gibson, Stephen E., 312, 316
Goldstein, Jeffrey H., ed., review, 151
Gomes, Peter J., 420
"Grant Proposal," 559
Grassmaster, 311
"Grateful to *News* for Good News on Teens," 513
Greenwood Village, 459, 475
Grossman, Arnie, 447

Hankins, Leslie, 180
Hard Times, "Nothing but Facts," 11
Harris, Margaret, 109
Harris, Robert, 77
"Hate Speech on Campus," 504
Hatfield, Jeff S., 154
Head, John, 447
Helgesen, Sally, 256
Henry, Reasie A., et al., 165
Hewlett-Packard, 337
"Hitchcock Final and Answers," 180
"Holiday Greetings," 308
hooks, bell, 22
"How to Make a Budget and Stick to It," 543
"How to Tell a Sea Monster: Molecular Discrimination of Large Marine Animals of the North Atlantic," 171
"How to Win the Blame Game," 298
Huey, John, 216
"Humor as a Double-Edged Sword: Four Functions of Humor in Communication," 119
Huntington, Susan L., 451
Hutton, Stan, 379

"The Ideal Community," 390
"I Have a Dream," 439

"Improving Understanding and Increasing Grades: 4 Tips for Fall Freshman at Columbus Day, An Open Letter to My Son at College," 96
"In Memoriam: Understanding Teaching as Public Service," 156
"In Praise of the Research University: Remarks at the Brandeis Commencement, May 1996, School of Science Ceremonies," 192
"Introduction to T-REX, Construction Photos, and Traffic Updates," 332
"Invitation to the 8th Annual Republican Senatorial Regain the Majority Dinner," 455
"Irony in the Morning," 512
"It's Okay to Be Anal Sometimes," 218

Jamieson, Kathleen Hall, 397
Jefferson, Thomas, 426
Johnstone, K. A., 171
Jones, Marty, 213
"Journalism & Democracy: On the Importance of Being a 'Public Nuisance,'" 366

Katz, Stanley N., 52
"Keeping Close to Home: Class and Education," 22
Kerry, John, 495
Kimbrough-Melton, Robin, 126
King, Martin Luther, Jr., 439
Korschgen, Ann J., 87
Kowalsky, James R., 154
Kush, Brooke, 133

Ladisch, Christine M., 477
"LaserJet Toner Cartridge Recycling Program," 337
"Learning, Understanding, and Meaning," 43
Lee, Linda, 73
Lesh-Laurie, Georgia, 307
Liberty Newport Tiger Fund, 312, 316
"Lilia," 19
Liu, Lisa, 205
"Living & Learning Program," 555
"The Logos, Constant Change, and Wisdom: Heraclitus and Unification," 101
Lutz, Robert A., 228

Mairson, Harry, 192
Malcolm X, 16
"Marketing Résumé," 284
Marriott, Bill, 308
Marshall, H. D., 171
McRae, Sandra S., 512
"Memo to CU-Denver Community," 307

Merrill, Ben, 555
"Message from Chris," 477
Meyer, John C., 119
Miller, Katharine S., 362
Million Mom March, 445
"Model Format for Cover Letter," 287
Mogelonsky, Marcia, 325
"Money Management Practices of College Students," 165
"A More Excellent Way," 420
Morgan, Betsy Levonian, 87
Morse, Suzanne W., 374
Moyers, Bill, 366
Muth, Anderson, 180
Muth, Anderson, et al., 555

National Fund for the United States Botanic Garden, 559
National Rifle Association Foundation, 449
Nelson, Jill, 386
"A New City?," 459
"The New Culture of Capitalism," 247
Newport Tiger Fund, 312, 316
"Newsletter," 475
Nolo: Law for All, 543
"Nothing but Facts," 11

Ohio State University, 451
Olive Garden Italian Restaurant, 289
Online Writing Lab (OWL), 197
"Orange You Feeling Threatened?," 513
"Organizer: Bill Talcott," 357
"Our Age of Propaganda," 412

Palmer, Parker J., 33
"The Pathbreaking, Fractionalized, Uncertain World of Knowledge," 52
Peet, Elizabeth, 101
Phillips, Frances, 379
Popenoe, David, 518
Porter, Michael E., 299
Pratkanis, Anthony R., 412
Pratt, Thane K., 154
Preface to *Everything You Think You Know About Politics . . . And Why You're Wrong*, 97
"President's Message, February 11, 2000," 312
"President's Message, February 12, 2001," 316
"Prison Studies," 16
"Pro & Con: Should Congress Set Higher MPG Requirements for Cars and Light Trucks?," 495
"Proposal for a Cornell College Living & Learning Group," 555
Purdue University, 197, 477
Pynn, L. M., 171

"The Quest for Community in Higher Education," 33

Republican Presidential Roundtable, 455
"Researching Bedlam and Madness in the Early Modern Era," 133
"Rethinking Justice," 126
Rhodes, Lynn K., 515
Rice for Peace, 471
Rifkin, Jeremy, 247, 431
Roepstorff, Brad, 285
"Romeo and J l et," 341
"The Roots of Debate in Education and the Hope of Dialogue," 65
Rose, Mike, 19
"Running a Successful Company: Ten Rules That Worked for Me," 216
Russell, Gordon W., review, 149

"SAFE Colorado: Sane Alternatives to the Firearms Epidemic," 447
Seabloom, Joe, 555
"Sex without Strings, Relationships without Rings: Today's Young Singles Talk about Mating and Dating," 518
Seybold, Patricia B., 298
Simon, John C., et al., 154
Simpson, Mark, 301
"Six Practices for Creating Communities of Value, Not Proximity," 221
Small, Mark A., 126
Smoke Free Movies, 566
"So Many Numbers—What Do You Do with the Data?," 109
Sorrells, Kathryn, 183
"The Standpoint: How Common Principles and Goals Can Save the World's Water," 479
Stanford University, 362
"Statement of Purpose," 189
States, Bert O., 112
"Steel Belvedere," 319
Stenson, G. B., 171
Sticks and Stones: The Troublesome Success of Children's Literature from Slovenly Peter to Harry Potter, review, 149
"The Story of a Garment Worker," 205
Stoscheck, Leo, 94
"Strategy and the Internet," 299
"Strickland Announces Candidacy for U.S. Senate," 468
Strickland, Tom, 468
Strutt, Peter, 555
Swanson, Jayne, 287

Tang, Cristina, 105

Tannen, Deborah, 65
"A Tax, Not a Fee," 514
Technical Standards, Inc., 347
"Technology Résumé," 285
"Temporal Variation in Bird Counts within a Hawaiian Rainforest," 154
Terkel, Studs, 357
"Think You Can Teach? Pass This Test," 515
"The Treaty Initiative to Share and Protect the Global Water Common," 431
T-REX Transportation Expansion Project, 332
"Troping through Proverbia," 112
"Tuning In to the World of Nonprofit Organizations," 379

Ulrich, Dave, 221
United Illuminating Company, 341
University of Colorado at Denver, 307, 515, 548
U.S. Army, 280

Vermette, Paul J., 96
VISTA, 552

Walton, Sam, 216

"Wanted: 'Civic Scientists' to Educate the Public, Press and Policy Makers," 362
Webb, Michael, 319
Weber, Janice G., 165
"Welcome to the Family," 289
"When Life Itself Becomes Incredibly Complex," 256
Whitehead, Barbara Dafoe, 518
Whittaker, Richard, 453
Why We Watch: The Attractions of Violent Entertainment, review, 151
"Why You Need to Vote," 443
Wilson Quarterly, 282
Woodard, Matt, 135
works + conversations, 453

Yarbrough, David, 165
"Young Adults: New Customers/New Foods," 325
"The Young Can't Wait," 355
"Your Driving Costs 2003: Figuring It Out," 530

Zielinski, Dave, 264
Zipes, Jack, review, 149
Zobel de Ayala, Jaime A., II, 405